CODE OF FEDERAL
REGULATIONS

Title 2
Grants and Agreements

Revised as of January 1, 2014

Containing a codification of documents
of general applicability and future effect

As of January 1, 2014

Published by the Office of the Federal Register
National Archives and Records Administration
as a Special Edition of the Federal Register

U.S. GOVERNMENT OFFICIAL EDITION NOTICE

Legal Status and Use of Seals and Logos

The seal of the National Archives and Records Administration (NARA) authenticates the Code of Federal Regulations (CFR) as the official codification of Federal regulations established under the Federal Register Act. Under the provisions of 44 U.S.C. 1507, the contents of the CFR, a special edition of the Federal Register, shall be judicially noticed. The CFR is prima facie evidence of the original documents published in the Federal Register (44 U.S.C. 1510).

It is prohibited to use NARA's official seal and the stylized Code of Federal Regulations logo on any republication of this material without the express, written permission of the Archivist of the United States or the Archivist's designee. Any person using NARA's official seals and logos in a manner inconsistent with the provisions of 36 CFR part 1200 is subject to the penalties specified in 18 U.S.C. 506, 701, and 1017.

Use of ISBN Prefix

This is the Official U.S. Government edition of this publication and is herein identified to certify its authenticity. Use of the 0–16 ISBN prefix is for U.S. Government Printing Office Official Editions only. The Superintendent of Documents of the U.S. Government Printing Office requests that any reprinted edition clearly be labeled as a copy of the authentic work with a new ISBN.

 U.S. GOVERNMENT PRINTING OFFICE

U.S. Superintendent of Documents • Washington, DC 20402–0001

http://bookstore.gpo.gov

Phone: toll-free (866) 512-1800; DC area (202) 512-1800

Table of Contents

iv

Cite this Code: **CFR**

To cite the regulations in this volume use title, part and section number. Thus, 2 CFR 1.100 refers to title 2, part 1, section 100.

Explanation

The Code of Federal Regulations is a codification of the general and permanent rules published in the Federal Register by the Executive departments and agencies of the Federal Government. The Code is divided into 50 titles which represent broad areas subject to Federal regulation. Each title is divided into chapters which usually bear the name of the issuing agency. Each chapter is further subdivided into parts covering specific regulatory areas.

Each volume of the Code is revised at least once each calendar year and issued on a quarterly basis approximately as follows:

Title 1 through Title 16...as of January 1
Title 17 through Title 27 ....as of April 1
Title 28 through Title 41 ....as of July 1
Title 42 through Title 50...as of October 1

The appropriate revision date is printed on the cover of each volume.

LEGAL STATUS

The contents of the Federal Register are required to be judicially noticed (44 U.S.C. 1507). The Code of Federal Regulations is prima facie evidence of the text of the original documents (44 U.S.C. 1510).

HOW TO USE THE CODE OF FEDERAL REGULATIONS

The Code of Federal Regulations is kept up to date by the individual issues of the Federal Register. These two publications must be used together to determine the latest version of any given rule.

To determine whether a Code volume has been amended since its revision date (in this case, January 1, 2014), consult the "List of CFR Sections Affected (LSA)," which is issued monthly, and the "Cumulative List of Parts Affected," which appears in the Reader Aids section of the daily Federal Register. These two lists will identify the Federal Register page number of the latest amendment of any given rule.

EFFECTIVE AND EXPIRATION DATES

Each volume of the Code contains amendments published in the Federal Register since the last revision of that volume of the Code. Source citations for the regulations are referred to by volume number and page number of the Federal Register and date of publication. Publication dates and effective dates are usually not the same and care must be exercised by the user in determining the actual effective date. In instances where the effective date is beyond the cut-off date for the Code a note has been inserted to reflect the future effective date. In those instances where a regulation published in the Federal Register states a date certain for expiration, an appropriate note will be inserted following the text.

OMB CONTROL NUMBERS

The Paperwork Reduction Act of 1980 (Pub. L. 96–511) requires Federal agencies to display an OMB control number with their information collection request.

vi

Many agencies have begun publishing numerous OMB control numbers as amendments to existing regulations in the CFR. These OMB numbers are placed as close as possible to the applicable recordkeeping or reporting requirements.

PAST PROVISIONS OF THE CODE

Provisions of the Code that are no longer in force and effect as of the revision date stated on the cover of each volume are not carried. Code users may find the text of provisions in effect on any given date in the past by using the appropriate List of CFR Sections Affected (LSA). For the convenience of the reader, a "List of CFR Sections Affected" is published at the end of each CFR volume. For changes to the Code prior to the LSA listings at the end of the volume, consult previous annual editions of the LSA. For changes to the Code prior to 2001, consult the List of CFR Sections Affected compilations, published for 1949-1963, 1964-1972, 1973-1985, and 1986-2000.

"[RESERVED]" TERMINOLOGY

The term "[Reserved]" is used as a place holder within the Code of Federal Regulations. An agency may add regulatory information at a "[Reserved]" location at any time. Occasionally "[Reserved]" is used editorially to indicate that a portion of the CFR was left vacant and not accidentally dropped due to a printing or computer error.

INCORPORATION BY REFERENCE

What is incorporation by reference? Incorporation by reference was established by statute and allows Federal agencies to meet the requirement to publish regulations in the Federal Register by referring to materials already published elsewhere. For an incorporation to be valid, the Director of the Federal Register must approve it. The legal effect of incorporation by reference is that the material is treated as if it were published in full in the Federal Register (5 U.S.C. 552(a)). This material, like any other properly issued regulation, has the force of law.

What is a proper incorporation by reference? The Director of the Federal Register will approve an incorporation by reference only when the requirements of 1 CFR part 51 are met. Some of the elements on which approval is based are:

(a) The incorporation will substantially reduce the volume of material published in the Federal Register.

(b) The matter incorporated is in fact available to the extent necessary to afford fairness and uniformity in the administrative process.

(c) The incorporating document is drafted and submitted for publication in accordance with 1 CFR part 51.

What if the material incorporated by reference cannot be found? If you have any problem locating or obtaining a copy of material listed as an approved incorporation by reference, please contact the agency that issued the regulation containing that incorporation. If, after contacting the agency, you find the material is not available, please notify the Director of the Federal Register, National Archives and Records Administration, 8601 Adelphi Road, College Park, MD 20740-6001, or call 202-741-6010.

CFR INDEXES AND TABULAR GUIDES

A subject index to the Code of Federal Regulations is contained in a separate volume, revised annually as of January 1, entitled CFR INDEX AND FINDING AIDS. This volume contains the Parallel Table of Authorities and Rules. A list of CFR titles, chapters, subchapters, and parts and an alphabetical list of agencies publishing in the CFR are also included in this volume.

An index to the text of "Title 3—The President" is carried within that volume.

The Federal Register Index is issued monthly in cumulative form. This index is based on a consolidation of the "Contents" entries in the daily Federal Register.

A List of CFR Sections Affected (LSA) is published monthly, keyed to the revision dates of the 50 CFR titles.

REPUBLICATION OF MATERIAL

There are no restrictions on the republication of material appearing in the Code of Federal Regulations.

INQUIRIES

For a legal interpretation or explanation of any regulation in this volume, contact the issuing agency. The issuing agency's name appears at the top of odd-numbered pages.

For inquiries concerning CFR reference assistance, call 202–741–6000 or write to the Director, Office of the Federal Register, National Archives and Records Administration, 8601 Adelphi Road, College Park, MD 20740-6001 or e-mail *fedreg.info@nara.gov*.

SALES

The Government Printing Office (GPO) processes all sales and distribution of the CFR. For payment by credit card, call toll-free, 866-512-1800, or DC area, 202-512-1800, M-F 8 a.m. to 4 p.m. e.s.t. or fax your order to 202-512-2104, 24 hours a day. For payment by check, write to: US Government Printing Office – New Orders, P.O. Box 979050, St. Louis, MO 63197-9000.

ELECTRONIC SERVICES

The full text of the Code of Federal Regulations, the LSA (List of CFR Sections Affected), The United States Government Manual, the Federal Register, Public Laws, Public Papers of the Presidents of the United States, Compilation of Presidential Documents and the Privacy Act Compilation are available in electronic format via *www.ofr.gov*. For more information, contact the GPO Customer Contact Center, U.S. Government Printing Office. Phone 202-512-1800, or 866-512-1800 (toll-free). E-mail, *ContactCenter@gpo.gov*.

The Office of the Federal Register also offers a free service on the National Archives and Records Administration's (NARA) World Wide Web site for public law numbers, Federal Register finding aids, and related information. Connect to NARA's web site at *www.archives.gov/federal-register*.

The e-CFR is a regularly updated, unofficial editorial compilation of CFR material and Federal Register amendments, produced by the Office of the Federal Register and the Government Printing Office. It is available at *www.ecfr.gov*.

CHARLES A. BARTH,
Director,
Office of the Federal Register.
January 1, 2014.

THIS TITLE

Title 2—GRANTS AND AGREEMENTS is composed of one volume. This volume is comprised of Subtitle A—Office of Management and Budget Guidance for Grants and Agreements and Subtitle B—Federal Agency Regulations for Grants and Agreements. The contents of this volume represents all current regulations codified under this title of the CFR as of January 1, 2014.

For this volume, Susannah C. Hurley was Chief Editor. The Code of Federal Regulations publication program is under the direction of the Managing Editor, assisted by Ann Worley.

Title 2—Grants and Agreements

1

Subtitle A—Office of Management and Budget Guidance for Grants and Agreements

PART 1—ABOUT TITLE 2 OF THE CODE OF FEDERAL REGULATIONS AND SUBTITLE A

AUTHORITY: 31 U.S.C. 503; 31 U.S.C. 1111; 41 U.S.C. 405; Reorganization Plan No. 2 of 1970; E.O. 11541, 35 FR 10737, 3 CFR, 1966–1970, p. 939.

SOURCE: 69 FR 26280, May 11, 2004, unless otherwise noted.

Subpart A—Introduction to Title 2 of the CFR

§ 1.100 Content of this title.

This title contains—

(a) Office of Management and Budget (OMB) guidance to Federal agencies on government-wide policies and procedures for the award and administration of grants and agreements; and

(b) Federal agency regulations implementing that OMB guidance.

§ 1.105 Organization and subtitle content.

(a) This title is organized into two subtitles.

(b) The OMB guidance described in § 1.100(a) is published in subtitle A. Publication of the OMB guidance in the CFR does not change its nature—it is guidance and not regulation.

(c) Each Federal agency that publishes regulations implementing the OMB guidance has a chapter in subtitle B in which it issues those regulations. The Federal agency regulations in subtitle B differ in nature from the OMB guidance in subtitle A because the OMB guidance is not regulatory (Federal agency regulations in subtitle B may give regulatory effect to the OMB guidance, to the extent that the agency regulations require compliance with all or portions of the guidance).

§ 1.110 Issuing authorities.

OMB issues this subtitle. Each Federal agency that has a chapter in subtitle B of this title issues that chapter.

Subpart B—Introduction to Subtitle A

§ 1.200 Purpose of chapters I and II.

(a) Chapters I and II of subtitle A provide OMB guidance to Federal agencies that helps ensure consistent and uniform government-wide policies and procedures for the management of the agencies' grants and agreements.

(b) There are two chapters for publication of the guidance because portions of it may be revised as a result of ongoing efforts to streamline and simplify requirements for the award and administration of grants and other financial assistance (and thereby implement the Federal Financial Assistance Management Improvement Act of 1999, Pub. L. 106–107).

(c) The OMB guidance in its initial form—before completion of revisions described in paragraph (b) of this section—is published in chapter II of this subtitle. When revisions to a part of the guidance are finalized, that part is published in chapter I and removed from chapter II.

§ 1.205 Applicability to grants and other funding instruments.

The types of instruments that are subject to the guidance in this subtitle vary from one portion of the guidance to another (note that each part identifies the types of instruments to which it applies). All portions of the guidance apply to grants and cooperative agreements, some portions also apply to other types of financial assistance or nonprocurement instruments, and some portions also apply to procurement contracts. For example, the:

(a) Guidance on debarment and suspension in part 180 of this subtitle applies broadly to all financial assistance and other nonprocurement transactions, and not just to grants and cooperative agreements.

(b) Cost principles in parts 220, 225 and 230 of this subtitle apply to procurement contracts, as well as to financial assistance, although those principles are implemented for procurement contracts through the Federal Acquisition Regulation in title 48 of the CFR, rather than through Federal agency regulations on grants and agreements in this title.

[70 FR 51863, Aug. 31, 2005]

§ 1.210 Applicability to Federal agencies and others.

(a) This subtitle contains guidance that directly applies only to Federal agencies.

(b) The guidance in this subtitle may affect others through each Federal agency's implementation of the guidance, portions of which may apply to—

(1) The agency's awarding or administering officials;

(2) Non-Federal entities that receive or apply for the agency's grants or agreements or receive subawards under those grants or agreements; or

(3) Any other entities involved in agency transactions subject to the guidance in this chapter.

§ 1.215 Relationship to previous issuances.

Although some of the guidance was organized differently within OMB circulars or other documents, much of the guidance in this subtitle existed prior to the establishment of title 2 of the CFR. Specifically:

Guidance in * * *	On * * *	Previously was in * * *
(a) Chapter I, part 180	Nonprocurement debarment and suspension.	OMB guidance that conforms with the government-wide common rule (see 60 FR 33036, June 26, 1995).
(b) Chapter I, part 182	Drug-free workplace requirements	OMB guidance (54 FR 4946, January 31, 1989) and a government-wide common rule (as amended at 68 FR 66534, November 26, 2003).
(c) Chapter II, part 215	Administrative requirements for grants and agreements.	OMB Circular A–110.
(d) Chapter II, part 220	Cost principles for educational institutions.	OMB Circular A–21.
(e) Chapter II, part 225	Cost principles for State, local, and Indian tribal governments.	OMB Circular A–87.
(f) Chapter II, part 230	Cost principles for non-profit organizations.	OMB Circular A–122.
(g) [Reserved]		

[74 FR 28149, June 15, 2009]

§ 1.220 Federal agency implementation of this subtitle.

A Federal agency that awards grants and agreements subject to the guidance in this subtitle implements the guidance in agency regulations in subtitle B of this title and/or in policy and procedural issuances, such as internal instructions to the agency's awarding and administering officials. An applicant or recipient would see the effect of that implementation in the organization and content of the agency's announcements of funding opportunities and in its award terms and conditions.

§ 1.230 Maintenance of this subtitle.

OMB issues guidance in this subtitle after publication in the FEDERAL REGISTER. Any portion of the guidance that has a potential impact on the public is published with an opportunity for public comment.

Subpart C—Responsibilities of OMB and Federal Agencies

§ 1.300 OMB responsibilities.

OMB is responsible for:

(a) Issuing and maintaining the guidance in this subtitle, as described in § 1.230.

(b) Interpreting the policy requirements in this subtitle.

(c) Reviewing Federal agency regulations implementing the requirements of this subtitle, as required by Executive Order 12866.

(d) Conducting broad oversight of government-wide compliance with the guidance in this subtitle.

(e) Performing other OMB functions specified in this subtitle.

§ 1.305   Federal agency responsibilities.

The head of each Federal agency that awards and administers grants and agreements subject to the guidance in this subtitle is responsible for:

(a) Implementing the guidance in this subtitle.

(b) Ensuring that the agency's components and subcomponents comply with the agency's implementation of the guidance.

(c) Performing other functions specified in this subtitle.

CHAPTER I—OFFICE OF MANAGEMENT AND BUDGET GOVERNMENTWIDE GUIDANCE FOR GRANTS AND AGREEMENTS

PARTS 2–24 [RESERVED]

PART 25—UNIVERSAL IDENTIFIER AND CENTRAL CONTRACTOR REGISTRATION

Subpart A—General

Authority: Pub. L. 109–282; 31 U.S.C. 6102.

Source: 75 FR 55673, Sept. 14, 2010, unless otherwise noted.

Subpart A—General

§ 25.100 Purposes of this part.

This part provides guidance to agencies to establish:

(a) The Dun and Bradstreet (D&B) Data Universal Numbering System (DUNS) number as a universal identifier for Federal financial assistance applicants, as well as recipients and their direct subrecipients.

(b) The Central Contractor Registration (CCR) as the repository for standard information about applicants and recipients.

§ 25.105 Types of awards to which this part applies.

This part applies to an agency's grants, cooperative agreements, loans, and other types of Federal financial assistance included in the definition of "award" in § 25.305. The requirements in this part must be implemented for grants and cooperative agreements by October 1, 2010. The requirements in this part must be implemented for all other award forms listed in § 25.200 requirement at a date to be specified in the future.

§ 25.110 Types of recipient and subrecipient entities to which this part applies.

(a) *General.* Through an agency's implementation of the guidance in this part, this part applies to all entities, other than those exempted in paragraphs (b), (c), and (d) of this section, that—

(1) Apply for or receive agency awards; or

(2) Receive subawards directly from recipients of those agency awards.

(b) *Exemptions for individuals.* None of the requirements in this part apply to an individual who applies for or receives Federal financial assistance as a natural person (*i.e.,* unrelated to any business or non-profit organization he or she may own or operate in his or her name).

(c) *Exemptions for Federal agencies.* The requirement in this part to maintain a current registration in the CCR does not apply to an agency of the Federal Government that receives an award from another agency.

(d) *Other exemptions.* (1) Under a condition identified in paragraph (d)(2) of this section, an agency may exempt an entity from an applicable requirement to obtain a DUNS number, register in the CCR, or both.

(i) In that case, the agency must use a generic DUNS number in data it reports to USASpending.gov if reporting for a prime award to the entity is required by the Federal Funding Accountability and Transparency Act (Pub. L. 109–282, hereafter cited as "Transparency Act").

(ii) Agency use of a generic DUNS should be used rarely for prime award reporting because it prevents prime awardees from being able to fulfill the subward or executive compensation reporting required by the Transparency Act.

(2) The conditions under which an agency may exempt an entity are—

(i) For any entity, if the agency determines that it must protect information about the entity from disclosure, to avoid compromising classified information or national security or jeopardizing the personal safety of the entity's clients.

(ii) For a foreign entity applying for or receiving an award or subaward for a project or program performed outside the United States valued at less than $25,000, if the agency deems it to be impractical for the entity to comply with the requirement(s).

(3) Agencies' use of generic DUNS numbers, as described in paragraphs (d)(1) and (2) of this section, should be rare. Having a generic DUNS number limits a recipient's ability to use Governmentwide systems that are needed to comply with some reporting requirements.

§ 25.115   Deviations.

Deviations from this part require the prior approval of the Office of Management and Budget (OMB).

Subpart B—Policy

§ 25.200   Requirements for program announcements, regulations, and application instructions.

(a) Each agency that awards types of Federal financial assistance included in the definition of "award" in § 25.305 must include the requirements described in paragraph (b) of this section in each program announcement, regu-

lation, or other issuance containing instructions for applicants that either:

(1) Is issued on or after the effective date of this part; or

(2) Has application or plan due dates after October 1, 2010.

(b) The program announcement, regulation, or other issuance must require each entity that applies and does not have an exemption under § 25.110 to:

(1) Be registered in the CCR prior to submitting an application or plan;

(2) Maintain an active CCR registration with current information at all times during which it has an active Federal award or an application or plan under consideration by an agency; and

(3) Provide its DUNS number in each application or plan it submits to the agency.

(c) For purposes of this policy:

(1) The applicant is the entity that meets the agency's or program's eligibility criteria and has the legal authority to apply and to receive the award. For example, if a consortium applies for an award to be made to the consortium as the recipient, the consortium must have a DUNS number. If a consortium is eligible to receive funding under an agency program but the agency's policy is to make the award to a lead entity for the consortium, the DUNS number of the lead entity will be used.

(2) A "program announcement" is any paper or electronic issuance that an agency uses to announce a funding opportunity, whether it is called a "program announcement," "notice of funding availability," "broad agency announcement," "research announcement," "solicitation," or some other term.

(3) To remain registered in the CCR database after the initial registration, the applicant is required to review and update on an annual basis from the date of initial registration or subsequent updates its information in the CCR database to ensure it is current, accurate and complete.

§ 25.205   Effect of noncompliance with a requirement to obtain a DUNS number or register in the CCR.

(a) An agency may not make an award to an entity until the entity has complied with the requirements described in § 25.200 to provide a valid DUNS number and maintain an active CCR registration with current information (other than any requirement that is not applicable because the entity is exempted under § 25.110).

(b) At the time an agency is ready to make an award, if the intended recipient has not complied with an applicable requirement to provide a DUNS number or maintain an active CCR registration with current information, the agency:

(1) May determine that the applicant is not qualified to receive an award; and

(2) May use that determination as a basis for making an award to another applicant.

§ 25.210 Authority to modify agency application forms or formats.

To implement the policies in §§ 25.200 and 25.205, an agency may add a DUNS number field to application forms or formats previously approved by OMB, without having to obtain further approval to add the field.

§ 25.215 Requirements for agency information systems.

Each agency that makes awards (as defined in § 25.325) must ensure that systems processing information related to the awards, and other systems as appropriate, are able to accept and use the DUNS number as the universal identifier for financial assistance applicants and recipients.

§ 25.220 Use of award term.

(a) To accomplish the purposes described in § 25.100, an agency must include in each award (as defined in § 25.305) the award term in Appendix A to this part.

(b) An agency may use different letters and numbers than those in Appendix A to this part to designate the paragraphs of the award term, if necessary, to conform the system of paragraph designations with the one used in other terms and conditions in the agency's awards.

Subpart C—Definitions

§ 25.300 Agency.

Agency means a Federal agency as defined at 5 U.S.C. 551(1) and further clarified by 5 U.S.C. 552(f).

§ 25.305 Award.

(a) *Award*, for the purposes of this part, means an award of Federal financial assistance that a non-Federal entity described in § 25.110(a) receives or administers in the form of—

(1) A grant;

(2) A cooperative agreement (which does not include a cooperative research and development agreement pursuant to the Federal Technology Transfer Act of 1986, as amended (15 U.S.C. 3710a));

(3) A loan;

(4) A loan guarantee;

(5) A subsidy;

(6) Insurance;

(7) Food commodities;

(8) A direct appropriation;

(9) Assessed or voluntary contributions; or

(10) Any other financial assistance transaction that authorizes the non-Federal entity's expenditure of Federal funds.

(b) An *Award* does not include:

(1) Technical assistance, which provides services in lieu of money; and

(2) A transfer of title to Federally owned property provided in lieu of money, even if the award is called a grant.

§ 25.310 Central Contractor Registration (CCR).

Central Contractor Registration (CCR) has the meaning given in paragraph C.1 of the award term in Appendix A to this part.

§ 25.315 Data Universal Numbering System (DUNS) Number.

Data Universal Numbering System (DUNS) Number has the meaning given in paragraph C.2 of the award term in Appendix A to this part.

§ 25.320 Entity.

Entity, as it is used in this part, has the meaning given in paragraph C.3 of the award term in Appendix A to this part.

§ 25.325   For-profit organization.

For-profit organization means a non-Federal entity organized for profit. It includes, but is not limited to:

(a) An "S corporation" incorporated under Subchapter S of the Internal Revenue Code;

(b) A corporation incorporated under another authority;

(c) A partnership;

(d) A limited liability corporation or partnership; and

(e) A sole proprietorship.

§ 25.330   Foreign public entity.

Foreign public entity means:

(a) A foreign government or foreign governmental entity;

(b) A public international organization, which is an organization entitled to enjoy privileges, exemptions, and immunities as an international organization under the International Organizations Immunities Act (22 U.S.C. 288–288f);

(c) An entity owned (in whole or in part) or controlled by a foreign government; and

(d) Any other entity consisting wholly or partially of one or more foreign governments or foreign governmental entities.

§ 25.335   Indian Tribe (or "Federally recognized Indian Tribe").

Indian Tribe (or "*Federally recognized Indian Tribe*") means any Indian Tribe, band, nation, or other organized group or community, including any Alaskan Native village or regional or village corporation (as defined in, or established under, the Alaskan Native Claims Settlement Act (43 U.S.C. 1601, *et seq.*)) that is recognized by the United States as eligible for the special programs and services provided by the United States to Indians because of their status as Indians.

§ 25.340   Local government.

Local government means a:

(a) County;

(b) Borough;

(c) Municipality;

(d) City;

(e) Town;

(f) Township;

(g) Parish;

(h) Local public authority, including any public housing agency under the United States Housing Act of 1937;

(i) Special district;

(j) School district;

(k) Intrastate district;

(l) Council of governments, whether or not incorporated as a nonprofit corporation under State law; and

(m) Any other instrumentality of a local government.

§ 25.345   Nonprofit organization.

Nonprofit organization—

(a) Means any corporation, trust, association, cooperative, or other organization that—

(1) Is operated primarily for scientific, educational, service, charitable, or similar purposes in the public interest;

(2) Is not organized primarily for profit; and

(3) Uses net proceeds to maintain, improve, or expand the operations of the organization.

(b) Includes nonprofit—

(1) Institutions of higher education;

(2) Hospitals; and

(3) Tribal organizations other than those included in the definition of "Indian Tribe."

§ 25.350   State.

State means—

(a) Any State of the United States;

(b) The District of Columbia;

(c) Any agency or instrumentality of a State other than a local government or State-controlled institution of higher education;

(d) The Commonwealths of Puerto Rico and the Northern Mariana Islands; and

(e) The United States Virgin Islands, Guam, American Samoa, and a territory or possession of the United States.

§ 25.355   Subaward.

Subaward has the meaning given in paragraph C.4 of the award term in Appendix A to this part.

§ 25.360   Subrecipient.

Subrecipient has the meaning given in paragraph C.5 of the award term in Appendix A to this part.

APPENDIX A TO PART 25—AWARD TERM

I. CENTRAL CONTRACTOR REGISTRATION AND UNIVERSAL IDENTIFIER REQUIREMENTS

A. *Requirement for Central Contractor Registration (CCR)*

Unless you are exempted from this requirement under 2 CFR 25.110, you as the recipient must maintain the currency of your information in the CCR until you submit the final financial report required under this award or receive the final payment, whichever is later. This requires that you review and update the information at least annually after the initial registration, and more frequently if required by changes in your information or another award term.

B. *Requirement for Data Universal Numbering System (DUNS) Numbers*

If you are authorized to make subawards under this award, you:

1. Must notify potential subrecipients that no entity (*see* definition in paragraph C of this award term) may receive a subaward from you unless the entity has provided its DUNS number to you.

2. May not make a subaward to an entity unless the entity has provided its DUNS number to you.

C. *Definitions*

For purposes of this award term:

1. *Central Contractor Registration (CCR)* means the Federal repository into which an entity must provide information required for the conduct of business as a recipient. Additional information about registration procedures may be found at the CCR Internet site (currently at *http://www.ccr.gov*).

2. *Data Universal Numbering System (DUNS) number* means the nine-digit number established and assigned by Dun and Bradstreet, Inc. (D&B) to uniquely identify business entities. A DUNS number may be obtained from D&B by telephone (currently 866–705–5711) or the Internet (currently at *http://fedgov.dnb.com/webform*).

3. *Entity,* as it is used in this award term, means all of the following, as defined at 2 CFR part 25, subpart C:

a. A Governmental organization, which is a State, local government, or Indian Tribe;

b. A foreign public entity;

c. A domestic or foreign nonprofit organization;

d. A domestic or foreign for-profit organization; and

e. A Federal agency, but only as a subrecipient under an award or subaward to a non-Federal entity.

4. *Subaward:*

a. This term means a legal instrument to provide support for the performance of any portion of the substantive project or program for which you received this award and that you as the recipient award to an eligible subrecipient.

b. The term does not include your procurement of property and services needed to carry out the project or program (for further explanation, *see* Sec. ____.210 of the attachment to OMB Circular A–133, "Audits of States, Local Governments, and Non-Profit Organizations").

c. A subaward may be provided through any legal agreement, including an agreement that you consider a contract.

5. *Subrecipient* means an entity that:

a. Receives a subaward from you under this award; and

b. Is accountable to you for the use of the Federal funds provided by the subaward.

PARTS 26–169 [RESERVED]

PART 170—REPORTING SUBAWARD AND EXECUTIVE COMPENSATION INFORMATION

Subpart A—General

Sec.
170.100 Purposes of this part.
170.105 Types of awards to which this part applies.
170.110 Types of entities to which this part applies.
170.115 Deviations.

Subpart B—Policy

170.200 Requirements for program announcements, regulations, and application instructions.
170.220 Award term

Subpart C—Definitions

170.300 Agency.
170.305 Award.
170.310 Entity.
170.315 Executive
170.320 Federal financial assistance subject to the Transparency Act.
170.325 Subaward.
170.330 Total compensation.

APPENDIX A TO PART 170—AWARD TERM

AUTHORITY: Pub. L. 109–282; 31 U.S.C. 6102.

SOURCE: 75 FR 55669, Sept. 14, 2010, unless otherwise noted.

Subpart A—General

§ 170.100 Purposes of this part.

This part provides guidance to agencies to establish requirements for recipients' reporting of information on subawards and executive total compensation, as required by the Federal Funding Accountability and Transparency Act of 2006 (Pub. L. 109–282), as amended by section 6202 of Public Law 110–252, hereafter referred to as "the Transparency Act".

§ 170.105 Types of awards to which this part applies.

This part applies to an agency's grants, cooperative agreements, loans, and other forms of Federal financial assistance subject to the Transparency Act, as defined in § 170.320.

§ 170.110 Types of entities to which this part applies.

(a) *General.* Through an agency's implementation of the guidance in this part, this part applies to all entities, other than those excepted in paragraph (b) of this section, that—

(1) Apply for or receive agency awards; or

(2) Receive subawards under those awards.

(b) *Exceptions.* (1) None of the requirements in this part apply to an individual who applies for or receives an award as a natural person (*i.e.,* unrelated to any business or non-profit organization he or she may own or operate in his or her name).

(2) None of the requirements regarding reporting names and total compensation of an entity's five most highly compensated executives apply unless in the entity's preceding fiscal year, it received—

(i) 80 percent or more of its annual gross revenue in Federal procurement contracts (and subcontracts) and Federal financial assistance awards subject to the Transparency Act, as defined at § 170.320 (and subawards); and

(ii) $25,000,000 or more in annual gross revenue from Federal procurement contracts (and subcontracts) and Federal financial assistance awards subject to the Transparency Act, as defined at § 170.320; and

(3) The public does not have access to information about the compensation of the senior executives through periodic reports filed under section 13(a) or 15(d) of the Securities Exchange Act of 1934 (15 U.S.C. 78m(a), 78o(d)) or section 6104 of the Internal Revenue Code of 1986.

§ 170.115 Deviations.

Deviations from this part require the prior approval of the Office of Management and Budget (OMB).

Subpart B—Policy

§ 170.200 Requirements for program announcements, regulations, and application instructions.

(a) Each agency that makes awards of Federal financial assistance subject to the Transparency Act must include the requirements described in paragraph (b) of this section in each program announcement, regulation, or other issuance containing instructions for applicants:

(1) Under which awards may be made that are subject to Transparency Act reporting requirements; and

(2) That either:

(i) Is issued on or after the effective date of this part; or

(ii) Has application or plan due dates after October 1, 2010.

(b) The program announcement, regulation, or other issuance must require each entity that applies and does not have an exception under § 170.110(b) to ensure they have the necessary processes and systems in place to comply with the reporting requirements should they receive funding.

(c) Federal agencies that obtain post-award data on subaward obligations outside of this policy should take the necessary steps to ensure that their recipients are not required, due to the combination of agency-specific and Transparency Act reporting requirements, to submit the same or similar data multiple times during a given reporting period.

§ 170.220 Award term.

(a) To accomplish the purposes described in § 170.100, an agency must include the award term in Appendix A to this part in each award to a non-Federal entity under which the total funding will include $25,000 or more in Federal funding at any time during the project or program period.

(b) An agency—

(1) Consistent with paragraph (a) of this section, is not required to include the award term in Appendix A to this part if it determines that there is no

possibility that the total amount of Federal funding under the award will equal or exceed $25,000. However, the agency must subsequently amend the award to add the award term if changes in circumstances increase the total Federal funding under the award to $25,000 or more during the project or program period.

Subpart C—Definitions

§ 170.300 Agency.

Agency means a Federal agency as defined at 5 U.S.C. 551(1) and further clarified by 5 U.S.C. 552(f).

§ 170.305 Award.

Award, for the purposes of this part, effective October 1, 2010, means a grant or cooperative agreement. On future dates to be specified by OMB in policy memoranda available at the OMB Web site, award also will include other types of awards of Federal financial assistance subject to the Transparency Act, as defined in § 170.320.

§ 170.310 Entity.

Entity has the meaning given in 2 CFR part 25.

§ 170.315 Executive.

Executive means officers, managing partners, or any other employees in management positions.

§ 170.320 Federal financial assistance subject to the Transparency Act.

Federal financial assistance subject to the Transparency Act means assistance that non-Federal entities described in § 170.105 receive or administer in the form of—

(a) Grants;

(b) Cooperative agreements (which does not include cooperative research and development agreements pursuant to the Federal Technology Transfer Act of 1986, as amended (15 U.S.C. 3710a));

(c) Loans;

(d) Loan guarantees;

(e) Subsidies;

(f) Insurance;

(g) Food commodities;

(h) Direct appropriations;

(i) Assessed and voluntary contributions; and

(j) Other financial assistance transactions that authorize the non-Federal entities' expenditure of Federal funds.

(b) Does not include—

(1) Technical assistance, which provides services in lieu of money;

(2) A transfer of title to Federally owned property provided in lieu of money, even if the award is called a grant;

(3) Any classified award; or

(4) Any award funded in whole or in part with Recovery funds, as defined in section 1512 of the American Recovery and Reinvestment Act of 2009 (Pub. L. 111–5).

EDITORIAL NOTE: At 75 FR 55669, Sept. 14, 2010, § 170.320 was added with two paragraph (b)s.

§ 170.325 Subaward.

Subaward has the meaning given in paragraph e.3 of the award term in Appendix A to this part.

§ 170.330 Total compensation.

Total Compensation has the meaning given in paragraph e.5 of the award term in Appendix A to this part.

APPENDIX A TO PART 170—AWARD TERM

I. Reporting Subawards and Executive Compensation.

a. *Reporting of first-tier subawards.*

1. *Applicability.* Unless you are exempt as provided in paragraph d. of this award term, you must report each action that obligates $25,000 or more in Federal funds that does not include Recovery funds (as defined in section 1512(a)(2) of the American Recovery and Reinvestment Act of 2009, Pub. L. 111–5) for a subaward to an entity (see definitions in paragraph e. of this award term).

2. *Where and when to report.*

i. You must report each obligating action described in paragraph a.1. of this award term to *http://www.fsrs.gov.*

ii. For subaward information, report no later than the end of the month following the month in which the obligation was made. (For example, if the obligation was made on November 7, 2010, the obligation must be reported by no later than December 31, 2010.)

3. *What to report.* You must report the information about each obligating action that the submission instructions posted at *http://www.fsrs.gov* specify.

b. *Reporting Total Compensation of Recipient Executives.*

1. *Applicability and what to report.* You must report total compensation for each of your

five most highly compensated executives for the preceding completed fiscal year, if—

i. the total Federal funding authorized to date under this award is $25,000 or more;

ii. in the preceding fiscal year, you received—

(A) 80 percent or more of your annual gross revenues from Federal procurement contracts (and subcontracts) and Federal financial assistance subject to the Transparency Act, as defined at 2 CFR 170.320 (and subawards); and

(B) $25,000,000 or more in annual gross revenues from Federal procurement contracts (and subcontracts) and Federal financial assistance subject to the Transparency Act, as defined at 2 CFR 170.320 (and subawards); and

iii. The public does not have access to information about the compensation of the executives through periodic reports filed under section 13(a) or 15(d) of the Securities Exchange Act of 1934 (15 U.S.C. 78m(a), 78o(d)) or section 6104 of the Internal Revenue Code of 1986. (To determine if the public has access to the compensation information, see the U.S. Security and Exchange Commission total compensation filings at *http:// www.sec.gov/answers/execomp.htm.*)

2. *Where and when to report.* You must report executive total compensation described in paragraph b.1. of this award term:

i. As part of your registration profile at *http://www.ccr.gov.*

ii. By the end of the month following the month in which this award is made, and annually thereafter.

c. *Reporting of Total Compensation of Subrecipient Executives.*

1. *Applicability and what to report.* Unless you are exempt as provided in paragraph d. of this award term, for each first-tier subrecipient under this award, you shall report the names and total compensation of each of the subrecipient's five most highly compensated executives for the subrecipient's preceding completed fiscal year, if—

i. in the subrecipient's preceding fiscal year, the subrecipient received—

(A) 80 percent or more of its annual gross revenues from Federal procurement contracts (and subcontracts) and Federal financial assistance subject to the Transparency Act, as defined at 2 CFR 170.320 (and subawards); and

(B) $25,000,000 or more in annual gross revenues from Federal procurement contracts (and subcontracts), and Federal financial assistance subject to the Transparency Act (and subawards); and

ii. The public does not have access to information about the compensation of the executives through periodic reports filed under section 13(a) or 15(d) of the Securities Exchange Act of 1934 (15 U.S.C. 78m(a), 78o(d)) or section 6104 of the Internal Revenue Code of 1986. (To determine if the public has access to the compensation information, see the

U.S. Security and Exchange Commission total compensation filings at *http:// www.sec.gov/answers/execomp.htm.*)

2. *Where and when to report.* You must report subrecipient executive total compensation described in paragraph c.1. of this award term:

i. To the recipient.

ii. By the end of the month following the month during which you make the subaward. For example, if a subaward is obligated on any date during the month of October of a given year (*i.e.,* between October 1 and 31), you must report any required compensation information of the subrecipient by November 30 of that year.

d. *Exemptions*

If, in the previous tax year, you had gross income, from all sources, under $300,000, you are exempt from the requirements to report:

i. Subawards, and

ii. The total compensation of the five most highly compensated executives of any subrecipient.

e. *Definitions.* For purposes of this award term:

1. *Entity* means all of the following, as defined in 2 CFR part 25:

i. A Governmental organization, which is a State, local government, or Indian tribe;

ii. A foreign public entity;

iii. A domestic or foreign nonprofit organization;

iv. A domestic or foreign for-profit organization;

v. A Federal agency, but only as a subrecipient under an award or subaward to a non-Federal entity.

2. *Executive* means officers, managing partners, or any other employees in management positions.

3. *Subaward:*

i. This term means a legal instrument to provide support for the performance of any portion of the substantive project or program for which you received this award and that you as the recipient award to an eligible subrecipient.

ii. The term does not include your procurement of property and services needed to carry out the project or program (for further explanation, see Sec. ___ .210 of the attachment to OMB Circular A–133, "Audits of States, Local Governments, and Non-Profit Organizations").

iii. A subaward may be provided through any legal agreement, including an agreement that you or a subrecipient considers a contract.

4. *Subrecipient* means an entity that:

i. Receives a subaward from you (the recipient) under this award; and

ii. Is accountable to you for the use of the Federal funds provided by the subaward.

5. *Total compensation* means the cash and noncash dollar value earned by the executive

during the recipient's or subrecipient's preceding fiscal year and includes the following (for more information see 17 CFR 229.402(c)(2)):

i. *Salary and bonus.*

ii. *Awards of stock, stock options, and stock appreciation rights.* Use the dollar amount recognized for financial statement reporting purposes with respect to the fiscal year in accordance with the Statement of Financial Accounting Standards No. 123 (Revised 2004) (FAS 123R), Shared Based Payments.

iii. *Earnings for services under non-equity incentive plans.* This does not include group life, health, hospitalization or medical reimbursement plans that do not discriminate in favor of executives, and are available generally to all salaried employees.

iv. *Change in pension value.* This is the change in present value of defined benefit and actuarial pension plans.

v. *Above-market earnings on deferred compensation which is not tax-qualified.*

vi. Other compensation, if the aggregate value of all such other compensation (e.g. severance, termination payments, value of life insurance paid on behalf of the employee, perquisites or property) for the executive exceeds $10,000.

PARTS 171–174 [RESERVED]

PART 175—AWARD TERM FOR TRAFFICKING IN PERSONS

Sec.
175.5 Purpose of this part.
175.10 Statutory requirement.
175.15 Award term.
175.20 Referral.
175.25 Definitions.

AUTHORITY: 22 U.S.C. 7104(g); 31 U.S.C. 503; 31 U.S.C. 1111; 41 U.S.C. 405; Reorganization Plan No. 2 of 1970; E.O. 11541, 35 FR 10737, 3 CFR, 1966–1970, p. 939.

SOURCE: 72 FR 63783, Nov. 13, 2007, unless otherwise noted.

§ 175.5 Purpose of this part.

This part establishes a Government-wide award term for grants and cooperative agreements to implement the requirement in paragraph (g) of section 106 of the Trafficking Victims Protection Act of 2000 (TVPA), as amended (22 U.S.C. 7104(g)).

§ 175.10 Statutory requirement.

In each agency award (i.e., grant or cooperative agreement) under which funding is provided to a private entity, section 106(g) of the TVPA, as amended, requires the agency to include a condition that authorizes the agency to terminate the award, without penalty, if the recipient or a subrecipient—

(a) Engages in severe forms of trafficking in persons during the period of time that the award is in effect;

(b) Procures a commercial sex act during the period of time that the award is in effect; or

(c) Uses forced labor in the performance of the award or subawards under the award.

§ 175.15 Award term.

(a) To implement the trafficking in persons requirement in section 106(g) of the TVPA, as amended, a Federal awarding agency must include the award term in paragraph (b) of this section in—

(1) A grant or cooperative agreement to a private entity, as defined in § 175.25(d); and

(2) A grant or cooperative agreement to a State, local government, Indian tribe or foreign public entity, if funding could be provided under the award to a private entity as a subrecipient.

(b) The award term that an agency must include, as described in paragraph (a) of this section, is:

I. Trafficking in persons.

a. *Provisions applicable to a recipient that is a private entity.*

1. You as the recipient, your employees, subrecipients under this award, and subrecipients' employees may not—

i. Engage in severe forms of trafficking in persons during the period of time that the award is in effect;

ii. Procure a commercial sex act during the period of time that the award is in effect; or

iii. Use forced labor in the performance of the award or subawards under the award.

2. We as the Federal awarding agency may unilaterally terminate this award, without penalty, if you or a subrecipient that is a private entity —

i. Is determined to have violated a prohibition in paragraph a.1 of this award term; or

ii. Has an employee who is determined by the agency official authorized to terminate the award to have violated a prohibition in paragraph a.1 of this award term through conduct that is either—

A. Associated with performance under this award; or

B. Imputed to you or the subrecipient using the standards and due process for imputing the conduct of an individual to an organization that are provided in 2 CFR part 180, "OMB Guidelines to Agencies on Governmentwide Debarment and Suspension (Nonprocurement)," as implemented by our agency at *[agency must insert reference here to its regulatory implementation of the OMB guidelines in 2 CFR part 180 (e.g., "2 CFR part XX")].*

b. *Provision applicable to a recipient other than a private entity.* We as the Federal awarding agency may unilaterally terminate this award, without penalty, if a subrecipient that is a private entity—

1. Is determined to have violated an applicable prohibition in paragraph a.1 of this award term; or

2. Has an employee who is determined by the agency official authorized to terminate the award to have violated an applicable prohibition in paragraph a.1 of this award term through conduct that is either—

i. Associated with performance under this award; or

ii. Imputed to the subrecipient using the standards and due process for imputing the conduct of an individual to an organization that are provided in 2 CFR part 180, "OMB Guidelines to Agencies on Governmentwide Debarment and Suspension (Nonprocurement)," as implemented by our agency at *[agency must insert reference here to its regulatory implementation of the OMB guidelines in 2 CFR part 180 (e.g., "2 CFR part XX")].*

c. *Provisions applicable to any recipient.*

1. You must inform us immediately of any information you receive from any source alleging a violation of a prohibition in paragraph a.1 of this award term.

2. Our right to terminate unilaterally that is described in paragraph a.2 or b of this section:

i. Implements section 106(g) of the Trafficking Victims Protection Act of 2000 (TVPA), as amended (22 U.S.C. 7104(g)), and

ii. Is in addition to all other remedies for noncompliance that are available to us under this award.

3. You must include the requirements of paragraph a.1 of this award term in any subaward you make to a private entity.

d. *Definitions.* For purposes of this award term:

1. "Employee" means either:

i. An individual employed by you or a subrecipient who is engaged in the performance of the project or program under this award; or

ii. Another person engaged in the performance of the project or program under this award and not compensated by you including, but not limited to, a volunteer or individual whose services are contributed by a third party as an in-kind contribution toward cost sharing or matching requirements.

2. "Forced labor" means labor obtained by any of the following methods: the recruitment, harboring, transportation, provision, or obtaining of a person for labor or services, through the use of force, fraud, or coercion for the purpose of subjection to involuntary servitude, peonage, debt bondage, or slavery.

3. "Private entity":

i. Means any entity other than a State, local government, Indian tribe, or foreign public entity, as those terms are defined in 2 CFR 175.25.

ii. Includes:

A. A nonprofit organization, including any nonprofit institution of higher education, hospital, or tribal organization other than one included in the definition of Indian tribe at 2 CFR 175.25(b).

B. A for-profit organization.

4. "Severe forms of trafficking in persons," "commercial sex act," and "coercion" have the meanings given at section 103 of the TVPA, as amended (22 U.S.C. 7102).

(c) An agency may use different letters and numbers to designate the paragraphs of the award term in paragraph (b) of this section, if necessary, to conform the system of paragraph designations with the one used in other terms and conditions in the agency's awards.

§ 175.20   Referral.

An agency official should inform the agency's suspending or debarring official if he or she terminates an award based on a violation of a prohibition contained in the award term under § 175.15.

§ 175.25   Definitions.

Terms used in this part are defined as follows:

(a) *Foreign public entity* means:

(1) A foreign government or foreign governmental entity;

(2) A public international organization, which is an organization entitled to enjoy privileges, exemptions, and immunities as an international organization under the International Organizations Immunities Act (22 U.S.C. 288–288f);

(3) An entity owned (in whole or in part) or controlled by a foreign government; and

(4) Any other entity consisting wholly or partially of one or more foreign governments or foreign governmental entities.

(b) *Indian tribe* means any Indian tribe, band, nation, or other organized group or community, including any Alaskan Native village or regional or village corporation (as defined in, or established under, the Alaskan Native Claims Settlement Act (43 U.S.C. 1601, *et seq.*)) that is recognized by the United States as eligible for the special programs and services provided by the United States to Indians because of their status as Indians.

(c) *Local government* means a:

(1) County;

(2) Borough;

(3) Municipality;

(4) City;

(5) Town;

(6) Township;

(7) Parish;

(8) Local public authority, including any public housing agency under the United States Housing Act of 1937;

(9) Special district;

(10) School district;

(11) Intrastate district;

(12) Council of governments, whether or not incorporated as a nonprofit corporation under State law; and

(13) Any other instrumentality of a local government.

(d) *Private entity.* (1) This term means any entity other than a State, local government, Indian tribe, or foreign public entity.

(2) This term includes:

(i) A nonprofit organization, including any nonprofit institution of higher education, hospital, or tribal organization other than one included in the definition of Indian tribe in paragraph (b) of this section.

(ii) A for-profit organization.

(e) *State,* consistent with the definition in section 103 of the TVPA, as amended (22 U.S.C. 7102), means:

(1) Any State of the United States;

(2) The District of Columbia;

(3) Any agency or instrumentality of a State other than a local government or State-controlled institution of higher education;

(4) The Commonwealths of Puerto Rico and the Northern Mariana Islands; and

(5) The United States Virgin Islands, Guam, American Samoa, and a territory or possession of the United States.

PART 176—AWARD TERMS FOR ASSISTANCE AGREEMENTS THAT INCLUDE FUNDS UNDER THE AMERICAN RECOVERY AND REINVESTMENT ACT OF 2009, PUBLIC LAW 111-5

U.S. OBLIGATIONS UNDER INTERNATIONAL
AGREEMENTS (AS OF FEBRUARY 16, 2010)

Subpart C—Wage Rate Requirements under Section 1606 of the American Recovery and Reinvestment Act of 2009

Subpart D—Single Audit Information for Recipients of Recovery Act Funds

AUTHORITY: American Recovery and Reinvestment Act of 2009, Public Law 111–5; Federal Funding Accountability and Transparency Act of 2006, (Pub. L. 109–282), as amended.

SOURCE: 74 FR 18450, Apr. 23, 2009, unless otherwise noted.

§ 176.10 Purpose of this part.

This part establishes Federal Governmentwide award terms for financial assistance awards, namely, grants, cooperative agreements, and loans, to implement the cross-cutting requirements of the American Recovery and Reinvestment Act of 2009, Public Law 111–5 (Recovery Act). These requirements are cross-cutting in that they apply to more than one agency's awards.

§ 176.20 Agency responsibilities (general).

(a) In any assistance award funded in whole or in part by the Recovery Act, the award official shall indicate that the award is being made under the Recovery Act, and indicate what projects and/or activities are being funded under the Recovery Act. This requirement applies whenever Recovery Act funds are used, regardless of the assistance type.

(b) To maximize transparency of Recovery Act funds required for reporting by the assistance recipient, the award official shall consider structuring assistance awards to allow for separately tracking Recovery Act funds.

(c) Award officials shall ensure that recipients comply with the Recovery Act requirements of Subpart A. If the recipient fails to comply with the reporting requirements or other award terms, the award official or other authorized agency action official shall take the appropriate enforcement or termination action in accordance with 2 CFR 215.62 or the agency's implementation of the OMB Circular A–102 grants management common rule. OMB Circular A–102 is available at *http://www.whitehouse.gov/omb/circulars/a102/a102.html.*

(d) The award official shall make the recipient's failure to comply with the reporting requirements a part of the recipient's performance record.

§ 176.30 Definitions.

As used in this part—

Award means any grant, cooperative agreement or loan made with Recovery Act funds. Award official means a person with the authority to enter into, administer, and/or terminate financial assistance awards and make related determinations and findings.

Classified or *"classified information"* means any knowledge that can be communicated or any documentary material, regardless of its physical form or characteristics, that—

(1)(i) Is owned by, is produced by or for, or is under the control of the United States Government; or

(ii) Has been classified by the Department of Energy as privately generated restricted data following the procedures in 10 CFR 1045.21; and

(2) Must be protected against unauthorized disclosure according to Executive Order 12958, Classified National Security Information, April 17, 1995, or classified in accordance with the Atomic Energy Act of 1954.

Recipient means any entity other than an individual that receives Recovery Act funds in the form of a grant, cooperative agreement or loan directly from the Federal Government.

Recovery funds or *Recovery Act funds* are funds made available through the appropriations of the American Recovery and Reinvestment Act of 2009, Public Law 111–5.

Subaward means—

(1) A legal instrument to provide support for the performance of any portion of the substantive project or program for which the recipient received this award and that the recipient awards to an eligible subrecipient;

(2) The term does not include the recipient's procurement of property and services needed to carry out the project or program (for further explanation, see § ___.210 of the attachment to OMB Circular A–133, "Audits of States, Local Governments, and Non-Profit Organizations"). OMB Circular A–133 is available at *http://www.whitehouse.gov/omb/circulars/a133/a133.html.*

(3) A subaward may be provided through any legal agreement, including an agreement that the recipient or a subrecipient considers a contract.

Subcontract means a legal instrument used by a recipient for procurement of property and services needed to carry out the project or program.

Subrecipient or *Subawardee* means a non-Federal entity that expends Federal awards received from a pass-through entity to carry out a Federal program, but does not include an individual that is a beneficiary of such a program. A subrecipient may also be a recipient of other Federal awards directly from a Federal awarding agency. Guidance on distinguishing between a subrecipient and a vendor is provided in § ___.210 of OMB Circular A–133.

Subpart A—Reporting and Registration Requirements Under Section 1512 of the American Recovery and Reinvestment Act of 2009

§ 176.40 Procedure.

The award official shall insert the standard award term in this subpart in all awards funded in whole or in part with Recovery Act funds, except for those that are classified, awarded to individuals, or awarded under mandatory and entitlement programs, except as specifically required by OMB, or expressly exempted from the reporting requirement in the Recovery Act.

§ 176.50 Award term—Reporting and registration requirements under section 1512 of the Recovery Act.

Agencies are responsible for ensuring that their recipients report information required under the Recovery Act in a timely manner. The following award term shall be used by agencies to implement the recipient reporting and registration requirements in section 1512:

(a) This award requires the recipient to complete projects or activities which are funded under the American Recovery and Reinvestment Act of 2009 (Recovery Act) and to report on use of Recovery Act funds provided through this award. Information from these reports will be made available to the public.

(b) The reports are due no later than ten calendar days after each calendar quarter in which the recipient receives the assistance award funded in whole or in part by the Recovery Act.

(c) Recipients and their first-tier recipients must maintain current registrations in the Central Contractor Registration (*http://www.ccr.gov*) at all times during which they have active federal awards funded with Recovery Act funds. A Dun and Bradstreet Data Universal Numbering System (DUNS) Number (*http://www.dnb.com*) is one of the requirements for registration in the Central Contractor Registration.

(d) The recipient shall report the information described in section 1512(c) of the Recovery Act using the reporting instructions and data elements that will be provided online at *http://www.FederalReporting.gov* and ensure that any information that is pre-filled is corrected or updated as needed.

Subpart B—Buy American Requirement Under Section 1605 of the American Recovery and Reinvestment Act of 2009

§ 176.60 Statutory requirement.

Section 1605 of the Recovery Act prohibits use of recovery funds for a project for the construction, alteration, maintenance, or repair of a public building or public work unless all of the iron, steel, and manufactured goods used in the project are produced in the United States. The law requires that this prohibition be applied in a manner consistent with U.S. obligations under international agreements, and it provides for waiver under three circumstances:

(a) Iron, steel, or relevant manufactured goods are not produced in the United States in sufficient and reasonably available quantities and of a satisfactory quality;

(b) Inclusion of iron, steel, or manufactured goods produced in the United States will increase the cost of the overall project by more than 25 percent; or

(c) Applying the domestic preference would be inconsistent with the public interest.

§ 176.70 Policy.

Except as provided in § 176.80 or § 176.90—

(a) None of the funds appropriated or otherwise made available by the Recovery Act may be used for a project for the construction, alteration, maintenance, or repair of a public building or public work (see definitions at §§ 176.140 and 176.160) unless—

(1) The public building or public work is located in the United States; and

(2) All of the iron, steel, and manufactured goods used in the project are produced or manufactured in the United States.

(i) Production in the United States of the iron or steel used in the project requires that all manufacturing processes must take place in the United States, except metallurgical processes involving refinement of steel additives. These requirements do not apply to iron or steel used as components or subcomponents of manufactured goods used in the project.

(ii) There is no requirement with regard to the origin of components or subcomponents in manufactured goods used in the project, as long as the manufacturing occurs in the United States.

(b) Paragraph (a) of this section shall not apply where the Recovery Act requires the application of alternative Buy American requirements for iron, steel, and manufactured goods.

§ 176.80 Exceptions.

(a) When one of the following exceptions applies in a case or category of cases, the award official may allow the recipient to use foreign iron, steel and/or manufactured goods in the project without regard to the restrictions of section 1605 of the Recovery Act:

(1) *Nonavailability.* The head of the Federal department or agency may determine that the iron, steel or relevant manufactured good is not produced or manufactured in the United States in sufficient and reasonably available commercial quantities of a satisfactory quality. The determinations of nonavailability of the articles listed at 48 CFR 25.104(a) and the procedures at 48 CFR 25.103(b)(1) also apply if any of those articles are manufactured goods needed in the project.

(2) *Unreasonable cost.* The head of the Federal department or agency may determine that the cost of domestic iron, steel, or relevant manufactured goods will increase the cost of the overall project by more than 25 percent in accordance with § 176.110.

(3) *Inconsistent with public interest.* The head of the Federal department or agency may determine that application of the restrictions of section 1605 of the Recovery Act would be inconsistent with the public interest.

(b) When a determination is made for any of the reasons stated in this section that certain foreign iron, steel, and/or manufactured goods may be used—

(1) The award official shall list the excepted materials in the award; and

(2) The head of the Federal department or agency shall publish a notice in the FEDERAL REGISTER within two weeks after the determination is made, unless the item has already been determined to be domestically nonavailable. A list of items that are not domestically available is at 48 CFR 25.104(a). The FEDERAL REGISTER notice or information from the notice may be posted by OMB to Recovery.gov. The notice shall include—

(i) The title "Buy American Exception under the American Recovery and Reinvestment Act of 2009";

(ii) The dollar value and brief description of the project; and

(iii) A detailed written justification as to why the restriction is being waived.

§ 176.90 Acquisitions covered under international agreements.

Section 1605(d) of the Recovery Act provides that the Buy American requirement in section 1605 shall be applied in a manner consistent with U.S. obligations under international agreements.

(a) The Buy American requirement set out in § 176.70 shall not be applied where the iron, steel, or manufactured goods used in the project are from a Party to an international agreement, listed in paragraph (b) of this section, and the recipient is required under an international agreement, described in the appendix to this subpart, to treat the goods and services of that Party the same as domestic goods and services. As of January 1, 2010, this obligation shall only apply to projects with an estimated value of $7,804,000 or more and projects that are not specifically excluded from the application of those agreements.

(b) The international agreements that obligate recipients that are covered under an international agreement to treat the goods and services of a Party the same as domestic goods and services and the respective Parties to the agreements are:

(1) The World Trade Organization Government Procurement Agreement (Aruba, Austria, Belgium, Bulgaria, Canada, Chinese Taipei (Taiwan), Cyprus, Czech Republic, Denmark, Estonia, Finland, France, Germany, Greece, Hong Kong, Hungary, Iceland, Ireland, Israel, Italy, Japan, Korea (Republic of), Latvia, Liechtenstein, Lithuania, Luxembourg, Malta, Netherlands, Norway, Poland, Portugal, Romania, Singapore, Slovak Republic, Slovenia, Spain, Sweden, Switzerland, and United Kingdom);

(2) The following Free Trade Agreements:

(i) Dominican Republic-Central America-United States Free Trade Agreement (Costa Rica, Dominican Republic, El Salvador, Guatemala, Honduras, Nicaragua);

(ii) North American Free Trade Agreement (NAFTA) (Canada and Mexico);

(iii) United States-Australia Free Trade Agreement;

(iv) United States-Bahrain Free Trade Agreement;

(v) United States-Chile Free Trade Agreement;

(vi) United States-Israel Free Trade Agreement;

(vii) United States-Morocco Free Trade Agreement;

(viii) United States-Oman Free Trade Agreement;

(ix) United States-Peru Trade Promotion Agreement; and

(x) United States-Singapore Free Trade Agreement.

(3) United States-European Communities Exchange of Letters (May 15, 1995): Austria, Belgium, Bulgaria, Cyprus, Czech Republic, Denmark, Estonia, Finland, France, Germany, Greece, Hungary, Ireland, Italy, Latvia, Lithuania, Luxembourg, Malta, Netherlands, Poland, Portugal, Romania, Slovak Republic, Slovenia, Spain, Sweden, and United Kingdom; and

(4) Agreement between the Government of Canada and the Government of the United States of America on Government Procurement.

[74 FR 18450, Apr. 23, 2009, as amended at 75 FR 14323, Mar. 25, 2010]

§ 176.100 Timely determination concerning the inapplicability of section 1605 of the Recovery Act.

(a) The head of the Federal department or agency involved may make a determination regarding inapplicability of section 1605 to a particular case or to a category of cases.

(b) Before Recovery Act funds are awarded by the Federal agency or obligated by the recipient for a project for the construction, alteration, maintenance, or repair of a public building or public work, an applicant or recipient may request from the award official a determination concerning the inapplicability of section 1605 of the Recovery Act for specifically identified items.

(c) The time for submitting the request and the information and supporting data that must be included in the request are to be specified in the agency's and recipient's request for applications and/or proposals, and as appropriate, in other written communications. The content of those communications should be consistent with the notice in § 176.150 or § 176.170, whichever applies.

(d) The award official must evaluate all requests based on the information provided and may supplement this information with other readily available information.

(e) In making a determination based on the increased cost to the project of using domestic iron, steel, and/or manufactured goods, the award official must compare the total estimated cost of the project using foreign iron, steel and/or relevant manufactured goods to the estimated cost if all domestic iron, steel, and/or relevant manufactured goods were used. If use of domestic iron, steel, and/or relevant manufactured goods would increase the cost of the overall project by more than 25 percent, then the award official shall determine that the cost of the domestic iron, steel, and/or relevant manufactured goods is unreasonable.

§ 176.110 Evaluating proposals of foreign iron, steel, and/or manufactured goods.

(a) If the award official receives a request for an exception based on the cost of certain domestic iron, steel, and/or manufactured goods being unreasonable, in accordance with § 176.80, then the award official shall apply evaluation factors to the proposal to use such foreign iron, steel, and/or manufactured goods as follows:

(1) Use an evaluation factor of 25 percent, applied to the total estimated cost of the project, if the foreign iron, steel, and/or manufactured goods are to be used in the project based on an exception for unreasonable cost requested by the applicant.

(2) Total evaluated cost = project cost estimate + (.25 × project cost estimate, if paragraph (a)(1) of this section applies).

(b) Applicants or recipients also may submit alternate proposals based on use of equivalent domestic iron, steel, and/or manufactured goods to avoid possible denial of Recovery Act funding for the proposal if the Federal Government determines that an exception permitting use of the foreign item(s) does not apply.

(c) If the award official makes an award to an applicant that proposed foreign iron, steel, and/or manufactured goods not listed in the applicable notice in the request for applications or proposals, then the award official must add the excepted materials to the list in the award term.

§ 176.120 Determinations on late requests.

(a) If a recipient requests a determination regarding the inapplicability of section 1605 of the Recovery Act after obligating Recovery Act funds for a project for construction, alteration, maintenance, or repair (late request), the recipient must explain why it could not request the determination before making the obligation or why the need for such determination otherwise was not reasonably foreseeable. If the award official concludes that the recipient should have made the request before making the obligation, the award official may deny the request.

(b) The award official must base evaluation of any late request for a determination regarding the inapplicability of section 1605 of the Recovery Act on information required by § 176.150(c) and (d) or § 176.170(c) and (d) and/or other readily available information.

(c) If a determination, under § 176.80 is made after Recovery Act funds were obligated for a project for construction, alteration, maintenance, or repair that an exception to section 1605 of the Recovery Act applies, the award official must amend the award to allow use of the foreign iron, steel, and/or relevant manufactured goods. When the basis of the exception is nonavailability or public interest, the amended award shall reflect adjustment of the award amount, redistribution of budgeted funds, and/or other appropriate actions taken to cover costs associated with acquiring or using the foreign iron, steel, and/or manufactured goods. When the basis for the exception is the unreasonable cost of domestic iron, steel, and/or manufactured goods the award official shall adjust the award amount or the budget, as appropriate, by at least the differential established in § 176.110(a).

§ 176.130 Noncompliance.

The award official must—

(a) Review allegations of violations of section 1605 of the Recovery Act;

(b) Unless fraud is suspected, notify the recipient of the apparent unauthorized use of foreign iron, steel, and/or manufactured goods and request a reply, to include proposed corrective action;

(c) If the review reveals that a recipient or subrecipient has used foreign iron, steel, and/or manufactured goods without authorization, take appropriate action, including one or more of the following:

(1) Process a determination concerning the inapplicability of section 1605 of the Recovery Act in accordance with § 176.120.

(2) Consider requiring the removal and replacement of the unauthorized foreign iron, steel, and/or manufactured goods.

(3) If removal and replacement of foreign iron, steel, and/or manufactured goods used in a public building or a public work would be impracticable, cause undue delay, or otherwise be detrimental to the interests of the Federal Government, the award official may determine in writing that the foreign iron, steel, and/or manufactured goods need not be removed and replaced. A determination to retain foreign iron, steel, and/or manufactured goods does not constitute a determination that an exception to section 1605 of the Recovery Act applies, and this should be stated in the determination. Further, a determination to retain foreign iron, steel, and/or manufactured goods does not affect the Federal Government's right to reduce the amount of the award by the cost of the steel, iron, or manufactured goods that are used in the project or to take enforcement or termination action in accordance with the agency's grants management regulations.

(4) If the noncompliance is sufficiently serious, consider exercising appropriate remedies, such as withholding cash payments pending correction of the deficiency, suspending or terminating the award, and withholding further awards for the project. Also consider preparing and forwarding a report to the agency suspending or debarring official in accordance with the agency's debarment rule implementing 2 CFR part 180. If the noncompliance appears to be fraudulent, refer the matter to other appropriate agency officials, such as the officer responsible for criminal investigation.

§ 176.140 Award term—Required Use of American Iron, Steel, and Manufactured Goods—Section 1605 of the American Recovery and Reinvestment Act of 2009.

When awarding Recovery Act funds for construction, alteration, maintenance, or repair of a public building or public work that does not involve iron, steel, and/or manufactured goods covered under international agreements, the agency shall use the award term described in the following paragraphs:

(a) *Definitions.* As used in this award term and condition—

(1) *Manufactured good* means a good brought to the construction site for incorporation into the building or work that has been—

(i) Processed into a specific form and shape; or

(ii) Combined with other raw material to create a material that has different properties than the properties of the individual raw materials.

(2) *Public building and public work* means a public building of, and a public work of, a governmental entity (the United States; the District of Columbia; commonwealths, territories, and minor outlying islands of the United States; State and local governments; and multi-State, regional, or interstate entities which have governmental functions). These buildings and works may include, without limitation, bridges, dams, plants, highways, parkways, streets, subways, tunnels, sewers, mains, power lines, pumping stations, heavy generators, railways, airports, terminals, docks, piers, wharves, ways, lighthouses, buoys, jetties, breakwaters, levees, and canals, and the construction, alteration, maintenance, or repair of such buildings and works.

(3) *Steel* means an alloy that includes at least 50 percent iron, between .02

and 2 percent carbon, and may include other elements.

(b) *Domestic preference.* (1) This award term and condition implements Section 1605 of the American Recovery and Reinvestment Act of 2009 (Recovery Act) (Pub. L. 111–5), by requiring that all iron, steel, and manufactured goods used in the project are produced in the United States except as provided in paragraph (b)(3) and (b)(4) of this section and condition.

(2) This requirement does not apply to the material listed by the Federal Government as follows:

[*Award official to list applicable excepted materials or indicate "none"*]

(3) The award official may add other iron, steel, and/or manufactured goods to the list in paragraph (b)(2) of this section and condition if the Federal Government determines that—

(i) The cost of the domestic iron, steel, and/or manufactured goods would be unreasonable. The cost of domestic iron, steel, or manufactured goods used in the project is unreasonable when the cumulative cost of such material will increase the cost of the overall project by more than 25 percent;

(ii) The iron, steel, and/or manufactured good is not produced, or manufactured in the United States in sufficient and reasonably available quantities and of a satisfactory quality; or

(iii) The application of the restriction of section 1605 of the Recovery Act would be inconsistent with the public interest.

(c) *Request for determination of inapplicability of Section 1605 of the Recovery Act.* (1)(i) Any recipient request to use foreign iron, steel, and/or manufactured goods in accordance with paragraph (b)(3) of this section shall include adequate information for Federal Government evaluation of the request, including—

(A) A description of the foreign and domestic iron, steel, and/or manufactured goods;

(B) Unit of measure;

(C) Quantity;

(D) Cost;

(E) Time of delivery or availability;

(F) Location of the project;

(G) Name and address of the proposed supplier; and

(H) A detailed justification of the reason for use of foreign iron, steel, and/or manufactured goods cited in accordance with paragraph (b)(3) of this section.

(ii) A request based on unreasonable cost shall include a reasonable survey of the market and a completed cost comparison table in the format in paragraph (d) of this section.

(iii) The cost of iron, steel, and/or manufactured goods material shall include all delivery costs to the construction site and any applicable duty.

(iv) Any recipient request for a determination submitted after Recovery Act funds have been obligated for a project for construction, alteration, maintenance, or repair shall explain why the recipient could not reasonably foresee the need for such determination and could not have requested the determination before the funds were obligated. If the recipient does not submit a satisfactory explanation, the award official need not make a determination.

(2) If the Federal Government determines after funds have been obligated for a project for construction, alteration, maintenance, or repair that an exception to section 1605 of the Recovery Act applies, the award official will amend the award to allow use of the foreign iron, steel, and/or relevant manufactured goods. When the basis for the exception is nonavailability or public interest, the amended award shall reflect adjustment of the award amount, redistribution of budgeted funds, and/or other actions taken to cover costs associated with acquiring or using the foreign iron, steel, and/or relevant manufactured goods. When the basis for the exception is the unreasonable cost of the domestic iron, steel, or manufactured goods, the award official shall adjust the award amount or redistribute budgeted funds by at least the differential established in 2 CFR 176.110(a).

(3) Unless the Federal Government determines that an exception to section 1605 of the Recovery Act applies, use of foreign iron, steel, and/or manufactured goods is noncompliant with

section 1605 of the American Recovery and Reinvestment Act.

(d) *Data.* To permit evaluation of requests under paragraph (b) of this section based on unreasonable cost, the Recipient shall include the following information and any applicable supporting data based on the survey of suppliers:

FOREIGN AND DOMESTIC ITEMS COST COMPARISON

Description	Unit of measure	Quantity	Cost (dollars)*
Item 1:.			
Foreign steel, iron, or manufactured good			
Domestic steel, iron, or manufactured good			
Item 2:.			
Foreign steel, iron, or manufactured good			
Domestic steel, iron, or manufactured good			

[List name, address, telephone number, email address, and contact for suppliers surveyed. Attach copy of response; if oral, attach summary.]
[Include other applicable supporting information.]
[*Include all delivery costs to the construction site.]

§ 176.150 Notice of Required Use of American Iron, Steel, and Manufactured Goods—Section 1605 of the American Recovery and Reinvestment Act of 2009.

When requesting applications or proposals for Recovery Act programs or activities that may involve construction, alteration, maintenance, or repair of a public building or public work, and do not involve iron, steel, and/or manufactured goods covered under international agreements, the agency shall use the notice described in the following paragraphs in their solicitations:

(a) *Definitions.* Manufactured good, public building and public work, and steel, as used in this notice, are defined in the 2 CFR 176.140.

(b) *Requests for determinations of inapplicability.* A prospective applicant requesting a determination regarding the inapplicability of section 1605 of the American Recovery and Reinvestment Act of 2009 (Pub. L. 111–5) (Recovery Act) should submit the request to the award official in time to allow a determination before submission of applications or proposals. The prospective applicant shall include the information and applicable supporting data required by paragraphs at 2 CFR 176.140(c) and (d) in the request. If an applicant has not requested a determination regarding the inapplicability of 1605 of the Recovery Act before submitting its application or proposal, or has not received a response to a previous request, the applicant shall include the information and supporting data in the application or proposal.

(c) *Evaluation of project proposals.* If the Federal Government determines that an exception based on unreasonable cost of domestic iron, steel, and/or manufactured goods applies, the Federal Government will evaluate a project requesting exception to the requirements of section 1605 of the Recovery Act by adding to the estimated total cost of the project 25 percent of the project cost, if foreign iron, steel, or manufactured goods are used in the project based on unreasonable cost of comparable manufactured domestic iron, steel, and/or manufactured goods.

(d) *Alternate project proposals.* (1) When a project proposal includes foreign iron, steel, and/or manufactured goods not listed by the Federal Government at 2 CFR 176.140(b)(2), the applicant also may submit an alternate proposal based on use of equivalent domestic iron, steel, and/or manufactured goods.

(2) If an alternate proposal is submitted, the applicant shall submit a separate cost comparison table prepared in accordance with 2 CFR 176.140(c) and (d) for the proposal that is based on the use of any foreign iron, steel, and/or manufactured goods for which the Federal Government has not yet determined an exception applies.

(3) If the Federal Government determines that a particular exception requested in accordance with 2 CFR 176.140(b) does not apply, the Federal Government will evaluate only those

proposals based on use of the equivalent domestic iron, steel, and/or manufactured goods, and the applicant shall be required to furnish such domestic items.

§ 176.160 **Award term—Required Use of American Iron, Steel, and Manufactured Goods (covered under International Agreements)—Section 1605 of the American Recovery and Reinvestment Act of 2009.**

When awarding Recovery Act funds for construction, alteration, maintenance, or repair of a public building or public work that involves iron, steel, and/or manufactured goods materials covered under international agreements, the agency shall use the award term described in the following paragraphs:

(a) *Definitions.* As used in this award term and condition—

Designated country—(1) A World Trade Organization Government Procurement Agreement country (Aruba, Austria, Belgium, Bulgaria, Canada, Chinese Taipei (Taiwan), Cyprus, Czech Republic, Denmark, Estonia, Finland, France, Germany, Greece, Hong Kong, Hungary, Iceland, Ireland, Israel, Italy, Japan, Korea (Republic of), Latvia, Liechtenstein, Lithuania, Luxembourg, Malta, Netherlands, Norway, Poland, Portugal, Romania, Singapore, Slovak Republic, Slovenia, Spain, Sweden, Switzerland, and United Kingdom;

(2) A Free Trade Agreement (FTA) country (Australia, Bahrain, Canada, Chile, Costa Rica, Dominican Republic, El Salvador, Guatemala, Honduras, Israel, Mexico, Morocco, Nicaragua, Oman, Peru, or Singapore);

(3) A United States-European Communities Exchange of Letters (May 15, 1995) country: Austria, Belgium, Bulgaria, Cyprus, Czech Republic, Denmark, Estonia, Finland, France, Germany, Greece, Hungary, Ireland, Italy, Latvia, Lithuania, Luxembourg, Malta, Netherlands, Poland, Portugal, Romania, Slovak Republic, Slovenia, Spain, Sweden, and United Kingdom; or

(4) An Agreement between Canada and the United States of America on Government Procurement country (Canada).

Designated country iron, steel, and/or manufactured goods—(1) Is wholly the growth, product, or manufacture of a designated country; or

(2) In the case of a manufactured good that consist in whole or in part of materials from another country, has been substantially transformed in a designated country into a new and different manufactured good distinct from the materials from which it was transformed.

Domestic iron, steel, and/or manufactured good—(1) Is wholly the growth, product, or manufacture of the United States; or

(2) In the case of a manufactured good that consists in whole or in part of materials from another country, has been substantially transformed in the United States into a new and different manufactured good distinct from the materials from which it was transformed. There is no requirement with regard to the origin of components or subcomponents in manufactured goods or products, as long as the manufacture of the goods occurs in the United States.

Foreign iron, steel, and/or manufactured good means iron, steel and/or manufactured good that is not domestic or designated country iron, steel, and/or manufactured good.

Manufactured good means a good brought to the construction site for incorporation into the building or work that has been—

(1) Processed into a specific form and shape; or

(2) Combined with other raw material to create a material that has different properties than the properties of the individual raw materials.

Public building and *public work* means a public building of, and a public work of, a governmental entity (the United States; the District of Columbia; commonwealths, territories, and minor outlying islands of the United States; State and local governments; and multi-State, regional, or interstate entities which have governmental functions). These buildings and works may include, without limitation, bridges, dams, plants, highways, parkways, streets, subways, tunnels, sewers, mains, power lines, pumping stations, heavy generators, railways, airports, terminals, docks, piers, wharves, ways, lighthouses, buoys, jetties, break-waters, levees, and canals, and the con-struction, alteration, maintenance, or repair of such buildings and works.

Steel means an alloy that includes at least 50 percent iron, between .02 and 2 percent carbon, and may include other elements.

(b) *Iron, steel, and manufactured goods.* (1) The award term and condition de-scribed in this section implements—

(i) Section 1605(a) of the American Recovery and Reinvestment Act of 2009 (Pub. L. 111–5) (Recovery Act), by re-quiring that all iron, steel, and manu-factured goods used in the project are produced in the United States; and

(ii) Section 1605(d), which requires application of the Buy American re-quirement in a manner consistent with U.S. obligations under international agreements. The restrictions of section 1605 of the Recovery Act do not apply to designated country iron, steel, and/or manufactured goods. The Buy Amer-ican requirement in section 1605 shall not be applied where the iron, steel or manufactured goods used in the project are from a Party to an international agreement that obligates the recipient to treat the goods and services of that Party the same as domestic goods and services. As of January 1, 2010, this ob-ligation shall only apply to projects with an estimated value of $7,804,000 or more.

(2) The recipient shall use only do-mestic or designated country iron, steel, and manufactured goods in per-forming the work funded in whole or part with this award, except as pro-vided in paragraphs (b)(3) and (b)(4) of this section.

(3) The requirement in paragraph (b)(2) of this section does not apply to the iron, steel, and manufactured goods listed by the Federal Government as follows:

_____

[*Award official to list applicable excepted ma-terials or indicate "none"*]

(4) The award official may add other iron, steel, and manufactured goods to the list in paragraph (b)(3) of this sec-tion if the Federal Government deter-mines that—

(i) The cost of domestic iron, steel, and/or manufactured goods would be unreasonable. The cost of domestic iron, steel, and/or manufactured goods used in the project is unreasonable when the cumulative cost of such ma-terial will increase the overall cost of the project by more than 25 percent;

(ii) The iron, steel, and/or manufac-tured good is not produced, or manu-factured in the United States in suffi-cient and reasonably available com-mercial quantities of a satisfactory quality; or

(iii) The application of the restric-tion of section 1605 of the Recovery Act would be inconsistent with the public interest.

(c) *Request for determination of inappli-cability of section 1605 of the Recovery Act or the Buy American Act.* (1)(i) Any recipient request to use foreign iron, steel, and/or manufactured goods in ac-cordance with paragraph (b)(4) of this section shall include adequate informa-tion for Federal Government evalua-tion of the request, including—

(A) A description of the foreign and domestic iron, steel, and/or manufac-tured goods;

(B) Unit of measure;

(C) Quantity;

(D) Cost;

(E) Time of delivery or availability;

(F) Location of the project;

(G) Name and address of the proposed supplier; and

(H) A detailed justification of the reason for use of foreign iron, steel, and/or manufactured goods cited in ac-cordance with paragraph (b)(4) of this section.

(ii) A request based on unreasonable cost shall include a reasonable survey of the market and a completed cost comparison table in the format in para-graph (d) of this section.

(iii) The cost of iron, steel, or manu-factured goods shall include all deliv-ery costs to the construction site and any applicable duty.

(iv) Any recipient request for a deter-mination submitted after Recovery Act funds have been obligated for a project for construction, alteration, mainte-nance, or repair shall explain why the recipient could not reasonably foresee the need for such determination and could not have requested the deter-mination before the funds were obli-gated. If the recipient does not submit a satisfactory explanation, the award official need not make a determination.

(2) If the Federal Government determines after funds have been obligated for a project for construction, alteration, maintenance, or repair that an exception to section 1605 of the Recovery Act applies, the award official will amend the award to allow use of the foreign iron, steel, and/or relevant manufactured goods. When the basis for the exception is nonavailability or public interest, the amended award shall reflect adjustment of the award amount, redistribution of budgeted funds, and/or other appropriate actions taken to cover costs associated with acquiring or using the foreign iron, steel, and/or relevant manufactured goods.. When the basis for the exception is the unreasonable cost of the domestic iron, steel, or manufactured goods, the award official shall adjust the award amount or redistribute budgeted funds, as appropriate, by at least the differential established in 2 CFR 176.110(a).

(3) Unless the Federal Government determines that an exception to section 1605 of the Recovery Act applies, use of foreign iron, steel, and/or manufactured goods other than designated country iron, steel, and/or manufactured goods is noncompliant with the applicable Act.

(d) *Data.* To permit evaluation of requests under paragraph (b) of this section based on unreasonable cost, the applicant shall include the following information and any applicable supporting data based on the survey of suppliers:

FOREIGN AND DOMESTIC ITEMS COST COMPARISON

Description	Unit of measure	Quantity	Cost (dollars)*
Item 1:			
Foreign steel, iron, or manufactured good			
Domestic steel, iron, or manufactured good			
Item 2:			
Foreign steel, iron, or manufactured good			
Domestic steel, iron, or manufactured good			

[List name, address, telephone number, email address, and contact for suppliers surveyed. Attach copy of response; if oral, attach summary.]
[Include other applicable supporting information.]
[*Include all delivery costs to the construction site.]

[74 FR 18450, Apr. 23, 2009, as amended at 75 FR 14323, Mar. 25, 2010]

§ 176.170 Notice of Required Use of American Iron, Steel, and Manufactured Goods (covered under International Agreements)—Section 1605 of the American Recovery and Reinvestment Act of 2009.

When requesting applications or proposals for Recovery Act programs or activities that may involve construction, alteration, maintenance, or repair of a public building or public work, and involve iron, steel, and/or manufactured goods covered under international agreements, the agency shall use the notice described in the following paragraphs in the solicitation:

(a) *Definitions. Designated country iron, steel, and/or manufactured goods, foreign iron, steel, and/or manufactured good, manufactured good, public building* and *public work,* and *steel,* as used in this provision, are defined in 2 CFR 176.160(a).

(b) *Requests for determinations of inapplicability.* A prospective applicant requesting a determination regarding the inapplicability of section 1605 of the American Recovery and Reinvestment Act of 2009 (Pub. L. 111–5) (Recovery Act) should submit the request to the award official in time to allow a determination before submission of applications or proposals. The prospective applicant shall include the information and applicable supporting data required by 2 CFR 176.160 (c) and (d) in the request. If an applicant has not requested a determination regarding the inapplicability of section 1605 of the Recovery Act before submitting its application or proposal, or has not received a response to a previous request, the applicant shall include the information and supporting data in the application or proposal.

(c) *Evaluation of project proposals.* If the Federal Government determines that an exception based on unreasonable cost of domestic iron, steel, and/or manufactured goods applies, the Federal Government will evaluate a project requesting exception to the requirements of section 1605 of the Recovery Act by adding to the estimated total cost of the project 25 percent of the project cost if foreign iron, steel, or manufactured goods are used based on unreasonable cost of comparable domestic iron, steel, or manufactured goods.

(d) *Alternate project proposals.* (1) When a project proposal includes foreign iron, steel, and/or manufactured goods, other than designated country iron, steel, and/or manufactured goods, that are not listed by the Federal Government in this Buy American notice in the request for applications or proposals, the applicant may submit an alternate proposal based on use of equivalent domestic or designated country iron, steel, and/or manufactured goods.

(2) If an alternate proposal is submitted, the applicant shall submit a separate cost comparison table prepared in accordance with paragraphs 2 CFR 176.160(c) and (d) for the proposal that is based on the use of any foreign iron, steel, and/or manufactured goods for which the Federal Government has not yet determined an exception applies.

(3) If the Federal Government determines that a particular exception requested in accordance with 2 CFR 176.160(b) does not apply, the Federal Government will evaluate only those proposals based on use of the equivalent domestic or designated country iron, steel, and/or manufactured goods, and the applicant shall be required to furnish such domestic or designated country items.

APPENDIX TO SUBPART B OF 2 CFR PART 176—U.S. STATES, OTHER SUB-FEDERAL ENTITIES, AND OTHER ENTITIES SUBJECT TO U.S. OBLIGATIONS UNDER INTERNATIONAL AGREEMENTS (AS OF FEBRUARY 16, 2010)

States	Entities covered	Exclusions	Relevant international agreements
Arizona	Executive branch agencies	....	—WTO GPA. —U.S.-Chile FTA. —U.S.-Singapore FTA.
Arkansas	Executive branch agencies, including universities but excluding the Office of Fish and Game.	Construction services	—WTO GPA. —DR-CAFTA. —U.S.-Australia FTA. —U.S.-Chile FTA. —U.S.-Morocco FTA. —U.S.-Peru TPA. —U.S.-Singapore FTA.
California	Executive branch agencies	....	—WTO GPA. —U.S.-Australia FTA. —U.S.-Chile FTA. —U.S.-Singapore FTA.
Colorado	Executive branch agencies	....	—WTO GPA. —DR-CAFTA. —U.S.-Australia FTA. —U.S.-Chile FTA. —U.S.-Morocco FTA. —U.S.-Peru TPA. —U.S.-Singapore FTA.
Connecticut	—Department of Administrative Services —Department of Transportation.. —Department of Public Works.. —Constituent Units of Higher Education.	....	—WTO GPA. —DR-CAFTA. —U.S.-Australia FTA. —U.S.-Chile FTA. —U.S.-Morocco FTA. —U.S.-Singapore FTA.

States	Entities covered	Exclusions	Relevant international agreements
Delaware	—Administrative Services (Central Procurement Agency). —State Universities. —State Colleges.	Construction-grade steel (including requirements on subcontracts); motor vehicles; coal.	—WTO GPA. —DR-CAFTA (except Honduras). —U.S.-Australia FTA. —U.S.-Chile FTA. —U.S.-Morocco FTA. —U.S.-Singapore FTA.
Florida	Executive branch agencies	Construction-grade steel (including requirements on subcontracts); motor vehicles; coal.	—WTO GPA. —DR-CAFTA. —U.S.-Australia FTA. —U.S.-Chile FTA. —U.S.-Morocco FTA. —U.S.-Peru TPA. —U.S.-Singapore FTA.
Georgia	—Department of Administrative Services. —Georgia Technology Authority.	Beef; compost; mulch	—U.S.-Australia FTA.
Hawaii	Department of Accounting and General Services.	Software developed in the State; construction.	—WTO GPA. —DR-CAFTA (except Honduras). —U.S.-Australia FTA. —U.S.-Chile FTA. —U.S.-Morocco FTA. —U.S.-Singapore FTA.
Idaho	Central Procurement Agency (including all colleges and universities subject to central purchasing oversight).	....	—WTO GPA. —DR-CAFTA (except Honduras). —U.S.-Australia FTA. —U.S.-Chile FTA. —U.S.-Morocco FTA. —U.S.-Singapore FTA.
Illinois	—Department of Central Management Services.	Construction-grade steel (including requirements on subcontracts); motor vehicles; coal.	—WTO GPA. —U.S.-Australia FTA. —U.S.-Chile FTA. —U.S.-Peru TPA. —U.S.-Singapore FTA. —U.S.-EC. Exchange of Letters (applies to EC Member States for procurement not covered by WTO GPA and only where the State considers out-of-State suppliers).
Iowa	—Department of General Services —Department of Transportation. —Board of Regents' Institutions (universities).	Construction-grade steel (including requirements on subcontracts); motor vehicles; coal.	—WTO GPA. —U.S.-Chile FTA. —U.S.-Singapore FTA.
Kansas	Executive branch agencies	Construction services; automobiles; aircraft.	—WTO GPA. —U.S.-Australia FTA. —U.S.-Chile FTA. —U.S.-Morocco FTA. —U.S.-Singapore FTA.
Kentucky	Division of Purchases, Finance and Administration Cabinet.	Construction projects	—WTO GPA. —DR-CAFTA. —U.S.-Australia FTA. —U.S.-Chile FTA. —U.S.-Morocco FTA. —U.S.-Singapore FTA.
Louisiana	Executive branch agencies	....	—WTO GPA. —DR-CAFTA. —U.S.-Australia FTA. —U.S.-Chile FTA. —U.S.-Morocco FTA. —U.S.-Singapore FTA.

34

States	Entities covered	Exclusions	Relevant international agreements
Maine	—Department of Administrative and Financial Services —Bureau of General Services (covering State government agencies and school construction). — Department of Transportation..	Construction-grade steel (including requirements on subcontracts); motor vehicles; coal.	—WTO GPA. —U.S.-Australia FTA. —U.S.-Chile FTA. —U.S.-Singapore FTA.
Maryland	—Office of the Treasury —Department of the Environment.. —Department of General Services.. —Department of Housing and Community Development.. —Department of Human Resources.. —Department of Licensing and Regulation.. —Department of Natural Resources.. —Department of Public Safety and Correctional Services.. —Department of Personnel. .. —Department of Transportation..	Construction-grade steel (including requirements on subcontracts); motor vehicles; coal.	—WTO GPA. —DR-CAFTA. —U.S.-Australia FTA. —U.S.-Chile FTA. —U.S.-Morocco FTA. —U.S.-Singapore FTA.
Massachusetts	—Executive Office for Administration and Finance. —Executive Office of Communities and Development. —Executive Office of Consumer Affairs. —Executive Office of Economic Affairs. —Executive Office of Education. —Executive Office of Elder Affairs. —Executive Office of Environmental Affairs. —Executive Office of Health and Human Service. —Executive Office of Labor. —Executive Office of Public Safety. —Executive Office of Transportation and Construction.	....	—WTO GPA. —U.S.-Chile FTA. —U.S.-Singapore FTA.
Michigan	Department of Management and Budget.	Construction-grade steel (including requirements on subcontracts); motor vehicles; coal.	—WTO GPA. —U.S.-Australia FTA. —U.S.-Chile FTA. —U.S.-Singapore FTA.
Minnesota	Executive branch agencies	....	—WTO GPA. —U.S.-Chile FTA. —U.S.-Singapore FTA.
Mississippi	Department of Finance and Administration.	Services	—WTO GPA. —DR-CAFTA. —U.S.-Australia FTA. —U.S.-Chile FTA. —U.S.-Morocco FTA. —U.S.-Peru TPA. —U.S.-Singapore FTA.
Missouri	—Office of Administration ...... —Division of Purchasing and Materials Management.	....	—WTO GPA. —U.S.-Chile FTA. —U.S.-Singapore FTA.
Montana	Executive branch agencies	Goods	—WTO GPA. —U.S.-Chile FTA. —U.S.-Singapore FTA.
Nebraska	Central Procurement Agency	....	—WTO GPA. —DR-CAFTA. —U.S.-Australia FTA. —U.S.-Chile FTA. —U.S.-Morocco FTA.

States	Entities covered	Exclusions	Relevant international agreements
New Hampshire	Central Procurement Agency	Construction-grade steel (including requirements on subcontracts), motor vehicles; coal.	—U.S.-Singapore FTA. —WTO GPA. —DR-CAFTA. —U.S.-Australia FTA. —U.S.-Chile FTA. —U.S.-Morocco FTA. —U.S.-Singapore FTA.
New York	—State agencies —State university system. —Public authorities and public benefit corporations, with the exception of those entities with multi-State mandates.	Construction-grade steel (including requirements on subcontracts); motor vehicles; coal; transit cars, buses and related equipment.	—WTO GPA. —DR-CAFTA. —U.S.-Australia FTA. —U.S.-Chile FTA. —U.S.-Morocco FTA. —U.S.-Peru TPA. —U.S.-Singapore FTA.
North Dakota	....	....	—U.S.-EC Exchange of Letters (applies to EC Member States and only where the State considers out-of-State suppliers).
Oklahoma	Department of Central Services and all State agencies and departments subject to the Oklahoma Central Purchasing Act.	Construction services; construction-grade steel (including requirements on subcontracts); motor vehicles; coal.	—WTO GPA. —U.S.-Australia FTA. —U.S.-Chile FTA. —U.S.-Peru TPA. —U.S.-Singapore FTA.
Oregon	Department of Administrative Services.	....	—WTO GPA. —DR-CAFTA (except Honduras). —U.S.-Australia FTA. —U.S.-Chile FTA. —U.S.-Morocco FTA. —U.S.-Singapore FTA.
Pennsylvania	Executive branch agencies, including: —Governor's Office. —Department of the Auditor General.. —Treasury Department. —Department of Agriculture. —Department of Banking. —Pennsylvania Securities Commission. —Department of Health. —Department of Transportation. —Insurance Department. —Department of Aging. —Department of Correction. —Department of Labor and Industry. —Department of Military Affairs. —Office of Attorney General. —Department of General Services. —Department of Education. —Public Utility Commission. —Department of Revenue. —Department of State. —Pennsylvania State Police. —Department of Public Welfare. —Fish Commission. —Game Commission. —Department of Commerce. —Board of Probation and Parole. —Liquor Control Board. —Milk Marketing Board. —Lieutenant Governor's Office. —Department of Community Affairs.	Construction-grade steel (including requirements on subcontracts); motor vehicles; coal.	—WTO GPA. —U.S.-Australia FTA. —U.S.-Chile FTA. —U.S.-Singapore FTA.

States	Entities covered	Exclusions	Relevant international agreements
	—Pennsylvania Historical and Museum Commission. —Pennsylvania Emergency Management Agency. —State Civil Service Commission. —Pennsylvania Public Television Network. —Department of Environmental Resources. —State Tax Equalization Board. —Department of Public Welfare. —State Employees' Retirement System. —Pennsylvania Municipal Retirement Board. —Public School Employees' Retirement System. —Pennsylvania Crime Commission. —Executive Offices.		
Rhode Island	Executive branch agencies	Boats, automobiles, buses and related equipment.	—WTO GPA. —DR-CAFTA (except Honduras). —U.S.-Australia FTA. —U.S.-Chile FTA. —U.S.-Morocco FTA. —U.S.-Singapore FTA.
South Dakota	Central Procuring Agency (including universities and penal institutions).	Beef	—WTO GPA. —DR-CAFTA. —U.S.-Australia FTA. —U.S.-Chile FTA. —U.S.-Morocco FTA. —U.S.-Singapore FTA.
Tennessee	Executive branch agencies	Services; construction	—WTO GPA-U.S.-Australia FTA. —U.S.-Chile FTA. —U.S.-Singapore FTA.
Texas	Texas Building and Procurement Commission.	....	—WTO GPA. —DR-CAFTA. —U.S.-Australia FTA. —U.S.-Chile FTA. —U.S.-Morocco FTA. —U.S.-Peru TPA. —U.S.-Singapore FTA.
Utah	Executive branch agencies	....	—WTO GPA. —DR-CAFTA (except Honduras). —U.S.-Australia FTA. —U.S.-Chile FTA. —U.S.-Morocco FTA. —U.S.-Peru TPA. —U.S.-Singapore FTA.
Vermont	Executive branch agencies	....	—WTO GPA. —DR-CAFTA. —U.S.-Australia FTA. —U.S.-Chile FTA. —U.S.-Morocco FTA. —U.S.-Singapore FTA.
Washington	Executive branch agencies, including: —General Administration. —Department of Transportation. —State Universities.	Fuel; paper products; boats; ships; and vessels.	—WTO GPA. —DR-CAFTA. —U.S.-Australia FTA. —U.S.-Chile FTA. —U.S.-Morocco FTA. —U.S.-Singapore FTA.
West Virginia	....	....	—U.S.-EC Exchange of Letters (applies to EC Member States and only where the State considers out-of-State suppliers).

States	Entities covered	Exclusions	Relevant international agreements
Wisconsin	Executive branch agencies, including: —Department of Administration. —State Correctional Institutions. —Department of Development. —Educational Communications Board. —Department of Employment Relations. —State Historical Society. —Department of Health and Social Services. —Insurance Commissioner. —Department of Justice. —Lottery Board. —Department of Natural Resources. —Administration for Public Instruction. —Racing Board. —Department of Revenue. —State Fair Park Board. —Department of Transportation. —State University System.		—WTO GPA. —U.S.-Chile FTA. —U.S.-Singapore FTA.
Wyoming	—Procurement Services Division —Wyoming Department of Transportation. —University of Wyoming.	Construction-grade steel (including requirements on subcontracts); motor vehicles; coal.	—WTO GPA. —DR-CAFTA. —U.S.-Australia FTA. —U.S.-Chile FTA. —U.S.-Morocco FTA. —U.S.-Singapore FTA.

Other sub-federal entities	Entities covered	Exclusions	Relevant international agreements
Puerto Rico	—Department of State —Department of Justice. —Department of the Treasury. —Department of Labor and Human Resources. —Department of Natural and Environmental Resources. —Department of Consumer Affairs. —Department of Sports and Recreation.	Construction services —Department of Economic Development and Commerce.	—DR-CAFTA. —U.S.-Peru TPA.
Port Authority of New York and New Jersey.		Restrictions attached to Federal funds for airport projects; maintenance, repair and operating materials and supplies.	—WTO GPA (except Canada). —U.S.-Chile FTA. —U.S.-Singapore FTA.
Port of Baltimore		Restrictions attached to Federal funds for airport projects.	—WTO GPA (except Canada). —U.S.-Chile FTA. —U.S.-Singapore FTA.
New York Power Authority		Restrictions attached to Federal funds for airport projects; conditions specified for the State of New York	—WTO GPA (except Canada). —U.S.-Chile FTA. —U.S.-Singapore FTA.
Massachusetts Port Authority			U.S.-EC Exchange of Letters (applies to EC Member States and only where the Port Authority considers out-of-State suppliers).

States	Entities covered	Exclusions	Relevant international agreements
Boston, Chicago, Dallas, Detroit, Indianapolis, Nashville, and San Antonio.	....	....	U.S.-EC Exchange of Letters (only applies to EC Member States and where the city considers out-of-city suppliers).

Other entities	Entities covered	Exclusions	Relevant international agreements
Rural Utilities Service (waiver of Buy American restriction on financing for all power generation projects).	Any recipient	....	—WTO GPA. —DR-CAFTA. —NAFTA. —U.S.-Australia FTA. —U.S.-Bahrain FTA. —U.S.-Chile FTA. —U.S.-Morocco FTA. —U.S.-Oman FTA. —U.S.-Peru TPA. —U.S.-Singapore FTA.
Rural Utilities Service (waiver of Buy American restriction on financing for tele-communications projects).	Any recipient	....	—NAFTA. —U.S.-Israel FTA.
U.S. Department of Agriculture, Rural Utilities Services, *Water and Waste Disposal Programs* (exclusion of Canadian iron, steel and manufactured products from domestic purchasing restriction in Section 1605 of American Recovery and Reinvestment Act of 2009).	Any recipient	....	U.S.-Canada Agreement.
U.S. Department of Agriculture, Rural Housing Service, *Community Facilities Program* (exclusion of Canadian iron, steel and manufactured products from domestic purchasing restriction in Section 1605 of American Recovery and Reinvestment Act of 2009).	Any recipient	....	U.S.-Canada Agreement.
U.S. Department of Energy, Office of Energy Efficiency and Renewable Energy, *Energy Efficiency and Conservation Block Grants* (exclusion of Canadian iron, steel and manufactured products from domestic purchasing restriction in Section 1605 of American Recovery and Reinvestment Act of 2009).	Any recipient	....	U.S.-Canada Agreement.
U.S. Department of Energy, Office of Energy Efficiency and Renewable Energy, *State Energy Program* (exclusion of Canadian iron, steel and manufactured products from domestic purchasing restriction in Section 1605 of American Recovery and Reinvestment Act of 2009 (ARRA).	Any recipient	....	U.S.-Canada Agreement.

States	Entities covered	Exclusions	Relevant international agreements
U.S. Department of Housing and Urban Development, Office of Community Planning and Development, *Community Development Block Grants Recovery* (CDBG–R) (exclusion of Canadian iron, steel and manufactured products from domestic purchasing restriction in Section 1605 of American Recovery and Reinvestment Act of 2009).	Any recipient	....	U.S.-Canada Agreement.
U.S. Department of Housing and Urban Development, Office of Public and Indian Housing, *Public Housing Capital Fund* (exclusion of Canadian iron, steel and manufactured products from domestic purchasing restriction in Section 1605 of American Recovery and Reinvestment Act of 2009).	Any recipient	....	U.S.-Canada Agreement.
U.S. Environmental Protection *Clean Water and Drinking Water State Revolving Funds* Agency for projects funded by reallocated ARRA funds where the contracts are signed after February 17, 2010 (exclusion of Canadian iron, steel and manufactured products from domestic purchasing restriction in Section 1605 of American Recovery and Reinvestment Act of 2009).	Any recipient	....	U.S.-Canada Agreement.

General Exceptions: The following restrictions and exceptions are excluded from U.S. obligations under international agreements:

1. The restrictions attached to Federal funds to States for mass transit and highway projects.

2. Dredging.

The World Trade Organization Government Procurement Agreement (WTO GPA) Parties: Aruba, Austria, Belgium, Bulgaria, Canada, Chinese Taipei (Taiwan), Cyprus, Czech Republic, Denmark, Estonia, Finland, France, Germany, Greece, Hong Kong, Hungary, Iceland, Ireland, Israel, Italy, Japan, Korea (Republic of), Latvia, Liechtenstein, Lithuania, Luxembourg, Malta, Netherlands, Norway, Poland, Portugal, Romania, Singapore, Slovak Republic, Slovenia, Spain, Sweden, Switzerland, and United Kingdom.

The Free Trade Agreements and the respective Parties to the agreements are:

(1) Dominican Republic-Central America-United States Free Trade Agreement (DR–CAFTA): Costa Rica, Dominican Republic, El Salvador, Guatemala, Honduras, and Nicaragua;

(2) North American Free Trade Agreement (NAFTA): Canada and Mexico;

(3) United States-Australia Free Trade Agreement (U.S.-Australia FTA);

(4) United States-Bahrain Free Trade Agreement (U.S.-Bahrain FTA);

(5) United States-Chile Free Trade Agreement (U.S.-Chile FTA);

(6) United States-Israel Free Trade Agreement (U.S.-Israel FTA);

(7) United States-Morocco Free Trade Agreement (U.S.-Morocco FTA);

(8) United States-Oman Free Trade Agreement (U.S.-Oman FTA);

(9) United States-Peru Trade Promotion Agreement (U.S.-Peru TPA); and

(10) United States-Singapore Free Trade Agreement (U.S.-Singapore FTA).

United States-European Communities Exchange of Letters (May 30, 1995) (U.S.-EC Exchange of Letters) applies to EC Member States: Austria, Belgium, Bulgaria, Cyprus, Czech Republic, Denmark, Estonia, Finland, France, Germany, Greece, Hungary, Ireland, Italy, Latvia, Lithuania, Luxembourg, Malta, Netherlands, Poland, Portugal, Romania, Slovak Republic, Slovenia, Spain, Sweden, and United Kingdom.

Agreement between the Government of Canada and the Government of the United States of

40

America on Government Procurement (Feb. 10, 2010) (U.S.-Canada Agreement): Applies only to Canada.

[75 FR 14324, Mar. 25, 2010]

Subpart C—Wage Rate Requirements Under Section 1606 of the American Recovery and Reinvestment Act of 2009

§ 176.180 Procedure.

The award official shall insert the standard award term in this subpart in all awards funded in whole or in part with Recovery Act funds.

§ 176.190 Award term—Wage rate requirements under Section 1606 of the Recovery Act.

When issuing announcements or requesting applications for Recovery Act programs or activities that may involve construction, alteration, maintenance, or repair the agency shall use the award term described in the following paragraphs:

(a) Section 1606 of the Recovery Act requires that all laborers and mechanics employed by contractors and subcontractors on projects funded directly by or assisted in whole or in part by and through the Federal Government pursuant to the Recovery Act shall be paid wages at rates not less than those prevailing on projects of a character similar in the locality as determined by the Secretary of Labor in accordance with subchapter IV of chapter 31 of title 40, United States Code.

Pursuant to Reorganization Plan No. 14 and the Copeland Act, 40 U.S.C. 3145, the Department of Labor has issued regulations at 29 CFR parts 1, 3, and 5 to implement the Davis-Bacon and related Acts. Regulations in 29 CFR 5.5 instruct agencies concerning application of the standard Davis-Bacon contract clauses set forth in that section. Federal agencies providing grants, cooperative agreements, and loans under the Recovery Act shall ensure that the standard Davis-Bacon contract clauses found in 29 CFR 5.5(a) are incorporated in any resultant covered contracts that are in excess of $2,000 for construction, alteration or repair (including painting and decorating).

(b) For additional guidance on the wage rate requirements of section 1606, contact your awarding agency. Recipients of grants, cooperative agreements and loans should direct their initial inquiries concerning the application of Davis-Bacon requirements to a particular federally assisted project to the Federal agency funding the project. The Secretary of Labor retains final coverage authority under Reorganization Plan Number 14.

Subpart D—Single Audit Information for Recipients of Recovery Act Funds

§ 176.200 Procedure.

The award official shall insert the standard award term in this subpart in all awards funded in whole or in part with Recovery Act funds.

§ 176.210 Award term—Recovery Act transactions listed in Schedule of Expenditures of Federal Awards and Recipient Responsibilities for Informing Subrecipients.

The award term described in this section shall be used by agencies to clarify recipient responsibilities regarding tracking and documenting Recovery Act expenditures:

(a) To maximize the transparency and accountability of funds authorized under the American Recovery and Reinvestment Act of 2009 (Pub. L. 111–5) (Recovery Act) as required by Congress and in accordance with 2 CFR 215.21 "Uniform Administrative Requirements for Grants and Agreements" and OMB Circular A–102 Common Rules provisions, recipients agree to maintain records that identify adequately the source and application of Recovery Act funds. OMB Circular A–102 is available at *http://www.whitehouse.gov/omb/circulars/a102/a102.html.*

(b) For recipients covered by the Single Audit Act Amendments of 1996 and OMB Circular A–133, "Audits of States, Local Governments, and Non-Profit Organizations," recipients agree to separately identify the expenditures for Federal awards under the Recovery Act on the Schedule of Expenditures of Federal Awards (SEFA) and the Data Collection Form (SF–SAC) required by OMB Circular A–133. OMB Circular A–133 is available at *http://www.whitehouse.gov/omb/circulars/a133/*

a133.html. This shall be accomplished by identifying expenditures for Federal awards made under the Recovery Act separately on the SEFA, and as separate rows under Item 9 of Part III on the SF–SAC by CFDA number, and inclusion of the prefix "ARRA-" in identifying the name of the Federal program on the SEFA and as the first characters in Item 9d of Part III on the SF–SAC.

(c) Recipients agree to separately identify to each subrecipient, and document at the time of subaward and at the time of disbursement of funds, the Federal award number, CFDA number, and amount of Recovery Act funds. When a recipient awards Recovery Act funds for an existing program, the information furnished to subrecipients shall distinguish the subawards of incremental Recovery Act funds from regular subawards under the existing program.

(d) Recipients agree to require their subrecipients to include on their SEFA information to specifically identify Recovery Act funding similar to the requirements for the recipient SEFA described above. This information is needed to allow the recipient to properly monitor subrecipient expenditure of ARRA funds as well as oversight by the Federal awarding agencies, Offices of Inspector General and the Government Accountability Office.

PARTS 177–179 [RESERVED]

PART 180—OMB GUIDELINES TO AGENCIES ON GOVERNMENT-WIDE DEBARMENT AND SUSPENSION (NONPROCUREMENT)

180.315 May I use the services of an excluded person as a principal under a covered transaction?

180.320 Must I verify that principals of my covered transactions are eligible to participate?

180.325 What happens if I do business with an excluded person in a covered transaction?

180.330 What requirements must I pass down to persons at lower tiers with whom I intend to do business?

DISCLOSING INFORMATION—PRIMARY TIER PARTICIPANTS

180.335 What information must I provide before entering into a covered transaction with a Federal agency?

180.340 If I disclose unfavorable information required under § 180.335 will I be prevented from participating in the transaction?

180.345 What happens if I fail to disclose information required under § 180.335?

180.350 What must I do if I learn of information required under § 180.335 after entering into a covered transaction with a Federal agency?

DISCLOSING INFORMATION—LOWER TIER PARTICIPANTS

180.355 What information must I provide to a higher tier participant before entering into a covered transaction with that participant?

180.360 What happens if I fail to disclose information required under § 180.355?

180.365 What must I do if I learn of information required under § 180.355 after entering into a covered transaction with a higher tier participant?

Subpart D—Responsibilities of Federal Agency Officials Regarding Transactions

180.400 May I enter into a transaction with an excluded or disqualified person?

180.405 May I enter into a covered transaction with a participant if a principal of the transaction is excluded?

180.410 May I approve a participant's use of the services of an excluded person?

180.415 What must I do if a Federal agency excludes the participant or a principal after I enter into a covered transaction?

180.420 May I approve a transaction with an excluded or disqualified person at a lower tier?

180.425 When do I check to see if a person is excluded or disqualified?

180.430 How do I check to see if a person is excluded or disqualified?

180.435 What must I require of a primary tier participant?

180.440 What action may I take if a primary tier participant knowingly does business with an excluded or disqualified person?

180.445 What action may I take if a primary tier participant fails to disclose the information required under § 180.335?

180.450 What may I do if a lower tier participant fails to disclose the information required under § 180.355 to the next higher tier?

Subpart E—Excluded Parties List System

180.500 What is the purpose of the Excluded Parties List System (EPLS)?

180.505 Who uses the EPLS?

180.510 Who maintains the EPLS?

180.515 What specific information is in the EPLS?

180.520 Who places the information into the EPLS?

180.525 Whom do I ask if I have questions about a person in the EPLS?

180.530 Where can I find the EPLS?

Subpart F—General Principles Relating to Suspension and Debarment Actions

180.600 How do suspension and debarment actions start?

180.605 How does suspension differ from debarment?

180.610 What procedures does a Federal agency use in suspension and debarment actions?

180.615 How does a Federal agency notify a person of a suspension or debarment action?

180.620 Do Federal agencies coordinate suspension and debarment actions?

180.625 What is the scope of a suspension or debarment?

180.630 May a Federal agency impute the conduct of one person to another?

180.635 May a Federal agency settle a debarment or suspension action?

180.640 May a settlement include a voluntary exclusion?

180.645 Do other Federal agencies know if an agency agrees to a voluntary exclusion?

Subpart G—Suspension

180.700 When may the suspending official issue a suspension?

180.705 What does the suspending official consider in issuing a suspension?

180.710 When does a suspension take effect?

180.715 What notice does the suspending official give me if I am suspended?

180.720 How may I contest a suspension?

180.725 How much time do I have to contest a suspension?

180.730 What information must I provide to the suspending official if I contest the suspension?

180.735 Under what conditions do I get an additional opportunity to challenge the facts on which the suspension is based?

AUTHORITY: Sec. 2455, Pub. L. 103–355, 108 Stat. 3327; E.O. 12549, 3 CFR, 1986 Comp., p.189; E.O. 12689, 3 CFR, 1989 Comp., p. 235.

SOURCE: 70 FR 51865, Aug. 31, 2005, unless otherwise noted.

§ 180.5 What does this part do?

This part provides Office of Management and Budget (OMB) guidance for Federal agencies on the governmentwide debarment and suspension system for nonprocurement programs and activities.

§ 180.10 How is this part organized?

This part is organized in two segments.

(a) Sections 180.5 through 180.45 contain general policy direction for Federal agencies' use of the standards in subparts A through I of this part.

(b) Subparts A through I of this part contain uniform governmentwide standards that Federal agencies are to use to specify—

(1) The types of transactions that are covered by the nonprocurement debarment and suspension system;

(2) The effects of an exclusion under that nonprocurement system, including reciprocal effects with the governmentwide debarment and suspension system for procurement;

(3) The criteria and minimum due process to be used in nonprocurement debarment and suspension actions; and

(4) Related policies and procedures to ensure the effectiveness of those actions.

§ 180.15 To whom does the guidance apply?

The guidance provides OMB guidance only to Federal agencies. Publication of the guidance in the CFR does not change its nature—it is guidance and not regulation. Federal agencies' implementation of the guidance governs the rights and responsibilities of other persons affected by the nonprocurement debarment and suspension system.

§180.20 What must a Federal agency do to implement these guidelines?

As required by Section 3 of E.O. 12549, each Federal agency with nonprocurement programs and activities covered by subparts A through I of the guidance must issue regulations consistent with those subparts.

§180.25 What must a Federal agency address in its implementation of the guidance?

Each Federal agency implementing regulation:

(a) Must establish policies and procedures for that agency's nonprocurement debarment and suspension programs and activities that are consistent with the guidance. When adopted by a Federal agency, the provisions of the guidance has regulatory effect for that agency's programs and activities.

(b) Must address some matters for which these guidelines give each Federal agency some discretion. Specifically, the regulation must—

(1) Identify either the Federal agency head or the title of the designated official who is authorized to grant exceptions under §180.135 to let an excluded person participate in a covered transaction.

(2) State whether the agency includes as covered transactions an additional tier of contracts awarded under covered nonprocurement transactions, as permitted under §180.220(c).

(3) Identify the method(s) an agency official may use, when entering into a covered transaction with a primary tier participant, to communicate to the participant the requirements described in §180.435. Examples of methods are an award term that requires compliance as a condition of the award; an assurance of compliance obtained at time of application; or a certification.

(4) State whether the Federal agency specifies a particular method that participants must use to communicate compliance requirements to lower-tier participants, as described in §180.330(a). If there is a specified method, the regulation needs to require agency officials,

when entering into covered transactions with primary tier participants, to communicate that requirement.

(c) May also, at the agency's option:

(1) Identify any specific types of transactions that the Federal agency includes as "nonprocurement transactions" in addition to the examples provided in §180.970.

(2) Identify any types of nonprocurement transactions that the Federal agency exempts from coverage under these guidelines, as authorized under §180.215(g)(2).

(3) Identify specific examples of types of individuals who would be "principals" under the Federal agency's nonprocurement programs and transactions, in addition to the types of individuals described at §180.995.

(4) Specify the Federal agency's procedures, if any, by which a respondent may appeal a suspension or debarment decision.

(5) Identify by title the officials designated by the Federal agency head as debarring officials under §180.930 or suspending officials under §180.1010.

(6) Include a subpart covering disqualifications, as authorized in §180.45.

(7) Include any provisions authorized by OMB.

[70 FR 51865, Aug. 31, 2005, as amended at 71 FR 66432, Nov. 15, 2006]

§180.30 Where does a Federal agency implement these guidelines?

Each Federal agency that participates in the governmentwide nonprocurement debarment and suspension system must issue a regulation implementing these guidelines within its chapter in subtitle B of this title of the Code of Federal Regulations.

§180.35 By when must a Federal agency implement these guidelines?

Federal agencies must submit proposed regulations to the OMB for review within nine months of the issuance of these guidelines and issue final regulations within eighteen months of these guidelines.

§180.40 How are these guidelines maintained?

The Interagency Committee on Debarment and Suspension established by section 4 of E.O. 12549 recommends to the OMB any needed revisions to the guidelines in this part. The OMB publishes proposed changes to the guidelines in the FEDERAL REGISTER for public comment, considers comments with the help of the Interagency Committee on Debarment and Suspension, and issues the final guidelines.

§ 180.45 Do these guidelines cover persons who are disqualified, as well as those who are excluded from nonprocurement transactions?

A Federal agency may add a subpart covering disqualifications to its regulation implementing these guidelines, but the guidelines in subparts A through I of this part—

(a) Address disqualified persons only to—

(1) Provide for their inclusion in the EPLS; and

(2) State responsibilities of Federal agencies and participants to check for disqualified persons before entering into covered transactions.

(b) Do not specify the—

(1) Transactions for which a disqualified person is ineligible. Those transactions vary on a case-by-case basis, because they depend on the language of the specific statute, Executive order or regulation that caused the disqualification;

(2) Entities to which a disqualification applies; or

(3) Process that a Federal agency uses to disqualify a person. Unlike exclusion under subparts A through I of this part, disqualification is frequently not a discretionary action that a Federal agency takes, and may include special procedures.

Subpart A—General

§ 180.100 How are subparts A through I organized?

(a) Each subpart contains information related to a broad topic or specific audience with special responsibilities, as shown in the following table:

In subpart . . .	You will find provisions related to . . .
A	general information about Subparts A through I of this part.
B	the types of transactions that are covered by the Governmentwide nonprocurement suspension and debarment system.
C	the responsibilities of persons who participate in covered transactions.
D	the responsibilities of Federal agency officials who are authorized to enter into covered transactions.
E	the responsibilities of Federal agencies for entering information into the EPLS
F	the general principles governing suspension, debarment, voluntary exclusion and settlement.
G	suspension actions.
H	debarment actions.
I	definitions of terms used in this part.

(b) The following table shows which subparts may be of special interest to you, depending on who you are:

If you are . . .	See Subpart(s) . . .
(1) a participant or principal in a nonprocurement transaction	A, B, C and I.
(2) a respondent in a suspension action	A, B, F, G and I.
(3) a respondent in a debarment action	A, B, F, H and I.
(4) a suspending official	A, B, E, F, G and I.
(5) a debarring official	A, B, D, F, H and I.
(6) an Federal agency official authorized to enter into a covered transaction	A, B, D, E and I.

§ 180.105 How is this part written?

(a) This part uses a "plain language" format to make it easier for the general public and business community to use. The section headings and text, often in the form of questions and answers, must be read together.

(b) Pronouns used within this part, such as "I" and "you," change from subpart to subpart depending on the audience being addressed.

(c) The "Covered Transactions" diagram in the appendix to this part shows the levels or "tiers" at which a Federal agency may enforce an exclusion.

§ 180.110 Do terms in this part have special meanings?

This part uses terms throughout the text that have special meaning. Those terms are defined in subpart I of this part. For example, three important terms are—

(a) *Exclusion or excluded,* which refers only to discretionary actions taken by a suspending or debarring official under Executive Order 12549 and Executive Order 12689 or under the Federal Acquisition Regulation (48 CFR part 9, subpart 9.4);

(b) *Disqualification or disqualified,* which refers to prohibitions under specific statutes, executive orders (other than Executive Order 12549 and Executive Order 12689), or other authorities. Disqualifications frequently are not subject to the discretion of a Federal agency official, may have a different scope than exclusions, or have special conditions that apply to the disqualification; and

(c) *Ineligibility or ineligible,* which generally refers to a person who is either excluded or disqualified.

§ 180.115 What do Subparts A through I of this part do?

Subparts A through I of this part provide for reciprocal exclusion of persons who have been excluded under the Federal Acquisition Regulation, and provide for the consolidated listing of all persons who are excluded, or disqualified by statute, executive order or other legal authority.

§ 180.120 Do subparts A through I of this part apply to me?

Portions of subparts A through I of this part (see table at § 180.100(b)) apply to you if you are a—

(a) Person who has been, is, or may reasonably be expected to be, a participant or principal in a covered transaction;

(b) Respondent (a person against whom a Federal agency has initiated a debarment or suspension action);

(c) Federal agency debarring or suspending official; or

(d) Federal agency official who is authorized to enter into covered transactions with non-Federal parties.

§ 180.125 What is the purpose of the nonprocurement debarment and suspension system?

(a) To protect the public interest, the Federal Government ensures the integrity of Federal programs by conducting business only with responsible persons.

(b) A Federal agency uses the nonprocurement debarment and suspension system to exclude from Federal programs persons who are not presently responsible.

(c) An exclusion is a serious action that a Federal agency may take only to protect the public interest. A Federal agency may not exclude a person or commodity for the purposes of punishment.

§ 180.130 How does an exclusion restrict a person's involvement in covered transactions?

With the exceptions stated in §§ 180.135, 315, and 420, a person who is excluded by any Federal agency may not:

(a) Be a participant in a Federal agency transaction that is a covered transaction; or

(b) Act as a principal of a person participating in one of those covered transactions.

§ 180.135 May a Federal agency grant an exception to let an excluded person participate in a covered transaction?

(a) A Federal agency head or designee may grant an exception permitting an excluded person to participate in a particular covered transaction. If the agency head or designee grants an exception, the exception must be in writing and state the reason(s) for deviating from the governmentwide policy in Executive Order 12549.

(b) An exception granted by one Federal agency for an excluded person does not extend to the covered transactions of another Federal agency.

§ 180.140 Does an exclusion under the nonprocurement system affect a person's eligibility for Federal procurement contracts?

If any Federal agency excludes a person under Executive Order 12549 or Executive Order 12689, on or after August

25, 1995, the excluded person is also ineligible for Federal procurement transactions under the FAR. Therefore, an exclusion under this part has reciprocal effect in Federal procurement transactions.

§ 180.145 Does an exclusion under the Federal procurement system affect a person's eligibility to participate in nonprocurement transactions?

If any Federal agency excludes a person under the FAR on or after August 25, 1995, the excluded person is also ineligible to participate in Federal agencies' nonprocurement covered transactions. Therefore, an exclusion under the FAR has reciprocal effect in Federal nonprocurement transactions.

§ 180.150 Against whom may a Federal agency take an exclusion action?

Given a cause that justifies an exclusion under this part, a Federal agency may exclude any person who has been, is, or may reasonably be expected to be a participant or principal in a covered transaction.

§ 180.155 How do I know if a person is excluded?

Check the Governmentwide Excluded Parties List System (EPLS) to determine whether a person is excluded. The General Services Administration (GSA) maintains the EPLS and makes it available, as detailed in Subpart E of this part. When a Federal agency takes an action to exclude a person under the nonprocurement or procurement debarment and suspension system, the agency enters the information about the excluded person into the EPLS.

Subpart B—Covered Transactions

§ 180.200 What is a covered transaction?

A covered transaction is a nonprocurement or procurement transaction that is subject to the prohibitions of this part. It may be a transaction at—

(a) The primary tier, between a Federal agency and a person (see appendix to this part); or

(b) A lower tier, between a participant in a covered transaction and another person.

§ 180.205 Why is it important if a particular transaction is a covered transaction?

The importance of whether a transaction is a covered transaction depends upon who you are.

(a) As a participant in the transaction, you have the responsibilities laid out in subpart C of this part. Those include responsibilities to the person or Federal agency at the next higher tier from whom you received the transaction, if any. They also include responsibilities if you subsequently enter into other covered transactions with persons at the next lower tier.

(b) As a Federal official who enters into a primary tier transaction, you have the responsibilities laid out in subpart D of this part.

(c) As an excluded person, you may not be a participant or principal in the transaction unless—

(1) The person who entered into the transaction with you allows you to continue your involvement in a transaction that predates your exclusion, as permitted under § 180.310 or § 180.415; or

(2) A Federal agency official obtains an exception from the agency head or designee to allow you to be involved in the transaction, as permitted under § 180.135.

§ 180.210 Which nonprocurement transactions are covered transactions?

All nonprocurement transactions, as defined in § 180.970, are covered transactions unless listed in the exemptions under § 180.215.

§ 180.215 Which nonprocurement transactions are not covered transactions?

The following types of nonprocurement transactions are not covered transactions:

(a) A direct award to—

(1) A foreign government or foreign governmental entity;

(2) A public international organization;

(3) An entity owned (in whole or in part) or controlled by a foreign government; or

(4) Any other entity consisting wholly or partially of one or more foreign

governments or foreign governmental entities.

(b) A benefit to an individual as a personal entitlement without regard to the individual's present responsibility (but benefits received in an individual's business capacity are not excepted). For example, if a person receives social security benefits under the Supplemental Security Income provisions of the Social Security Act, 42 U.S.C. 1301 *et seq.*, those benefits are not covered transactions and, therefore, are not affected if the person is excluded.

(c) Federal employment.

(d) A transaction that a Federal agency needs to respond to a national or agency-recognized emergency or disaster.

(e) A permit, license, certificate or similar instrument issued as a means to regulate public health, safety or the environment, unless a Federal agency specifically designates it to be a covered transaction.

(f) An incidental benefit that results from ordinary governmental operations.

(g) Any other transaction if—

(1) The application of an exclusion to the transaction is prohibited by law; or

(2) A Federal agency's regulation exempts it from coverage under this part.

§ 180.220 Are any procurement contracts included as covered transactions?

(a) Covered transactions under this part—

(1) Do not include any procurement contracts awarded directly by a Federal agency; but

(2) Do include some procurement contracts awarded by non-Federal participants in nonprocurement covered transactions.

(b) Specifically, a contract for goods or services is a covered transaction if any of the following applies:

(1) The contract is awarded by a participant in a nonprocurement transaction that is covered under § 180.210, and the amount of the contract is expected to equal or exceed $25,000.

(2) The contract requires the consent of an official of a Federal agency. In that case, the contract, regardless of the amount, always is a covered transaction, and it does not matter who

awarded it. For example, it could be a subcontract awarded by a contractor at a tier below a nonprocurement transaction, as shown in the appendix to this part.

(3) The contract is for Federally-required audit services.

(c) A subcontract also is a covered transaction if,—

(1) It is awarded by a participant in a procurement transaction under a nonprocurement transaction of a Federal agency that extends the coverage of paragraph (b)(1) of this section to additional tiers of contracts (see the diagram in the appendix to this part showing that optional lower tier coverage); and

(2) The value of the subcontract is expected to equal or exceed $25,000.

[70 FR 51865, Aug. 31, 2005, as amended at 71 FR 66432, Nov. 15, 2006]

§ 180.225 How do I know if a transaction in which I may participate is a covered transaction?

As a participant in a transaction, you will know that it is a covered transaction because the Federal agency regulations governing the transaction, the appropriate Federal agency official or participant at the next higher tier who enters into the transaction with you, will tell you that you must comply with applicable portions of this part.

Subpart C—Responsibilities of Participants Regarding Transactions Doing Business With Other Persons

§ 180.300 What must I do before I enter into a covered transaction with another person at the next lower tier?

When you enter into a covered transaction with another person at the next lower tier, you must verify that the person with whom you intend to do business is not excluded or disqualified. You do this by:

(a) Checking the EPLS; or

(b) Collecting a certification from that person; or

49

(c) Adding a clause or condition to the covered transaction with that person.

[70 FR 51865, Aug. 31, 2005, as amended at 71 FR 66432, Nov. 15, 2006]

§ 180.305 May I enter into a covered transaction with an excluded or disqualified person?

(a) You as a participant may not enter into a covered transaction with an excluded person, unless the Federal agency responsible for the transaction grants an exception under § 180.135.

(b) You may not enter into any transaction with a person who is disqualified from that transaction, unless you have obtained an exception under the disqualifying statute, Executive order, or regulation.

§ 180.310 What must I do if a Federal agency excludes a person with whom I am already doing business in a covered transaction?

(a) You as a participant may continue covered transactions with an excluded person if the transactions were in existence when the agency excluded the person. However, you are not required to continue the transactions, and you may consider termination. You should make a decision about whether to terminate and the type of termination action, if any, only after a thorough review to ensure that the action is proper and appropriate.

(b) You may not renew or extend covered transactions (other than no-cost time extensions) with any excluded person, unless the Federal agency responsible for the transaction grants an exception under § 180.135.

§ 180.315 May I use the services of an excluded person as a principal under a covered transaction?

(a) You as a participant may continue to use the services of an excluded person as a principal under a covered transaction if you were using the services of that person in the transaction before the person was excluded. However, you are not required to continue using that person's services as a principal. You should make a decision about whether to discontinue that person's services only after a thorough re-

view to ensure that the action is proper and appropriate.

(b) You may not begin to use the services of an excluded person as a principal under a covered transaction unless the Federal agency responsible for the transaction grants an exception under § 180.135.

§ 180.320 Must I verify that principals of my covered transactions are eligible to participate?

Yes, you as a participant are responsible for determining whether any of your principals of your covered transactions is excluded or disqualified from participating in the transaction.

You may decide the method and frequency by which you do so. You may, but you are not required to, check the EPLS.

§ 180.325 What happens if I do business with an excluded person in a covered transaction?

If as a participant you knowingly do business with an excluded person, the Federal agency responsible for your transaction may disallow costs, annul or terminate the transaction, issue a stop work order, debar or suspend you, or take other remedies as appropriate.

§ 180.330 What requirements must I pass down to persons at lower tiers with whom I intend to do business?

Before entering into a covered transaction with a participant at the next lower tier, you must require that participant to—

(a) Comply with this subpart as a condition of participation in the transaction. You may do so using any method(s), unless the regulation of the Federal agency responsible for the transaction requires you to use specific methods.

(b) Pass the requirement to comply with this subpart to each person with whom the participant enters into a covered transaction at the next lower tier.

DISCLOSING INFORMATION—PRIMARY TIER PARTICIPANTS

§180.335 What information must I provide before entering into a covered transaction with a Federal agency?

Before you enter into a covered transaction at the primary tier, you as the participant must notify the Federal agency office that is entering into the transaction with you, if you know that you or any of the principals for that covered transaction:

(a) Are presently excluded or disqualified;

(b) Have been convicted within the preceding three years of any of the offenses listed in §180.800(a) or had a civil judgment rendered against you for one of those offenses within that time period;

(c) Are presently indicted for or otherwise criminally or civilly charged by a governmental entity (Federal, State or local) with commission of any of the offenses listed in §180.800(a); or

(d) Have had one or more public transactions (Federal, State, or local) terminated within the preceding three years for cause or default.

§180.340 If I disclose unfavorable information required under §180.335, will I be prevented from participating in the transaction?

As a primary tier participant, your disclosure of unfavorable information about yourself or a principal under §180.335 will not necessarily cause a Federal agency to deny your participation in the covered transaction. The agency will consider the information when it determines whether to enter into the covered transaction. The agency will also consider any additional information or explanation that you elect to submit with the disclosed information.

§180.345 What happens if I fail to disclose information required under §180.335?

If a Federal agency later determines that you failed to disclose information under §180.335 that you knew at the time you entered into the covered transaction, the agency may—

(a) Terminate the transaction for material failure to comply with the terms and conditions of the transaction; or

(b) Pursue any other available remedies, including suspension and debarment.

§180.350 What must I do if I learn of information required under §180.335 after entering into a covered transaction with a Federal agency?

At any time after you enter into a covered transaction, you must give immediate written notice to the Federal agency office with which you entered into the transaction if you learn either that—

(a) You failed to disclose information earlier, as required by §180.335; or

(b) Due to changed circumstances, you or any of the principals for the transaction now meet any of the criteria in §180.335.

DISCLOSING INFORMATION—LOWER TIER PARTICIPANTS

§180.355 What information must I provide to a higher tier participant before entering into a covered transaction with that participant?

Before you enter into a covered transaction with a person at the next higher tier, you as a lower tier participant must notify that person if you know that you or any of the principals are presently excluded or disqualified.

§180.360 What happens if I fail to disclose information required under §180.355?

If a Federal agency later determines that you failed to tell the person at the higher tier that you were excluded or disqualified at the time you entered into the covered transaction with that person, the agency may pursue any available remedies, including suspension and debarment.

§180.365 What must I do if I learn of information required under §180.355 after entering into a covered transaction with a higher tier participant?

At any time after you enter into a lower tier covered transaction with a person at a higher tier, you must provide immediate written notice to that person if you learn either that—

(a) You failed to disclose information earlier, as required by § 180.355; or

(b) Due to changed circumstances, you or any of the principals for the transaction now meet any of the criteria in § 180.355.

Subpart D—Responsibilities of Federal Agency Officials Regarding Transactions

§ 180.400 May I enter into a transaction with an excluded or disqualified person?

(a) You as a Federal agency official may not enter into a covered transaction with an excluded person unless you obtain an exception under § 180.135.

(b) You may not enter into any transaction with a person who is disqualified from that transaction, unless you obtain a waiver or exception under the statute, Executive order, or regulation that is the basis for the person's disqualification.

§ 180.405 May I enter into a covered transaction with a participant if a principal of the transaction is excluded?

As a Federal agency official, you may not enter into a covered transaction with a participant if you know that a principal of the transaction is excluded, unless you obtain an exception under § 180.135.

§ 180.410 May I approve a participant's use of the services of an excluded person?

After entering into a covered transaction with a participant, you as a Federal agency official may not approve a participant's use of an excluded person as a principal under that transaction, unless you obtain an exception under § 180.135.

§ 180.415 What must I do if a Federal agency excludes the participant or a principal after I enter into a covered transaction?

(a) You as a Federal agency official may continue covered transactions with an excluded person, or under which an excluded person is a principal, if the transactions were in existence when the person was excluded. You are not required to continue the

transactions, however, and you may consider termination. You should make a decision about whether to terminate and the type of termination action, if any, only after a thorough review to ensure that the action is proper.

(b) You may not renew or extend covered transactions (other than no-cost time extensions) with any excluded person, or under which an excluded person is a principal, unless you obtain an exception under § 180.135.

§ 180.420 May I approve a transaction with an excluded or disqualified person at a lower tier?

If a transaction at a lower tier is subject to your approval, you as a Federal agency official may not approve—

(a) A covered transaction with a person who is currently excluded, unless you obtain an exception under § 180.135; or

(b) A transaction with a person who is disqualified from that transaction, unless you obtain a waiver or exception under the statute, Executive order, or regulation that is the basis for the person's disqualification.

§ 180.425 When do I check to see if a person is excluded or disqualified?

As a Federal agency official, you must check to see if a person is excluded or disqualified before you—

(a) Enter into a primary tier covered transaction;

(b) Approve a principal in a primary tier covered transaction;

(c) Approve a lower tier participant if your agency's approval of the lower tier participant is required; or

(d) Approve a principal in connection with a lower tier transaction if your agency's approval of the principal is required.

§ 180.430 How do I check to see if a person is excluded or disqualified?

You check to see if a person is excluded or disqualified in two ways:

(a) You as a Federal agency official must check the EPLS when you take any action listed in § 180.425.

(b) You must review information that a participant gives you, as required by § 180.335, about its status or the status of the principals of a transaction.

§ 180.435 What must I require of a primary tier participant?

You as a Federal agency official must require each participant in a primary tier covered transaction to—

(a) Comply with subpart C of this part as a condition of participation in the transaction; and

(b) Communicate the requirement to comply with subpart C of this part to persons at the next lower tier with whom the primary tier participant enters into covered transactions.

§ 180.440 What action may I take if a primary tier participant knowingly does business with an excluded or disqualified person?

If a participant knowingly does business with an excluded or disqualified person, you as a Federal agency official may refer the matter for suspension and debarment consideration. You may also disallow costs, annul or terminate the transaction, issue a stop work order, or take any other appropriate remedy.

§ 180.445 What action may I take if a primary tier participant fails to disclose the information required under § 180.335?

If you as a Federal agency official determine that a participant failed to disclose information, as required by § 180.335, at the time it entered into a covered transaction with you, you may—

(a) Terminate the transaction for material failure to comply with the terms and conditions of the transaction; or

(b) Pursue any other available remedies, including suspension and debarment.

§ 180.450 What action may I take if a lower tier participant fails to disclose the information required under § 180.355 to the next higher tier?

If you as a Federal agency official determine that a lower tier participant failed to disclose information, as required by § 180.355, at the time it entered into a covered transaction with a participant at the next higher tier, you may pursue any remedies available to you, including the initiation of a suspension or debarment action.

Subpart E—Excluded Parties List System

§ 180.500 What is the purpose of the Excluded Parties List System (EPLS)?

The EPLS is a widely available source of the most current information about persons who are excluded or disqualified from covered transactions.

§ 180.505 Who uses the EPLS?

(a) Federal agency officials use the EPLS to determine whether to enter into a transaction with a person, as required under § 180.430.

(b) Participants also may, but are not required to, use the EPLS to determine if—

(1) Principals of their transactions are excluded or disqualified, as required under § 180.320; or

(2) Persons with whom they are entering into covered transactions at the next lower tier are excluded or disqualified.

(c) The EPLS is available to the general public.

§ 180.510 Who maintains the EPLS?

The General Services Administration (GSA) maintains the EPLS. When a Federal agency takes an action to exclude a person under the nonprocurement or procurement debarment and suspension system, the agency enters the information about the excluded person into the EPLS.

§ 180.515 What specific information is in the EPLS?

(a) At a minimum, the EPLS indicates—

(1) The full name (where available) and address of each excluded and disqualified person, in alphabetical order, with cross references if more than one name is involved in a single action;

(2) The type of action;

(3) The cause for the action;

(4) The scope of the action;

(5) Any termination date for the action;

(6) The Federal agency and name and telephone number of the agency point of contact for the action; and

(7) The Dun and Bradstreet Number (DUNS), or other similar code approved

by the GSA, of the excluded or disqualified person, if available.

(b)(1) The database for the EPLS includes a field for the Taxpayer Identification Number (TIN) (the social security number (SSN) for an individual) of an excluded or disqualified person.

(2) Agencies disclose the SSN of an individual to verify the identity of an individual, only if permitted under the Privacy Act of 1974 and, if appropriate, the Computer Matching and Privacy Protection Act of 1988, as codified in 5 U.S.C. 552(a).

§ 180.520 Who places the information into the EPLS?

Federal agency officials who take actions to exclude persons under this part or officials who are responsible for identifying disqualified persons must enter the following information about those persons into the EPLS:

(a) Information required by § 180.515(a);

(b) The Taxpayer Identification Number (TIN) of the excluded or disqualified person, including the social security number (SSN) for an individual, if the number is available and may be disclosed under law;

(c) Information about an excluded or disqualified person, generally within five working days, after—

(1) Taking an exclusion action;

(2) Modifying or rescinding an exclusion action;

(3) Finding that a person is disqualified; or

(4) Finding that there has been a change in the status of a person who is listed as disqualified.

§ 180.525 Whom do I ask if I have questions about a person in the EPLS?

If you have questions about a listed person in the EPLS, ask the point of contact for the Federal agency that placed the person's name into the EPLS. You may find the agency point of contact from the EPLS.

§ 180.530 Where can I find the EPLS?

You may access the EPLS through the Internet, currently at *http://epls.arnet.gov* or *http://www.epls.gov*.

Subpart F—General Principles Relating to Suspension and Debarment Actions

§ 180.600 How do suspension and debarment actions start?

When Federal agency officials receive information from any source concerning a cause for suspension or debarment, they will promptly report it and the agency will investigate. The officials refer the question of whether to suspend or debar you to their suspending or debarring official for consideration, if appropriate.

§ 180.605 How does suspension differ from debarment?

Suspension differs from debarment in that—

A suspending official . . .	A debarring official . . .
(a) Imposes suspension as a temporary status of in eligibility for procurement and nonprocurement transactions, pending completion of an investigation or legal proceedings.	Imposes debarment for a specified period as a final determination that a person is not presently responsible.
(b) Must—	
(1) Have *adequate evidence* that there may be a cause for debarment of a person; and	
(2) Conclude that *immediate action* is necessary to protect the Federal interest	Must conclude, based on a *preponderance of the evidence,* that the person has engaged in conduct that warrants debarment.
(c) Usually imposes the suspension *first,* and then promptly notifies the suspended person, giving the person an opportunity to contest the suspension and have it lifted.	Imposes debarment *after* giving the respondent notice of the action and an opportunity to contest the proposed debarment.

§ 180.610 What procedures does a Federal agency use in suspension and debarment actions?

In deciding whether to suspend or debar you, a Federal agency handles the actions as informally as practicable, consistent with principles of fundamental fairness.

(a) For suspension actions, a Federal agency uses the procedures in this subpart and subpart G of this part.

(b) For debarment actions, a Federal agency uses the procedures in this subpart and subpart H of this part.

§ 180.615 How does a Federal agency notify a person of a suspension or debarment action?

(a) The suspending or debarring official sends a written notice to the last known street address, facsimile number, or e-mail address of—

(1) You or your identified counsel; or

(2) Your agent for service of process, or any of your partners, officers, directors, owners, or joint venturers.

(b) The notice is effective if sent to any of these persons.

§ 180.620 Do Federal agencies coordinate suspension and debarment actions?

Yes, when more than one Federal agency has an interest in a suspension or debarment, the agencies may consider designating one agency as the lead agency for making the decision. Agencies are encouraged to establish methods and procedures for coordinating their suspension and debarment actions.

§ 180.625 What is the scope of a suspension or debarment?

If you are suspended or debarred, the suspension or debarment is effective as follows:

(a) Your suspension or debarment constitutes suspension or debarment of all of your divisions and other organizational elements from all covered transactions, unless the suspension or debarment decision is limited—

(1) By its terms to one or more specifically identified individuals, divisions, or other organizational elements; or

(2) To specific types of transactions.

(b) Any affiliate of a participant may be included in a suspension or debarment action if the suspending or debarring official—

(1) Officially names the affiliate in the notice; and

(2) Gives the affiliate an opportunity to contest the action.

§ 180.630 May a Federal agency impute the conduct of one person to another?

For purposes of actions taken under this part, a Federal agency may impute conduct as follows:

(a) *Conduct imputed from an individual to an organization.* A Federal agency may impute the fraudulent, criminal, or other improper conduct of any officer, director, shareholder, partner, employee, or other individual associated with an organization, to that organization when the improper conduct occurred in connection with the individual's performance of duties for or on behalf of that organization, or with the organization's knowledge, approval or acquiescence. The organization's acceptance of the benefits derived from the conduct is evidence of knowledge, approval or acquiescence.

(b) *Conduct imputed from an organization to an individual, or between individuals.* A Federal agency may impute the fraudulent, criminal, or other improper conduct of any organization to an individual, or from one individual to another individual, if the individual to whom the improper conduct is imputed either participated in, had knowledge of, or reason to know of the improper conduct.

(c) *Conduct imputed from one organization to another organization.* A Federal agency may impute the fraudulent, criminal, or other improper conduct of one organization to another organization when the improper conduct occurred in connection with a partnership, joint venture, joint application, association or similar arrangement, or when the organization to whom the improper conduct is imputed has the power to direct, manage, control or influence the activities of the organization responsible for the improper conduct. Acceptance of the benefits derived from the conduct is evidence of knowledge, approval or acquiescence.

§ 180.635 May a Federal agency settle a debarment or suspension action?

Yes, a Federal agency may settle a debarment or suspension action at any time if it is in the best interest of the Federal Government.

§ 180.640 May a settlement include a voluntary exclusion?

Yes, if a Federal agency enters into a settlement with you in which you agree to be excluded, it is called a voluntary exclusion and has government-wide effect.

§ 180.645 Do other Federal agencies know if an agency agrees to a voluntary exclusion?

(a) Yes, the Federal agency agreeing to the voluntary exclusion enters information about it into the EPLS.

(b) Also, any agency or person may contact the Federal agency that agreed to the voluntary exclusion to find out the details of the voluntary exclusion.

Subpart G—Suspension

§ 180.700 When may the suspending official issue a suspension?

Suspension is a serious action. Using the procedures of this subpart and subpart F of this part, the suspending official may impose suspension only when that official determines that—

(a) There exists an indictment for, or other adequate evidence to suspect, an offense listed under § 180.800(a), or

(b) There exists adequate evidence to suspect any other cause for debarment listed under § 180.800(b) through (d); and

(c) Immediate action is necessary to protect the public interest.

§ 180.705 What does the suspending official consider in issuing a suspension?

(a) In determining the adequacy of the evidence to support the suspension, the suspending official considers how much information is available, how credible it is given the circumstances, whether or not important allegations are corroborated, and what inferences can reasonably be drawn as a result. During this assessment, the suspending official may examine the basic documents, including grants, cooperative agreements, loan authorizations, contracts, and other relevant documents.

(b) An indictment, conviction, civil judgment, or other official findings by Federal, State, or local bodies that determine factual and/or legal matters, constitutes adequate evidence for purposes of suspension actions.

(c) In deciding whether immediate action is needed to protect the public interest, the suspending official has wide discretion. For example, the suspending official may infer the necessity for immediate action to protect the public interest either from the nature of the circumstances giving rise to a cause for suspension or from potential business relationships or involvement with a program of the Federal Government.

§ 180.710 When does a suspension take effect?

A suspension is effective when the suspending official signs the decision to suspend.

§ 180.715 What notice does the suspending official give me if I am suspended?

After deciding to suspend you, the suspending official promptly sends you a Notice of Suspension advising you—

(a) That you have been suspended;

(b) That your suspension is based on—

(1) An indictment;

(2) A conviction;

(3) Other adequate evidence that you have committed irregularities which seriously reflect on the propriety of further Federal Government dealings with you; or

(4) Conduct of another person that has been imputed to you, or your affiliation with a suspended or debarred person;

(c) Of any other irregularities in terms sufficient to put you on notice without disclosing the Federal Government's evidence;

(d) Of the cause(s) upon which the suspending official relied under § 180.700 for imposing suspension;

(e) That your suspension is for a temporary period pending the completion of an investigation or resulting legal or debarment proceedings;

(f) Of the applicable provisions of this subpart, subpart F of this part, and any other agency procedures governing suspension decisionmaking; and

(g) Of the governmentwide effect of your suspension from procurement and nonprocurement programs and activities.

§ 180.720 How may I contest a suspension?

If you as a respondent wish to contest a suspension, you or your representative must provide the suspending official with information in opposition to the suspension. You may do this orally or in writing, but any information provided orally that you consider important must also be submitted in writing for the official record.

§ 180.725 How much time do I have to contest a suspension?

(a) As a respondent you or your representative must either send, or make arrangements to appear and present, the information and argument to the suspending official within 30 days after you receive the Notice of Suspension.

(b) The Federal agency taking the action considers the notice to be received by you—

(1) When delivered, if the agency mails the notice to the last known street address, or five days after the agency sends it if the letter is undeliverable;

(2) When sent, if the agency sends the notice by facsimile or five days after the agency sends it if the facsimile is undeliverable; or

(3) When delivered, if the agency sends the notice by e-mail or five days after the agency sends it if the e-mail is undeliverable.

§ 180.730 What information must I provide to the suspending official if I contest the suspension?

(a) In addition to any information and argument in opposition, as a respondent your submission to the suspending official must identify—

(1) Specific facts that contradict the statements contained in the Notice of Suspension. A general denial is insufficient to raise a genuine dispute over facts material to the suspension;

(2) All existing, proposed, or prior exclusions under regulations implementing Executive Order 12549 and all similar actions taken by Federal, State, or local agencies, including administrative agreements that affect only those agencies;

(3) All criminal and civil proceedings not included in the Notice of Suspension that grew out of facts relevant to the cause(s) stated in the notice; and

(4) All of your affiliates.

(b) If you fail to disclose this information, or provide false information, the Federal agency taking the action may seek further criminal, civil or administrative action against you, as appropriate.

§ 180.735 Under what conditions do I get an additional opportunity to challenge the facts on which the suspension is based?

(a) You as a respondent will not have an additional opportunity to challenge the facts if the suspending official determines that—

(1) Your suspension is based upon an indictment, conviction, civil judgment, or other finding by a Federal, State, or local body for which an opportunity to contest the facts was provided;

(2) Your presentation in opposition contains only general denials to information contained in the Notice of Suspension;

(3) The issues raised in your presentation in opposition to the suspension are not factual in nature, or are not material to the suspending official's initial decision to suspend, or the official's decision whether to continue the suspension; or

(4) On the basis of advice from the Department of Justice, an office of the United States Attorney, a State attorney general's office, or a State or local prosecutor's office, that substantial interests of the government in pending or contemplated legal proceedings based on the same facts as the suspension would be prejudiced by conducting fact-finding.

(b) You will have an opportunity to challenge the facts if the suspending official determines that—

(1) The conditions in paragraph (a) of this section do not exist; and

(2) Your presentation in opposition raises a genuine dispute over facts material to the suspension.

(c) If you have an opportunity to challenge disputed material facts under this section, the suspending official or designee must conduct additional proceedings to resolve those facts.

§ 180.740 Are suspension proceedings formal?

(a) Suspension proceedings are conducted in a fair and informal manner. The suspending official may use flexible procedures to allow you to present matters in opposition. In so doing, the suspending official is not required to follow formal rules of evidence or procedure in creating an official record upon which the official will base a final suspension decision.

(b) You as a respondent or your representative must submit any documentary evidence you want the suspending official to consider.

§ 180.745 How is fact-finding conducted?

(a) If fact-finding is conducted—

(1) You may present witnesses and other evidence, and confront any witness presented; and

(2) The fact-finder must prepare written findings of fact for the record.

(b) A transcribed record of fact-finding proceedings must be made, unless you as a respondent and the Federal agency agree to waive it in advance. If you want a copy of the transcribed record, you may purchase it.

§ 180.750 What does the suspending official consider in deciding whether to continue or terminate my suspension?

(a) The suspending official bases the decision on all information contained in the official record. The record includes—

(1) All information in support of the suspending official's initial decision to suspend you;

(2) Any further information and argument presented in support of, or opposition to, the suspension; and

(3) Any transcribed record of fact-finding proceedings.

(b) The suspending official may refer disputed material facts to another official for findings of fact. The suspending official may reject any resulting findings, in whole or in part, only after specifically determining them to be arbitrary, capricious, or clearly erroneous.

§ 180.755 When will I know whether the suspension is continued or terminated?

The suspending official must make a written decision whether to continue, modify, or terminate your suspension within 45 days of closing the official record. The official record closes upon the suspending official's receipt of final submissions, information and findings of fact, if any. The suspending official may extend that period for good cause.

§ 180.760 How long may my suspension last?

(a) If legal or debarment proceedings are initiated at the time of, or during your suspension, the suspension may continue until the conclusion of those proceedings. However, if proceedings are not initiated, a suspension may not exceed 12 months.

(b) The suspending official may extend the 12 month limit under paragraph (a) of this section for an additional 6 months if an office of a U.S. Assistant Attorney General, U.S. Attorney, or other responsible prosecuting official requests an extension in writing. In no event may a suspension exceed 18 months without initiating proceedings under paragraph (a) of this section.

(c) The suspending official must notify the appropriate officials under paragraph (b) of this section of an impending termination of a suspension at least 30 days before the 12 month period expires to allow the officials an opportunity to request an extension.

Subpart H—Debarment

§ 180.800 What are the causes for debarment?

A Federal agency may debar a person for—

(a) Conviction of or civil judgment for—

(1) Commission of fraud or a criminal offense in connection with obtaining, attempting to obtain, or performing a public or private agreement or transaction;

(2) Violation of Federal or State antitrust statutes, including those proscribing price fixing between competitors, allocation of customers between competitors, and bid rigging;

(3) Commission of embezzlement, theft, forgery, bribery, falsification or destruction of records, making false statements, tax evasion, receiving stolen property, making false claims, or obstruction of justice; or

(4) Commission of any other offense indicating a lack of business integrity or business honesty that seriously and directly affects your present responsibility;

(b) Violation of the terms of a public agreement or transaction so serious as to affect the integrity of an agency program, such as—

(1) A willful failure to perform in accordance with the terms of one or more public agreements or transactions;

(2) A history of failure to perform or of unsatisfactory performance of one or more public agreements or transactions; or

(3) A willful violation of a statutory or regulatory provision or requirement applicable to a public agreement or transaction;

(c) Any of the following causes:

(1) A nonprocurement debarment by any Federal agency taken before October 1, 1988, or a procurement debarment by any Federal agency taken pursuant to 48 CFR part 9, subpart 9.4, before August 25, 1995;

(2) Knowingly doing business with an ineligible person, except as permitted under §180.135;

(3) Failure to pay a single substantial debt, or a number of outstanding debts (including disallowed costs and overpayments, but not including sums owed the Federal Government under the Internal Revenue Code) owed to any Federal agency or instrumentality, provided the debt is uncontested by the debtor or, if contested, provided that the debtor's legal and administrative remedies have been exhausted;

(4) Violation of a material provision of a voluntary exclusion agreement entered into under §180.640 or of any settlement of a debarment or suspension action; or

(5) Violation of the provisions of the Drug-Free Workplace Act of 1988 (41 U.S.C. 701); or

(d) Any other cause of so serious or compelling a nature that it affects your present responsibility.

§180.805 What notice does the debarring official give me if I am proposed for debarment?

After consideration of the causes in §180.800, if the debarring official proposes to debar you, the official sends you a Notice of Proposed Debarment, pursuant to §180.615, advising you—

(a) That the debarring official is considering debarring you;

(b) Of the reasons for proposing to debar you in terms sufficient to put you on notice of the conduct or transactions upon which the proposed debarment is based;

(c) Of the cause(s) under §180.800 upon which the debarring official relied for proposing your debarment;

(d) Of the applicable provisions of this subpart, subpart F of this part, and any other agency procedures governing debarment; and

(e) Of the governmentwide effect of a debarment from procurement and nonprocurement programs and activities.

§180.810 When does a debarment take effect?

Unlike suspension, a debarment is not effective until the debarring official issues a decision. The debarring official does not issue a decision until the respondent has had an opportunity to contest the proposed debarment.

§180.815 How may I contest a proposed debarment?

If you as a respondent wish to contest a proposed debarment, you or your representative must provide the debarring official with information in opposition to the proposed debarment. You may do this orally or in writing, but any information provided orally that you consider important must also be submitted in writing for the official record.

§180.820 How much time do I have to contest a proposed debarment?

(a) As a respondent you or your representative must either send, or make arrangements to appear and present, the information and argument to the debarring official within 30 days after you receive the Notice of Proposed Debarment.

(b) The Federal agency taking the action considers the Notice of Proposed Debarment to be received by you—

(1) When delivered, if the agency mails the notice to the last known street address, or five days after the agency sends it if the letter is undeliverable;

(2) When sent, if the agency sends the notice by facsimile or five days after the agency sends it if the facsimile is undeliverable; or

(3) When delivered, if the agency sends the notice by e-mail or five days after the agency sends it if the e-mail is undeliverable.

§ 180.825 What information must I provide to the debarring official if I contest the proposed debarment?

(a) In addition to any information and argument in opposition, as a respondent your submission to the debarring official must identify—

(1) Specific facts that contradict the statements contained in the Notice of Proposed Debarment. Include any information about any of the factors listed in § 180.860. A general denial is insufficient to raise a genuine dispute over facts material to the debarment;

(2) All existing, proposed, or prior exclusions under regulations implementing Executive Order 12549 and all similar actions taken by Federal, State, or local agencies, including administrative agreements that affect only those agencies;

(3) All criminal and civil proceedings not included in the Notice of Proposed Debarment that grew out of facts relevant to the cause(s) stated in the notice; and

(4) All of your affiliates.

(b) If you fail to disclose this information, or provide false information, the Federal agency taking the action may seek further criminal, civil or administrative action against you, as appropriate.

§ 180.830 Under what conditions do I get an additional opportunity to challenge the facts on which the proposed debarment is based?

(a) You as a respondent will not have an additional opportunity to challenge the facts if the debarring official determines that—

(1) Your debarment is based upon a conviction or civil judgment;

(2) Your presentation in opposition contains only general denials to information contained in the Notice of Proposed Debarment; or

(3) The issues raised in your presentation in opposition to the proposed debarment are not factual in nature, or are not material to the debarring official's decision whether to debar.

(b) You will have an additional opportunity to challenge the facts if the debarring official determines that—

(1) The conditions in paragraph (a) of this section do not exist; and

(2) Your presentation in opposition raises a genuine dispute over facts material to the proposed debarment.

(c) If you have an opportunity to challenge disputed material facts under this section, the debarring official or designee must conduct additional proceedings to resolve those facts.

§ 180.835 Are debarment proceedings formal?

(a) Debarment proceedings are conducted in a fair and informal manner. The debarring official may use flexible procedures to allow you as a respondent to present matters in opposition. In so doing, the debarring official is not required to follow formal rules of evidence or procedure in creating an official record upon which the official will base the decision whether to debar.

(b) You or your representative must submit any documentary evidence you want the debarring official to consider.

§ 180.840 How is fact-finding conducted?

(a) If fact-finding is conducted—

(1) You may present witnesses and other evidence, and confront any witness presented; and

(2) The fact-finder must prepare written findings of fact for the record.

(b) A transcribed record of fact-finding proceedings must be made, unless you as a respondent and the Federal agency agree to waive it in advance. If you want a copy of the transcribed record, you may purchase it.

§ 180.845 What does the debarring official consider in deciding whether to debar me?

(a) The debarring official may debar you for any of the causes in § 180.800. However, the official need not debar you even if a cause for debarment exists. The official may consider the seriousness of your acts or omissions and the mitigating or aggravating factors set forth at § 180.860.

(b) The debarring official bases the decision on all information contained in the official record. The record includes—

(1) All information in support of the debarring official's proposed debarment;

(2) Any further information and argument presented in support of, or in opposition to, the proposed debarment; and

(3) Any transcribed record of fact-finding proceedings.

(c) The debarring official may refer disputed material facts to another official for findings of fact. The debarring official may reject any resultant findings, in whole or in part, only after specifically determining them to be arbitrary, capricious, or clearly erroneous.

§ 180.850 What is the standard of proof in a debarment action?

(a) In any debarment action, the Federal agency must establish the cause for debarment by a preponderance of the evidence.

(b) If the proposed debarment is based upon a conviction or civil judgment, the standard of proof is met.

§ 180.855 Who has the burden of proof in a debarment action?

(a) The Federal agency has the burden to prove that a cause for debarment exists.

(b) Once a cause for debarment is established, you as a respondent have the burden of demonstrating to the satisfaction of the debarring official that you are presently responsible and that debarment is not necessary.

§ 180.860 What factors may influence the debarring official's decision?

This section lists the mitigating and aggravating factors that the debarring official may consider in determining whether to debar you and the length of your debarment period. The debarring official may consider other factors if appropriate in light of the circumstances of a particular case. The existence or nonexistence of any factor, such as one of those set forth in this section, is not necessarily determinative of your present responsibility. In making a debarment decision, the debarring official may consider the following factors:

(a) The actual or potential harm or impact that results or may result from the wrongdoing.

(b) The frequency of incidents and/or duration of the wrongdoing.

(c) Whether there is a pattern or prior history of wrongdoing. For example, if you have been found by another Federal agency or a State agency to have engaged in wrongdoing similar to that found in the debarment action, the existence of this fact may be used by the debarring official in determining that you have a pattern or prior history of wrongdoing.

(d) Whether you are or have been excluded or disqualified by an agency of the Federal Government or have not been allowed to participate in State or local contracts or assistance agreements on a basis of conduct similar to one or more of the causes for debarment specified in this part.

(e) Whether you have entered into an administrative agreement with a Federal agency or a State or local government that is not governmentwide but is based on conduct similar to one or more of the causes for debarment specified in this part.

(f) Whether and to what extent you planned, initiated, or carried out the wrongdoing.

(g) Whether you have accepted responsibility for the wrongdoing and recognize the seriousness of the misconduct that led to the cause for debarment.

(h) Whether you have paid or agreed to pay all criminal, civil and administrative liabilities for the improper activity, including any investigative or administrative costs incurred by the government, and have made or agreed to make full restitution.

(i) Whether you have cooperated fully with the government agencies during the investigation and any court or administrative action. In determining the extent of cooperation, the debarring official may consider when the cooperation began and whether you disclosed all pertinent information known to you.

(j) Whether the wrongdoing was pervasive within your organization.

(k) The kind of positions held by the individuals involved in the wrongdoing.

(l) Whether your organization took appropriate corrective action or remedial measures, such as establishing ethics training and implementing programs to prevent recurrence.

(m) Whether your principals tolerated the offense.

(n) Whether you brought the activity cited as a basis for the debarment to the attention of the appropriate government agency in a timely manner.

(o) Whether you have fully investigated the circumstances surrounding the cause for debarment and, if so, made the result of the investigation available to the debarring official.

(p) Whether you had effective standards of conduct and internal control systems in place at the time the questioned conduct occurred.

(q) Whether you have taken appropriate disciplinary action against the individuals responsible for the activity which constitutes the cause for debarment.

(r) Whether you have had adequate time to eliminate the circumstances within your organization that led to the cause for the debarment.

(s) Other factors that are appropriate to the circumstances of a particular case.

§ 180.865   How long may my debarment last?

(a) If the debarring official decides to debar you, your period of debarment will be based on the seriousness of the cause(s) upon which your debarment is based. Generally, debarment should not exceed three years. However, if circumstances warrant, the debarring official may impose a longer period of debarment.

(b) In determining the period of debarment, the debarring official may consider the factors in § 180.860. If a suspension has preceded your debarment, the debarring official must consider the time you were suspended.

(c) If the debarment is for a violation of the provisions of the Drug-Free Workplace Act of 1988, your period of debarment may not exceed five years.

§ 180.870   When do I know if the debarring official debars me?

(a) The debarring official must make a written decision whether to debar within 45 days of closing the official record. The official record closes upon the debarring official's receipt of final submissions, information and findings of fact, if any. The debarring official may extend that period for good cause.

(b) The debarring official sends you written notice, pursuant to § 180.615 that the official decided, either—

(1) Not to debar you; or

(2) To debar you. In this event, the notice:

(i) Refers to the Notice of Proposed Debarment;

(ii) Specifies the reasons for your debarment;

(iii) States the period of your debarment, including the effective dates; and

(iv) Advises you that your debarment is effective for covered transactions and contracts that are subject to the Federal Acquisition Regulation (48 CFR chapter 1), throughout the executive branch of the Federal Government unless an agency head or an authorized designee grants an exception.

§ 180.875   May I ask the debarring official to reconsider a decision to debar me?

Yes, as a debarred person you may ask the debarring official to reconsider the debarment decision or to reduce the time period or scope of the debarment. However, you must put your request in writing and support it with documentation.

§ 180.880   What factors may influence the debarring official during reconsideration?

The debarring official may reduce or terminate your debarment based on—

(a) Newly discovered material evidence;

(b) A reversal of the conviction or civil judgment upon which your debarment was based;

(c) A bona fide change in ownership or management;

(d) Elimination of other causes for which the debarment was imposed; or

(e) Other reasons the debarring official finds appropriate.

§180.885   May the debarring official extend a debarment?

(a) Yes, the debarring official may extend a debarment for an additional period, if that official determines that an extension is necessary to protect the public interest.

(b) However, the debarring official may not extend a debarment solely on the basis of the facts and circumstances upon which the initial debarment action was based.

(c) If the debarring official decides that a debarment for an additional period is necessary, the debarring official must follow the applicable procedures in this subpart, and subpart F of this part, to extend the debarment.

Subpart I—Definitions

§180.900   Adequate evidence.

Adequate evidence means information sufficient to support the reasonable belief that a particular act or omission has occurred.

§180.905   Affiliate.

Persons are *affiliates* of each other if, directly or indirectly, either one controls or has the power to control the other or a third person controls or has the power to control both. The ways a Federal agency may determine control include, but are not limited to—

(a) Interlocking management or ownership;

(b) Identity of interests among family members;

(c) Shared facilities and equipment;

(d) Common use of employees; or

(e) A business entity which has been organized following the exclusion of a person which has the same or similar management, ownership, or principal employees as the excluded person.

§180.910   Agent or representative.

Agent or representative means any person who acts on behalf of, or who is authorized to commit a participant in a covered transaction.

§180.915   Civil judgment.

Civil judgment means the disposition of a civil action by any court of competent jurisdiction, whether by verdict, decision, settlement, stipulation, other disposition which creates a civil liability for the complained of wrongful acts, or a final determination of liability under the Program Fraud Civil Remedies Act of 1988 (31 U.S.C. 3801–3812).

§180.920   Conviction.

Conviction means—

(a) A judgment or any other determination of guilt of a criminal offense by any court of competent jurisdiction, whether entered upon a verdict or plea, including a plea of nolo contendere; or

(b) Any other resolution that is the functional equivalent of a judgment, including probation before judgment and deferred prosecution. A disposition without the participation of the court is the functional equivalent of a judgment only if it includes an admission of guilt.

§180.925   Debarment.

Debarment means an action taken by a debarring official under Subpart H of this part to exclude a person from participating in covered transactions and transactions covered under the Federal Acquisition Regulation (48 CFR chapter 1). A person so excluded is debarred.

§180.930   Debarring official.

Debarring official means an agency official who is authorized to impose debarment. A debarring official is either—

(a) The agency head; or

(b) An official designated by the agency head.

§180.935   Disqualified.

Disqualified means that a person is prohibited from participating in specified Federal procurement or nonprocurement transactions as required under a statute, Executive order (other than Executive Orders 12549 and 12689) or other authority. Examples of disqualifications include persons prohibited under—

(a) The Davis-Bacon Act (40 U.S.C. 276(a));

(b) The equal employment opportunity acts and Executive orders; or

(c) The Clean Air Act (42 U.S.C. 7606), Clean Water Act (33 U.S.C. 1368) and Executive Order 11738 (3 CFR, 1973 Comp., p. 799).

§ 180.940   Excluded or exclusion.

Excluded or exclusion means—

(a) That a person or commodity is prohibited from being a participant in covered transactions, whether the person has been suspended; debarred; proposed for debarment under 48 CFR part 9, subpart 9.4; voluntarily excluded; or

(b) The act of excluding a person.

§ 180.945   Excluded Parties List System (EPLS).

Excluded Parties List System (EPLS) means the list maintained and disseminated by the General Services Administration (GSA) containing the names and other information about persons who are ineligible.

§ 180.950   Federal agency.

Federal agency means any United States executive department, military department, defense agency or any other agency of the executive branch. Other agencies of the Federal government are not considered "agencies" for the purposes of this part unless they issue regulations adopting the governmentwide Debarment and Suspension system under Executive Orders 12549 and 12689.

§ 180.955   Indictment.

Indictment means an indictment for a criminal offense. A presentment, information, or other filing by a competent authority charging a criminal offense shall be given the same effect as an indictment.

§ 180.960   Ineligible or ineligibility.

Ineligible or ineligibility means that a person or commodity is prohibited from covered transactions because of an exclusion or disqualification.

§ 180.965   Legal proceedings.

Legal proceedings means any criminal proceeding or any civil judicial proceeding, including a proceeding under the Program Fraud Civil Remedies Act (31 U.S.C. 3801–3812), to which the Federal Government or a State or local government or quasi-governmental authority is a party. The term also includes appeals from those proceedings.

§ 180.970   Nonprocurement transaction.

(a) *Nonprocurement transaction* means any transaction, regardless of type (except procurement contracts), including, but not limited to the following:

(1) Grants.

(2) Cooperative agreements.

(3) Scholarships.

(4) Fellowships.

(5) Contracts of assistance.

(6) Loans.

(7) Loan guarantees.

(8) Subsidies.

(9) Insurances.

(10) Payments for specified uses.

(11) Donation agreements.

(b) A nonprocurement transaction at any tier does not require the transfer of Federal funds.

§ 180.975   Notice.

Notice means a written communication served in person, sent by certified mail or its equivalent, or sent electronically by e-mail or facsimile. (See § 180. 615.)

§ 180.980   Participant.

Participant means any person who submits a proposal for or who enters into a covered transaction, including an agent or representative of a participant.

§ 180.985   Person.

Person means any individual, corporation, partnership, association, unit of government, or legal entity, however organized.

§ 180.990   Preponderance of the evidence.

Preponderance of the evidence means proof by information that, compared with information opposing it, leads to the conclusion that the fact at issue is more probably true than not.

§ 180.995 **Principal.**

Principal means—

(a) An officer, director, owner, partner, principal investigator, or other person within a participant with management or supervisory responsibilities related to a covered transaction; or

(b) A consultant or other person, whether or not employed by the participant or paid with Federal funds, who—

(1) Is in a position to handle Federal funds;

(2) Is in a position to influence or control the use of those funds; or,

(3) Occupies a technical or professional position capable of substantially influencing the development or outcome of an activity required to perform the covered transaction.

§ 180.1000 **Respondent.**

Respondent means a person against whom an agency has initiated a debarment or suspension action.

§ 180.1005 **State.**

(a) *State* means—

(1) Any of the states of the United States;

(2) The District of Columbia;

(3) The Commonwealth of Puerto Rico;

(4) Any territory or possession of the United States; or

(5) Any agency or instrumentality of a state.

(b) For purposes of this part, *State* does not include institutions of higher education, hospitals, or units of local government.

§ 180.1010 **Suspending official.**

(a) *Suspending official* means an agency official who is authorized to impose suspension. The suspending official is either:

(1) The agency head; or

(2) An official designated by the agency head.

§ 180.1015 **Suspension.**

Suspension is an action taken by a suspending official under subpart G of this part that immediately prohibits a person from participating in covered transactions and transactions covered under the Federal Acquisition Regulation (48 CFR chapter 1) for a temporary period, pending completion of an agency investigation and any judicial or administrative proceedings that may ensue. A person so excluded is suspended.

§ 180.1020 **Voluntary exclusion or voluntarily excluded.**

(a) *Voluntary exclusion* means a person's agreement to be excluded under the terms of a settlement between the person and one or more agencies. Voluntary exclusion must have governmentwide effect.

(b) *Voluntarily excluded* means the status of a person who has agreed to a voluntary exclusion.

APPENDIX TO PART 180—COVERED
TRANSACTIONS

COVERED TRANSACTIONS

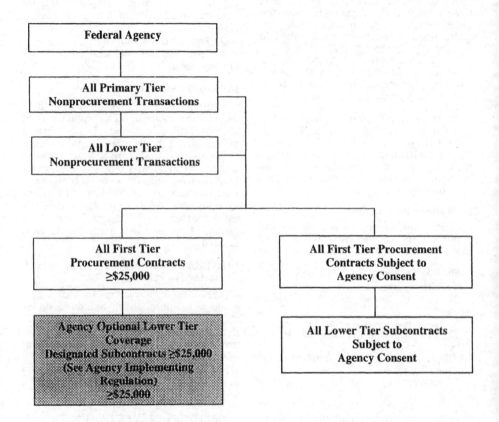

PART 181 [RESERVED]

PART 182—GOVERNMENTWIDE RE-QUIREMENTS FOR DRUG-FREE WORKPLACE (FINANCIAL ASSIST-ANCE)

Sec.
182.5 What does this part do?
182.10 How is this part organized?
182.15 To whom does the guidance apply?
182.20 What must a Federal agency do to implement the guidance?
182.25 What must a Federal agency address in its implementation of the guidance?
182.30 Where does a Federal agency implement the guidance?
182.35 By when must a Federal agency implement the guidance?
182.40 How is the guidance maintained?

Subpart A—Purpose and Coverage

182.100 How is this part written?
182.105 Do terms in this part have special meanings?
182.110 What do subparts A through F of this part do?
182.115 Does this part apply to me?
182.120 Are any of my Federal assistance awards exempt from this part?
182.125 Does this part affect the Federal contracts that I receive?

Subpart B—Requirements for Recipients Other Than Individuals

182.200 What must I do to comply with this part?
182.205 What must I include in my drug-free workplace statement?
182.210 To whom must I distribute my drug-free workplace statement?

AUTHORITY: 41 U.S.C. 701, *et seq.*

SOURCE: 74 FR 28150, June 15, 2009, unless otherwise noted.

§ **182.5 What does this part do?**

This part provides Office of Management and Budget (OMB) guidance for Federal agencies on the portion of the Drug-Free Workplace Act of 1988 (41 U.S.C. 701–707, as amended) that applies to grants. It also applies the provisions of the Act to cooperative agreements and other financial assistance awards, as a matter of Federal Government policy.

§ **182.10 How is this part organized?**

This part is organized in two segments.

(a) Sections 182.5 through 182.40 contain general policy direction for Federal agencies' use of the uniform policies and procedures in subparts A through F of this part.

(b) Subparts A through F of this part contain uniform governmentwide policies and procedures for Federal agency use to specify the—

(1) Types of awards that are covered by drug-free workplace requirements;

(2) Drug-free workplace requirements with which a recipient must comply;

(3) Actions required of an agency awarding official; and

(4) Consequences of a violation of drug-free workplace requirements.

§ **182.15 To whom does the guidance apply?**

This part provides OMB guidance only to Federal agencies. Publication of this guidance in the Code of Federal Regulations does not change its nature—it is guidance and not regulation. Federal agencies' implementation of the guidance governs the rights and responsibilities of other persons affected by the drug-free workplace requirements.

§ **182.20 What must a Federal agency do to implement the guidance?**

To comply with the requirement in Section 41 U.S.C. 705 for Government-wide regulations, each Federal agency that awards grants or cooperative agreements or makes other financial assistance awards that are subject to the drug-free workplace requirements in subparts A through F of the guidance must issue a regulation consistent with those subparts.

§ **182.25 What must a Federal agency address in its implementation of the guidance?**

Each Federal agency's implementing regulation:

(a) Must establish drug-free workplace policies and procedures for that agency's awards that are consistent with the guidance in this part. When adopted by a Federal agency, the provisions of the guidance have regulatory effect for that agency's awards.

(b) Must address some matters for which the guidance in this part gives the agency discretion. Specifically, the regulation must—

(1) State whether the agency:

(i) Has a central point to which a recipient may send the notification of a conviction that is required under § 182.225(a) or § 182.300(b); or

(ii) Requires the recipient to send the notification to the awarding official for each agency award, or to his or her official designee.

(2) Either:

(i) State that the agency head is the official authorized to determine under § 182.500 or § 182.505 that a recipient has violated the drug-free workplace requirements; or

(ii) Provide the title of the official designated to make that determination.

(c) May also, at the agency's option, identify any specific types of financial assistance awards, in addition to grants and cooperative agreements, to which the Federal agency makes this guidance applicable.

§ 182.30 Where does a Federal agency implement the guidance?

Each Federal agency that awards grants or cooperative agreements or makes other financial assistance awards that are subject to the drug-free workplace guidance in this part must issue a regulation implementing the guidance within its chapter in subtitle B of this title of the Code of Federal Regulations.

§ 182.35 By when must a Federal agency implement the guidance?

Federal agencies must submit proposed regulations to the OMB for review within nine months of the issuance of this part and issue final regulations within eighteen months of the guidance.

§ 182.40 How is the guidance maintained?

The OMB publishes proposed changes to the guidance in the FEDERAL REG-ISTER for public comment, considers comments with the help of appropriate interagency working groups, and then issues any changes to the guidance in final form.

Subpart A—Purpose and Coverage

§ 182.100 How is this part written?

(a) This part uses a "plain language" format to make it easier for the general public and business community to use and understand. The section headings and text, often in the form of questions and answers, must be read together.

(b) Pronouns used within this part, such as "I" and "you," change from subpart to subpart depending on the audience being addressed.

§ 182.105 Do terms in this part have special meanings?

This part uses terms that have special meanings. Those terms are defined in subpart F of this part.

§ 182.110 What do subparts A through F of this part do?

Subparts A through F of this part specify standard policies and procedures to carry out the Drug-Free Workplace Act of 1988 for financial assistance awards.

§ 182.115 Does this part apply to me?

(a) Portions of this part apply to you if you are either—

(1) A recipient of a Federal assistance award (see definitions of award and recipient in §§ 182.605 and 182.660, respectively); or

(2) A Federal agency awarding official.

(b) The following table shows the subparts that apply to you:

If you are * * *	See subparts * * *
(1) a recipient who is not an individual ..	A, B and E.
(2) a recipient who is an individual	A, C and E.
(3) a Federal agency awarding official ...	A, D and E.

§ 182.120 Are any of my Federal assistance awards exempt from this part?

This part does not apply to any award to which the agency head, or his or her designee, determines that the application of this part would be inconsistent with the international obligations of the United States or the laws or regulations of a foreign government.

§ 182.125 Does this part affect the Federal contracts that I receive?

This part will affect future contract awards indirectly if you are debarred or suspended for a violation of the requirements of this part, as described in § 182.510(c). However, this part does not apply directly to procurement contracts. The portion of the Drug-Free Workplace Act of 1988 that applies to Federal procurement contracts is carried out through the Federal Acquisition Regulation in chapter 1 of Title 48 of the Code of Federal Regulations (the drug-free workplace coverage currently is in 48 CFR part 23, subpart 23.5).

Subpart B—Requirements for Recipients Other Than Individuals

§ 182.200 What must I do to comply with this part?

There are two general requirements if you are a recipient other than an individual.

(a) First, you must make a good faith effort, on a continuing basis, to maintain a drug-free workplace. You must agree to do so as a condition for receiving any award covered by this part. The specific measures that you must take in this regard are described in more detail in subsequent sections of this subpart. Briefly, those measures are to—

(1) Publish a drug-free workplace statement and establish a drug-free awareness program for your employees (see §§ 182.205 through 182.220); and

(2) Take actions concerning employees who are convicted of violating drug statutes in the workplace (see § 182.225).

(b) Second, you must identify all known workplaces under your Federal awards (see § 182.230).

§ 182.205 What must I include in my drug-free workplace statement?

You must publish a statement that—

(a) Tells your employees that the unlawful manufacture, distribution, dispensing, possession, or use of a controlled substance is prohibited in your workplace;

(b) Specifies the actions that you will take against employees for violating that prohibition; and

(c) Lets each employee know that, as a condition of employment under any award, he or she:

(1) Will abide by the terms of the statement; and

(2) Must notify you in writing if he or she is convicted for a violation of a criminal drug statute occurring in the workplace and must do so no more than five calendar days after the conviction.

§ 182.210 To whom must I distribute my drug-free workplace statement?

You must require that a copy of the statement described in § 182.205 be given to each employee who will be engaged in the performance of any Federal award.

§ 182.215 What must I include in my drug-free awareness program?

You must establish an ongoing drug-free awareness program to inform employees about—

(a) The dangers of drug abuse in the workplace;

(b) Your policy of maintaining a drug-free workplace;

(c) Any available drug counseling, rehabilitation, and employee assistance programs; and

(d) The penalties that you may impose upon them for drug abuse violations occurring in the workplace.

§ 182.220 By when must I publish my drug-free workplace statement and establish my drug-free awareness program?

If you are a new recipient that does not already have a policy statement as described in § 182.205 and an ongoing awareness program as described in § 182.215, you must publish the statement and establish the program by the time given in the following table:

If * * *	Then you * * *
(a) the performance period of the award is less than 30 days ...	must have the policy statement and program in place as soon as possible, but before the date on which performance is expected to be completed.
(b) the performance period of the award is 30 days or more	must have the policy statement and program in place within 30 days after award.
(c) you believe there are extraordinary circumstances that will require more than 30 days for you to publish the policy statement and establish the awareness program.	may ask the agency awarding official to give you more time to do so. The amount of additional time, if any, to be given is at the discretion of the awarding official.

§ 182.225 What actions must I take concerning employees who are convicted of drug violations in the workplace?

There are two actions you must take if an employee is convicted of a drug violation in the workplace:

(a) First, you must notify Federal agencies if an employee who is engaged in the performance of an award informs you about a conviction, as required by § 182.205(c)(2), or you otherwise learn of the conviction. Your notification to the Federal agencies must—

(1) Be in writing;

(2) Include the employee's position title;

(3) Include the identification number(s) of each affected award;

(4) Be sent within ten calendar days after you learn of the conviction; and

(5) Be sent to every Federal agency on whose award the convicted employee was working. It must be sent to every awarding official or his or her official designee, unless the Federal agency has specified a central point for the receipt of the notices.

(b) Second, within 30 calendar days of learning about an employee's conviction, you must either—

(1) Take appropriate personnel action against the employee, up to and including termination, consistent with the requirements of the Rehabilitation Act of 1973 (29 U.S.C. 794), as amended; or

(2) Require the employee to participate satisfactorily in a drug abuse assistance or rehabilitation program approved for these purposes by a Federal, State or local health, law enforcement, or other appropriate agency.

§ 182.230 How and when must I identify workplaces?

(a) You must identify all known workplaces under each agency award. A failure to do so is a violation of your drug-free workplace requirements. You may identify the workplaces—

(1) To the agency official that is making the award, either at the time of application or upon award; or

(2) In documents that you keep on file in your offices during the performance of the award, in which case you must make the information available for inspection upon request by agency officials or their designated representatives.

(b) Your workplace identification for an award must include the actual address of buildings (or parts of buildings) or other sites where work under the award takes place. Categorical descriptions may be used (e.g., all vehicles of a mass transit authority or State highway department while in operation, State employees in each local unemployment office, performers in concert halls or radio studios).

(c) If you identified workplaces to the agency awarding official at the time of application or award, as described in paragraph (a)(1) of this section, and any workplace that you identified changes during the performance of the award, you must inform the agency awarding official.

Subpart C—Requirements for Recipients Who Are Individuals

§ 182.300 What must I do to comply with this part if I am an individual recipient?

As a condition of receiving a Federal agency award, if you are an individual recipient, you must agree that—

(a) You will not engage in the unlawful manufacture, distribution, dispensing, possession, or use of a controlled substance in conducting any activity related to the award; and

(b) If you are convicted of a criminal drug offense resulting from a violation occurring during the conduct of any award activity, you will report the conviction:

(1) In writing.

(2) Within 10 calendar days of the conviction.

(3) To the Federal agency awarding official or other designee for each award that you currently have, unless the agency designates a central point for the receipt of the notices, either in the award document or its regulation implementing the guidance in this part. When notice is made to a central point, it must include the identification number(s) of each affected award.

Subpart D—Responsibilities of Agency Awarding Officials

§182.400 What are my responsibilities as an agency awarding official?

As a Federal agency awarding official, you must obtain each recipient's agreement, as a condition of the award, to comply with the requirements in—

(a) Subpart B of this part, if the recipient is not an individual; or

(b) Subpart C of this part, if the recipient is an individual.

Subpart E—Violations of This Part and Consequences

§182.500 How are violations of this part determined for recipients other than individuals?

A recipient other than an individual is in violation of the requirements of this part if the agency head or his or her designee determines, in writing, that—

(a) The recipient has violated the requirements of subpart B of this part; or

(b) The number of convictions of the recipient's employees for violating criminal drug statutes in the workplace is large enough to indicate that the recipient has failed to make a good faith effort to provide a drug-free workplace.

§182.505 How are violations of this part determined for recipients who are individuals?

An individual recipient is in violation of the requirements of this part if the agency head or his or her designee determines, in writing, that—

(a) The recipient has violated the requirements of subpart C of this part; or

(b) The recipient is convicted of a criminal drug offense resulting from a violation occurring during the conduct of any award activity.

§182.510 What actions will the Federal Government take against a recipient determined to have violated this part?

If a recipient is determined to have violated this part, as described in §182.500 or §182.505, the agency may take one or more of the following actions—

(a) Suspension of payments under the award;

(b) Suspension or termination of the award; and

(c) Suspension or debarment of the recipient under the agency's regulation implementing the OMB guidance on nonprocurement debarment and suspension (2 CFR part 180), for a period not to exceed five years.

§182.515 Are there any exceptions to those actions?

The agency head may waive with respect to a particular award, in writing, a suspension of payments under an award, suspension or termination of an award, or suspension or debarment of a recipient if the agency head determines that such a waiver would be in the public interest. This exception authority cannot be delegated to any other official.

Subpart F—Definitions

§182.605 Award.

Award means an award of financial assistance by a Federal agency directly to a recipient.

(a) The term award includes:

(1) A Federal grant or cooperative agreement, in the form of money or property in lieu of money.

(2) A block grant or a grant in an entitlement program, whether or not the grant is exempted from coverage under the Governmentwide rule that implements OMB Circular A–102 (for availability of OMB circulars, see 5 CFR 1310.3) and specifies uniform administrative requirements.

(b) The term award does not include:

(1) Technical assistance that provides services instead of money.

(2) Loans.

(3) Loan guarantees.

(4) Interest subsidies.

(5) Insurance.

(6) Direct appropriations.

(7) Veterans' benefits to individuals (i.e., any benefit to veterans, their families, or survivors by virtue of the service of a veteran in the Armed Forces of the United States).

§ 182.610 Controlled substance.

Controlled substance means a controlled substance in schedules I through V of the Controlled Substances Act (21 U.S.C. 812), and as further defined by regulation at 21 CFR 1308.11 through 1308.15.

§ 182.615 Conviction.

Conviction means a finding of guilt (including a plea of nolo contendere) or imposition of sentence, or both, by any judicial body charged with the responsibility to determine violations of the Federal or State criminal drug statutes.

§ 182.620 Cooperative agreement.

Cooperative agreement means an award of financial assistance that, consistent with 31 U.S.C. 6305, is used to enter into the same kind of relationship as a grant (see definition of grant in § 182.650), except that substantial involvement is expected between the Federal agency and the recipient when carrying out the activity contemplated by the award. The term does not include cooperative research and development agreements as defined in 15 U.S.C. 3710a.

§ 182.625 Criminal drug statute.

Criminal drug statute means a Federal or non-Federal criminal statute involving the manufacture, distribution, dispensing, use, or possession of any controlled substance.

§ 182.630 Debarment.

Debarment means an action taken by a Federal agency to prohibit a recipient from participating in Federal Government procurement contracts and covered nonprocurement transactions. A recipient so prohibited is debarred, in accordance with the Federal Acquisition Regulation for procurement contracts (48 CFR part 9, subpart 9.4) and agency regulations implementing the OMB guidance on nonprocurement debarment and suspension (2 CFR part 180, which implements Executive Orders 12549 and 12689).

§ 182.635 Drug-free workplace.

Drug-free workplace means a site for the performance of work done in connection with a specific award at which employees of the recipient are prohibited from engaging in the unlawful manufacture, distribution, dispensing, possession, or use of a controlled substance.

§ 182.640 Employee.

(a) Employee means the employee of a recipient directly engaged in the performance of work under the award, including—

(1) All direct charge employees;

(2) All indirect charge employees, unless their impact or involvement in the performance of work under the award is insignificant to the performance of the award; and

(3) Temporary personnel and consultants who are directly engaged in the performance of work under the award and who are on the recipient's payroll.

(b) This definition does not include workers not on the payroll of the recipient (e.g., volunteers, even if used to meet a matching requirement; consultants or independent contractors not on the payroll; or employees of subrecipients or subcontractors in covered workplaces).

§ 182.645 Federal agency or agency.

Federal agency or agency means any United States executive department, military department, government corporation, government controlled corporation, any other establishment in the executive branch (including the Executive Office of the President), or any independent regulatory agency.

§ 182.650 Grant.

Grant means an award of financial assistance that, consistent with 31 U.S.C. 6304, is used to enter into a relationship—

(a) The principal purpose of which is to transfer a thing of value to the recipient to carry out a public purpose of support or stimulation authorized by a law of the United States, rather than to acquire property or services for the Federal Government's direct benefit or use; and

(b) In which substantial involvement is not expected between the Federal agency and the recipient when carrying out the activity contemplated by the award.

§ 182.655 Individual.

Individual means a natural person.

§ 182.660 Recipient.

Recipient means any individual, corporation, partnership, association, unit of government (except a Federal agency) or legal entity, however organized, that receives an award directly from a Federal agency.

§ 182.665 State.

State means any of the States of the United States, the District of Columbia, the Commonwealth of Puerto Rico, or any territory or possession of the United States.

§ 182.670 Suspension.

Suspension means an action taken by a Federal agency that immediately prohibits a recipient from participating in Federal Government procurement contracts and covered nonprocurement transactions for a temporary period, pending completion of an investigation and any judicial or administrative proceedings that may ensue. A recipient so prohibited is suspended, in accordance with the Federal Acquisition Regulation for procurement contracts (48 CFR part 9, subpart 9.4) and agency regulations implementing the OMB guidance on nonprocurement debarment and suspension (2 CFR part 180, which implements Executive Orders 12549 and 12689). Suspension of a recipient is a distinct and separate action from suspension of an award or suspension of payments under an award.

PARTS 183–199 [RESERVED]

CHAPTER II—OFFICE OF MANAGEMENT AND BUDGET GUIDANCE

PART 200—UNIFORM ADMINISTRATIVE REQUIREMENTS, COST PRINCIPLES, AND AUDIT REQUIREMENTS FOR FEDERAL AWARDS

Subpart A—Acronyms and Definitions

ACRONYMS

200.510 Financial statements.
200.511 Audit findings follow-up.
200.512 Report submission.

FEDERAL AGENCIES

200.513 Responsibilities.

AUDITORS

200.514 Scope of audit.
200.515 Audit reporting.
200.516 Audit findings.
200.517 Audit documentation.
200.518 Major program determination.
200.519 Criteria for Federal program risk.
200.520 Criteria for a low-risk auditee.

MANAGEMENT DECISIONS

200.521 Management decision.
APPENDIX I TO PART 200—FULL TEXT OF NO-
  TICE OF FUNDING OPPORTUNITY
APPENDIX II TO PART 200—CONTRACT PROVI-
  SIONS FOR NON-FEDERAL ENTITY CON-
  TRACTS UNDER FEDERAL AWARDS
APPENDIX III TO PART 200—INDIRECT (F&A)
  COSTS IDENTIFICATION AND ASSIGNMENT,
  AND RATE DETERMINATION FOR INSTITU-
  TIONS OF HIGHER EDUCATION (IHES)
APPENDIX IV TO PART 200—INDIRECT (F&A)
  COSTS IDENTIFICATION AND ASSIGNMENT,
  AND RATE DETERMINATION FOR NONPROFIT
  ORGANIZATIONS
APPENDIX V TO PART 200—STATE/LOCAL GOV-
  ERNMENT AND INDIAN TRIBE-WIDE CEN-
  TRAL SERVICE COST ALLOCATION PLANS
APPENDIX VI TO PART 200—PUBLIC ASSIST-
  ANCE COST ALLOCATION PLANS
APPENDIX VII TO PART 220—STATES AND
  LOCAL GOVERNMENT AND INDIAN TRIBE IN-
  DIRECT COST PROPOSALS
APPENDIX VIII TO PART 200—NONPROFIT OR-
  GANIZATIONS EXEMPTED FROM SUBPART
  E—COST PRINCIPLES OF PART 200
APPENDIX IX TO PART 200—HOSPITAL COST
  PRINCIPLES
APPENDIX X TO PART 200—DATA COLLECTION
  FORM (FORM SF-SAC)
APPENDIX XI TO PART 200—COMPLIANCE SUP-
  PLEMENT

AUTHORITY: 31 U.S.C. 503

SOURCE: 78 FR 78608, Dec. 26, 2013, unless
otherwise noted.

Subpart A—Acronyms and Definitions

ACRONYMS

§ 200.0 Acronyms.

ACRONYM   TERM

CAS Cost Accounting Standards
CFDA Catalog of Federal Domestic
  Assistance

CFR Code of Federal Regulations
CMIA Cash Management Improve-
  ment Act
COG Councils Of Governments
COSO Committee of Sponsoring Orga-
  nizations of the Treadway Commis-
  sion
D&B Dun and Bradstreet
DUNS Data Universal Numbering
  System
EPA Environmental Protection Agen-
  cy
ERISA Employee Retirement Income
  Security Act of 1974 (29 U.S.C. 1301–
  1461)
EUI Energy Usage Index
F&A Facilities and Administration
FAC Federal Audit Clearinghouse
FAIN Federal Award Identification
  Number
FAPIIS Federal Awardee Perform-
  ance and Integrity Information Sys-
  tem
FAR Federal Acquisition Regulation
FFATA Federal Funding Account-
  ability and Transparency Act of 2006
  or Transparency Act—Public Law
  109–282, as amended by section 6202(a)
  of Public Law 110–252 (31 U.S.C. 6101)
FICA Federal Insurance Contribu-
  tions Act
FOIA Freedom of Information Act
FR Federal Register
FTE Full-time equivalent
GAAP Generally Accepted Account-
  ing Principles
GAGAS Generally Accepted Govern-
  ment Accounting Standards
GAO General Accounting Office
GOCO Government owned, contractor
  operated
GSA General Services Administration
IBS Institutional Base Salary
IHE Institutions of Higher Education
IRC Internal Revenue Code
ISDEAA Indian Self-Determination
  and Education and Assistance Act
MTC Modified Total Cost
MTDC Modified Total Direct Cost
OMB Office of Management and Budg-
  et
PII Personally Identifiable Informa-
  tion
PRHP Post-retirement Health Plans
PTE Pass-through Entity
REUI Relative Energy Usage Index
SAM System for Award Management
SFA Student Financial Aid
SNAP Supplemental Nutrition Assist-
  ance Program

SPOC   Single Point of Contact
TANF   Temporary   Assistance   for
  Needy Families
TFM   Treasury Financial Manual
U.S.C.   United States Code
VAT   Value Added Tax

§200.1   Definitions.

These are the definitions for terms used in this part. Different definitions may be found in Federal statutes or regulations that apply more specifically to particular programs or activities. These definitions could be supplemented by additional instructional information provided in governmentwide standard information collections.

§200.2   Acquisition cost.

Acquisition cost means the cost of the asset including the cost to ready the asset for its intended use. Acquisition cost for equipment, for example, means the net invoice price of the equipment, including the cost of any modifications, attachments, accessories, or auxiliary apparatus necessary to make it usable for the purpose for which it is acquired. Acquisition costs for software includes those development costs capitalized in accordance with generally accepted accounting principles (GAAP). Ancillary charges, such as taxes, duty, protective in transit insurance, freight, and installation may be included in or excluded from the acquisition cost in accordance with the non-Federal entity's regular accounting practices.

§200.3   Advance payment.

Advance payment means a payment that a Federal awarding agency or pass-through entity makes by any appropriate payment mechanism, including a predetermined payment schedule, before the non-Federal entity disburses the funds for program purposes.

§200.4   Allocation.

Allocation means the process of assigning a cost, or a group of costs, to one or more cost objective(s), in reasonable proportion to the benefit provided or other equitable relationship. The process may entail assigning a cost(s) directly to a final cost objective or through one or more intermediate cost objectives.

§200.5   Audit finding.

Audit finding means deficiencies which the auditor is required by §200.516 Audit findings, paragraph (a) to report in the schedule of findings and questioned costs.

§200.6   Auditee.

Auditee means any non-Federal entity that expends Federal awards which must be audited under Subpart F—Audit Requirements of this part.

§200.7   Auditor.

Auditor means an auditor who is a public accountant or a Federal, state or local government audit organization, which meets the general standards specified in generally accepted government auditing standards (GAGAS). The term auditor does not include internal auditors of nonprofit organizations.

§200.8   Budget.

Budget means the financial plan for the project or program that the Federal awarding agency or pass-through entity approves during the Federal award process or in subsequent amendments to the Federal award. It may include the Federal and non-Federal share or only the Federal share, as determined by the Federal awarding agency or pass-through entity.

§200.9   Central service cost allocation plan.

Central service cost allocation plan means the documentation identifying, accumulating, and allocating or developing billing rates based on the allowable costs of services provided by a state, local government, or Indian tribe on a centralized basis to its departments and agencies. The costs of these services may be allocated or billed to users.

§200.10   Catalog of Federal Domestic Assistance (CFDA) number.

CFDA number means the number assigned to a Federal program in the CFDA.

§ 200.11 CFDA program title.

CFDA program title means the title of the program under which the Federal award was funded in the CFDA.

§ 200.12 Capital assets.

Capital assets means tangible or intangible assets used in operations having a useful life of more than one year which are capitalized in accordance with GAAP. Capital assets include:

(a) Land, buildings (facilities), equipment, and intellectual property (including software) whether acquired by purchase, construction, manufacture, lease-purchase, exchange, or through capital leases; and

(b) Additions, improvements, modifications, replacements, rearrangements, reinstallations, renovations or alterations to capital assets that materially increase their value or useful life (not ordinary repairs and maintenance).

§ 200.13 Capital expenditures.

Capital expenditures means expenditures to acquire capital assets or expenditures to make additions, improvements, modifications, replacements, rearrangements, reinstallations, renovations, or alterations to capital assets that materially increase their value or useful life.

§ 200.14 Claim.

Claim means, depending on the context, either:

(a) A written demand or written assertion by one of the parties to a Federal award seeking as a matter of right:

(1) The payment of money in a sum certain;

(2) The adjustment or interpretation of the terms and conditions of the Federal award; or

(3) Other relief arising under or relating to a Federal award.

(b) A request for payment that is not in dispute when submitted.

§ 200.15 Class of Federal awards.

Class of Federal awards means a group of Federal awards either awarded under a specific program or group of programs or to a specific type of non-Federal entity or group of non-Federal entities to which specific provisions or exceptions may apply.

§ 200.16 Closeout.

Closeout means the process by which the Federal awarding agency or pass-through entity determines that all applicable administrative actions and all required work of the Federal award have been completed and takes actions as described in § 200.343 Closeout.

§ 200.17 Cluster of programs.

Cluster of programs means a grouping of closely related programs that share common compliance requirements. The types of clusters of programs are research and development (R&D), student financial aid (SFA), and other clusters. "Other clusters" are as defined by OMB in the compliance supplement or as designated by a state for Federal awards the state provides to its subrecipients that meet the definition of a cluster of programs. When designating an "other cluster," a state must identify the Federal awards included in the cluster and advise the subrecipients of compliance requirements applicable to the cluster, consistent with § 200.331 Requirements for pass-through entities, paragraph (a). A cluster of programs must be considered as one program for determining major programs, as described in § 200.518 Major program determination, and, with the exception of R&D as described in § 200.501 Audit requirements, paragraph (c), whether a program-specific audit may be elected.

§ 200.18 Cognizant agency for audit.

Cognizant agency for audit means the Federal agency designated to carry out the responsibilities described in § 200.513 Responsibilities, paragraph (a). The cognizant agency for audit is not necessarily the same as the cognizant agency for indirect costs. A list of cognizant agencies for audit may be found at the FAC Web site.

§ 200.19 Cognizant agency for indirect costs.

Cognizant agency for indirect costs means the Federal agency responsible for reviewing, negotiating, and approving cost allocation plans or indirect cost proposals developed under this part on behalf of all Federal agencies.

The cognizant agency for indirect cost is not necessarily the same as the cognizant agency for audit. For assignments of cognizant agencies see the following:

(a) For IHEs: Appendix III to Part 200—Indirect (F&A) Costs Identification and Assignment, and Rate Determination for Institutions of Higher Education (IHEs), paragraph C.10.

(b) For nonprofit organizations: Appendix IV to Part 200—Indirect (F&A) Costs Identification and Assignment, and Rate Determination for Nonprofit Organizations, paragraph C.1.

(c) For state and local governments: Appendix V to Part 200—State/Local Government and Indian Tribe-Wide Central Service Cost Allocation Plans, paragraph F.1.

§ 200.20 Computing devices.

Computing devices means machines used to acquire, store, analyze, process, and publish data and other information electronically, including accessories (or "peripherals") for printing, transmitting and receiving, or storing electronic information. See also §§ 200.94 Supplies and 200.58 Information technology systems.

§ 200.21 Compliance supplement.

Compliance supplement means Appendix XI to Part 200—Compliance Supplement (previously known as the Circular A–133 Compliance Supplement).

§ 200.22 Contract.

Contract means a legal instrument by which a non-Federal entity purchases property or services needed to carry out the project or program under a Federal award. The term as used in this part does not include a legal instrument, even if the non-Federal entity considers it a contract, when the substance of the transaction meets the definition of a Federal award or subaward (see § 200.92 Subaward).

§ 200.23 Contractor.

Contractor means an entity that receives a contract as defined in § 200.22 Contract.

§ 200.24 Cooperative agreement.

Cooperative agreement means a legal instrument of financial assistance between a Federal awarding agency or pass-through entity and a non-Federal entity that, consistent with 31 U.S.C. 6302–6305:

(a) Is used to enter into a relationship the principal purpose of which is to transfer anything of value from the Federal awarding agency or pass-through entity to the non-Federal entity to carry out a public purpose authorized by a law of the United States (see 31 U.S.C. 6101(3)); and not to acquire property or services for the Federal government or pass-through entity's direct benefit or use;

(b) Is distinguished from a grant in that it provides for substantial involvement between the Federal awarding agency or pass-through entity and the non-Federal entity in carrying out the activity contemplated by the Federal award.

(c) The term does not include:

(1) A cooperative research and development agreement as defined in 15 U.S.C. 3710a; or

(2) An agreement that provides only:

(i) Direct United States Government cash assistance to an individual;

(ii) A subsidy;

(iii) A loan;

(iv) A loan guarantee; or

(v) Insurance.

§ 200.25 Cooperative audit resolution.

Cooperative audit resolution means the use of audit follow-up techniques which promote prompt corrective action by improving communication, fostering collaboration, promoting trust, and developing an understanding between the Federal agency and the non-Federal entity. This approach is based upon:

(a) A strong commitment by Federal agency and non-Federal entity leadership to program integrity;

(b) Federal agencies strengthening partnerships and working cooperatively with non-Federal entities and their auditors; and non-Federal entities and their auditors working cooperatively with Federal agencies;

(c) A focus on current conditions and corrective action going forward;

(d) Federal agencies offering appropriate relief for past noncompliance when audits show prompt corrective action has occurred; and

(e) Federal agency leadership sending a clear message that continued failure to correct conditions identified by audits which are likely to cause improper payments, fraud, waste, or abuse is unacceptable and will result in sanctions.

§ 200.26   Corrective action.

Corrective action means action taken by the auditee that:
(a) Corrects identified deficiencies;
(b) Produces recommended improvements; or
(c) Demonstrates that audit findings are either invalid or do not warrant auditee action.

§ 200.27   Cost allocation plan.

Cost allocation plan means central service cost allocation plan or public assistance cost allocation plan.

§ 200.28   Cost objective.

Cost objective means a program, function, activity, award, organizational subdivision, contract, or work unit for which cost data are desired and for which provision is made to accumulate and measure the cost of processes, products, jobs, capital projects, etc. A cost objective may be a major function of the non-Federal entity, a particular service or project, a Federal award, or an indirect (Facilities & Administrative (F&A)) cost activity, as described in Subpart E—Cost Principles of this Part. See also §§ 200.44 Final cost objective and 200.60 Intermediate cost objective.

§ 200.29   Cost sharing or matching.

Cost sharing or matching means the portion of project costs not paid by Federal funds (unless otherwise authorized by Federal statute). See also § 200.306 Cost sharing or matching.

§ 200.30   Cross-cutting audit finding.

Cross-cutting audit finding means an audit finding where the same underlying condition or issue affects Federal awards of more than one Federal awarding agency or pass-through entity.

§ 200.31   Disallowed costs.

Disallowed costs means those charges to a Federal award that the Federal awarding agency or pass-through enti-ty determines to be unallowable, in accordance with the applicable Federal statutes, regulations, or the terms and conditions of the Federal award.

§ 200.32   Data Universal Numbering System (DUNS) number.

DUNS number means the nine-digit number established and assigned by Dun and Bradstreet, Inc. (D&B) to uniquely identify entities. A non-Federal entity is required to have a DUNS number in order to apply for, receive, and report on a Federal award. A DUNS number may be obtained from D&B by telephone (currently 866–705–5711) or the Internet (currently at *http:// fedgov.dnb.com/webform*).

§ 200.33   Equipment.

Equipment means tangible personal property (including information technology systems) having a useful life of more than one year and a per-unit acquisition cost which equals or exceeds the lesser of the capitalization level established by the non-Federal entity for financial statement purposes, or $5,000. See also §§ 200.12 Capital assets, 200.20 Computing devices, 200.48 General purpose equipment, 200.58 Information technology systems, 200.89 Special purpose equipment, and 200.94 Supplies.

§ 200.34   Expenditures.

Expenditures means charges made by a non-Federal entity to a project or program for which a Federal award was received.
(a) The charges may be reported on a cash or accrual basis, as long as the methodology is disclosed and is consistently applied.
(b) For reports prepared on a cash basis, expenditures are the sum of:
(1) Cash disbursements for direct charges for property and services;
(2) The amount of indirect expense charged;
(3) The value of third-party in-kind contributions applied; and
(4) The amount of cash advance payments and payments made to subrecipients.
(c) For reports prepared on an accrual basis, expenditures are the sum of:
(1) Cash disbursements for direct charges for property and services;

(2) The amount of indirect expense incurred;

(3) The value of third-party in-kind contributions applied; and

(4) The net increase or decrease in the amounts owed by the non-Federal entity for:

(i) Goods and other property received;

(ii) Services performed by employees, contractors, subrecipients, and other payees; and

(iii) Programs for which no current services or performance are required such as annuities, insurance claims, or other benefit payments.

§200.35 Federal agency.

Federal agency means an "agency" as defined at 5 U.S.C. 551(1) and further clarified by 5 U.S.C. 552(f).

§200.36 Federal Audit Clearinghouse (FAC).

FAC means the clearinghouse designated by OMB as the repository of record where non-Federal entities are required to transmit the reporting packages required by Subpart F—Audit Requirements of this part. The mailing address of the FAC is Federal Audit Clearinghouse, Bureau of the Census, 1201 E. 10th Street, Jeffersonville, IN 47132 and the web address is: *http://harvester.census.gov/sac/*. Any future updates to the location of the FAC may be found at the OMB Web site.

§200.37 Federal awarding agency.

Federal awarding agency means the Federal agency that provides a Federal award directly to a non-Federal entity.

§200.38 Federal award.

Federal award has the meaning, depending on the context, in either paragraph (a) or (b) of this section:

(a)(1) The Federal financial assistance that a non-Federal entity receives directly from a Federal awarding agency or indirectly from a pass-through entity, as described in §200.101 Applicability; or

(2) The cost-reimbursement contract under the Federal Acquisition Regulations that a non-Federal entity receives directly from a Federal awarding agency or indirectly from a pass-through entity, as described in §200.101 Applicability.

(b) The instrument setting forth the terms and conditions. The instrument is the grant agreement, cooperative agreement, other agreement for assistance covered in paragraph (b) of §200.40 Federal financial assistance, or the cost-reimbursement contract awarded under the Federal Acquisition Regulations.

(c) Federal award does not include other contracts that a Federal agency uses to buy goods or services from a contractor or a contract to operate Federal government owned, contractor operated facilities (GOCOs).

(d) See also definitions of Federal financial assistance, grant agreement, and cooperative agreement.

§200.39 Federal award date.

Federal award date means the date when the Federal award is signed by the authorized official of the Federal awarding agency.

§200.40 Federal financial assistance.

(a) For grants and cooperative agreements, *Federal financial assistance* means assistance that non-Federal entities receive or administer in the form of:

(1) Grants;

(2) Cooperative agreements;

(3) Non-cash contributions or donations of property (including donated surplus property);

(4) Direct appropriations;

(5) Food commodities; and

(6) Other financial assistance (except assistance listed in paragraph (b) of this section).

(b) For Subpart F—Audit Requirements of this part, *Federal financial assistance* also includes assistance that non-Federal entities receive or administer in the form of:

(1) Loans;

(2) Loan Guarantees;

(3) Interest subsidies; and

(4) Insurance.

(c) *Federal financial assistance* does not include amounts received as reimbursement for services rendered to individuals as described in §200.502 Basis for determining Federal awards *expended*, paragraph (h) and (i) of this part.

§ 200.41 Federal interest.

Federal interest means, for purposes of § 200.329 Reporting on real property or when used in connection with the acquisition or improvement of real property, equipment, or supplies under a Federal award, the dollar amount that is the product of the:

(a) Federal share of total project costs; and

(b) Current fair market value of the property, improvements, or both, to the extent the costs of acquiring or improving the property were included as project costs.

§ 200.42 Federal program.

Federal program means:

(a) All Federal awards which are assigned a single number in the CFDA.

(b) When no CFDA number is assigned, all Federal awards to non-Federal entities from the same agency made for the same purpose should be combined and considered one program.

(c) Notwithstanding paragraphs (a) and (b) of this definition, a cluster of programs. The types of clusters of programs are:

(1) Research and development (R&D);

(2) Student financial aid (SFA); and

(3) "Other clusters," as described in the definition of Cluster of Programs.

§ 200.43 Federal share.

Federal share means the portion of the total project costs that are paid by Federal funds.

§ 200.44 Final cost objective.

Final cost objective means a cost objective which has allocated to it both direct and indirect costs and, in the non-Federal entity's accumulation system, is one of the final accumulation points, such as a particular award, internal project, or other direct activity of a non-Federal entity. See also §§ 200.28 Cost objective and 200.60 Intermediate cost objective.

§ 200.45 Fixed amount awards.

Fixed amount awards means a type of grant agreement under which the Federal awarding agency or pass-through entity provides a specific level of support without regard to actual costs incurred under the Federal award. This type of Federal award reduces some of the administrative burden and record-keeping requirements for both the non-Federal entity and Federal awarding agency or pass-through entity. Accountability is based primarily on performance and results. See §§ 200.201 Use of grant agreements (including fixed amount awards), cooperative agreements, and contracts, paragraph (b) and 200.332 Fixed amount subawards.

§ 200.46 Foreign public entity.

Foreign public entity means:

(a) A foreign government or foreign governmental entity;

(b) A public international organization, which is an organization entitled to enjoy privileges, exemptions, and immunities as an international organization under the International Organizations Immunities Act (22 U.S.C. 288–288f);

(c) An entity owned (in whole or in part) or controlled by a foreign government; or

(d) Any other entity consisting wholly or partially of one or more foreign governments or foreign governmental entities.

§ 200.47 Foreign organization.

Foreign organization means an entity that is:

(a) A public or private organization located in a country other than the United States and its territories that are subject to the laws of the country in which it is located, irrespective of the citizenship of project staff or place of performance;

(b) A private nongovernmental organization located in a country other than the United States that solicits and receives cash contributions from the general public;

(c) A charitable organization located in a country other than the United States that is nonprofit and tax exempt under the laws of its country of domicile and operation, and is not a university, college, accredited degree-granting institution of education, private foundation, hospital, organization engaged exclusively in research or scientific activities, church, synagogue, mosque or other similar entities organized primarily for religious purposes; or

(d) An organization located in a country other than the United States not recognized as a Foreign Public Entity.

§ 200.48 General purpose equipment.

General purpose equipment means equipment which is not limited to research, medical, scientific or other technical activities. Examples include office equipment and furnishings, modular offices, telephone networks, information technology equipment and systems, air conditioning equipment, reproduction and printing equipment, and motor vehicles. See also Equipment and Special Purpose Equipment.

§ 200.49 Generally Accepted Accounting Principles (GAAP).

GAAP has the meaning specified in accounting standards issued by the Government Accounting Standards Board (GASB) and the Financial Accounting Standards Board (FASB).

§ 200.50 Generally Accepted Government Auditing Standards (GAGAS).

GAGAS means generally accepted government auditing standards issued by the Comptroller General of the United States, which are applicable to financial audits.

§ 200.51 Grant agreement.

Grant agreement means a legal instrument of financial assistance between a Federal awarding agency or pass-through entity and a non-Federal entity that, consistent with 31 U.S.C. 6302, 6304:

(a) Is used to enter into a relationship the principal purpose of which is to transfer anything of value from the Federal awarding agency or pass-through entity to the non-Federal entity to carry out a public purpose authorized by a law of the United States (see 31 U.S.C. 6101(3)); and not to acquire property or services for the Federal awarding agency or pass-through entity's direct benefit or use;

(b) Is distinguished from a cooperative agreement in that it does not provide for substantial involvement between the Federal awarding agency or pass-through entity and the non-Federal entity in carrying out the activity contemplated by the Federal award.

(c) Does not include an agreement that provides only:
(1) Direct United States Government cash assistance to an individual;
(2) A subsidy;
(3) A loan;
(4) A loan guarantee; or
(5) Insurance.

§ 200.52 Hospital.

Hospital means a facility licensed as a hospital under the law of any state or a facility operated as a hospital by the United States, a state, or a subdivision of a state.

§ 200.53 Improper payment.

(a) *Improper payment* means any payment that should not have been made or that was made in an incorrect amount (including overpayments and underpayments) under statutory, contractual, administrative, or other legally applicable requirements; and

(b) *Improper payment* includes any payment to an ineligible party, any payment for an ineligible good or service, any duplicate payment, any payment for a good or service not received (except for such payments where authorized by law), any payment that does not account for credit for applicable discounts, and any payment where insufficient or lack of documentation prevents a reviewer from discerning whether a payment was proper.

§ 200.54 Indian tribe (or "federally recognized Indian tribe").

Indian tribe means any Indian tribe, band, nation, or other organized group or community, including any Alaska Native village or regional or village corporation as defined in or established pursuant to the Alaska Native Claims Settlement Act (43 U.S.C. Chapter 33), which is recognized as eligible for the special programs and services provided by the United States to Indians because of their status as Indians (25 U.S.C. 450b(e)). See annually published Bureau of Indian Affairs list of Indian Entities Recognized and Eligible to Receive Services.

§ 200.55 Institutions of Higher Education (IHEs).

IHE is defined at 20 U.S.C. 1001.

§ 200.56 Indirect (facilities & administrative (F&A)) costs.

Indirect (F&A) costs means those costs incurred for a common or joint purpose benefitting more than one cost objective, and not readily assignable to the cost objectives specifically benefitted, without effort disproportionate to the results achieved. To facilitate equitable distribution of indirect expenses to the cost objectives served, it may be necessary to establish a number of pools of indirect (F&A) costs. Indirect (F&A) cost pools should be distributed to benefitted cost objectives on bases that will produce an equitable result in consideration of relative benefits derived.

§ 200.57 Indirect cost rate proposal.

Indirect cost rate proposal means the documentation prepared by a non-Federal entity to substantiate its request for the establishment of an indirect cost rate as described in Appendix III to Part 200—Indirect (F&A) Costs Identification and Assignment, and Rate Determination for Institutions of Higher Education (IHEs) through Appendix VII to Part 200—States and Local Government and Indian Tribe Indirect Cost Proposals of this part.

§ 200.58 Information technology systems.

Information technology systems means computing devices, ancillary equipment, software, firmware, and similar procedures, services (including support services), and related resources. See also §§ 200.20 Computing devices and 200.33 Equipment.

§ 200.59 Intangible property.

Intangible property means property having no physical existence, such as trademarks, copyrights, patents and patent applications and property, such as loans, notes and other debt instruments, lease agreements, stock and other instruments of property ownership (whether the property is tangible or intangible).

§ 200.60 Intermediate cost objective.

Intermediate cost objective means a cost objective that is used to accumulate indirect costs or service center costs that are subsequently allocated to one or more indirect cost pools or final cost objectives. See also § 200.28 Cost objective and § 200.44 Final cost objective.

§ 200.61 Internal controls.

Internal controls means a process, implemented by a non-Federal entity, designed to provide reasonable assurance regarding the achievement of objectives in the following categories:

(a) Effectiveness and efficiency of operations;

(b) Reliability of reporting for internal and external use; and

(c) Compliance with applicable laws and regulations.

§ 200.62 Internal control over compliance requirements for Federal awards.

Internal control over compliance requirements for Federal awards means a process implemented by a non-Federal entity designed to provide reasonable assurance regarding the achievement of the following objectives for Federal awards:

(a) Transactions are properly recorded and accounted for, in order to:

(1) Permit the preparation of reliable financial statements and Federal reports;

(2) Maintain accountability over assets; and

(3) Demonstrate compliance with Federal statutes, regulations, and the terms and conditions of the Federal award;

(b) Transactions are executed in compliance with:

(1) Federal statutes, regulations, and the terms and conditions of the Federal award that could have a direct and material effect on a Federal program; and

(2) Any other Federal statutes and regulations that are identified in the Compliance Supplement; and

(c) Funds, property, and other assets are safeguarded against loss from unauthorized use or disposition.

§ 200.63 Loan.

Loan means a Federal loan or loan guarantee received or administered by a non-Federal entity, except as used in the definition of § 200.80 Program income.

(a) The term "direct loan" means a disbursement of funds by the Federal government to a non-Federal borrower under a contract that requires the repayment of such funds with or without interest. The term includes the purchase of, or participation in, a loan made by another lender and financing arrangements that defer payment for more than 90 days, including the sale of a Federal government asset on credit terms. The term does not include the acquisition of a federally guaranteed loan in satisfaction of default claims or the price support loans of the Commodity Credit Corporation.

(b) The term "direct loan obligation" means a binding agreement by a Federal awarding agency to make a direct loan when specified conditions are fulfilled by the borrower.

(c) The term "loan guarantee" means any Federal government guarantee, insurance, or other pledge with respect to the payment of all or a part of the principal or interest on any debt obligation of a non-Federal borrower to a non-Federal lender, but does not include the insurance of deposits, shares, or other withdrawable accounts in financial institutions.

(d) The term "loan guarantee commitment" means a binding agreement by a Federal awarding agency to make a loan guarantee when specified conditions are fulfilled by the borrower, the lender, or any other party to the guarantee agreement.

§ 200.64 Local government.

Local government means any unit of government within a state, including a:

(a) County;
(b) Borough;
(c) Municipality;
(d) City;
(e) Town;
(f) Township;
(g) Parish;
(h) Local public authority, including any public housing agency under the United States Housing Act of 1937;
(i) Special district;
(j) School district;
(k) Intrastate district;
(l) Council of governments, whether or not incorporated as a nonprofit corporation under state law; and

(m) Any other agency or instrumentality of a multi-, regional, or intrastate or local government.

§ 200.65 Major program.

Major program means a Federal program determined by the auditor to be a major program in accordance with § 200.518 Major program determination or a program identified as a major program by a Federal awarding agency or pass-through entity in accordance with § 200.503 Relation to other audit requirements, paragraph (e).

§ 200.66 Management decision.

Management decision means the evaluation by the Federal awarding agency or pass-through entity of the audit findings and corrective action plan and the issuance of a written decision to the auditee as to what corrective action is necessary.

§ 200.67 Micro-purchase.

Micro-purchase means a purchase of supplies or services using simplified acquisition procedures, the aggregate amount of which does not exceed the micro-purchase threshold. Micro-purchase procedures comprise a subset of a non-Federal entity's small purchase procedures. The non-Federal entity uses such procedures in order to expedite the completion of its lowest-dollar small purchase transactions and minimize the associated administrative burden and cost. The micro-purchase threshold is set by the Federal Acquisition Regulation at 48 CFR Subpart 2.1 (Definitions). It is $3,000 except as otherwise discussed in Subpart 2.1 of that regulation, but this threshold is periodically adjusted for inflation.

§ 200.68 Modified Total Direct Cost (MTDC).

MTDC means all direct salaries and wages, applicable fringe benefits, materials and supplies, services, travel, and subawards and subcontracts up to the first $25,000 of each subaward or subcontract (regardless of the period of performance of the subawards and subcontracts under the award). MTDC excludes equipment, capital expenditures, charges for patient care, rental costs, tuition remission, scholarships and fellowships, participant support costs and the portion of each subaward and subcontract in excess of $25,000. Other items may only be excluded when necessary to avoid a serious inequity in the distribution of indirect costs, and with the approval of the cognizant agency for indirect costs.

§ 200.69 Non-Federal entity.

Non-Federal entity means a state, local government, Indian tribe, institution of higher education (IHE), or nonprofit organization that carries out a Federal award as a recipient or subrecipient.

§ 200.70 Nonprofit organization.

Nonprofit organization means any corporation, trust, association, cooperative, or other organization, not including IHEs, that:

(a) Is operated primarily for scientific, educational, service, charitable, or similar purposes in the public interest;

(b) Is not organized primarily for profit; and

(c) Uses net proceeds to maintain, improve, or expand the operations of the organization.

§ 200.71 Obligations.

When used in connection with a non-Federal entity's utilization of funds under a Federal award, obligations means orders placed for property and services, contracts and subawards made, and similar transactions during a given period that require payment by the non-Federal entity during the same or a future period.

§ 200.72 Office of Management and Budget (OMB).

OMB means the Executive Office of the President, Office of Management and Budget.

§ 200.73 Oversight agency for audit.

Oversight agency for audit means the Federal awarding agency that provides the predominant amount of funding directly to a non-Federal entity not assigned a cognizant agency for audit. When there is no direct funding, the Federal awarding agency which is the predominant source of pass-through funding must assume the oversight responsibilities. The duties of the over-

sight agency for audit and the process for any reassignments are described in § 200.513 Responsibilities, paragraph (b).

§ 200.74 Pass-through entity.

Pass-through entity means a non-Federal entity that provides a subaward to a subrecipient to carry out part of a Federal program.

§ 200.75 Participant support costs.

Participant support costs means direct costs for items such as stipends or subsistence allowances, travel allowances, and registration fees paid to or on behalf of participants or trainees (but not employees) in connection with conferences, or training projects.

§ 200.76 Performance goal.

Performance goal means a target level of performance expressed as a tangible, measurable objective, against which actual achievement can be compared, including a goal expressed as a quantitative standard, value, or rate. In some instances (e.g., discretionary research awards), this may be limited to the requirement to submit technical performance reports (to be evaluated in accordance with agency policy).

§ 200.77 Period of performance.

Period of performance means the time during which the non-Federal entity may incur new obligations to carry out the work authorized under the Federal award. The Federal awarding agency or pass-through entity must include start and end dates of the period of performance in the Federal award (see §§ 200.210 Information contained in a Federal award paragraph (a)(5) and 200.331 Requirements for pass-through entities, paragraph (a)(1)(iv)).

§ 200.78 Personal property.

Personal property means property other than real property. It may be tangible, having physical existence, or intangible.

§ 200.79 Personally Identifiable Information (PII).

PII means information that can be used to distinguish or trace an individual's identity, either alone or when combined with other personal or identifying information that is linked or linkable to a specific individual. Some information that is considered to be PII is available in public sources such as telephone books, public Web sites, and university listings. This type of information is considered to be Public PII and includes, for example, first and last name, address, work telephone number, email address, home telephone number, and general educational credentials. The definition of PII is not anchored to any single category of information or technology. Rather, it requires a case-by-case assessment of the specific risk that an individual can be identified. Non-PII can become PII whenever additional information is made publicly available, in any medium and from any source, that, when combined with other available information, could be used to identify an individual.

§ 200.80 Program income.

Program income means gross income earned by the non-Federal entity that is directly generated by a supported activity or earned as a result of the Federal award during the period of performance. (See § 200.77 Period of performance.) Program income includes but is not limited to income from fees for services performed, the use or rental or real or personal property acquired under Federal awards, the sale of commodities or items fabricated under a Federal award, license fees and royalties on patents and copyrights, and principal and interest on loans made with Federal award funds. Interest earned on advances of Federal funds is not program income. Except as otherwise provided in Federal statutes, regulations, or the terms and conditions of the Federal award, program income does not include rebates, credits, discounts, and interest earned on any of them. See also § 200.407 Prior written approval (prior approval). See also 35 U.S.C. 200–212 "Disposition of Rights in Educational Awards" applies to inventions made under Federal awards.

§ 200.81 Property.

Property means real property or personal property.

§ 200.82 Protected Personally Identifiable Information (Protected PII).

Protected PII means an individual's first name or first initial and last name in combination with any one or more of types of information, including, but not limited to, social security number, passport number, credit card numbers, clearances, bank numbers, biometrics, date and place of birth, mother's maiden name, criminal, medical and financial records, educational transcripts. This does not include PII that is required by law to be disclosed. (See also § 200.79 Personally Identifiable Information (PII)).

§ 200.83 Project cost.

Project cost means total allowable costs incurred under a Federal award and all required cost sharing and voluntary committed cost sharing, including third-party contributions.

§ 200.84 Questioned cost.

Questioned cost means a cost that is questioned by the auditor because of an audit finding:

(a) Which resulted from a violation or possible violation of a statute, regulation, or the terms and conditions of a Federal award, including for funds used to match Federal funds;

(b) Where the costs, at the time of the audit, are not supported by adequate documentation; or

(c) Where the costs incurred appear unreasonable and do not reflect the actions a prudent person would take in the circumstances.

§ 200.85 Real property.

Real property means land, including land improvements, structures and appurtenances thereto, but excludes moveable machinery and equipment.

§ 200.86 Recipient.

Recipient means a non-Federal entity that receives a Federal award directly from a Federal awarding agency to carry out an activity under a Federal program. The term recipient does not include subrecipients. See also § 200.69 Non-Federal entity.

§ 200.87 Research and Development (R&D).

R&D means all research activities, both basic and applied, and all development activities that are performed by non-Federal entities. The term research also includes activities involving the training of individuals in research techniques where such activities utilize the same facilities as other research and development activities and where such activities are not included in the instruction function.

"Research" is defined as a systematic study directed toward fuller scientific knowledge or understanding of the subject studied. "Development" is the systematic use of knowledge and understanding gained from research directed toward the production of useful materials, devices, systems, or methods, including design and development of prototypes and processes.

§ 200.88 Simplified acquisition threshold.

Simplified acquisition threshold means the dollar amount below which a non-Federal entity may purchase property or services using small purchase methods. Non-Federal entities adopt small purchase procedures in order to expedite the purchase of items costing less than the simplified acquisition threshold. The simplified acquisition threshold is set by the Federal Acquisition Regulation at 48 CFR Subpart 2.1 (Definitions) and in accordance with 41 U.S.C. 1908. As of the publication of this part, the simplified acquisition threshold is $150,000, but this threshold is periodically adjusted for inflation. (Also see definition of § 200.67 Micropurchase.)

§ 200.89 Special purpose equipment.

Special purpose equipment means equipment which is used only for research, medical, scientific, or other technical activities. Examples of special purpose equipment include microscopes, x-ray machines, surgical instruments, and spectrometers. See also §§ 200.33 Equipment and 200.48 General purpose equipment.

§ 200.90 State.

State means any state of the United States, the District of Columbia, the Commonwealth of Puerto Rico, the Virgin Islands, Guam, American Samoa, the Commonwealth of the Northern Mariana Islands, and any agency or instrumentality thereof exclusive of local governments.

§ 200.91 Student Financial Aid (SFA).

SFA means Federal awards under those programs of general student assistance, such as those authorized by Title IV of the Higher Education Act of 1965, as amended, (20 U.S.C. 1070–1099d), which are administered by the U.S. Department of Education, and similar programs provided by other Federal agencies. It does not include Federal awards under programs that provide fellowships or similar Federal awards to students on a competitive basis, or for specified studies or research.

§ 200.92 Subaward.

Subaward means an award provided by a pass-through entity to a subrecipient for the subrecipient to carry out part of a Federal award received by the pass-through entity. It does not include payments to a contractor or payments to an individual that is a beneficiary of a Federal program. A subaward may be provided through any form of legal agreement, including an agreement that the pass-through entity considers a contract.

§ 200.93 Subrecipient.

Subrecipient means a non-Federal entity that receives a subaward from a pass-through entity to carry out part of a Federal program; but does not include an individual that is a beneficiary of such program. A subrecipient may also be a recipient of other Federal awards directly from a Federal awarding agency.

§ 200.94 Supplies.

Supplies means all tangible personal property other than those described in § 200.33 Equipment. A computing device is a supply if the acquisition cost is less than the lesser of the capitalization level established by the non-Federal entity for financial statement purposes or $5,000, regardless of the length of its useful life. See also §§ 200.20 Computing devices and 200.33 Equipment.

§ 200.95 Termination.

Termination means the ending of a Federal award, in whole or in part at any time prior to the planned end of period of performance.

§ 200.96 Third-party in-kind contributions.

Third-party in-kind contributions means the value of non-cash contributions (i.e., property or services) that—
(a) Benefit a federally assisted project or program; and
(b) Are contributed by non-Federal third parties, without charge, to a non-Federal entity under a Federal award.

§ 200.97 Unliquidated obligations.

Unliquidated obligations means, for financial reports prepared on a cash basis, obligations incurred by the non-Federal entity that have not been paid (liquidated). For reports prepared on an accrual expenditure basis, these are obligations incurred by the non-Federal entity for which an expenditure has not been recorded.

§ 200.98 Unobligated balance.

Unobligated balance means the amount of funds under a Federal award that the non-Federal entity has not obligated. The amount is computed by subtracting the cumulative amount of the non-Federal entity's unliquidated obligations and expenditures of funds under the Federal award from the cumulative amount of the funds that the Federal awarding agency or pass-through entity authorized the non-Federal entity to obligate.

§ 200.99 Voluntary committed cost sharing.

Voluntary committed cost sharing means cost sharing specifically pledged on a voluntary basis in the proposal's budget or the Federal award on the part of the non-Federal entity and that becomes a binding requirement of Federal award.

Subpart B—General Provisions

§ 200.100 Purpose.

(a)(1) This part establishes uniform administrative requirements, cost principles, and audit requirements for Federal awards to non-Federal entities, as described in § 200.101 Applicability. Federal awarding agencies must not impose additional or inconsistent requirements, except as provided in §§ 200.102 Exceptions and 200.210 Information contained in a Federal award, or unless specifically required by Federal statute, regulation, or Executive Order.

(2) This part provides the basis for a systematic and periodic collection and uniform submission by Federal agencies of information on all Federal financial assistance programs to the Office of Management and Budget (OMB). It also establishes Federal policies related to the delivery of this information to the public, including through the use of electronic media. It prescribes the manner in which General Services Administration (GSA), OMB, and Federal agencies that administer Federal financial assistance programs are to carry out their statutory responsibilities under the Federal Program Information Act (31 U.S.C. 6101–6106).

(b) Administrative requirements. Subparts B through D of this part set forth the uniform administrative requirements for grant and cooperative agreements, including the requirements for Federal awarding agency management of Federal grant programs before the Federal award has been made, and the requirements Federal awarding agencies may impose on non-Federal entities in the Federal award.

(c) Cost Principles. Subpart E—Cost Principles of this part establishes principles for determining the allowable costs incurred by non-Federal entities under Federal awards. The principles are for the purpose of cost determination and are not intended to identify the circumstances or dictate the extent of Federal government participation in the financing of a particular program or project. The principles are designed to provide that Federal awards bear their fair share of cost recognized under these principles except where restricted or prohibited by statute.

(d) Single Audit Requirements and Audit Follow-up. Subpart F—Audit Requirements of this part is issued pursuant to the Single Audit Act Amendments of 1996, (31 U.S.C. 7501–7507). It sets forth standards for obtaining consistency and uniformity among Federal agencies for the audit of non-Federal entities expending Federal awards. These provisions also provide the policies and procedures for Federal awarding agencies and pass-through entities when using the results of these audits.

(e) For OMB guidance to Federal awarding agencies on Challenges and Prizes, please see M–10–11 Guidance on the Use of Challenges and Prizes to Promote Open Government, issued March 8, 2010, or its successor.

§ 200.101 Applicability.

(a) *General applicability to Federal agencies.* The requirements established in this part apply to Federal agencies that make Federal awards to non-Federal entities. These requirements are applicable to all costs related to Federal awards.

(b)(1) *Applicability to different types of Federal awards.* The following table describes what portions of this part apply to which types of Federal awards. The terms and conditions of Federal awards (including this part) flow down to subawards to subrecipients unless a particular section of this part or the terms and conditions of the Federal award specifically indicate otherwise. This means that non-Federal entities must comply with requirements in this part regardless of whether the non-Federal entity is a recipient or subrecipient of a Federal award. Pass-through entities must comply with the requirements described in Subpart D—Post Federal Award Requirements of this part, §§ 200.330 Subrecipient and contractor determinations through 200.332 Fixed amount Subawards, but not any requirements in this part directed towards Federal awarding agencies unless the requirements of this part or the terms and conditions of the Federal award indicate otherwise.

The following portions of the part:	Are applicable to the following types of Federal Awards (except as noted in paragraphs (d) and (e) of this section):	Are NOT applicable to the following types of Federal Awards:
This table must be read along with the other provisions of this section		
Authority: 31 U.S.C. 503		
Subpart A—Acronyms and Definitions	—All.	
Subpart B—General Provisions, except for §§ § 200.111 English *language*, § 200.112 Conflict of *interest*, § 200.113 Mandatory *disclosures*	—All.	
§ 200.111 English *language*, § 200.112 Conflict of *interest*, and § 200.113	—Grant agreements and cooperative agreements	—Agreements for: loans, loan guarantees, interest subsidies, and insurance.
Mandatory *disclosures*		—Cost-reimbursement contracts awarded under the Federal Acquisition Regulations and cost-reimbursement subcontracts under these contracts.
Subparts C–D, except for Subrecipient Monitoring and Management	—Grant agreements and cooperative agreements	—Agreements for: loans, loan guarantees, interest subsidies, and insurance. —Cost-reimbursement contracts awarded under the Federal Acquisition Regulations and cost-reimbursement subcontracts under these contracts.
Subpart D—Post Federal Award Requirements, Subrecipient Monitoring and Management	—All.	
Subpart E—Cost Principles	—Grant agreements and cooperative agreements, except those providing food commodities —Cost-reimbursement contracts awarded under the Federal Acquisition Regulations and cost-reimbursement subcontracts under these contracts in accordance with the FAR	—Grant agreements and cooperative agreements providing food commodities. —Fixed amount awards. —Agreements for: loans, loan guarantees, interest subsidies, insurance. —Federal awards to hospitals (see Appendix IX to Part 200—Hospital Cost Principles).
Subpart F—Audit Requirements	—All.	

(2) *Federal award of cost-reimbursement contract under the FAR to a non-Federal entity.* When a non-Federal entity is awarded a cost-reimbursement contract, only Subpart D—Post Federal Award Requirements of this part, §§ 200.330 Subrecipient and contractor determinations through 200.332 Fixed amount Subawards (in addition to any FAR related requirements for subaward monitoring), Subpart E—Cost Principles of this part and Subpart F—Audit Requirements of this part are incorporated by reference into the contract. However, when the Cost Accounting Standards (CAS) are applicable to the contract, they take precedence over the requirements of this part except for Subpart F—Audit Requirements of this part when they are in conflict. In addition, costs that are made unallowable under 10 U.S.C. 2324(e) and 41 U.S.C. 4304(a) as described in the FAR subpart 31.2 and subpart 31.603 are always unallowable. For requirements other than those covered in Subpart D—Post Federal Award Requirements of this part, §§ 200.330 Subrecipient and contractor determinations through 200.332 Fixed amount Subawards, Subpart E—Cost Principles of this part and Subpart F—Audit Requirements of this part, the terms of the contract and the FAR apply.

(3) With the exception of Subpart F—Audit Requirements of this part, which is required by the Single Audit Act, in any circumstances where the provisions of Federal statutes or regulations differ from the provisions of this part, the provision of the Federal statutes or regulations govern. This includes, for agreements with Indian tribes, the provisions of the Indian Self-Determination and Education and Assistance Act (ISDEAA), as amended, 25 U.S.C 450–458ddd–2.

(c) Federal agencies may apply subparts A through E of this part to for-profit entities, foreign public entities, or foreign organizations, except where the Federal awarding agency determines that the application these subparts would be inconsistent with the international obligations of the United States or the statute or regulations of a foreign government.

(d) Except for § 200.202 Requirement to provide public notice of Federal financial assistance programs and §§ 200.330 Subrecipient and contractor determinations through 200.332 Fixed amount Subawards of Subpart D—Post Federal Award Requirements of this part, the requirements in Subpart C—Pre-Federal Award Requirements and Contents of Federal Awards, Subpart D—Post Federal Award Requirements of this part, and Subpart E—Cost Principles of this part do not apply to the following programs:

(1) The block grant awards authorized by the Omnibus Budget Reconciliation Act of 1981 (including Community Services; Preventive Health and Health Services; Alcohol, Drug Abuse, and Mental Health Services; Maternal and Child Health Services; Social Services; Low-Income Home Energy Assistance; States' Program of Community Development Block Grant Awards for Small Cities; and Elementary and Secondary Education other than programs administered by the Secretary of Education under title V, subtitle D, chapter 2, section 583—the Secretary's discretionary award program) and both the Alcohol and Drug Abuse Treatment and Rehabilitation Block Grant Award (42 U.S.C. 300x–21 to 300x–35 and 42 U.S.C. 300x–51 to 300x64) and the Mental Health Service for the Homeless Block Grant Award (42 U.S.C. 300x to 300x–9) under the Public Health Services Act.

(2) Federal awards to local education agencies under 20 U.S.C. 7702–7703b, (portions of the Impact Aid program);

(3) Payments under the Department of Veterans Affairs' State Home Per Diem Program (38 U.S.C. 1741); and

(4) Federal awards authorized under the Child Care and Development Block Grant Act of 1990, as amended:

(i) Child Care and Development Block Grant (42 U.S.C. 9858)

(ii) Child Care Mandatory and Matching Funds of the Child Care and Development Fund (42 U.S.C. 9858)

(e) Except for § 200.202 Requirement to provide public notice of Federal financial assistance programs the guidance in Subpart C—Pre-Federal Award Requirements and Contents of Federal Awards of this part does not apply to the following programs:

(1) Entitlement Federal awards to carry out the following programs of the Social Security Act:

(i) Temporary Assistance to Needy Families (title IV–A of the Social Security Act, 42 U.S.C. 601–619);

(ii) Child Support Enforcement and Establishment of Paternity (title IV–D of the Social Security Act, 42 U.S.C. 651–669b);

(iii) Foster Care and Adoption Assistance (title IV–E of the Act, 42 U.S.C. 670–679c);

(iv) Aid to the Aged, Blind, and Disabled (titles I, X, XIV, and XVI–AABD of the Act, as amended); and

(v) Medical Assistance (Medicaid) (title XIX of the Act, 42 U.S.C. 1396–1396w–5) not including the State Medicaid Fraud Control program authorized by section 1903(a)(6)(B) of the Social Security Act (42 U.S.C. 1396b(a)(6)(B)).

(2) A Federal award for an experimental, pilot, or demonstration project that is also supported by a Federal award listed in paragraph (e)(1) of this section;

(3) Federal awards under subsection 412(e) of the Immigration and Nationality Act and subsection 501(a) of the Refugee Education Assistance Act of 1980 (Pub. L. 96–422, 94 Stat. 1809), for cash assistance, medical assistance, and supplemental security income benefits to refugees and entrants and the administrative costs of providing the assistance and benefits (8 U.S.C. 1522(e));

(4) Entitlement awards under the following programs of The National School Lunch Act:

(i) National School Lunch Program (section 4 of the Act, 42 U.S.C. 1753),

(ii) Commodity Assistance (section 6 of the Act, 42 U.S.C. 1755),

(iii) Special Meal Assistance (section 11 of the Act, 42 U.S.C. 1759a),

(iv) Summer Food Service Program for Children (section 13 of the Act, 42 U.S.C. 1761), and

(v) Child and Adult Care Food Program (section 17 of the Act, 42 U.S.C. 1766).

(5) Entitlement awards under the following programs of The Child Nutrition Act of 1966:

(i) Special Milk Program (section 3 of the Act, 42 U.S.C. 1772),

(ii) School Breakfast Program (section 4 of the Act, 42 U.S.C. 1773), and

(iii) State Administrative Expenses (section 7 of the Act, 42 U.S.C. section 1776).

(6) Entitlement awards for State Administrative Expenses under The Food and Nutrition Act of 2008 (section 16 of the Act, 7 U.S.C. 2025).

(7) Non-discretionary Federal awards under the following non-entitlement programs:

(i) Special Supplemental Nutrition Program for Women, Infants and Children (section 17 of the Child Nutrition Act of 1966) 42 U.S.C. section 1786;

(ii) The Emergency Food Assistance Programs (Emergency Food Assistance Act of 1983) 7 U.S.C. section 7501 note; and

(iii) Commodity Supplemental Food Program (section 5 of the Agriculture and Consumer Protection Act of 1973) 7 U.S.C. section 612c note.

§ 200.102 Exceptions.

(a) With the exception of Subpart F—Audit Requirements of this part, OMB may allow exceptions for classes of Federal awards or non-Federal entities subject to the requirements of this part when exceptions are not prohibited by statute. However, in the interest of maximum uniformity, exceptions from the requirements of this part will be permitted only in unusual circumstances. Exceptions for classes of Federal awards or non-Federal entities will be published on the OMB Web site at www.whitehouse.gov/omb.

(b) Exceptions on a case-by-case basis for individual non-Federal entities may be authorized by the Federal awarding agency or cognizant agency for indirect costs except where otherwise required by law or where OMB or other approval is expressly required by this part. No case-by-case exceptions may be granted to the provisions of Subpart F—Audit Requirements of this part.

(c) The Federal awarding agency may apply more restrictive requirements to a class of Federal awards or non-Federal entities when approved by OMB, required by Federal statutes or regulations except for the requirements in Subpart F—Audit Requirements of this part. A Federal awarding agency may apply less restrictive requirements when making fixed amount awards as defined in Subpart A—Acronyms and

Definitions of this part, except for those requirements imposed by statute or in Subpart F—Audit Requirements of this part.

(d) On a case-by-case basis, OMB will approve new strategies for Federal awards when proposed by the Federal awarding agency in accordance with OMB guidance (such as M–13–17) to develop additional evidence relevant to addressing important policy challenges or to promote cost-effectiveness in and across Federal programs. Proposals may draw on the innovative program designs discussed in M–13–17 to expand or improve the use of effective practices in delivering Federal financial assistance while also encouraging innovation in service delivery. Proposals submitted to OMB in accordance with M–13–17 may include requests to waive requirements other than those in Subpart F—Audit Requirements of this part.

§ 200.103 Authorities.

This part is issued under the following authorities.

(a) Subpart B—General Provisions of this part through Subpart D—Post Federal Award Requirements of this part are authorized under 31 U.S.C. 503 (the Chief Financial Officers Act, Functions of the Deputy Director for Management), 31 U.S.C. 1111 (Improving Economy and Efficiency of the United States Government), 41 U.S.C. 1101–1131 (the Office of Federal Procurement Policy Act), Reorganization Plan No. 2 of 1970, and Executive Order 11541 ("Prescribing the Duties of the Office of Management and Budget and the Domestic Policy Council in the Executive Office of the President"), the Single Audit Act Amendments of 1996, (31 U.S.C. 7501–7507), as well as The Federal Program Information Act (Public Law 95–220 and Public Law 98–169, as amended, codified at 31 U.S.C. 6101–6106).

(b) Subpart E—Cost Principles of this part is authorized under the Budget and Accounting Act of 1921, as amended; the Budget and Accounting Procedures Act of 1950, as amended (31 U.S.C. 1101–1125); the Chief Financial Officers Act of 1990 (31 U.S.C. 503–504); Reorganization Plan No. 2 of 1970; and Executive Order No. 11541, "Prescribing the Duties of the Office of Management

and Budget and the Domestic Policy Council in the Executive Office of the President."

(c) Subpart F—Audit Requirements of this part is authorized under the Single Audit Act Amendments of 1996, (31 U.S.C. 7501–7507).

§ 200.104 Supersession.

As described in § 200.110 Effective/applicability date, this part supersedes the following OMB guidance documents and regulations under Title 2 of the Code of Federal Regulations:

(a) A–21, "Cost Principles for Educational Institutions" (2 CFR part 220);

(b) A–87, "Cost Principles for State, Local and Indian Tribal Governments" (2 CFR part 225) and also FEDERAL REGISTER notice 51 FR 552 (January 6, 1986);

(c) A–89, "Federal Domestic Assistance Program Information";

(d) A–102, "Grant Awards and Cooperative Agreements with State and Local Governments";

(e) A–110, "Uniform Administrative Requirements for Awards and Other Agreements with Institutions of Higher Education, Hospitals, and Other Nonprofit Organizations" (codified at 2 CFR 215);

(f) A–122, "Cost Principles for Non-Profit Organizations" (2 CFR part 230);

(g) A–133, "Audits of States, Local Governments and Non-Profit Organizations,"; and

(h) Those sections of A–50 related to audits performed under Subpart F—Audit Requirements of this part.

§ 200.105 Effect on other issuances.

For Federal awards subject to this part, all administrative requirements, program manuals, handbooks and other non-regulatory materials that are inconsistent with the requirements of this part must be superseded upon implementation of this part by the Federal agency, except to the extent they are required by statute or authorized in accordance with the provisions in § 200.102 Exceptions.

§ 200.106 Agency implementation.

The specific requirements and responsibilities of Federal agencies and non-Federal entities are set forth in this part. Federal agencies making Federal awards to non-Federal entities must implement the language in the Subpart C—Pre-Federal Award Requirements and Contents of Federal Awards of this part through Subpart F—Audit Requirements of this part in codified regulations unless different provisions are required by Federal statute or are approved by OMB.

§ 200.107   OMB responsibilities.

OMB will review Federal agency regulations and implementation of this part, and will provide interpretations of policy requirements and assistance to ensure effective and efficient implementation. Any exceptions will be subject to approval by OMB. Exceptions will only be made in particular cases where adequate justification is presented.

§ 200.108   Inquiries.

Inquiries concerning this part may be directed to the Office of Federal Financial Management Office of Management and Budget, in Washington, DC. Non-Federal entities' inquiries should be addressed to the Federal awarding agency, cognizant agency for indirect costs, cognizant or oversight agency for audit, or pass-through entity as appropriate.

§ 200.109   Review date.

OMB will review this part at least every five years after December 26, 2013.

§ 200.110   Effective/applicability date.

(a) The standards set forth in this part which affect administration of Federal awards issued by Federal agencies become effective once implemented by Federal agencies or when any future amendment to this part becomes final. Federal agencies must implement the policies and procedures applicable to Federal awards by promulgating a regulation to be effective by December 26, 2014 unless different provisions are required by statute or approved by OMB.

(b) The standards set forth in Subpart F—Audit Requirements of this part and any other standards which apply directly to Federal agencies will be effective December 26, 2013 and will apply to audits of fiscal years beginning on or after December 26, 2014.

§ 200.111   English language.

(a) All Federal financial assistance announcements and Federal award information must be in the English language. Applications must be submitted in the English language and must be in the terms of U.S. dollars. If the Federal awarding agency receives applications in another currency, the Federal awarding agency will evaluate the application by converting the foreign currency to United States currency using the date specified for receipt of the application.

(b) Non-Federal entities may translate the Federal award and other documents into another language. In the event of inconsistency between any terms and conditions of the Federal award and any translation into another language, the English language meaning will control. Where a significant portion of the non-Federal entity's employees who are working on the Federal award are not fluent in English, the non-Federal entity must provide the Federal award in English and the language(s) with which employees are more familiar.

§ 200.112   Conflict of interest.

The Federal awarding agency must establish conflict of interest policies for Federal awards. The non-Federal entity must disclose in writing any potential conflict of interest to the Federal awarding agency or pass-through entity in accordance with applicable Federal awarding agency policy.

§ 200.113   Mandatory disclosures.

The non-Federal entity or applicant for a Federal award must disclose, in a timely manner, in writing to the Federal awarding agency or pass-through entity all violations of Federal criminal law involving fraud, bribery, or gratuity violations potentially affecting the Federal award. Failure to make required disclosures can result in any of the remedies described in § 200.338 Remedies for noncompliance, including suspension or debarment. (See also 2 CFR part 180 and 31 U.S.C. 3321).

Subpart C—Pre-Federal Award Requirements and Contents of Federal Awards

§ 200.200 Purpose.

(a) Sections 200.201 Use of grant agreements (including fixed amount awards), cooperative agreements, and contracts through 200.208 Certifications and representations. Prescribe instructions and other pre-award matters to be used in the announcement and application process.

(b) Use of §§ 200.203 Notices of funding opportunities, 200.204 Federal awarding agency review of merit of proposals, 200.205 Federal awarding agency review of risk posed by applicants, and 200.207 Specific conditions, is required only for competitive Federal awards, but may also be used by the Federal awarding agency for non-competitive awards where appropriate or where required by Federal statute.

§ 200.201 Use of grant agreements (including fixed amount awards), cooperative agreements, and contracts.

(a) The Federal awarding agency or pass-through entity must decide on the appropriate instrument for the Federal award (i.e., grant agreement, cooperative agreement, or contract) in accordance with the Federal Grant and Cooperative Agreement Act (31 U.S.C. 6301–08).

(b) Fixed Amount Awards. In addition to the options described in paragraph (a) of this section, Federal awarding agencies, or pass-through entities as permitted in § 200.332 Fixed amount subawards, may use fixed amount awards (see § 200.45 Fixed amount awards) to which the following conditions apply:

(1) Payments are based on meeting specific requirements of the Federal award. Accountability is based on performance and results. The Federal award amount is negotiated using the cost principles (or other pricing information) as a guide. Except in the case of termination before completion of the Federal award, there is no governmental review of the actual costs incurred by the non-Federal entity in performance of the award. The Federal awarding agency or pass-through enti-

ty may use fixed amount awards if the project scope is specific and if adequate cost, historical, or unit pricing data is available to establish a fixed amount award with assurance that the non-Federal entity will realize no increment above actual cost. Some of the ways in which the Federal award may be paid include, but are not limited to:

(i) In several partial payments, the amount of each agreed upon in advance, and the "milestone" or event triggering the payment also agreed upon in advance, and set forth in the Federal award;

(ii) On a unit price basis, for a defined unit or units, at a defined price or prices, agreed to in advance of performance of the Federal award and set forth in the Federal award; or,

(iii) In one payment at Federal award completion.

(2) A fixed amount award cannot be used in programs which require mandatory cost sharing or match.

(3) The non-Federal entity must certify in writing to the Federal awarding agency or pass-through entity at the end of the Federal award that the project or activity was completed or the level of effort was expended. If the required level of activity or effort was not carried out, the amount of the Federal award must be adjusted.

(4) Periodic reports may be established for each Federal award.

(5) Changes in principal investigator, project leader, project partner, or scope of effort must receive the prior written approval of the Federal awarding agency or pass-through entity.

§ 200.202 Requirement to provide public notice of Federal financial assistance programs.

(a) The Federal awarding agency must notify the public of Federal programs in the Catalog of Federal Domestic Assistance (CFDA), maintained by the General Services Administration (GSA).

(1) The CFDA, or any OMB-designated replacement, is the single, authoritative, governmentwide comprehensive source of Federal financial assistance program information produced by the executive branch of the Federal government.

99

(2) The information that the Federal awarding agency must submit to GSA for approval by OMB is listed in paragraph (b) of this section. GSA must prescribe the format for the submission.

(3) The Federal awarding agency may not award Federal financial assistance without assigning it to a program that has been included in the CFDA as required in this section unless there are exigent circumstances requiring otherwise, such as timing requirements imposed by statute.

(b) For each program that awards discretionary Federal awards, non-discretionary Federal awards, loans, insurance, or any other type of Federal financial assistance, the Federal awarding agency must submit the following information to GSA:

(1) Program Description, Purpose, Goals and Measurement. A brief summary of the statutory or regulatory requirements of the program and its intended outcome. Where appropriate, the Program Description, Purpose, Goals, and Measurement should align with the strategic goals and objectives within the Federal awarding agency's performance plan and should support the Federal awarding agency's performance measurement, management, and reporting as required by Part 6 of OMB Circular A-11;

(2) Identification of whether the program makes Federal awards on a discretionary basis or the Federal awards are prescribed by Federal statute, such as in the case of formula grants.

(3) Projected total amount of funds available for the program. Estimates based on previous year funding are acceptable if current appropriations are not available at the time of the submission;

(4) Anticipated Source of Available Funds: The statutory ·authority for funding the program and, to the extent possible, agency, sub-agency, or, if known, the specific program unit that will issue the Federal awards, and associated funding identifier (e.g., Treasury Account Symbol(s));

(5) General Eligibility Requirements: The statutory, regulatory or other eligibility factors or considerations that determine the applicant's qualification

for Federal awards under the program (e.g., type of non-Federal entity); and

(6) Applicability of Single Audit Requirements as required by Subpart F—Audit Requirements of this part.

§ 200.203 Notices of funding opportunities.

For competitive grants and cooperative agreements, the Federal awarding agency must announce specific funding opportunities by providing the following information in a public notice:

(a) *Summary Information in Notices of Funding Opportunities.* The Federal awarding agency must display the following information posted on the OMB-designated governmentwide Web site for finding and applying for Federal financial assistance, in a location preceding the full text of the announcement:

(1) Federal Awarding Agency Name;

(2) Funding Opportunity Title;

(3) Announcement Type (whether the funding opportunity is the initial announcement of this funding opportunity or a modification of a previously announced opportunity);

(4) Funding Opportunity Number (required, if applicable). If the Federal awarding agency has assigned or will assign a number to the funding opportunity announcement, this number must be provided;

(5) Catalog of Federal Financial Assistance (CFDA) Number(s);

(6) Key Dates. Key dates include due dates for applications or Executive Order 12372 submissions, as well as for any letters of intent or pre-applications. For any announcement issued before a program's application materials are available, key dates also include the date on which those materials will be released; and any other additional information, as deemed applicable by the relevant Federal awarding agency.

(b) The Federal awarding agency must generally make all funding opportunities available for application for at least 60 calendar days. The Federal awarding agency may make a determination to have a less than 60 calendar day availability period but no funding opportunity should be available for less than 30 calendar days unless exigent circumstances require as determined by the Federal awarding agency head or delegate.

(c) *Full Text of Funding Opportunities.* The Federal awarding agency must include the following information in the full text of each funding opportunity. For specific instructions on the content required in this section, refer to Appendix I to Part 200—Full Text of Notice of Funding Opportunity to this part.

(1) Full programmatic description of the funding opportunity.

(2) Federal award information, including sufficient information to help an applicant make an informed decision about whether to submit an application. (See also § 200.414 Indirect (F&A) costs, paragraph (b)).

(3) Specific eligibility information, including any factors or priorities that affect an applicant's or its application's eligibility for selection.

(4) Application Preparation and Submission Information, including the applicable submission dates and time.

(5) Application Review Information including the criteria and process to be used to evaluate applications. See also § 200.205 Federal awarding agency review of risk posed by applicants. See also 2 CFR part 27.

(6) Federal Award Administration Information. See also § 200.210 Information contained in a Federal award.

§ 200.204 Federal awarding agency review of merit of proposals.

For competitive grants or cooperative agreements, unless prohibited by Federal statute, the Federal awarding agency must design and execute a merit review process for applications. This process must be described or incorporated by reference in the applicable funding opportunity (see Appendix I to this part, Full text of the Funding Opportunity.) See also § 200.203 Notices of funding opportunities.

§ 200.205 Federal awarding agency review of risk posed by applicants.

(a) Prior to making a Federal award, the Federal awarding agency is required by 31 U.S.C. 3321 and 41 U.S.C. 2313 note to review information available through any OMB-designated repositories of governmentwide eligibility qualification or financial integrity information, such as Federal Awardee Performance and Integrity Information System (FAPIIS), Dun and Bradstreet, and "Do Not Pay". See also suspension and debarment requirements at 2 CFR part 180 as well as individual Federal agency suspension and debarment regulations in title 2 of the Code of Federal Regulations.

(b) In addition, for competitive grants or cooperative agreements, the Federal awarding agency must have in place a framework for evaluating the risks posed by applicants before they receive Federal awards. This evaluation may incorporate results of the evaluation of the applicant's eligibility or the quality of its application. If the Federal awarding agency determines that a Federal award will be made, special conditions that correspond to the degree of risk assessed may be applied to the Federal award. Criteria to be evaluated must be described in the announcement of funding opportunity described in § 200.203 Notices of funding opportunities.

(c) In evaluating risks posed by applicants, the Federal awarding agency may use a risk-based approach and may consider any items such as the following:

(1) Financial stability;

(2) Quality of management systems and ability to meet the management standards prescribed in this part;

(3) History of performance. The applicant's record in managing Federal awards, if it is a prior recipient of Federal awards, including timeliness of compliance with applicable reporting requirements, conformance to the terms and conditions of previous Federal awards, and if applicable, the extent to which any previously awarded amounts will be expended prior to future awards;

(4) Reports and findings from audits performed under Subpart F—Audit Requirements of this part or the reports and findings of any other available audits; and

(5) The applicant's ability to effectively implement statutory, regulatory, or other requirements imposed on non-Federal entities.

(d) In addition to this review, the Federal awarding agency must comply with the guidelines on governmentwide suspension and debarment in 2 CFR part 180, and must require non-Federal entities to comply with these provisions. These provisions restrict Federal awards, subawards and contracts with certain parties that are debarred, suspended or otherwise excluded from or ineligible for participation in Federal programs or activities.

§ 200.206 Standard application requirements.

(a) *Paperwork clearances.* The Federal awarding agency may only use application information collections approved by OMB under the Paperwork Reduction Act of 1995 and OMB's implementing regulations in 5 CFR part 1320, Controlling Paperwork Burdens on the Public. Consistent with these requirements, OMB will authorize additional information collections only on a limited basis.

(b) If applicable, the Federal awarding agency may inform applicants and recipients that they do not need to provide certain information otherwise required by the relevant information collection.

§ 200.207 Specific conditions.

(a) Based on the criteria set forth in § 200.205 Federal awarding agency review of risk posed by applicants or when an applicant or recipient has a history of failure to comply with the general or specific terms and conditions of a Federal award, or failure to meet expected performance goals as described in § 200.210 Information contained in a Federal award, or is not otherwise responsible, the Federal awarding agency or pass-through entity may impose additional specific award conditions as needed under the procedure specified in paragraph (b) of this section. These additional Federal award conditions may include items such as the following:

(1) Requiring payments as reimbursements rather than advance payments;

(2) Withholding authority to proceed to the next phase until receipt of evidence of acceptable performance within a given period of performance;

(3) Requiring additional, more detailed financial reports;

(4) Requiring additional project monitoring;

(5) Requiring the non-Federal entity to obtain technical or management assistance; or

(6) Establishing additional prior approvals.

(b) The Federal awarding agency or pass-through entity must notify the applicant or non-Federal entity as to:

(1) The nature of the additional requirements;

(2) The reason why the additional requirements are being imposed;

(3) The nature of the action needed to remove the additional requirement, if applicable;

(4) The time allowed for completing the actions if applicable, and

(5) The method for requesting reconsideration of the additional requirements imposed.

(c) Any special conditions must be promptly removed once the conditions that prompted them have been corrected.

§ 200.208 Certifications and representations.

Unless prohibited by Federal statutes or regulations, each Federal awarding agency or pass-through entity is authorized to require the non-Federal entity to submit certifications and representations required by Federal statutes, or regulations on an annual basis. Submission may be required more frequently if the non-Federal entity fails to meet a requirement of a Federal award.

§ 200.209 Pre-award costs.

For requirements on costs incurred by the applicant prior to the start date of the period of performance of the Federal award, see § 200.458 Pre-award costs.

§ 200.210 Information contained in a Federal award.

A Federal award must include the following information:

(a) *General Federal Award Information.* The Federal awarding agency must include the following general Federal award information in each Federal award:

(1) Recipient name (which must match registered name in DUNS);

(2) Recipient's DUNS number (see §200.32 Data Universal Numbering System (DUNS) number);

(3) Unique Federal Award Identification Number (FAIN);

(4) Federal Award Date (see §200.39 Federal award date);

(5) Period of Performance Start and End Date;

(6) Amount of Federal Funds Obligated by this action;

(7) Total Amount of Federal Funds Obligated;

(8) Total Amount of the Federal Award;

(9) Budget Approved by the Federal Awarding Agency;

(10) Total Approved Cost Sharing or Matching, where applicable;

(11) Federal award project description, (to comply with statutory requirements (e.g., FFATA));

(12) Name of Federal awarding agency and contact information for awarding official,

(13) CFDA Number and Name;

(14) Identification of whether the award is R&D; and

(15) Indirect cost rate for the Federal award (including if the de minimis rate is charged per §200.414 Indirect (F&A) costs).

(b) *General Terms and Conditions* (1) Federal awarding agencies must incorporate the following general terms and conditions either in the Federal award or by reference, as applicable:

(i) Administrative requirements implemented by the Federal awarding agency as specified in this part.

(ii) National policy requirements. These include statutory, executive order, other Presidential directive, or regulatory requirements that apply by specific reference and are not program-specific. See §200.300 Statutory and national policy requirements.

(2) The Federal award must include wording to incorporate, by reference, the applicable set of general terms and conditions. The reference must be to the Web site at which the Federal awarding agency maintains the general terms and conditions.

(3) If a non-Federal entity requests a copy of the full text of the general terms and conditions, the Federal awarding agency must provide it.

(4) Wherever the general terms and conditions are publicly available, the Federal awarding agency must maintain an archive of previous versions of the general terms and conditions, with effective dates, for use by the non-Federal entity, auditors, or others.

(c) *Federal Awarding Agency, Program, or Federal Award Specific Terms and Conditions.* The Federal awarding agency may include with each Federal award any terms and conditions necessary to communicate requirements that are in addition to the requirements outlined in the Federal awarding agency's general terms and conditions. Whenever practicable, these specific terms and conditions also should be shared on a public Web site and in notices of funding opportunities (as outlined in §200.203 Notices of funding opportunities) in addition to being included in a Federal award. See also §200.206 Standard application requirements.

(d) *Federal Award Performance Goals.* The Federal awarding agency must include in the Federal award an indication of the timing and scope of expected performance by the non-Federal entity as related to the outcomes intended to be achieved by the program. In some instances (e.g., discretionary research awards), this may be limited to the requirement to submit technical performance reports (to be evaluated in accordance with Federal awarding agency policy). Where appropriate, the Federal award may include specific performance goals, indicators, milestones, or expected outcomes (such as outputs, or services performed or public impacts of any of these) with an expected timeline for accomplishment. Reporting requirements must be clearly articulated such that, where appropriate, performance during the execution of the Federal award has a standard against which non-Federal entity performance can be measured. The Federal awarding agency may include program-specific requirements, as applicable. These requirements should be aligned with agency strategic goals, strategic objectives or performance goals that are relevant to the program. See also OMB Circular A–11, Preparation, Submission and Execution of the

Budget Part 6 for definitions of strategic objectives and performance goals.

(e) Any other information required by the Federal awarding agency.

§ 200.211 Public access to Federal award information.

(a) In accordance with statutory requirements for Federal spending transparency (e.g., FFATA), except as noted in this section, for applicable Federal awards the Federal awarding agency must announce all Federal awards publicly and publish the required information on a publicly available OMB-designated governmentwide Web site (at time of publication, *www.USAspending.gov*).

(b) Nothing in this section may be construed as requiring the publication of information otherwise exempt under the Freedom of Information Act (5 U.S.C 552), or controlled unclassified information pursuant to Executive Order 13556.

Subpart D—Post Federal Award Requirements

STANDARDS FOR FINANCIAL AND PROGRAM MANAGEMENT

§ 200.300 Statutory and national policy requirements.

(a) The Federal awarding agency must manage and administer the Federal award in a manner so as to ensure that Federal funding is expended and associated programs are implemented in full accordance with U.S. statutory and public policy requirements: including, but not limited to, those protecting public welfare, the environment, and prohibiting discrimination. The Federal awarding agency must communicate to the non-Federal entity all relevant public policy requirements, including those in general appropriations provisions, and incorporate them either directly or by reference in the terms and conditions of the Federal award.

(b) The non-Federal entity is responsible for complying with all requirements of the Federal award. For all Federal awards, this includes the provisions of FFATA, which includes requirements on executive compensation, and also requirements implementing

the Act for the non-Federal entity at 2 CFR part 25 Financial Assistance Use of Universal Identifier and Central Contractor Registration and 2 CFR part 170 Reporting Subaward and Executive Compensation Information. See also statutory requirements for whistleblower protections at 10 U.S.C. 2409, 41 U.S.C. 4712, and 10 U.S.C. 2324, 41 U.S.C. 4304 and 4310.

§ 200.301 Performance measurement.

The Federal awarding agency must require the recipient to use OMB-approved governmentwide standard information collections when providing financial and performance information. As appropriate and in accordance with above mentioned information collections, the Federal awarding agency must require the recipient to relate financial data to performance accomplishments of the Federal award. Also, in accordance with above mentioned governmentwide standard information collections, and when applicable, recipients must also provide cost information to demonstrate cost effective practices (e.g., through unit cost data). The recipient's performance should be measured in a way that will help the Federal awarding agency and other non-Federal entities to improve program outcomes, share lessons learned, and spread the adoption of promising practices. The Federal awarding agency should provide recipients with clear performance goals, indicators, and milestones as described in § 200.210 Information contained in a Federal award. Performance reporting frequency and content should be established to not only allow the Federal awarding agency to understand the recipient progress but also to facilitate identification of promising practices among recipients and build the evidence upon which the Federal awarding agency's program and performance decisions are made.

§ 200.302 Financial management.

(a) Each state must expend and account for the Federal award in accordance with state laws and procedures for expending and accounting for the state's own funds. In addition, the state's and the other non-Federal entity's financial management systems, including records documenting compliance with Federal statutes, regulations, and the terms and conditions of the Federal award, must be sufficient to permit the preparation of reports required by general and program-specific terms and conditions; and the tracing of funds to a level of expenditures adequate to establish that such funds have been used according to the Federal statutes, regulations, and the terms and conditions of the Federal award. See also § 200.450 Lobbying.

(b) The financial management system of each non-Federal entity must provide for the following (see also §§ 200.333 Retention requirements for records, 200.334 Requests for transfer of records, 200.335 Methods for collection, transmission and storage of information, 200.336 Access to records, and 200.337 Restrictions on public access to records):

(1) Identification, in its accounts, of all Federal awards received and expended and the Federal programs under which they were received. Federal program and Federal award identification must include, as applicable, the CFDA title and number, Federal award identification number and year, name of the Federal agency, and name of the pass-through entity, if any.

(2) Accurate, current, and complete disclosure of the financial results of each Federal award or program in accordance with the reporting requirements set forth in §§ 200.327 Financial reporting and 200.328 Monitoring and reporting program performance. If a Federal awarding agency requires reporting on an accrual basis from a recipient that maintains its records on other than an accrual basis, the recipient must not be required to establish an accrual accounting system. This recipient may develop accrual data for its reports on the basis of an analysis of the documentation on hand. Similarly, a pass-through entity must not require a subrecipient to establish an accrual accounting system and must allow the subrecipient to develop accrual data for its reports on the basis of an analysis of the documentation on hand.

(3) Records that identify adequately the source and application of funds for federally-funded activities. These records must contain information pertaining to Federal awards, authorizations, obligations, unobligated balances, assets, expenditures, income and interest and be supported by source documentation.

(4) Effective control over, and accountability for, all funds, property, and other assets. The non-Federal entity must adequately safeguard all assets and assure that they are used solely for authorized purposes. See § 200.303 Internal controls.

(5) Comparison of expenditures with budget amounts for each Federal award.

(6) Written procedures to implement the requirements of § 200.305 Payment.

(7) Written procedures for determining the allowability of costs in accordance with Subpart E—Cost Principles of this part and the terms and conditions of the Federal award.

§ 200.303 Internal controls.

The non-Federal entity must:

(a) Establish and maintain effective internal control over the Federal award that provides reasonable assurance that the non-Federal entity is managing the Federal award in compliance with Federal statutes, regulations, and the terms and conditions of the Federal award. These internal controls should be in compliance with guidance in "Standards for Internal Control in the Federal Government" issued by the Comptroller General of the United States and the "Internal Control Integrated Framework", issued by the Committee of Sponsoring Organizations of the Treadway Commission (COSO).

(b) Comply with Federal statutes, regulations, and the terms and conditions of the Federal awards.

(c) Evaluate and monitor the non-Federal entity's compliance with statute, regulations and the terms and conditions of Federal awards.

(d) Take prompt action when instances of noncompliance are identified including noncompliance identified in audit findings.

(e) Take reasonable measures to safeguard protected personally identifiable information and other information the Federal awarding agency or pass-through entity designates as sensitive or the non-Federal entity considers sensitive consistent with applicable Federal, state and local laws regarding privacy and obligations of confidentiality.

§ 200.304 Bonds.

The Federal awarding agency may include a provision on bonding, insurance, or both in the following circumstances:

(a) Where the Federal government guarantees or insures the repayment of money borrowed by the recipient, the Federal awarding agency, at its discretion, may require adequate bonding and insurance if the bonding and insurance requirements of the non-Federal entity are not deemed adequate to protect the interest of the Federal government.

(b) The Federal awarding agency may require adequate fidelity bond coverage where the non-Federal entity lacks sufficient coverage to protect the Federal government's interest.

(c) Where bonds are required in the situations described above, the bonds must be obtained from companies holding certificates of authority as acceptable sureties, as prescribed in 31 CFR Part 223, "Surety Companies Doing Business with the United States."

§ 200.305 Payment.

(a) For states, payments are governed by Treasury-State CMIA agreements and default procedures codified at 31 CFR Part 205 "Rules and Procedures for Efficient Federal-State Funds Transfers" and TFM 4A–2000 Overall Disbursing Rules for All Federal Agencies.

(b) For non-Federal entities other than states, payments methods must minimize the time elapsing between the transfer of funds from the United States Treasury or the pass-through entity and the disbursement by the non-Federal entity whether the payment is made by electronic funds transfer, or issuance or redemption of checks, warrants, or payment by other means. See also § 200.302 Financial management paragraph (f). Except as noted elsewhere in this part, Federal

agencies must require recipients to use only OMB-approved standard governmentwide information collection requests to request payment.

(1) The non-Federal entity must be paid in advance, provided it maintains or demonstrates the willingness to maintain both written procedures that minimize the time elapsing between the transfer of funds and disbursement by the non-Federal entity, and financial management systems that meet the standards for fund control and accountability as established in this part. Advance payments to a non-Federal entity must be limited to the minimum amounts needed and be timed to be in accordance with the actual, immediate cash requirements of the non-Federal entity in carrying out the purpose of the approved program or project. The timing and amount of advance payments must be as close as is administratively feasible to the actual disbursements by the non-Federal entity for direct program or project costs and the proportionate share of any allowable indirect costs. The non-Federal entity must make timely payment to contractors in accordance with the contract provisions.

(2) Whenever possible, advance payments must be consolidated to cover anticipated cash needs for all Federal awards made by the Federal awarding agency to the recipient.

(i) Advance payment mechanisms include, but are not limited to, Treasury check and electronic funds transfer and should comply with applicable guidance in 31 CFR part 208.

(ii) Non-Federal entities must be authorized to submit requests for advance payments and reimbursements at least monthly when electronic fund transfers are not used, and as often as they like when electronic transfers are used, in accordance with the provisions of the Electronic Fund Transfer Act (15 U.S.C. 1601).

(3) Reimbursement is the preferred method when the requirements in paragraph (b) cannot be met, when the Federal awarding agency sets a specific condition per § 200.207 Specific conditions, or when the non-Federal entity requests payment by reimbursement. This method may be used on any Federal award for construction, or if the

major portion of the construction project is accomplished through private market financing or Federal loans, and the Federal award constitutes a minor portion of the project. When the reimbursement method is used, the Federal awarding agency or pass-through entity must make payment within 30 calendar days after receipt of the billing, unless the Federal awarding agency or pass-through entity reasonably believes the request to be improper.

(4) If the non-Federal entity cannot meet the criteria for advance payments and the Federal awarding agency or pass-through entity has determined that reimbursement is not feasible because the non-Federal entity lacks sufficient working capital, the Federal awarding agency or pass-through entity may provide cash on a working capital advance basis. Under this procedure, the Federal awarding agency or pass-through entity must advance cash payments to the non-Federal entity to cover its estimated disbursement needs for an initial period generally geared to the non-Federal entity's disbursing cycle. Thereafter, the Federal awarding agency or pass-through entity must reimburse the non-Federal entity for its actual cash disbursements. Use of the working capital advance method of payment requires that the pass-through entity provide timely advance payments to any subrecipients in order to meet the subrecipient's actual cash disbursements. The working capital advance method of payment must not be used by the pass-through entity if the reason for using this method is the unwillingness or inability of the pass-through entity to provide timely advance payments to the subrecipient to meet the subrecipient's actual cash disbursements.

(5) Use of resources before requesting cash advance payments. To the extent available, the non-Federal entity must disburse funds available from program income (including repayments to a revolving fund), rebates, refunds, contract settlements, audit recoveries, and interest earned on such funds before requesting additional cash payments.

(6) Unless otherwise required by Federal statutes, payments for allowable costs by non-Federal entities must not

be withheld at any time during the period of performance unless the conditions of §§ 200.207 Specific conditions, Subpart D—Post Federal Award Requirements of this part, 200.338 Remedies for Noncompliance, or the following apply:

(i) The non-Federal entity has failed to comply with the project objectives, Federal statutes, regulations, or the terms and conditions of the Federal award.

(ii) The non-Federal entity is delinquent in a debt to the United States as defined in OMB Guidance A–129, "Policies for Federal Credit Programs and Non-Tax Receivables." Under such conditions, the Federal awarding agency or pass-through entity may, upon reasonable notice, inform the non-Federal entity that payments must not be made for obligations incurred after a specified date until the conditions are corrected or the indebtedness to the Federal government is liquidated.

(iii) A payment withheld for failure to comply with Federal award conditions, but without suspension of the Federal award, must be released to the non-Federal entity upon subsequent compliance. When a Federal award is suspended, payment adjustments will be made in accordance with § 200.342 Effects of suspension and termination.

(iv) A payment must not be made to a non-Federal entity for amounts that are withheld by the non-Federal entity from payment to contractors to assure satisfactory completion of work. A payment must be made when the non-Federal entity actually disburses the withheld funds to the contractors or to escrow accounts established to assure satisfactory completion of work.

(7) Standards governing the use of banks and other institutions as depositories of advance payments under Federal awards are as follows.

(i) The Federal awarding agency and pass-through entity must not require separate depository accounts for funds provided to a non-Federal entity or establish any eligibility requirements for depositories for funds provided to the non-Federal entity. However, the non-Federal entity must be able to account for the receipt, obligation and expenditure of funds.

(ii) Advance payments of Federal funds must be deposited and maintained in insured accounts whenever possible.

(8) The non-Federal entity must maintain advance payments of Federal awards in interest-bearing accounts, unless the following apply.

(i) The non-Federal entity receives less than $120,000 in Federal awards per year.

(ii) The best reasonably available interest-bearing account would not be expected to earn interest in excess of $500 per year on Federal cash balances.

(iii) The depository would require an average or minimum balance so high that it would not be feasible within the expected Federal and non-Federal cash resources.

(iv) A foreign government or banking system prohibits or precludes interest bearing accounts.

(9) Interest earned on Federal advance payments deposited in interest-bearing accounts must be remitted annually to the Department of Health and Human Services, Payment Management System, Rockville, MD 20852. Interest amounts up to $500 per year may be retained by the non-Federal entity for administrative expense.

§ 200.306   Cost sharing or matching.

(a) Under Federal research proposals, voluntary committed cost sharing is not expected. It cannot be used as a factor during the merit review of applications or proposals, but may be considered if it is both in accordance with Federal awarding agency regulations and specified in a notice of funding opportunity. Criteria for considering voluntary committed cost sharing and any other program policy factors that may be used to determine who may receive a Federal award must be explicitly described in the notice of funding opportunity. Furthermore, only mandatory cost sharing or cost sharing specifically committed in the project budget must be included in the organized research base for computing the indirect (F&A) cost rate or reflected in any allocation of indirect costs. See also §§ 200.414 Indirect (F&A) costs, 200.203 Notices of funding opportunities, and Appendix I to Part 200—Full Text of Notice of Funding Opportunity.

(b) For all Federal awards, any shared costs or matching funds and all contributions, including cash and third party in-kind contributions, must be accepted as part of the non-Federal entity's cost sharing or matching when such contributions meet all of the following criteria:

(1) Are verifiable from the non-Federal entity's records;

(2) Are not included as contributions for any other Federal award;

(3) Are necessary and reasonable for accomplishment of project or program objectives;

(4) Are allowable under Subpart E—Cost Principles of this part;

(5) Are not paid by the Federal government under another Federal award, except where the Federal statute authorizing a program specifically provides that Federal funds made available for such program can be applied to matching or cost sharing requirements of other Federal programs;

(6) Are provided for in the approved budget when required by the Federal awarding agency; and

(7) Conform to other provisions of this part, as applicable.

(c) Unrecovered indirect costs, including indirect costs on cost sharing or matching may be included as part of cost sharing or matching only with the prior approval of the Federal awarding agency. Unrecovered indirect cost means the difference between the amount charged to the Federal award and the amount which could have been to the Federal award under the non-Federal entity's approved negotiated indirect cost rate.

(d) Values for non-Federal entity contributions of services and property must be established in accordance with § 200.434 Contributions and donations. If a Federal awarding agency authorizes the non-Federal entity to donate buildings or land for construction/facilities acquisition projects or long-term use, the value of the donated property for cost sharing or matching must be the lesser of paragraphs (d)(1) or (2) of this section.

(1) The value of the remaining life of the property recorded in the non-Federal entity's accounting records at the time of donation.

(2) The current fair market value. However, when there is sufficient justification, the Federal awarding agency may approve the use of the current fair market value of the donated property, even if it exceeds the value described in (1) above at the time of donation.

(e) Volunteer services furnished by third-party professional and technical personnel, consultants, and other skilled and unskilled labor may be counted as cost sharing or matching if the service is an integral and necessary part of an approved project or program. Rates for third-party volunteer services must be consistent with those paid for similar work by the non-Federal entity. In those instances in which the required skills are not found in the non-Federal entity, rates must be consistent with those paid for similar work in the labor market in which the non-Federal entity competes for the kind of services involved. In either case, paid fringe benefits that are reasonable, necessary, allocable, and otherwise allowable may be included in the valuation.

(f) When a third-party organization furnishes the services of an employee, these services must be valued at the employee's regular rate of pay plus an amount of fringe benefits that is reasonable, necessary, allocable, and otherwise allowable, and indirect costs at either the third-party organization's approved federally negotiated indirect cost rate or, a rate in accordance with §200.414 Indirect (F&A) costs, paragraph (d), provided these services employ the same skill(s) for which the employee is normally paid. Where donated services are treated as indirect costs, indirect cost rates will separate the value of the donated services so that reimbursement for the donated services will not be made.

(g) Donated property from third parties may include such items as equipment, office supplies, laboratory supplies, or workshop and classroom supplies. Value assessed to donated property included in the cost sharing or matching share must not exceed the fair market value of the property at the time of the donation.

(h) The method used for determining cost sharing or matching for third-party-donated equipment, buildings and land for which title passes to the non-Federal entity may differ according to the purpose of the Federal award, if paragraph (h)(1) or (2) of this section applies.

(1) If the purpose of the Federal award is to assist the non-Federal entity in the acquisition of equipment, buildings or land, the aggregate value of the donated property may be claimed as cost sharing or matching.

(2) If the purpose of the Federal award is to support activities that require the use of equipment, buildings or land, normally only depreciation charges for equipment and buildings may be made. However, the fair market value of equipment or other capital assets and fair rental charges for land may be allowed, provided that the Federal awarding agency has approved the charges. See also §200.420 Considerations for selected items of cost.

(i) The value of donated property must be determined in accordance with the usual accounting policies of the non-Federal entity, with the following qualifications:

(1) The value of donated land and buildings must not exceed its fair market value at the time of donation to the non-Federal entity as established by an independent appraiser (e.g., certified real property appraiser or General Services Administration representative) and certified by a responsible official of the non-Federal entity as required by the Uniform Relocation Assistance and Real Property Acquisition Policies Act of 1970, as amended, (42 U.S.C. 4601–4655) (Uniform Act) except as provided in the implementing regulations at 49 CFR part 24.

(2) The value of donated equipment must not exceed the fair market value of equipment of the same age and condition at the time of donation.

(3) The value of donated space must not exceed the fair rental value of comparable space as established by an independent appraisal of comparable space and facilities in a privately-owned building in the same locality.

(4) The value of loaned equipment must not exceed its fair rental value.

(j) For third-party in-kind contributions, the fair market value of goods and services must be documented and to the extent feasible supported by the same methods used internally by the non-Federal entity.

§ 200.307 Program income.

(a) *General.* Non-Federal entities are encouraged to earn income to defray program costs where appropriate.

(b) *Cost of generating program income.* If authorized by Federal regulations or the Federal award, costs incidental to the generation of program income may be deducted from gross income to determine program income, provided these costs have not been charged to the Federal award.

(c) *Governmental revenues.* Taxes, special assessments, levies, fines, and other such revenues raised by a non-Federal entity are not program income unless the revenues are specifically identified in the Federal award or Federal awarding agency regulations as program income.

(d) *Property.* Proceeds from the sale of real property or equipment are not program income; such proceeds will be handled in accordance with the requirements of Subpart D—Post Federal Award Requirements of this part, Property Standards §§ 200.311 Real property and 200.313 Equipment, or as specifically identified in Federal statutes, regulations, or the terms and conditions of the Federal award.

(e) *Use of program income.* If the Federal awarding agency does not specify in its regulations or the terms and conditions of the Federal award, or give prior approval for how program income is to be used, paragraph (e)(1) of this section must apply. For Federal awards made to IHEs and nonprofit research institutions, if the Federal awarding agency does not specify in its regulations or the terms and conditions of the Federal award how program income is to be used, paragraph (e)(2) of this section must apply. In specifying alternatives to paragraphs (e)(1) and (2) of this section, the Federal awarding agency may distinguish between income earned by the recipient and income earned by subrecipients and between the sources, kinds, or amounts of income. When the Federal awarding agency authorizes the approaches in paragraphs (e)(2) and (3) of this section, program income in excess of any amounts specified must also be deducted from expenditures.

(1) *Deduction.* Ordinarily program income must be deducted from total allowable costs to determine the net allowable costs. Program income must be used for current costs unless the Federal awarding agency authorizes otherwise. Program income that the non-Federal entity did not anticipate at the time of the Federal award must be used to reduce the Federal award and non-Federal entity contributions rather than to increase the funds committed to the project.

(2) *Addition.* With prior approval of the Federal awarding agency, program income may be added to the Federal award by the Federal agency and the non-Federal entity. The program income must be used for the purposes and under the conditions of the Federal award.

(3) *Cost sharing or matching.* With prior approval of the Federal awarding agency, program income may be used to meet the cost sharing or matching requirement of the Federal award. The amount of the Federal award remains the same.

(f) *Income after the period of performance.* There are no Federal requirements governing the disposition of income earned after the end of the period of performance for the Federal award, unless the Federal awarding agency regulations or the terms and conditions of the Federal award provide otherwise. The Federal awarding agency may negotiate agreements with recipients regarding appropriate uses of income earned after the period of performance as part of the grant closeout process. See also § 200.343 Closeout.

§ 200.308 Revision of budget and program plans.

(a) The approved budget for the Federal award summarizes the financial aspects of the project or program as approved during the Federal award process. It may include either the Federal and non-Federal share (see § 200.43 Federal share) or only the Federal share, depending upon Federal awarding agency requirements. It must be related to performance for program evaluation purposes whenever appropriate.

(b) Recipients are required to report deviations from budget or project scope or objective, and request prior approvals from Federal awarding agencies for budget and program plan revisions, in accordance with this section.

(c) For non-construction Federal awards, recipients must request prior approvals from Federal awarding agencies for one or more of the following program or budget-related reasons:

(1) Change in the scope or the objective of the project or program (even if there is no associated budget revision requiring prior written approval).

(2) Change in a key person specified in the application or the Federal award.

(3) The disengagement from the project for more than three months, or a 25 percent reduction in time devoted to the project, by the approved project director or principal investigator.

(4) The inclusion, unless waived by the Federal awarding agency, of costs that require prior approval in accordance with Subpart E—Cost Principles of this part or 45 CFR Part 74 Appendix E, "Principles for Determining Costs Applicable to Research and Development under Awards and Contracts with Hospitals," or 48 CFR Part 31, "Contract Cost Principles and Procedures," as applicable.

(5) The transfer of funds budgeted for participant support costs as defined in §200.75 Participant support costs to other categories of expense.

(6) Unless described in the application and funded in the approved Federal awards, the subawarding, transferring or contracting out of any work under a Federal award. This provision does not apply to the acquisition of supplies, material, equipment or general support services.

(7) Changes in the amount of approved cost-sharing or matching provided by the non-Federal entity. No other prior approval requirements for specific items may be imposed unless a deviation has been approved by OMB. See also §§200.102 Exceptions and 200.407 Prior written approval (prior approval).

(d) Except for requirements listed in paragraph (c)(1) of this section, the Federal awarding agency are authorized, at their option, to waive prior written approvals required by paragraph (c) this section. Such waivers may include authorizing recipients to do any one or more of the following:

(1) Incur project costs 90 calendar days before the Federal awarding agency makes the Federal award. Expenses more than 90 calendar days pre-award require prior approval of the Federal awarding agency. All costs incurred before the Federal awarding agency makes the Federal award are at the recipient's risk (i.e., the Federal awarding agency is under no obligation to reimburse such costs if for any reason the recipient does not receive a Federal award or if the Federal award is less than anticipated and inadequate to cover such costs). See also §200.458 Pre-award costs.

(2) Initiate a one-time extension of the period of performance by up to 12 months unless one or more of the conditions outlined in paragraphs (d)(2)(i) through (iii) of this section apply. For one-time extensions, the recipient must notify the Federal awarding agency in writing with the supporting reasons and revised period of performance at least 10 calendar days before the end of the period of performance specified in the Federal award. This one-time extension may not be exercised merely for the purpose of using unobligated balances. Extensions require explicit prior Federal awarding agency approval when:

(i) The terms and conditions of the Federal award prohibit the extension.

(ii) The extension requires additional Federal funds.

(iii) The extension involves any change in the approved objectives or scope of the project.

(3) Carry forward unobligated balances to subsequent periods of performance.

(4) For Federal awards that support research, unless the Federal awarding agency provides otherwise in the Federal award or in the Federal awarding agency's regulations, the prior approval requirements described in paragraph (d) are automatically waived (i.e., recipients need not obtain such prior approvals) unless one of the conditions included in paragraph (d)(2) applies.

111

(e) The Federal awarding agency may, at its option, restrict the transfer of funds among direct cost categories or programs, functions and activities for Federal awards in which the Federal share of the project exceeds the Simplified Acquisition Threshold and the cumulative amount of such transfers exceeds or is expected to exceed 10 percent of the total budget as last approved by the Federal awarding agency. The Federal awarding agency cannot permit a transfer that would cause any Federal appropriation to be used for purposes other than those consistent with the appropriation.

(f) All other changes to non-construction budgets, except for the changes described in paragraph (c) of this section, do not require prior approval (see also § 200.407 Prior written approval (prior approval)).

(g) For construction Federal awards, the recipient must request prior written approval promptly from the Federal awarding agency for budget revisions whenever paragraph (g)(1), (2), or (3) of this section applies.

(1) The revision results from changes in the scope or the objective of the project or program.

(2) The need arises for additional Federal funds to complete the project.

(3) A revision is desired which involves specific costs for which prior written approval requirements may be imposed consistent with applicable OMB cost principles listed in Subpart E—Cost Principles of this part.

(4) No other prior approval requirements for budget revisions may be imposed unless a deviation has been approved by OMB.

(5) When a Federal awarding agency makes a Federal award that provides support for construction and non-construction work, the Federal awarding agency may require the recipient to obtain prior approval from the Federal awarding agency before making any fund or budget transfers between the two types of work supported.

(h) When requesting approval for budget revisions, the recipient must use the same format for budget information that was used in the application, unless the Federal awarding agency indicates a letter of request suffices.

(i) Within 30 calendar days from the date of receipt of the request for budget revisions, the Federal awarding agency must review the request and notify the recipient whether the budget revisions have been approved. If the revision is still under consideration at the end of 30 calendar days, the Federal awarding agency must inform the recipient in writing of the date when the recipient may expect the decision.

§ 200.309　Period of performance.

A non-Federal entity may charge to the Federal award only allowable costs incurred during the period of performance and any costs incurred before the Federal awarding agency or pass-through entity made the Federal award that were authorized by the Federal awarding agency or pass-through entity.

PROPERTY STANDARDS

§ 200.310　Insurance coverage.

The non-Federal entity must, at a minimum, provide the equivalent insurance coverage for real property and equipment acquired or improved with Federal funds as provided to property owned by the non-Federal entity. Federally-owned property need not be insured unless required by the terms and conditions of the Federal award.

§ 200.311　Real property.

(a) *Title.* Subject to the obligations and conditions set forth in this section, title to real property acquired or improved under a Federal award will vest upon acquisition in the non-Federal entity.

(b) *Use.* Except as otherwise provided by Federal statutes or by the Federal awarding agency, real property will be used for the originally authorized purpose as long as needed for that purpose, during which time the non-Federal entity must not dispose of or encumber its title or other interests.

(c) *Disposition.* When real property is no longer needed for the originally authorized purpose, the non-Federal entity must obtain disposition instructions from the Federal awarding agency or pass-through entity. The instructions must provide for one of the following alternatives:

(1) Retain title after compensating the Federal awarding agency. The amount paid to the Federal awarding agency will be computed by applying the Federal awarding agency's percentage of participation in the cost of the original purchase (and costs of any improvements) to the fair market value of the property. However, in those situations where non-Federal entity is disposing of real property acquired or improved with a Federal award and acquiring replacement real property under the same Federal award, the net proceeds from the disposition may be used as an offset to the cost of the replacement property.

(2) Sell the property and compensate the Federal awarding agency. The amount due to the Federal awarding agency will be calculated by applying the Federal awarding agency's percentage of participation in the cost of the original purchase (and cost of any improvements) to the proceeds of the sale after deduction of any actual and reasonable selling and fixing-up expenses. If the Federal award has not been closed out, the net proceeds from sale may be offset against the original cost of the property. When non-Federal entity is directed to sell property, sales procedures must be followed that provide for competition to the extent practicable and result in the highest possible return.

(3) Transfer title to the Federal awarding agency or to a third party designated/approved by the Federal awarding agency. The non-Federal entity is entitled to be paid an amount calculated by applying the non-Federal entity's percentage of participation in the purchase of the real property (and cost of any improvements) to the current fair market value of the property.

§200.312 Federally-owned and exempt property.

(a) Title to federally-owned property remains vested in the Federal government. The non-Federal entity must submit annually an inventory listing of federally-owned property in its custody to the Federal awarding agency. Upon completion of the Federal award or when the property is no longer needed, the non-Federal entity must report the property to the Federal awarding agency for further Federal agency utilization.

(b) If the Federal awarding agency has no further need for the property, it must declare the property excess and report it for disposal to the appropriate Federal disposal authority, unless the Federal awarding agency has statutory authority to dispose of the property by alternative methods (e.g., the authority provided by the Federal Technology Transfer Act (15 U.S.C. 3710 (i)) to donate research equipment to educational and non-profit organizations in accordance with Executive Order 12999, "Educational Technology: Ensuring Opportunity for All Children in the Next Century."). The Federal awarding agency must issue appropriate instructions to the non-Federal entity.

(c) Exempt federally-owned property means property acquired under a Federal award the title based upon the explicit terms and conditions of the Federal award that indicate the Federal awarding agency has chosen to vest in the non-Federal entity without further obligation to the Federal government or under conditions the Federal agency considers appropriate. The Federal awarding agency may exercise this option when statutory authority exists. Absent statutory authority and specific terms and conditions of the Federal award, title to exempt federally-owned property acquired under the Federal award remains with the Federal government.

§200.313 Equipment.

See also §200.439 Equipment and other capital expenditures.

(a) *Title.* Subject to the obligations and conditions set forth in this section, title to equipment acquired under a Federal award will vest upon acquisition in the non-Federal entity. Unless a statute specifically authorizes the Federal agency to vest title in the non-Federal entity without further obligation to the Federal government, and the Federal agency elects to do so, the title must be a conditional title. Title must vest in the non-Federal entity subject to the following conditions:

(1) Use the equipment for the authorized purposes of the project until funding for the project ceases, or until the

property is no longer needed for the purposes of the project.

(2) Not encumber the property without approval of the Federal awarding agency or pass-through entity.

(3) Use and dispose of the property in accordance with paragraphs (b), (c) and (e) of this section.

(b) A state must use, manage and dispose of equipment acquired under a Federal award by the state in accordance with state laws and procedures. Other non-Federal entities must follow paragraphs (c) through (e) of this section.

(c) *Use.* (1) Equipment must be used by the non-Federal entity in the program or project for which it was acquired as long as needed, whether or not the project or program continues to be supported by the Federal award, and the non-Federal entity must not encumber the property without prior approval of the Federal awarding agency. When no longer needed for the original program or project, the equipment may be used in other activities supported by the Federal awarding agency, in the following order of priority:

(i) Activities under a Federal award from the Federal awarding agency which funded the original program or project, then

(ii) Activities under Federal awards from other Federal awarding agencies. This includes consolidated equipment for information technology systems.

(2) During the time that equipment is used on the project or program for which it was acquired, the non-Federal entity must also make equipment available for use on other projects or programs currently or previously supported by the Federal government, provided that such use will not interfere with the work on the projects or program for which it was originally acquired. First preference for other use must be given to other programs or projects supported by Federal awarding agency that financed the equipment and second preference must be given to programs or projects under Federal awards from other Federal awarding agencies. Use for non-federally-funded programs or projects is also permissible. User fees should be considered if appropriate.

(3) Notwithstanding the encouragement in § 200.307 Program income to earn program income, the non-Federal entity must not use equipment acquired with the Federal award to provide services for a fee that is less than private companies charge for equivalent services unless specifically authorized by Federal statute for as long as the Federal government retains an interest in the equipment.

(4) When acquiring replacement equipment, the non-Federal entity may use the equipment to be replaced as a trade-in or sell the property and use the proceeds to offset the cost of the replacement property.

(d) *Management requirements.* Procedures for managing equipment (including replacement equipment), whether acquired in whole or in part under a Federal award, until disposition takes place will, as a minimum, meet the following requirements:

(1) Property records must be maintained that include a description of the property, a serial number or other identification number, the source of funding for the property (including the FAIN), who holds title, the acquisition date, and cost of the property, percentage of Federal participation in the project costs for the Federal award under which the property was acquired, the location, use and condition of the property, and any ultimate disposition data including the date of disposal and sale price of the property.

(2) A physical inventory of the property must be taken and the results reconciled with the property records at least once every two years.

(3) A control system must be developed to ensure adequate safeguards to prevent loss, damage, or theft of the property. Any loss, damage, or theft must be investigated.

(4) Adequate maintenance procedures must be developed to keep the property in good condition.

(5) If the non-Federal entity is authorized or required to sell the property, proper sales procedures must be established to ensure the highest possible return.

(e) *Disposition.* When original or replacement equipment acquired under a Federal award is no longer needed for the original project or program or for other activities currently or previously supported by a Federal awarding agency, except as otherwise provided in Federal statutes, regulations, or Federal awarding agency disposition instructions, the non-Federal entity must request disposition instructions from the Federal awarding agency if required by the terms and conditions of the Federal award. Disposition of the equipment will be made as follows, in accordance with Federal awarding agency disposition instructions:

(1) Items of equipment with a current per unit fair market value of $5,000 or less may be retained, sold or otherwise disposed of with no further obligation to the Federal awarding agency.

(2) Except as provided in § 200.312 Federally-owned and exempt property, paragraph (b), or if the Federal awarding agency fails to provide requested disposition instructions within 120 days, items of equipment with a current per-unit fair-market value in excess of $5,000 may be retained by the non-Federal entity or sold. The Federal awarding agency is entitled to an amount calculated by multiplying the current market value or proceeds from sale by the Federal awarding agency's percentage of participation in the cost of the original purchase. If the equipment is sold, the Federal awarding agency may permit the non-Federal entity to deduct and retain from the Federal share $500 or ten percent of the proceeds, whichever is less, for its selling and handling expenses.

(3) The non-Federal entity may transfer title to the property to the Federal Government or to an eligible third party provided that, in such cases, the non-Federal entity must be entitled to compensation for its attributable percentage of the current fair market value of the property.

(4) In cases where a non-Federal entity fails to take appropriate disposition actions, the Federal awarding agency may direct the non-Federal entity to take disposition actions.

§ 200.314 Supplies.

See also § 200.453 Materials and supplies costs, including costs of computing devices.

(a) Title to supplies will vest in the non-Federal entity upon acquisition. If there is a residual inventory of unused supplies exceeding $5,000 in total aggregate value upon termination or completion of the project or program and the supplies are not needed for any other Federal award, the non-Federal entity must retain the supplies for use on other activities or sell them, but must, in either case, compensate the Federal government for its share. The amount of compensation must be computed in the same manner as for equipment. See § 200.313 Equipment, paragraph (e)(2) for the calculation methodology.

(b) As long as the Federal government retains an interest in the supplies, the non-Federal entity must not use supplies acquired under a Federal award to provide services to other organizations for a fee that is less than private companies charge for equivalent services, unless specifically authorized by Federal statute.

§ 200.315 Intangible property.

(a) Title to intangible property (see § 200.59 Intangible property) acquired under a Federal award vests upon acquisition in the non-Federal entity. The non-Federal entity must use that property for the originally-authorized purpose, and must not encumber the property without approval of the Federal awarding agency. When no longer needed for the originally authorized purpose, disposition of the intangible property must occur in accordance with the provisions in § 200.313 Equipment paragraph (e).

(b) The non-Federal entity may copyright any work that is subject to copyright and was developed, or for which ownership was acquired, under a Federal award. The Federal awarding agency reserves a royalty-free, nonexclusive and irrevocable right to reproduce, publish, or otherwise use the work for Federal purposes, and to authorize others to do so.

(c) The non-Federal entity is subject to applicable regulations governing patents and inventions, including governmentwide regulations issued by the Department of Commerce at 37 CFR Part 401, "Rights to Inventions Made by Nonprofit Organizations and Small Business Firms Under Government

Awards, Contracts and Cooperative Agreements."

(d) The Federal government has the right to:

(1) Obtain, reproduce, publish, or otherwise use the data produced under a Federal award; and

(2) Authorize others to receive, reproduce, publish, or otherwise use such data for Federal purposes.

(e) Freedom of Information Act (FOIA).

(1) In addition, in response to a Freedom of Information Act (FOIA) request for research data relating to published research findings produced under a Federal award that were used by the Federal government in developing an agency action that has the force and effect of law, the Federal awarding agency must request, and the non-Federal entity must provide, within a reasonable time, the research data so that they can be made available to the public through the procedures established under the FOIA. If the Federal awarding agency obtains the research data solely in response to a FOIA request, the Federal awarding agency may charge the requester a reasonable fee equaling the full incremental cost of obtaining the research data. This fee should reflect costs incurred by the Federal agency and the non-Federal entity. This fee is in addition to any fees the Federal awarding agency may assess under the FOIA (5 U.S.C. 552(a)(4)(A)).

(2) Published research findings means when:

(i) Research findings are published in a peer-reviewed scientific or technical journal; or

(ii) A Federal agency publicly and officially cites the research findings in support of an agency action that has the force and effect of law. "Used by the Federal government in developing an agency action that has the force and effect of law" is defined as when an agency publicly and officially cites the research findings in support of an agency action that has the force and effect of law.

(3) Research data means the recorded factual material commonly accepted in the scientific community as necessary to validate research findings, but not any of the following: preliminary analyses, drafts of scientific papers, plans for future research, peer reviews, or communications with colleagues. This "recorded" material excludes physical objects (e.g., laboratory samples). Research data also do not include:

(i) Trade secrets, commercial information, materials necessary to be held confidential by a researcher until they are published, or similar information which is protected under law; and

(ii) Personnel and medical information and similar information the disclosure of which would constitute a clearly unwarranted invasion of personal privacy, such as information that could be used to identify a particular person in a research study.

§ 200.316   Property trust relationship.

Real property, equipment, and intangible property, that are acquired or improved with a Federal award must be held in trust by the non-Federal entity as trustee for the beneficiaries of the project or program under which the property was acquired or improved. The Federal awarding agency may require the non-Federal entity to record liens or other appropriate notices of record to indicate that personal or real property has been acquired or improved with a Federal award and that use and disposition conditions apply to the property.

PROCUREMENT STANDARDS

§ 200.317   Procurements by states.

When procuring property and services under a Federal award, a state must follow the same policies and procedures it uses for procurements from its non-Federal funds. The state will comply with § 200.322 Procurement of recovered *materials* and ensure that every purchase order or other contract includes any clauses required by section § 200.326 Contract provisions. All other non-Federal entities, including subrecipients of a state, will follow §§ 200.318 General procurement standards through 200.326 Contract provisions.

§ 200.318 General procurement standards.

(a) The non-Federal entity must use its own documented procurement procedures which reflect applicable State and local laws and regulations, provided that the procurements conform to applicable Federal law and the standards identified in this section.

(b) Non-Federal entities must maintain oversight to ensure that contractors perform in accordance with the terms, conditions, and specifications of their contracts or purchase orders.

(c)(1) The non-Federal entity must maintain written standards of conduct covering conflicts of interest and governing the performance of its employees engaged in the selection, award and administration of contracts. No employee, officer, or agent must participate in the selection, award, or administration of a contract supported by a Federal award if he or she has a real or apparent conflict of interest. Such a conflict of interest would arise when the employee, officer, or agent, any member of his or her immediate family, his or her partner, or an organization which employs or is about to employ any of the parties indicated herein, has a financial or other interest in or a tangible personal benefit from a firm considered for a contract. The officers, employees, and agents of the non-Federal entity must neither solicit nor accept gratuities, favors, or anything of monetary value from contractors or parties to subcontracts. However, non-Federal entities may set standards for situations in which the financial interest is not substantial or the gift is an unsolicited item of nominal value. The standards of conduct must provide for disciplinary actions to be applied for violations of such standards by officers, employees, or agents of the non-Federal entity.

(2) If the non-Federal entity has a parent, affiliate, or subsidiary organization that is not a state, local government, or Indian tribe, the non-Federal entity must also maintain written standards of conduct covering organizational conflicts of interest. Organizational conflicts of interest means that because of relationships with a parent company, affiliate, or subsidiary organization, the non-Federal entity is unable or appears to be unable to be impartial in conducting a procurement action involving a related organization.

(d) The non-Federal entity's procedures must avoid acquisition of unnecessary or duplicative items. Consideration should be given to consolidating or breaking out procurements to obtain a more economical purchase. Where appropriate, an analysis will be made of lease versus purchase alternatives, and any other appropriate analysis to determine the most economical approach.

(e) To foster greater economy and efficiency, and in accordance with efforts to promote cost-effective use of shared services across the Federal government, the non-Federal entity is encouraged to enter into state and local intergovernmental agreements or inter-entity agreements where appropriate for procurement or use of common or shared goods and services.

(f) The non-Federal entity is encouraged to use Federal excess and surplus property in lieu of purchasing new equipment and property whenever such use is feasible and reduces project costs.

(g) The non-Federal entity is encouraged to use value engineering clauses in contracts for construction projects of sufficient size to offer reasonable opportunities for cost reductions. Value engineering is a systematic and creative analysis of each contract item or task to ensure that its essential function is provided at the overall lower cost.

(h) The non-Federal entity must award contracts only to responsible contractors possessing the ability to perform successfully under the terms and conditions of a proposed procurement. Consideration will be given to such matters as contractor integrity, compliance with public policy, record of past performance, and financial and technical resources.

(i) The non-Federal entity must maintain records sufficient to detail the history of procurement. These records will include, but are not necessarily limited to the following: rationale for the method of procurement, selection of contract type, contractor selection or rejection, and the basis for the contract price.

(j)(1) The non-Federal entity may use time and material type contracts only after a determination that no other contract is suitable and if the contract includes a ceiling price that the contractor exceeds at its own risk. Time and material type contract means a contract whose cost to a non-Federal entity is the sum of:

(i) The actual cost of materials; and

(ii) Direct labor hours charged at fixed hourly rates that reflect wages, general and administrative expenses, and profit.

(2) Since this formula generates an open-ended contract price, a time-and-materials contract provides no positive profit incentive to the contractor for cost control or labor efficiency. Therefore, each contract must set a ceiling price that the contractor exceeds at its own risk. Further, the non-Federal entity awarding such a contract must assert a high degree of oversight in order to obtain reasonable assurance that the contractor is using efficient methods and effective cost controls.

(k) The non-Federal entity alone must be responsible, in accordance with good administrative practice and sound business judgment, for the settlement of all contractual and administrative issues arising out of procurements. These issues include, but are not limited to, source evaluation, protests, disputes, and claims. These standards do not relieve the non-Federal entity of any contractual responsibilities under its contracts. The Federal awarding agency will not substitute its judgment for that of the non-Federal entity unless the matter is primarily a Federal concern. Violations of law will be referred to the local, state, or Federal authority having proper jurisdiction.

§ 200.319 Competition.

(a) All procurement transactions must be conducted in a manner providing full and open competition consistent with the standards of this section. In order to ensure objective contractor performance and eliminate unfair competitive advantage, contractors that develop or draft specifications, requirements, statements of work, and invitations for bids or requests for proposals must be excluded from competing for such procurements. Some of the situations considered to be restrictive of competition include but are not limited to:

(1) Placing unreasonable requirements on firms in order for them to qualify to do business;

(2) Requiring unnecessary experience and excessive bonding;

(3) Noncompetitive pricing practices between firms or between affiliated companies;

(4) Noncompetitive contracts to consultants that are on retainer contracts;

(5) Organizational conflicts of interest;

(6) Specifying only a "brand name" product instead of allowing "an equal" product to be offered and describing the performance or other relevant requirements of the procurement; and

(7) Any arbitrary action in the procurement process.

(b) The non-Federal entity must conduct procurements in a manner that prohibits the use of statutorily or administratively imposed state or local geographical preferences in the evaluation of bids or proposals, except in those cases where applicable Federal statutes expressly mandate or encourage geographic preference. Nothing in this section preempts state licensing laws. When contracting for architectural and engineering (A/E) services, geographic location may be a selection criterion provided its application leaves an appropriate number of qualified firms, given the nature and size of the project, to compete for the contract.

(c) The non-Federal entity must have written procedures for procurement transactions. These procedures must ensure that all solicitations:

(1) Incorporate a clear and accurate description of the technical requirements for the material, product, or service to be procured. Such description must not, in competitive procurements, contain features which unduly restrict competition. The description may include a statement of the qualitative nature of the material, product or service to be procured and, when necessary, must set forth those minimum essential characteristics and

standards to which it must conform if it is to satisfy its intended use. Detailed product specifications should be avoided if at all possible. When it is impractical or uneconomical to make a clear and accurate description of the technical requirements, a "brand name or equivalent" description may be used as a means to define the performance or other salient requirements of procurement. The specific features of the named brand which must be met by offers must be clearly stated; and

(2) Identify all requirements which the offerors must fulfill and all other factors to be used in evaluating bids or proposals.

(d) The non-Federal entity must ensure that all prequalified lists of persons, firms, or products which are used in acquiring goods and services are current and include enough qualified sources to ensure maximum open and free competition. Also, the non-Federal entity must not preclude potential bidders from qualifying during the solicitation period.

§200.320 Methods of procurement to be followed.

The non-Federal entity must use one of the following methods of procurement.

(a) Procurement by micro-purchases. Procurement by micro-purchase is the acquisition of supplies or services, the aggregate dollar amount of which does not exceed $3,000 (or $2,000 in the case of acquisitions for construction subject to the Davis-Bacon Act). To the extent practicable, the non-Federal entity must distribute micro-purchases equitably among qualified suppliers. Micro-purchases may be awarded without soliciting competitive quotations if the non-Federal entity considers the price to be reasonable.

(b) Procurement by small purchase procedures. Small purchase procedures are those relatively simple and informal procurement methods for securing services, supplies, or other property that do not cost more than the Simplified Acquisition Threshold. If small purchase procedures are used, price or rate quotations must be obtained from an adequate number of qualified sources.

(c) Procurement by sealed bids (formal advertising). Bids are publicly solicited and a firm fixed price contract (lump sum or unit price) is awarded to the responsible bidder whose bid, conforming with all the material terms and conditions of the invitation for bids, is the lowest in price. The sealed bid method is the preferred method for procuring construction, if the conditions in paragraph (c)(1) of this section apply.

(1) In order for sealed bidding to be feasible, the following conditions should be present:

(i) A complete, adequate, and realistic specification or purchase description is available;

(ii) Two or more responsible bidders are willing and able to compete effectively for the business; and

(iii) The procurement lends itself to a firm fixed price contract and the selection of the successful bidder can be made principally on the basis of price.

(2) If sealed bids are used, the following requirements apply:

(i) The invitation for bids will be publicly advertised and bids must be solicited from an adequate number of known suppliers, providing them sufficient response time prior to the date set for opening the bids;

(ii) The invitation for bids, which will include any specifications and pertinent attachments, must define the items or services in order for the bidder to properly respond;

(iii) All bids will be publicly opened at the time and place prescribed in the invitation for bids;

(iv) A firm fixed price contract award will be made in writing to the lowest responsive and responsible bidder. Where specified in bidding documents, factors such as discounts, transportation cost, and life cycle costs must be considered in determining which bid is lowest. Payment discounts will only be used to determine the low bid when prior experience indicates that such discounts are usually taken advantage of; and

(v) Any or all bids may be rejected if there is a sound documented reason.

(d) Procurement by competitive proposals. The technique of competitive proposals is normally conducted with more than one source submitting an offer, and either a fixed price or cost-reimbursement type contract is awarded. It is generally used when conditions are not appropriate for the use of sealed bids. If this method is used, the following requirements apply:

(1) Requests for proposals must be publicized and identify all evaluation factors and their relative importance. Any response to publicized requests for proposals must be considered to the maximum extent practical;

(2) Proposals must be solicited from an adequate number of qualified sources;

(3) The non-Federal entity must have a written method for conducting technical evaluations of the proposals received and for selecting recipients;

(4) Contracts must be awarded to the responsible firm whose proposal is most advantageous to the program, with price and other factors considered; and

(5) The non-Federal entity may use competitive proposal procedures for qualifications-based procurement of architectural/engineering (A/E) professional services whereby competitors' qualifications are evaluated and the most qualified competitor is selected, subject to negotiation of fair and reasonable compensation. The method, where price is not used as a selection factor, can only be used in procurement of A/E professional services. It cannot be used to purchase other types of services though A/E firms are a potential source to perform the proposed effort.

(e) [Reserved]

(f) Procurement by noncompetitive proposals. Procurement by noncompetitive proposals is procurement through solicitation of a proposal from only one source and may be used only when one or more of the following circumstances apply:

(1) The item is available only from a single source;

(2) The public exigency or emergency for the requirement will not permit a delay resulting from competitive solicitation;

(3) The Federal awarding agency or pass-through entity expressly authorizes noncompetitive proposals in response to a written request from the non-Federal entity; or

(4) After solicitation of a number of sources, competition is determined inadequate.

§ 200.321 Contracting with small and minority businesses, women's business enterprises, and labor surplus area firms.

(a) The non-Federal entity must take all necessary affirmative steps to assure that minority businesses, women's business enterprises, and labor surplus area firms are used when possible.

(b) Affirmative steps must include:

(1) Placing qualified small and minority businesses and women's business enterprises on solicitation lists;

(2) Assuring that small and minority businesses, and women's business enterprises are solicited whenever they are potential sources;

(3) Dividing total requirements, when economically feasible, into smaller tasks or quantities to permit maximum participation by small and minority businesses, and women's business enterprises;

(4) Establishing delivery schedules, where the requirement permits, which encourage participation by small and minority businesses, and women's business enterprises;

(5) Using the services and assistance, as appropriate, of such organizations as the Small Business Administration and the Minority Business Development Agency of the Department of Commerce; and

(6) Requiring the prime contractor, if subcontracts are to be let, to take the affirmative steps listed in paragraphs (1) through (5) of this section.

§ 200.322 Procurement of recovered materials.

A non-Federal entity that is a state agency or agency of a political subdivision of a state and its contractors must comply with section 6002 of the Solid Waste Disposal Act, as amended by the Resource Conservation and Recovery Act. The requirements of Section 6002 include procuring only items designated in guidelines of the Environmental Protection Agency (EPA) at 40 CFR part 247 that contain the highest percentage of recovered materials practicable, consistent with maintaining a satisfactory level of competition, where the purchase price of the item exceeds $10,000 or the value of the quantity acquired by the preceding fiscal year exceeded $10,000; procuring solid waste management services in a manner that maximizes energy and resource recovery; and establishing an affirmative procurement program for procurement of recovered materials identified in the EPA guidelines.

§200.323 Contract cost and price.

(a) The non-Federal entity must perform a cost or price analysis in connection with every procurement action in excess of the Simplified Acquisition Threshold including contract modifications. The method and degree of analysis is dependent on the facts surrounding the particular procurement situation, but as a starting point, the non-Federal entity must make independent estimates before receiving bids or proposals.

(b) The non-Federal entity must negotiate profit as a separate element of the price for each contract in which there is no price competition and in all cases where cost analysis is performed. To establish a fair and reasonable profit, consideration must be given to the complexity of the work to be performed, the risk borne by the contractor, the contractor's investment, the amount of subcontracting, the quality of its record of past performance, and industry profit rates in the surrounding geographical area for similar work.

(c) Costs or prices based on estimated costs for contracts under the Federal award are allowable only to the extent that costs incurred or cost estimates included in negotiated prices would be allowable for the non-Federal entity under Subpart E—Cost Principles of this part. The non-Federal entity may reference its own cost principles that comply with the Federal cost principles.

(d) The cost plus a percentage of cost and percentage of construction cost methods of contracting must not be used.

§200.324 Federal awarding agency or pass-through entity review.

(a) The non-Federal entity must make available, upon request of the Federal awarding agency or pass-through entity, technical specifications on proposed procurements where the Federal awarding agency or pass-through entity believes such review is needed to ensure that the item or service specified is the one being proposed for acquisition. This review generally will take place prior to the time the specification is incorporated into a solicitation document. However, if the non-Federal entity desires to have the review accomplished after a solicitation has been developed, the Federal awarding agency or pass-through entity may still review the specifications, with such review usually limited to the technical aspects of the proposed purchase.

(b) The non-Federal entity must make available upon request, for the Federal awarding agency or pass-through entity pre-procurement review, procurement documents, such as requests for proposals or invitations for bids, or independent cost estimates, when:

(1) The non-Federal entity's procurement procedures or operation fails to comply with the procurement standards in this part;

(2) The procurement is expected to exceed the Simplified Acquisition Threshold and is to be awarded without competition or only one bid or offer is received in response to a solicitation;

(3) The procurement, which is expected to exceed the Simplified Acquisition Threshold, specifies a "brand name" product;

(4) The proposed contract is more than the Simplified Acquisition Threshold and is to be awarded to other than the apparent low bidder under a sealed bid procurement; or

(5) A proposed contract modification changes the scope of a contract or increases the contract amount by more than the Simplified Acquisition Threshold.

(c) The non-Federal entity is exempt from the pre-procurement review in paragraph (b) of this section if the Federal awarding agency or pass-through entity determines that its procurement systems comply with the standards of this part.

(1) The non-Federal entity may request that its procurement system be

reviewed by the Federal awarding agency or pass-through entity to determine whether its system meets these standards in order for its system to be certified. Generally, these reviews must occur where there is continuous high-dollar funding, and third party contracts are awarded on a regular basis;

(2) The non-Federal entity may self-certify its procurement system. Such self-certification must not limit the Federal awarding agency's right to survey the system. Under a self-certification procedure, the Federal awarding agency may rely on written assurances from the non-Federal entity that it is complying with these standards. The non-Federal entity must cite specific policies, procedures, regulations, or standards as being in compliance with these requirements and have its system available for review.

§ 200.325   Bonding requirements.

For construction or facility improvement contracts or subcontracts exceeding the Simplified Acquisition Threshold, the Federal awarding agency or pass-through entity may accept the bonding policy and requirements of the non-Federal entity provided that the Federal awarding agency or pass-through entity has made a determination that the Federal interest is adequately protected. If such a determination has not been made, the minimum requirements must be as follows:

(a) A bid guarantee from each bidder equivalent to five percent of the bid price. The "bid guarantee" must consist of a firm commitment such as a bid bond, certified check, or other negotiable instrument accompanying a bid as assurance that the bidder will, upon acceptance of the bid, execute such contractual documents as may be required within the time specified.

(b) A performance bond on the part of the contractor for 100 percent of the contract price. A "performance bond" is one executed in connection with a contract to secure fulfillment of all the contractor's obligations under such contract.

(c) A payment bond on the part of the contractor for 100 percent of the contract price. A "payment bond" is one executed in connection with a contract

to assure payment as required by law of all persons supplying labor and material in the execution of the work provided for in the contract.

§ 200.326   Contract provisions.

The non-Federal entity's contracts must contain the applicable provisions described in Appendix II to Part 200— Contract Provisions for non-Federal Entity Contracts Under Federal Awards.

PERFORMANCE AND FINANCIAL MONITORING AND REPORTING

§ 200.327   Financial reporting.

Unless otherwise approved by OMB, the Federal awarding agency may solicit only the standard, OMB-approved governmentwide data elements for collection of financial information (at time of publication the Federal Financial Report or such future collections as may be approved by OMB and listed on the OMB Web site). This information must be collected with the frequency required by the terms and conditions of the Federal award, but no less frequently than annually nor more frequently than quarterly except in unusual circumstances, for example where more frequent reporting is necessary for the effective monitoring of the Federal award or could significantly affect program outcomes, and preferably in coordination with performance reporting.

200.328   Monitoring and reporting program performance.

(a) *Monitoring by the non-Federal entity.* The non-Federal entity is responsible for oversight of the operations of the Federal award supported activities. The non-Federal entity must monitor its activities under Federal awards to assure compliance with applicable Federal requirements and performance expectations are being achieved. Monitoring by the non-Federal entity must cover each program, function or activity. See also § 200.331 Requirements for pass-through *entities.*

(b) *Non-construction performance reports.* The Federal awarding agency must use standard, OMB-approved data elements for collection of performance information (including performance progress reports, Research Performance Progress Report, or such future collections as may be approved by OMB and listed on the OMB Web site).

(1) The non-Federal entity must submit performance reports at the interval required by the Federal awarding agency or pass-through entity to best inform improvements in program outcomes and productivity. Intervals must be no less frequent than annually nor more frequent than quarterly except in unusual circumstances, for example where more frequent reporting is necessary for the effective monitoring of the Federal award or could significantly affect program outcomes. Annual reports must be due 90 calendar days after the reporting period; quarterly or semiannual reports must be due 30 calendar days after the reporting period. Alternatively, the Federal awarding agency or pass-through entity may require annual reports before the anniversary dates of multiple year Federal awards. The final performance report will be due 90 calendar days after the period of performance end date. If a justified request is submitted by a non-Federal entity, the Federal agency may extend the due date for any performance report.

(2) The non-Federal entity must submit performance reports using OMB-approved governmentwide standard information collections when providing performance information. As appropriate in accordance with above mentioned information collections, these reports will contain, for each Federal award, brief information on the following unless other collections are approved by OMB:

(i) A comparison of actual accomplishments to the objectives of the Federal award established for the period. Where the accomplishments of the Federal award can be quantified, a computation of the cost (for example, related to units of accomplishment) may be required if that information will be useful. Where performance trend data and analysis would be informative to the Federal awarding agency program, the Federal awarding agency should include this as a performance reporting requirement.

(ii) The reasons why established goals were not met, if appropriate.

(iii) Additional pertinent information including, when appropriate, analysis and explanation of cost overruns or high unit costs.

(c) *Construction performance reports.* For the most part, onsite technical inspections and certified percentage of completion data are relied on heavily by Federal awarding agencies and pass-through entities to monitor progress under Federal awards and subawards for construction. The Federal awarding agency may require additional performance reports only when considered necessary.

(d) *Significant developments.* Events may occur between the scheduled performance reporting dates that have significant impact upon the supported activity. In such cases, the non-Federal entity must inform the Federal awarding agency or pass-through entity as soon as the following types of conditions become known:

(1) Problems, delays, or adverse conditions which will materially impair the ability to meet the objective of the Federal award. This disclosure must include a statement of the action taken, or contemplated, and any assistance needed to resolve the situation.

(2) Favorable developments which enable meeting time schedules and objectives sooner or at less cost than anticipated or producing more or different beneficial results than originally planned.

(e) The Federal awarding agency may make site visits as warranted by program needs.

(f) The Federal awarding agency may waive any performance report required by this part if not needed.

§ 200.329 **Reporting on real property.**

The Federal awarding agency or pass-through entity must require a non-Federal entity to submit reports at least annually on the status of real property in which the Federal government retains an interest, unless the Federal interest in the real property extends 15 years or longer. In those instances where the Federal interest attached is for a period of 15 years or more, the Federal awarding agency or pass-through entity, at its option, may require the non-Federal entity to report at various multi-year frequencies (e.g., every two years or every three years, not to exceed a five-year reporting period; or a Federal awarding agency or pass-through entity may require annual reporting for the first three years of a Federal award and thereafter require reporting every five years).

SUBRECIPIENT MONITORING AND MANAGEMENT

§ 200.330 Subrecipient and contractor determinations.

The non-Federal entity may concurrently receive Federal awards as a recipient, a subrecipient, and a contractor, depending on the substance of its agreements with Federal awarding agencies and pass-through entities. Therefore, a pass-through entity must make case-by-case determinations whether each agreement it makes for the disbursement of Federal program funds casts the party receiving the funds in the role of a subrecipient or a contractor. The Federal awarding agency may supply and require recipients to comply with additional guidance to support these determinations provided such guidance does not conflict with this section.

(a) *Subrecipients.* A subaward is for the purpose of carrying out a portion of a Federal award and creates a Federal assistance relationship with the subrecipient. See § 200.92 Subaward. Characteristics which support the classification of the non-Federal entity as a subrecipient include when the non-Federal entity:

(1) Determines who is eligible to receive what Federal assistance;

(2) Has its performance measured in relation to whether objectives of a Federal program were met;

(3) Has responsibility for programmatic decision making;

(4) Is responsible for adherence to applicable Federal program requirements specified in the Federal award; and

(5) In accordance with its agreement, uses the Federal funds to carry out a program for a public purpose specified in authorizing statute, as opposed to providing goods or services for the benefit of the pass-through entity.

(b) *Contractors.* A contract is for the purpose of obtaining goods and services for the non-Federal entity's own use and creates a procurement relationship with the contractor. See § 200.22 Contract. Characteristics indicative of a procurement relationship between the non-Federal entity and a contractor are when the non-Federal entity receiving the Federal funds:

(1) Provides the goods and services within normal business operations;

(2) Provides similar goods or services to many different purchasers;

(3) Normally operates in a competitive environment;

(4) Provides goods or services that are ancillary to the operation of the Federal program; and

(5) Is not subject to compliance requirements of the Federal program as a result of the agreement, though similar requirements may apply for other reasons.

(c) *Use of judgment in making determination.* In determining whether an agreement between a pass-through entity and another non-Federal entity casts the latter as a subrecipient or a contractor, the substance of the relationship is more important than the form of the agreement. All of the characteristics listed above may not be present in all cases, and the pass-through entity must use judgment in classifying each agreement as a subaward or a procurement contract.

§ 200.331 Requirements for pass-through entities.

All pass-through entities must:

(a) Ensure that every subaward is clearly identified to the subrecipient as a subaward and includes the following information at the time of the subaward and if any of these data elements change, include the changes in subsequent subaward modification. When some of this information is not available, the pass-through entity must provide the best information available to describe the Federal award and subaward. Required information includes:

(1) Federal Award Identification.

(i) Subrecipient name (which must match registered name in DUNS);

(ii) Subrecipient's DUNS number (see § 200.32 Data Universal Numbering System (DUNS) *number*);

(iii) Federal Award Identification Number (FAIN);

(iv) Federal Award Date (see §200.39 Federal award date);

(v) Subaward Period of Performance Start and End Date;

(vi) Amount of Federal Funds Obligated by this action;

(vii) Total Amount of Federal Funds Obligated to the subrecipient;

(viii) Total Amount of the Federal Award;

(ix) Federal award project description, as required to be responsive to the Federal Funding Accountability and Transparency Act (FFATA);

(x) Name of Federal awarding agency, pass-through entity, and contact information for awarding official,

(xi) CFDA Number and Name; the pass-through entity must identify the dollar amount made available under each Federal award and the CFDA number at time of disbursement;

(xii) Identification of whether the award is R&D; and

(xiii) Indirect cost rate for the Federal award (including if the de minimis rate is charged per §200.414 Indirect (F&A) costs).

(2) All requirements imposed by the pass-through entity on the subrecipient so that the Federal award is used in accordance with Federal statutes, regulations and the terms and conditions of the Federal award.

(3) Any additional requirements that the pass-through entity imposes on the subrecipient in order for the pass-through entity to meet its own responsibility to the Federal awarding agency including identification of any required financial and performance reports;

(4) An approved federally recognized indirect cost rate negotiated between the subrecipient and the Federal government or, if no such rate exists, either a rate negotiated between the pass-through entity and the subrecipient (in compliance with this part), or a de minimis indirect cost rate as defined in §200.414 Indirect (F&A) costs, paragraph (b) of this part.

(5) A requirement that the subrecipient permit the pass-through entity and auditors to have access to the subrecipient's records and financial statements as necessary for the pass-through entity to meet the requirements of this section, §§200.300 Statutory and national policy requirements through 200.309 Period of performance, and Subpart F—Audit Requirements of this part; and

(6) Appropriate terms and conditions concerning closeout of the subaward.

(b) Evaluate each subrecipient's risk of noncompliance with Federal statutes, regulations, and the terms and conditions of the subaward for purposes of determining the appropriate subrecipient monitoring described in paragraph (e) of this section, which may include consideration of such factors as:

(1) The subrecipient's prior experience with the same or similar subawards;

(2) The results of previous audits including whether or not the subrecipient receives a Single Audit in accordance with Subpart F—Audit Requirements of this part, and the extent to which the same or similar subaward has been audited as a major program;

(3) Whether the subrecipient has new personnel or new or substantially changed systems; and

(4) The extent and results of Federal awarding agency monitoring (e.g., if the subrecipient also receives Federal awards directly from a Federal awarding agency).

(c) Consider imposing specific subaward conditions upon a subrecipient if appropriate as described in §200.207 Specific conditions.

(d) Monitor the activities of the subrecipient as necessary to ensure that the subaward is used for authorized purposes, in compliance with Federal statutes, regulations, and the terms and conditions of the subaward; and that subaward performance goals are achieved. Pass-through entity monitoring of the subrecipient must include:

(1) Reviewing financial and programmatic reports required by the pass-through entity.

(2) Following-up and ensuring that the subrecipient takes timely and appropriate action on all deficiencies pertaining to the Federal award provided to the subrecipient from the pass-through entity detected through audits, on-site reviews, and other means.

(3) Issuing a management decision for audit findings pertaining to the Federal award provided to the subrecipient

from the pass-through entity as required by § 200.521 Management decision.

(e) Depending upon the pass-through entity's assessment of risk posed by the subrecipient (as described in paragraph (b) of this section), the following monitoring tools may be useful for the pass-through entity to ensure proper accountability and compliance with program requirements and achievement of performance goals:

(1) Providing subrecipients with training and technical assistance on program-related matters; and

(2) Performing on-site reviews of the subrecipient's program operations;

(3) Arranging for agreed-upon-procedures engagements as described in § 200.425 Audit services.

(f) Verify that every subrecipient is audited as required by Subpart F—Audit Requirements of this part when it is expected that the subrecipient's Federal awards expended during the respective fiscal year equaled or exceeded the threshold set forth in § 200.501 Audit requirements.

(g) Consider whether the results of the subrecipient's audits, on-site reviews, or other monitoring indicate conditions that necessitate adjustments to the pass-through entity's own records.

(h) Consider taking enforcement action against noncompliant subrecipients as described in § 200.338 Remedies for noncompliance of this part and in program regulations.

§ 200.332 Fixed amount subawards.

With prior written approval from the Federal awarding agency, a pass-through entity may provide subawards based on fixed amounts up to the Simplified Acquisition Threshold, provided that the subawards meet the requirements for fixed amount awards in § 200.201 Use of grant agreements (including fixed amount awards), cooperative agreements, and contracts.

RECORD RETENTION AND ACCESS

§ 200.333 Retention requirements for records.

Financial records, supporting documents, statistical records, and all other non-Federal entity records pertinent to a Federal award must be retained for a period of three years from the date of submission of the final expenditure report or, for Federal awards that are renewed quarterly or annually, from the date of the submission of the quarterly or annual financial report, respectively, as reported to the Federal awarding agency or pass-through entity in the case of a subrecipient. Federal awarding agencies and pass-through entities must not impose any other record retention requirements upon non-Federal entities. The only exceptions are the following:

(a) If any litigation, claim, or audit is started before the expiration of the 3-year period, the records must be retained until all litigation, claims, or audit findings involving the records have been resolved and final action taken.

(b) When the non-Federal entity is notified in writing by the Federal awarding agency, cognizant agency for audit, oversight agency for audit, cognizant agency for indirect costs, or pass-through entity to extend the retention period.

(c) Records for real property and equipment acquired with Federal funds must be retained for 3 years after final disposition.

(d) When records are transferred to or maintained by the Federal awarding agency or pass-through entity, the 3-year retention requirement is not applicable to the non-Federal entity.

(e) Records for program income transactions after the period of performance. In some cases recipients must report program income after the period of performance. Where there is such a requirement, the retention period for the records pertaining to the earning of the program income starts from the end of the non-Federal entity's fiscal year in which the program income is earned.

(f) Indirect cost rate proposals and cost allocations plans. This paragraph applies to the following types of documents and their supporting records: indirect cost rate computations or proposals, cost allocation plans, and any similar accounting computations of the rate at which a particular group of costs is chargeable (such as computer usage chargeback rates or composite fringe benefit rates).

(1) *If submitted for negotiation.* If the proposal, plan, or other computation is required to be submitted to the Federal government (or to the pass-through entity) to form the basis for negotiation of the rate, then the 3-year retention period for its supporting records starts from the date of such submission.

(2) *If not submitted for negotiation.* If the proposal, plan, or other computation is not required to be submitted to the Federal government (or to the pass-through entity) for negotiation purposes, then the 3-year retention period for the proposal, plan, or computation and its supporting records starts from the end of the fiscal year (or other accounting period) covered by the proposal, plan, or other computation.

§ 200.334 Requests for transfer of records.

The Federal awarding agency must request transfer of certain records to its custody from the non-Federal entity when it determines that the records possess long-term retention value. However, in order to avoid duplicate recordkeeping, the Federal awarding agency may make arrangements for the non-Federal entity to retain any records that are continuously needed for joint use.

§ 200.335 Methods for collection, transmission and storage of information.

In accordance with the May 2013 Executive Order on Making Open and Machine Readable the New Default for Government Information, the Federal awarding agency and the non-Federal entity should, whenever practicable, collect, transmit, and store Federal award-related information in open and machine readable formats rather than in closed formats or on paper. The Federal awarding agency or pass-through entity must always provide or accept paper versions of Federal award-related information to and from the non-Federal entity upon request. If paper copies are submitted, the Federal awarding agency or pass-through entity must not require more than an original and two copies. When original records are electronic and cannot be altered, there is no need to create and retain paper copies. When original records are paper, electronic versions may be substituted through the use of duplication or other forms of electronic media provided that they are subject to periodic quality control reviews, provide reasonable safeguards against alteration, and remain readable.

§ 200.336 Access to records.

(a) *Records of non-Federal entities.* The Federal awarding agency, Inspectors General, the Comptroller General of the United States, and the pass-through entity, or any of their authorized representatives, must have the right of access to any documents, papers, or other records of the non-Federal entity which are pertinent to the Federal award, in order to make audits, examinations, excerpts, and transcripts. The right also includes timely and reasonable access to the non-Federal entity's personnel for the purpose of interview and discussion related to such documents.

(b) Only under extraordinary and rare circumstances would such access include review of the true name of victims of a crime. Routine monitoring cannot be considered extraordinary and rare circumstances that would necessitate access to this information. When access to the true name of victims of a crime is necessary, appropriate steps to protect this sensitive information must be taken by both the non-Federal entity and the Federal awarding agency. Any such access, other than under a court order or subpoena pursuant to a bona fide confidential investigation, must be approved by the head of the Federal awarding agency or delegate.

(c) *Expiration of right of access.* The rights of access in this section are not limited to the required retention period but last as long as the records are retained. Federal awarding agencies and pass-through entities must not impose any other access requirements upon non-Federal entities.

§ 200.337 Restrictions on public access to records.

No Federal awarding agency may place restrictions on the non-Federal entity that limit public access to the records of the non-Federal entity pertinent to a Federal award, except for protected personally identifiable information (PII) or when the Federal awarding agency can demonstrate that such records will be kept confidential and would have been exempted from disclosure pursuant to the Freedom of Information Act (5 U.S.C. 552) or controlled unclassified information pursuant to Executive Order 13556 if the records had belonged to the Federal awarding agency. The Freedom of Information Act (5 U.S.C. 552) (FOIA) does not apply to those records that remain under a non-Federal entity's control except as required under § 200.315 Intangible property. Unless required by Federal, state, or local statute, non-Federal entities are not required to permit public access to their records. The non-Federal entity's records provided to a Federal agency generally will be subject to FOIA and applicable exemptions.

REMEDIES FOR NONCOMPLIANCE

§ 200.338 Remedies for noncompliance.

If a non-Federal entity fails to comply with Federal statutes, regulations or the terms and conditions of a Federal award, the Federal awarding agency or pass-through entity may impose additional conditions, as described in § 200.207 Specific conditions. If the Federal awarding agency or pass-through entity determines that noncompliance cannot be remedied by imposing additional conditions, the Federal awarding agency or pass-through entity may take one or more of the following actions, as appropriate in the circumstances:

(a) Temporarily withhold cash payments pending correction of the deficiency by the non-Federal entity or more severe enforcement action by the Federal awarding agency or pass-through entity.

(b) Disallow (that is, deny both use of funds and any applicable matching credit for) all or part of the cost of the activity or action not in compliance.

(c) Wholly or partly suspend or terminate the Federal award.

(d) Initiate suspension or debarment proceedings as authorized under 2 CFR part 180 and Federal awarding agency

regulations (or in the case of a pass-through entity, recommend such a proceeding be initiated by a Federal awarding agency).

(e) Withhold further Federal awards for the project or program.

(f) Take other remedies that may be legally available.

§ 200.339 Termination.

(a) The Federal award may be terminated in whole or in part as follows:

(1) By the Federal awarding agency or pass-through entity, if a non-Federal entity fails to comply with the terms and conditions of a Federal award;

(2) By the Federal awarding agency or pass-through entity for cause;

(3) By the Federal awarding agency or pass-through entity with the consent of the non-Federal entity, in which case the two parties must agree upon the termination conditions, including the effective date and, in the case of partial termination, the portion to be terminated; or

(4) By the non-Federal entity upon sending to the Federal awarding agency or pass-through entity written notification setting forth the reasons for such termination, the effective date, and, in the case of partial termination, the portion to be terminated. However, if the Federal awarding agency or pass-through entity determines in the case of partial termination that the reduced or modified portion of the Federal award or subaward will not accomplish the purposes for which the Federal award was made, the Federal awarding agency or pass-through entity may terminate the Federal award in its entirety.

(b) When a Federal award is terminated or partially terminated, both the Federal awarding agency or pass-through entity and the non-Federal entity remain responsible for compliance with the requirements in §§ 200.343 Closeout and 200.344 Post-closeout adjustments and continuing responsibilities.

§ 200.340 Notification of termination requirement.

(a) The Federal agency or pass-through entity must provide to the non-Federal entity a notice of termination.

(b) If the Federal award is terminated for the non-Federal entity's failure to comply with the Federal statutes, regulations, or terms and conditions of the Federal award, the notification must state that the termination decision may be considered in evaluating future applications received from the non-Federal entity.

(c) Upon termination of a Federal award, the Federal awarding agency must provide the information required under FFATA to the Federal Web site established to fulfill the requirements of FFATA, and update or notify any other relevant governmentwide systems or entities of any indications of poor performance as required by 41 U.S.C. 417b and 31 U.S.C. 3321 and implementing guidance at 2 CFR part 77. See also the requirements for Suspension and Debarment at 2 CFR part 180.

§ 200.341 Opportunities to object, hearings and appeals.

Upon taking any remedy for noncompliance, the Federal awarding agency must provide the non-Federal entity an opportunity to object and provide information and documentation challenging the suspension or termination action, in accordance with written processes and procedures published by the Federal awarding agency. The Federal awarding agency or pass-through entity must comply with any requirements for hearings, appeals or other administrative proceedings which the non-Federal entity is entitled under any statute or regulation applicable to the action involved.

§ 200.342 Effects of suspension and termination.

Costs to the non-Federal entity resulting from obligations incurred by the non-Federal entity during a suspension or after termination of a Federal award or subaward are not allowable unless the Federal awarding agency or pass-through entity expressly authorizes them in the notice of suspension or termination or subsequently. However, costs during suspension or after termination are allowable if:

(a) The costs result from obligations which were properly incurred by the non-Federal entity before the effective date of suspension or termination, are not in anticipation of it; and

(b) The costs would be allowable if the Federal award was not suspended or expired normally at the end of the period of performance in which the termination takes effect.

CLOSEOUT

§ 200.343 Closeout.

The Federal agency or pass-through entity will close-out the Federal award when it determines that all applicable administrative actions and all required work of the Federal award have been completed by the non-Federal entity. This section specifies the actions the non-Federal entity and Federal awarding agency or pass-through entity must take to complete this process at the end of the period of performance.

(a) The non-Federal entity must submit, no later than 90 calendar days after the end date of the period of performance, all financial, performance, and other reports as required by or the terms and conditions of the Federal award. The Federal awarding agency or pass-through entity may approve extensions when requested by the non-Federal entity.

(b) Unless the Federal awarding agency or pass-through entity authorizes an extension, a non-Federal entity must liquidate all obligations incurred under the Federal award not later than 90 calendar days after the end date of the period of performance as specified in the terms and conditions of the Federal award.

(c) The Federal awarding agency or pass-through entity must make prompt payments to the non-Federal entity for allowable reimbursable costs under the Federal award being closed out.

(d) The non-Federal entity must promptly refund any balances of unobligated cash that the Federal awarding agency or pass-through entity paid in advance or paid and that is not authorized to be retained by the non-Federal entity for use in other projects. See OMB Circular A–129 and see § 200.345 Collection of amounts due for requirements regarding unreturned amounts that become delinquent debts.

(e) Consistent with the terms and conditions of the Federal award, the Federal awarding agency or pass-through entity must make a settlement for any upward or downward adjustments to the Federal share of costs after closeout reports are received.

(f) The non-Federal entity must account for any real and personal property acquired with Federal funds or received from the Federal government in accordance with §§ 200.310 Insurance coverage through 200.316 Property trust relationship and 200.329 Reporting on real property.

(g) The Federal awarding agency or pass-through entity should complete all closeout actions for Federal awards no later than one year after receipt and acceptance of all required final reports.

POST-CLOSEOUT ADJUSTMENTS AND CONTINUING RESPONSIBILITIES

§ 200.344 Post-closeout adjustments and continuing responsibilities.

(a) The closeout of a Federal award does not affect any of the following.

(1) The right of the Federal awarding agency or pass-through entity to disallow costs and recover funds on the basis of a later audit or other review. The Federal awarding agency or pass-through entity must make any cost disallowance determination and notify the non-Federal entity within the record retention period.

(2) The obligation of the non-Federal entity to return any funds due as a result of later refunds, corrections, or other transactions including final indirect cost rate adjustments.

(3) Audit requirements in Subpart F—Audit Requirements of this part.

(4) Property management and disposition requirements in Subpart D—Post Federal Award Requirements of this part, §§ 200.310 Insurance Coverage through 200.316 Property trust relationship.

(5) Records retention as required in Subpart D—Post Federal Award Requirements of this part, §§ 200.333 Retention requirements for records through 200.337 Restrictions on public access to records.

(b) After closeout of the Federal award, a relationship created under the Federal award may be modified or ended in whole or in part with the consent of the Federal awarding agency or pass-through entity and the non-Federal entity, provided the responsibilities of the non-Federal entity referred to in paragraph (a) of this section including those for property management as applicable, are considered and provisions made for continuing responsibilities of the non-Federal entity, as appropriate.

COLLECTION OF AMOUNTS DUE

§ 200.345 Collection of amounts due.

(a) Any funds paid to the non-Federal entity in excess of the amount to which the non-Federal entity is finally determined to be entitled under the terms of the Federal award constitute a debt to the Federal government. If not paid within 90 calendar days after demand, the Federal awarding agency may reduce the debt by:

(1) Making an administrative offset against other requests for reimbursements;

(2) Withholding advance payments otherwise due to the non-Federal entity; or

(3) Other action permitted by Federal statute.

(b) Except where otherwise provided by statutes or regulations, the Federal awarding agency will charge interest on an overdue debt in accordance with the Federal Claims Collection Standards (31 CFR parts 900 through 999). The date from which interest is computed is not extended by litigation or the filing of any form of appeal.

Subpart E—Cost Principles

GENERAL PROVISIONS

§ 200.400 Policy guide.

The application of these cost principles is based on the fundamental premises that:

(a) The non-Federal entity is responsible for the efficient and effective administration of the Federal award through the application of sound management practices.

(b) The non-Federal entity assumes responsibility for administering Federal funds in a manner consistent with underlying agreements, program objectives, and the terms and conditions of the Federal award.

(c) The non-Federal entity, in recognition of its own unique combination of staff, facilities, and experience, has the primary responsibility for employing whatever form of sound organization and management techniques may be necessary in order to assure proper and efficient administration of the Federal award.

(d) The application of these cost principles should require no significant changes in the internal accounting policies and practices of the non-Federal entity. However, the accounting practices of the non-Federal entity must be consistent with these cost principles and support the accumulation of costs as required by the principles, and must provide for adequate documentation to support costs charged to the Federal award.

(e) In reviewing, negotiating and approving cost allocation plans or indirect cost proposals, the cognizant agency for indirect costs should generally assure that the non-Federal entity is applying these cost accounting principles on a consistent basis during their review and negotiation of indirect cost proposals. Where wide variations exist in the treatment of a given cost item by the non-Federal entity, the reasonableness and equity of such treatments should be fully considered. See §200.56 Indirect (facilities & administrative (F&A)) costs.

(f) For non-Federal entities that educate and engage students in research, the dual role of students as both trainees and employees contributing to the completion of Federal awards for research must be recognized in the application of these principles.

(g) The non-Federal entity may not. earn or keep any profit resulting from Federal financial assistance, unless expressly authorized by the terms and conditions of the Federal award. See also §200.307 Program income.

§200.401 Application.

(a) *General.* These principles must be used in determining the allowable costs of work performed by the non-Federal entity under Federal awards. These principles also must be used by the non-Federal entity as a guide in the pricing of fixed-price contracts and subcontracts where costs are used in determining the appropriate price. The principles do not apply to:

(1) Arrangements under which Federal financing is in the form of loans, scholarships, fellowships, traineeships, or other fixed amounts based on such items as education allowance or published tuition rates and fees.

(2) For IHEs, capitation awards, which are awards based on case counts or number of beneficiaries according to the terms and conditions of the Federal award.

(3) Fixed amount awards. See also Subpart A—Acronyms and Definitions, §§200.45 Fixed amount awards and 200.201 Use of grant agreements (including fixed amount awards), cooperative agreements, and contracts.

(4) Federal awards to hospitals (see Appendix IX to Part 200—Hospital Cost Principles).

(5) Other awards under which the non-Federal entity is not required to account to the Federal government for actual costs incurred.

(b) *Federal Contract.* Where a Federal contract awarded to a non-Federal entity is subject to the Cost Accounting Standards (CAS), it incorporates the applicable CAS clauses, Standards, and CAS administration requirements per the 48 CFR Chapter 99 and 48 CFR part 30 (FAR Part 30). CAS applies directly to the CAS-covered contract and the Cost Accounting Standards at 48 CFR parts 9904 or 9905 takes precedence over the cost principles in this Subpart E—Cost Principles of this part with respect to the allocation of costs. When a contract with a non-Federal entity is subject to full CAS coverage, the allowability of certain costs under the cost principles will be affected by the allocation provisions of the Cost Accounting Standards (e.g., CAS 414—48 CFR 9904.414, Cost of Money as an Element of the Cost of Facilities Capital, and CAS 417—48 CFR 9904.417, Cost of Money as an Element of the Cost of Capital Assets Under Construction), apply rather the allowability provisions of §200.449 Interest. In complying with those requirements, the non-Federal entity's application of cost accounting practices for estimating, accumulating, and reporting costs for other Federal awards and other cost objectives under the CAS-covered contract still must be consistent with its cost accounting practices for the CAS-covered contracts. In all cases, only one set of accounting records needs to be maintained for the allocation of costs by the non-Federal entity.

(c) *Exemptions.* Some nonprofit organizations, because of their size and nature of operations, can be considered to be similar to for-profit entities for purpose of applicability of cost principles. Such nonprofit organizations must operate under Federal cost principles applicable to for-profit entities located at 48 CFR 31.2. A listing of these organizations is contained in Appendix VIII to Part 200—Nonprofit Organizations Exempted From Subpart E—Cost Principles of this part. Other organizations, as approved by the cognizant agency for indirect costs, may be added from time to time.

BASIC CONSIDERATIONS

§ 200.402   Composition of costs.

Total cost. The total cost of a Federal award is the sum of the allowable direct and allocable indirect costs less any applicable credits.

§ 200.403   Factors affecting allowability of costs.

Except where otherwise authorized by statute, costs must meet the following general criteria in order to be allowable under Federal awards:

(a) Be necessary and reasonable for the performance of the Federal award and be allocable thereto under these principles.

(b) Conform to any limitations or exclusions set forth in these principles or in the Federal award as to types or amount of cost items.

(c) Be consistent with policies and procedures that apply uniformly to both federally-financed and other activities of the non-Federal entity.

(d) Be accorded consistent treatment. A cost may not be assigned to a Federal award as a direct cost if any other cost incurred for the same purpose in like circumstances has been allocated to the Federal award as an indirect cost.

(e) Be determined in accordance with generally accepted accounting principles (GAAP), except, for state and local governments and Indian tribes only, as otherwise provided for in this part.

(f) Not be included as a cost or used to meet cost sharing or matching requirements of any other federally-financed program in either the current or a prior period. See also § 200.306 Cost sharing or matching paragraph (b).

(g) Be adequately documented. See also §§ 200.300 Statutory and national policy requirements through 200.309 Period of performance of this part.

§ 200.404   Reasonable costs.

A cost is reasonable if, in its nature and amount, it does not exceed that which would be incurred by a prudent person under the circumstances prevailing at the time the decision was made to incur the cost. The question of reasonableness is particularly important when the non-Federal entity is predominantly federally-funded. In determining reasonableness of a given cost, consideration must be given to:

(a) Whether the cost is of a type generally recognized as ordinary and necessary for the operation of the non-Federal entity or the proper and efficient performance of the Federal award.

(b) The restraints or requirements imposed by such factors as: sound business practices; arm's-length bargaining; Federal, state and other laws and regulations; and terms and conditions of the Federal award.

(c) Market prices for comparable goods or services for the geographic area.

(d) Whether the individuals concerned acted with prudence in the circumstances considering their responsibilities to the non-Federal entity, its employees, where applicable its students or membership, the public at large, and the Federal government.

(e) Whether the non-Federal entity significantly deviates from its established practices and policies regarding the incurrence of costs, which may unjustifiably increase the Federal award's cost.

§ 200.405 Allocable costs.

(a) A cost is allocable to a particular Federal award or other cost objective if the goods or services involved are chargeable or assignable to that Federal award or cost objective in accordance with relative benefits received. This standard is met if the cost:

(1) Is incurred specifically for the Federal award;

(2) Benefits both the Federal award and other work of the non-Federal entity and can be distributed in proportions that may be approximated using reasonable methods; and

(3) Is necessary to the overall operation of the non-Federal entity and is assignable in part to the Federal award in accordance with the principles in this subpart.

(b) All activities which benefit from the non-Federal entity's indirect (F&A) cost, including unallowable activities and donated services by the non-Federal entity or third parties, will receive an appropriate allocation of indirect costs.

(c) Any cost allocable to a particular Federal award under the principles provided for in this part may not be charged to other Federal awards to overcome fund deficiencies, to avoid restrictions imposed by Federal statutes, regulations, or terms and conditions of the Federal awards, or for other reasons. However, this prohibition would not preclude the non-Federal entity from shifting costs that are allowable under two or more Federal awards in accordance with existing Federal statutes, regulations, or the terms and conditions of the Federal awards.

(d) Direct cost allocation principles. If a cost benefits two or more projects or activities in proportions that can be determined without undue effort or cost, the cost should be allocated to the projects based on the proportional benefit. If a cost benefits two or more projects or activities in proportions that cannot be determined because of the interrelationship of the work involved, then, notwithstanding paragraph (c) of this section, the costs may be allocated or transferred to benefitted projects on any reasonable documented basis. Where the purchase of equipment or other capital asset is specifically authorized under a Federal award, the costs are assignable to the Federal award regardless of the use that may be made of the equipment or other capital asset involved when no longer needed for the purpose for which it was originally required. See also §§ 200.310 Insurance coverage through 200.316 Property trust relationship and 200.439 Equipment and other capital expenditures.

(e) If the contract is subject to CAS, costs must be allocated to the contract pursuant to the Cost Accounting Standards. To the extent that CAS is applicable, the allocation of costs in accordance with CAS takes precedence over the allocation provisions in this part.

§ 200.406 Applicable credits.

(a) Applicable credits refer to those receipts or reduction-of-expenditure-type transactions that offset or reduce expense items allocable to the Federal award as direct or indirect (F&A) costs. Examples of such transactions are: purchase discounts, rebates or allowances, recoveries or indemnities on losses, insurance refunds or rebates, and adjustments of overpayments or erroneous charges. To the extent that such credits accruing to or received by the non-Federal entity relate to allowable costs, they must be credited to the Federal award either as a cost reduction or cash refund, as appropriate.

(b) In some instances, the amounts received from the Federal government to finance activities or service operations of the non-Federal entity should be treated as applicable credits. Specifically, the concept of netting such credit items (including any amounts used to meet cost sharing or matching requirements) should be recognized in determining the rates or amounts to be charged to the Federal award. (See §§ 200.436 Depreciation and 200.468 Specialized service facilities, for areas of potential application in the matter of Federal financing of activities.)

§ 200.407 Prior written approval (prior approval).

Under any given Federal award, the reasonableness and allocability of certain items of costs may be difficult to determine. In order to avoid subsequent disallowance or dispute based on unreasonableness or nonallocability, the non-Federal entity may seek the prior written approval of the cognizant agency for indirect costs or the Federal awarding agency in advance of the incurrence of special or unusual costs. Prior written approval should include the timeframe or scope of the agreement. The absence of prior written approval on any element of cost will not, in itself, affect the reasonableness or allocability of that element, unless prior approval is specifically required for allowability as described under certain circumstances in the following sections of this part:

(a) § 200.201 Use of grant agreements (including fixed amount awards), cooperative agreements, and contracts, paragraph (b)(5);

(b) § 200.306 Cost sharing or matching;

(c) § 200.307 Program income;

(d) § 200.308 Revision of budget and program plans;

(e) § 200.332 Fixed amount subawards;

(f) § 200.413 Direct costs, paragraph (c);

(g) § 200.430 Compensation—personal services, paragraph (h);

(h) § 200.431 Compensation—fringe benefits;

(i) § 200.438 Entertainment costs;

(j) § 200.439 Equipment and other capital expenditures;

(k) § 200.440 Exchange rates;

(l) § 200.441 Fines, penalties, damages and other settlements;

(m) § 200.442 Fund raising and investment management costs;

(n) § 200.445 Goods or services for personal use;

(o) § 200.447 Insurance and indemnification;

(p) § 200.454 Memberships, subscriptions, and professional activity costs, paragraph (c);

(q) § 200.455 Organization costs;

(r) § 200.456 Participant support costs;

(s) § 200.458 Pre-award costs;

(t) § 200.462 Rearrangement and reconversion costs;

(u) § 200.467 Selling and marketing costs; and

(v) § 200.474 Travel costs.

§ 200.408 Limitation on allowance of costs.

The Federal award may be subject to statutory requirements that limit the allowability of costs. When the maximum amount allowable under a limitation is less than the total amount determined in accordance with the principles in this part, the amount not recoverable under the Federal award may not be charged to the Federal award.

§ 200.409 Special considerations.

In addition to the basic considerations regarding the allowability of costs highlighted in this subtitle, other subtitles in this part describe special considerations and requirements applicable to states, local governments, Indian tribes, and IHEs. In addition, certain provisions among the items of cost in this subpart, are only applicable to certain types of non-Federal entities, as specified in the following sections:

(a) Direct and Indirect (F&A) Costs (§§ 200.412 Classification of costs through 200.415 Required certifications) of this subpart;

(b) Special Considerations for States, Local Governments and Indian Tribes (§§ 200.416 Cost allocation plans and indirect cost proposals and 200.417 Interagency service) of this subpart; and

(c) Special Considerations for Institutions of Higher Education (§§ 200.418 Costs incurred by states and local governments and 200.419 Cost accounting standards and disclosure statement) of this subpart.

§ 200.410 Collection of unallowable costs.

Payments made for costs determined to be unallowable by either the Federal awarding agency, cognizant agency for indirect costs, or pass-through entity, either as direct or indirect costs, must be refunded (including interest) to the Federal government in accordance with instructions from the Federal agency that determined the costs are unallowable unless Federal statute or regulation directs otherwise. See also

Subpart D—Post Federal Award Requirements of this part, §§200.300 Statutory and national policy requirements through 200.309 Period of performance.

§200.411 **Adjustment of previously negotiated indirect (F&A) cost rates containing unallowable costs.**

(a) Negotiated indirect (F&A) cost rates based on a proposal later found to have included costs that:

(1) Are unallowable as specified by Federal statutes, regulations or the terms and conditions of a Federal award; or

(2) Are unallowable because they are not allocable to the Federal award(s), must be adjusted, or a refund must be made, in accordance with the requirements of this section. These adjustments or refunds are designed to correct the proposals used to establish the rates and do not constitute a reopening of the rate negotiation. The adjustments or refunds will be made regardless of the type of rate negotiated (predetermined, final, fixed, or provisional).

(b) For rates covering a future fiscal year of the non-Federal entity, the unallowable costs will be removed from the indirect (F&A) cost pools and the rates appropriately adjusted.

(c) For rates covering a past period, the Federal share of the unallowable costs will be computed for each year involved and a cash refund (including interest chargeable in accordance with applicable regulations) will be made to the Federal government. If cash refunds are made for past periods covered by provisional or fixed rates, appropriate adjustments will be made when the rates are finalized to avoid duplicate recovery of the unallowable costs by the Federal government.

(d) For rates covering the current period, either a rate adjustment or a refund, as described in paragraphs (b) and (c) of this section, must be required by the cognizant agency for indirect costs. The choice of method must be at the discretion of the cognizant agency for indirect costs, based on its judgment as to which method would be most practical.

(e) The amount or proportion of unallowable costs included in each year's rate will be assumed to be the same as the amount or proportion of unallowable costs included in the base year proposal used to establish the rate.

DIRECT AND INDIRECT (F&A) COSTS

§200.412 **Classification of costs.**

There is no universal rule for classifying certain costs as either direct or indirect (F&A) under every accounting system. A cost may be direct with respect to some specific service or function, but indirect with respect to the Federal award or other final cost objective. Therefore, it is essential that each item of cost incurred for the same purpose be treated consistently in like circumstances either as a direct or an indirect (F&A) cost in order to avoid possible double-charging of Federal awards. Guidelines for determining direct and indirect (F&A) costs charged to Federal awards are provided in this subpart.

§200.413 **Direct costs.**

(a) *General.* Direct costs are those costs that can be identified specifically with a particular final cost objective, such as a Federal award, or other internally or externally funded activity, or that can be directly assigned to such activities relatively easily with a high degree of accuracy. Costs incurred for the same purpose in like circumstances must be treated consistently as either direct or indirect (F&A) costs. See also §200.405 Allocable costs.

(b) *Application to Federal awards.* Identification with the Federal award rather than the nature of the goods and services involved is the determining factor in distinguishing direct from indirect (F&A) costs of Federal awards. Typical costs charged directly to a Federal award are the compensation of employees who work on that award, their related fringe benefit costs, the costs of materials and other items of expense incurred for the Federal award. If directly related to a specific award, certain costs that otherwise would be treated as indirect costs may also include extraordinary utility consumption, the cost of materials supplied from stock or services rendered by specialized facilities or other institutional service operations.

(c) The salaries of administrative and clerical staff should normally be treated as indirect (F&A) costs. Direct charging of these costs may be appropriate only if all of the following conditions are met:

(1) Administrative or clerical services are integral to a project or activity;

(2) Individuals involved can be specifically identified with the project or activity;

(3) Such costs are explicitly included in the budget or have the prior written approval of the Federal awarding agency; and

(4) The costs are not also recovered as indirect costs.

(d) *Minor items.* Any direct cost of minor amount may be treated as an indirect (F&A) cost for reasons of practicality where such accounting treatment for that item of cost is consistently applied to all Federal and non-Federal cost objectives.

(e) The costs of certain activities are not allowable as charges to Federal awards. However, even though these costs are unallowable for purposes of computing charges to Federal awards, they nonetheless must be treated as direct costs for purposes of determining indirect (F&A) cost rates and be allocated their equitable share of the non-Federal entity's indirect costs if they represent activities which:

(1) Include the salaries of personnel,

(2) Occupy space, and

(3) Benefit from the non-Federal entity's indirect (F&A) costs.

(f) For nonprofit organizations, the costs of activities performed by the non-Federal entity primarily as a service to members, clients, or the general public when significant and necessary to the non-Federal entity's mission must be treated as direct costs whether or not allowable, and be allocated an equitable share of indirect (F&A) costs. Some examples of these types of activities include:

(1) Maintenance of membership rolls, subscriptions, publications, and related functions. See also § 200.454 Memberships, subscriptions, and professional activity costs.

(2) Providing services and information to members, legislative or administrative bodies, or the public. See also §§ 200.454 Memberships, subscriptions, and professional activity costs and 200.450 Lobbying.

(3) Promotion, lobbying, and other forms of public relations. See also §§ 200.421 Advertising and public relations and 200.450 Lobbying.

(4) Conferences except those held to conduct the general administration of the non-Federal entity. See also § 200.432 Conferences.

(5) Maintenance, protection, and investment of special funds not used in operation of the non-Federal entity.

(6) Administration of group benefits on behalf of members or clients, including life and hospital insurance, annuity or retirement plans, and financial aid. See also § 200.431 Compensation—fringe benefits.

§ 200.414   Indirect (F&A) costs.

(a) *Facilities and Administration Classification.* For major IHEs and major nonprofit organizations, indirect (F&A) costs must be classified within two broad categories: "Facilities" and "Administration." "Facilities" is defined as depreciation on buildings, equipment and capital improvement, interest on debt associated with certain buildings, equipment and capital improvements, and operations and maintenance expenses. "Administration" is defined as general administration and general expenses such as the director's office, accounting, personnel and all other types of expenditures not listed specifically under one of the subcategories of "Facilities" (including cross allocations from other pools, where applicable). For nonprofit organizations, library expenses are included in the "Administration" category; for institutions of higher education, they are included in the "Facilities" category. Major IHEs are defined as those required to use the Standard Format for Submission as noted in Appendix III to Part 200—Indirect (F&A) Costs Identification and Assignment, and Rate Determination for Institutions of Higher Education (IHEs) paragraph C. 11. Major nonprofit organizations are those which receive more than $10 million dollars in direct Federal funding.

(b) *Diversity of nonprofit organizations.* Because of the diverse characteristics and accounting practices of nonprofit organizations, it is not possible to specify the types of cost which may be classified as indirect (F&A) cost in all situations. Identification with a Federal award rather than the nature of the goods and services involved is the determining factor in distinguishing direct from indirect (F&A) costs of Federal awards. However, typical examples of indirect (F&A) cost for many nonprofit organizations may include depreciation on buildings and equipment, the costs of operating and maintaining facilities, and general administration and general expenses, such as the salaries and expenses of executive officers, personnel administration, and accounting.

(c) *Federal Agency Acceptance of Negotiated Indirect Cost Rates.* (See also §200.306 Cost sharing or matching.)

(1) The negotiated rates must be accepted by all Federal awarding agencies. A Federal awarding agency may use a rate different from the negotiated rate for a class of Federal awards or a single Federal award only when required by Federal statute or regulation, or when approved by a Federal awarding agency head or delegate based on documented justification as described in paragraph (c)(3) of this section.

(2) The Federal awarding agency head or delegate must notify OMB of any approved deviations.

(3) The Federal awarding agency must implement, and make publicly available, the policies, procedures and general decision making criteria that their programs will follow to seek and justify deviations from negotiated rates.

(4) As required under §200.203 Notices of funding opportunities, the Federal awarding agency must include in the notice of funding opportunity the policies relating to indirect cost rate reimbursement, matching, or cost share as approved under paragraph (e)(1) of this section. As appropriate, the Federal agency should incorporate discussion of these policies into Federal awarding agency outreach activities with non-Federal entities prior to the posting of a notice of funding opportunity.

(d) Pass-through entities are subject to the requirements in §200.331 Re-

quirements for pass-through entities, paragraph (a)(4).

(e) Requirements for development and submission of indirect (F&A) cost rate proposals and cost allocation plans are contained in Appendices III–VII as follows:

(1) Appendix III to Part 200—Indirect (F&A) Costs Identification and Assignment, and Rate Determination for

(2) Appendix IV to Part 200—Indirect (F&A) Costs Identification and Assignment, and Rate Determination for Nonprofit Organizations;

(3) Appendix V to Part 200—State/Local Government and Indian Tribe-Wide Central Service Cost Allocation Plans;

(4) Appendix VI to Part 200—Public Assistance Cost Allocation Plans; and

(5) Appendix VII to Part 200—States and Local Government and Indian Tribe Indirect Cost Proposals.

(f) In addition to the procedures outlined in the appendices in paragraph (e) of this section, any non-Federal entity that has never received a negotiated indirect cost rate, except for those non-Federal entities described in Appendix VII to Part 200—States and Local Government and Indian Tribe Indirect Cost Proposals, paragraph (d)(1)(B) may elect to charge a de minimis rate of) 10% of modified total direct costs (MTDC) which may be used indefinitely. As described in §200.403 Factors affecting allowability of costs, costs must be consistently charged as either indirect or direct costs, but may not be double charged or inconsistently charged as both. If chosen, this methodology once elected must be used consistently for all Federal awards until such time as a non-Federal entity chooses to negotiate for a rate, which the non-Federal entity may apply to do at any time.

(g) Any non-Federal entity that has a federally negotiated indirect cost rate may apply for a one-time extension of a current negotiated indirect cost rates for a period of up to four years. This extension will be subject to the review and approval of the cognizant agency for indirect costs. If an extension is granted the non-Federal entity may not request a rate review until the extension period ends. At the end of the

4-year extension, the non-Federal entity must re-apply to negotiate a rate.

§ 200.415 Required certifications.

Required certifications include:

(a) To assure that expenditures are proper and in accordance with the terms and conditions of the Federal award and approved project budgets, the annual and final fiscal reports or vouchers requesting payment under the agreements must include a certification, signed by an official who is authorized to legally bind the non-Federal entity, which reads as follows: "By signing this report, I certify to the best of my knowledge and belief that the report is true, complete, and accurate, and the expenditures, disbursements and cash receipts are for the purposes and objectives set forth in the terms and conditions of the Federal award. I am aware that any false, fictitious, or fraudulent information, or the omission of any material fact, may subject me to criminal, civil or administrative penalties for fraud, false statements, false claims or otherwise. (U.S. Code Title 18, Section 1001 and Title 31, Sections 3729–3730 and 3801–3812)."

(b) Certification of cost allocation plan or indirect (F&A) cost rate proposal. Each cost allocation plan or indirect (F&A) cost rate proposal must comply with the following:

(1) A proposal to establish a cost allocation plan or an indirect (F&A) cost rate, whether submitted to a Federal cognizant agency for indirect costs or maintained on file by the non-Federal entity, must be certified by the non-Federal entity using the Certificate of Cost Allocation Plan or Certificate of Indirect Costs as set forth in Appendices III through VII. The certificate must be signed on behalf of the non-Federal entity by an individual at a level no lower than vice president or chief financial officer of the non-Federal entity that submits the proposal.

(2) Unless the non-Federal entity has elected the option under § 200.414 Indirect (F&A) costs, paragraph (f), the Federal government may either disallow all indirect (F&A) costs or unilaterally establish such a plan or rate when the non-Federal entity fails to submit a certified proposal for establishing such a plan or rate in accordance with the requirements. Such a plan or rate may be based upon audited historical data or such other data that have been furnished to the cognizant agency for indirect costs and for which it can be demonstrated that all unallowable costs have been excluded. When a cost allocation plan or indirect cost rate is unilaterally established by the Federal government because the non-Federal entity failed to submit a certified proposal, the plan or rate established will be set to ensure that potentially unallowable costs will not be reimbursed.

(c) Certifications by non-profit organizations as appropriate that they did not meet the definition of a major corporation as defined in § 200.414 Indirect (F&A) costs, paragraph (a).

(d) See also § 200.450 Lobbying for another required certification.

SPECIAL CONSIDERATIONS FOR STATES, LOCAL GOVERNMENTS AND INDIAN TRIBES

§ 200.416 Cost allocation plans and indirect cost proposals.

(a) For states, local governments and Indian tribes, certain services, such as motor pools, computer centers, purchasing, accounting, etc., are provided to operating agencies on a centralized basis. Since Federal awards are performed within the individual operating agencies, there needs to be a process whereby these central service costs can be identified and assigned to benefitted activities on a reasonable and consistent basis. The central service cost allocation plan provides that process.

(b) Individual operating agencies (governmental department or agency), normally charge Federal awards for indirect costs through an indirect cost rate. A separate indirect cost rate(s) proposal for each operating agency is usually necessary to claim indirect costs under Federal awards. Indirect costs include:

(1) The indirect costs originating in each department or agency of the governmental unit carrying out Federal awards and

(2) The costs of central governmental services distributed through the central service cost allocation plan and not otherwise treated as direct costs.

(c) The requirements for development and submission of cost allocation plans (for central service costs and public assistance programs) and indirect cost rate proposals are contained in appendices IV, V and VI to this part.

§200.417 Interagency service.

The cost of services provided by one agency to another within the governmental unit may include allowable direct costs of the service plus a prorated share of indirect costs. A standard indirect cost allowance equal to ten percent of the direct salary and wage cost of providing the service (excluding overtime, shift premiums, and fringe benefits) may be used in lieu of determining the actual indirect costs of the service. These services do not include centralized services included in central service cost allocation plans as described in Appendix V to Part 200—State/Local Government and Indian Tribe-Wide Central Service Cost Allocation Plans.

SPECIAL CONSIDERATIONS FOR
INSTITUTIONS OF HIGHER EDUCATION

§200.418 Costs incurred by states and local governments.

Costs incurred or paid by a state or local government on behalf of its IHEs for fringe benefit programs, such as pension costs and FICA and any other costs specifically incurred on behalf of, and in direct benefit to, the IHEs, are allowable costs of such IHEs whether or not these costs are recorded in the accounting records of the institutions, subject to the following:

(a) The costs meet the requirements of §§200.402 Composition of costs through 200.411 Adjustment of previously negotiated indirect (F&A) cost rates containing unallowable costs, of this subpart;

(b) The costs are properly supported by approved cost allocation plans in accordance with applicable Federal cost accounting principles in this part; and

(c) The costs are not otherwise borne directly or indirectly by the Federal government.

§200.419 Cost accounting standards and disclosure statement.

(a) An IHE that receives aggregate Federal awards totaling $50 million or more in Federal awards subject to this part in its most recently completed fiscal year must comply with the Cost Accounting Standards Board's cost accounting standards located at 48 CFR 9905.501, 9905.502, 9905.505, and 9905.506. CAS-covered contracts awarded to the IHEs are subject to the CAS requirements at 48 CFR 9900 through 9999 and 48 CFR part 30 (FAR Part 30).

(b) *Disclosure statement.* An IHE that receives aggregate Federal awards totaling $50 million or more subject to this part during its most recently completed fiscal year must disclose their cost accounting practices by filing a Disclosure Statement (DS–2), which is reproduced in Appendix III to Part 200—Indirect (F&A) Costs Identification and Assignment, and Rate Determination for Institutions of Higher Education (IHEs). With the approval of the cognizant agency for indirect costs, an IHE may meet the DS–2 submission by submitting the DS–2 for each business unit that received $50 million or more in Federal awards.

(1) The DS–2 must be submitted to the cognizant agency for indirect costs with a copy to the IHE's cognizant agency for audit.

(2) An IHE is responsible for maintaining an accurate DS–2 and complying with disclosed cost accounting practices. An IHE must file amendments to the DS–2 to the cognizant agency for indirect costs six months in advance of a disclosed practices being changed to comply with a new or modified standard, or when practices are changed for other reasons. An IHE may proceed with implementing the change only if it has not been notified by the Federal cognizant agency for indirect costs that either a longer period will be needed for review or there are concerns with the potential change within the six months period. Amendments of a DS–2 may be submitted at any time. Resubmission of a complete, updated DS–2 is discouraged except when there are extensive changes to disclosed practices.

(3) *Cost and funding adjustments.* Cost adjustments must be made by the cognizant agency for indirect costs if an IHE fails to comply with the cost policies in this part or fails to consistently follow its established or disclosed cost accounting practices when estimating, accumulating or reporting the costs of Federal awards, and the aggregate cost impact on Federal awards is material. The cost adjustment must normally be made on an aggregate basis for all affected Federal awards through an adjustment of the IHE's future F&A costs rates or other means considered appropriate by the cognizant agency for indirect costs. Under the terms of CAS covered contracts, adjustments in the amount of funding provided may also be required when the estimated proposal costs were not determined in accordance with established cost accounting practices.

(4) *Overpayments.* Excess amounts paid in the aggregate by the Federal government under Federal awards due to a noncompliant cost accounting practice used to estimate, accumulate, or report costs must be credited or refunded, as deemed appropriate by the cognizant agency for indirect costs. Interest applicable to the excess amounts paid in the aggregate during the period of noncompliance must also be determined and collected in accordance with applicable Federal agency regulations.

(5) *Compliant cost accounting practice changes.* Changes from one compliant cost accounting practice to another compliant practice that are approved by the cognizant agency for indirect costs may require cost adjustments if the change has a material effect on Federal awards and the changes are deemed appropriate by the cognizant agency for indirect costs.

(6) *Responsibilities.* The cognizant agency for indirect cost must:

(i) Determine cost adjustments for all Federal awards in the aggregate on behalf of the Federal Government. Actions of the cognizant agency for indirect cost in making cost adjustment determinations must be coordinated with all affected Federal awarding agencies to the extent necessary.

(ii) Prescribe guidelines and establish internal procedures to promptly determine on behalf of the Federal Government that a DS–2 adequately discloses the IHE's cost accounting practices and that the disclosed practices are compliant with applicable CAS and the requirements of this part.

(iii) Distribute to all affected Federal awarding agencies any DS–2 determination of adequacy or noncompliance.

GENERAL PROVISIONS FOR SELECTED ITEMS OF COST

§ 200.420   Considerations for selected items of cost.

This section provides principles to be applied in establishing the allowability of certain items involved in determining cost, in addition to the requirements of Subtitle II. Basic Considerations of this subpart. These principles apply whether or not a particular item of cost is properly treated as direct cost or indirect (F&A) cost. Failure to mention a particular item of cost is not intended to imply that it is either allowable or unallowable; rather, determination as to allowability in each case should be based on the treatment provided for similar or related items of cost, and based on the principles described in §§ 200.402 Composition of costs through 200.411 Adjustment of previously negotiated indirect (F&A) cost rates containing unallowable costs. In case of a discrepancy between the provisions of a specific Federal award and the provisions below, the Federal award governs. Criteria outlined in § 200.403 Factors affecting allowability of *costs* must be applied in determining allowability. See also § 200.102 Exceptions.

§ 200.421   Advertising and public relations.

(a) The term advertising costs means the costs of advertising media and corollary administrative costs. Advertising media include magazines, newspapers, radio and television, direct mail, exhibits, electronic or computer transmittals, and the like.

(b) The only allowable advertising costs are those which are solely for:

(1) The recruitment of personnel required by the non-Federal entity for performance of a Federal award (See also § 200.463 Recruiting costs);

(2) The procurement of goods and services for the performance of a Federal award;

(3) The disposal of scrap or surplus materials acquired in the performance of a Federal award except when non-Federal entities are reimbursed for disposal costs at a predetermined amount; or

(4) Program outreach and other specific purposes necessary to meet the requirements of the Federal award.

(c) The term "public relations" includes community relations and means those activities dedicated to maintaining the image of the non-Federal entity or maintaining or promoting understanding and favorable relations with the community or public at large or any segment of the public.

(d) The only allowable public relations costs are:

(1) Costs specifically required by the Federal award;

(2) Costs of communicating with the public and press pertaining to specific activities or accomplishments which result from performance of the Federal award (these costs are considered necessary as part of the outreach effort for the Federal award); or

(3) Costs of conducting general liaison with news media and government public relations officers, to the extent that such activities are limited to communication and liaison necessary to keep the public informed on matters of public concern, such as notices of funding opportunities, financial matters, etc.

(e) Unallowable advertising and public relations costs include the following:

(1) All advertising and public relations costs other than as specified in paragraphs (b) and (d) of this section;

(2) Costs of meetings, conventions, convocations, or other events related to other activities of the entity (see also §200.432 Conferences), including:

(i) Costs of displays, demonstrations, and exhibits;

(ii) Costs of meeting rooms, hospitality suites, and other special facilities used in conjunction with shows and other special events; and

(iii) Salaries and wages of employees engaged in setting up and displaying exhibits, making demonstrations, and providing briefings;

(3) Costs of promotional items and memorabilia, including models, gifts, and souvenirs;

(4) Costs of advertising and public relations designed solely to promote the non-Federal entity.

§200.422 Advisory councils.

Costs incurred by advisory councils or committees are unallowable unless authorized by statute, the Federal awarding agency or as an indirect cost where allocable to Federal awards. See §200.444 General costs of government, applicable to states, local governments and Indian tribes.

§200.423 Alcoholic beverages.

Costs of alcoholic beverages are unallowable.

§200.424 Alumni/ae activities.

Costs incurred by IHEs for, or in support of, alumni/ae activities are unallowable.

§200.425 Audit services.

(a) A reasonably proportionate share of the costs of audits required by, and performed in accordance with, the Single Audit Act Amendments of 1996 (31 U.S.C. 7501–7507), as implemented by requirements of this part, are allowable. However, the following audit costs are unallowable:

(1) Any costs when audits required by the Single Audit Act and Subpart F—Audit Requirements of this part have not been conducted or have been conducted but not in accordance therewith; and

(2) Any costs of auditing a non-Federal entity that is exempted from having an audit conducted under the Single Audit Act and Subpart F—Audit Requirements of this part because its expenditures under Federal awards are less than $750,000 during the non-Federal entity's fiscal year.

(b) The costs of a financial statement audit of a non-Federal entity that does not currently have a Federal award may be included in the indirect cost pool for a cost allocation plan or indirect cost proposal.

(c) Pass-through entities may charge Federal awards for the cost of agreed-upon-procedures engagements to monitor subrecipients (in accordance with Subpart D—Post Federal Award Requirements of this part, §§ 200.330 Subrecipient and contractor determinations through 200.332 Fixed Amount Subawards) who are exempted from the requirements of the Single Audit Act and Subpart F—Audit Requirements of this part. This cost is allowable only if the agreed-upon-procedures engagements are:

(1) Conducted in accordance with GAGAS attestation standards;

(2) Paid for and arranged by the pass-through entity; and

(3) Limited in scope to one or more of the following types of compliance requirements: activities allowed or unallowed; allowable costs/cost principles; eligibility; and reporting.

§ 200.426 Bad debts.

Bad debts (debts which have been determined to be uncollectable), including losses (whether actual or estimated) arising from uncollectable accounts and other claims, are unallowable. Related collection costs, and related legal costs, arising from such debts after they have been determined to be uncollectable are also unallowable. See also § 200.428 Collections of improper payments.

§ 200.427 Bonding costs.

(a) Bonding costs arise when the Federal awarding agency requires assurance against financial loss to itself or others by reason of the act or default of the non-Federal entity. They arise also in instances where the non-Federal entity requires similar assurance, including: bonds as bid, performance, payment, advance payment, infringement, and fidelity bonds for employees and officials.

(b) Costs of bonding required pursuant to the terms and conditions of the Federal award are allowable.

(c) Costs of bonding required by the non-Federal entity in the general conduct of its operations are allowable as an indirect cost to the extent that such bonding is in accordance with sound business practice and the rates and premiums are reasonable under the circumstances.

§ 200.428 Collections of improper payments.

The costs incurred by a non-Federal entity to recover improper payments are allowable as either direct or indirect costs, as appropriate. Amounts collected may be used by the non-Federal entity in accordance with cash management standards set forth in § 200.305 *Payment*.

§ 200.429 Commencement and convocation costs.

For IHEs, costs incurred for commencements and convocations are unallowable, except as provided for in Appendix III to Part 200—Indirect (F&A) Costs Identification and Assignment, and Rate Determination for Institutions of Higher Education (IHEs), paragraph (B)(9) Student Administration and Services, as student activity costs.

§ 200.430 Compensation—personal services.

(a) *General.* Compensation for personal services includes all remuneration, paid currently or accrued, for services of employees rendered during the period of performance under the Federal award, including but not necessarily limited to wages and salaries. Compensation for personal services may also include fringe benefits which are addressed in § 200.431 Compensation—fringe benefits. Costs of compensation are allowable to the extent that they satisfy the specific requirements of this part, and that the total compensation for individual employees:

(1) Is reasonable for the services rendered and conforms to the established written policy of the non-Federal entity consistently applied to both Federal and non-Federal activities;

(2) Follows an appointment made in accordance with a non-Federal entity's laws and/or rules or written policies and meets the requirements of Federal statute, where applicable; and

(3) Is determined and supported as provided in paragraph (i) of this section, Standards for Documentation of Personnel Expenses, when applicable.

(b) *Reasonableness.* Compensation for employees engaged in work on Federal awards will be considered reasonable to the extent that it is consistent with that paid for similar work in other activities of the non-Federal entity. In cases where the kinds of employees required for Federal awards are not found in the other activities of the non-Federal entity, compensation will be considered reasonable to the extent that it is comparable to that paid for similar work in the labor market in which the non-Federal entity competes for the kind of employees involved.

(c) *Professional activities outside the non-Federal entity.* Unless an arrangement is specifically authorized by a Federal awarding agency, a non-Federal entity must follow its written non-Federal entity-wide policies and practices concerning the permissible extent of professional services that can be provided outside the non-Federal entity for non-organizational compensation. Where such non-Federal entity-wide written policies do not exist or do not adequately define the permissible extent of consulting or other non-organizational activities undertaken for extra outside pay, the Federal government may require that the effort of professional staff working on Federal awards be allocated between:

(1) Non-Federal entity activities, and

(2) Non-organizational professional activities. If the Federal awarding agency considers the extent of non-organizational professional effort excessive or inconsistent with the conflicts-of-interest terms and conditions of the Federal award, appropriate arrangements governing compensation will be negotiated on a case-by-case basis.

(d) *Unallowable costs.* (1) Costs which are unallowable under other sections of these principles must not be allowable under this section solely on the basis that they constitute personnel compensation.

(2) The allowable compensation for certain employees is subject to a ceiling in accordance with statute. For the amount of the ceiling for cost-reimbursement contracts, the covered compensation subject to the ceiling, the covered employees, and other relevant provisions, see 10 U.S.C. 2324(e)(1)(P), and 41 U.S.C. 1127 and 4304(a)(16). For other types of Federal awards, other statutory ceilings may apply.

(e) *Special considerations.* Special considerations in determining allowability of compensation will be given to any change in a non-Federal entity's compensation policy resulting in a substantial increase in its employees' level of compensation (particularly when the change was concurrent with an increase in the ratio of Federal awards to other activities) or any change in the treatment of allowability of specific types of compensation due to changes in Federal policy.

(f) *Incentive compensation.* Incentive compensation to employees based on cost reduction, or efficient performance, suggestion awards, safety awards, etc., is allowable to the extent that the overall compensation is determined to be reasonable and such costs are paid or accrued pursuant to an agreement entered into in good faith between the non-Federal entity and the employees before the services were rendered, or pursuant to an established plan followed by the non-Federal entity so consistently as to imply, in effect, an agreement to make such payment.

(g) *Nonprofit organizations.* For compensation to members of nonprofit organizations, trustees, directors, associates, officers, or the immediate families thereof, determination should be made that such compensation is reasonable for the actual personal services rendered rather than a distribution of earnings in excess of costs. This may include director's and executive committee member's fees, incentive awards, allowances for off-site pay, incentive pay, location allowances, hardship pay, and cost-of-living differentials.

(h) *Institutions of higher education (IHEs).* (1) Certain conditions require special consideration and possible limitations in determining allowable personnel compensation costs under Federal awards. Among such conditions are the following:

(i) Allowable activities. Charges to Federal awards may include reasonable amounts for activities contributing and directly related to work under an agreement, such as delivering special lectures about specific aspects of the ongoing activity, writing reports and articles, developing and maintaining protocols (human, animals, etc.), managing substances/chemicals, managing

143

and securing project-specific data, co-ordinating research subjects, participating in appropriate seminars, consulting with colleagues and graduate students, and attending meetings and conferences.

(ii) *Incidental activities.* Incidental activities for which supplemental compensation is allowable under written institutional policy (at a rate not to exceed institutional base salary) need not be included in the records described in paragraph (h)(9) of this section to directly charge payments of incidental activities, such activities must either be specifically provided for in the Federal award budget or receive prior written approval by the Federal awarding agency.

(2) *Salary basis.* Charges for work performed on Federal awards by faculty members during the academic year are allowable at the IBS rate. Except as noted in paragraph (h)(1)(ii) of this section, in no event will charges to Federal awards, irrespective of the basis of computation, exceed the proportionate share of the IBS for that period. This principle applies to all members of faculty at an institution. IBS is defined as the annual compensation paid by an IHE for an individual's appointment, whether that individual's time is spent on research, instruction, administration, or other activities. IBS excludes any income that an individual earns outside of duties performed for the IHE. Unless there is prior approval by the Federal awarding agency, charges of a faculty member's salary to a Federal award must not exceed the proportionate share of the IBS for the period during which the faculty member worked on the award.

(3) *Intra-Institution of Higher Education (IHE) consulting.* Intra-IHE consulting by faculty is assumed to be undertaken as an IHE obligation requiring no compensation in addition to IBS. However, in unusual cases where consultation is across departmental lines or involves a separate or remote operation, and the work performed by the faculty member is in addition to his or her regular responsibilities, any charges for such work representing additional compensation above IBS are allowable provided that such consulting arrangements are specifically

provided for in the Federal award or approved in writing by the Federal awarding agency.

(4) Extra Service Pay normally represents overload compensation, subject to institutional compensation policies for services above and beyond IBS. Where extra service pay is a result of Intra-IHE consulting, it is subject to the same requirements of paragraph (b) above. It is allowable if all of the following conditions are met:

(i) The non-Federal entity establishes consistent written policies which apply uniformly to all faculty members, not just those working on Federal awards.

(ii) The non-Federal entity establishes a consistent written definition of work covered by IBS which is specific enough to determine conclusively when work beyond that level has occurred. This may be described in appointment letters or other documentations.

(iii) The supplementation amount paid is commensurate with the IBS rate of pay and the amount of additional work performed. See paragraph (h)(2) of this section.

(iv) The salaries, as supplemented, fall within the salary structure and pay ranges established by and documented in writing or otherwise applicable to the non-Federal entity.

(v) The total salaries charged to Federal awards including extra service pay are subject to the Standards of Documentation as described in paragraph (i) of this section.

(5) *Periods outside the academic year.* (i) Except as specified for teaching activity in paragraph (h)(5)(ii) of this section, charges for work performed by faculty members on Federal awards during periods not included in the base salary period will be at a rate not in excess of the IBS.

(ii) Charges for teaching activities performed by faculty members on Federal awards during periods not included in IBS period will be based on the normal written policy of the IHE governing compensation to faculty members for teaching assignments during such periods.

(6) *Part-time faculty.* Charges for work performed on Federal awards by faculty members having only part-time appointments will be determined at a

rate not in excess of that regularly paid for part-time assignments.

(7) *Sabbatical leave costs.* Rules for sabbatical leave are as follow:

(i) Costs of leaves of absence by employees for performance of graduate work or sabbatical study, travel, or research are allowable provided the IHE has a uniform written policy on sabbatical leave for persons engaged in instruction and persons engaged in research. Such costs will be allocated on an equitable basis among all related activities of the IHE.

(ii) Where sabbatical leave is included in fringe benefits for which a cost is determined for assessment as a direct charge, the aggregate amount of such assessments applicable to all work of the institution during the base period must be reasonable in relation to the IHE's actual experience under its sabbatical leave policy.

(8) *Salary rates for non-faculty members.* Non-faculty full-time professional personnel may also earn "extra service pay" in accordance with the non-Federal entity's written policy and consistent with paragraph (h)(1)(i) of this section.

(i) *Standards for Documentation of Personnel Expenses* (1) Charges to Federal awards for salaries and wages must be based on records that accurately reflect the work performed. These records must:

(i) Be supported by a system of internal control which provides reasonable assurance that the charges are accurate, allowable, and properly allocated;

(ii) Be incorporated into the official records of the non-Federal entity;

(iii) Reasonably reflect the total activity for which the employee is compensated by the non-Federal entity, not exceeding 100% of compensated activities (for IHE, this per the IHE's definition of IBS);

(iv) Encompass both federally assisted and all other activities compensated by the non-Federal entity on an integrated basis, but may include the use of subsidiary records as defined in the non-Federal entity's written policy;

(v) Comply with the established accounting policies and practices of the non-Federal entity (See paragraph (h)(1)(ii) above for treatment of incidental work for IHEs.); and

(vi) [Reserved]

(vii) Support the distribution of the employee's salary or wages among specific activities or cost objectives if the employee works on more than one Federal award; a Federal award and non-Federal award; an indirect cost activity and a direct cost activity; two or more indirect activities which are allocated using different allocation bases; or an unallowable activity and a direct or indirect cost activity.

(viii) Budget estimates (i.e., estimates determined before the services are performed) alone do not qualify as support for charges to Federal awards, but may be used for interim accounting purposes, provided that:

(A) The system for establishing the estimates produces reasonable approximations of the activity actually performed;

(B) Significant changes in the corresponding work activity (as defined by the non-Federal entity's written policies) are identified and entered into the records in a timely manner. Short term (such as one or two months) fluctuation between workload categories need not be considered as long as the distribution of salaries and wages is reasonable over the longer term; and

(C) The non-Federal entity's system of internal controls includes processes to review after-the-fact interim charges made to a Federal awards based on budget estimates. All necessary adjustment must be made such that the final amount charged to the Federal award is accurate, allowable, and properly allocated.

(ix) Because practices vary as to the activity constituting a full workload (for IHEs, IBS), records may reflect categories of activities expressed as a percentage distribution of total activities.

(x) It is recognized that teaching, research, service, and administration are often inextricably intermingled in an academic setting. When recording salaries and wages charged to Federal awards for IHEs, a precise assessment of factors that contribute to costs is therefore not always feasible, nor is it expected.

145

(2) For records which meet the standards required in paragraph (i)(1) of this section, the non-Federal entity will not be required to provide additional support or documentation for the work performed, other than that referenced in paragraph (i)(3) of this section.

(3) In accordance with Department of Labor regulations implementing the Fair Labor Standards Act (FLSA) (29 CFR part 516), charges for the salaries and wages of nonexempt employees, in addition to the supporting documentation described in this section, must also be supported by records indicating the total number of hours worked each day.

(4) Salaries and wages of employees used in meeting cost sharing or matching requirements on Federal awards must be supported in the same manner as salaries and wages claimed for reimbursement from Federal awards.

(5) For states, local governments and Indian tribes, substitute processes or systems for allocating salaries and wages to Federal awards may be used in place of or in addition to the records described in paragraph (1) if approved by the cognizant agency for indirect cost. Such systems may include, but are not limited to, random moment sampling, "rolling" time studies, case counts, or other quantifiable measures of work performed.

(i) Substitute systems which use sampling methods (primarily for Temporary Assistance for Needy Families (TANF), the Supplemental Nutrition Assistance Program (SNAP), Medicaid, and other public assistance programs) must meet acceptable statistical sampling standards including:

(A) The sampling universe must include all of the employees whose salaries and wages are to be allocated based on sample results except as provided in paragraph (i)(5)(iii) of this section;

(B) The entire time period involved must be covered by the sample; and

(C) The results must be statistically valid and applied to the period being sampled.

(ii) Allocating charges for the sampled employees' supervisors, clerical and support staffs, based on the results of the sampled employees, will be acceptable.

(iii) Less than full compliance with the statistical sampling standards noted in subsection (5)(i) may be accepted by the cognizant agency for indirect costs if it concludes that the amounts to be allocated to Federal awards will be minimal, or if it concludes that the system proposed by the non-Federal entity will result in lower costs to Federal awards than a system which complies with the standards.

(6) Cognizant agencies for indirect costs are encouraged to approve alternative proposals based on outcomes and milestones for program performance where these are clearly documented. Where approved by the Federal cognizant agency for indirect costs, these plans are acceptable as an alternative to the requirements of paragraph (i)(1) of this section.

(7) For Federal awards of similar purpose activity or instances of approved blended funding, a non-Federal entity may submit performance plans that incorporate funds from multiple Federal awards and account for their combined use based on performance-oriented metrics, provided that such plans are approved in advance by all involved Federal awarding agencies. In these instances, the non-Federal entity must submit a request for waiver of the requirements based on documentation that describes the method of charging costs, relates the charging of costs to the specific activity that is applicable to all fund sources, and is based on quantifiable measures of the activity in relation to time charged.

(8) For a non-Federal entity where the records do not meet the standards described in this section, the Federal government may require personnel activity reports, including prescribed certifications, or equivalent documentation that support the records as required in this section.

§ 200.431 Compensation—fringe benefits.

(a) Fringe benefits are allowances and services provided by employers to their employees as compensation in addition to regular salaries and wages. Fringe benefits include, but are not limited to, the costs of leave (vacation, family-related, sick or military), employee insurance, pensions, and unemployment benefit plans. Except as provided elsewhere in these principles, the costs of fringe benefits are allowable provided that the benefits are reasonable and are required by law, non-Federal entity-employee agreement, or an established policy of the non-Federal entity.

(b) *Leave.* The cost of fringe benefits in the form of regular compensation paid to employees during periods of authorized absences from the job, such as for annual leave, family-related leave, sick leave, holidays, court leave, military leave, administrative leave, and other similar benefits, are allowable if all of the following criteria are met:

(1) They are provided under established written leave policies;

(2) The costs are equitably allocated to all related activities, including Federal awards; and,

(3) The accounting basis (cash or accrual) selected for costing each type of leave is consistently followed by the non-Federal entity or specified grouping of employees.

(i) When a non-Federal entity uses the cash basis of accounting, the cost of leave is recognized in the period that the leave is taken and paid for. Payments for unused leave when an employee retires or terminates employment are allowable as indirect costs in the year of payment.

(ii) The accrual basis may be only used for those types of leave for which a liability as defined by GAAP exists when the leave is earned. When a non-Federal entity uses the accrual basis of accounting, allowable leave costs are the lesser of the amount accrued or funded.

(c) The cost of fringe benefits in the form of employer contributions or expenses for social security; employee life, health, unemployment, and worker's compensation insurance (except as indicated in §200.447 Insurance and indemnification); pension plan costs (see paragraph (i) of this section); and other similar benefits are allowable, provided such benefits are granted under established written policies. Such benefits, must be allocated to Federal awards and all other activities in a manner consistent with the pattern of benefits attributable to the individuals or group(s) of employees whose salaries and wages are chargeable to such Federal awards and other activities, and charged as direct or indirect costs in accordance with the non-Federal entity's accounting practices.

(d) Fringe benefits may be assigned to cost objectives by identifying specific benefits to specific individual employees or by allocating on the basis of entity-wide salaries and wages of the employees receiving the benefits. When the allocation method is used, separate allocations must be made to selective groupings of employees, unless the non-Federal entity demonstrates that costs in relationship to salaries and wages do not differ significantly for different groups of employees.

(e) *Insurance.* See also §200.447 Insurance and indemnification, paragraphs (d)(1) and (2).

(1) Provisions for a reserve under a self-insurance program for unemployment compensation or workers' compensation are allowable to the extent that the provisions represent reasonable estimates of the liabilities for such compensation, and the types of coverage, extent of coverage, and rates and premiums would have been allowable had insurance been purchased to cover the risks. However, provisions for self-insured liabilities which do not become payable for more than one year after the provision is made must not exceed the present value of the liability.

(2) Costs of insurance on the lives of trustees, officers, or other employees holding positions of similar responsibility are allowable only to the extent that the insurance represents additional compensation. The costs of such insurance when the non-Federal entity is named as beneficiary are unallowable.

(3) Actual claims paid to or on behalf of employees or former employees for workers' compensation, unemployment compensation, severance pay, and similar employee benefits (e.g., post-retirement health benefits), are allowable in the year of payment provided that the non-Federal entity follows a consistent costing policy and they are allocated as indirect costs.

(f) *Automobiles.* That portion of automobile costs furnished by the entity that relates to personal use by employees (including transportation to and from work) is unallowable as fringe benefit or indirect (F&A) costs regardless of whether the cost is reported as taxable income to the employees.

(g) *Pension Plan Costs.* Pension plan costs which are incurred in accordance with the established policies of the non-Federal entity are allowable, provided that:

(1) Such policies meet the test of reasonableness.

(2) The methods of cost allocation are not discriminatory.

(3) For entities using accrual based accounting, the cost assigned to each fiscal year is determined in accordance with GAAP.

(4) The costs assigned to a given fiscal year are funded for all plan participants within six months after the end of that year. However, increases to normal and past service pension costs caused by a delay in funding the actuarial liability beyond 30 calendar days after each quarter of the year to which such costs are assignable are unallowable. Non-Federal entity may elect to follow the "Cost Accounting Standard for Composition and Measurement of Pension Costs" (48 CFR 9904.412).

(5) Pension plan termination insurance premiums paid pursuant to the Employee Retirement Income Security Act (ERISA) of 1974 (29 U.S.C. 1301–1461) are allowable. Late payment charges on such premiums are unallowable. Excise taxes on accumulated funding deficiencies and other penalties imposed under ERISA are unallowable.

(6) Pension plan costs may be computed using a pay-as-you-go method or an acceptable actuarial cost method in accordance with established written policies of the non-Federal entity.

(i) For pension plans financed on a pay-as-you-go method, allowable costs will be limited to those representing actual payments to retirees or their beneficiaries.

(ii) Pension costs calculated using an actuarial cost-based method recognized by GAAP are allowable for a given fiscal year if they are funded for that year within six months after the end of that year. Costs funded after the six month period (or a later period agreed to by the cognizant agency for indirect costs) are allowable in the year funded. The cognizant agency for indirect costs may agree to an extension of the six month period if an appropriate adjustment is made to compensate for the timing of the charges to the Federal government and related Federal reimbursement and the non-Federal entity's contribution to the pension fund. Adjustments may be made by cash refund or other equitable procedures to compensate the Federal government for the time value of Federal reimbursements in excess of contributions to the pension fund.

(iii) Amounts funded by the non-Federal entity in excess of the actuarially determined amount for a fiscal year may be used as the non-Federal entity's contribution in future periods.

(iv) When a non-Federal entity converts to an acceptable actuarial cost method, as defined by GAAP, and funds pension costs in accordance with this method, the unfunded liability at the time of conversion is allowable if amortized over a period of years in accordance with GAAP.

(v) The Federal government must receive an equitable share of any previously allowed pension costs (including earnings thereon) which revert or inure to the non-Federal entity in the form of a refund, withdrawal, or other credit.

(h) *Post-Retirement Health.* Post-retirement health plans (PRHP) refers to costs of health insurance or health services not included in a pension plan covered by paragraph (g) of this section for retirees and their spouses, dependents, and survivors. PRHP costs may be computed using a pay-as-you-go method or an acceptable actuarial cost method in accordance with established written policies of the non-Federal entity.

(1) For PRHP financed on a pay-as-you-go method, allowable costs will be limited to those representing actual payments to retirees or their beneficiaries.

(2) PRHP costs calculated using an actuarial cost method recognized by GAAP are allowable if they are funded for that year within six months after the end of that year. Costs funded after

the six month period (or a later period agreed to by the cognizant agency) are allowable in the year funded. The Federal cognizant agency for indirect costs may agree to an extension of the six month period if an appropriate adjustment is made to compensate for the timing of the charges to the Federal government and related Federal reimbursements and the non-Federal entity's contributions to the PRHP fund. Adjustments may be made by cash refund, reduction in current year's PRHP costs, or other equitable procedures to compensate the Federal government for the time value of Federal reimbursements in excess of contributions to the PRHP fund.

(3) Amounts funded in excess of the actuarially determined amount for a fiscal year may be used as the Federal government's contribution in a future period.

(4) When a non-Federal entity converts to an acceptable actuarial cost method and funds PRHP costs in accordance with this method, the initial unfunded liability attributable to prior years is allowable if amortized over a period of years in accordance with GAAP, or, if no such GAAP period exists, over a period negotiated with the cognizant agency for indirect costs.

(5) To be allowable in the current year, the PRHP costs must be paid either to:

(i) An insurer or other benefit provider as current year costs or premiums, or

(ii) An insurer or trustee to maintain a trust fund or reserve for the sole purpose of providing post-retirement benefits to retirees and other beneficiaries.

(6) The Federal government must receive an equitable share of any amounts of previously allowed post-retirement benefit costs (including earnings thereon) which revert or inure to the entity in the form of a refund, withdrawal, or other credit.

(i) *Severance Pay.* (1) Severance pay, also commonly referred to as dismissal wages, is a payment in addition to regular salaries and wages, by non-Federal entities to workers whose employment is being terminated. Costs of severance pay are allowable only to the extent that in each case, it is required by (a) law, (b) employer-employee agreement,

(c) established policy that constitutes, in effect, an implied agreement on the non-Federal entity's part, or (d) circumstances of the particular employment.

(2) Costs of severance payments are divided into two categories as follows:

(i) Actual normal turnover severance payments must be allocated to all activities; or, where the non-Federal entity provides for a reserve for normal severances, such method will be acceptable if the charge to current operations is reasonable in light of payments actually made for normal severances over a representative past period, and if amounts charged are allocated to all activities of the non-Federal entity.

(ii) Measurement of costs of abnormal or mass severance pay by means of an accrual will not achieve equity to both parties. Thus, accruals for this purpose are not allowable. However, the Federal government recognizes its obligation to participate, to the extent of its fair share, in any specific payment. Prior approval by the Federal awarding agency or cognizant agency for indirect cost, as appropriate, is required.

(3) Costs incurred in certain severance pay packages which are in an amount in excess of the normal severance pay paid by the non-Federal entity to an employee upon termination of employment and are paid to the employee contingent upon a change in management control over, or ownership of, the non-Federal entity's assets, are unallowable.

(4) Severance payments to foreign nationals employed by the non-Federal entity outside the United States, to the extent that the amount exceeds the customary or prevailing practices for the non-Federal entity in the United States, are unallowable, unless they are necessary for the performance of Federal programs and approved by the Federal awarding agency.

(5) Severance payments to foreign nationals employed by the non-Federal entity outside the United States due to the termination of the foreign national as a result of the closing of, or curtailment of activities by, the non-Federal entity in that country, are unallowable, unless they are necessary for the

performance of Federal programs and approved by the Federal awarding agency.

(j)(1) *For IHEs only.* Fringe benefits in the form of tuition or remission of tuition for individual employees are allowable, provided such benefits are granted in accordance with established non-Federal entity policies, and are distributed to all non-Federal entity activities on an equitable basis. Tuition benefits for family members other than the employee are unallowable.

(2) Fringe benefits in the form of tuition or remission of tuition for individual employees not employed by IHEs are limited to the tax-free amount allowed per section 127 of the Internal Revenue Code as amended.

(3) IHEs may offer employees tuition waivers or tuition reductions for undergraduate education under IRC Section 117(d) as amended, provided that the benefit does not discriminate in favor of highly compensated employees. Federal reimbursement of tuition or remission of tuition is also limited to the institution for which the employee works. See § 200.466 Scholarships and student aid costs, for treatment of tuition remission provided to students.

(k) For IHEs whose costs are paid by state or local governments, fringe benefit programs (such as pension costs and FICA) and any other benefits costs specifically incurred on behalf of, and in direct benefit to, the non-Federal entity, are allowable costs of such non-Federal entities whether or not these costs are recorded in the accounting records of the non-Federal entities, subject to the following:

(1) The costs meet the requirements of Basic Considerations in §§ 200.402 Composition of costs through 200.411 Adjustment of previously negotiated indirect (F&A) cost rates containing unallowable costs of this subpart;

(2) The costs are properly supported by approved cost allocation plans in accordance with applicable Federal cost accounting principles; and

(3) The costs are not otherwise borne directly or indirectly by the Federal government.

§ 200.432 Conferences.

A conference is defined as a meeting, retreat, seminar, symposium, work-shop or event whose primary purpose is the dissemination of technical information beyond the non-Federal entity and is necessary and reasonable for successful performance under the Federal award. Allowable conference costs paid by the non-Federal entity as a sponsor or host of the conference may include rental of facilities, speakers' fees, costs of meals and refreshments, local transportation, and other items incidental to such conferences unless further restricted by the terms and conditions of the Federal award. As needed, the costs of identifying, but not providing, locally available dependent-care resources are allowable. Conference hosts/sponsors must exercise discretion and judgment in ensuring that conference costs are appropriate, necessary and managed in a manner that minimizes costs to the Federal award. The Federal awarding agency may authorize exceptions where appropriate for programs including Indian tribes, children, and the elderly. See also §§ 200.438 Entertainment costs, 200.456 Participant support costs, 200.474 Travel costs, and 200.475 Trustees.

§ 200.433 Contingency provisions.

(a) Contingency is that part of a budget estimate of future costs (typically of large construction projects, IT systems, or other items as approved by the Federal awarding agency) which is associated with possible events or conditions arising from causes the precise outcome of which is indeterminable at the time of estimate, and that experience shows will likely result, in aggregate, in additional costs for the approved activity or project. Amounts for major project scope changes, unforeseen risks, or extraordinary events may not be included.

(b) It is permissible for contingency amounts other than those excluded in paragraph (b)(1) of this section to be explicitly included in budget estimates, to the extent they are necessary to improve the precision of those estimates. Amounts must be estimated using broadly-accepted cost estimating methodologies, specified in the budget documentation of the Federal award, and accepted by the Federal awarding agency. As such, contingency amounts are to be included in the Federal award. In order for actual costs incurred to be allowable, they must comply with the cost principles and other requirements in this part (see also §§200.300 Statutory and national policy requirements through 200.309 Period of performance of Subpart D of this part and 200.403 Factors affecting allowability of costs); be necessary and reasonable for proper and efficient accomplishment of project or program objectives, and be verifiable from the non-Federal entity's records.

(c) Payments made by the Federal awarding agency to the non-Federal entity's "contingency reserve" or any similar payment made for events the occurrence of which cannot be foretold with certainty as to the time or intensity, or with an assurance of their happening, are unallowable, except as noted in §§200.431 Compensation—fringe benefits regarding self-insurance, pensions, severance and post-retirement health costs and 200.447 Insurance and indemnification.

§200.434 Contributions and donations.

(a) Costs of contributions and donations, including cash, property, and services, from the non-Federal entity to other entities, are unallowable.

(b) The value of services and property donated to the non-Federal entity may not be charged to the Federal award either as a direct or indirect (F&A) cost. The value of donated services and property may be used to meet cost sharing or matching requirements (see §200.306 Cost sharing or matching). Depreciation on donated assets is permitted in accordance with §200.436 Depreciation, as long as the donated property is not counted towards cost sharing or matching requirements.

(c) Services donated or volunteered to the non-Federal entity may be furnished to a non-Federal entity by professional and technical personnel, consultants, and other skilled and unskilled labor. The value of these services is not allowable either as a direct or indirect cost. However, the value of donated services may be used to meet cost sharing or matching requirements in accordance with the provisions of §200.306 Cost sharing or matching.

(d) To the extent feasible, services donated to the non-Federal entity will be supported by the same methods used to support the allocability of regular personnel services.

(e) The following provisions apply to nonprofit organizations. The value of services donated to the nonprofit organization utilized in the performance of a direct cost activity must be considered in the determination of the non-Federal entity's indirect cost rate(s) and, accordingly, must be allocated a proportionate share of applicable indirect costs when the following circumstances exist:

(1) The aggregate value of the services is material;

(2) The services are supported by a significant amount of the indirect costs incurred by the non-Federal entity;

(i) In those instances where there is no basis for determining the fair market value of the services rendered, the non-Federal entity and the cognizant agency for indirect costs must negotiate an appropriate allocation of indirect cost to the services.

(ii) Where donated services directly benefit a project supported by the Federal award, the indirect costs allocated to the services will be considered as a part of the total costs of the project. Such indirect costs may be reimbursed under the Federal award or used to meet cost sharing or matching requirements.

(f) Fair market value of donated services must be computed as described in §200.306 Cost sharing or matching.

(g) Personal Property and Use of Space.

(1) Donated personal property and use of space may be furnished to a non-Federal entity. The value of the personal property and space is not reimbursable either as a direct or indirect cost.

(2) The value of the donations may be used to meet cost sharing or matching share requirements under the conditions described in §§200.300 Statutory and national policy requirements through 200.309 Period of performance of subpart D of this part. The value of the donations must be determined in accordance with §§200.300 Statutory and national policy requirements

through 200.309 Period of performance. Where donations are treated as indirect costs, indirect cost rates will separate the value of the donations so that reimbursement will not be made.

§ 200.435 Defense and prosecution of criminal and civil proceedings, claims, appeals and patent infringements.

(a) Definitions for the purposes of this section.

(1) *Conviction* means a judgment or conviction of a criminal offense by any court of competent jurisdiction, whether entered upon verdict or a plea, including a conviction due to a plea of nolo contendere.

(2) *Costs* include the services of in-house or private counsel, accountants, consultants, or others engaged to assist the non-Federal entity before, during, and after commencement of a judicial or administrative proceeding, that bear a direct relationship to the proceeding.

(3) *Fraud* means:

(i) Acts of fraud or corruption or attempts to defraud the Federal government or to corrupt its agents,

(ii) Acts that constitute a cause for debarment or suspension (as specified in agency regulations), and

(iii) Acts which violate the False Claims Act (31 U.S.C. 3729-3732) or the Anti-kickback Act (41 U.S.C. 1320a-7b(b)).

(4) *Penalty* does not include restitution, reimbursement, or compensatory damages.

(5) *Proceeding* includes an investigation.

(b) *Costs.* (1) Except as otherwise described herein, costs incurred in connection with any criminal, civil or administrative proceeding (including filing of a false certification) commenced by the Federal government, a state, local government, or foreign government, or joined by the Federal government (including a proceeding under the False Claims Act), against the non-Federal entity, (or commenced by third parties or a current or former employee of the non-Federal entity who submits a whistleblower complaint of reprisal in accordance with 10 U.S.C. 2409 or 41 U.S.C. 4712), are not allowable if the proceeding:

(i) Relates to a violation of, or failure to comply with, a Federal, state, local or foreign statute, regulation or the terms and conditions of the Federal award, by the non-Federal entity (including its agents and employees); and

(ii) Results in any of the following dispositions:

(A) In a criminal proceeding, a conviction.

(B) In a civil or administrative proceeding involving an allegation of fraud or similar misconduct, a determination of non-Federal entity liability.

(C) In the case of any civil or administrative proceeding, the disallowance of costs or the imposition of a monetary penalty, or an order issued by the Federal awarding agency head or delegate to the non-Federal entity to take corrective action under 10 U.S.C. 2409 or 41 U.S.C. 4712.

(D) A final decision by an appropriate Federal official to debar or suspend the non-Federal entity, to rescind or void a Federal award, or to terminate a Federal award for default by reason of a violation or failure to comply with a statute, regulation, or the terms and conditions of the Federal award.

(E) A disposition by consent or compromise, if the action could have resulted in any of the dispositions described in paragraphs (b)(1)(ii)(A) through (D) of this section.

(2) If more than one proceeding involves the same alleged misconduct, the costs of all such proceedings are unallowable if any results in one of the dispositions shown in paragraph (b) of this section.

(c) If a proceeding referred to in paragraph (b) of this section is commenced by the Federal government and is resolved by consent or compromise pursuant to an agreement by the non-Federal entity and the Federal government, then the costs incurred may be allowed to the extent specifically provided in such agreement.

(d) If a proceeding referred to in paragraph (b) of this section is commenced by a state, local or foreign government, the authorized Federal official may allow the costs incurred if such authorized Federal official determines that the costs were incurred as a result of:

(1) A specific term or condition of the Federal award, or

(2) Specific written direction of an authorized official of the Federal awarding agency.

(e) Costs incurred in connection with proceedings described in paragraph (b) of this section, which are not made unallowable by that subsection, may be allowed but only to the extent that:

(1) The costs are reasonable and necessary in relation to the administration of the Federal award and activities required to deal with the proceeding and the underlying cause of action;

(2) Payment of the reasonable, necessary, allocable and otherwise allowable costs incurred is not prohibited by any other provision(s) of the Federal award;

(3) The costs are not recovered from the Federal Government or a third party, either directly as a result of the proceeding or otherwise; and,

(4) An authorized Federal official must determine the percentage of costs allowed considering the complexity of litigation, generally accepted principles governing the award of legal fees in civil actions involving the United States, and such other factors as may be appropriate. Such percentage must not exceed 80 percent. However, if an agreement reached under paragraph (c) of this section has explicitly considered this 80 percent limitation and permitted a higher percentage, then the full amount of costs resulting from that agreement are allowable.

(f) Costs incurred by the non-Federal entity in connection with the defense of suits brought by its employees or ex-employees under section 2 of the Major Fraud Act of 1988 (18 U.S.C. 1031), including the cost of all relief necessary to make such employee whole, where the non-Federal entity was found liable or settled, are unallowable.

(g) Costs of prosecution of claims against the Federal government, including appeals of final Federal agency decisions, are unallowable.

(h) Costs of legal, accounting, and consultant services, and related costs, incurred in connection with patent infringement litigation, are unallowable unless otherwise provided for in the Federal award.

(i) Costs which may be unallowable under this section, including directly associated costs, must be segregated and accounted for separately. During the pendency of any proceeding covered by paragraphs (b) and (f) of this section, the Federal government must generally withhold payment of such costs. However, if in its best interests, the Federal government may provide for conditional payment upon provision of adequate security, or other adequate assurance, and agreement to repay all unallowable costs, plus interest, if the costs are subsequently determined to be unallowable.

§200.436 Depreciation.

(a) Depreciation is the method for allocating the cost of fixed assets to periods benefitting from asset use. The non-Federal entity may be compensated for the use of its buildings, capital improvements, equipment, and software projects capitalized in accordance with GAAP, provided that they are used, needed in the non-Federal entity's activities, and properly allocated to Federal awards. Such compensation must be made by computing depreciation.

(b) The allocation for depreciation must be made in accordance with Appendices IV through VIII.

(c) Depreciation is computed applying the following rules. The computation of depreciation must be based on the acquisition cost of the assets involved. For an asset donated to the non-Federal entity by a third party, its fair market value at the time of the donation must be considered as the acquisition cost. Such assets may be depreciated or claimed as matching but not both. For this purpose, the acquisition cost will exclude:

(1) The cost of land;

(2) Any portion of the cost of buildings and equipment borne by or donated by the Federal government, irrespective of where title was originally vested or where it is presently located;

(3) Any portion of the cost of buildings and equipment contributed by or for the non-Federal entity, or where law or agreement prohibits recovery; and

(4) Any asset acquired solely for the performance of a non-Federal award.

153

(d) When computing depreciation charges, the following must be observed:

(1) The period of useful service or useful life established in each case for usable capital assets must take into consideration such factors as type of construction, nature of the equipment, technological developments in the particular area, historical data, and the renewal and replacement policies followed for the individual items or classes of assets involved.

(2) The depreciation method used to charge the cost of an asset (or group of assets) to accounting periods must reflect the pattern of consumption of the asset during its useful life. In the absence of clear evidence indicating that the expected consumption of the asset will be significantly greater in the early portions than in the later portions of its useful life, the straight-line method must be presumed to be the appropriate method. Depreciation methods once used may not be changed unless approved in advance by the cognizant agency. The depreciation methods used to calculate the depreciation amounts for indirect (F&A) rate purposes must be the same methods used by the non-Federal entity for its financial statements.

(3) The entire building, including the shell and all components, may be treated as a single asset and depreciated over a single useful life. A building may also be divided into multiple components. Each component item may then be depreciated over its estimated useful life. The building components must be grouped into three general components of a building: building shell (including construction and design costs), building services systems (e.g., elevators, HVAC, plumbing system and heating and air-conditioning system) and fixed equipment (e.g., sterilizers, casework, fume hoods, cold rooms and glassware/washers). In exceptional cases, a cognizant agency may authorize a non-Federal entity to use more than these three groupings. When a non-Federal entity elects to depreciate its buildings by its components, the same depreciation methods must be used for indirect (F&A) purposes and financial statements pur-

poses, as described in paragraphs (d)(1) and (2) of this section.

(4) No depreciation may be allowed on any assets that have outlived their depreciable lives.

(5) Where the depreciation method is introduced to replace the use allowance method, depreciation must be computed as if the asset had been depreciated over its entire life (i.e., from the date the asset was acquired and ready for use to the date of disposal or withdrawal from service). The total amount of use allowance and depreciation for an asset (including imputed depreciation applicable to periods prior to the conversion from the use allowance method as well as depreciation after the conversion) may not exceed the total acquisition cost of the asset.

(e) Charges for depreciation must be supported by adequate property records, and physical inventories must be taken at least once every two years to ensure that the assets exist and are usable, used, and needed. Statistical sampling techniques may be used in taking these inventories. In addition, adequate depreciation records showing the amount of depreciation taken each period must also be maintained.

§ 200.437 Employee health and welfare costs.

(a) Costs incurred in accordance with the non-Federal entity's documented policies for the improvement of working conditions, employer-employee relations, employee health, and employee performance are allowable.

(b) Such costs will be equitably apportioned to all activities of the non-Federal entity. Income generated from any of these activities will be credited to the cost thereof unless such income has been irrevocably sent to employee welfare organizations.

(c) Losses resulting from operating food services are allowable only if the non-Federal entity's objective is to operate such services on a break-even basis. Losses sustained because of operating objectives other than the above are allowable only:

(1) Where the non-Federal entity can demonstrate unusual circumstances; and

(2) With the approval of the cognizant agency for indirect costs.

§200.438 Entertainment costs.

Costs of entertainment, including amusement, diversion, and social activities and any associated costs are unallowable, except where specific costs that might otherwise be considered entertainment have a programmatic purpose and are authorized either in the approved budget for the Federal award or with prior written approval of the Federal awarding agency.

§200.439 Equipment and other capital expenditures.

(a) See §§200.13 Capital expenditures, 200.33 Equipment, 200.89 Special purpose equipment, 200.48 General purpose equipment, 200.2 Acquisition cost, and 200.12 Capital assets.

(b) The following rules of allowability must apply to equipment and other capital expenditures:

(1) Capital expenditures for general purpose equipment, buildings, and land are unallowable as direct charges, except with the prior written approval of the Federal awarding agency or pass-through entity.

(2) Capital expenditures for special purpose equipment are allowable as direct costs, provided that items with a unit cost of $5,000 or more have the prior written approval of the Federal awarding agency or pass-through entity.

(3) Capital expenditures for improvements to land, buildings, or equipment which materially increase their value or useful life are unallowable as a direct cost except with the prior written approval of the Federal awarding agency, or pass-through entity. See §200.436 Depreciation, for rules on the allowability of depreciation on buildings, capital improvements, and equipment. See also §200.465 Rental costs of real property and equipment.

(4) When approved as a direct charge pursuant to paragraphs (b)(1) through (3) of this section, capital expenditures will be charged in the period in which the expenditure is incurred, or as otherwise determined appropriate and negotiated with the Federal awarding agency.

(5) The unamortized portion of any equipment written off as a result of a change in capitalization levels may be recovered by continuing to claim the otherwise allowable depreciation on the equipment, or by amortizing the amount to be written off over a period of years negotiated with the Federal cognizant agency for indirect cost.

(6) Cost of equipment disposal. If the non-Federal entity is instructed by the Federal awarding agency to otherwise dispose of or transfer the equipment the costs of such disposal or transfer are allowable.

§200.440 Exchange rates.

(a) Cost increases for fluctuations in exchange rates are allowable costs subject to the availability of funding, and prior approval by the Federal awarding agency. The Federal awarding agency must however ensure that adequate funds are available to cover currency fluctuations in order to avoid a violation of the Anti-Deficiency Act.

(b) The non-Federal entity is required to make reviews of local currency gains to determine the need for additional federal funding before the expiration date of the Federal award. Subsequent adjustments for currency increases may be allowable only when the non-Federal entity provides the Federal awarding agency with adequate source documentation from a commonly used source in effect at the time the expense was made, and to the extent that sufficient Federal funds are available.

§200.441 Fines, penalties, damages and other settlements.

Costs resulting from non-Federal entity violations of, alleged violations of, or failure to comply with, Federal, state, tribal, local or foreign laws and regulations are unallowable, except when incurred as a result of compliance with specific provisions of the Federal award, or with prior written approval of the Federal awarding agency. See also §200.435 Defense and prosecution of criminal and civil proceedings, claims, appeals and patent infringements.

§200.442 Fund raising and investment management costs.

(a) Costs of organized fund raising, including financial campaigns, endowment drives, solicitation of gifts and bequests, and similar expenses incurred to raise capital or obtain contributions are unallowable. Fund raising costs for the purposes of meeting the Federal program objectives are allowable with prior written approval from the Federal awarding agency. Proposal costs are covered in § 200.460 Proposal costs.

(b) Costs of investment counsel and staff and similar expenses incurred to enhance income from investments are unallowable except when associated with investments covering pension, self-insurance, or other funds which include Federal participation allowed by this part.

(c) Costs related to the physical custody and control of monies and securities are allowable.

(d) Both allowable and unallowable fund raising and investment activities must be allocated as an appropriate share of indirect costs under the conditions described in § 200.413 Direct costs.

§ 200.443 Gains and losses on disposition of depreciable assets.

(a) Gains and losses on the sale, retirement, or other disposition of depreciable property must be included in the year in which they occur as credits or charges to the asset cost grouping(s) in which the property was included. The amount of the gain or loss to be included as a credit or charge to the appropriate asset cost grouping(s) is the difference between the amount realized on the property and the undepreciated basis of the property.

(b) Gains and losses from the disposition of depreciable property must not be recognized as a separate credit or charge under the following conditions:

(1) The gain or loss is processed through a depreciation account and is reflected in the depreciation allowable under §§ 200.436 Depreciation and 200.439 Equipment and other capital expenditures.

(2) The property is given in exchange as part of the purchase price of a similar item and the gain or loss is taken into account in determining the depreciation cost basis of the new item.

(3) A loss results from the failure to maintain permissible insurance, except as otherwise provided in § 46*200.447 Insurance and indemnification.

(4) Compensation for the use of the property was provided through use allowances in lieu of depreciation.

(5) Gains and losses arising from mass or extraordinary sales, retirements, or other dispositions must be considered on a case-by-case basis.

(c) Gains or losses of any nature arising from the sale or exchange of property other than the property covered in paragraph (a) of this section, e.g., land, must be excluded in computing Federal award costs.

(d) When assets acquired with Federal funds, in part or wholly, are disposed of, the distribution of the proceeds must be made in accordance with §§ 200.310 Insurance Coverage through 200.316 Property trust relationship.

§ 200.444 General costs of government.

(a) For states, local governments, and Indian Tribes, the general costs of government are unallowable (except as provided in § 200.474 Travel costs). Unallowable costs include:

(1) Salaries and expenses of the Office of the Governor of a state or the chief executive of a local government or the chief executive of an Indian tribe;

(2) Salaries and other expenses of a state legislature, tribal council, or similar local governmental body, such as a county supervisor, city council, school board, etc., whether incurred for purposes of legislation or executive direction;

(3) Costs of the judicial branch of a government;

(4) Costs of prosecutorial activities unless treated as a direct cost to a specific program if authorized by statute or regulation (however, this does not preclude the allowability of other legal activities of the Attorney General as described in § 200.435 Defense and prosecution of criminal and civil proceedings, claims, appeals and patent infringements); and

(5) Costs of other general types of government services normally provided to the general public, such as fire and police, unless provided for as a direct cost under a program statute or regulation.

(b) For Indian tribes and Councils Of Governments (COGs) (see § 200.64 Local government), the portion of salaries and expenses directly attributable to managing and operating Federal programs by the chief executive and his or her staff is allowable. Up to 50% of these costs can be included in the indirect cost calculation without documentation.

§ 200.445 Goods or services for personal use.

(a) Costs of goods or services for personal use of the non-Federal entity's employees are unallowable regardless of whether the cost is reported as taxable income to the employees.

(b) Costs of housing (e.g., depreciation, maintenance, utilities, furnishings, rent), housing allowances and personal living expenses are only allowable as direct costs regardless of whether reported as taxable income to the employees. In addition, to be allowable direct costs must be approved in advance by a Federal awarding agency.

§ 200.446 Idle facilities and idle capacity.

(a) As used in this section the following terms have the meanings set forth in this section:

(1) Facilities means land and buildings or any portion thereof, equipment individually or collectively, or any other tangible capital asset, wherever located, and whether owned or leased by the non-Federal entity.

(2) Idle facilities means completely unused facilities that are excess to the non-Federal entity's current needs.

(3) Idle capacity means the unused capacity of partially used facilities. It is the difference between:

(i) That which a facility could achieve under 100 percent operating time on a one-shift basis less operating interruptions resulting from time lost for repairs, setups, unsatisfactory materials, and other normal delays and;

(ii) The extent to which the facility was actually used to meet demands during the accounting period. A multishift basis should be used if it can be shown that this amount of usage would normally be expected for the type of facility involved.

(4) Cost of idle facilities or idle capacity means costs such as maintenance, repair, housing, rent, and other related costs, e.g., insurance, interest, and depreciation. These costs could in-

clude the costs of idle public safety emergency facilities, telecommunications, or information technology system capacity that is built to withstand major fluctuations in load, e.g., consolidated data centers.

(b) The costs of idle facilities are unallowable except to the extent that:

(1) They are necessary to meet workload requirements which may fluctuate and are allocated appropriately to all benefiting programs; or

(2) Although not necessary to meet fluctuations in workload, they were necessary when acquired and are now idle because of changes in program requirements, efforts to achieve more economical operations, reorganization, termination, or other causes which could not have been reasonably foreseen. Under the exception stated in this subsection, costs of idle facilities are allowable for a reasonable period of time, ordinarily not to exceed one year, depending on the initiative taken to use, lease, or dispose of such facilities.

(c) The costs of idle capacity are normal costs of doing business and are a factor in the normal fluctuations of usage or indirect cost rates from period to period. Such costs are allowable, provided that the capacity is reasonably anticipated to be necessary to carry out the purpose of the Federal award or was originally reasonable and is not subject to reduction or elimination by use on other Federal awards, subletting, renting, or sale, in accordance with sound business, economic, or security practices. Widespread idle capacity throughout an entire facility or among a group of assets having substantially the same function may be considered idle facilities.

§ 200.447 Insurance and indemnification.

(a) Costs of insurance required or approved and maintained, pursuant to the Federal award, are allowable.

(b) Costs of other insurance in connection with the general conduct of activities are allowable subject to the following limitations:

(1) Types and extent and cost of coverage are in accordance with the non-Federal entity's policy and sound business practice.

(2) Costs of insurance or of contributions to any reserve covering the risk of loss of, or damage to, Federal government property are unallowable except to the extent that the Federal awarding agency has specifically required or approved such costs.

(3) Costs allowed for business interruption or other similar insurance must exclude coverage of management fees.

(4) Costs of insurance on the lives of trustees, officers, or other employees holding positions of similar responsibilities are allowable only to the extent that the insurance represents additional compensation (see § 200.431 Compensation—fringe benefits). The cost of such insurance when the non-Federal entity is identified as the beneficiary is unallowable.

(5) Insurance against defects. Costs of insurance with respect to any costs incurred to correct defects in the non-Federal entity's materials or workmanship are unallowable.

(6) Medical liability (malpractice) insurance. Medical liability insurance is an allowable cost of Federal research programs only to the extent that the Federal research programs involve human subjects or training of participants in research techniques. Medical liability insurance costs must be treated as a direct cost and must be assigned to individual projects based on the manner in which the insurer allocates the risk to the population covered by the insurance.

(c) Actual losses which could have been covered by permissible insurance (through a self-insurance program or otherwise) are unallowable, unless expressly provided for in the Federal award. However, costs incurred because of losses not covered under nominal deductible insurance coverage provided in keeping with sound management practice, and minor losses not covered by insurance, such as spoilage, breakage, and disappearance of small hand tools, which occur in the ordinary course of operations, are allowable.

(d) Contributions to a reserve for certain self-insurance programs including workers' compensation, unemployment compensation, and severance pay are allowable subject to the following provisions:

(1) The type of coverage and the extent of coverage and the rates and premiums would have been allowed had insurance (including reinsurance) been purchased to cover the risks. However, provision for known or reasonably estimated self-insured liabilities, which do not become payable for more than one year after the provision is made, must not exceed the discounted present value of the liability. The rate used for discounting the liability must be determined by giving consideration to such factors as the non-Federal entity's settlement rate for those liabilities and its investment rate of return.

(2) Earnings or investment income on reserves must be credited to those reserves.

(3)(i) Contributions to reserves must be based on sound actuarial principles using historical experience and reasonable assumptions. Reserve levels must be analyzed and updated at least biennially for each major risk being insured and take into account any reinsurance, coinsurance, etc. Reserve levels related to employee-related coverages will normally be limited to the value of claims:

(A) Submitted and adjudicated but not paid;

(B) Submitted but not adjudicated; and

(C) Incurred but not submitted.

(ii) Reserve levels in excess of the amounts based on the above must be identified and justified in the cost allocation plan or indirect cost rate proposal.

(4) Accounting records, actuarial studies, and cost allocations (or billings) must recognize any significant differences due to types of insured risk and losses generated by the various insured activities or agencies of the non-Federal entity. If individual departments or agencies of the non-Federal entity experience significantly different levels of claims for a particular risk, those differences are to be recognized by the use of separate allocations or other techniques resulting in an equitable allocation.

(5) Whenever funds are transferred from a self-insurance reserve to other accounts (e.g., general fund or unrestricted account), refunds must be made to the Federal government for its

share of funds transferred, including earned or imputed interest from the date of transfer and debt interest, if applicable, chargeable in accordance with applicable Federal cognizant agency for indirect cost, claims collection regulations.

(e) Insurance refunds must be credited against insurance costs in the year the refund is received.

(f) Indemnification includes securing the non-Federal entity against liabilities to third persons and other losses not compensated by insurance or otherwise. The Federal government is obligated to indemnify the non-Federal entity only to the extent expressly provided for in the Federal award, except as provided in paragraph (c) of this section.

§ 200.448 Intellectual property.

(a) *Patent costs.* (1) The following costs related to securing patents and copyrights are allowable:

(i) Costs of preparing disclosures, reports, and other documents required by the Federal award, and of searching the art to the extent necessary to make such disclosures;

(ii) Costs of preparing documents and any other patent costs in connection with the filing and prosecution of a United States patent application where title or royalty-free license is required by the Federal government to be conveyed to the Federal government; and

(iii) General counseling services relating to patent and copyright matters, such as advice on patent and copyright laws, regulations, clauses, and employee intellectual property agreements (See also § 200.459 Professional service costs).

(2) The following costs related to securing patents and copyrights are unallowable:

(i) Costs of preparing disclosures, reports, and other documents, and of searching the art to make disclosures not required by the Federal award;

(ii) Costs in connection with filing and prosecuting any foreign patent application, or any United States patent application, where the Federal award does not require conveying title or a royalty-free license to the Federal government.

(b) *Royalties and other costs for use of patents and copyrights.* (1) Royalties on a patent or copyright or amortization of the cost of acquiring by purchase a copyright, patent, or rights thereto, necessary for the proper performance of the Federal award are allowable unless:

(i) The Federal government already has a license or the right to free use of the patent or copyright.

(ii) The patent or copyright has been adjudicated to be invalid, or has been administratively determined to be invalid.

(iii) The patent or copyright is considered to be unenforceable.

(iv) The patent or copyright is expired.

(2) Special care should be exercised in determining reasonableness where the royalties may have been arrived at as a result of less-than-arm's-length bargaining, such as:

(i) Royalties paid to persons, including corporations, affiliated with the non-Federal entity.

(ii) Royalties paid to unaffiliated parties, including corporations, under an agreement entered into in contemplation that a Federal award would be made.

(iii) Royalties paid under an agreement entered into after a Federal award is made to a non-Federal entity.

(3) In any case involving a patent or copyright formerly owned by the non-Federal entity, the amount of royalty allowed should not exceed the cost which would have been allowed had the non-Federal entity retained title thereto.

§ 200.449 Interest.

(a) *General.* Costs incurred for interest on borrowed capital, temporary use of endowment funds, or the use of the non-Federal entity's own funds, however represented, are unallowable. Financing costs (including interest) to acquire, construct, or replace capital assets are allowable, subject to the conditions in this section.

(b)(1) Capital assets is defined as noted in § 200.12 Capital assets. An asset cost includes (as applicable) acquisition costs, construction costs, and other costs capitalized in accordance with GAAP.

(2) For non-Federal entity fiscal years beginning on or after January 1, 2016, intangible assets include patents and computer software. For software development projects, only interest attributable to the portion of the project costs capitalized in accordance with GAAP is allowable.

(c) *Conditions for all non-Federal entities.* (1) The non-Federal entity uses the capital assets in support of Federal awards;

(2) The allowable asset costs to acquire facilities and equipment are limited to a fair market value available to the non-Federal entity from an unrelated (arm's length) third party.

(3) The non-Federal entity obtains the financing via an arm's-length transaction (that is, a transaction with an unrelated third party); or claims reimbursement of actual interest cost at a rate available via such a transaction.

(4) The non-Federal entity limits claims for Federal reimbursement of interest costs to the least expensive alternative. For example, a capital lease may be determined less costly than purchasing through debt financing, in which case reimbursement must be limited to the amount of interest determined if leasing had been used.

(5) The non-Federal entity expenses or capitalizes allowable interest cost in accordance with GAAP.

(6) Earnings generated by the investment of borrowed funds pending their disbursement for the asset costs are used to offset the current period's allowable interest cost, whether that cost is expensed or capitalized. Earnings subject to being reported to the Federal Internal Revenue Service under arbitrage requirements are excludable.

(7) The following conditions must apply to debt arrangements over $1 million to purchase or construct facilities, unless the non-Federal entity makes an initial equity contribution to the purchase of 25 percent or more. For this purpose, "initial equity contribution" means the amount or value of contributions made by the non-Federal entity for the acquisition of facilities prior to occupancy.

(i) The non-Federal entity must reduce claims for reimbursement of interest cost by an amount equal to imputed interest earnings on excess cash flow attributable to the portion of the facility used for Federal awards.

(ii) The non-Federal entity must impute interest on excess cash flow as follows:

(A) Annually, the non-Federal entity must prepare a cumulative (from the inception of the project) report of monthly cash inflows and outflows, regardless of the funding source. For this purpose, inflows consist of Federal reimbursement for depreciation, amortization of capitalized construction interest, and annual interest cost. Outflows consist of initial equity contributions, debt principal payments (less the pro-rata share attributable to the cost of land), and interest payments.

(B) To compute monthly cash inflows and outflows, the non-Federal entity must divide the annual amounts determined in step (i) by the number of months in the year (usually 12) that the building is in service.

(C) For any month in which cumulative cash inflows exceed cumulative outflows, interest must be calculated on the excess inflows for that month and be treated as a reduction to allowable interest cost. The rate of interest to be used must be the three-month Treasury bill closing rate as of the last business day of that month.

(8) Interest attributable to a fully depreciated asset is unallowable.

(d) Additional conditions for states, local governments and Indian tribes. For costs to be allowable, the non-Federal entity must have incurred the interest costs for buildings after October 1, 1980, or for land and equipment after September 1, 1995.

(1) The requirement to offset interest earned on borrowed funds against current allowable interest cost (paragraph (c)(5), above) also applies to earnings on debt service reserve funds.

(2) The non-Federal entity will negotiate the amount of allowable interest cost related to the acquisition of facilities with asset costs of $1 million or more, as outlined in paragraph (c)(7) of this section. For this purpose, a non-Federal entity must consider only cash inflows and outflows attributable to that portion of the real property used for Federal awards.

(e) Additional conditions for IHEs. For costs to be allowable, the IHE must have incurred the interest costs after September 23, 1982, in connection with acquisitions of capital assets that occurred after that date.

(f) Additional condition for nonprofit organizations. For costs to be allowable, the nonprofit organization incurred the interest costs after September 29, 1995, in connection with acquisitions of capital assets that occurred after that date.

(g) The interest allowability provisions of this section do not apply to a nonprofit organization subject to "full coverage" under the Cost Accounting Standards (CAS), as defined at 48 CFR 9903.201–2(a). The non-Federal entity's Federal awards are instead subject to CAS 414 (48 CFR 9904.414), "Cost of Money as an Element of the Cost of Facilities Capital", and CAS 417 (48 CFR 9904.417), "Cost of Money as an Element of the Cost of Capital Assets Under Construction".

§200.450 Lobbying.

(a) The cost of certain influencing activities associated with obtaining grants, contracts, cooperative agreements, or loans is an unallowable cost. Lobbying with respect to certain grants, contracts, cooperative agreements, and loans is governed by relevant statutes, including among others, the provisions of 31 U.S.C. 1352, as well as the common rule, "New Restrictions on Lobbying" published at 55 FR 6736 (February 26, 1990), including definitions, and the Office of Management and Budget "Governmentwide Guidance for New Restrictions on Lobbying" and notices published at 54 FR 52306 (December 20, 1989), 55 FR 24540 (June 15, 1990), 57 FR 1772 (January 15, 1992), and 61 FR 1412 (January 19, 1996).

(b) Executive lobbying costs. Costs incurred in attempting to improperly influence either directly or indirectly, an employee or officer of the executive branch of the Federal government to give consideration or to act regarding a Federal award or a regulatory matter are unallowable. Improper influence means any influence that induces or tends to induce a Federal employee or officer to give consideration or to act regarding a Federal award or regulatory matter on any basis other than the merits of the matter.

(c) In addition to the above, the following restrictions are applicable to nonprofit organizations and IHEs:

(1) Costs associated with the following activities are unallowable:

(i) Attempts to influence the outcomes of any Federal, state, or local election, referendum, initiative, or similar procedure, through in-kind or cash contributions, endorsements, publicity, or similar activity;

(ii) Establishing, administering, contributing to, or paying the expenses of a political party, campaign, political action committee, or other organization established for the purpose of influencing the outcomes of elections in the United States;

(iii) Any attempt to influence:

(A) The introduction of Federal or state legislation;

(B) The enactment or modification of any pending Federal or state legislation through communication with any member or employee of the Congress or state legislature (including efforts to influence state or local officials to engage in similar lobbying activity);

(C) The enactment or modification of any pending Federal or state legislation by preparing, distributing, or using publicity or propaganda, or by urging members of the general public, or any segment thereof, to contribute to or participate in any mass demonstration, march, rally, fund raising drive, lobbying campaign or letter writing or telephone campaign; or

(D) Any government official or employee in connection with a decision to sign or veto enrolled legislation;

(iv) Legislative liaison activities, including attendance at legislative sessions or committee hearings, gathering information regarding legislation, and analyzing the effect of legislation, when such activities are carried on in support of or in knowing preparation for an effort to engage in unallowable lobbying.

(2) The following activities are excepted from the coverage of paragraph (c)(1) of this section:

(i) Technical and factual presentations on topics directly related to the performance of a grant, contract, or other agreement (through hearing testimony, statements, or letters to the Congress or a state legislature, or subdivision, member, or cognizant staff member thereof), in response to a documented request (including a Congressional Record notice requesting testimony or statements for the record at a regularly scheduled hearing) made by the non-Federal entity's member of congress, legislative body or a subdivision, or a cognizant staff member thereof, provided such information is readily obtainable and can be readily put in deliverable form, and further provided that costs under this section for travel, lodging or meals are unallowable unless incurred to offer testimony at a regularly scheduled Congressional hearing pursuant to a written request for such presentation made by the Chairman or Ranking Minority Member of the Committee or Subcommittee conducting such hearings;

(ii) Any lobbying made unallowable by paragraph (c)(1)(iii) of this section to influence state legislation in order to directly reduce the cost, or to avoid material impairment of the non-Federal entity's authority to perform the grant, contract, or other agreement; or

(iii) Any activity specifically authorized by statute to be undertaken with funds from the Federal award.

(iv) Any activity excepted from the definitions of "lobbying" or "influencing legislation" by the Internal Revenue Code provisions that require nonprofit organizations to limit their participation in direct and "grass roots" lobbying activities in order to retain their charitable deduction status and avoid punitive excise taxes, I.R.C. §§ 501(c)(3), 501(h), 4911(a), including:

(A) Nonpartisan analysis, study, or research reports;

(B) Examinations and discussions of broad social, economic, and similar problems; and

(C) Information provided upon request by a legislator for technical advice and assistance, as defined by I.R.C. § 4911(d)(2) and 26 CFR 56.4911–2(c)(1)–(c)(3).

(v) When a non-Federal entity seeks reimbursement for indirect (F&A) costs, total lobbying costs must be separately identified in the indirect (F&A) cost rate proposal, and thereafter treated as other unallowable activity costs in accordance with the procedures of § 200.413 Direct costs.

(vi) The non-Federal entity must submit as part of its annual indirect (F&A) cost rate proposal a certification that the requirements and standards of this section have been complied with. (See also § 200.415 Required certifications.)

(vii)(A) Time logs, calendars, or similar records are not required to be created for purposes of complying with the record keeping requirements in § 200.302 Financial management with respect to lobbying costs during any particular calendar month when:

(1) The employee engages in lobbying (as defined in paragraphs (c)(1) and (c)(2) of this section) 25 percent or less of the employee's compensated hours of employment during that calendar month; and

(2) Within the preceding five-year period, the non-Federal entity has not materially misstated allowable or unallowable costs of any nature, including legislative lobbying costs.

(B) When conditions in paragraph (c)(2)(vii)(A)(1) and (2) of this section are met, non-Federal entities are not required to establish records to support the allowability of claimed costs in addition to records already required or maintained. Also, when conditions in paragraphs (c)(2)(vii)(A)(1) and (2) of this section are met, the absence of time logs, calendars, or similar records will not serve as a basis for disallowing costs by contesting estimates of lobbying time spent by employees during a calendar month.

(viii) The Federal awarding agency must establish procedures for resolving in advance, in consultation with OMB, any significant questions or disagreements concerning the interpretation or application of this section. Any such advance resolutions must be binding in any subsequent settlements, audits, or investigations with respect to that grant or contract for purposes of interpretation of this part, provided, however, that this must not be construed to prevent a contractor or non-Federal entity from contesting the lawfulness of such a determination.

§ 200.451 Losses on other awards or contracts.

Any excess of costs over income under any other award or contract of any nature is unallowable. This includes, but is not limited to, the non-Federal entity's contributed portion by reason of cost-sharing agreements or any under-recoveries through negotiation of flat amounts for indirect (F&A) costs. Also, any excess of costs over authorized funding levels transferred from any award or contract to another award or contract is unallowable. All losses are not allowable indirect (F&A) costs and are required to be included in the appropriate indirect cost rate base for allocation of indirect costs.

§ 200.452 Maintenance and repair costs.

Costs incurred for utilities, insurance, security, necessary maintenance, janitorial services, repair, or upkeep of buildings and equipment (including Federal property unless otherwise provided for) which neither add to the permanent value of the property nor appreciably prolong its intended life, but keep it in an efficient operating condition, are allowable. Costs incurred for improvements which add to the permanent value of the buildings and equipment or appreciably prolong their intended life must be treated as capital expenditures (see § 200.439 Equipment and other capital expenditures). These costs are only allowable to the extent not paid through rental or other agreements.

§ 200.453 Materials and supplies costs, including costs of computing devices.

(a) Costs incurred for materials, supplies, and fabricated parts necessary to carry out a Federal award are allowable.

(b) Purchased materials and supplies must be charged at their actual prices, net of applicable credits. Withdrawals from general stores or stockrooms should be charged at their actual net cost under any recognized method of pricing inventory withdrawals, consistently applied. Incoming transportation charges are a proper part of materials and supplies costs.

(c) Materials and supplies used for the performance of a Federal award may be charged as direct costs. In the specific case of computing devices, charging as direct costs is allowable for devices that are essential and allocable, but not solely dedicated, to the performance of a Federal award.

(d) Where federally-donated or furnished materials are used in performing the Federal award, such materials will be used without charge.

§ 200.454 Memberships, subscriptions, and professional activity costs.

(a) Costs of the non-Federal entity's membership in business, technical, and professional organizations are allowable.

(b) Costs of the non-Federal entity's subscriptions to business, professional, and technical periodicals are allowable.

(c) Costs of membership in any civic or community organization are allowable with prior approval by the Federal awarding agency or pass-through entity.

(d) Costs of membership in any country club or social or dining club or organization are unallowable.

(e) Costs of membership in organizations whose primary purpose is lobbying are unallowable. See also § 200.450 Lobbying.

§ 200.455 Organization costs.

Costs such as incorporation fees, brokers' fees, fees to promoters, organizers or management consultants, attorneys, accountants, or investment counselor, whether or not employees of the non-Federal entity in connection with establishment or reorganization of an organization, are unallowable except with prior approval of the Federal awarding agency.

§ 200.456 Participant support costs.

Participant support costs as defined in § 200.75 Participant support costs are allowable with the prior approval of the Federal awarding agency.

§ 200.457 Plant and security costs.

Necessary and reasonable expenses incurred for routine and security to protect facilities, personnel, and work products are allowable. Such costs include, but are not limited to, wages and uniforms of personnel engaged in security activities; equipment; barriers; protective (non-military) gear, devices, and equipment; contractual security services; and consultants. Capital expenditures for plant security purposes are subject to § 200.439 Equipment and other capital expenditures.

§ 200.458   Pre-award costs.

Pre-award costs are those incurred prior to the effective date of the Federal award directly pursuant to the negotiation and in anticipation of the Federal award where such costs are necessary for efficient and timely performance of the scope of work. Such costs are allowable only to the extent that they would have been allowable if incurred after the date of the Federal award and only with the written approval of the Federal awarding agency.

§ 200.459   Professional service costs.

(a) Costs of professional and consultant services rendered by persons who are members of a particular profession or possess a special skill, and who are not officers or employees of the non-Federal entity, are allowable, subject to paragraphs (b) and (c) when reasonable in relation to the services rendered and when not contingent upon recovery of the costs from the Federal government. In addition, legal and related services are limited under § 200.435 Defense and prosecution of criminal and civil proceedings, claims, appeals and patent infringements.

(b) In determining the allowability of costs in a particular case, no single factor or any special combination of factors is necessarily determinative. However, the following factors are relevant:

(1) The nature and scope of the service rendered in relation to the service required.

(2) The necessity of contracting for the service, considering the non-Federal entity's capability in the particular area.

(3) The past pattern of such costs, particularly in the years prior to Federal awards.

(4) The impact of Federal awards on the non-Federal entity's business (i.e., what new problems have arisen).

(5) Whether the proportion of Federal work to the non-Federal entity's total business is such as to influence the non-Federal entity in favor of incurring the cost, particularly where the services rendered are not of a continuing nature and have little relationship to work under Federal awards.

(6) Whether the service can be performed more economically by direct employment rather than contracting.

(7) The qualifications of the individual or concern rendering the service and the customary fees charged, especially on non-federally funded activities.

(8) Adequacy of the contractual agreement for the service (e.g., description of the service, estimate of time required, rate of compensation, and termination provisions).

(c) In addition to the factors in paragraph (b) of this section, to be allowable, retainer fees must be supported by evidence of bona fide services available or rendered.

§ 200.460   Proposal costs.

Proposal costs are the costs of preparing bids, proposals, or applications on potential Federal and non-Federal awards or projects, including the development of data necessary to support the non-Federal entity's bids or proposals. Proposal costs of the current accounting period of both successful and unsuccessful bids and proposals normally should be treated as indirect (F&A) costs and allocated currently to all activities of the non-Federal entity. No proposal costs of past accounting periods will be allocable to the current period.

§ 200.461   Publication   and   printing costs.

(a) Publication costs for electronic and print media, including distribution, promotion, and general handling are allowable. If these costs are not identifiable with a particular cost objective, they should be allocated as indirect costs to all benefiting activities of the non-Federal entity.

(b) Page charges for professional journal publications are allowable where:

(1) The publications report work supported by the Federal government; and

(2) The charges are levied impartially on all items published by the journal, whether or not under a Federal award.

(3) The non-Federal entity may charge the Federal award before close-out for the costs of publication or sharing of research results if the costs are not incurred during the period of performance of the Federal award.

§ 200.462 Rearrangement and reconversion costs.

(a) Costs incurred for ordinary and normal rearrangement and alteration of facilities are allowable as indirect costs. Special arrangements and alterations costs incurred specifically for a Federal award are allowable as a direct cost with the prior approval of the Federal awarding agency or pass-through entity.

(b) Costs incurred in the restoration or rehabilitation of the non-Federal entity's facilities to approximately the same condition existing immediately prior to commencement of Federal awards, less costs related to normal wear and tear, are allowable.

§ 200.463 Recruiting costs.

(a) Subject to paragraphs (b) and (c) of this section, and provided that the size of the staff recruited and maintained is in keeping with workload requirements, costs of "help wanted" advertising, operating costs of an employment office necessary to secure and maintain an adequate staff, costs of operating an aptitude and educational testing program, travel costs of employees while engaged in recruiting personnel, travel costs of applicants for interviews for prospective employment, and relocation costs incurred incident to recruitment of new employees, are allowable to the extent that such costs are incurred pursuant to the non-Federal entity's standard recruitment program. Where the non-Federal entity uses employment agencies, costs not in excess of standard commercial rates for such services are allowable.

(b) Special emoluments, fringe benefits, and salary allowances incurred to attract professional personnel that do not meet the test of reasonableness or do not conform with the established practices of the non-Federal entity, are unallowable.

(c) Where relocation costs incurred incident to recruitment of a new employee have been funded in whole or in part as a direct cost to a Federal award, and the newly hired employee resigns for reasons within the employee's control within 12 months after hire, the non-Federal entity will be required to refund or credit the Federal share of such relocation costs to the Federal government. See also § 200.464 Relocation costs of employees.

(d) Short-term, travel visa costs (as opposed to longer-term, immigration visas) are generally allowable expenses that may be proposed as a direct cost. Since short-term visas are issued for a specific period and purpose, they can be clearly identified as directly connected to work performed on a Federal award. For these costs to be directly charged to a Federal award, they must:

(1) Be critical and necessary for the conduct of the project;

(2) Be allowable under the applicable cost principles;

(3) Be consistent with the non-Federal entity's cost accounting practices and non-Federal entity policy; and

(4) Meet the definition of "direct cost" as described in the applicable cost principles.

§ 200.464 Relocation costs of employees.

(a) Relocation costs are costs incident to the permanent change of duty assignment (for an indefinite period or for a stated period of not less than 12 months) of an existing employee or upon recruitment of a new employee. Relocation costs are allowable, subject to the limitations described in paragraphs (b), (c), and (d) of this section, provided that:

(1) The move is for the benefit of the employer.

(2) Reimbursement to the employee is in accordance with an established written policy consistently followed by the employer.

(3) The reimbursement does not exceed the employee's actual (or reasonably estimated) expenses.

(b) Allowable relocation costs for current employees are limited to the following:

165

(1) The costs of transportation of the employee, members of his or her immediate family and his household, and personal effects to the new location.

(2) The costs of finding a new home, such as advance trips by employees and spouses to locate living quarters and temporary lodging during the transition period, up to maximum period of 30 calendar days.

(3) Closing costs, such as brokerage, legal, and appraisal fees, incident to the disposition of the employee's former home. These costs, together with those described in (4), are limited to 8 per cent of the sales price of the employee's former home.

(4) The continuing costs of ownership (for up to six months) of the vacant former home after the settlement or lease date of the employee's new permanent home, such as maintenance of buildings and grounds (exclusive of fixing-up expenses), utilities, taxes, and property insurance.

(5) Other necessary and reasonable expenses normally incident to relocation, such as the costs of canceling an unexpired lease, transportation of personal property, and purchasing insurance against loss of or damages to personal property. The cost of canceling an unexpired lease is limited to three times the monthly rental.

(c) Allowable relocation costs for new employees are limited to those described in paragraphs (b)(1) and (2) of this section. When relocation costs incurred incident to the recruitment of new employees have been allowed either as a direct or indirect cost and the employee resigns for reasons within the employee's control within 12 months after hire, the non-Federal entity must refund or credit the Federal government for its share of the cost. However, the costs of travel to an overseas location must be considered travel costs in accordance with § 200.474 Travel costs, and not this § 200.464 Relocation costs of employees, for the purpose of this paragraph if dependents are not permitted at the location for any reason and the costs do not include costs of transporting household goods.

(d) The following costs related to relocation are unallowable:

(1) Fees and other costs associated with acquiring a new home.

(2) A loss on the sale of a former home.

(3) Continuing mortgage principal and interest payments on a home being sold.

(4) Income taxes paid by an employee related to reimbursed relocation costs.

§ 200.465 Rental costs of real property and equipment.

(a) Subject to the limitations described in paragraphs (b) through (d) of this section, rental costs are allowable to the extent that the rates are reasonable in light of such factors as: rental costs of comparable property, if any; market conditions in the area; alternatives available; and the type, life expectancy, condition, and value of the property leased. Rental arrangements should be reviewed periodically to determine if circumstances have changed and other options are available.

(b) Rental costs under "sale and lease back" arrangements are allowable only up to the amount that would be allowed had the non-Federal entity continued to own the property. This amount would include expenses such as depreciation, maintenance, taxes, and insurance.

(c) Rental costs under "less-than-arm's-length" leases are allowable only up to the amount (as explained in paragraph (b) of this section). For this purpose, a less-than-arm's-length lease is one under which one party to the lease agreement is able to control or substantially influence the actions of the other. Such leases include, but are not limited to those between:

(1) Divisions of the non-Federal entity;

(2) The non-Federal entity under common control through common officers, directors, or members; and

(3) The non-Federal entity and a director, trustee, officer, or key employee of the non-Federal entity or an immediate family member, either directly or through corporations, trusts, or similar arrangements in which they hold a controlling interest. For example, the non-Federal entity may establish a separate corporation for the sole purpose of owning property and leasing it back to the non-Federal entity.

(4) Family members include one party with any of the following relationships to another party:

(i) Spouse, and parents thereof;

(ii) Children, and spouses thereof;

(iii) Parents, and spouses thereof;

(iv) Siblings, and spouses thereof;

(v) Grandparents and grandchildren, and spouses thereof;

(vi) Domestic partner and parents thereof, including domestic partners of any individual in 2 through 5 of this definition; and

(vii) Any individual related by blood or affinity whose close association with the employee is the equivalent of a family relationship.

(5) Rental costs under leases which are required to be treated as capital leases under GAAP are allowable only up to the amount (as explained in paragraph (b) of this section) that would be allowed had the non-Federal entity purchased the property on the date the lease agreement was executed. The provisions of GAAP must be used to determine whether a lease is a capital lease. Interest costs related to capital leases are allowable to the extent they meet the criteria in § 200.449 Interest. Unallowable costs include amounts paid for profit, management fees, and taxes that would not have been incurred had the non-Federal entity purchased the property.

(6) The rental of any property owned by any individuals or entities affiliated with the non-Federal entity, to include commercial or residential real estate, for purposes such as the home office workspace is unallowable.

§ 200.466   Scholarships and student aid costs.

(a) Costs of scholarships, fellowships, and other programs of student aid at IHEs are allowable only when the purpose of the Federal award is to provide training to selected participants and the charge is approved by the Federal awarding agency. However, tuition remission and other forms of compensation paid as, or in lieu of, wages to students performing necessary work are allowable provided that:

(1) The individual is conducting activities necessary to the Federal award;

(2) Tuition remission and other support are provided in accordance with established policy of the IHE and consistently provided in a like manner to students in return for similar activities conducted under Federal awards as well as other activities; and

(3) During the academic period, the student is enrolled in an advanced degree program at a non-Federal entity or affiliated institution and the activities of the student in relation to the Federal award are related to the degree program;

(4) The tuition or other payments are reasonable compensation for the work performed and are conditioned explicitly upon the performance of necessary work; and

(5) It is the IHE's practice to similarly compensate students under Federal awards as well as other activities.

(b) Charges for tuition remission and other forms of compensation paid to students as, or in lieu of, salaries and wages must be subject to the reporting requirements in § 200.430 Compensation—personal services, and must be treated as direct or indirect cost in accordance with the actual work being performed. Tuition remission may be charged on an average rate basis. See also § 200.431 Compensation—fringe benefits.

§ 200.467   Selling and marketing costs.

Costs of selling and marketing any products or services of the non-Federal entity (unless allowed under § 200.421 Advertising and public relations.) are unallowable, except as direct costs, with prior approval by the Federal awarding agency when necessary for the performance of the Federal award.

§ 200.468   Specialized service facilities.

(a) The costs of services provided by highly complex or specialized facilities operated by the non-Federal entity, such as computing facilities, wind tunnels, and reactors are allowable, provided the charges for the services meet the conditions of either paragraphs (b) or (c) of this section, and, in addition, take into account any items of income or Federal financing that qualify as applicable credits under § 200.406 Applicable credits.

(b) The costs of such services, when material, must be charged directly to applicable awards based on actual usage of the services on the basis of a schedule of rates or established methodology that:

(1) Does not discriminate between activities under Federal awards and other activities of the non-Federal entity, including usage by the non-Federal entity for internal purposes, and

(2) Is designed to recover only the aggregate costs of the services. The costs of each service must consist normally of both its direct costs and its allocable share of all indirect (F&A) costs. Rates must be adjusted at least biennially, and must take into consideration over/under applied costs of the previous period(s).

(c) Where the costs incurred for a service are not material, they may be allocated as indirect (F&A) costs.

(d) Under some extraordinary circumstances, where it is in the best interest of the Federal government and the non-Federal entity to establish alternative costing arrangements, such arrangements may be worked out with the Federal cognizant agency for indirect costs.

§ 200.469 Student activity costs.

Costs incurred for intramural activities, student publications, student clubs, and other student activities, are unallowable, unless specifically provided for in the Federal award.

§ 200.470 Taxes (including Value Added Tax).

(a) For states, local governments and Indian tribes:

(1) Taxes that a governmental unit is legally required to pay are allowable, except for self-assessed taxes that disproportionately affect Federal programs or changes in tax policies that disproportionately affect Federal programs.

(2) Gasoline taxes, motor vehicle fees, and other taxes that are in effect user fees for benefits provided to the Federal government are allowable.

(3) This provision does not restrict the authority of the Federal awarding agency to identify taxes where Federal participation is inappropriate. Where the identification of the amount of un-allowable taxes would require an inordinate amount of effort, the cognizant agency for indirect costs may accept a reasonable approximation thereof.

(b) For nonprofit organizations and IHEs:

(1) In general, taxes which the non-Federal entity is required to pay and which are paid or accrued in accordance with GAAP, and payments made to local governments in lieu of taxes which are commensurate with the local government services received are allowable, except for:

(i) Taxes from which exemptions are available to the non-Federal entity directly or which are available to the non-Federal entity based on an exemption afforded the Federal government and, in the latter case, when the Federal awarding agency makes available the necessary exemption certificates,

(ii) Special assessments on land which represent capital improvements, and

(iii) Federal income taxes.

(2) Any refund of taxes, and any payment to the non-Federal entity of interest thereon, which were allowed as Federal award costs, will be credited either as a cost reduction or cash refund, as appropriate, to the Federal government. However, any interest actually paid or credited to an non-Federal entity incident to a refund of tax, interest, and penalty will be paid or credited to the Federal government only to the extent that such interest accrued over the period during which the non-Federal entity has been reimbursed by the Federal government for the taxes, interest, and penalties.

(c) Value Added Tax (VAT) Foreign taxes charged for the purchase of goods or services that a non-Federal entity is legally required to pay in country is an allowable expense under Federal awards. Foreign tax refunds or applicable credits under Federal awards refer to receipts, or reduction of expenditures, which operate to offset or reduce expense items that are allocable to Federal awards as direct or indirect costs. To the extent that such credits accrued or received by the non-Federal entity relate to allowable cost, these costs must be credited to the Federal awarding agency either as costs or cash refunds. If the costs are credited back to the Federal award, the non-Federal entity may reduce the Federal share of costs by the amount of the foreign tax reimbursement, or where Federal award has not expired, use the foreign government tax refund for approved activities under the Federal award with prior approval of the Federal awarding agency.

§200.471 Termination costs.

Termination of a Federal award generally gives rise to the incurrence of costs, or the need for special treatment of costs, which would not have arisen had the Federal award not been terminated. Cost principles covering these items are set forth in this section. They are to be used in conjunction with the other provisions of this part in termination situations.

(a) The cost of items reasonably usable on the non-Federal entity's other work must not be allowable unless the non-Federal entity submits evidence that it would not retain such items at cost without sustaining a loss. In deciding whether such items are reasonably usable on other work of the non-Federal entity, the Federal awarding agency should consider the non-Federal entity's plans and orders for current and scheduled activity. Contemporaneous purchases of common items by the non-Federal entity must be regarded as evidence that such items are reasonably usable on the non-Federal entity's other work. Any acceptance of common items as allocable to the terminated portion of the Federal award must be limited to the extent that the quantities of such items on hand, in transit, and on order are in excess of the reasonable quantitative requirements of other work.

(b) If in a particular case, despite all reasonable efforts by the non-Federal entity, certain costs cannot be discontinued immediately after the effective date of termination, such costs are generally allowable within the limitations set forth in this part, except that any such costs continuing after termination due to the negligent or willful failure of the non-Federal entity to discontinue such costs must be unallowable.

(c) Loss of useful value of special tooling, machinery, and equipment is generally allowable if:

(1) Such special tooling, special machinery, or equipment is not reasonably capable of use in the other work of the non-Federal entity,

(2) The interest of the Federal government is protected by transfer of title or by other means deemed appropriate by the Federal awarding agency (see also §200.313 Equipment, paragraph (d), and

(3) The loss of useful value for any one terminated Federal award is limited to that portion of the acquisition cost which bears the same ratio to the total acquisition cost as the terminated portion of the Federal award bears to the entire terminated Federal award and other Federal awards for which the special tooling, machinery, or equipment was acquired.

(d) Rental costs under unexpired leases are generally allowable where clearly shown to have been reasonably necessary for the performance of the terminated Federal award less the residual value of such leases, if:

(1) The amount of such rental claimed does not exceed the reasonable use value of the property leased for the period of the Federal award and such further period as may be reasonable, and

(2) The non-Federal entity makes all reasonable efforts to terminate, assign, settle, or otherwise reduce the cost of such lease. There also may be included the cost of alterations of such leased property, provided such alterations were necessary for the performance of the Federal award, and of reasonable restoration required by the provisions of the lease.

(e) Settlement expenses including the following are generally allowable:

(1) Accounting, legal, clerical, and similar costs reasonably necessary for:

(i) The preparation and presentation to the Federal awarding agency of settlement claims and supporting data with respect to the terminated portion of the Federal award, unless the termination is for cause (see Subpart D—Post Federal Award Requirements of this part, §§200.338 Remedies for Noncompliance through 200.342 Effects of Suspension and termination); and

(ii) The termination and settlement of subawards.

(2) Reasonable costs for the storage, transportation, protection, and disposition of property provided by the Federal government or acquired or produced for the Federal award.

(f) Claims under subawards, including the allocable portion of claims which are common to the Federal award and to other work of the non-Federal entity, are generally allowable. An appropriate share of the non-Federal entity's indirect costs may be allocated to the amount of settlements with contractors and/or subrecipients, provided that the amount allocated is otherwise consistent with the basic guidelines contained in § 200.414 Indirect (F&A) costs. The indirect costs so allocated must exclude the same and similar costs claimed directly or indirectly as settlement expenses.

§ 200.472 Training and education costs.

The cost of training and education provided for employee development is allowable.

§ 200.473 Transportation costs.

Costs incurred for freight, express, cartage, postage, and other transportation services relating either to goods purchased, in process, or delivered, are allowable. When such costs can readily be identified with the items involved, they may be charged directly as transportation costs or added to the cost of such items. Where identification with the materials received cannot readily be made, inbound transportation cost may be charged to the appropriate indirect (F&A) cost accounts if the non-Federal entity follows a consistent, equitable procedure in this respect. Outbound freight, if reimbursable under the terms and conditions of the Federal award, should be treated as a direct cost.

§ 200.474 Travel costs.

(a) *General.* Travel costs are the expenses for transportation, lodging, subsistence, and related items incurred by employees who are in travel status on official business of the non-Federal entity. Such costs may be charged on an actual cost basis, on a per diem or mileage basis in lieu of actual costs incurred, or on a combination of the two, provided the method used is applied to an entire trip and not to selected days of the trip, and results in charges consistent with those normally allowed in like circumstances in the non-Federal entity's non-federally-funded activities and in accordance with non-Federal entity's written travel reimbursement policies. Notwithstanding the provisions of § 200.444 General costs of government, travel costs of officials covered by that section are allowable with the prior written approval of the Federal awarding agency or pass-through entity when they are specifically related to the Federal award.

(b) *Lodging and subsistence.* Costs incurred by employees and officers for travel, including costs of lodging, other subsistence, and incidental expenses, must be considered reasonable and otherwise allowable only to the extent such costs do not exceed charges normally allowed by the non-Federal entity in its regular operations as the result of the non-Federal entity's written travel policy. In addition, if these costs are charged directly to the Federal award documentation must justify that:

(1) Participation of the individual is necessary to the Federal award; and

(2) The costs are reasonable and consistent with non-Federal entity's established travel policy.

(c)(1) Temporary dependent care costs (as dependent is defined in 26 U.S.C. 152) above and beyond regular dependent care that directly results from travel to conferences is allowable provided that:

(i) The costs are a direct result of the individual's travel for the Federal award;

(ii) The costs are consistent with the non-Federal entity's documented travel policy for all entity travel; and

(iii) Are only temporary during the travel period.

(2) Travel costs for dependents are unallowable, except for travel of duration of six months or more with prior approval of the Federal awarding agency. See also § 200.432 Conferences.

(3) In the absence of an acceptable, written non-Federal entity policy regarding travel costs, the rates and amounts established under 5 U.S.C.

5701–11, ("Travel and Subsistence Expenses; Mileage Allowances"), or by the Administrator of General Services, or by the President (or his or her designee) pursuant to any provisions of such subchapter must apply to travel under Federal awards (48 CFR 31.205–46(a)).

(d) *Commercial air travel.* (1) Airfare costs in excess of the basic least expensive unrestricted accommodations class offered by commercial airlines are unallowable except when such accommodations would:

(i) Require circuitous routing;

(ii) Require travel during unreasonable hours;

(iii) Excessively prolong travel;

(iv) Result in additional costs that would offset the transportation savings; or

(v) Offer accommodations not reasonably adequate for the traveler's medical needs. The non-Federal entity must justify and document these conditions on a case-by-case basis in order for the use of first-class or business-class airfare to be allowable in such cases.

(2) Unless a pattern of avoidance is detected, the Federal government will generally not question a non-Federal entity's determinations that customary standard airfare or other discount airfare is unavailable for specific trips if the non-Federal entity can demonstrate that such airfare was not available in the specific case.

(e) *Air travel by other than commercial carrier.* Costs of travel by non-Federal entity-owned, -leased, or -chartered aircraft include the cost of lease, charter, operation (including personnel costs), maintenance, depreciation, insurance, and other related costs. The portion of such costs that exceeds the cost of airfare as provided for in paragraph (d) of this section, is unallowable.

§ 200.475   Trustees.

Travel and subsistence costs of trustees (or directors) at IHEs and nonprofit organizations are allowable. See also § 200.474 Travel costs.

Subpart F—Audit Requirements

GENERAL

§ 200.500   Purpose.

This part sets forth standards for obtaining consistency and uniformity among Federal agencies for the audit of non-Federal entities expending Federal awards.

AUDITS

§ 200.501   Audit requirements.

(a) *Audit required.* A non-Federal entity that expends $750,000 or more during the non-Federal entity's fiscal year in Federal awards must have a single or program-specific audit conducted for that year in accordance with the provisions of this part.

(b) *Single audit.* A non-Federal entity that expends $750,000 or more during the non-Federal entity's fiscal year in Federal awards must have a single audit conducted in accordance with § 200.514 Scope of audit except when it elects to have a program-specific audit conducted in accordance with paragraph (c) of this section.

(c) *Program-specific audit election.* When an auditee expends Federal awards under only one Federal program (excluding R&D) and the Federal program's statutes, regulations, or the terms and conditions of the Federal award do not require a financial statement audit of the auditee, the auditee may elect to have a program-specific audit conducted in accordance with § 200.507 Program-specific audits. A program-specific audit may not be elected for R&D unless all of the Federal awards expended were received from the same Federal agency, or the same Federal agency and the same pass-through entity, and that Federal agency, or pass-through entity in the case of a subrecipient, approves in advance a program-specific audit.

(d) *Exemption when Federal awards expended are less than $750,000.* A non-Federal entity that expends less than $750,000 during the non-Federal entity's fiscal year in Federal awards is exempt from Federal audit requirements for that year, except as noted in § 200.503 Relation to other audit requirements, but records must be available for review or audit by appropriate officials of the Federal agency, pass-through entity, and Government Accountability Office (GAO).

(e) *Federally Funded Research and Development Centers (FFRDC).* Management of an auditee that owns or operates a FFRDC may elect to treat the FFRDC as a separate entity for purposes of this part.

(f) *Subrecipients and Contractors.* An auditee may simultaneously be a recipient, a subrecipient, and a contractor. Federal awards expended as a recipient or a subrecipient are subject to audit under this part. The payments received for goods or services provided as a contractor are not Federal awards. Section § 200.330 Subrecipient and contractor determinations should be considered in determining whether payments constitute a Federal award or a payment for goods or services provided as a contractor.

(g) *Compliance responsibility for contractors.* In most cases, the auditee's compliance responsibility for contractors is only to ensure that the procurement, receipt, and payment for goods and services comply with Federal statutes, regulations, and the terms and conditions of Federal awards. Federal award compliance requirements normally do not pass through to contractors. However, the auditee is responsible for ensuring compliance for procurement transactions which are structured such that the contractor is responsible for program compliance or the contractor's records must be reviewed to determine program compliance. Also, when these procurement transactions relate to a major program, the scope of the audit must include determining whether these transactions are in compliance with Federal statutes, regulations, and the terms and conditions of Federal awards.

(h) *For-profit subrecipient.* Since this part does not apply to for-profit subrecipients, the pass-through entity is responsible for establishing requirements, as necessary, to ensure compliance by for-profit subrecipients. The agreement with the for-profit subrecipient should describe applicable compliance requirements and the for-profit subrecipient's compliance re-

sponsibility. Methods to ensure compliance for Federal awards made to for-profit subrecipients may include pre-award audits, monitoring during the agreement, and post-award audits. See also § 200.331 Requirements for pass-through entities.

§ 200.502 **Basis for determining Federal awards expended.**

(a) *Determining Federal awards expended.* The determination of when a Federal award is expended should be based on when the activity related to the Federal award occurs. Generally, the activity pertains to events that require the non-Federal entity to comply with Federal statutes, regulations, and the terms and conditions of Federal awards, such as: expenditure/expense transactions associated with awards including grants, cost-reimbursement contracts under the FAR, compacts with Indian Tribes, cooperative agreements, and direct appropriations; the disbursement of funds to subrecipients; the use of loan proceeds under loan and loan guarantee programs; the receipt of property; the receipt of surplus property; the receipt or use of program income; the distribution or use of food commodities; the disbursement of amounts entitling the non-Federal entity to an interest subsidy; and the period when insurance is in force.

(b) *Loan and loan guarantees (loans).* Since the Federal government is at risk for loans until the debt is repaid, the following guidelines must be used to calculate the value of Federal awards expended under loan programs, except as noted in paragraphs (c) and (d) of this section:

(1) Value of new loans made or received during the audit period; plus

(2) Beginning of the audit period balance of loans from previous years for which the Federal government imposes continuing compliance requirements; plus

(3) Any interest subsidy, cash, or administrative cost allowance received.

(c) *Loan and loan guarantees (loans) at IHEs.* When loans are made to students of an IHE but the IHE does not make the loans, then only the value of loans made during the audit period must be considered Federal awards expended in that audit period. The balance of loans

172

for previous audit periods is not included as Federal awards expended because the lender accounts for the prior balances.

(d) *Prior loan and loan guarantees (loans).* Loans, the proceeds of which were received and expended in prior years, are not considered Federal awards expended under this part when the Federal statutes, regulations, and the terms and conditions of Federal awards pertaining to such loans impose no continuing compliance requirements other than to repay the loans.

(e) *Endowment funds.* The cumulative balance of Federal awards for endowment funds that are federally restricted are considered Federal awards expended in each audit period in which the funds are still restricted.

(f) *Free rent.* Free rent received by itself is not considered a Federal award expended under this part. However, free rent received as part of a Federal award to carry out a Federal program must be included in determining Federal awards expended and subject to audit under this part.

(g) *Valuing non-cash assistance.* Federal non-cash assistance, such as free rent, food commodities, donated property, or donated surplus property, must be valued at fair market value at the time of receipt or the assessed value provided by the Federal agency.

(h) *Medicare.* Medicare payments to a non-Federal entity for providing patient care services to Medicare-eligible individuals are not considered Federal awards expended under this part.

(i) *Medicaid.* Medicaid payments to a subrecipient for providing patient care services to Medicaid-eligible individuals are not considered Federal awards expended under this part unless a state requires the funds to be treated as Federal awards expended because reimbursement is on a cost-reimbursement basis.

(j) *Certain loans provided by the National Credit Union Administration.* For purposes of this part, loans made from the National Credit Union Share Insurance Fund and the Central Liquidity Facility that are funded by contributions from insured non-Federal entities are not considered Federal awards expended.

§ 200.503 Relation to other audit requirements.

(a) An audit conducted in accordance with this part must be in lieu of any financial audit of Federal awards which a non-Federal entity is required to undergo under any other Federal statute or regulation. To the extent that such audit provides a Federal agency with the information it requires to carry out its responsibilities under Federal statute or regulation, a Federal agency must rely upon and use that information.

(b) Notwithstanding subsection (a), a Federal agency, Inspectors General, or GAO may conduct or arrange for additional audits which are necessary to carry out its responsibilities under Federal statute or regulation. The provisions of this part do not authorize any non-Federal entity to constrain, in any manner, such Federal agency from carrying out or arranging for such additional audits, except that the Federal agency must plan such audits to not be duplicative of other audits of Federal awards. Prior to commencing such an audit, the Federal agency or pass-through entity must review the FAC for recent audits submitted by the non-Federal entity, and to the extent such audits meet a Federal agency or pass-through entity's needs, the Federal agency or pass-through entity must rely upon and use such audits. Any additional audits must be planned and performed in such a way as to build upon work performed, including the audit documentation, sampling, and testing already performed, by other auditors.

(c) The provisions of this part do not limit the authority of Federal agencies to conduct, or arrange for the conduct of, audits and evaluations of Federal awards, nor limit the authority of any Federal agency Inspector General or other Federal official. For example, requirements that may be applicable under the FAR or CAS and the terms and conditions of a cost-reimbursement contract may include additional applicable audits to be conducted or arranged for by Federal agencies.

(d) Federal agency to pay for additional audits. A Federal agency that conducts or arranges for additional audits must, consistent with other applicable Federal statutes and regulations, arrange for funding the full cost of such additional audits.

(e) Request for a program to be audited as a major program. A Federal awarding agency may request that an auditee have a particular Federal program audited as a major program in lieu of the Federal awarding agency conducting or arranging for the additional audits. To allow for planning, such requests should be made at least 180 calendar days prior to the end of the fiscal year to be audited. The auditee, after consultation with its auditor, should promptly respond to such a request by informing the Federal awarding agency whether the program would otherwise be audited as a major program using the risk-based audit approach described in § 200.518 Major program determination and, if not, the estimated incremental cost. The Federal awarding agency must then promptly confirm to the auditee whether it wants the program audited as a major program. If the program is to be audited as a major program based upon this Federal awarding agency request, and the Federal awarding agency agrees to pay the full incremental costs, then the auditee must have the program audited as a major program. A pass-through entity may use the provisions of this paragraph for a subrecipient.

§ 200.504   Frequency of audits.

Except for the provisions for biennial audits provided in paragraphs (a) and (b) of this section, audits required by this part must be performed annually. Any biennial audit must cover both years within the biennial period.

(a) A state, local government, or Indian tribe that is required by constitution or statute, in effect on January 1, 1987, to undergo its audits less frequently than annually, is permitted to undergo its audits pursuant to this part biennially. This requirement must still be in effect for the biennial period.

(b) Any nonprofit organization that had biennial audits for all biennial periods ending between July 1, 1992, and January 1, 1995, is permitted to undergo its audits pursuant to this part biennially.

§ 200.505   Sanctions.

In cases of continued inability or unwillingness to have an audit conducted in accordance with this part, Federal agencies and pass-through entities must take appropriate action as provided in § 200.338 Remedies for noncompliance.

§ 200.506   Audit costs.

See § 200.425 Audit services.

§ 200.507   Program-specific audits.

(a) *Program-specific audit guide available.* In many cases, a program-specific audit guide will be available to provide specific guidance to the auditor with respect to internal controls, compliance requirements, suggested audit procedures, and audit reporting requirements. A listing of current program-specific audit guides can be found in the compliance supplement beginning with the 2014 supplement including Federal awarding agency contact information and a Web site where a copy of the guide can be obtained. When a current program-specific audit guide is available, the auditor must follow GAGAS and the guide when performing a program-specific audit.

(b) *Program-specific audit guide not available.* (1) When a program-specific audit guide is not available, the auditee and auditor must have basically the same responsibilities for the Federal program as they would have for an audit of a major program in a single audit.

(2) The auditee must prepare the financial statement(s) for the Federal program that includes, at a minimum, a schedule of expenditures of Federal awards for the program and notes that describe the significant accounting policies used in preparing the schedule, a summary schedule of prior audit findings consistent with the requirements of § 200.511 Audit findings follow-up, paragraph (b), and a corrective action plan consistent with the requirements of § 200.511 Audit findings follow-up, paragraph (c).

(3) The auditor must:

(i) Perform an audit of the financial statement(s) for the Federal program in accordance with GAGAS;

(ii) Obtain an understanding of internal controls and perform tests of internal controls over the Federal program consistent with the requirements of §200.514 Scope of audit, paragraph (c) for a major program;

(iii) Perform procedures to determine whether the auditee has complied with Federal statutes, regulations, and the terms and conditions of Federal awards that could have a direct and material effect on the Federal program consistent with the requirements of §200.514 Scope of audit, paragraph (d) for a major program;

(iv) Follow up on prior audit findings, perform procedures to assess the reasonableness of the summary schedule of prior audit findings prepared by the auditee in accordance with the requirements of §200.511 Audit findings follow-up, and report, as a current year audit finding, when the auditor concludes that the summary schedule of prior audit findings materially misrepresents the status of any prior audit finding; and

(v) Report any audit findings consistent with the requirements of §200.516 Audit findings.

(4) The auditor's report(s) may be in the form of either combined or separate reports and may be organized differently from the manner presented in this section. The auditor's report(s) must state that the audit was conducted in accordance with this part and include the following:

(i) An opinion (or disclaimer of opinion) as to whether the financial statement(s) of the Federal program is presented fairly in all material respects in accordance with the stated accounting policies;

(ii) A report on internal control related to the Federal program, which must describe the scope of testing of internal control and the results of the tests;

(iii) A report on compliance which includes an opinion (or disclaimer of opinion) as to whether the auditee complied with laws, regulations, and the terms and conditions of Federal awards which could have a direct and material effect on the Federal program; and

(iv) A schedule of findings and questioned costs for the Federal program that includes a summary of the auditor's results relative to the Federal program in a format consistent with §200.515 Audit reporting, paragraph (d)(1) and findings and questioned costs consistent with the requirements of §200.515 Audit reporting, paragraph (d)(3).

(c) *Report submission for program-specific audits.* (1) The audit must be completed and the reporting required by paragraph (c)(2) or (c)(3) of this section submitted within the earlier of 30 calendar days after receipt of the auditor's report(s), or nine months after the end of the audit period, unless a different period is specified in a program-specific audit guide. Unless restricted by Federal law or regulation, the auditee must make report copies available for public inspection. Auditees and auditors must ensure that their respective parts of the reporting package do not include protected personally identifiable information.

(2) When a program-specific audit guide is available, the auditee must electronically submit to the FAC the data collection form prepared in accordance with §200.512 Report submission, paragraph (b), as applicable to a program-specific audit, and the reporting required by the program-specific audit guide.

(3) When a program-specific audit guide is not available, the reporting package for a program-specific audit must consist of the financial statement(s) of the Federal program, a summary schedule of prior audit findings, and a corrective action plan as described in paragraph (b)(2) of this section, and the auditor's report(s) described in paragraph (b)(4) of this section. The data collection form prepared in accordance with §200.512 Report submission, paragraph (b), as applicable to a program-specific audit, and one copy of this reporting package must be electronically submitted to the FAC.

(d) *Other sections of this part may apply.* Program-specific audits are subject to:

(1) 200.500 Purpose through 200.503 Relation to other audit requirements, paragraph (d);

(2) 200.504 Frequency of audits through 200.506 Audit costs;

(3) 200.508 Auditee responsibilities through 200.509 Auditor selection;

(4) 200.511 Audit findings follow-up;

(5) 200.512 Report submission, paragraphs (e) through (h);

(6) 200.513 Responsibilities;

(7) 200.516 Audit findings through 200.517 Audit documentation;

(8) 200.521 Management decision, and

(9) Other referenced provisions of this part unless contrary to the provisions of this section, a program-specific audit guide, or program statutes and regulations.

AUDITEES

§ 200.508 Auditee responsibilities.

The auditee must:

(a) Procure or otherwise arrange for the audit required by this part in accordance with § 200.509 Auditor selection, and ensure it is properly performed and submitted when due in accordance with § 200.512 Report submission.

(b) Prepare appropriate financial statements, including the schedule of expenditures of Federal awards in accordance with § 200.510 Financial statements.

(c) Promptly follow up and take corrective action on audit findings, including preparation of a summary schedule of prior audit findings and a corrective action plan in accordance with § 200.511 Audit findings follow-up, paragraph (b) and § 200.511 Audit findings follow-up, paragraph (c), respectively.

(d) Provide the auditor with access to personnel, accounts, books, records, supporting documentation, and other information as needed for the auditor to perform the audit required by this part.

§ 200.509 Auditor selection.

(a) *Auditor procurement.* In procuring audit services, the auditee must follow the procurement standards prescribed by the Procurement Standards in §§ 200.317 Procurement by states through 20.326 Contract provisions of

Subpart D- Post Federal Award Requirements of this part or the FAR (48 CFR part 42), as applicable. When procuring audit services, the objective is to obtain high-quality audits. In requesting proposals for audit services, the objectives and scope of the audit must be made clear and the non-Federal entity must request a copy of the audit organization's peer review report which the auditor is required to provide under GAGAS. Factors to be considered in evaluating each proposal for audit services include the responsiveness to the request for proposal, relevant experience, availability of staff with professional qualifications and technical abilities, the results of peer and external quality control reviews, and price. Whenever possible, the auditee must make positive efforts to utilize small businesses, minority-owned firms, and women's business enterprises, in procuring audit services as stated in § 200.321 Contracting with small and minority businesses, women's business enterprises, and labor surplus area firms, or the FAR (48 CFR part 42), as applicable.

(b) *Restriction on auditor preparing indirect cost proposals.* An auditor who prepares the indirect cost proposal or cost allocation plan may not also be selected to perform the audit required by this part when the indirect costs recovered by the auditee during the prior year exceeded $1 million. This restriction applies to the base year used in the preparation of the indirect cost proposal or cost allocation plan and any subsequent years in which the resulting indirect cost agreement or cost allocation plan is used to recover costs.

(c) *Use of Federal auditors.* Federal auditors may perform all or part of the work required under this part if they comply fully with the requirements of this part.

§ 200.510 Financial statements.

(a) *Financial statements.* The auditee must prepare financial statements that reflect its financial position, results of operations or changes in net assets, and, where appropriate, cash flows for the fiscal year audited. The financial statements must be for the same organizational unit and fiscal year that is chosen to meet the requirements of this part. However, non-Federal entity-wide financial statements may also include departments, agencies, and other organizational units that have separate audits in accordance with § 200.514 Scope of audit, paragraph (a) and prepare separate financial statements.

(b) *Schedule of expenditures of Federal awards.* The auditee must also prepare a schedule of expenditures of Federal awards for the period covered by the auditee's financial statements which must include the total Federal awards expended as determined in accordance with § 200.502 Basis for determining Federal awards expended. While not required, the auditee may choose to provide information requested by Federal awarding agencies and pass-through entities to make the schedule easier to use. For example, when a Federal program has multiple Federal award years, the auditee may list the amount of Federal awards expended for each Federal award year separately. At a minimum, the schedule must:

(1) List individual Federal programs by Federal agency. For a cluster of programs, provide the cluster name, list individual Federal programs within the cluster of programs, and provide the applicable Federal agency name. For R&D, total Federal awards expended must be shown either by individual Federal award or by Federal agency and major subdivision within the Federal agency. For example, the National Institutes of Health is a major subdivision in the Department of Health and Human Services.

(2) For Federal awards received as a subrecipient, the name of the pass-through entity and identifying number assigned by the pass-through entity must be included.

(3) Provide total Federal awards expended for each individual Federal program and the CFDA number or other identifying number when the CFDA information is not available. For a cluster of programs also provide the total for the cluster.

(4) Include the total amount provided to subrecipients from each Federal program.

(5) For loan or loan guarantee programs described in § 200.502 Basis for determining Federal awards expended, paragraph (b), identify in the notes to the schedule the balances outstanding at the end of the audit period. This is in addition to including the total Federal awards expended for loan or loan guarantee programs in the schedule.

(6) Include notes that describe that significant accounting policies used in preparing the schedule, and note whether or not the non-Federal entity elected to use the 10% de minimis cost rate as covered in § 200.414 Indirect (F&A) costs.

§ 200.511 Audit findings follow-up.

(a) *General.* The auditee is responsible for follow-up and corrective action on all audit findings. As part of this responsibility, the auditee must prepare a summary schedule of prior audit findings. The auditee must also prepare a corrective action plan for current year audit findings. The summary schedule of prior audit findings and the corrective action plan must include the reference numbers the auditor assigns to audit findings under § 200.516 Audit findings, paragraph (c). Since the summary schedule may include audit findings from multiple years, it must include the fiscal year in which the finding initially occurred. The corrective action plan and summary schedule of prior audit findings must include findings relating to the financial statements which are required to be reported in accordance with GAGAS.

(b) *Summary schedule of prior audit findings.* The summary schedule of prior audit findings must report the status of all audit findings included in the prior audit's schedule of findings and questioned costs. The summary schedule must also include audit findings reported in the prior audit's summary schedule of prior audit findings except audit findings listed as corrected in accordance with paragraph (b)(1) of this section, or no longer valid or not warranting further action in accordance with paragraph (b)(3) of this section.

(1) When audit findings were fully corrected, the summary schedule need only list the audit findings and state that corrective action was taken.

(2) When audit findings were not corrected or were only partially corrected, the summary schedule must describe the reasons for the finding's recurrence

and planned corrective action, and any partial corrective action taken. When corrective action taken is significantly different from corrective action previously reported in a corrective action plan or in the Federal agency's or pass-through entity's management decision, the summary schedule must provide an explanation.

(3) When the auditee believes the audit findings are no longer valid or do not warrant further action, the reasons for this position must be described in the summary schedule. A valid reason for considering an audit finding as not warranting further action is that all of the following have occurred:

(i) Two years have passed since the audit report in which the finding occurred was submitted to the FAC;

(ii) The Federal agency or pass-through entity is not currently following up with the auditee on the audit finding; and

(iii) A management decision was not issued.

(c) *Corrective action plan.* At the completion of the audit, the auditee must prepare, in a document separate from the auditor's findings described in § 200.516 Audit findings, a corrective action plan to address each audit finding included in the current year auditor's reports. The corrective action plan must provide the name(s) of the contact person(s) responsible for corrective action, the corrective action planned, and the anticipated completion date. If the auditee does not agree with the audit findings or believes corrective action is not required, then the corrective action plan must include an explanation and specific reasons.

§ 200.512 Report submission.

(a) *General.* (1) The audit must be completed and the data collection form described in paragraph (b) of this section and reporting package described in paragraph (c) of this section must be submitted within the earlier of 30 calendar days after receipt of the auditor's report(s), or nine months after the end of the audit period. If the due date falls on a Saturday, Sunday, or Federal holiday, the reporting package is due the next business day.

(2) Unless restricted by Federal statutes or regulations, the auditee must make copies available for public inspection. Auditees and auditors must ensure that their respective parts of the reporting package do not include protected personally identifiable information.

(b) *Data Collection.* The FAC is the repository of record for Subpart F—Audit Requirements of this part reporting packages and the data collection form. All Federal agencies, pass-through entities and others interested in a reporting package and data collection form must obtain it by accessing the FAC.

(1) The auditee must submit required data elements described in Appendix X to Part 200—Data Collection Form (Form SF-SAC), which state whether the audit was completed in accordance with this part and provides information about the auditee, its Federal programs, and the results of the audit. The data must include information available from the audit required by this part that is necessary for Federal agencies to use the audit to ensure integrity for Federal programs. The data elements and format must be approved by OMB, available from the FAC, and include collections of information from the reporting package described in paragraph (c) of this section. A senior level representative of the auditee (e.g., state controller, director of finance, chief executive officer, or chief financial officer) must sign a statement to be included as part of the data collection that says that the auditee complied with the requirements of this part, the data were prepared in accordance with this part (and the instructions accompanying the form), the reporting package does not include protected personally identifiable information, the information included in its entirety is accurate and complete, and that the FAC is authorized to make the reporting package and the form publicly available on a Web site.

(2) *Exception for Indian Tribes.* An auditee that is an Indian tribe may opt not to authorize the FAC to make the reporting package publicly available on a Web site, by excluding the authorization for the FAC publication in the statement described in paragraph (b)(1) of this section. If this option is exercised, the auditee becomes responsible for submitting the reporting package

directly to any pass-through entities through which it has received a Federal award and to pass-through entities for which the summary schedule of prior audit findings reported the status of any findings related to Federal awards that the pass-through entity provided. Unless restricted by Federal statute or regulation, if the auditee opts not to authorize publication, it must make copies of the reporting package available for public inspection.

(3) Using the information included in the reporting package described in paragraph (c) of this section, the auditor must complete the applicable data elements of the data collection form. The auditor must sign a statement to be included as part of the data collection form that indicates, at a minimum, the source of the information included in the form, the auditor's responsibility for the information, that the form is not a substitute for the reporting package described in paragraph (c) of this section, and that the content of the form is limited to the collection of information prescribed by OMB.

(c) *Reporting package.* The reporting package must include the:

(1) Financial statements and schedule of expenditures of Federal awards discussed in §200.510 Financial statements, paragraphs (a) and (b), respectively;

(2) Summary schedule of prior audit findings discussed in §200.511 Audit findings follow-up, paragraph (b);

(3) Auditor's report(s) discussed in §200.515 Audit reporting; and

(4) Corrective action plan discussed in §200.511 Audit findings follow-up, paragraph (c).

(d) *Submission to FAC.* The auditee must electronically submit to the FAC the data collection form described in paragraph (b) of this section and the reporting package described in paragraph (c) of this section.

(e) *Requests for management letters issued by the auditor.* In response to requests by a Federal agency or pass-through entity, auditees must submit a copy of any management letters issued by the auditor.

(f) *Report retention requirements.* Auditees must keep one copy of the data collection form described in para-

graph (b) of this section and one copy of the reporting package described in paragraph (c) of this section on file for three years from the date of submission to the FAC.

(g) *FAC responsibilities.* The FAC must make available the reporting packages received in accordance with paragraph (c) of this section and §200.507 Program-specific audits, paragraph (c) to the public, except for Indian tribes exercising the option in (b)(2) of this section, and maintain a data base of completed audits, provide appropriate information to Federal agencies, and follow up with known auditees that have not submitted the required data collection forms and reporting packages.

(h) *Electronic filing.* Nothing in this part must preclude electronic submissions to the FAC in such manner as may be approved by OMB.

§ 200.513 **Responsibilities.**

(a)(1) Cognizant agency for audit responsibilities. A non-Federal entity expending more than $50 million a year in Federal awards must have a cognizant agency for audit. The designated cognizant agency for audit must be the Federal awarding agency that provides the predominant amount of direct funding to a non-Federal entity unless OMB designates a specific cognizant agency for audit.

(2) To provide for continuity of cognizance, the determination of the predominant amount of direct funding must be based upon direct Federal awards expended in the non-Federal entity's fiscal years ending in 2009, 2014, 2019 and every fifth year thereafter. For example, audit cognizance for periods ending in 2011 through 2015 will be determined based on Federal awards expended in 2009.

(3) Notwithstanding the manner in which audit cognizance is determined, a Federal awarding agency with cognizance for an auditee may reassign cognizance to another Federal awarding agency that provides substantial funding and agrees to be the cognizant agency for audit. Within 30 calendar days after any reassignment, both the old and the new cognizant agency for audit must provide notice of the

change to the FAC, the auditee, and, if known, the auditor. The cognizant agency for audit must:

(i) Provide technical audit advice and liaison assistance to auditees and auditors.

(ii) Obtain or conduct quality control reviews on selected audits made by non-Federal auditors, and provide the results to other interested organizations. Cooperate and provide support to the Federal agency designated by OMB to lead a governmentwide project to determine the quality of single audits by providing a statistically reliable estimate of the extent that single audits conform to applicable requirements, standards, and procedures; and to make recommendations to address noted audit quality issues, including recommendations for any changes to applicable requirements, standards and procedures indicated by the results of the project. This governmentwide audit quality project must be performed once every 6 years beginning in 2018 or at such other interval as determined by OMB, and the results must be public.

(iii) Promptly inform other affected Federal agencies and appropriate Federal law enforcement officials of any direct reporting by the auditee or its auditor required by GAGAS or statutes and regulations.

(iv) Advise the community of independent auditors of any noteworthy or important factual trends related to the quality of audits stemming from quality control reviews. Significant problems or quality issues consistently identified through quality control reviews of audit reports must be referred to appropriate state licensing agencies and professional bodies.

(v) Advise the auditor, Federal awarding agencies, and, where appropriate, the auditee of any deficiencies found in the audits when the deficiencies require corrective action by the auditor. When advised of deficiencies, the auditee must work with the auditor to take corrective action. If corrective action is not taken, the cognizant agency for audit must notify the auditor, the auditee, and applicable Federal awarding agencies and pass-through entities of the facts and make recommendations for follow-up action. Major inadequacies or repetitive sub-standard performance by auditors must be referred to appropriate state licensing agencies and professional bodies for disciplinary action.

(vi) Coordinate, to the extent practical, audits or reviews made by or for Federal agencies that are in addition to the audits made pursuant to this part, so that the additional audits or reviews build upon rather than duplicate audits performed in accordance with this part.

(vii) Coordinate a management decision for cross-cutting audit findings (as defined in § 200.30 Cross-cutting audit finding) that affect the Federal programs of more than one agency when requested by any Federal awarding agency whose awards are included in the audit finding of the auditee.

(viii) Coordinate the audit work and reporting responsibilities among auditors to achieve the most cost-effective audit.

(ix) Provide advice to auditees as to how to handle changes in fiscal years.

(b) Oversight agency for audit responsibilities. An auditee who does not have a designated cognizant agency for audit will be under the general oversight of the Federal agency determined in accordance with § 200.73 Oversight agency for audit. A Federal agency with oversight for an auditee may reassign oversight to another Federal agency that agrees to be the oversight agency for audit. Within 30 calendar days after any reassignment, both the old and the new oversight agency for audit must provide notice of the change to the FAC, the auditee, and, if known, the auditor. The oversight agency for audit:

(1) Must provide technical advice to auditees and auditors as requested.

(2) May assume all or some of the responsibilities normally performed by a cognizant agency for audit.

(c) Federal awarding agency responsibilities. The Federal awarding agency must perform the following for the Federal awards it makes (See also the requirements of § 200.210 Information contained in a Federal award):

(1) Ensure that audits are completed and reports are received in a timely manner and in accordance with the requirements of this part.

(2) Provide technical advice and counsel to auditees and auditors as requested.

(3) Follow-up on audit findings to ensure that the recipient takes appropriate and timely corrective action. As part of audit follow-up, the Federal awarding agency must:

(i) Issue a management decision as prescribed in §200.521 Management decision;

(ii) Monitor the recipient taking appropriate and timely corrective action;

(iii) Use cooperative audit resolution mechanisms (see §200.25 Cooperative audit resolution) to improve Federal program outcomes through better audit resolution, follow-up, and corrective action; and

(iv) Develop a baseline, metrics, and targets to track, over time, the effectiveness of the Federal agency's process to follow-up on audit findings and on the effectiveness of Single Audits in improving non-Federal entity accountability and their use by Federal awarding agencies in making award decisions.

(4) Provide OMB annual updates to the compliance supplement and work with OMB to ensure that the compliance supplement focuses the auditor to test the compliance requirements most likely to cause improper payments, fraud, waste, abuse or generate audit finding for which the Federal awarding agency will take sanctions.

(5) Provide OMB with the name of a single audit accountable official from among the senior policy officials of the Federal awarding agency who must be:

(i) Responsible for ensuring that the agency fulfills all the requirement of §200.513 Responsibilities and effectively uses the single audit process to reduce improper payments and improve Federal program outcomes.

(ii) Held accountable to improve the effectiveness of the single audit process based upon metrics as described in paragraph (c)(3)(iv) of this section.

(iii) Responsible for designating the Federal agency's key management single audit liaison.

(6) Provide OMB with the name of a key management single audit liaison who must:

(i) Serve as the Federal awarding agency's management point of contact for the single audit process both within and outside the Federal government.

(ii) Promote interagency coordination, consistency, and sharing in areas such as coordinating audit follow-up; identifying higher-risk non-Federal entities; providing input on single audit and follow-up policy; enhancing the utility of the FAC; and studying ways to use single audit results to improve Federal award accountability and best practices.

(iii) Oversee training for the Federal awarding agency's program management personnel related to the single audit process.

(iv) Promote the Federal awarding agency's use of cooperative audit resolution mechanisms.

(v) Coordinate the Federal awarding agency's activities to ensure appropriate and timely follow-up and corrective action on audit findings.

(vi) Organize the Federal cognizant agency for audit's follow-up on cross-cutting audit findings that affect the Federal programs of more than one Federal awarding agency.

(vii) Ensure the Federal awarding agency provides annual updates of the compliance supplement to OMB.

(viii) Support the Federal awarding agency's single audit accountable official's mission.

AUDITORS

§200.514 Scope of audit.

(a) *General.* The audit must be conducted in accordance with GAGAS. The audit must cover the entire operations of the auditee, or, at the option of the auditee, such audit must include a series of audits that cover departments, agencies, and other organizational units that expended or otherwise administered Federal awards during such audit period, provided that each such audit must encompass the financial statements and schedule of expenditures of Federal awards for each such department, agency, and other organizational unit, which must be considered to be a non-Federal entity. The financial statements and schedule of expenditures of Federal awards must be for the same audit period.

(b) *Financial statements.* The auditor must determine whether the financial statements of the auditee are presented fairly in all material respects in accordance with generally accepted accounting principles. The auditor must also determine whether the schedule of expenditures of Federal awards is stated fairly in all material respects in relation to the auditee's financial statements as a whole.

(c) *Internal control.* (1) The compliance supplement provides guidance on internal controls over Federal programs based upon the guidance in Standards for Internal Control in the Federal Government issued by the Comptroller General of the United States and the Internal Control—Integrated Framework, issued by the Committee of Sponsoring Organizations of the Treadway Commission (COSO).

(2) In addition to the requirements of GAGAS, the auditor must perform procedures to obtain an understanding of internal control over Federal programs sufficient to plan the audit to support a low assessed level of control risk of noncompliance for major programs.

(3) Except as provided in paragraph (c)(4) of this section, the auditor must:

(i) Plan the testing of internal control over compliance for major programs to support a low assessed level of control risk for the assertions relevant to the compliance requirements for each major program; and

(ii) Perform testing of internal control as planned in paragraph (c)(3)(i) of this section.

(4) When internal control over some or all of the compliance requirements for a major program are likely to be ineffective in preventing or detecting noncompliance, the planning and performing of testing described in paragraph (c)(3) of this section are not required for those compliance requirements. However, the auditor must report a significant deficiency or material weakness in accordance with §200.516 Audit findings, assess the related control risk at the maximum, and consider whether additional compliance tests are required because of ineffective internal control.

(d) *Compliance.* (1) In addition to the requirements of GAGAS, the auditor must determine whether the auditee has complied with Federal statutes, regulations, and the terms and condi-

tions of Federal awards that may have a direct and material effect on each of its major programs.

(2) The principal compliance requirements applicable to most Federal programs and the compliance requirements of the largest Federal programs are included in the compliance supplement.

(3) For the compliance requirements related to Federal programs contained in the compliance supplement, an audit of these compliance requirements will meet the requirements of this part. Where there have been changes to the compliance requirements and the changes are not reflected in the compliance supplement, the auditor must determine the current compliance requirements and modify the audit procedures accordingly. For those Federal programs not covered in the compliance supplement, the auditor should follow the compliance supplement's guidance for programs not included in the supplement.

(4) The compliance testing must include tests of transactions and such other auditing procedures necessary to provide the auditor sufficient appropriate audit evidence to support an opinion on compliance.

(e) *Audit follow-up.* The auditor must follow-up on prior audit findings, perform procedures to assess the reasonableness of the summary schedule of prior audit findings prepared by the auditee in accordance with §200.511 Audit findings follow-up paragraph (b), and report, as a current year audit finding, when the auditor concludes that the summary schedule of prior audit findings materially misrepresents the status of any prior audit finding. The auditor must perform audit follow-up procedures regardless of whether a prior audit finding relates to a major program in the current year.

(f) *Data Collection Form.* As required in §200.512 Report submission paragraph (b)(3), the auditor must complete and sign specified sections of the data collection form.

§ 200.515 Audit reporting.

The auditor's report(s) may be in the form of either combined or separate reports and may be organized differently from the manner presented in this section. The auditor's report(s) must state that the audit was conducted in accordance with this part and include the following:

(a) An opinion (or disclaimer of opinion) as to whether the financial statements are presented fairly in all material respects in accordance with generally accepted accounting principles and an opinion (or disclaimer of opinion) as to whether the schedule of expenditures of Federal awards is fairly stated in all material respects in relation to the financial statements as a whole.

(b) A report on internal control over financial reporting and compliance with Federal statutes, regulations, and the terms and conditions of the Federal award, noncompliance with which could have a material effect on the financial statements. This report must describe the scope of testing of internal control and compliance and the results of the tests, and, where applicable, it will refer to the separate schedule of findings and questioned costs described in paragraph (d) of this section.

(c) A report on compliance for each major program and report and internal control over compliance. This report must describe the scope of testing of internal control over compliance, include an opinion or modified opinion as to whether the auditee complied with Federal statutes, regulations, and the terms and conditions of Federal awards which could have a direct and material effect on each major program and refer to the separate schedule of findings and questioned costs described in paragraph (d) of this section.

(d) A schedule of findings and questioned costs which must include the following three components:

(1) A summary of the auditor's results, which must include:

(i) The type of report the auditor issued on whether the financial statements audited were prepared in accordance with GAAP (i.e., unmodified opinion, qualified opinion, adverse opinion, or disclaimer of opinion);

(ii) Where applicable, a statement about whether significant deficiencies or material weaknesses in internal control were disclosed by the audit of the financial statements;

(iii) A statement as to whether the audit disclosed any noncompliance that is material to the financial statements of the auditee;

(iv) Where applicable, a statement about whether significant deficiencies or material weaknesses in internal control over major programs were disclosed by the audit;

(v) The type of report the auditor issued on compliance for major programs (i.e., unmodified opinion, qualified opinion, adverse opinion, or disclaimer of opinion);

(vi) A statement as to whether the audit disclosed any audit findings that the auditor is required to report under § 200.516 Audit findings paragraph (a);

(vii) An identification of major programs by listing each individual major program; however in the case of a cluster of programs only the cluster name as shown on the Schedule of Expenditures of Federal Awards is required;

(viii) The dollar threshold used to distinguish between Type A and Type B programs, as described in § 200.518 Major program determination paragraph (b)(1), or (b)(3) when a recalculation of the Type A threshold is required for large loan or loan guarantees; and

(ix) A statement as to whether the auditee qualified as a low-risk auditee under § 200.520 Criteria for a low-risk auditee.

(2) Findings relating to the financial statements which are required to be reported in accordance with GAGAS.

(3) Findings and questioned costs for Federal awards which must include audit findings as defined in § 200.516 Audit findings, paragraph (a).

(i) Audit findings (e.g., internal control findings, compliance findings, questioned costs, or fraud) that relate to the same issue should be presented as a single audit finding. Where practical, audit findings should be organized by Federal agency or pass-through entity.

(ii) Audit findings that relate to both the financial statements and Federal awards, as reported under paragraphs (d)(2) and (d)(3) of this section, respectively, should be reported in both sections of the schedule. However, the reporting in one section of the schedule may be in summary form with a reference to a detailed reporting in the other section of the schedule.

(e) Nothing in this part precludes combining of the audit reporting required by this section with the reporting required by § 200.512 Report submission, paragraph (b) Data Collection when allowed by GAGAS and Appendix X to Part 200—Data Collection Form (Form SF–SAC).

§ 200.516 Audit findings.

(a) *Audit findings reported.* The auditor must report the following as audit findings in a schedule of findings and questioned costs:

(1) Significant deficiencies and material weaknesses in internal control over major programs and significant instances of abuse relating to major programs. The auditor's determination of whether a deficiency in internal control is a significant deficiency or material weakness for the purpose of reporting an audit finding is in relation to a type of compliance requirement for a major program identified in the Compliance Supplement.

(2) Material noncompliance with the provisions of Federal statutes, regulations, or the terms and conditions of Federal awards related to a major program. The auditor's determination of whether a noncompliance with the provisions of Federal statutes, regulations, or the terms and conditions of Federal awards is material for the purpose of reporting an audit finding is in relation to a type of compliance requirement for a major program identified in the compliance supplement.

(3) Known questioned costs that are greater than $25,000 for a type of compliance requirement for a major program. Known questioned costs are those specifically identified by the auditor. In evaluating the effect of questioned costs on the opinion on compliance, the auditor considers the best estimate of total costs questioned (likely questioned costs), not just the questioned costs specifically identified (known questioned costs). The auditor must also report known questioned costs when likely questioned costs are greater than $25,000 for a type of compliance requirement for a major program. In reporting questioned costs,

the auditor must include information to provide proper perspective for judging the prevalence and consequences of the questioned costs.

(4) Known questioned costs that are greater than $25,000 for a Federal program which is not audited as a major program. Except for audit follow-up, the auditor is not required under this part to perform audit procedures for such a Federal program; therefore, the auditor will normally not find questioned costs for a program that is not audited as a major program. However, if the auditor does become aware of questioned costs for a Federal program that is not audited as a major program (e.g., as part of audit follow-up or other audit procedures) and the known questioned costs are greater than $25,000, then the auditor must report this as an audit finding.

(5) The circumstances concerning why the auditor's report on compliance for each major program is other than an unmodified opinion, unless such circumstances are otherwise reported as audit findings in the schedule of findings and questioned costs for Federal awards.

(6) Known or likely fraud affecting a Federal award, unless such fraud is otherwise reported as an audit finding in the schedule of findings and questioned costs for Federal awards. This paragraph does not require the auditor to report publicly information which could compromise investigative or legal proceedings or to make an additional reporting when the auditor confirms that the fraud was reported outside the auditor's reports under the direct reporting requirements of GAGAS.

(7) Instances where the results of audit follow-up procedures disclosed that the summary schedule of prior audit findings prepared by the auditee in accordance with § 200.511 Audit findings follow-up, paragraph (b) materially misrepresents the status of any prior audit finding.

(b) *Audit finding detail and clarity.* Audit findings must be presented in sufficient detail and clarity for the auditee to prepare a corrective action plan and take corrective action, and for Federal agencies and pass-through entities to arrive at a management decision. The following specific information must be included, as applicable, in audit findings:

(1) Federal program and specific Federal award identification including the CFDA title and number, Federal award identification number and year, name of Federal agency, and name of the applicable pass-through entity. When information, such as the CFDA title and number or Federal award identification number, is not available, the auditor must provide the best information available to describe the Federal award.

(2) The criteria or specific requirement upon which the audit finding is based, including the Federal statutes, regulations, or the terms and conditions of the Federal awards. Criteria generally identify the required or desired state or expectation with respect to the program or operation. Criteria provide a context for evaluating evidence and understanding findings.

(3) The condition found, including facts that support the deficiency identified in the audit finding.

(4) A statement of cause that identifies the reason or explanation for the condition or the factors responsible for the difference between the situation that exists (condition) and the required or desired state (criteria), which may also serve as a basis for recommendations for corrective action.

(5) The possible asserted effect to provide sufficient information to the auditee and Federal agency, or pass-through entity in the case of a subrecipient, to permit them to determine the cause and effect to facilitate prompt and proper corrective action. A statement of the effect or potential effect should provide a clear, logical link to establish the impact or potential impact of the difference between the condition and the criteria.

(6) Identification of questioned costs and how they were computed. Known questioned costs must be identified by applicable CFDA number(s) and applicable Federal award identification number(s).

(7) Information to provide proper perspective for judging the prevalence and consequences of the audit findings, such as whether the audit findings represent an isolated instance or a systemic problem. Where appropriate, instances identified must be related to the universe and the number of cases examined and be quantified in terms of dollar value. The auditor should report whether the sampling was a statistically valid sample.

(8) Identification of whether the audit finding was a repeat of a finding in the immediately prior audit and if so any applicable prior year audit finding numbers.

(9) Recommendations to prevent future occurrences of the deficiency identified in the audit finding.

(10) Views of responsible officials of the auditee.

(c) *Reference numbers.* Each audit finding in the schedule of findings and questioned costs must include a reference number in the format meeting the requirements of the data collection form submission required by §200.512 Report submission, paragraph (b) to allow for easy referencing of the audit findings during follow-up.

§200.517 Audit documentation.

(a) *Retention of audit documentation.* The auditor must retain audit documentation and reports for a minimum of three years after the date of issuance of the auditor's report(s) to the auditee, unless the auditor is notified in writing by the cognizant agency for audit, oversight agency for audit, cognizant agency for indirect costs, or pass-through entity to extend the retention period. When the auditor is aware that the Federal agency, pass-through entity, or auditee is contesting an audit finding, the auditor must contact the parties contesting the audit finding for guidance prior to destruction of the audit documentation and reports.

(b) *Access to audit documentation.* Audit documentation must be made available upon request to the cognizant or oversight agency for audit or its designee, cognizant agency for indirect cost, a Federal agency, or GAO at the completion of the audit, as part of a quality review, to resolve audit findings, or to carry out oversight responsibilities consistent with the purposes of this part. Access to audit documentation includes the right of Federal agencies to obtain copies of audit documentation, as is reasonable and necessary.

§ 200.518 **Major program determination.**

(a) *General.* The auditor must use a risk-based approach to determine which Federal programs are major programs. This risk-based approach must include consideration of: current and prior audit experience, oversight by Federal agencies and pass-through entities, and the inherent risk of the Federal program. The process in paragraphs (b) through (i) of this section must be followed.

(b) *Step one.*(1) The auditor must identify the larger Federal programs, which must be labeled Type A programs. Type A programs are defined as Federal programs with Federal awards expended during the audit period exceeding the levels outlined in the table in this paragraph (b)(1):

Total Federal awards expended	Type A/B threshold
Equal to $750,000 but less than or equal to $25 million.	$750,000.
Exceed $25 million but less than or equal to $100 million.	Total Federal awards expended times .03.
Exceed $100 million but less than or equal to $1 billion.	$3 million.
Exceed $1 billion but less than or equal to $10 billion.	Total Federal awards expended times .003.
Exceed $10 billion but less than or equal to $20 billion.	$30 million.
Exceed $20 billion	Total Federal awards expended times .0015.

(2) Federal programs not labeled Type A under paragraph (b)(1) of this section must be labeled Type B programs.

(3) The inclusion of large loan and loan guarantees (loans) should not result in the exclusion of other programs as Type A programs. When a Federal program providing loans exceeds four times the largest non-loan program it is considered a large loan program, and the auditor must consider this Federal program as a Type A program and exclude its values in determining other Type A programs. This recalculation of the Type A program is performed after removing the total of all large loan programs. For the purposes of this paragraph a program is only considered to be a Federal program providing

loans if the value of Federal awards expended for loans within the program comprises fifty percent or more of the total Federal awards expended for the program. A cluster of programs is treated as one program and the value of Federal awards expended under a loan program is determined as described in § 200.502 Basis for determining Federal awards *expended.*

(4) For biennial audits permitted under § 200.504 Frequency of audits, the determination of Type A and Type B programs must be based upon the Federal awards expended during the two-year period.

(c) *Step two.* (1) The auditor must identify Type A programs which are low-risk. In making this determination, the auditor must consider whether the requirements in § 200.519 Criteria for Federal program risk paragraph (c), the results of audit follow-up, or any changes in personnel or systems affecting the program indicate significantly increased risk and preclude the program from being low risk. For a Type A program to be considered low-risk, it must have been audited as a major program in at least one of the two most recent audit periods (in the most recent audit period in the case of a biennial audit), and, in the most recent audit period, the program must have not had:

(i) Internal control deficiencies which were identified as material weaknesses in the auditor's report on internal control for major programs as required under § 200.515 Audit reporting, paragraph (c);

(ii) A modified opinion on the program in the auditor's report on major programs as required under § 200.515 Audit reporting, paragraph (c); or

(iii) Known or likely questioned costs that exceed five percent of the total Federal awards expended for the program.

(2) Notwithstanding paragraph (c)(1) of this section, OMB may approve a Federal awarding agency's request that a Type A program may not be considered low risk for a certain recipient. For example, it may be necessary for a large Type A program to be audited as a major program each year at a particular recipient to allow the Federal awarding agency to comply with 31

U.S.C. 3515. The Federal awarding agency must notify the recipient and, if known, the auditor of OMB's approval at least 180 calendar days prior to the end of the fiscal year to be audited.

(d) *Step three.* (1) The auditor must identify Type B programs which are high-risk using professional judgment and the criteria in §200.519 Criteria for Federal program risk. However, the auditor is not required to identify more high-risk Type B programs than at least one fourth the number of low-risk Type A programs identified as low-risk under Step 2 (paragraph (c) of this section). Except for known material weakness in internal control or compliance problems as discussed in §200.519 Criteria for Federal program risk paragraphs (b)(1), (b)(2), and (c)(1), a single criteria in risk would seldom cause a Type B program to be considered high-risk. When identifying which Type B programs to risk assess, the auditor is encouraged to use an approach which provides an opportunity for different high-risk Type B programs to be audited as major over a period of time.

(2) The auditor is not expected to perform risk assessments on relatively small Federal programs. Therefore, the auditor is only required to perform risk assessments on Type B programs that exceed twenty-five percent (0.25) of the Type A threshold determined in Step 1 (paragraph (b) of this section).

(e) *Step four.* At a minimum, the auditor must audit all of the following as major programs:

(1) All Type A programs not identified as low risk under step two (paragraph (c)(1) of this section).

(2) All Type B programs identified as high-risk under step three (paragraph (d) of this section).

(3) Such additional programs as may be necessary to comply with the percentage of coverage rule discussed in paragraph (f) of this section. This may require the auditor to audit more programs as major programs than the number of Type A programs.

(f) *Percentage of coverage rule.* If the auditee meets the criteria in §200.520 Criteria for a low-risk auditee, the auditor need only audit the major programs identified in Step 4 (paragraph (e)(1) and (2) of this section) and such

additional Federal programs with Federal awards expended that, in aggregate, all major programs encompass at least 20 percent (0.20) of total Federal awards expended. Otherwise, the auditor must audit the major programs identified in Step 4 (paragraphs (e)(1) and (2) of this section) and such additional Federal programs with Federal awards expended that, in aggregate, all major programs encompass at least 40 percent (0.40) of total Federal awards expended.

(g) *Documentation of risk.* The auditor must include in the audit documentation the risk analysis process used in determining major programs.

(h) *Auditor's judgment.* When the major program determination was performed and documented in accordance with this Subpart, the auditor's judgment in applying the risk-based approach to determine major programs must be presumed correct. Challenges by Federal agencies and pass-through entities must only be for clearly improper use of the requirements in this part. However, Federal agencies and pass-through entities may provide auditors guidance about the risk of a particular Federal program and the auditor must consider this guidance in determining major programs in audits not yet completed.

§200.519 Criteria for Federal program risk.

(a) *General.* The auditor's determination should be based on an overall evaluation of the risk of noncompliance occurring that could be material to the Federal program. The auditor must consider criteria, such as described in paragraphs (b), (c), and (d) of this section, to identify risk in Federal programs. Also, as part of the risk analysis, the auditor may wish to discuss a particular Federal program with auditee management and the Federal agency or pass-through entity.

(b) *Current and prior audit experience.* (1) Weaknesses in internal control over Federal programs would indicate higher risk. Consideration should be given to the control environment over Federal programs and such factors as the expectation of management's adherence to Federal statutes, regulations, and the terms and conditions of Federal awards and the competence and experience of personnel who administer the Federal programs.

(i) A Federal program administered under multiple internal control structures may have higher risk. When assessing risk in a large single audit, the auditor must consider whether weaknesses are isolated in a single operating unit (e.g., one college campus) or pervasive throughout the entity.

(ii) When significant parts of a Federal program are passed through to subrecipients, a weak system for monitoring subrecipients would indicate higher risk.

(2) Prior audit findings would indicate higher risk, particularly when the situations identified in the audit findings could have a significant impact on a Federal program or have not been corrected.

(3) Federal programs not recently audited as major programs may be of higher risk than Federal programs recently audited as major programs without audit findings.

(c) *Oversight exercised by Federal agencies and pass-through entities.* (1) Oversight exercised by Federal agencies or pass-through entities could be used to assess risk. For example, recent monitoring or other reviews performed by an oversight entity that disclosed no significant problems would indicate lower risk, whereas monitoring that disclosed significant problems would indicate higher risk.

(2) Federal agencies, with the concurrence of OMB, may identify Federal programs that are higher risk. OMB will provide this identification in the compliance supplement.

(d) *Inherent risk of the Federal program.* (1) The nature of a Federal program may indicate risk. Consideration should be given to the complexity of the program and the extent to which the Federal program contracts for goods and services. For example, Federal programs that disburse funds through third party contracts or have eligibility criteria may be of higher risk. Federal programs primarily involving staff payroll costs may have high risk for noncompliance with requirements of § 200.430 Compensation—

personal services, but otherwise be at low risk.

(2) The phase of a Federal program in its life cycle at the Federal agency may indicate risk. For example, a new Federal program with new or interim regulations may have higher risk than an established program with time-tested regulations. Also, significant changes in Federal programs, statutes, regulations, or the terms and conditions of Federal awards may increase risk.

(3) The phase of a Federal program in its life cycle at the auditee may indicate risk. For example, during the first and last years that an auditee participates in a Federal program, the risk may be higher due to start-up or close-out of program activities and staff.

(4) Type B programs with larger Federal awards expended would be of higher risk than programs with substantially smaller Federal awards expended.

§ 200.520 Criteria for a low-risk auditee.

An auditee that meets all of the following conditions for each of the preceding two audit periods must qualify as a low-risk auditee and be eligible for reduced audit coverage in accordance with § 200.518 Major program determination.

(a) Single audits were performed on an annual basis in accordance with the provisions of this Subpart, including submitting the data collection form and the reporting package to the FAC within the timeframe specified in § 200.512 Report submission. A non-Federal entity that has biennial audits does not qualify as a low-risk auditee.

(b) The auditor's opinion on whether the financial statements were prepared in accordance with GAAP, or a basis of accounting required by state law, and the auditor's in relation to opinion on the schedule of expenditures of Federal awards were unmodified.

(c) There were no deficiencies in internal control which were identified as material weaknesses under the requirements of GAGAS.

(d) The auditor did not report a substantial doubt about the auditee's ability to continue as a going concern.

(e) None of the Federal programs had audit findings from any of the following in either of the preceding two audit periods in which they were classified as Type A programs:

(1) Internal control deficiencies that were identified as material weaknesses in the auditor's report on internal control for major programs as required under §200.515 Audit reporting, paragraph (c);

(2) A modified opinion on a major program in the auditor's report on major programs as required under §200.515 Audit reporting, paragraph (c); or

(3) Known or likely questioned costs that exceeded five percent of the total Federal awards expended for a Type A program during the audit period.

MANAGEMENT DECISIONS

§ 200.521 Management decision.

(a) *General.* The management decision must clearly state whether or not the audit finding is sustained, the reasons for the decision, and the expected auditee action to repay disallowed costs, make financial adjustments, or take other action. If the auditee has not completed corrective action, a timetable for follow-up should be given. Prior to issuing the management decision, the Federal agency or pass-through entity may request additional information or documentation from the auditee, including a request for auditor assurance related to the documentation, as a way of mitigating disallowed costs. The management decision should describe any appeal process available to the auditee. While not required, the Federal agency or pass-through entity may also issue a management decision on findings relating to the financial statements which are required to be reported in accordance with GAGAS.

(b) *Federal agency.* As provided in §200.513 Responsibilities, paragraph (a)(7), the cognizant agency for audit must be responsible for coordinating a management decision for audit findings that affect the programs of more than one Federal agency. As provided in §200.513 Responsibilities, paragraph (c)(3), a Federal awarding agency is responsible for issuing a management decision for findings that relate to Federal awards it makes to non-Federal entities.

(c) *Pass-through entity.* As provided in §200.331 Requirements for pass-through entities, paragraph (d), the pass-through entity must be responsible for issuing a management decision for audit findings that relate to Federal awards it makes to subrecipients.

(d) *Time requirements.* The Federal awarding agency or pass-through entity responsible for issuing a management decision must do so within six months of acceptance of the audit report by the FAC. The auditee must initiate and proceed with corrective action as rapidly as possible and corrective action should begin no later than upon receipt of the audit report.

(e) *Reference numbers.* Management decisions must include the reference numbers the auditor assigned to each audit finding in accordance with §200.516 Audit findings paragraph (c).

APPENDIX I TO PART 200—FULL TEXT OF NOTICE OF FUNDING OPPORTUNITY

The full text of the notice of funding opportunity is organized in sections. The required format outlined in this appendix indicates immediately following the title of each section whether that section is required in every announcement or is a Federal awarding agency option. The format is designed so that similar types of information will appear in the same sections in announcements of different Federal funding opportunities. Toward that end, there is text in each of the following sections to describe the types of information that a Federal awarding agency would include in that section of an actual announcement.

A Federal awarding agency that wishes to include information that the format does not specifically discuss may address that subject in whatever section(s) is most appropriate. For example, if a Federal awarding agency chooses to address performance goals in the announcement, it might do so in the funding opportunity description, the application content, or the reporting requirements.

Similarly, when this format calls for a type of information to be in a particular section, a Federal awarding agency wishing to address that subject in other sections may elect to repeat the information in those sections or use cross references between the sections (there should be hyperlinks for cross-references in any electronic versions of the announcement). For example, a Federal awarding agency may want to include in Section I information about the types of non-Federal entities who are eligible to apply. The format specifies a standard location for that information in Section III.1 but that does not preclude repeating the information in Section I or creating a cross reference between Sections I and III.1, as long as a potential applicant can find the information quickly and easily from the standard location.

The sections of the full text of the announcement are described in the following paragraphs.

A. PROGRAM DESCRIPTION—REQUIRED

This section contains the full program description of the funding opportunity. It may be as long as needed to adequately communicate to potential applicants the areas in which funding may be provided. It describes the Federal awarding agency's funding priorities or the technical or focus areas in which the Federal awarding agency intends to provide assistance. As appropriate, it may include any program history (e.g., whether this is a new program or a new or changed area of program emphasis). This section may communicate indicators of successful projects (e.g., if the program encourages collaborative efforts) and may include examples of projects that have been funded previously. This section also may include other information the Federal awarding agency deems necessary, and must at a minimum include citations for authorizing statutes and regulations for the funding opportunity.

B. FEDERAL AWARD INFORMATION—REQUIRED

This section provides sufficient information to help an applicant make an informed decision about whether to submit a proposal. Relevant information could include the total amount of funding that the Federal awarding agency expects to award through the announcement; the anticipated number of Federal awards; the expected amounts of individual Federal awards (which may be a range); the amount of funding per Federal award, on average, experienced in previous years; and the anticipated start dates and periods of performance for new Federal awards. This section also should address whether applications for renewal or supplementation of existing projects are eligible to compete with applications for new Federal awards.

This section also must indicate the type(s) of assistance instrument (e.g., grant, cooperative agreement) that may be awarded if applications are successful. If cooperative agreements may be awarded, this section either should describe the "substantial involvement" that the Federal awarding agency expects to have or should reference where the potential applicant can find that information (e.g., in the funding opportunity description in A. Program Description—Required or Federal award administration information in section D. Application and Submission Information). If procurement contracts also may be awarded, this must be stated.

C. ELIGIBILITY INFORMATION

This section addresses the considerations or factors that determine applicant or application eligibility. This includes the eligibility of particular types of applicant organizations, any factors affecting the eligibility of the principal investigator or project director, and any criteria that make particular projects ineligible. Federal agencies should make clear whether an applicant's failure to meet an eligibility criterion by the time of an application deadline will result in the Federal awarding agency returning the application without review or, even though an application may be reviewed, will preclude the Federal awarding agency from making a Federal award. Key elements to be addressed are:

1. *Eligible Applicants—Required.* Announcements must clearly identify the types of entities that are eligible to apply. If there are no restrictions on eligibility, this section may simply indicate that all potential applicants are eligible. If there are restrictions on eligibility, it is important to be clear about the specific types of entities that are eligible, not just the types that are ineligible. For example, if the program is limited to nonprofit organizations subject to 26 U.S.C. 501(c)(3) of the tax code (26 U.S.C. 501(c)(3)), the announcement should say so. Similarly, it is better to state explicitly that Native American tribal organizations are eligible than to assume that they can unambiguously infer that from a statement that nonprofit organizations may apply. Eligibility also can be expressed by exception, (e.g., open to all types of domestic applicants other than individuals). This section should refer to any portion of Section IV specifying documentation that must be submitted to support an eligibility determination (e.g., proof of 501(c)(3) status as determined by the Internal Revenue Service or an authorizing tribal resolution). To the extent that any funding restriction in Section IV.5 could affect the eligibility of an applicant or project, the announcement must either restate that restriction in this section or provide a cross-reference to its description in Section IV.5.

2. *Cost Sharing or Matching—Required.* Announcements must state whether there is required cost sharing, matching, or cost participation without which an application would be ineligible (if cost sharing is not required, the announcement must explicitly say so). Required cost sharing may be a certain percentage or amount, or may be in the form of contributions of specified items or activities (e.g., provision of equipment). It is

important that the announcement be clear about any restrictions on the types of cost (e.g., in-kind contributions) that are acceptable as cost sharing. Cost sharing as an eligibility criterion includes requirements based in statute or regulation, as described in § 200.306 Cost sharing or matching of this Part. This section should refer to the appropriate portion(s) of section D. Application and Submission Information stating any pre-award requirements for submission of letters or other documentation to verify commitments to meet cost-sharing requirements if a Federal award is made.

3. *Other—Required, if applicable.* If there are other eligibility criteria (i.e., criteria that have the effect of making an application or project ineligible for Federal awards, whether referred to as "responsiveness" criteria, "go-no go" criteria, "threshold" criteria, or in other ways), must be clearly stated and must include a reference to the regulation of requirement that describes the restriction, as applicable. For example, if entities that have been found to be in violation of a particular Federal statute are ineligible, it is important to say so. This section must also state any limit on the number of applications an applicant may submit under the announcement and make clear whether the limitation is on the submitting organization, individual investigator/program director, or both. This section should also address any eligibility criteria for beneficiaries or for program participants other than Federal award recipients.

D. APPLICATION AND SUBMISSION INFORMATION

1. *Address to Request Application Package—Required.* Potential applicants must be told how to get application forms, kits, or other materials needed to apply (if this announcement contains everything needed, this section need only say so). An Internet address where the materials can be accessed is acceptable. However, since high-speed Internet access is not yet universally available for downloading documents, and applicants may have additional accessibility requirements, there also should be a way for potential applicants to request paper copies of materials, such as a U.S. Postal Service mailing address, telephone or FAX number, Telephone Device for the Deaf (TDD), Text Telephone (TTY) number, and/or Federal Information Relay Service (FIRS) number.

2. *Content and Form of Application Submission—Required.* This section must identify the required content of an application and the forms or formats that an applicant must use to submit it. If any requirements are stated elsewhere because they are general requirements that apply to multiple programs or funding opportunities, this section should refer to where those requirements may be found. This section also should include required forms or formats as part of the announcement or state where the applicant may obtain them.

This section should specifically address content and form or format requirements for:

i. Pre-applications, letters of intent, or white papers required or encouraged (see Section IV.3), including any limitations on the number of pages or other formatting requirements similar to those for full applications.

ii. The application as a whole. For all submissions, this would include any limitations on the number of pages, font size and typeface, margins, paper size, number of copies, and sequence or assembly requirements. If electronic submission is permitted or required, this could include special requirements for formatting or signatures.

iii. Component pieces of the application (e.g., if all copies of the application must bear original signatures on the face page or the program narrative may not exceed 10 pages). This includes any pieces that may be submitted separately by third parties (e.g., references or letters confirming commitments from third parties that will be contributing a portion of any required cost sharing).

iv. Information that successful applicants must submit after notification of intent to make a Federal award, but prior to a Federal award. This could include evidence of compliance with requirements relating to human subjects or information needed to comply with the National Environmental Policy Act (NEPA) (42 U.S.C. 4321–4370h).

3. *Dun and Bradstreet Universal Numbering System (DUNS) Number and System for Award Management (SAM)—Required.*

This paragraph must state clearly that each applicant (unless the applicant is an individual or Federal awarding agency is excepted from those requirements under 2 CFR § 25.110(b) or (c), or has an exception approved by the Federal awarding agency under 2 CFR § 25.110(d)) is required to: (i) Be registered in SAM before submitting its application; (ii) provide a valid DUNS number in its application; and (iii) continue to maintain an active SAM registration with current information at all times during which it has an active Federal award or an application or plan under consideration by a Federal awarding agency. It also must state that the Federal awarding agency may not make a Federal award to an applicant until the applicant has complied with all applicable DUNS and SAM requirements and, if an applicant has not fully complied with the requirements by the time the Federal awarding agency is ready to make a Federal award, the Federal awarding agency may determine that the applicant is not qualified to receive a Federal award and use that determination as a basis

191

for making a Federal award to another applicant.

4. Submission Dates and Times—Required. Announcements must identify due dates and times for all submissions. This includes not only the full applications but also any preliminary submissions (e.g., letters of intent, white papers, or pre-applications). It also includes any other submissions of information before Federal award that are separate from the full application. If the funding opportunity is a general announcement that is open for a period of time with no specific due dates for applications, this section should say so. Note that the information on dates that is included in this section also must appear with other overview information in a location preceding the full text of the announcement (see §200.203 Notices of funding opportunities of this Part).

Each type of submission should be designated as encouraged or required and, if required, any deadline date (or dates, if the Federal awarding agency plans more than one cycle of application submission, review, and Federal award under the announcement) should be specified. The announcement must state (or provide a reference to another document that states):

i. Any deadline in terms of a date and local time. If the due date falls on a Saturday, Sunday, or Federal holiday, the reporting package is due the next business day.

ii. What the deadline means (e.g., whether it is the date and time by which the Federal awarding agency must receive the application, the date by which the application must be postmarked, or something else) and how that depends, if at all, on the submission method (e.g., mail, electronic, or personal/courier delivery).

iii. The effect of missing a deadline (e.g., whether late applications are neither reviewed nor considered or are reviewed and considered under some circumstances).

iv. How the receiving Federal office determines whether an application or pre-application has been submitted before the deadline. This includes the form of acceptable proof of mailing or system-generated documentation of receipt date and time.

This section also may indicate whether, when, and in what form the applicant will receive an acknowledgement of receipt. This information should be displayed in ways that will be easy to understand and use. It can be difficult to extract all needed information from narrative paragraphs, even when they are well written. A tabular form for providing a summary of the information may help applicants for some programs and give them what effectively could be a checklist to verify the completeness of their application package before submission.

5. Intergovernmental Review—Required, if applicable. If the funding opportunity is subject to Executive Order 12372, "Intergovern-

mental Review of Federal Programs," the notice must say so. In alerting applicants that they must contact their state's Single Point of Contact (SPOC) to find out about and comply with the state's process under Executive Order 12372, it may be useful to inform potential applicants that the names and addresses of the SPOCs are listed in the Office of Management and Budget's Web site. *www.whitehouse.gov/omb/grants/spoc.html.*

6. Funding Restrictions—Required. Notices must include information on funding restrictions in order to allow an applicant to develop an application and budget consistent with program requirements. Examples are whether construction is an allowable activity, if there are any limitations on direct costs such as foreign travel or equipment purchases, and if there are any limits on indirect costs (or facilities and administrative costs). Applicants must be advised if Federal awards will not allow reimbursement of pre-Federal award costs.

7. Other Submission Requirements— Required. This section must address any other submission requirements not included in the other paragraphs of this section. This might include the format of submission, i.e., paper or electronic, for each type of required submission. Applicants should not be required to submit in more than one format and this section should indicate whether they may choose whether to submit applications in hard copy or electronically, may submit only in hard copy, or may submit only electronically.

This section also must indicate where applications (and any pre-applications) must be submitted if sent by postal mail, electronic means, or hand-delivery. For postal mail submission, this must include the name of an office, official, individual or function (e.g., application receipt center) and a complete mailing address. For electronic submission, this must include the URL or email address; whether a password(s) is required; whether particular software or other electronic capabilities are required; what to do in the event of system problems and a point of contact who will be available in the event the applicant experiences technical difficulties.[1]

E. APPLICATION REVIEW INFORMATION

1. Criteria—Required. This section must address the criteria that the Federal awarding agency will use to evaluate applications.

---

[1] With respect to electronic methods for providing information about funding opportunities or accepting applicants' submissions of information, each Federal awarding agency is responsible for compliance with Section 508 of the Rehabilitation Act of 1973 (29 U.S.C. 794d).

This includes the merit and other review criteria that evaluators will use to judge applications, including any statutory, regulatory, or other preferences (e.g., minority status or Native American tribal preferences) that will be applied in the review process. These criteria are distinct from eligibility criteria that are addressed before an application is accepted for review and any program policy or other factors that are applied during the selection process, after the review process is completed. The intent is to make the application process transparent so applicants can make informed decisions when preparing their applications to maximize fairness of the process. The announcement should clearly describe all criteria, including any sub-criteria. If criteria vary in importance, the announcement should specify the relative percentages, weights, or other means used to distinguish among them. For statutory, regulatory, or other preferences, the announcement should provide a detailed explanation of those preferences with an explicit indication of their effect (e.g., whether they result in additional points being assigned).

If an applicant's proposed cost sharing will be considered in the review process (as opposed to being an eligibility criterion described in Section III.2), the announcement must specifically address how it will be considered (e.g., to assign a certain number of additional points to applicants who offer cost sharing, or to break ties among applications with equivalent scores after evaluation against all other factors). If cost sharing will not be considered in the evaluation, the announcement should say so, so that there is no ambiguity for potential applicants. Vague statements that cost sharing is encouraged, without clarification as to what that means, are unhelpful to applicants. It also is important that the announcement be clear about any restrictions on the types of cost (e.g., in-kind contributions) that are acceptable as cost sharing.

2. *Review and Selection Process—Required.* This section may vary in the level of detail provided. The announcement must list any program policy or other factors or elements, other than merit criteria, that the selecting official may use in selecting applications for Federal award (e.g., geographical dispersion, program balance, or diversity). The Federal awarding agency may also include other appropriate details. For example, this section may indicate who is responsible for evaluation against the merit criteria (e.g., peers external to the Federal awarding agency or Federal awarding agency personnel) and/or who makes the final selections for Federal awards. If there is a multi-phase review process (e.g., an external panel advising internal Federal awarding agency personnel who make final recommendations to the deciding official), the announcement may describe the phases. It also may include: the number of

people on an evaluation panel and how it operates, the way reviewers are selected, reviewer qualifications, and the way that conflicts of interest are avoided. With respect to electronic methods for providing information about funding opportunities or accepting applicants' submissions of information, each Federal awarding agency is responsible for compliance with Section 508 of the Rehabilitation Act of 1973 (29 U.S.C. 794d).

In addition, if the Federal awarding agency permits applicants to nominate suggested reviewers of their applications or suggest those they feel may be inappropriate due to a conflict of interest, that information should be included in this section.

3. *Anticipated Announcement and Federal Award Dates—Optional.* This section is intended to provide applicants with information they can use for planning purposes. If there is a single application deadline followed by the simultaneous review of all applications, the Federal awarding agency can include in this section information about the anticipated dates for announcing or notifying successful and unsuccessful applicants and for having Federal awards in place. If applications are received and evaluated on a "rolling" basis at different times during an extended period, it may be appropriate to give applicants an estimate of the time needed to process an application and notify the applicant of the Federal awarding agency's decision.

F. FEDERAL AWARD ADMINISTRATION
INFORMATION

1. *Federal Award Notices—Required.* This section must address what a successful applicant can expect to receive following selection. If the Federal awarding agency's practice is to provide a separate notice stating that an application has been selected before it actually makes the Federal award, this section would be the place to indicate that the letter is not an authorization to begin performance (to the extent that it allows charging to Federal awards of pre-award costs at the non-Federal entity's own risk). This section should indicate that the notice of Federal award signed by the grants officer (or equivalent) is the authorizing document, and whether it is provided through postal mail or by electronic means and to whom. It also may address the timing, form, and content of notifications to unsuccessful applicants. See also § 200.210 Information contained in a Federal award.

2. *Administrative and National Policy Requirements—Required.* This section must identify the usual administrative and national policy requirements the Federal awarding agency's Federal awards may include. Providing this information lets a potential applicant identify any requirements with which it would have difficulty complying if its application is successful. In those cases,

193

early notification about the requirements allows the potential applicant to decide not to apply or to take needed actions before receiving the Federal award. The announcement need not include all of the terms and conditions of the Federal award, but may refer to a document (with information about how to obtain it) or Internet site where applicants can see the terms and conditions. If this funding opportunity will lead to Federal awards with some special terms and conditions that differ from the Federal awarding agency's usual (sometimes called "general") terms and conditions, this section should highlight those special terms and conditions. Doing so will alert applicants that have received Federal awards from the Federal awarding agency previously and might not otherwise expect different terms and conditions. For the same reason, the announcement should inform potential applicants about special requirements that could apply to particular Federal awards after the review of applications and other information, based on the particular circumstances of the effort to be supported (e.g., if human subjects were to be involved or if some situations may justify special terms on intellectual property, data sharing or security requirements).

3. Reporting—Required. This section must include general information about the type (e.g., financial or performance), frequency, and means of submission (paper or electronic) of post-Federal award reporting requirements. Highlight any special reporting requirements for Federal awards under this funding opportunity that differ (e.g., by report type, frequency, form/format, or circumstances for use) from what the Federal awarding agency's Federal awards usually require.

G. FEDERAL AWARDING AGENCY CONTACT(S)— REQUIRED

The announcement must give potential applicants a point(s) of contact for answering questions or helping with problems while the funding opportunity is open. The intent of this requirement is to be as helpful as possible to potential applicants, so the Federal awarding agency should consider approaches such as giving:

i. Points of contact who may be reached in multiple ways (e.g., by telephone, FAX, and/or email, as well as regular mail).

ii. A fax or email address that multiple people access, so that someone will respond even if others are unexpectedly absent during critical periods.

iii. Different contacts for distinct kinds of help (e.g., one for questions of programmatic content and a second for administrative questions).

H. OTHER INFORMATION—OPTIONAL

This section may include any additional information that will assist a potential applicant. For example, the section might:

i. Indicate whether this is a new program or a one-time initiative.

ii. Mention related programs or other upcoming or ongoing Federal awarding agency funding opportunities for similar activities.

iii. Include current Internet addresses for Federal awarding agency Web sites that may be useful to an applicant in understanding the program.

iv. Alert applicants to the need to identify proprietary information and inform them about the way the Federal awarding agency will handle it.

v. Include certain routine notices to applicants (e.g., that the Federal government is not obligated to make any Federal award as a result of the announcement or that only grants officers can bind the Federal government to the expenditure of funds).

APPENDIX II TO PART 200—CONTRACT PROVISIONS FOR NON-FEDERAL ENTITY CONTRACTS UNDER FEDERAL AWARDS

In addition to other provisions required by the Federal agency or non-Federal entity, all contracts made by the non-Federal entity under the Federal award must contain provisions covering the following, as applicable.

(A) Contracts for more than the simplified acquisition threshold currently set at $150,000, which is the inflation adjusted amount determined by the Civilian Agency Acquisition Council and the Defense Acquisition Regulations Council (Councils) as authorized by 41 U.S.C. 1908, must address administrative, contractual, or legal remedies in instances where contractors violate or breach contract terms, and provide for such sanctions and penalties as appropriate.

(B) All contracts in excess of $10,000 must address termination for cause and for convenience by the non-Federal entity including the manner by which it will be effected and the basis for settlement.

(C) Equal Employment Opportunity. Except as otherwise provided under 41 CFR Part 60, all contracts that meet the definition of "federally assisted construction contract" in 41 CFR Part 60–1.3 must include the equal opportunity clause provided under 41 CFR 60–1.4(b), in accordance with Executive Order 11246, "Equal Employment Opportunity" (30 FR 12319, 12935, 3 CFR Part, 1964– 1965 Comp., p. 339), as amended by Executive Order 11375, "Amending Executive Order 11246 Relating to Equal Employment Opportunity," and implementing regulations at 41 CFR part 60, "Office of Federal Contract Compliance Programs, Equal Employment Opportunity, Department of Labor."

194

(D) Davis-Bacon Act, as amended (40 U.S.C. 3141–3148). When required by Federal program legislation, all prime construction contracts in excess of $2,000 awarded by non-Federal entities must include a provision for compliance with the Davis-Bacon Act (40 U.S.C. 3141–3144, and 3146–3148) as supplemented by Department of Labor regulations (29 CFR Part 5, "Labor Standards Provisions Applicable to Contracts Covering Federally Financed and Assisted Construction"). In accordance with the statute, contractors must be required to pay wages to laborers and mechanics at a rate not less than the prevailing wages specified in a wage determination made by the Secretary of Labor. In addition, contractors must be required to pay wages not less than once a week. The non-Federal entity must place a copy of the current prevailing wage determination issued by the Department of Labor in each solicitation. The decision to award a contract or subcontract must be conditioned upon the acceptance of the wage determination. The non-Federal entity must report all suspected or reported violations to the Federal awarding agency. The contracts must also include a provision for compliance with the Copeland "Anti-Kickback" Act (40 U.S.C. 3145), as supplemented by Department of Labor regulations (29 CFR Part 3, "Contractors and Subcontractors on Public Building or Public Work Financed in Whole or in Part by Loans or Grants from the United States"). The Act provides that each contractor or subrecipient must be prohibited from inducing, by any means, any person employed in the construction, completion, or repair of public work, to give up any part of the compensation to which he or she is otherwise entitled. The non-Federal entity must report all suspected or reported violations to the Federal awarding agency.

(E) Contract Work Hours and Safety Standards Act (40 U.S.C. 3701–3708). Where applicable, all contracts awarded by the non-Federal entity in excess of $100,000 that involve the employment of mechanics or laborers must include a provision for compliance with 40 U.S.C. 3702 and 3704, as supplemented by Department of Labor regulations (29 CFR Part 5). Under 40 U.S.C. 3702 of the Act, each contractor must be required to compute the wages of every mechanic and laborer on the basis of a standard work week of 40 hours. Work in excess of the standard work week is permissible provided that the worker is compensated at a rate of not less than one and a half times the basic rate of pay for all hours worked in excess of 40 hours in the work week. The requirements of 40 U.S.C. 3704 are applicable to construction work and provide that no laborer or mechanic must be required to work in surroundings or under working conditions which are unsanitary, hazardous or dangerous. These requirements do not apply to the purchases of supplies or materials or articles ordinarily available on the open market, or contracts for transportation or transmission of intelligence.

(F) Rights to Inventions Made Under a Contract or Agreement. If the Federal award meets the definition of "funding agreement" under 37 CFR § 401.2 (a) and the recipient or subrecipient wishes to enter into a contract with a small business firm or nonprofit organization regarding the substitution of parties, assignment or performance of experimental, developmental, or research work under that "funding agreement," the recipient or subrecipient must comply with the requirements of 37 CFR Part 401, "Rights to Inventions Made by Nonprofit Organizations and Small Business Firms Under Government Grants, Contracts and Cooperative Agreements," and any implementing regulations issued by the awarding agency.

(G) Clean Air Act (42 U.S.C. 7401–7671q.) and the Federal Water Pollution Control Act (33 U.S.C. 1251–1387), as amended—Contracts and subgrants of amounts in excess of $150,000 must contain a provision that requires the non-Federal award to agree to comply with all applicable standards, orders or regulations issued pursuant to the Clean Air Act (42 U.S.C. 7401–7671q) and the Federal Water Pollution Control Act as amended (33 U.S.C. 1251–1387). Violations must be reported to the Federal awarding agency and the Regional Office of the Environmental Protection Agency (EPA).

(H) Mandatory standards and policies relating to energy efficiency which are contained in the state energy conservation plan issued in compliance with the Energy Policy and Conservation Act (42 U.S.C. 6201).

(I) Debarment and Suspension (Executive Orders 12549 and 12689)—A contract award (see 2 CFR 180.220) must not be made to parties listed on the governmentwide Excluded Parties List System in the System for Award Management (SAM), in accordance with the OMB guidelines at 2 CFR 180 that implement Executive Orders 12549 (3 CFR Part 1986 Comp., p. 189) and 12689 (3 CFR Part 1989 Comp., p. 235), "Debarment and Suspension." The Excluded Parties List System in SAM contains the names of parties debarred, suspended, or otherwise excluded by agencies, as well as parties declared ineligible under statutory or regulatory authority other than Executive Order 12549.

(J) Byrd Anti-Lobbying Amendment (31 U.S.C. 1352)—Contractors that apply or bid for an award of $100,000 or more must file the required certification. Each tier certifies to the tier above that it will not and has not used Federal appropriated funds to pay any person or organization for influencing or attempting to influence an officer or employee of any agency, a member of Congress, officer or employee of Congress, or an employee of a member of Congress in connection with obtaining any Federal contract, grant or any other award covered by 31 U.S.C. 1352. Each tier must also disclose any lobbying with non-Federal funds that takes place in connection with obtaining any Federal award. Such disclosures are forwarded from tier to tier up to the non-Federal award.

(K) See § 200.322 Procurement of recovered materials.

APPENDIX III TO PART 200—INDIRECT (F&A) COSTS IDENTIFICATION AND ASSIGNMENT, AND RATE DETERMINATION FOR INSTITUTIONS OF HIGHER EDUCATION (IHES)

A. GENERAL

This appendix provides criteria for identifying and computing indirect (or indirect (F&A)) rates at IHEs (institutions). Indirect (F&A) costs are those that are incurred for common or joint objectives and therefore cannot be identified readily and specifically with a particular sponsored project, an instructional activity, or any other institutional activity. See subsection B.1, Definition of Facilities and Administration, for a discussion of the components of indirect (F&A) costs.

1. Major Functions of an Institution

Refers to instruction, organized research, other sponsored activities and other institutional activities as defined in this section:

a. *Instruction* means the teaching and training activities of an institution. Except for research training as provided in subsection b, this term includes all teaching and training activities, whether they are offered for credits toward a degree or certificate or on a non-credit basis, and whether they are offered through regular academic departments or separate divisions, such as a summer school division or an extension division. Also considered part of this major function are departmental research, and, where agreed to, university research.

(1) *Sponsored instruction and training* means specific instructional or training activity established by grant, contract, or cooperative agreement. For purposes of the cost principles, this activity may be considered a major function even though an institution's accounting treatment may include it in the instruction function.

(2) *Departmental research* means research, development and scholarly activities that are not organized research and, consequently, are not separately budgeted and accounted for. Departmental research, for purposes of this document, is not considered as a major function, but as a part of the instruction function of the institution.

b. *Organized research* means all research and development activities of an institution that are separately budgeted and accounted for. It includes:

(1) *Sponsored research* means all research and development activities that are sponsored by Federal and non-Federal agencies and organizations. This term includes activities involving the training of individuals in research techniques (commonly called research training) where such activities utilize the same facilities as other research and development activities and where such activities are not included in the instruction function.

(2) *University research* means all research and development activities that are separately budgeted and accounted for by the institution under an internal application of institutional funds. University research, for purposes of this document, must be combined with sponsored research under the function of organized research.

c. *Other sponsored activities* means programs and projects financed by Federal and non-Federal agencies and organizations which involve the performance of work other than instruction and organized research. Examples of such programs and projects are health service projects and community service programs. However, when any of these activities are undertaken by the institution without outside support, they may be classified as other institutional activities.

d. *Other institutional activities* means all activities of an institution except for instruction, departmental research, organized research, and other sponsored activities, as defined in this section; indirect (F&A) cost activities identified in this Appendix paragraph B, Identification and assignment of indirect (F&A) costs; and specialized services facilities described in § 200.468 Specialized service facilities of this Part.

Examples of other institutional activities include operation of residence halls, dining halls, hospitals and clinics, student unions, intercollegiate athletics, bookstores, faculty housing, student apartments, guest houses, chapels, theaters, public museums, and other similar auxiliary enterprises. This definition also includes any other categories of activities, costs of which are "unallowable" to Federal awards, unless otherwise indicated in an award.

2. Criteria for Distribution

a. *Base period.* A base period for distribution of indirect (F&A) costs is the period during which the costs are incurred. The base period normally should coincide with the fiscal year established by the institution, but in any event the base period should be so selected as to avoid inequities in the distribution of costs.

b. *Need for cost groupings.* The overall objective of the indirect (F&A) cost allocation process is to distribute the indirect (F&A) costs described in Section B, Identification and assignment of indirect (F&A) costs, to

196

the major functions of the institution in proportions reasonably consistent with the nature and extent of their use of the institution's resources. In order to achieve this objective, it may be necessary to provide for selective distribution by establishing separate groupings of cost within one or more of the indirect (F&A) cost categories referred to in subsection B.1, Definition of Facilities and Administration. In general, the cost groupings established within a category should constitute, in each case, a pool of those items of expense that are considered to be of like nature in terms of their relative contribution to (or degree of remoteness from) the particular cost objectives to which distribution is appropriate. Cost groupings should be established considering the general guides provided in subsection c of this section. Each such pool or cost grouping should then be distributed individually to the related cost objectives, using the distribution base or method most appropriate in light of the guidelines set forth in subsection d of this section.

c. *General considerations on cost groupings.* The extent to which separate cost groupings and selective distribution would be appropriate at an institution is a matter of judgment to be determined on a case-by-case basis. Typical situations which may warrant the establishment of two or more separate cost groupings (based on account classification or analysis) within an indirect (F&A) cost category include but are not limited to the following:

(1) If certain items or categories of expense relate solely to one of the major functions of the institution or to less than all functions, such expenses should be set aside as a separate cost grouping for direct assignment or selective allocation in accordance with the guides provided in subsections b and d.

(2) If any types of expense ordinarily treated as general administration or departmental administration are charged to Federal awards as direct costs, expenses applicable to other activities of the institution when incurred for the same purposes in like circumstances must, through separate cost groupings, be excluded from the indirect (F&A) costs allocable to those Federal awards and included in the direct cost of other activities for cost allocation purposes.

(3) If it is determined that certain expenses are for the support of a service unit or facility whose output is susceptible of measurement on a workload or other quantitative basis, such expenses should be set aside as a separate cost grouping for distribution on such basis to organized research, instructional, and other activities at the institution or within the department.

(4) If activities provide their own purchasing, personnel administration, building maintenance or similar service, the distribution of general administration and general

expenses, or operation and maintenance expenses to such activities should be accomplished through cost groupings which include only that portion of central indirect (F&A) costs (such as for overall management) which are properly allocable to such activities.

(5) If the institution elects to treat fringe benefits as indirect (F&A) charges, such costs should be set aside as a separate cost grouping for selective distribution to related cost objectives.

(6) The number of separate cost groupings within a category should be held within practical limits, after taking into consideration the materiality of the amounts involved and the degree of precision attainable through less selective methods of distribution.

d. Selection of distribution method.

(1) Actual conditions must be taken into account in selecting the method or base to be used in distributing individual cost groupings. The essential consideration in selecting a base is that it be the one best suited for assigning the pool of costs to cost objectives in accordance with benefits derived; with a traceable cause-and-effect relationship; or with logic and reason, where neither benefit nor a cause-and-effect relationship is determinable.

(2) If a cost grouping can be identified directly with the cost objective benefitted, it should be assigned to that cost objective.

(3) If the expenses in a cost grouping are more general in nature, the distribution may be based on a cost analysis study which results in an equitable distribution of the costs. Such cost analysis studies may take into consideration weighting factors, population, or space occupied if appropriate. Cost analysis studies, however, must (a) be appropriately documented in sufficient detail for subsequent review by the cognizant agency for indirect costs, (b) distribute the costs to the related cost objectives in accordance with the relative benefits derived, (c) be statistically sound, (d) be performed specifically at the institution at which the results are to be used, and (e) be reviewed periodically, but not less frequently than rate negotiations, updated if necessary, and used consistently. Any assumptions made in the study must be stated and explained. The use of cost analysis studies and periodic changes in the method of cost distribution must be fully justified.

(4) If a cost analysis study is not performed, or if the study does not result in an equitable distribution of the costs, the distribution must be made in accordance with the appropriate base cited in Section B, Identification and assignment of indirect (F&A) costs, unless one of the following conditions is met:

(a) It can be demonstrated that the use of a different base would result in a more equitable allocation of the costs, or that a more readily available base would not increase the costs charged to Federal awards, or

(b) The institution qualifies for, and elects to use, the simplified method for computing indirect (F&A) cost rates described in Section D, Simplified method for small institutions.

(5) Notwithstanding subsection (3), effective July 1, 1998, a cost analysis or base other than that in Section B must not be used to distribute utility or student services costs. Instead, subsections B.4.c Operation and maintenance expenses, may be used in the recovery of utility costs.

e. Order of distribution.

(1) Indirect (F&A) costs are the broad categories of costs discussed in Section B.1, Definitions of Facilities and Administration

(2) Depreciation, interest expenses, operation and maintenance expenses, and general administrative and general expenses should be allocated in that order to the remaining indirect (F&A) cost categories as well as to the major functions and specialized service facilities of the institution. Other cost categories may be allocated in the order determined to be most appropriate by the institutions. When cross allocation of costs is made as provided in subsection (3), this order of allocation does not apply.

(3) Normally an indirect (F&A) cost category will be considered closed once it has been allocated to other cost objectives, and costs may not be subsequently allocated to it. However, a cross allocation of costs between two or more indirect (F&A) cost categories may be used if such allocation will result in a more equitable allocation of costs. If a cross allocation is used, an appropriate modification to the composition of the indirect (F&A) cost categories described in Section B is required.

B. IDENTIFICATION AND ASSIGNMENT OF INDIRECT (F&A) COSTS

1. Definition of Facilities and Administration

See § 200.414 Indirect (F&A) costs which provides the basis for this indirect cost requirements.

2. Depreciation

a. The expenses under this heading are the portion of the costs of the institution's buildings, capital improvements to land and buildings, and equipment which are computed in accordance with § 200.436 Depreciation.

b. In the absence of the alternatives provided for in Section A.2.d, Selection of distribution method, the expenses included in this category must be allocated in the following manner:

(1) Depreciation on buildings used exclusively in the conduct of a single function, and on capital improvements and equipment used in such buildings, must be assigned to that function.

(2) Depreciation on buildings used for more than one function, and on capital improvements and equipment used in such buildings, must be allocated to the individual functions performed in each building on the basis of usable square feet of space, excluding common areas such as hallways, stairwells, and rest rooms.

(3) Depreciation on buildings, capital improvements and equipment related to space (e.g., individual rooms, laboratories) used jointly by more than one function (as determined by the users of the space) must be treated as follows. The cost of each jointly used unit of space must be allocated to benefitting functions on the basis of:

(a) The employee full-time equivalents (FTEs) or salaries and wages of those individual functions benefitting from the use of that space; or

(b) Institution-wide employee FTEs or salaries and wages applicable to the benefitting major functions (see Section A.1) of the institution.

(4) Depreciation on certain capital improvements to land, such as paved parking areas, fences, sidewalks, and the like, not included in the cost of buildings, must be allocated to user categories of students and employees on a full-time equivalent basis. The amount allocated to the student category must be assigned to the instruction function of the institution. The amount allocated to the employee category must be further allocated to the major functions of the institution in proportion to the salaries and wages of all employees applicable to those functions.

3. Interest

Interest on debt associated with certain buildings, equipment and capital improvements, as defined in § 200.449 Interest, must be classified as an expenditure under the category Facilities. These costs must be allocated in the same manner as the depreciation on the buildings, equipment and capital improvements to which the interest relates.

4. Operation and Maintenance Expenses

a. The expenses under this heading are those that have been incurred for the administration, supervision, operation, maintenance, preservation, and protection of the institution's physical plant. They include expenses normally incurred for such items as janitorial and utility services; repairs and ordinary or normal alterations of buildings, furniture and equipment; care of grounds; maintenance and operation of buildings and other plant facilities; security; earthquake and disaster preparedness; environmental safety; hazardous waste disposal; property, liability and all other insurance relating to property; space and capital leasing; facility planning and management; and central receiving. The operation and maintenance expense category should also include its allocable share of fringe benefit costs, depreciation, and interest costs.

b. In the absence of the alternatives provided for in Section A.2.d, the expenses included in this category must be allocated in the same manner as described in subsection 2.b for depreciation.

c. A utility cost adjustment of up to 1.3 percentage points may be included in the negotiated indirect cost rate of the IHE for organized research, per the computation alternatives in paragraphs (c)(1) and (2) of this section:

(1) Where space is devoted to a single function and metering allows unambiguous measurement of usage related to that space, costs must be assigned to the function located in that space.

(2) Where space is allocated to different functions and metering does not allow unambiguous measurement of usage by function, costs must be allocated as follows:

(i) Utilities costs should be apportioned to functions in the same manner as depreciation, based on the calculated difference between the site or building actual square footage for monitored research laboratory space (site, building, floor, or room), and a separate calculation prepared by the IHE using the "effective square footage" described in subsection (c)(2)(ii) of this section.

(ii) "Effective square footage" allocated to research laboratory space must be calculated as the actual square footage times the relative energy utilization index (REUI) posted on the OMB Web site at the time of a rate determination.

A. This index is the ratio of a laboratory energy use index (lab EUI) to the corresponding index for overall average college or university space (college EUI).

B. In July 2012, values for these two indices (taken respectively from the Lawrence Berkeley Laboratory "Labs for the 21st Century" benchmarking tool *http:// labs21benchmarking.lbl.gov/CompareData.php* and the US Department of Energy "Buildings Energy Databook" and *http:// buildingsdatabook.eren.doe.gov/CBECS.aspx*) were 310 kBtu/sq ft-yr. and 155 kBtu/sq ft-yr., so that the adjustment ratio is 2.0 by this methodology. To retain currency, OMB will adjust the EUI numbers from time to time (no more often than annually nor less often than every 5 years), using reliable and publicly disclosed data. Current values of both the EUIs and the REUI will be posted on the OMB Web site.

5. General Administration and General Expenses

a. The expenses under this heading are those that have been incurred for the general executive and administrative offices of educational institutions and other expenses of a general character which do not relate solely to any major function of the institution; i.e., solely to (1) instruction, (2) organized research, (3) other sponsored activities, or (4) other institutional activities. The general administration and general expense category should also include its allocable share of fringe benefit costs, operation and maintenance expense, depreciation, and interest costs. Examples of general administration and general expenses include: those expenses incurred by administrative offices that serve the entire university system of which the institution is a part; central offices of the institution such as the President's or Chancellor's office, the offices for institution-wide financial management, business services, budget and planning, personnel management, and safety and risk management; the office of the General Counsel; and the operations of the central administrative management information systems. General administration and general expenses must not include expenses incurred within non-university-wide deans' offices, academic departments, organized research units, or similar organizational units. (See subsection 6, Departmental administration expenses.)

b. In the absence of the alternatives provided for in Section A.2.d, the expenses included in this category must be grouped first according to common major functions of the institution to which they render services or provide benefits. The aggregate expenses of each group must then be allocated to serviced or benefitted functions on the modified total cost basis. Modified total costs consist of the same elements as those in Section C.2. When an activity included in this indirect (F&A) cost category provides a service or product to another institution or organization, an appropriate adjustment must be made to either the expenses or the basis of allocation or both, to assure a proper allocation of costs.

6. Departmental Administration Expenses

a. The expenses under this heading are those that have been incurred for administrative and supporting services that benefit common or joint departmental activities or objectives in academic deans' offices, academic departments and divisions, and organized research units. Organized research units include such units as institutes, study centers, and research centers. Departmental administration expenses are subject to the following limitations.

(1) Academic deans' offices. Salaries and operating expenses are limited to those attributable to administrative functions.

(2) Academic departments:

(a) Salaries and fringe benefits attributable to the administrative work (including bid and proposal preparation) of faculty (including department heads) and other professional personnel conducting research and/or instruction, must be allowed at a rate of 3.6 percent of modified total direct costs. This category does not include professional business or professional administrative officers. This allowance must be added to the computation of the indirect (F&A) cost rate for major functions in Section C, Determination and application of indirect (F&A) cost rate or rates; the expenses covered by the allowance must be excluded from the departmental administration cost pool. No documentation is required to support this allowance.

(b) Other administrative and supporting expenses incurred within academic departments are allowable provided they are treated consistently in like circumstances. This would include expenses such as the salaries of secretarial and clerical staffs, the salaries of administrative officers and assistants, travel, office supplies, stockrooms, and the like.

(3) Other fringe benefit costs applicable to the salaries and wages included in subsections (1) and (2) are allowable, as well as an appropriate share of general administration and general expenses, operation and maintenance expenses, and depreciation.

(4) Federal agencies may authorize reimbursement of additional costs for department heads and faculty only in exceptional cases where an institution can demonstrate undue hardship or detriment to project performance.

b. The following guidelines apply to the determination of departmental administrative costs as direct or indirect (F&A) costs.

(1) In developing the departmental administration cost pool, special care should be exercised to ensure that costs incurred for the same purpose in like circumstances are treated consistently as either direct or indirect (F&A) costs. For example, salaries of technical staff, laboratory supplies (e.g., chemicals), telephone toll charges, animals, animal care costs, computer costs, travel costs, and specialized shop costs must be treated as direct costs wherever identifiable to a particular cost objective. Direct charging of these costs may be accomplished through specific identification of individual costs to benefitting cost objectives, or through recharge centers or specialized service facilities, as appropriate under the circumstances. See §§ 200.413 Direct costs, paragraph (c) and 200.468 Specialized service facilities.

(2) Items such as office supplies, postage, local telephone costs, and memberships must normally be treated as indirect (F&A) costs.

c. In the absence of the alternatives provided for in Section A.2.d, the expenses included in this category must be allocated as follows:

(1) The administrative expenses of the dean's office of each college and school must be allocated to the academic departments within that college or school on the modified total cost basis.

(2) The administrative expenses of each academic department, and the department's share of the expenses allocated in subsection (1) must be allocated to the appropriate functions of the department on the modified total cost basis.

7. Sponsored Projects Administration

a. The expenses under this heading are limited to those incurred by a separate organization(s) established primarily to administer sponsored projects, including such functions as grant and contract administration (Federal and non-Federal), special security, purchasing, personnel, administration, and editing and publishing of research and other reports. They include the salaries and expenses of the head of such organization, assistants, and immediate staff, together with the salaries and expenses of personnel engaged in supporting activities maintained by the organization, such as stock rooms, print shops, and the like. This category also includes an allocable share of fringe benefit costs, general administration and general expenses, operation and maintenance expenses, and depreciation. Appropriate adjustments will be made for services provided to other functions or organizations.

b. In the absence of the alternatives provided for in Section A.2.d, the expenses included in this category must be allocated to the major functions of the institution under which the sponsored projects are conducted on the basis of the modified total cost of sponsored projects.

c. An appropriate adjustment must be made to eliminate any duplicate charges to Federal awards when this category includes similar or identical activities as those included in the general administration and general expense category or other indirect (F&A) cost items, such as accounting, procurement, or personnel administration.

8. Library Expenses

a. The expenses under this heading are those that have been incurred for the operation of the library, including the cost of books and library materials purchased for the library, less any items of library income that qualify as applicable credits under § 200.406 Applicable credits. The library expense category should also include the fringe benefits applicable to the salaries and wages included therein, an appropriate share of general administration and general expense, operation and maintenance expense, and depreciation. Costs incurred in the purchases of rare books (museum-type books) with no value to Federal awards should not be allocated to them.

b. In the absence of the alternatives provided for in Section A.2.d, the expenses included in this category must be allocated first on the basis of primary categories of users, including students, professional employees, and other users.

(1) The student category must consist of full-time equivalent students enrolled at the institution, regardless of whether they earn credits toward a degree or certificate.

(2) The professional employee category must consist of all faculty members and other professional employees of the institution, on a full-time equivalent basis. This category may also include post-doctorate fellows and graduate students.

(3) The other users category must consist of a reasonable factor as determined by institutional records to account for all other users of library facilities.

c. Amount allocated in paragraph b of this section must be assigned further as follows:

(1) The amount in the student category must be assigned to the instruction function of the institution.

(2) The amount in the professional employee category must be assigned to the major functions of the institution in proportion to the salaries and wages of all faculty members and other professional employees applicable to those functions.

(3) The amount in the other users category must be assigned to the other institutional activities function of the institution.

9. Student Administration and Services

a. The expenses under this heading are those that have been incurred for the administration of student affairs and for services to students, including expenses of such activities as deans of students, admissions, registrar, counseling and placement services, student advisers, student health and infirmary services, catalogs, and commencements and convocations. The salaries of members of the academic staff whose responsibilities to the institution require administrative work that benefits sponsored projects may also be included to the extent that the portion charged to student administration is determined in accordance with Subpart E— Cost Principles of this Part. This expense category also includes the fringe benefit costs applicable to the salaries and wages included therein, an appropriate share of general administration and general expenses, operation and maintenance, interest expense, and depreciation.

b. In the absence of the alternatives provided for in Section A.2.d, the expenses in this category must be allocated to the instruction function, and subsequently to Federal awards in that function.

10. Offset for Indirect (F&A) Expenses Otherwise Provided for by the Federal Government

a. The items to be accumulated under this heading are the reimbursements and other payments from the Federal government which are made to the institution to support solely, specifically, and directly, in whole or in part, any of the administrative or service activities described in subsections 2 through 9.

b. The items in this group must be treated as a credit to the affected individual indirect (F&A) cost category before that category is allocated to benefitting functions.

C. DETERMINATION AND APPLICATION OF INDIRECT (F&A) COST RATE OR RATES

1. Indirect (F&A) Cost Pools

a. (1) Subject to subsection b, the separate categories of indirect (F&A) costs allocated to each major function of the institution as prescribed in paragraph B of this paragraph C.1 Identification and assignment of indirect (F&A) costs, must be aggregated and treated as a common pool for that function. The amount in each pool must be divided by the distribution base described in subsection 2 to arrive at a single indirect (F&A) cost rate for each function.

(2) The rate for each function is used to distribute indirect (F&A) costs to individual Federal awards of that function. Since a common pool is established for each major function of the institution, a separate indirect (F&A) cost rate would be established for each of the major functions described in Section A.1 under which Federal awards are carried out.

(3) Each institution's indirect (F&A) cost rate process must be appropriately designed to ensure that Federal sponsors do not in any way subsidize the indirect (F&A) costs of other sponsors, specifically activities sponsored by industry and foreign governments. Accordingly, each allocation method used to identify and allocate the indirect (F&A) cost pools, as described in Sections A.2, Criteria for distribution, and B.2 through B.9, must contain the full amount of the institution's modified total costs or other appropriate units of measurement used to make the computations. In addition, the final rate distribution base (as defined in subsection 2) for each major function (organized research, instruction, etc., as described in Section A.1, Major functions of an institution) must contain all the programs or activities which utilize the indirect (F&A) costs allocated to that major function. At the time an indirect (F&A) cost proposal is submitted to a cognizant agency for indirect costs, each institution must describe the process it uses to

ensure that Federal funds are not used to subsidize industry and foreign government funded programs.

b. In some instances a single rate basis for use across the board on all work within a major function at an institution may not be appropriate. A single rate for research, for example, might not take into account those different environmental factors and other conditions which may affect substantially the indirect (F&A) costs applicable to a particular segment of research at the institution. A particular segment of research may be that performed under a single sponsored agreement or it may consist of research under a group of Federal awards performed in a common environment. The environmental factors are not limited to the physical location of the work. Other important factors are the level of the administrative support required, the nature of the facilities or other resources employed, the scientific disciplines or technical skills involved, the organizational arrangements used, or any combination thereof. If a particular segment of a sponsored agreement is performed within an environment which appears to generate a significantly different level of indirect (F&A) costs, provisions should be made for a separate indirect (F&A) cost pool applicable to such work. The separate indirect (F&A) cost pool should be developed during the regular course of the rate determination process and the separate indirect (F&A) cost rate resulting therefrom should be utilized; provided it is determined that (1) such indirect (F&A) cost rate differs significantly from that which would have been obtained under subsection a, and (2) the volume of work to which such rate would apply is material in relation to other Federal awards at the institution.

2. The Distribution Basis

Indirect (F&A) costs must be distributed to applicable Federal awards and other benefitting activities within each major function (see section A.1, Major functions of an institution) on the basis of modified total direct costs (MTDC), consisting of all salaries and wages, fringe benefits, materials and supplies, services, travel, and subgrants and subcontracts up to the first $25,000 of each subaward (regardless of the period covered by the subaward). MTDC is defined in §200.68 Modified Total Direct Cost (MTDC). For this purpose, an indirect (F&A) cost rate should be determined for each of the separate indirect (F&A) cost pools developed pursuant to subsection 1. The rate in each case should be stated as the percentage which the amount of the particular indirect (F&A) cost pool is of the modified total direct costs identified with such pool.

3. Negotiated Lump Sum for Indirect (F&A) Costs

A negotiated fixed amount in lieu of indirect (F&A) costs may be appropriate for self-contained, off-campus, or primarily subcontracted activities where the benefits derived from an institution's indirect (F&A) services cannot be readily determined. Such negotiated indirect (F&A) costs will be treated as an offset before allocation to instruction, organized research, other sponsored activities, and other institutional activities. The base on which such remaining expenses are allocated should be appropriately adjusted.

4. Predetermined Rates for Indirect (F&A) Costs

Public Law 87-638 (76 Stat. 437) as amended (41 U.S.C. 4708) authorizes the use of predetermined rates in determining the "indirect costs" (indirect (F&A) costs) applicable under research agreements with educational institutions. The stated objectives of the law are to simplify the administration of cost-type research and development contracts (including grants) with educational institutions, to facilitate the preparation of their budgets, and to permit more expeditious closeout of such contracts when the work is completed. In view of the potential advantages offered by this procedure, negotiation of predetermined rates for indirect (F&A) costs for a period of two to four years should be the norm in those situations where the cost experience and other pertinent facts available are deemed sufficient to enable the parties involved to reach an informed judgment as to the probable level of indirect (F&A) costs during the ensuing accounting periods.

5. Negotiated Fixed Rates and Carry-Forward Provisions

When a fixed rate is negotiated in advance for a fiscal year (or other time period), the over- or under-recovery for that year may be included as an adjustment to the indirect (F&A) cost for the next rate negotiation. When the rate is negotiated before the carry-forward adjustment is determined, the carry-forward amount may be applied to the next subsequent rate negotiation. When such adjustments are to be made, each fixed rate negotiated in advance for a given period will be computed by applying the expected indirect (F&A) costs allocable to Federal awards for the forecast period plus or minus the carry-forward adjustment (over- or under-recovery) from the prior period, to the forecast distribution base. Unrecovered amounts under lump-sum agreements or cost-sharing provisions of prior years must not be carried forward for consideration in the new rate negotiation. There must, however, be an advance understanding in each case between the institution and the cognizant agency for indirect costs as to whether these differences will be considered in the rate negotiation rather than making the determination after the differences are known. Further, institutions electing to use this carry-forward provision may not subsequently change without prior approval of the cognizant agency for indirect costs. In the event that an institution returns to a post-determined rate, any over- or under-recovery during the period in which negotiated fixed rates and carry-forward provisions were followed will be included in the subsequent post-determined rates. Where multiple rates are used, the same procedure will be applicable for determining each rate.

6. Provisional and Final Rates for Indirect (F&A) Costs

Where the cognizant agency for indirect costs determines that cost experience and other pertinent facts do not justify the use of predetermined rates, or a fixed rate with a carry-forward, or if the parties cannot agree on an equitable rate, a provisional rate must be established. To prevent substantial overpayment or underpayment, the provisional rate may be adjusted by the cognizant agency for indirect costs during the institution's fiscal year. Predetermined or fixed rates may replace provisional rates at any time prior to the close of the institution's fiscal year. If a provisional rate is not replaced by a predetermined or fixed rate prior to the end of the institution's fiscal year, a final rate will be established and upward or downward adjustments will be made based on the actual allowable costs incurred for the period involved.

7. Fixed Rates for the Life of the Sponsored Agreement

Federal agencies must use the negotiated rates except as provided in paragraph (e) of § 200.414 Indirect (F&A) costs, must paragraph (b)(1) for indirect (F&A) costs in effect at the time of the initial award throughout the life of the Federal award. Award levels for Federal awards may not be adjusted in future years as a result of changes in negotiated rates. "Negotiated rates" per the rate agreement include final, fixed, and predetermined rates and exclude provisional rates. "Life" for the purpose of this subsection means each competitive segment of a project. A competitive segment is a period of years approved by the Federal awarding agency at the time of the Federal award. If negotiated rate agreements do not extend through the life of the Federal award at the time of the initial award, then the negotiated rate for the last year of the Federal award must be extended through the end of the life of the Federal award.

b. Except as provided in § 200.414 Indirect (F&A) costs, when an educational institution does not have a negotiated rate with the Federal government at the time of an award (because the educational institution is a new recipient or the parties cannot reach agreement on a rate), the provisional rate used at the time of the award must be adjusted once a rate is negotiated and approved by the cognizant agency for indirect costs.

8. Limitation on Reimbursement of Administrative Costs

a. Notwithstanding the provisions of subsection C.1.a, the administrative costs charged to Federal awards awarded or amended (including continuation and renewal awards) with effective dates beginning on or after the start of the institution's first fiscal year which begins on or after October 1, 1991, must be limited to 26% of modified total direct costs (as defined in subsection 2) for the total of General Administration and General Expenses, Departmental Administration, Sponsored Projects Administration, and Student Administration and Services (including their allocable share of depreciation, interest costs, operation and maintenance expenses, and fringe benefits costs, as provided by Section B, Identification and assignment of indirect (F&A) costs, and all other types of expenditures not listed specifically under one of the subcategories of facilities in Section B.

b. Institutions should not change their accounting or cost allocation methods if the effect is to change the charging of a particular type of cost from F&A to direct, or to reclassify costs, or increase allocations from the administrative pools identified in paragraph B.1 of this Appendix to the other F&A cost pools or fringe benefits. Cognizant agencies for indirect cost are authorized to allow changes where an institution's charging practices are at variance with acceptable practices followed by a substantial majority of other institutions.

9. Alternative Method for Administrative Costs

a. Notwithstanding the provisions of subsection 1.a, an institution may elect to claim a fixed allowance for the "Administration" portion of indirect (F&A) costs. The allowance could be either 24% of modified total direct costs or a percentage equal to 95% of the most recently negotiated fixed or predetermined rate for the cost pools included under "Administration" as defined in Section B.1, whichever is less. Under this alternative, no cost proposal need be prepared for the "Administration" portion of the indirect (F&A) cost rate nor is further identification or documentation of these costs required (see subsection c). Where a negotiated indirect (F&A) cost agreement includes this alternative, an institution must make no further charges for the expenditure categories described in Section B.5, General administration and general expenses, Section B.6, Departmental administration expenses, Section B.7, Sponsored projects administration, and Section B.9, Student administration and services.

b. In negotiations of rates for subsequent periods, an institution that has elected the option of subsection a may continue to exercise it at the same rate without further identification or documentation of costs.

c. If an institution elects to accept a threshold rate as defined in subsection a of this section, it is not required to perform a detailed analysis of its administrative costs. However, in order to compute the facilities components of its indirect (F&A) cost rate, the institution must reconcile its indirect (F&A) cost proposal to its financial statements and make appropriate adjustments and reclassifications to identify the costs of each major function as defined in Section A.1, as well as to identify and allocate the facilities components. Administrative costs that are not identified as such by the institution's accounting system (such as those incurred in academic departments) will be classified as instructional costs for purposes of reconciling indirect (F&A) cost proposals to financial statements and allocating facilities costs.

10. Individual Rate Components

In order to provide mutually agreed-upon information for management purposes, each indirect (F&A) cost rate negotiation or determination shall include development of a rate for each indirect (F&A) cost pool as well as the overall indirect (F&A) cost rate.

11. Negotiation and Approval of Indirect (F&A) Rate

a. Cognizant agency for indirect costs is defined in Subpart A—Acronyms and Definitions.

(1) Cost negotiation cognizance is assigned to the Department of Health and Human Services (HHS) or the Department of Defense's Office of Naval Research (DOD), normally depending on which of the two agencies (HHS or DOD) provides more funds to the educational institution for the most recent three years. Information on funding must be derived from relevant data gathered by the National Science Foundation. In cases where neither HHS nor DOD provides Federal funding to an educational institution, the cognizant agency for indirect costs assignment must default to HHS. Notwithstanding the method for cognizance determination described in this section, other arrangements for cognizance of a particular educational institution may also be based in part on the types of research performed at the educational institution and must be de-

cided based on mutual agreement between HHS and DOD.

(2) After cognizance is established, it must continue for a five-year period.

b. Acceptance of rates. See §200.414 Indirect (F&A) costs.

c. Correcting deficiencies. The cognizant agency for indirect costs must negotiate changes needed to correct systems deficiencies relating to accountability for Federal awards. Cognizant agencies for indirect costs must address the concerns of other affected agencies, as appropriate, and must negotiate special rates for Federal agencies that are required to limit recovery of indirect costs by statute.

d. Resolving questioned costs. The cognizant agency for indirect costs must conduct any necessary negotiations with an educational institution regarding amounts questioned by audit that are due the Federal government related to costs covered by a negotiated agreement.

e. Reimbursement. Reimbursement to cognizant agencies for indirect costs for work performed under this Part may be made by reimbursement billing under the Economy Act, 31 U.S.C. 1535.

f. Procedure for establishing facilities and administrative rates must be established by one of the following methods:

(1) Formal negotiation. The cognizant agency for indirect costs is responsible for negotiating and approving rates for an educational institution on behalf of all Federal agencies. Non-cognizant Federal agencies for indirect costs, which make Federal awards to an educational institution, must notify the cognizant agency for indirect costs of specific concerns (i.e., a need to establish special cost rates) which could affect the negotiation process. The cognizant agency for indirect costs must address the concerns of all interested agencies, as appropriate. A pre-negotiation conference may be scheduled among all interested agencies, if necessary. The cognizant agency for indirect costs must then arrange a negotiation conference with the educational institution.

(2) Other than formal negotiation. The cognizant agency for indirect costs and educational institution may reach an agreement on rates without a formal negotiation conference; for example, through correspondence or use of the simplified method described in this section D of this Appendix.

g. Formalizing determinations and agreements. The cognizant agency for indirect costs must formalize all determinations or agreements reached with an educational institution and provide copies to other agencies having an interest. Determinations should include a description of any adjustments, the actual amount, both dollar and percentage adjusted, and the reason for making adjustments.

h. Disputes and disagreements. Where the cognizant agency for indirect costs is unable to reach agreement with an educational institution with regard to rates or audit resolution, the appeal system of the cognizant agency for indirect costs must be followed for resolution of the disagreement.

12. Standard Format for Submission

For facilities and administrative (indirect (F&A)) rate proposals, educational institutions must use the standard format, shown in section E of this appendix, to submit their indirect (F&A) rate proposal to the cognizant agency for indirect costs. The cognizant agency for indirect costs may, on an institution-by-institution basis, grant exceptions from all or portions of Part II of the standard format requirement. This requirement does not apply to educational institutions that use the simplified method for calculating indirect (F&A) rates, as described in Section D of this Appendix.

In order to provide mutually agreed upon information for management purposes, each F&A cost rate negotiation or determination must include development of a rate for each F&A cost pool as well as the overall F&A rate.

D. SIMPLIFIED METHOD FOR SMALL INSTITUTIONS

1. General

a. Where the total direct cost of work covered by this Part at an institution does not exceed $10 million in a fiscal year, the simplified procedure described in subsections 2 or 3 may be used in determining allowable indirect (F&A) costs. Under this simplified procedure, the institution's most recent annual financial report and immediately available supporting information must be utilized as a basis for determining the indirect (F&A) cost rate applicable to all Federal awards. The institution may use either the salaries and wages (see subsection 2) or modified total direct costs (see subsection 3) as the distribution basis.

b. The simplified procedure should not be used where it produces results which appear inequitable to the Federal government or the institution. In any such case, indirect (F&A) costs should be determined through use of the regular procedure.

2. Simplified Procedure—Salaries and Wages Base

a. Establish the total amount of salaries and wages paid to all employees of the institution.

b. Establish an indirect (F&A) cost pool consisting of the expenditures (exclusive of capital items and other costs specifically identified as unallowable) which customarily are classified under the following titles or their equivalents:

(1) General administration and general expenses (exclusive of costs of student administration and services, student activities, student aid, and scholarships).

(2) Operation and maintenance of physical plant and depreciation (after appropriate adjustment for costs applicable to other institutional activities).

(3) Library.

(4) Department administration expenses, which will be computed as 20 percent of the salaries and expenses of deans and heads of departments.

In those cases where expenditures classified under subsection (1) have previously been allocated to other institutional activities, they may be included in the indirect (F&A) cost pool. The total amount of salaries and wages included in the indirect (F&A) cost pool must be separately identified.

c. Establish a salary and wage distribution base, determined by deducting from the total of salaries and wages as established in subsection a from the amount of salaries and wages included under subsection b.

d. Establish the indirect (F&A) cost rate, determined by dividing the amount in the indirect (F&A) cost pool, subsection b, by the amount of the distribution base, subsection c.

e. Apply the indirect (F&A) cost rate to direct salaries and wages for individual agreements to determine the amount of indirect (F&A) costs allocable to such agreements.

3. Simplified Procedure—Modified Total Direct Cost Base

a. Establish the total costs incurred by the institution for the base period.

b. Establish an indirect (F&A) cost pool consisting of the expenditures (exclusive of capital items and other costs specifically identified as unallowable) which customarily are classified under the following titles or their equivalents:

(1) General administration and general expenses (exclusive of costs of student administration and services, student activities, student aid, and scholarships).

(2) Operation and maintenance of physical plant and depreciation (after appropriate adjustment for costs applicable to other institutional activities).

(3) Library.

(4) Department administration expenses, which will be computed as 20 percent of the salaries and expenses of deans and heads of departments. In those cases where expenditures classified under subsection (1) have previously been allocated to other institutional activities, they may be included in the indirect (F&A) cost pool. The modified total direct costs amount included in the indirect (F&A) cost pool must be separately identified.

c. Establish a modified total direct cost distribution base, as defined in Section C.2, The distribution basis, that consists of all institution's direct functions.

d. Establish the indirect (F&A) cost rate, determined by dividing the amount in the indirect (F&A) cost pool, subsection b, by the amount of the distribution base, subsection c.

e. Apply the indirect (F&A) cost rate to the modified total direct costs for individual agreements to determine the amount of indirect (F&A) costs allocable to such agreements.

E. DOCUMENTATION REQUIREMENTS

The standard format for documentation requirements for indirect (indirect (F&A)) rate proposals for claiming costs under the regular method is available on the OMB Web site here: *http://www.whitehouse.gov/omb/grants_forms.*

F. CERTIFICATION

1. Certification of Charges

To assure that expenditures for Federal awards are proper and in accordance with the agreement documents and approved project budgets, the annual and/or final fiscal reports or vouchers requesting payment under the agreements will include a certification, signed by an authorized official of the university, which reads "By signing this report, I certify to the best of my knowledge and belief that the report is true, complete, and accurate, and the expenditures, disbursements and cash receipts are for the purposes and intent set forth in the award documents. I am aware that any false, fictitious, or fraudulent information, or the omission of any material fact, may subject me to criminal, civil or administrative penalties for fraud, false statements, false claims or otherwise. (U.S. Code, Title 18, Section 1001 and Title 31, Sections 3729–3733 and 3801–3812)".

2. Certification of Indirect (F&A) Costs

a. *Policy.* Cognizant agencies must not accept a proposed indirect cost rate must unless such costs have been certified by the educational institution using the Certificate of indirect (F&A) Costs set forth in subsection F.2.c

b. The certificate must be signed on behalf of the institution by the chief financial officer or an individual designated by an individual at a level no lower than vice president or chief financial officer.

(1) No indirect (F&A) cost rate must be binding upon the Federal government if the most recent required proposal from the institution has not been certified. Where it is necessary to establish indirect (F&A) cost rates, and the institution has not submitted a certified proposal for establishing such

rates in accordance with the requirements of this section, the Federal government must unilaterally establish such rates. Such rates may be based upon audited historical data or such other data that have been furnished to the cognizant agency for indirect costs and for which it can be demonstrated that all unallowable costs have been excluded. When indirect (F&A) cost rates are unilaterally established by the Federal government because of failure of the institution to submit a certified proposal for establishing such rates in accordance with this section, the rates established will be set at a level low enough to ensure that potentially unallowable costs will not be reimbursed.

c. *Certificate.* The certificate required by this section must be in the following form:

CERTIFICATE OF INDIRECT (F&A) COSTS

This is to certify that to the best of my knowledge and belief:

(1) I have reviewed the indirect (F&A) cost proposal submitted herewith;

(2) All costs included in this proposal [identify date] to establish billing or final indirect (F&A) costs rate for [identify period covered by rate] are allowable in accordance with the requirements of the Federal agreement(s) to which they apply and with the cost principles applicable to those agreements.

(3) This proposal does not include any costs which are unallowable under applicable cost principles such as (without limitation): public relations costs, contributions and donations, entertainment costs, fines and penalties, lobbying costs, and defense of fraud proceedings; and

(4) All costs included in this proposal are properly allocable to Federal agreements on the basis of a beneficial or causal relationship between the expenses incurred and the agreements to which they are allocated in accordance with applicable requirements.

I declare that the foregoing is true and correct.

Institution of Higher Education:
Signature: _____
Name of Official: _____
Title: _____
Date of Execution: _____

APPENDIX IV TO PART 200—INDIRECT (F&A) COSTS IDENTIFICATION AND ASSIGNMENT, AND RATE DETERMINATION FOR NONPROFIT ORGANIZATIONS

A. GENERAL

1. Indirect costs are those that have been incurred for common or joint objectives and cannot be readily identified with a particular final cost objective. Direct cost of minor amounts may be treated as indirect

costs under the conditions described in §200.413 Direct costs paragraph (d) of this Part. After direct costs have been determined and assigned directly to awards or other work as appropriate, indirect costs are those remaining to be allocated to benefitting cost objectives. A cost may not be allocated to a Federal award as an indirect cost if any other cost incurred for the same purpose, in like circumstances, has been assigned to a Federal award as a direct cost. "Major nonprofit organizations" are defined in §200.414 Indirect (F&A) costs. See indirect cost rate reporting requirements in sections B.2.e and B.3.g of this Appendix.

B. ALLOCATION OF INDIRECT COSTS AND DETERMINATION OF INDIRECT COST RATES

1. General

a. If a nonprofit organization has only one major function, or where all its major functions benefit from its indirect costs to approximately the same degree, the allocation of indirect costs and the computation of an indirect cost rate may be accomplished through simplified allocation procedures, as described in section B.2 of this Appendix.

b. If an organization has several major functions which benefit from its indirect costs in varying degrees, allocation of indirect costs may require the accumulation of such costs into separate cost groupings which then are allocated individually to benefitting functions by means of a base which best measures the relative degree of benefit. The indirect costs allocated to each function are then distributed to individual Federal awards and other activities included in that function by means of an indirect cost rate(s).

c. The determination of what constitutes an organization's major functions will depend on its purpose in being; the types of services it renders to the public, its clients, and its members; and the amount of effort it devotes to such activities as fundraising, public information and membership activities.

d. Specific methods for allocating indirect costs and computing indirect cost rates along with the conditions under which each method should be used are described in section B.2 through B.5 of this Appendix.

e. The base period for the allocation of indirect costs is the period in which such costs are incurred and accumulated for allocation to work performed in that period. The base period normally should coincide with the organization's fiscal year but, in any event, must be so selected as to avoid inequities in the allocation of the costs.

2. Simplified Allocation Method

a. Where an organization's major functions benefit from its indirect costs to approximately the same degree, the allocation of indirect costs may be accomplished by (i) separating the organization's total costs for the base period as either direct or indirect, and (ii) dividing the total allowable indirect costs (net of applicable credits) by an equitable distribution base. The result of this process is an indirect cost rate which is used to distribute indirect costs to individual Federal awards. The rate should be expressed as the percentage which the total amount of allowable indirect costs bears to the base selected. This method should also be used where an organization has only one major function encompassing a number of individual projects or activities, and may be used where the level of Federal awards to an organization is relatively small.

b. Both the direct costs and the indirect costs must exclude capital expenditures and unallowable costs. However, unallowable costs which represent activities must be included in the direct costs under the conditions described in §200.413 Direct costs, paragraph (e) of this Part.

c. The distribution base may be total direct costs (excluding capital expenditures and other distorting items, such as contracts or subawards for $25,000 or more), direct salaries and wages, or other base which results in an equitable distribution. The distribution base must exclude participant support costs as defined in §200.75 Participant support costs.

d. Except where a special rate(s) is required in accordance with section B.5 of this Appendix, the indirect cost rate developed under the above principles is applicable to all Federal awards of the organization. If a special rate(s) is required, appropriate modifications must be made in order to develop the special rate(s).

e. For an organization that receives more than $10 million in Federal funding of direct costs in a fiscal year, a breakout of the indirect cost component into two broad categories, Facilities and Administration as defined in section A.3 of this Appendix, is required. The rate in each case must be stated as the percentage which the amount of the particular indirect cost category (i.e., Facilities or Administration) is of the distribution base identified with that category.

3. Multiple Allocation Base Method

a. General. Where an organization's indirect costs benefit its major functions in varying degrees, indirect costs must be accumulated into separate cost groupings, as described in subparagraph b. Each grouping must then be allocated individually to benefitting functions by means of a base which best measures the relative benefits. The default allocation bases by cost pool are described in section B.3.c of this Appendix.

b. Identification of indirect costs. Cost groupings must be established so as to permit the allocation of each grouping on the basis of benefits provided to the major functions. Each grouping must constitute a pool of expenses that are of like character in terms of functions they benefit and in terms of the allocation base which best measures the relative benefits provided to each function. The groupings are classified within the two broad categories: "Facilities" and "Administration," as described in section A.3 of this Appendix. The indirect cost pools are defined as follows:

(1) Depreciation. The expenses under this heading are the portion of the costs of the organization's buildings, capital improvements to land and buildings, and equipment which are computed in accordance with § 200.436 Depreciation.

(2) Interest. Interest on debt associated with certain buildings, equipment and capital improvements are computed in accordance with § 200.449 Interest.

(3) Operation and maintenance expenses. The expenses under this heading are those that have been incurred for the administration, operation, maintenance, preservation, and protection of the organization's physical plant. They include expenses normally incurred for such items as: janitorial and utility services; repairs and ordinary or normal alterations of buildings, furniture and equipment; care of grounds; maintenance and operation of buildings and other plant facilities; security; earthquake and disaster preparedness; environmental safety; hazardous waste disposal; property, liability and other insurance relating to property; space and capital leasing; facility planning and management; and central receiving. The operation and maintenance expenses category must also include its allocable share of fringe benefit costs, depreciation, and interest costs.

(4) General administration and general expenses. The expenses under this heading are those that have been incurred for the overall general executive and administrative offices of the organization and other expenses of a general nature which do not relate solely to any major function of the organization. This category must also include its allocable share of fringe benefit costs, operation and maintenance expense, depreciation, and interest costs. Examples of this category include central offices, such as the director's office, the office of finance, business services, budget and planning, personnel, safety and risk management, general counsel, management information systems, and library costs.

In developing this cost pool, special care should be exercised to ensure that costs incurred for the same purpose in like circumstances are treated consistently as either direct or indirect costs. For example, salaries of technical staff, project supplies, project publication, telephone toll charges, computer costs, travel costs, and specialized services costs must be treated as direct costs wherever identifiable to a particular program. The salaries and wages of administrative and pooled clerical staff should normally be treated as indirect costs. Direct charging of these costs may be appropriate where a major project or activity explicitly requires and budgets for administrative or clerical services and other individuals involved can be identified with the program or activity. Items such as office supplies, postage, local telephone costs, periodicals and memberships should normally be treated as indirect costs.

c. Allocation bases. Actual conditions must be taken into account in selecting the base to be used in allocating the expenses in each grouping to benefitting functions. The essential consideration in selecting a method or a base is that it is the one best suited for assigning the pool of costs to cost objectives in accordance with benefits derived; a traceable cause and effect relationship; or logic and reason, where neither the cause nor the effect of the relationship is determinable. When an allocation can be made by assignment of a cost grouping directly to the function benefitted, the allocation must be made in that manner. When the expenses in a cost grouping are more general in nature, the allocation must be made through the use of a selected base which produces results that are equitable to both the Federal government and the organization. The distribution must be made in accordance with the bases described herein unless it can be demonstrated that the use of a different base would result in a more equitable allocation of the costs, or that a more readily available base would not increase the costs charged to Federal awards. The results of special cost studies (such as an engineering utility study) must not be used to determine and allocate the indirect costs to Federal awards.

(1) Depreciation. Depreciation expenses must be allocated in the following manner:

(a) Depreciation on buildings used exclusively in the conduct of a single function, and on capital improvements and equipment used in such buildings, must be assigned to that function.

(b) Depreciation on buildings used for more than one function, and on capital improvements and equipment used in such buildings, must be allocated to the individual functions performed in each building on the basis of usable square feet of space, excluding common areas, such as hallways, stairwells, and restrooms.

(c) Depreciation on buildings, capital improvements and equipment related space (e.g., individual rooms, and laboratories) used jointly by more than one function (as determined by the users of the space) must be treated as follows. The cost of each jointly used unit of space must be allocated to the benefitting functions on the basis of:

(i) the employees and other users on a full-time equivalent (FTE) basis or salaries and wages of those individual functions benefitting from the use of that space; or

(ii) organization-wide employee FTEs or salaries and wages applicable to the benefitting functions of the organization.

(d) Depreciation on certain capital improvements to land, such as paved parking areas, fences, sidewalks, and the like, not included in the cost of buildings, must be allocated to user categories on a FTE basis and distributed to major functions in proportion to the salaries and wages of all employees applicable to the functions.

(2) Interest. Interest costs must be allocated in the same manner as the depreciation on the buildings, equipment and capital equipment to which the interest relates.

(3) Operation and maintenance expenses. Operation and maintenance expenses must be allocated in the same manner as the depreciation.

(4) General administration and general expenses. General administration and general expenses must be allocated to benefitting functions based on modified total costs (MTC). The MTC is the modified total direct costs (MTDC), as described in Subpart A—Acronyms and Definitions of Part 200, plus the allocated indirect cost proportion. The expenses included in this category could be grouped first according to major functions of the organization to which they render services or provide benefits. The aggregate expenses of each group must then be allocated to benefitting functions based on MTC.

d. Order of distribution.

(1) Indirect cost categories consisting of depreciation, interest, operation and maintenance, and general administration and general expenses must be allocated in that order to the remaining indirect cost categories as well as to the major functions of the organization. Other cost categories should be allocated in the order determined to be most appropriate by the organization. This order of allocation does not apply if cross allocation of costs is made as provided in section B.3.d.2 of this Appendix.

(2) Normally, an indirect cost category will be considered closed once it has been allocated to other cost objectives, and costs must not be subsequently allocated to it. However, a cross allocation of costs between two or more indirect costs categories could be used if such allocation will result in a more equitable allocation of costs. If a cross allocation is used, an appropriate modification to the composition of the indirect cost categories is required.

e. Application of indirect cost rate or rates. Except where a special indirect cost rate(s) is required in accordance with section B.5 of this Appendix, the separate groupings of indirect costs allocated to each major function must be aggregated and treated as a common pool for that function. The costs in the common pool must then be distributed to individual Federal awards included in that function by use of a single indirect cost rate.

f. Distribution basis. Indirect costs must be distributed to applicable Federal awards and other benefitting activities within each major function on the basis of MTDC (see definition in §200.68 Modified Total Direct Cost (MTDC) of Part 200.

g. Individual Rate Components. An indirect cost rate must be determined for each separate indirect cost pool developed. The rate in each case must be stated as the percentage which the amount of the particular indirect cost pool is of the distribution base identified with that pool. Each indirect cost rate negotiation or determination agreement must include development of the rate for each indirect cost pool as well as the overall indirect cost rate. The indirect cost pools must be classified within two broad categories: "Facilities" and "Administration," as described in section A.3 of this Appendix.

4. Direct Allocation Method

a. Some nonprofit organizations treat all costs as direct costs except general administration and general expenses. These organizations generally separate their costs into three basic categories: (i) General administration and general expenses, (ii) fundraising, and (iii) other direct functions (including projects performed under Federal awards). Joint costs, such as depreciation, rental costs, operation and maintenance of facilities, telephone expenses, and the like are prorated individually as direct costs to each category and to each Federal award or other activity using a base most appropriate to the particular cost being prorated.

b. This method is acceptable, provided each joint cost is prorated using a base which accurately measures the benefits provided to each Federal award or other activity. The bases must be established in accordance with reasonable criteria, and be supported by current data. This method is compatible with the Standards of Accounting and Financial Reporting for Voluntary Health and Welfare Organizations issued jointly by the National Health Council, Inc., the National Assembly of Voluntary Health and Social Welfare Organizations, and the United Way of America.

c. Under this method, indirect costs consist exclusively of general administration and general expenses. In all other respects, the organization's indirect cost rates must be computed in the same manner as that described in section B.2 Simplified allocation method of this Appendix.

5. Special Indirect Cost Rates

In some instances, a single indirect cost rate for all activities of an organization or for each major function of the organization may not be appropriate, since it would not take into account those different factors which may substantially affect the indirect costs applicable to a particular segment of work. For this purpose, a particular segment of work may be that performed under a single Federal award or it may consist of work under a group of Federal awards performed in a common environment. These factors may include the physical location of the work, the level of administrative support required, the nature of the facilities or other resources employed, the scientific disciplines or technical skills involved, the organizational arrangements used, or any combination thereof. When a particular segment of work is performed in an environment which appears to generate a significantly different level of indirect costs, provisions should be made for a separate indirect cost pool applicable to such work. The separate indirect cost pool should be developed during the course of the regular allocation process, and the separate indirect cost rate resulting therefrom should be used, provided it is determined that (i) the rate differs significantly from that which would have been obtained under sections B.2, B.3, and B.4 of this Appendix, and (ii) the volume of work to which the rate would apply is material.

C. NEGOTIATION AND APPROVAL OF INDIRECT COST RATES

1. Definitions

As used in this section, the following terms have the meanings set forth in this section:

a. *Cognizant agency for indirect costs* means the Federal agency responsible for negotiating and approving indirect cost rates for a nonprofit organization on behalf of all Federal agencies.

b. *Predetermined rate* means an indirect cost rate, applicable to a specified current or future period, usually the organization's fiscal year. The rate is based on an estimate of the costs to be incurred during the period. A predetermined rate is not subject to adjustment.

c. *Fixed rate* means an indirect cost rate which has the same characteristics as a predetermined rate, except that the difference between the estimated costs and the actual costs of the period covered by the rate is carried forward as an adjustment to the rate computation of a subsequent period.

d. *Final rate* means an indirect cost rate applicable to a specified past period which is based on the actual costs of the period. A final rate is not subject to adjustment.

e. *Provisional rate or billing rate* means a temporary indirect cost rate applicable to a specified period which is used for funding, interim reimbursement, and reporting indirect costs on Federal awards pending the establishment of a final rate for the period.

f. *Indirect cost proposal* means the documentation prepared by an organization to substantiate its claim for the reimbursement of indirect costs. This proposal provides the basis for the review and negotiation leading to the establishment of an organization's indirect cost rate.

g. *Cost objective* means a function, organizational subdivision, contract, Federal award, or other work unit for which cost data are desired and for which provision is made to accumulate and measure the cost of processes, projects, jobs and capitalized projects.

2. Negotiation and Approval of Rates

a. Unless different arrangements are agreed to by the Federal agencies concerned, the Federal agency with the largest dollar value of Federal awards with an organization will be designated as the cognizant agency for indirect costs for the negotiation and approval of the indirect cost rates and, where necessary, other rates such as fringe benefit and computer charge-out rates. Once an agency is assigned cognizance for a particular nonprofit organization, the assignment will not be changed unless there is a shift in the dollar volume of the Federal awards to the organization for at least three years. All concerned Federal agencies must be given the opportunity to participate in the negotiation process but, after a rate has been agreed upon, it will be accepted by all Federal agencies. When a Federal agency has reason to believe that special operating factors affecting its Federal awards necessitate special indirect cost rates in accordance with section B.5 of this Appendix, it will, prior to the time the rates are negotiated, notify the cognizant agency for indirect costs. (See also § 200.414 Indirect (F&A) costs of Part 200.)

b. Except as otherwise provided in § 200.414 Indirect (F&A) costs paragraph (e) of this Part, a nonprofit organization which has not previously established an indirect cost rate with a Federal agency must submit its initial indirect cost proposal immediately after the organization is advised that a Federal award will be made and, in no event, later than three months after the effective date of the Federal award.

c. Unless approved by the cognizant agency for indirect costs in accordance with § 200.414 Indirect (F&A) costs paragraph (f) of this Part, organizations that have previously established indirect cost rates must submit a new indirect cost proposal to the cognizant agency for indirect costs within six months after the close of each fiscal year.

d. A predetermined rate may be negotiated for use on Federal awards where there is reasonable assurance, based on past experience and reliable projection of the organization's costs, that the rate is not likely to exceed a rate based on the organization's actual costs.

e. Fixed rates may be negotiated where predetermined rates are not considered appropriate. A fixed rate, however, must not be negotiated if (i) all or a substantial portion of the organization's Federal awards are expected to expire before the carry-forward adjustment can be made; (ii) the mix of Federal and non-Federal work at the organization is too erratic to permit an equitable carry-forward adjustment; or (iii) the organization's operations fluctuate significantly from year to year.

f. Provisional and final rates must be negotiated where neither predetermined nor fixed rates are appropriate. Predetermined or fixed rates may replace provisional rates at any time prior to the close of the organization's fiscal year. If that event does not occur, a final rate will be established and upward or downward adjustments will be made based on the actual allowable costs incurred for the period involved.

g. The results of each negotiation must be formalized in a written agreement between the cognizant agency for indirect costs and the nonprofit organization. The cognizant agency for indirect costs must make available copies of the agreement to all concerned Federal agencies.

h. If a dispute arises in a negotiation of an indirect cost rate between the cognizant agency for indirect costs and the nonprofit organization, the dispute must be resolved in accordance with the appeals procedures of the cognizant agency for indirect costs.

i. To the extent that problems are encountered among the Federal agencies in connection with the negotiation and approval process, OMB will lend assistance as required to resolve such problems in a timely manner.

D. Certification of Indirect (F&A) Costs

Required Certification. No proposal to establish indirect (F&A) cost rates must be acceptable unless such costs have been certified by the non-profit organization using the Certificate of Indirect (F&A) Costs set forth in section j. of this appendix. The certificate must be signed on behalf of the organization by an individual at a level no lower than vice president or chief financial officer for the organization.

j. Each indirect cost rate proposal must be accompanied by a certification in the following form:

Certificate of Indirect (F&A) Costs

This is to certify that to the best of my knowledge and belief:

(1) I have reviewed the indirect (F&A) cost proposal submitted herewith;

(2) All costs included in this proposal [identify date] to establish billing or final indirect (F&A) costs rate for [identify period covered by rate] are allowable in accordance with the requirements of the Federal awards to which they apply and with Subpart E—Cost Principles of Part 200.

(3) This proposal does not include any costs which are unallowable under Subpart E—Cost Principles of Part 200 such as (without limitation): public relations costs, contributions and donations, entertainment costs, fines and penalties, lobbying costs, and defense of fraud proceedings; and

(4) All costs included in this proposal are properly allocable to Federal awards on the basis of a beneficial or causal relationship between the expenses incurred and the Federal awards to which they are allocated in accordance with applicable requirements.

I declare that the foregoing is true and correct.

Nonprofit Organization: _____
Signature: _____
Name of Official: _____
Title: _____
Date of Execution: _____

APPENDIX V TO PART 200—STATE/LOCAL GOVERNMENT AND INDIAN TRIBE-WIDE CENTRAL SERVICE COST ALLOCATION PLANS

A. GENERAL

1. Most governmental units provide certain services, such as motor pools, computer centers, purchasing, accounting, etc., to operating agencies on a centralized basis. Since federally-supported awards are performed within the individual operating agencies, there needs to be a process whereby these central service costs can be identified and assigned to benefitted activities on a reasonable and consistent basis. The central service cost allocation plan provides that process. All costs and other data used to distribute the costs included in the plan should be supported by formal accounting and other records that will support the propriety of the costs assigned to Federal awards.

2. Guidelines and illustrations of central service cost allocation plans are provided in a brochure published by the Department of Health and Human Services entitled "A Guide for State, Local and Indian Tribal Governments: Cost Principles and Procedures for Developing Cost Allocation Plans and Indirect Cost Rates for Agreements with the Federal Government." A copy of this brochure may be obtained from the Superintendent of Documents, U.S. Government Printing Office.

B. DEFINITIONS

1. *Agency or operating agency* means an organizational unit or sub-division within a governmental unit that is responsible for the performance or administration of Federal awards or activities of the governmental unit.

211

2. *Allocated central services* means central services that benefit operating agencies but are not billed to the agencies on a fee-for-service or similar basis. These costs are allocated to benefitted agencies on some reasonable basis. Examples of such services might include general accounting, personnel administration, purchasing, etc.

3. *Billed central services* means central services that are billed to benefitted agencies or programs on an individual fee-for-service or similar basis. Typical examples of billed central services include computer services, transportation services, insurance, and fringe benefits.

4. *Cognizant agency for indirect costs* is defined in § 200.19 Cognizant agency for indirect costs of this Part. The determination of cognizant agency for indirect costs for states and local governments is described in section F.1, Negotiation and Approval of Central Service Plans.

5. *Major local government* means local government that receives more than $100 million in direct Federal awards subject to this Part.

C. SCOPE OF THE CENTRAL SERVICE COST ALLOCATION PLANS

The central service cost allocation plan will include all central service costs that will be claimed (either as a billed or an allocated cost) under Federal awards and will be documented as described in section E. Costs of central services omitted from the plan will not be reimbursed.

D. SUBMISSION REQUIREMENTS

1. Each state will submit a plan to the Department of Health and Human Services for each year in which it claims central service costs under Federal awards. The plan should include (a) a projection of the next year's allocated central service cost (based either on actual costs for the most recently completed year or the budget projection for the coming year), and (b) a reconciliation of actual allocated central service costs to the estimated costs used for either the most recently completed year or the year immediately preceding the most recently completed year.

2. Each major local government is also required to submit a plan to its cognizant agency for indirect costs annually.

3. All other local governments claiming central service costs must develop a plan in accordance with the requirements described in this Part and maintain the plan and related supporting documentation for audit. These local governments are not required to submit their plans, for Federal approval unless they are specifically requested to do so by the cognizant agency for indirect costs. Where a local government only receives funds as a subrecipient, the pass-through entity will be responsible for monitoring the subrecipient's plan.

4. All central service cost allocation plans will be prepared and, when required, submitted within six months prior to the beginning of each of the governmental unit's fiscal years in which it proposes to claim central service costs. Extensions may be granted by the cognizant agency for indirect costs on a case-by-case basis.

E. DOCUMENTATION REQUIREMENTS FOR SUBMITTED PLANS

The documentation requirements described in this section may be modified, expanded, or reduced by the cognizant agency for indirect costs on a case-by-case basis. For example, the requirements may be reduced for those central services which have little or no impact on Federal awards. Conversely, if a review of a plan indicates that certain additional information is needed, and will likely be needed in future years, it may be routinely requested in future plan submissions. Items marked with an asterisk (*) should be submitted only once; subsequent plans should merely indicate any changes since the last plan.

1. General

All proposed plans must be accompanied by the following: an organization chart sufficiently detailed to show operations including the central service activities of the state/local government whether or not they are shown as benefitting from central service functions; a copy of the Comprehensive Annual Financial Report (or a copy of the Executive Budget if budgeted costs are being proposed) to support the allowable costs of each central service activity included in the plan; and, a certification (see subsection 4.) that the plan was prepared in accordance with this Part, contains only allowable costs, and was prepared in a manner that treated similar costs consistently among the various Federal awards and between Federal and non-Federal awards/activities.

2. Allocated Central Services

For each allocated central service, the plan must also include the following: a brief description of the service, an identification of the unit rendering the service and the operating agencies receiving the service, the items of expense included in the cost of the service, the method used to distribute the cost of the service to benefitted agencies, and a summary schedule showing the allocation of each service to the specific benefitted agencies. If any self-insurance funds or fringe benefits costs are treated as allocated (rather than billed) central services, documentation discussed in subsections 3.b. and c. must also be included.

3. Billed Services

a. *General.* The information described in this section must be provided for all billed central services, including internal service funds, self-insurance funds, and fringe benefit funds.

b. Internal service funds.

(1) For each internal service fund or similar activity with an operating budget of $5 million or more, the plan must include: a brief description of each service; a balance sheet for each fund based on individual accounts contained in the governmental unit's accounting system; a revenue/expenses statement, with revenues broken out by source, e.g., regular billings, interest earned, etc.; a listing of all non-operating transfers (as defined by Generally Accepted Accounting Principles (GAAP)) into and out of the fund; a description of the procedures (methodology) used to charge the costs of each service to users, including how billing rates are determined; a schedule of current rates; and, a schedule comparing total revenues (including imputed revenues) generated by the service to the allowable costs of the service, as determined under this Part, with an explanation of how variances will be handled.

(2) Revenues must consist of all revenues generated by the service, including unbilled and uncollected revenues. If some users were not billed for the services (or were not billed at the full rate for that class of users), a schedule showing the full imputed revenues associated with these users must be provided. Expenses must be broken out by object cost categories (e.g., salaries, supplies, etc.).

c. *Self-insurance funds.* For each self-insurance fund, the plan must include: the fund balance sheet; a statement of revenue and expenses including a summary of billings and claims paid by agency; a listing of all non-operating transfers into and out of the fund; the type(s) of risk(s) covered by the fund (e.g., automobile liability, workers' compensation, etc.); an explanation of how the level of fund contributions are determined, including a copy of the current actuarial report (with the actuarial assumptions used) if the contributions are determined on an actuarial basis; and, a description of the procedures used to charge or allocate fund contributions to benefitted activities. Reserve levels in excess of claims (1) submitted and adjudicated but not paid, (2) submitted but not adjudicated, and (3) incurred but not submitted must be identified and explained.

d. *Fringe benefits.* For fringe benefit costs, the plan must include: a listing of fringe benefits provided to covered employees, and the overall annual cost of each type of benefit; current fringe benefit policies; and procedures used to charge or allocate the costs of the benefits to benefitted activities. In addition, for pension and post-retirement health insurance plans, the following information must be provided: the governmental unit's funding policies, e.g., legislative bills, trust agreements, or state-mandated contribution rules, if different from actuarially determined rates; the pension plan's costs accrued for the year; the amount funded, and date(s) of funding; a copy of the current actuarial report (including the actuarial assumptions); the plan trustee's report; and, a schedule from the activity showing the value of the interest cost associated with late funding.

4. Required Certification

Each central service cost allocation plan will be accompanied by a certification in the following form:

CERTIFICATE OF COST ALLOCATION PLAN

This is to certify that I have reviewed the cost allocation plan submitted herewith and to the best of my knowledge and belief:

(1) All costs included in this proposal [identify date] to establish cost allocations or billings for [identify period covered by plan] are allowable in accordance with the requirements of this Part and the Federal award(s) to which they apply. Unallowable costs have been adjusted for in allocating costs as indicated in the cost allocation plan.

(2) All costs included in this proposal are properly allocable to Federal awards on the basis of a beneficial or causal relationship between the expenses incurred and the Federal awards to which they are allocated in accordance with applicable requirements. Further, the same costs that have been treated as indirect costs have not been claimed as direct costs. Similar types of costs have been accounted for consistently.

I declare that the foregoing is true and correct.

Governmental Unit: _____
Signature: _____
Name of Official: _____
Title: _____
Date of Execution: _____

F. NEGOTIATION AND APPROVAL OF CENTRAL SERVICE PLANS

1. Federal Cognizant Agency for Indirect Costs Assignments for Cost Negotiation

In general, unless different arrangements are agreed to by the concerned Federal agencies, for central service cost allocation plans, the cognizant agency responsible for review and approval is the Federal agency with the largest dollar value of total Federal awards with a governmental unit. For indirect cost rates and departmental indirect cost allocation plans, the cognizant agency is the Federal agency with the largest dollar value of direct Federal awards with a governmental unit or component, as appropriate.

Once designated as the cognizant agency for indirect costs, the Federal agency must remain so for a period of five years. In addition, the following Federal agencies continue to be responsible for the indicated governmental entities:

Department of Health and Human Services— Public assistance and state-wide cost allocation plans for all states (including the District of Columbia and Puerto Rico), state and local hospitals, libraries and health districts.

Department of the Interior—Indian tribal governments, territorial governments, and state and local park and recreational districts.

Department of Labor—State and local labor departments.

Department of Education—School districts and state and local education agencies.

Department of Agriculture—State and local agriculture departments.

Department of Transportation—State and local airport and port authorities and transit districts.

Department of Commerce—State and local economic development districts.

Department of Housing and Urban Development—State and local housing and development districts.

Environmental Protection Agency—State and local water and sewer districts.

2. Review

All proposed central service cost allocation plans that are required to be submitted will be reviewed, negotiated, and approved by the cognizant agency for indirect costs on ·a timely basis. The cognizant agency for indirect costs will review the proposal within six months of receipt of the proposal and either negotiate/approve the proposal or advise the governmental unit of the additional documentation needed to support/evaluate the proposed plan or the changes required to make the proposal acceptable. Once an agreement with the governmental unit has been reached, the agreement will be accepted and used by all Federal agencies, unless prohibited or limited by statute. Where a Federal awarding agency has reason to believe that special operating factors affecting its Federal awards necessitate special consideration, the funding agency will, prior to the time the plans are negotiated, notify the cognizant agency for indirect costs.

3. Agreement

The results of each negotiation must be formalized in a written agreement between the cognizant agency for indirect costs and the governmental unit. This agreement will be subject to re-opening if the agreement is subsequently found to violate a statute or the information upon which the plan was negotiated is later found to be materially in-

complete or inaccurate. The results of the negotiation must be made available to all Federal agencies for their use.

4. Adjustments

Negotiated cost allocation plans based on a proposal later found to have included costs that: (a) are unallowable (i) as specified by law or regulation, (ii) as identified in subpart F, General Provisions for selected Items of Cost of this Part, or (iii) by the terms and conditions of Federal awards, or (b) are unallowable because they are clearly not allocable to Federal awards, must be adjusted, or a refund must be made at the option of the cognizant agency for indirect costs, including earned or imputed interest from the date of transfer and debt interest, if applicable, chargeable in accordance with applicable Federal cognizant agency for indirect costs regulations. Adjustments or cash refunds may include, at the option of the cognizant agency for indirect costs, earned or imputed interest from the date of expenditure and delinquent debt interest, if applicable, chargeable in accordance with applicable cognizant agency claims collection regulations. These adjustments or refunds are designed to correct the plans and do not constitute a re-opening of the negotiation.

G. OTHER POLICIES

1. Billed Central Service Activities

Each billed central service activity must separately account for all revenues (including imputed revenues) generated by the service, expenses incurred to furnish the service, and profit/loss.

2. Working Capital Reserves

Internal service funds are dependent upon a reasonable level of working capital reserve to operate from one billing cycle to the next. Charges by an internal service activity to provide for the establishment and maintenance of a reasonable level of working capital reserve, in addition to the full recovery of costs, are allowable. A working capital reserve as part of retained earnings of up to 60 calendar days cash expenses for normal operating purposes is considered reasonable. A working capital reserve exceeding 60 calendar days may be approved by the cognizant agency for indirect costs in exceptional cases.

3. Carry-Forward Adjustments of Allocated Central Service Costs

Allocated central service costs are usually negotiated and approved for a future fiscal year on a "fixed with carry-forward" basis. Under this procedure, the fixed amounts for the future year covered by agreement are not subject to adjustment for that year. However, when the actual costs of the year

214

involved become known, the differences between the fixed amounts previously approved and the actual costs will be carried forward and used as an adjustment to the fixed amounts established for a later year. This "carry-forward" procedure applies to all central services whose costs were fixed in the approved plan. However, a carry-forward adjustment is not permitted, for a central service activity that was not included in the approved plan, or for unallowable costs that must be reimbursed immediately.

4. Adjustments of Billed Central Services

Billing rates used to charge Federal awards must be based on the estimated costs of providing the services, including an estimate of the allocable central service costs. A comparison of the revenue generated by each billed service (including total revenues whether or not billed or collected) to the actual allowable costs of the service will be made at least annually, and an adjustment will be made for the difference between the revenue and the allowable costs. These adjustments will be made through one of the following adjustment methods: (a) a cash refund including earned or imputed interest from the date of transfer and debt interest, if applicable, chargeable in accordance with applicable Federal cognizant agency for indirect costs regulations to the Federal Government for the Federal share of the adjustment, (b) credits to the amounts charged to the individual programs, (c) adjustments to future billing rates, or (d) adjustments to allocated central service costs. Adjustments to allocated central services will not be permitted where the total amount of the adjustment for a particular service (Federal share and non-Federal) share exceeds $500,000. Adjustment methods may include, at the option of the cognizant agency, earned or imputed interest from the date of expenditure and delinquent debt interest, if applicable, chargeable in accordance with applicable cognizant agency claims collection regulations.

5. Records Retention

All central service cost allocation plans and related documentation used as a basis for claiming costs under Federal awards must be retained for audit in accordance with the records retention requirements contained in Subpart D—Post Federal Award Requirements, of Part 200.

6. Appeals

If a dispute arises in the negotiation of a plan between the cognizant agency for indirect costs and the governmental unit, the dispute must be resolved in accordance with the appeals procedures of the cognizant agency for indirect costs.

7. OMB Assistance

To the extent that problems are encountered among the Federal agencies or governmental units in connection with the negotiation and approval process, OMB will lend assistance, as required, to resolve such problems in a timely manner.

APPENDIX VI TO PART 200—PUBLIC ASSISTANCE COST ALLOCATION PLANS

A. GENERAL

Federally-financed programs administered by state public assistance agencies are funded predominately by the Department of Health and Human Services (HHS). In support of its stewardship requirements, HHS has published requirements for the development, documentation, submission, negotiation, and approval of public assistance cost allocation plans in Subpart E of 45 CFR Part 95. All administrative costs (direct and indirect) are normally charged to Federal awards by implementing the public assistance cost allocation plan. This Appendix extends these requirements to all Federal agencies whose programs are administered by a state public assistance agency. Major federally-financed programs typically administered by state public assistance agencies include: Temporary Aid to Needy Families (TANF), Medicaid, Food Stamps, Child Support Enforcement, Adoption Assistance and Foster Care, and Social Services Block Grant.

B. DEFINITIONS

1. *State public assistance agency* means a state agency administering or supervising the administration of one or more public assistance programs operated by the state as identified in Subpart E of 45 CFR Part 95. For the purpose of this Appendix, these programs include all programs administered by the state public assistance agency.

2. *State public assistance agency costs* means all costs incurred by, or allocable to, the state public assistance agency, except expenditures for financial assistance, medical contractor payments, food stamps, and payments for services and goods provided directly to program recipients.

C. POLICY

State public assistance agencies will develop, document and implement, and the Federal Government will review, negotiate, and approve, public assistance cost allocation plans in accordance with Subpart E of 45 CFR Part 95. The plan will include all programs administered by the state public assistance agency. Where a letter of approval or disapproval is transmitted to a state public assistance agency in accordance with Subpart E, the letter will apply to all Federal agencies and programs. The remaining sections of this Appendix (except for the requirement for certification) summarize the provisions of Subpart E of 45 CFR Part 95.

D. SUBMISSION, DOCUMENTATION, AND APPROVAL OF PUBLIC ASSISTANCE COST ALLOCATION PLANS

1. State public assistance agencies are required to promptly submit amendments to the cost allocation plan to HHS for review and approval.

2. Under the coordination process outlined in section E, Review of Implementation of Approved Plans, affected Federal agencies will review all new plans and plan amendments and provide comments, as appropriate, to HHS. The effective date of the plan or plan amendment will be the first day of the calendar quarter following the event that required the amendment, unless another date is specifically approved by HHS. HHS, as the cognizant agency for indirect costs acting on behalf of all affected Federal agencies, will, as necessary, conduct negotiations with the state public assistance agency and will inform the state agency of the action taken on the plan or plan amendment.

E. REVIEW OF IMPLEMENTATION OF APPROVED PLANS

1. Since public assistance cost allocation plans are of a narrative nature, the review during the plan approval process consists of evaluating the appropriateness of the proposed groupings of costs (cost centers) and the related allocation bases. As such, the Federal government needs some assurance that the cost allocation plan has been implemented as approved. This is accomplished by reviews by the funding agencies, single audits, or audits conducted by the cognizant audit agency.

2. Where inappropriate charges affecting more than one funding agency are identified, the cognizant HHS cost negotiation office will be advised and will take the lead in resolving the issue(s) as provided for in Subpart E of 45 CFR Part 95.

3. If a dispute arises in the negotiation of a plan or from a disallowance involving two or more funding agencies, the dispute must be resolved in accordance with the appeals procedures set out in 45 CFR Part 16. Disputes involving only one funding agency will be resolved in accordance with the Federal awarding agency's appeal process.

4. To the extent that problems are encountered among the Federal agencies or governmental units in connection with the negotiation and approval process, the Office of Management and Budget will lend assistance, as required, to resolve such problems in a timely manner.

F. UNALLOWABLE COSTS

Claims developed under approved cost allocation plans will be based on allowable costs as identified in this Part. Where unallowable costs have been claimed and reimbursed, they will be refunded to the program that reimbursed the unallowable cost using one of the following methods: (a) a cash refund, (b) offset to a subsequent claim, or (c) credits to the amounts charged to individual Federal awards. Cash refunds, offsets, and credits may include at the option of the cognizant agency for indirect cost, earned or imputed interest from the date of expenditure and delinquent debt interest, if applicable, chargeable in accordance with applicable cognizant agency for indirect cost claims collection regulations.

APPENDIX VII TO PART 200—STATES AND LOCAL GOVERNMENT AND INDIAN TRIBE INDIRECT COST PROPOSALS

A. GENERAL

1. Indirect costs are those that have been incurred for common or joint purposes. These costs benefit more than one cost objective and cannot be readily identified with a particular final cost objective without effort disproportionate to the results achieved. After direct costs have been determined and assigned directly to Federal awards and other activities as appropriate, indirect costs are those remaining to be allocated to benefitted cost objectives. A cost may not be allocated to a Federal award as an indirect cost if any other cost incurred for the same purpose, in like circumstances, has been assigned to a Federal award as a direct cost.

2. Indirect costs include (a) the indirect costs originating in each department or agency of the governmental unit carrying out Federal awards and (b) the costs of central governmental services distributed through the central service cost allocation plan (as described in Appendix V to Part 200—State/Local Government and Indian Tribe-Wide Central Service Cost Allocation Plans) and not otherwise treated as direct costs.

3. Indirect costs are normally charged to Federal awards by the use of an indirect cost rate. A separate indirect cost rate(s) is usually necessary for each department or agency of the governmental unit claiming indirect costs under Federal awards. Guidelines and illustrations of indirect cost proposals are provided in a brochure published by the Department of Health and Human Services entitled "*A Guide for States and Local Government Agencies: Cost Principles and Procedures for Establishing Cost Allocation Plans and Indirect Cost Rates for Grants and Contracts with*

the Federal Government." A copy of this brochure may be obtained from the Superintendent of Documents, U.S. Government Printing Office.

4. Because of the diverse characteristics and accounting practices of governmental units, the types of costs which may be classified as indirect costs cannot be specified in all situations. However, typical examples of indirect costs may include certain state/local-wide central service costs, general administration of the non-Federal entity accounting and personnel services performed within the non-Federal entity, depreciation on buildings and equipment, the costs of operating and maintaining facilities.

5. This Appendix does not apply to state public assistance agencies. These agencies should refer instead to Appendix VII to Part 200—States and Local Government and Indian Tribe Indirect Cost Proposals.

B. DEFINITIONS

1. *Base* means the accumulated direct costs (normally either total direct salaries and wages or total direct costs exclusive of any extraordinary or distorting expenditures) used to distribute indirect costs to individual Federal awards. The direct cost base selected should result in each Federal award bearing a fair share of the indirect costs in reasonable relation to the benefits received from the costs.

2. *Base period* for the allocation of indirect costs is the period in which such costs are incurred and accumulated for allocation to activities performed in that period. The base period normally should coincide with the governmental unit's fiscal year, but in any event, must be so selected as to avoid inequities in the allocation of costs.

3. *Cognizant agency for indirect costs* means the Federal agency responsible for reviewing and approving the governmental unit's indirect cost rate(s) on the behalf of the Federal government. The cognizant agency for indirect costs assignment is described in Appendix VI, section F, Negotiation and Approval of Central Service Plans.

4. *Final rate* means an indirect cost rate applicable to a specified past period which is based on the actual allowable costs of the period. A final audited rate is not subject to adjustment.

5. *Fixed rate* means an indirect cost rate which has the same characteristics as a predetermined rate, except that the difference between the estimated costs and the actual, allowable costs of the period covered by the rate is carried forward as an adjustment to the rate computation of a subsequent period.

6. *Indirect cost pool* is the accumulated costs that jointly benefit two or more programs or other cost objectives.

7. *Indirect cost rate* is a device for determining in a reasonable manner the proportion of indirect costs each program should

bear. It is the ratio (expressed as a percentage) of the indirect costs to a direct cost base.

8. *Indirect cost rate proposal* means the documentation prepared by a governmental unit or subdivision thereof to substantiate its request for the establishment of an indirect cost rate.

9. *Predetermined rate* means an indirect cost rate, applicable to a specified current or future period, usually the governmental unit's fiscal year. This rate is based on an estimate of the costs to be incurred during the period. Except under very unusual circumstances, a predetermined rate is not subject to adjustment. (Because of legal constraints, predetermined rates are not permitted for Federal contracts; they may, however, be used for grants or cooperative agreements.) Predetermined rates may not be used by governmental units that have not submitted and negotiated the rate with the cognizant agency for indirect costs. In view of the potential advantages offered by this procedure, negotiation of predetermined rates for indirect costs for a period of two to four years should be the norm in those situations where the cost experience and other pertinent facts available are deemed sufficient to enable the parties involved to reach an informed judgment as to the probable level of indirect costs during the ensuing accounting periods.

10. *Provisional rate* means a temporary indirect cost rate applicable to a specified period which is used for funding, interim reimbursement, and reporting indirect costs on Federal awards pending the establishment of a "final" rate for that period.

C. ALLOCATION OF INDIRECT COSTS AND DETERMINATION OF INDIRECT COST RATES

1. General

a. Where a governmental unit's department or agency has only one major function, or where all its major functions benefit from the indirect costs to approximately the same degree, the allocation of indirect costs and the computation of an indirect cost rate may be accomplished through simplified allocation procedures as described in subsection 2.

b. Where a governmental unit's department or agency has several major functions which benefit from its indirect costs in varying degrees, the allocation of indirect costs may require the accumulation of such costs into separate cost groupings which then are allocated individually to benefitted functions by means of a base which best measures the relative degree of benefit. The indirect costs allocated to each function are then distributed to individual Federal awards and other activities included in that function by means of an indirect cost rate(s).

c. Specific methods for allocating indirect costs and computing indirect cost rates along with the conditions under which each method should be used are described in subsections 2, 3 and 4.

2. Simplified Method

a. Where a non-Federal entity's major functions benefit from its indirect costs to approximately the same degree, the allocation of indirect costs may be accomplished by (1) classifying the non-Federal entity's total costs for the base period as either direct or indirect, and (2) dividing the total allowable indirect costs (net of applicable credits) by an equitable distribution base. The result of this process is an indirect cost rate which is used to distribute indirect costs to individual Federal awards. The rate should be expressed as the percentage which the total amount of allowable indirect costs bears to the base selected. This method should also be used where a governmental unit's department or agency has only one major function encompassing a number of individual projects or activities, and may be used where the level of Federal awards to that department or agency is relatively small.

b. Both the direct costs and the indirect costs must exclude capital expenditures and unallowable costs. However, unallowable costs must be included in the direct costs if they represent activities to which indirect costs are properly allocable.

c. The distribution base may be (1) total direct costs (excluding capital expenditures and other distorting items, such as pass-through funds, subcontracts in excess of $25,000, participant support costs, etc.), (2) direct salaries and wages, or (3) another base which results in an equitable distribution.

3. Multiple Allocation Base Method

a. Where a non-Federal entity's indirect costs benefit its major functions in varying degrees, such costs must be accumulated into separate cost groupings. Each grouping must then be allocated individually to benefitted functions by means of a base which best measures the relative benefits.

b. The cost groupings should be established so as to permit the allocation of each grouping on the basis of benefits provided to the major functions. Each grouping should constitute a pool of expenses that are of like character in terms of the functions they benefit and in terms of the allocation base which best measures the relative benefits provided to each function. The number of separate groupings should be held within practical limits, taking into consideration the materiality of the amounts involved and the degree of precision needed.

c. Actual conditions must be taken into account in selecting the base to be used in allocating the expenses in each grouping to benefitted functions. When an allocation can be made by assignment of a cost grouping directly to the function benefitted, the allocation must be made in that manner. When the expenses in a grouping are more general in nature, the allocation should be made through the use of a selected base which produces results that are equitable to both the Federal government and the governmental unit. In general, any cost element or related factor associated with the governmental unit's activities is potentially adaptable for use as an allocation base provided that: (1) it can readily be expressed in terms of dollars or other quantitative measures (total direct costs, direct salaries and wages, staff hours applied, square feet used, hours of usage, number of documents processed, population served, and the like), and (2) it is common to the benefitted functions during the base period.

d. Except where a special indirect cost rate(s) is required in accordance with paragraph (C)(4) of this Appendix, the separate groupings of indirect costs allocated to each major function must be aggregated and treated as a common pool for that function. The costs in the common pool must then be distributed to individual Federal awards included in that function by use of a single indirect cost rate.

e. The distribution base used in computing the indirect cost rate for each function may be (1) total direct costs (excluding capital expenditures and other distorting items such as pass-through funds, subcontracts in excess of $25,000, participant support costs, etc.), (2) direct salaries and wages, or (3) another base which results in an equitable distribution. An indirect cost rate should be developed for each separate indirect cost pool developed. The rate in each case should be stated as the percentage relationship between the particular indirect cost pool and the distribution base identified with that pool.

4. Special Indirect Cost Rates

a. In some instances, a single indirect cost rate for all activities of a non-Federal entity or for each major function of the agency may not be appropriate. It may not take into account those different factors which may substantially affect the indirect costs applicable to a particular program or group of programs. The factors may include the physical location of the work, the level of administrative support required, the nature of the facilities or other resources employed, the organizational arrangements used, or any combination thereof. When a particular Federal award is carried out in an environment which appears to generate a significantly different level of indirect costs, provisions should be made for a separate indirect cost pool applicable to that Federal award. The separate indirect cost pool should be developed during the course of the regular allocation process, and the separate indirect cost rate resulting therefrom should be used, provided that: (1) The rate differs significantly from the rate which would have been developed under paragraphs (C)(2) and (C)(3) of this Appendix, and (2) the Federal award to which the rate would apply is material in amount.

b. Where Federal statutes restrict the reimbursement of certain indirect costs, it may be necessary to develop a special rate for the affected Federal award. Where a "restricted rate" is required, the same procedure for developing a non-restricted rate will be used except for the additional step of the elimination from the indirect cost pool those costs for which the law prohibits reimbursement.

D. SUBMISSION AND DOCUMENTATION OF PROPOSALS

1. Submission of Indirect Cost Rate Proposals

a. All departments or agencies of the governmental unit desiring to claim indirect costs under Federal awards must prepare an indirect cost rate proposal and related documentation to support those costs. The proposal and related documentation must be retained for audit in accordance with the records retention requirements contained in the Common Rule.

b. A governmental department or agency unit that receives more than $35 million in direct Federal funding must submit its indirect cost rate proposal to its cognizant agency for indirect costs. Other governmental department or agency must develop an indirect cost proposal in accordance with the requirements of this Part and maintain the proposal and related supporting documentation for audit. These governmental departments or agencies are not required to submit their proposals unless they are specifically requested to do so by the cognizant agency for indirect costs. Where a non-Federal entity only receives funds as a subrecipient, the pass-through entity will be responsible for negotiating and/or monitoring the subrecipient's indirect costs.

c. Each Indian tribal government desiring reimbursement of indirect costs must submit its indirect cost proposal to the Department of the Interior (its cognizant agency for indirect costs).

d. Indirect cost proposals must be developed (and, when required, submitted) within six months after the close of the governmental unit's fiscal year, unless an exception is approved by the cognizant agency for indirect costs. If the proposed central service cost allocation plan for the same period has not been approved by that time, the indirect cost proposal may be prepared including an amount for central services that is based on the latest federally-approved central service cost allocation plan. The difference between these central service amounts and the

amounts ultimately approved will be compensated for by an adjustment in a subsequent period.

2. Documentation of Proposals

The following must be included with each indirect cost proposal:

a. The rates proposed, including subsidiary work sheets and other relevant data, cross referenced and reconciled to the financial data noted in subsection b. Allocated central service costs will be supported by the summary table included in the approved central service cost allocation plan. This summary table is not required to be submitted with the indirect cost proposal if the central service cost allocation plan for the same fiscal year has been approved by the cognizant agency for indirect costs and is available to the funding agency.

b. A copy of the financial data (financial statements, comprehensive annual financial report, executive budgets, accounting reports, etc.) upon which the rate is based. Adjustments resulting from the use of unaudited data will be recognized, where appropriate, by the Federal cognizant agency for indirect costs in a subsequent proposal.

c. The approximate amount of direct base costs incurred under Federal awards. These costs should be broken out between salaries and wages and other direct costs.

d. A chart showing the organizational structure of the agency during the period for which the proposal applies, along with a functional statement(s) noting the duties and/or responsibilities of all units that comprise the agency. (Once this is submitted, only revisions need be submitted with subsequent proposals.)

3. Required certification.

Each indirect cost rate proposal must be accompanied by a certification in the following form:

CERTIFICATE OF INDIRECT COSTS

This is to certify that I have reviewed the indirect cost rate proposal submitted herewith and to the best of my knowledge and belief:

(1) All costs included in this proposal [identify date] to establish billing or final indirect costs rates for [identify period covered by rate] are allowable in accordance with the requirements of the Federal award(s) to which they apply and the provisions of this Part. Unallowable costs have been adjusted for in allocating costs as indicated in the indirect cost proposal

(2) All costs included in this proposal are properly allocable to Federal awards on the basis of a beneficial or causal relationship between the expenses incurred and the agreements to which they are allocated in accordance with applicable requirements. Further,

the same costs that have been treated as indirect costs have not been claimed as direct costs. Similar types of costs have been accounted for consistently and the Federal government will be notified of any accounting changes that would affect the predetermined rate.

I declare that the foregoing is true and correct.

Governmental Unit: _____
Signature: _____
Name of Official: _____
Title: _____
Date of Execution: _____

E. NEGOTIATION AND APPROVAL OF RATES.

1. Indirect cost rates will be reviewed, negotiated, and approved by the cognizant agency on a timely basis. Once a rate has been agreed upon, it will be accepted and used by all Federal agencies unless prohibited or limited by statute. Where a Federal awarding agency has reason to believe that special operating factors affecting its Federal awards necessitate special indirect cost rates, the funding agency will, prior to the time the rates are negotiated, notify the cognizant agency for indirect costs.

2. The use of predetermined rates, if allowed, is encouraged where the cognizant agency for indirect costs has reasonable assurance based on past experience and reliable projection of the non-Federal entity's costs, that the rate is not likely to exceed a rate based on actual costs. Long-term agreements utilizing predetermined rates extending over two or more years are encouraged, where appropriate.

3. The results of each negotiation must be formalized in a written agreement between the cognizant agency for indirect costs and the governmental unit. This agreement will be subject to re-opening if the agreement is subsequently found to violate a statute, or the information upon which the plan was negotiated is later found to be materially incomplete or inaccurate. The agreed upon rates must be made available to all Federal agencies for their use.

4. Refunds must be made if proposals are later found to have included costs that (a) are unallowable (i) as specified by law or regulation, (ii) as identified in § 200.420 Considerations for selected items of cost, of this Part, or (iii) by the terms and conditions of Federal awards, or (b) are unallowable because they are clearly not allocable to Federal awards. These adjustments or refunds will be made regardless of the type of rate negotiated (predetermined, final, fixed, or provisional).

F. OTHER POLICIES

1. Fringe Benefit Rates

If overall fringe benefit rates are not approved for the governmental unit as part of the central service cost allocation plan, these rates will be reviewed, negotiated and approved for individual recipient agencies during the indirect cost negotiation process. In these cases, a proposed fringe benefit rate computation should accompany the indirect cost proposal. If fringe benefit rates are not used at the recipient agency level (i.e., the agency specifically identifies fringe benefit costs to individual employees), the governmental unit should so advise the cognizant agency for indirect costs.

2. Billed Services Provided by the Recipient Agency

In some cases, governmental departments or agencies (components of the governmental unit) provide and bill for services similar to those covered by central service cost allocation plans (e.g., computer centers). Where this occurs, the governmental departments or agencies (components of the governmental unit)should be guided by the requirements in Appendix VI relating to the development of billing rates and documentation requirements, and should advise the cognizant agency for indirect costs of any billed services. Reviews of these types of services (including reviews of costing/billing methodology, profits or losses, etc.) will be made on a case-by-case basis as warranted by the circumstances involved.

3. Indirect Cost Allocations Not Using Rates

In certain situations, governmental departments or agencies (components of the governmental unit), because of the nature of their Federal awards, may be required to develop a cost allocation plan that distributes indirect (and, in some cases, direct) costs to the specific funding sources. In these cases, a narrative cost allocation methodology should be developed, documented, maintained for audit, or submitted, as appropriate, to the cognizant agency for indirect costs for review, negotiation, and approval.

4. Appeals

If a dispute arises in a negotiation of an indirect cost rate (or other rate) between the cognizant agency for indirect costs and the governmental unit, the dispute must be resolved in accordance with the appeals procedures of the cognizant agency for indirect costs.

5. Collection of Unallowable Costs and Erroneous Payments

Costs specifically identified as unallowable and charged to Federal awards either directly or indirectly will be refunded (including interest chargeable in accordance with applicable Federal cognizant agency for indirect costs regulations).

6. OMB Assistance

To the extent that problems are encountered among the Federal agencies or governmental units in connection with the negotiation and approval process, OMB will lend assistance, as required, to resolve such problems in a timely manner.

APPENDIX VIII TO PART 200—NONPROFIT ORGANIZATIONS EXEMPTED FROM SUBPART E—COST PRINCIPLES OF PART 200

1. Advance Technology Institute (ATI), Charleston, South Carolina
2. Aerospace Corporation, El Segundo, California
3. American Institutes of Research (AIR), Washington, DC
4. Argonne National Laboratory, Chicago, Illinois
5. Atomic Casualty Commission, Washington, DC
6. Battelle Memorial Institute, Headquartered in Columbus, Ohio
7. Brookhaven National Laboratory, Upton, New York
8. Charles Stark Draper Laboratory, Incorporated, Cambridge, Massachusetts
9. CNA Corporation (CNAC), Alexandria, Virginia
10. Environmental Institute of Michigan, Ann Arbor, Michigan
11. Georgia Institute of Technology/Georgia Tech Applied Research Corporation/Georgia Tech Research Institute, Atlanta, Georgia
12. Hanford Environmental Health Foundation, Richland, Washington
13. IIT Research Institute, Chicago, Illinois
14. Institute of Gas Technology, Chicago, Illinois
15. Institute for Defense Analysis, Alexandria, Virginia
16. LMI, McLean, Virginia
17. Mitre Corporation, Bedford, Massachusetts
18. Noblis, Inc., Falls Church, Virginia

19. National Radiological Astronomy Observatory, Green Bank, West Virginia
20. National Renewable Energy Laboratory, Golden, Colorado
21. Oak Ridge Associated Universities, Oak Ridge, Tennessee
22. Rand Corporation, Santa Monica, California
23. Research Triangle Institute, Research Triangle Park, North Carolina
24. Riverside Research Institute, New York, New York
25. South Carolina Research Authority (SCRA), Charleston, South Carolina
26. Southern Research Institute, Birmingham, Alabama
27. Southwest Research Institute, San Antonio, Texas
28. SRI International, Menlo Park, California
29. Syracuse Research Corporation, Syracuse, New York
30. Universities Research Association, Incorporated (National Acceleration Lab), Argonne, Illinois
31. Urban Institute, Washington DC
32. Non-profit insurance companies, such as Blue Cross and Blue Shield Organizations
33. Other non-profit organizations as negotiated with Federal awarding agencies

APPENDIX IX TO PART 200—HOSPITAL COST PRINCIPLES

Based on initial feedback, OMB proposes to establish a review process to consider existing hospital cost determine how best to update and align them with this Part. Until such time as revised guidance is proposed and implemented for hospitals, the existing principles located at 45 CFR Part 74 Appendix E, entitled "Principles for Determining Cost Applicable to Research and Development Under Grants and Contracts with Hospitals," remain in effect.

APPENDIX X TO PART 200—DATA COLLECTION FORM (FORM SF–SAC)

The Data Collection Form SF–SAC is available on the FAC Web site.

APPENDIX XI TO PART 200—COMPLIANCE SUPPLEMENT

The compliance supplement is available on the OMB Web site: (e.g. for 2013 here *http://www.whitehouse.gov/omb/circulars/*)

Subtitle B—Federal Agency Regulations for Grants and Agreements

CHAPTER III—DEPARTMENT OF HEALTH AND HUMAN SERVICES

225

PART 376—NONPROCUREMENT DEBARMENT AND SUSPENSION

Sec.
376.10 What does this part do?
376.20 Does this part apply to me?
376.30 What policies and procedures must I follow?

Subpart A—General

376.137 Who in the Department of Health and Human Services (HHS) may grant an exception to let an excluded person participate in a covered transaction?
376.147 Does an exclusion from participation in Federal health care programs under Title XI of the Social Security Act affect a person's eligibility to participate in nonprocurement and procurement transactions?

Subpart B—Covered Transactions

376.220 What contracts and subcontracts, in addition to those listed in 2 CFR 180.220, are covered transactions?

Subpart C—Responsibilities of Participants Regarding Transactions

376.332 What methods must I use to pass requirements down to participants at lower tiers with whom I intend to do business?
376.370 What are the obligations of Medicare carriers and intermediaries?

Subpart D—Responsibilities of Federal Agency Officials Regarding Transactions

376.437 What method do I use to communicate to a participant the requirements described in the OMB guidance at 2 CFR 180.435?

Subpart E—Excluded Parties List System [Reserved]

Subpart F—General Principles Relating to Suspension and Debarment Actions [Reserved]

Subpart G—Suspension [Reserved]

Subpart H—Debarment [Reserved]

Subpart I—Definitions

376.935 Disqualified (HHS supplement to government-wide definition at 2 CFR 180.935).
376.995 Principal (HHS supplement to government-wide definition at 2 CFR 180.995).

Subpart J [Reserved]

AUTHORITY: 5 U.S.C. 301; 31 U.S.C. 6101 (note); E.O. 12689 (3 CFR, 1989 Comp., p. 235); E.O. 12549 (3 CFR, 1986 Comp., p. 189); E.O. 11738 (3 CFR, 1973 Comp., p. 799).

SOURCE: 72 FR 9234, Mar. 1, 2007, unless otherwise noted.

§ 376.10 What does this part do?

This part adopts the Office of Management and Budget (OMB) guidance in subparts A through I of 2 CFR part 180, as supplemented by this part, as the Department of Health and Human Services (HHS or Department) policies and procedures for nonprocurement debarment and suspension. HHS thereby gives regulatory effect to the OMB guidance as supplemented by this part. This part satisfies the requirements in 2 CFR 180.20, section 3 of Executive Order 12549, "Debarment and Suspension" (3 CFR 1986 Comp., p. 189), Executive Order 12689, "Debarment and Suspension" (3 CFR 1989 Comp., p. 235) and 31 U.S.C. 6101 note (Section 2455, Pub. L. 103–355, 108 Stat. 3327).

§ 376.20 Does this part apply to me?

This part and, through this part, pertinent portions of the OMB guidance in subparts A through I of 2 CFR part 180 (see table at 2 CFR 180.100(b)), apply to you if you are a—

(a) Participant or principal in a "covered transaction" under subpart B of 2 CFR part 180, as supplemented by this part, and the definition of nonprocurement transaction" at 2 CFR 180.970.

(b) Respondent in HHS suspension or debarment action;

(c) HHS debarment or suspension official;

(d) HHS grants officer, agreements officer, or other HHS official authorized to enter into any type of nonprocurement transaction that is a covered transaction.

§ 376.30 What policies and procedures must I follow?

The policies and procedures that you must follow are the policies and procedures specified in each applicable section of the OMB guidance in subparts A through I of 2 CFR part 180, including the corresponding section that HHS published in 2 CFR part 376 identified by the same section number. The contracts under a nonprocurement transaction, that are covered transactions, for example, are specified by section 220 of the OMB guidance (*i.e.*, 2 CFR 180.220) as supplemented by section 220 in this part (*i.e.*, 2 CFR 376.220). For any section of OMB guidance in subparts A through I of 2 CFR part 180 that has no corresponding section in this part, HHS policies and procedures are those in the OMB guidance at 2 CFR part 180.

Subpart A—General

§ 376.137 Who in the Department of Health and Human Services (HHS) may grant an exception to let an excluded person participate in a covered transaction?

The HHS Debarring/Suspension Official has the authority to grant an exception to let an excluded person participate in a covered transaction as provided at 2 CFR 180.135.

§ 376.147 Does an exclusion from participation in Federal health care programs under Title XI of the Social Security Act affect a person's eligibility to participate in nonprocurement and procurement transactions?

Any individual or entity excluded from participation in Medicare, Medicaid, and other Federal health care programs under Title XI of the Social Security Act, 42 U.S.C. 1320a-7, 1320a-7a, 1320c-5, or 1395ccc, and implementing regulation at 42 CFR part 1001, will be subject to the prohibitions against participating in covered transactions, as set forth in this part and part 180, and is prohibited from participating in all Federal government procurement programs and nonprocurement programs. For example, if an individual or entity is excluded by the HHS Office of the Inspector General from participation in Medicare, Medicaid, and/or other Federal health care programs, in accordance with 42 U.S.C. 1320a-7, then that individual or entity is prohibited from participating in all Federal government procurement and nonprocurement programs (42 CFR part 1001).

Subpart B—Covered Transactions

§ 376.220 What contracts and subcontracts, in addition to those listed in 2 CFR 180.220, are covered transactions?

In addition to the contracts covered under 2 CFR 180.220(b), this part also applies to all lower tiers of subcontracts under covered nonprocurement transactions, as permitted under the OMB guidance at 2 CFR 180.220(c). (See optional lower tier coverage in the diagram in the appendix to 2 CFR part 180.)

Subpart C—Responsibilities of Participants Regarding Transactions

§ 376.332 What methods must I use to pass requirements down to participants at lower tiers with whom I intend to do business?

To communicate the requirements to lower-tier participants, you must include a term or condition in the lower-tier transaction requiring the lower-tier participant's compliance with 2 CFR part 180, as supplemented by this subpart.

§ 376.370 What are the obligations of Medicare carriers and intermediaries?

Because Medicare carriers, intermediaries and other Medicare contractors undertake responsibilities on behalf of the Medicare program (Title XVIII of the Social Security Act), these entities assume the same obligations and responsibilities as the HHS Medicare officials responsible for the Medicare Program with respect to actions under 2 CFR part 376. This would include the requirement for these entities to check the Excluded Parties List System (EPLS) and take necessary steps to effect this part.

Subpart D—Responsibilities of Federal Agency Officials Regarding Transactions

§ 376.437 What method do I use to communicate to a participant the requirements described in the OMB guidance at 2 CFR 180.435?

To communicate to a participant the requirements described in 2 CFR 180.435, you must include a term or condition in the transaction that requires the participant's compliance with subpart C of 2 CFR part 180, as supplemented by subpart C of this part, and require the participant to include a similar term or condition in lower-tier covered transactions.

Subpart E—Excluded Parties List System [Reserved]

Subpart F—General Principles Relating to Suspension and Debarment Actions [Reserved]

Subpart G—Suspension [Reserved]

Subpart H—Debarment [Reserved]

Subpart I—Definitions

§ 376.935 Disqualified. (HHS supplement to government-wide definition at 2 CFR 180.935).

Disqualified means persons prohibited from participating in specified federal procurement and nonprocurement transactions pursuant to the statutes listed in 2 CFR 180.935, and pursuant to Title XI of the Social Security Act (42 U.S.C. 1320a–7, 1320a–7a, 1320c–5, and 1395ccc) as enforced by the HHS Office of the Inspector General.

§ 376.995 Principal (HHS supplement to government-wide definition at 2 CFR 180.995).

Principal means individuals, in addition to those listed at 2 CFR 180.995, who participate in HHS covered transactions including:

(a) Providers of federally required audit services; and

(b) Researchers.

Subpart J [Reserved]

PART 382—REQUIREMENTS FOR DRUG-FREE WORKPLACE (FINANCIAL ASSISTANCE)

Sec.
382.10 What does this part do?
382.20 Does this part apply to me?
382.30 What policies and procedures must I follow?

Subpart A [Reserved]

Subpart B—Requirements for Recipients Other Than Individuals

382.225 Whom in HHS does a recipient other than an individual notify about a criminal drug conviction?

Subpart C—Requirements for Recipients Who Are Individuals

382.300 Whom in HHS does a recipient who is an individual notify about a criminal drug conviction?

Subpart D—Responsibilities of Agency Awarding Officials

382.400 What method do I use as an agency awarding official to obtain a recipient's agreement to comply with the OMB guidance?

Subpart E—Violations of This Part and Consequences

382.500 Who in HHS determines that a recipient other than an individual violated the requirements of this part?
382.505 Who in HHS determines that a recipient who is an individual violated requirements of this part?

Subpart F [Reserved]

AUTHORITY: 41 U.S.C. 701–707.

SOURCE: 74 FR 58190, Nov. 12, 2009, unless otherwise noted.

§ 382.10 What does this part do?

This part requires that the award and administration of HHS grants and cooperative agreements comply with Office of Management and Budget (OMB) guidance implementing the portion of the Drug-Free Workplace Act of 1988 (41 U.S.C. 701–707, as amended, hereafter referred to as "the Act") that applies to grants. It thereby—

(a) Gives regulatory effect to the OMB guidance (Subparts A through F of 2 CFR part 182) for the HHS grants and cooperative agreements; and

(b) Establishes HHS policies and procedures for compliance with the Act that are the same as those of other Federal agencies, in conformance with the requirement in 41 U.S.C. 705 for Governmentwide implementing regulations.

§ 382.20 Does this part apply to me?

This part and, through this part, pertinent portions of the OMB guidance in subparts A through F of 2 CFR part 182 (see table at 2 CFR 182.115(b)) apply to you if you are a—

(a) Recipient of an HHS grant or cooperative agreement; or

(b) HHS awarding official.

§ 382.30 What policies and procedures must I follow?

(a) *General.* You must follow the policies and procedures specified in applicable sections of the OMB guidance in subparts A through F of 2 CFR part 182, as implemented by this part.

(b) *Specific sections of OMB guidance that this part supplements.* In implementing the OMB guidance in 2 CFR part 182, this part supplements four sections of the guidance, as shown in the following table. For each of those sections, you must follow the policies and procedures in the OMB guidance, as supplemented by this part.

Section of OMB guidance	Section in this part where supplemented	What the supplementation clarifies
(1) 2 CFR 182.225(a)	§ 382.225	Whom in HHS a recipient other than an individual must notify if an employee is convicted for a violation of a criminal drug statute in the workplace.
(2) 2 CFR 182.300(b)	§ 382.300	Whom in HHS a recipient who is an individual must notify if he or she is convicted of a criminal drug offense resulting from a violation occurring during the conduct of any award activity.
(3) 2 CFR 182.500 ...	§ 382.500	Who in HHS is authorized to determine that a recipient other than an individual is in violation of the requirements of 2 CFR part 182, as implemented by this part.
(4) 2 CFR 182.505 ...	§ 382.505	Who in HHS is authorized to determine that a recipient who is an individual is in violation of the requirements of 2 CFR part 182, as implemented by this part.

(c) *Sections of the OMB guidance that this part does not supplement.* For any section of OMB guidance in subparts A through F of 2 CFR part 182 that is not listed in paragraph (b) of this section, HHS policies and procedures are the same as those in the OMB guidance.

Subpart A [Reserved]

Subpart B—Requirements for Recipients Other Than Individuals

§ 382.225 Whom in HHS does a recipient other than an individual notify about a criminal drug conviction?

A recipient other than an individual that is required under 2 CFR 182.225(a) to notify Federal agencies about an employee's conviction for a criminal drug offense must notify each HHS office from which it currently has an award.

Subpart C—Requirements for Recipients Who Are Individuals

§ 382.300 Whom in HHS does a recipient who is an individual notify about a criminal drug conviction?

A recipient who is an individual and is required under 2 CFR 182.300(b) to notify Federal agencies about a conviction for a criminal drug offense must notify each HHS office from which it currently has an award.

Subpart D—Responsibilities of Agency Awarding Officials

§ 382.400 What method do I use as an agency awarding official to obtain a recipient's agreement to comply with the OMB guidance?

To obtain a recipient's agreement to comply with applicable requirements in the OMB guidance at 2 CFR part 182, you must include the following term or condition in the award:

Drug-free workplace. You as the recipient must comply with drug-free workplace requirements in Subpart B (or Subpart C, if the recipient is an individual) of part 382, which adopts the Governmentwide implementation (2 CFR part 182) of sec. 5152–5158 of the Drug-Free Workplace Act of 1988 (Pub. L. 100–690, Title V, Subtitle D; 41 U.S.C. 701–707).

Subpart E—Violations of This Part and Consequences

§382.500 Who in HHS determines that a recipient other than an individual violated the requirements of this part?

The agency head is the official authorized to make the determination under 2 CFR 182.500.

§382.505 Who in HHS determines that a recipient who is an individual violated the requirements of this part?

The agency head is the official authorized to make the determination under 2 CFR 182.505.

Subpart F [Reserved]

CHAPTER IV—DEPARTMENT OF AGRICULTURE

PART 417—NONPROCUREMENT DEBARMENT AND SUSPENSION

Sec.
417.10 What does this part do?
417.20 Does this part apply to me?
417.30 What policies and procedures must I follow?

Subpart A—General

417.137 Who in the USDA may grant an exception to let an excluded person participate in a covered transaction?

Subpart B—Covered Transactions

417.210 Which nonprocurement transactions are covered transactions?
417.215 Which nonprocurement transactions, in addition to those listed in 2 CFR 180.215, are not covered transactions?
417.220 Are any procurement contracts included as covered transactions?
417.221 How would the exclusions from coverage for the USDA's foreign assistance programs apply?
417.222 How would the exclusions from coverage for the USDA's export credit guarantee and direct credit programs apply?

Subpart C—Responsibilities of Participants Regarding Transactions

417.332 What methods must I use to pass down requirements to participants in lower-tier covered transactions with whom I intend to do business?

Subpart D—Responsibilities of Department of Agriculture Officials Regarding Transactions

417.437 What method do I use to communicate to a participant the requirements described in the OMB guidance at 2 CFR 180.435?

Subparts E, F [Reserved]

Subpart G—Suspension

417.755 When will I know whether the USDA suspension is continued or terminated?

Subpart H—Debarment

417.800 What are the USDA causes for debarment?
417.865 How long may my debarment last?
417.870 When do I know if the USDA debarring official debars me?

Subpart I—Definitions

417.930 Debarring official (USDA supplement to governmentwide definition at 2 CFR 180.930).
417.1010 Suspending official (USDA supplement to governmentwide definition at 2 CFR 180.1010).

Subpart J [Reserved]

AUTHORITY: 5 U.S.C. 301; Pub. L. 101–576, 104 Stat. 2838; Sec. 2455, Pub. L. 103–355, 108 Stat. 3327 (31 U.S.C. 6101 note); 7 U.S.C. 2209j; E.O. 12549 (3 CFR, 1986 Comp., p. 189); E.O. 12698 (3 CFR, Comp., p. 235); 7 CFR 2.28.

SOURCE: 75 FR 29185, May 25, 2010, unless otherwise noted.

§ 417.10 What does this part do?

This part adopts the OMB guidance in subparts A through I of 2 CFR part 180, as supplemented by this part, as the USDA policies and procedures for nonprocurement debarment and suspension. It thereby gives regulatory effect for the USDA to the OMB guidance, as supplemented by this part. This part satisfies the requirements in section 3 of Executive Order 12549, "Debarment and Suspension" (3 CFR 1986 Comp., p. 189), Executive Order 12689, "Debarment and Suspension" (3 CFR 1989 Comp., p. 235) and 31 U.S.C. 6101 note (Section 2455, Pub. L. 103–355, 108 Stat. 3327).

§ 417.20 Does this part apply to me?

Through this part, pertinent portions of the OMB guidance in subparts A through I of 2 CFR part 180 (see table at 2 CFR 180.100(b)) apply to you if you are a:

(a) Participant or principal in a "covered transaction" (see subpart B of 2 CFR part 180 and the definition of "nonprocurement transaction" at 2 CFR 180.970, as supplemented by §§ 417.215 and 417.220 of this part);

(b) Respondent in a USDA debarment and suspension action;

(c) USDA debarment or suspension official; or

(d) USDA grants officer, agreements officer, or other official authorized to enter into any type of nonprocurement transaction that is a covered transaction.

235

§ 417.30　What policies and procedures must I follow?

The USDA policies and procedures that you must follow are the policies and procedures specified in this regulation and each applicable section of the OMB guidance in subparts A through I of 2 CFR part 180, as that section is supplemented by the section in this part with the same section number. The contracts that are covered transactions, for example, are specified by section 220 of the OMB guidance (*i.e.*, 2 CFR 180.220) as supplemented by section 220 in this part (*i.e.*, § 417.220). For any section of OMB guidance in subparts A through I of 2 CFR part 180 that has no corresponding section in this part, USDA policies and procedures are those in the OMB guidance.

Subpart A—General

§ 417.137　Who in the USDA may grant an exception to let an excluded person participate in a covered transaction?

Within the USDA, a debarring official may grant an exception to let an excluded person participate in a covered transaction as provided under 2 CFR 180.135.

Subpart B—Covered Transactions

§ 417.210　Which nonprocurement transactions are covered transactions?

All nonprocurement transactions, as defined in § 417.970, are covered transactions unless listed in § 417.215.

§ 417.215　Which nonprocurement transactions, in addition to those listed in 2 CFR 180.215, are not covered transactions?

(a) *Transactions not covered.* In addition to the nonprocurement transactions listed in 2 CFR 180.215, the following nonprocurement transactions are not covered transactions:

(1) An entitlement or mandatory award required by a statute, including a lower tier entitlement or mandatory award that is required by a statute.

(2) The export or substitution of Federal timber governed by the Forest Resources Conservation and Shortage Relief Act of 1990, 16 U.S.C. 620 *et seq.* (The

"Export Act"), which prevents a debarred person from entering into any contract for the purchase of unprocessed timber from Federal lands. *See* 16 U.S.C. 620d(d)(1)(A).

(3) The receipt of licenses, permits, certificates, and indemnification under regulatory programs conducted in the interest of public health and safety, and animal and plant health and safety.

(4) The receipt of official grading and inspection services, animal damage control services, public health and safety inspection services, and animal and plant health and safety inspection services.

(5) If the person is a State or local government, the provision of official grading and inspection services, animal damage control services, animal and plant health and safety inspection services.

(6) The receipt of licenses, permits, or certificates under regulatory programs conducted in the interest of ensuring fair trade practices.

(7) Permits, licenses, exchanges and other acquisitions of real property, rights of way, and easements under natural resource management programs.

(8) Any transaction to be implemented outside the United States that is below the primary tier covered transaction in a USDA foreign assistance program.

(9) Any transaction to be implemented outside the United States that is below the primary tier covered transaction in a USDA export credit guarantee program or direct credit program.

(b) *Limited requirement to check EPLS.* Notwithstanding the fact that transactions to be implemented outside the United States that are below the primary tier covered transaction in a USDA foreign assistance program, export credit guarantee program or direct credit program are not covered transactions, pursuant to paragraphs (a)(8) and (9) of this section, primary tier participants under these programs must check the EPLS prior to entering into any transaction with a person at the first lower tier and shall not enter into such a transaction if the person is excluded or disqualified under the EPLS.

(c) *Exception.* A cause for suspension or debarment under §180.700 or §180.800 of this title (as supplemented by §417.800) may be based on the actions of a person with respect to a procurement or nonprocurement transaction under a USDA program even if such transaction has been excluded from covered transaction status by this section or §417.220.

§417.220 Are any procurement contracts included as covered transactions?

(a) Covered transactions under this part:

(1) Do not include any procurement contracts awarded directly by a Federal agency; but

(2) Do include some procurement contracts awarded by non-Federal participants in nonprocurement covered transactions (*see* appendix to this part).

(b) Specifically, a contract for goods or services is a covered transaction if any of the following applies:

(1) The contract is awarded by a participant in a nonprocurement transaction that is covered under §417.210, and the amount of the contract is expected to equal or exceed $25,000.

(2) The contract requires the consent of a USDA official. In that case, the contract, regardless of the amount, always is a covered transaction, and it does not matter who awarded it. For example, it could be a subcontract awarded by a contractor at a tier below a nonprocurement transaction, as shown in the appendix to this part.

(3) The contract is for federally-required audit services.

(c) Any procurement contract to be implemented outside the United States that is below the primary tier covered transaction in a USDA foreign assistance program is not a covered transaction, notwithstanding the provisions in paragraphs (a) and (b) of this section.

(d) Any procurement contract to be implemented outside the United States that is below the primary tier covered transaction in a USDA export credit guarantee program or direct credit program is not a covered transaction, notwithstanding the provisions in paragraphs (a) and (b) of this section.

(e) Notwithstanding the fact that procurement contracts to be implemented outside the United States that are below the primary tier covered transaction in a USDA foreign assistance program, export credit guarantee program or direct credit program are not covered transactions, pursuant to paragraphs (c) and (d) of this section, primary tier participants under these programs must check the EPLS prior to entering into any procurement contract that is expected to equal or exceed $25,000 with a person at the first lower tier and shall not enter into such a procurement contract if the person is excluded or disqualified under the EPLS.

§417.221 How would the exclusions from coverage for the USDA's foreign assistance programs apply?

The primary tier covered transaction would be the food aid grant agreement entered into between USDA and a program participant, such as a U.S. private voluntary organization. USDA would have to check the EPLS before entering into the food aid grant agreement to ensure that the U.S. private voluntary organization that would be the primary tier participant is not excluded or disqualified. A transaction at the first lower tier might be a subrecipient agreement between the U.S. private voluntary organization and a foreign subrecipient of the commodities that were provided under the food aid grant agreement. Pursuant to §417.215(a)(8), this nonprocurement transaction would not be a covered transaction. In addition, a transaction at the first lower tier might be a procurement contract entered into between the U.S. private voluntary organization and a foreign entity to provide supplies or services that are expected to equal or exceed $25,000 in value and that are needed by such organization to implement activities under the food aid grant agreement. Pursuant to §417.220(c), this procurement contract would not be a covered transaction. However, pursuant to §§417.215(b) and 417.220(e), the U.S. private voluntary organization would be prohibited from entering into, at the first lower tier, an agreement with a subrecipient or a procurement contract that is expected to equal or exceed $25,000 with an entity that appears on the EPLS as excluded or disqualified.

§ 417.222 How would the exclusions from coverage for USDA's export credit guarantee and direct credit programs apply?

(a) *Export credit guarantee program.* In the case of the export credit guarantee program, the primary tier covered transaction would be the guarantee issued by the USDA to a U.S. exporter. The U.S. exporter usually assigns the guarantee to a U.S. financial institution, and this would create another primary tier covered transaction between USDA and the U.S. financial institution. USDA would have to check the EPLS before issuing a guarantee or accepting a guarantee assignment to ensure that the U.S. exporter or financial institution that would be the primary tier participant is not excluded or disqualified. A transaction at the first lower tier under the export credit guarantee program might be a payment obligation of a foreign bank to the U.S. exporter to pay on behalf of the importer for the exported U.S. commodities that are covered by the guarantee. Similarly, a transaction at the first lower tier might be a payment obligation of a foreign bank under an instrument, such as a loan agreement or letter of credit, to the U.S. financial institution assigned the guarantee, which has paid the exporter for the exported U.S. commodities and, in so doing, issued a loan to the foreign bank, which the foreign bank is obligated to repay on deferred payment terms. Pursuant to § 417.215(a)(9), these nonprocurement transactions would not be covered transactions. In addition, a transaction at the first lower tier under the export credit guarantee program might be a procurement contract (*i.e.,* a contract for the purchase and sale of goods) that is expected to equal or exceed $25,000 entered into between the U.S. exporter and the foreign importer for the U.S. commodities, the payment for which is covered by the guarantee. Pursuant to § 417.220(d), this procurement contract would not be a covered transaction. However, pursu-

ant to §§ 417.215(b) and 417.220(e), the U.S. exporter or U.S. financial institution would be prohibited from entering into, at the first lower tier, an agreement with an importer (or intervening purchaser) or foreign bank or a procurement contract that is expected to equal or exceed $25,000 with an entity that appears on the EPLS as excluded or disqualified.

(b) *Direct credit program.* In the case of the direct credit program, the primary tier covered transaction would be the financing agreement between the USDA and the U.S. exporter. USDA purchases the exporter's account receivable in a particular transaction pursuant to the financing agreement. On occasion, such transaction may contemplate a payment obligation of a U.S. or foreign bank to make the required payments. USDA would have to check the EPLS before entering into a financing agreement or accepting such a payor to ensure that the U.S. exporter or the bank, if any, that would be the primary tier participant is not excluded or disqualified. A transaction at the first lower tier might be a payment obligation of the importer to pay the exporter for the exported U.S. commodities that are covered by the financing agreement. Pursuant to § 417.215(a)(9), this nonprocurement transaction would not be a covered transaction. In addition, a transaction at the first lower tier might be a procurement contract that is expected to equal or exceed $25,000 entered into between the U.S. exporter and the foreign importer for the U.S. commodities, the payment for which is covered by the financing agreement. Pursuant to § 417.220(d), this procurement contract would not be a covered transaction. However, pursuant to §§ 417.215(b) and 417.220(e), the U.S. exporter would be prohibited from entering into, at the first lower tier, an agreement with an importer (or intervening purchaser) or bank, or a procurement contract that is expected to equal or exceed $25,000 with an entity that appears on the EPLS as excluded or disqualified.

Subpart C—Responsibilities of Participants Regarding Transactions

§417.332 What methods must I use to pass down requirements to participants in lower tier covered transactions with whom I intend to do business?

You as a participant must include a term or condition in lower tier covered transactions requiring lower tier participants to comply with subpart C of the OMB guidance in 2 CFR part 180, as supplemented by subpart C of this part.

Subpart D—Responsibilities of Department of Agriculture Officials Regarding Transactions

§417.437 What method do I use to communicate to a participant the requirements described in the OMB guidance at 2 CFR 180.435?

To communicate to a participant the requirements described in 2 CFR 180.435, you must include a term or condition in the transaction that requires the participant's compliance with subpart C of 2 CFR part 180, as supplemented by subpart C of this part, and requires the participant to include a similar term or condition in lower tier covered transactions.

Subparts E–F [Reserved]

Subpart G—Suspension

§417.755 When will I know whether the USDA suspension is continued or terminated?

The suspending official must make a written decision whether to continue, modify, or terminate your suspension within 45 days of closing the official record. The official record closes upon the suspending official's receipt of final submissions, information and findings of fact, if any. The suspending official may extend that period for good cause. However, the record will remain open for the full 30 days, as called for in §180.725, even when you make a submission before the 30 days expire.

Subpart H—Debarment

§417.800 What are the USDA causes for debarment?

A Federal agency may debar a person for—

(a) Conviction of or civil judgment for—

(1) Commission of fraud or a criminal offense in connection with obtaining, attempting to obtain, or performing a public or private agreement or transaction;

(2) Violation of Federal or State antitrust statutes, including those proscribing price fixing between competitors, allocation of customers between competitors, and bid rigging;

(3) Commission of embezzlement, theft, forgery, bribery, falsification or destruction of records, making false statements, tax evasion, receiving stolen property, making false claims, or obstruction of justice; or

(4) Commission of any other offense indicating a lack of business integrity or business honesty that seriously and directly affects your present responsibility;

(b) Violation of the terms of a public agreement or transaction so serious as to affect the integrity of an agency program, such as—

(1) A willful failure to perform in accordance with the terms of one or more public agreements or transactions;

(2) A history of failure to perform or of unsatisfactory performance of one or more public agreements or transactions; or

(3) A willful violation of a statutory or regulatory provision or requirement applicable to a public agreement or transaction;

(c) Any of the following causes:

(1) A nonprocurement debarment by any Federal agency taken before March 1, 1989, or a procurement debarment by any Federal agency taken pursuant to 48 CFR part 9, subpart 9.4, before August 25, 1995;

(2) Knowingly doing business with an ineligible person, except as permitted under §180.135;

(3) Failure to pay a single substantial debt, or a number of outstanding debts (including disallowed costs and overpayments, but not including sums owed

the Federal Government under the Internal Revenue Code) owed to any Federal agency or instrumentality, provided the debt is uncontested by the debtor or, if contested, provided that the debtor's legal and administrative remedies have been exhausted;

(4) Violation of a material provision of a voluntary exclusion agreement entered into under §180.640 or of any settlement of a debarment or suspension action; or

(5) Violation of the provisions of the Drug-Free Workplace Act of 1988 (41 U.S.C. 701); or

(d) Any other cause of so serious or compelling a nature that it affects your present responsibility.

§417.865 How long may my debarment last?

(a) If the debarring official decides to debar you, your period of debarment will be based on the seriousness of the cause(s) upon which your debarment is based. Generally, debarment should not exceed 3 years. However, if circumstances warrant, the debarring official may impose a longer period of debarment.

(b) In determining the period of debarment, the debarring official may consider the factors in 2 CFR 180.860. If a suspension has preceded your debarment, the debarring official must consider the time you were suspended.

(c) If the debarment is for a violation of the provisions of the Drug-Free Workplace Act of 1988, your period of debarment may not exceed 5 years.

(d) The Secretary shall permanently debar from participation in USDA programs any individual, organization, corporation, or other entity convicted of a felony for knowingly defrauding the United States in connection with any program administered by USDA.

(1) *Reduction.* If the Secretary considers it appropriate s/he may reduce a debarment under this subsection to a period of not less than 10 years.

(2) *Exemption.* A debarment under this subsection shall not apply with regard to participation in USDA domestic food assistance programs. For purposes of this paragraph, participation in a domestic food assistance program does not include acting as an authorized retail food store in the Supple-

mental Nutrition Assistance Program (SNAP), the Special Supplemental Nutrition Assistance Program for Women, Infants, and Children (WIC), or as a nonbeneficiary entity in any of the domestic food assistance programs. The programs include:

(i) Special Nutrition Assistance Program, 7 U.S.C. 2011, *et seq.;*

(ii) Food Distribution Program on Indian Reservations, 7 U.S.C. 2013(b);

(iii) National School Lunch Program, 42 U.S.C. 1751, *et seq.;*

(iv) Summer Food Service Program for Children, 42 U.S.C. 1761; Child and Adult Care Food Program, 42 U.S.C. 1766;

(v) Special Milk Program for Children, 42 U.S.C. 1772; School Breakfast Program, 42 U.S.C. 1773;

(vi) Special Supplemental Nutrition Program for Women, Infants, and Children, 42 U.S.C. 1786;

(vii) Commodity Supplemental Food Program, 42 U.S.C. 612c note;

(viii) WIC Farmers Market Nutrition Program, 42 U.S.C. 1786;

(ix) Senior Farmers' Market Nutrition Program, 7 U.S.C. 3007; and

(x) Emergency Food Assistance Program, 7 U.S.C. 7501, *et. seq.*

§417.870 When do I know if the USDA debarring official debars me?

(a) The debarring official must make a written decision whether to debar within 45 days of closing the official record. The official record closes upon the debarring official's receipt of final submissions, information and findings of fact, if any. The debarring official may extend that period for good cause. However, the record will remain open for the full 30 days, as called for in §180.820, even when you make a submission before the 30 days expire.

(b) The debarring official sends you written notice, pursuant to §180.615, that the official decided, either:

(1) Not to debar you; or

(2) To debar you. In this event, the notice:

(i) Refers to the Notice of Proposed Debarment;

(ii) Specifies the reasons for your debarment;

(iii) States the period of your debarment, including the effective dates; and

(iv) Advises you that your debarment is effective for covered transactions and contracts that are subject to the Federal Acquisition Regulation (48 CFR chapter 1), throughout the Executive Branch of the Federal Government unless an agency head or an authorized designee grants an exception.

Subpart I—Definitions

§ 417.930 Debarring official (USDA supplement to governmentwide definition at 2 CFR 180.930).

(a) Debarring official means an agency official who is authorized to impose debarment. The debarring official is either:

(1) The agency head; or

(2) An official designated by the agency head.

(b) The head of an organizational unit within USDA (*e.g.*, Administrator, Food and Nutrition Service), who has been delegated authority in 7 CFR part 2 to carry out a covered transaction, is delegated authority to act as the debarring official in connection with such transaction. This authority to act as a debarring official may not be redelegated below the head of the organizational unit, except that, in the case of the Forest Service, the Chief may redelegate the authority to act as a debarring official to the Deputy Chief for the National Forest System or an Associate Deputy Chief for the National Forest System.

§ 417.1010 Suspending official (USDA supplement to governmentwide definition at 2 CFR 180.1010).

(a) Suspending official means an agency official who is authorized to impose suspension. The suspending official is either:

(1) The agency head; or

(2) An official designated by the agency head.

(b) The head of an organizational unit within USDA (*e.g.*, Administrator, Food and Nutrition Service), who has been delegated authority in 7 CFR part 2 of this title to carry out a covered transaction, is delegated authority to act as the suspending official in connection with such transaction. This authority to act as a suspending official may not be redelegated below the head of the organizational unit, except that, in the case of the Forest Service, the Chief may redelegate the authority to act as a suspending official to the Deputy Chief for the National Forest System or an Associate Deputy Chief for the National Forest System.

Subpart J [Reserved]

PART 421—REQUIREMENTS FOR DRUG-FREE WORKPLACE (FINANCIAL ASSISTANCE)

AUTHORITY: 41 U.S.C. 701–707.

SOURCE: 76 FR 76610, Dec. 8, 2011, unless otherwise noted.

§ 421.10 What does this part do?

This part requires that the award and administration of USDA grants and cooperative agreements comply with Office of Management and Budget (OMB) guidance implementing the portion of the Drug-Free Workplace Act of 1988 (41 U.S.C. 701–707, as amended, hereafter referred to as "the Act") that applies to grants. It thereby—

(a) Gives regulatory effect to the OMB guidance (Subparts A through F of 2 CFR part 182) for USDA's grants and cooperative agreements; and

(b) Establishes USDA policies and procedures for compliance with the Act that are the same as those of other Federal agencies, in conformance with the requirement in 41 U.S.C. 705 for Governmentwide implementing regulations.

§ 421.20 Does this part apply to me?

This part and, through this part, pertinent portions of the OMB guidance in Subparts A through F of 2 CFR part 182

(see table at 2 CFR 182.115(b)) apply to you if you are a—

(a) Recipient of a USDA grant or cooperative agreement; or

(b) USDA awarding official.

§ 421.30 What policies and procedures must I follow?

(a) *General.* You must follow the policies and procedures specified in applicable sections of the OMB guidance in Subparts A through F of 2 CFR part 182, as implemented by this part.

(b) *Specific sections of OMB guidance that this part supplements.* In implementing the OMB guidance in 2 CFR part 182, this part supplements four sections of the guidance, as shown in the following table. For each of those sections, you must follow the policies and procedures in the OMB guidance, as supplemented by this part.

Section of OMB guidance	Section in this part where supplemented	What the supplementation clarifies
(1) 2 CFR 182.225(a)	§ 421.225	Whom in the USDA a recipient other than an individual must notify if an employee is convicted for a violation of a criminal drug statute in the workplace.
(2) 2 CFR 182.300(b)	§ 421.300	Whom in the USDA a recipient who is an individual must notify if he or she is convicted of a criminal drug offense resulting from a violation occurring during the conduct of any award activity.
(3) 2 CFR 182.500	§ 421.500	Who in the USDA is authorized to determine that a recipient other than an individual is in violation of the requirements of 2 CFR part 182, as implemented by this part.
(4) 2 CFR 182.505	§ 421.505	Who in the USDA is authorized to determine that a recipient who is an individual is in violation of the requirements of 2 CFR part 182, as implemented by this part.

(c) *Sections of the OMB guidance that this part does not supplement.* For any section of OMB guidance in Subparts A through F of 2 CFR part 182 that is not listed in paragraph (b) of this section, USDA policies and procedures are the same as those in the OMB guidance.

Subpart A—Purpose and Coverage [Reserved]

Subpart B—Requirements for Recipients Other Than Individuals

§ 421.225 Whom in the USDA does a recipient other than an individual notify about a criminal drug conviction?

A recipient other than an individual that is required under 2 CFR 182.225(a) to notify Federal agencies about an employee's conviction for a criminal

drug offense must notify the awarding official for each USDA agency from which the recipient currently has an award.

Subpart C—Requirements for Recipients Who Are Individuals

§ 421.300 Whom in the USDA does a recipient who is an individual notify about a criminal drug conviction?

A recipient who is an individual that is required under 2 CFR 182.300(b) to notify Federal agencies about a conviction for a criminal drug offense must notify the awarding official for each USDA agency from which the recipient currently has an award.

Subpart D—Responsibilities of Agency Awarding Officials

§ 421.400 What method do I use as an agency awarding official to obtain a recipient's agreement to comply with the OMB guidance?

To obtain a recipient's agreement to comply with applicable requirements in the OMB guidance at 2 CFR part 182, you must include the following term or condition in the award:

Drug-free workplace. You as the recipient must comply with drug-free workplace requirements in Subpart B (or Subpart C, if the recipient is an individual) of part 421, which adopts the Governmentwide implementation (2 CFR part 182) of sec. 5152–5158 of the Drug-Free Workplace Act of 1988 (Pub. L. 100–690, Title V, Subtitle D; 41 U.S.C. 701–707).

Subpart E—Violations of This Part and Consequences

§ 421.500 Who in the USDA determines that a recipient other than an individual violated the requirements of this part?

The Secretary of Agriculture and the Secretary's designee or designees are authorized to make the determination under 2 CFR 182.500.

§ 421.505 Who in the USDA determines that a recipient who is an individual violated the requirements of this part?

The Secretary of Agriculture and the Secretary's designee or designees are authorized to make the determination under 2 CFR 182.505.

CHAPTER VI—DEPARTMENT OF STATE

PART 601—NONPROCUREMENT DEBARMENT AND SUSPENSION

Sec.
601.10 What does this part do?
601.20 Does this part apply to me?
601.30 What policies and procedures must I follow?

Subpart A—General

601.137 Who in the Department of State may grant an exception to let an excluded person participate in a covered transaction?

Subpart B—Covered Transactions

601.220 What contracts and subcontracts, in addition to those listed in 2 CFR 180.220, are covered transactions?

Subpart C—Responsibilities of Participants Regarding Transactions

601.332 What methods must I use to pass requirements down to participants at lower tiers with whom I intend to do business?

Subpart D—Responsibilities of Federal Agency Officials Regarding Transactions

601.437 What method do I use to communicate to a participant the requirements described in the OMB guidance at 2 CFR 180.435?

Subparts E–H [Reserved]

Subpart I—Definitions

601.930 Debarring Official (Department of State supplement to government-wide definition at 2 CFR 180.930).
601.1010 Suspending Official (Department of State supplement to government-wide definition at 2 CFR 180.1010).

Subpart J [Reserved]

AUTHORITY: Sec. 2455, Pub. L. 103–355, 108; Stat. 3327 (31 U.S.C. 6101 note); E.O. 12549; (3 CFR, 1986 Comp., p. 189); E.O. 12689 (3); CFR, 1989 Comp., p. 235).

SOURCE: 72 FR 10034, Mar. 7, 2007, unless otherwise noted.

§ 601.10 What does this part do?

This part adopts the Office of Management and Budget (OMB) guidance in subparts A through I of 2 CFR part 180, as supplemented by this part, as the DOS policies and procedures for nonprocurement debarment and suspension. It thereby gives regulatory effect for DOS to the OMB guidance as supplemented by this part. This part satisfies the requirements in section 3 of Executive Order 12549, "Debarment and Suspension" (3 CFR 1986 Comp., p. 189); Executive Order 12689, "Debarment and Suspension" (3 CFR 1989 Comp., p. 235); and section 2455 of the Federal Acquisition Streamlining Act of 1994, Pub. L. 103–355 (31 U.S.C. 6101 note).

§ 601.20 Does this part apply to me?

This part and, through this part, pertinent portions of the OMB guidance in subparts A through I of 2 CFR part 180 (see table at 2 CFR 180.100(b)) apply to you if you are a—

(a) Participant or principal in a "covered transaction" (see subpart B of 2 CFR part 180 and the definition of "nonprocurement transaction" at 2 CFR 180.970);

(b) Respondent in a DOS suspension or debarment action;

(c) DOS debarment or suspension official; and

(d) DOS grants officer, agreements officer, or other official authorized to enter into any type of nonprocurement transaction that is a covered transaction.

§ 601.30 What policies and procedures must I follow?

The DOS policies and procedures that you must follow are the policies and procedures specified in each applicable section of the OMB guidance in subparts A through I of 2 CFR part 180 and any supplemental policies and procedures set forth in this part.

Subpart A—General

§ 601.137 Who in the Department of State may grant an exception to let an excluded person participate in a covered transaction?

The Procurement Executive, Office of the Procurement Executive, DOS, may grant an exception permitting an excluded person to participate in a particular covered transaction. If the Procurement Executive, Office of the Procurement Executive, DOS, grants an exception, the exception must be in writing and state the reason(s) for deviating from the government-wide policy in Executive Order 12549.

Subpart B—Covered Transactions

§ 601.220 What contracts and subcontracts, in addition to those listed in 2 CFR 180.220, are covered transactions?

In addition to the contracts covered under 2 CFR 180.220(b) of the OMB guidance, this part applies to any contract, regardless of tier, that is awarded by a contractor, subcontractor, supplier, consultant, or its agent or representative in any transaction, if the contract is to be funded or provided by the DOS under a covered nonprocurement transaction and the amount of the contract is expected to equal or exceed $25,000. This extends the coverage of the DOS nonprocurement suspension and debarment requirements to all lower tiers of subcontracts under covered nonprocurement transactions, as permitted under the OMB guidance at 2 CFR 180.220(c) (see optional lower tier coverage in the figure in the appendix to 2 CFR part 180).

Subpart C—Responsibilities of Participants Regarding Transactions

§ 601.332 What methods must I use to pass requirements down to participants at lower tiers with whom I intend to do business?

You, as a participant, must include a term or condition in lower-tier transactions requiring lower-tier participants to comply with subpart C of the OMB guidance in 2 CFR part 180, as supplemented by this subpart.

Subpart D—Responsibilities of Federal Agency Officials Regarding Transactions

§ 601.437 What method do I use to communicate to a participant the requirements described in the OMB guidance at 2 CFR 180.435?

To communicate to a participant the requirements described in 2 CFR 180.435 of the OMB guidance, you must include a term or condition in the transaction that requires the participant's compliance with subpart C of 2 CFR part 180, as supplemented by subpart C of this part, and requires the participant to include a similar term or condition in lower-tier covered transactions.

Subparts E–H [Reserved]

Subpart I—Definitions

§ 601.930 Debarring Official (Department of State supplement to government-wide definition at 2 CFR 180.930).

The Debarring Official for the Department of State is the Procurement Executive, Office of the Procurement Executive (A/OPE).

§ 601.1010 Suspending Official (Department of Energy supplement to government-wide definition at 2 CFR 180.1010).

The Debarring Official for the Department of State is the Procurement Executive, Office of the Procurement Executive (A/OPE).

Subpart J [Reserved]

CHAPTER VII—AGENCY FOR INTERNATIONAL DEVELOPMENT

PART 780—NONPROCUREMENT DEBARMENT AND SUSPENSION

Sec.
780.10 What does this part do?
780.20 Does this part apply to me?
780.30 What policies and procedures must I follow?

Subpart A—General

780.137 Who in the Agency for International Development may grant an exception to let an excluded person participate in a covered transaction?

Subpart B—Covered Transactions

780.220 What contracts and subcontracts, in addition to those listed in 2 CFR 180.220, are covered transactions?

Subpart C—Responsibilities of Participants Regarding Transactions

780.332 What methods must I use to pass requirements down to participants at lower tiers with whom I intend to do business?

Subpart D—Responsibilities of Federal Agency Officials Regarding Transactions

780.437 What method do I use to communicate to a participant the requirements described in the OMB guidance at 2 CFR 180.435?

Subparts E–H [Reserved]

Subpart I—Definitions

780.930 Debarring Official (Agency for International Development supplement to government-wide definition at 2 CFR 180.930).
780.1010 Suspending Official (Agency for International Development supplement to government-wide definition at 2 CFR 180.1010).

Subpart J [Reserved]

AUTHORITY: Sec. 2455, Pub. L. 103–355, 108 Stat. 3327; E.O. 12549, 3 CFR, 1986 Comp., p. 189; E.O. 12689, 3 CFR, 1989 Comp., p. 235.

SOURCE: 76 FR 34144, June 13, 2011, unless otherwise noted.

§ 780.10 What does this part do?

This part adopts the Office of Management and Budget (OMB) guidance in subparts A through I of 2 CFR part 180, as supplemented by this part, as the USAID policies and procedures for nonprocurement debarment and suspension. It thereby gives regulatory effect for USAID to the OMB guidance as supplemented by this part. This part satisfies the requirements in section 3 of Executive Order 12549, "Debarment and Suspension" (3 CFR 1986 Comp., p. 189); Executive Order 12689, "Debarment and Suspension" (3 CFR 1989 Comp., p. 235); and section 2455 of the Federal Acquisition Streamlining Act of 1994, Public Law 103–355 (31 U.S.C. 6101 note).

§ 780.20 Does this part apply to me?

This part and, through this part, pertinent portions of the OMB guidance in subparts A through I of 2 CFR part 180 (see table at 2 CFR 180.100(b)) apply to you if you are a—
(a) Participant or principal in a "covered transaction" (see subpart B of 2 CFR part 180 and the definition of "non-procurement transaction" at 2 CFR 180.970);
(b) Respondent in a USAID suspension or debarment action;
(c) USAID debarment or suspension official; and
(d) USAID grants officer, agreements officer, or other official authorized to enter into any type of non-procurement transaction that is a covered transaction.

§ 780.30 What policies and procedures must I follow?

The USAID policies and procedures that you must follow are the policies and procedures specified in each applicable section of the OMB guidance in subparts A through I of 2 CFR part 180 and any supplemental policies and procedures set forth in this part.

Subpart A—General

§ 780.137 Who in USAID may grant an exception to let an excluded person participate in a covered transaction?

The Director, Office of Acquisition and Assistance or designee, may grant an exception permitting an excluded person to participate in a particular covered transaction. If the Director, Office of Acquisition and Assistance or designee grants an exception, the exception must be in writing and state the reason(s) for deviating from the

251

government-wide policy in Executive Order 12549.

Subpart B—Covered Transactions

§ 780.220 What contracts and subcontracts, in addition to those listed in 2 CFR 180.220, are covered transactions?

In addition to the contracts covered under 2 CFR 180.220(b) of the OMB guidance, this part applies to any contract, regardless of tier, that is awarded by a contractor, subcontractor, supplier, consultant, or its agent or representative in any transaction, if the contract is to be funded or provided by the USAID under a covered non-procurement transaction and the amount of the contract is expected to equal or exceed $25,000. This extends the coverage of the USAID non-procurement suspension and debarment requirements to all lower tiers of subcontracts under covered non-procurement transactions, as permitted under the OMB guidance at 2 CFR 180.220(c) (see optional lower tier coverage in the figure in the appendix to 2 CFR part 180).

Subpart C—Responsibilities of Participants Regarding Transactions

§ 780.332 What requirements must I pass down to persons at lower tiers with whom I intend to do business?

You, as a participant, must include a term or condition in lower-tier transactions requiring lower-tier participants to comply with subpart C of the OMB guidance in 2 CFR part 180, as supplemented by this subpart.

Subpart D—Responsibilities of Federal Agency Officials Regarding Transactions

§ 780.437 What method do I use to communicate to a participant the requirements described in the OMB guidance at 2 CFR 180.435?

To communicate to a participant the requirements described in 2 CFR 180.435 of the OMB guidance, you must include a term or condition in the transaction that requires the participant's compliance with subpart C of 2 CFR part 180, and supplemented by subpart C of this part, and requires the participant to include a similar term or condition in lower-tier covered transactions.

Subparts E–H [Reserved]

Subpart I—Definitions

§ 780.930 Debarring Official (Agency for International Development supplement to government-wide definition at 2 CFR 180.930).

The Debarring Official for USAID is the Director of the Office of Acquisition and Assistance.

§ 780.1010 Suspending Official (Agency for International Development supplement to government-wide definition at 2 CFR 180.1010).

The Suspending Official for USAID is the Director of the Office of Acquisition and Assistance.

Subpart J [Reserved]

PART 782—REQUIREMENTS FOR DRUG-FREE WORKPLACE (FINANCIAL ASSISTANCE)

Sec.
782.10   What does this part do?
782.20   Does this part apply to me?
782.30   What policies and procedures must I follow?

Subpart A—Purpose and Coverage [Reserved]

Subpart B—Requirements for Recipients Other Than Individuals

782.225   Whom in USAID does a recipient other than an individual notify about a criminal drug conviction?

Subpart C—Requirements for Recipients Who Are Individuals

782.300   Whom in USAID does a recipient who is an individual notify about a criminal drug conviction?

Subpart D—Responsibilities of Agency Awarding Officials

782.400   What method do I use as an agency awarding official to obtain a recipient's agreement to comply with the OMB guidance?

Subpart E—Violations of This Part and Consequences

782.500 Who in USAID determines that a recipient other than an individual violated the requirements of this part?
782.505 Who in USAID determines that a recipient who is an individual violated the requirements of this part?

Subpart F—Definitions

782.605 Award (USAID Supplement to Government Wide Definition at 2 CFR 182.605).

AUTHORITY: 41 U.S.C. 701–707.

SOURCE: 76 FR 34574, June 14, 2011, unless otherwise noted.

§782.10 What does this part do?

This part requires that the award and administration of USAID grants and cooperative agreements comply with Office of Management and Budget (OMB) guidance implementing the portion of the Drug-Free Workplace Act of 1988 (41 U.S.C. 701–707, as amended, hereafter referred to as "the Act") that applies to grants. It thereby—

(a) Gives regulatory effect to the OMB guidance (Subparts A through F of 2 CFR Part 182) for USAID's grants and cooperative agreements; and

(b) Establishes USAID policies and procedures for compliance with the Act that are the same as those of other Federal agencies, in conformance with the requirement in 41 U.S.C. 705 for Government wide implementing regulations.

§782.20 Does this part apply to me?

This part and, through this part, pertinent portions of the OMB guidance in subparts A through F of 2 CFR part 182 (see table at 2 CFR 182.115(b)) apply to you if you are a—

(a) Recipient of a USAID grant or cooperative agreement; or

(b) USAID awarding official.

§782.30 What policies and procedures must I follow?

(a) *General.* You must follow the policies and procedures specified in applicable sections of the OMB guidance in Subparts A through F of 2 CFR part 182, as implemented by this part.

(b) *Specific sections of OMB guidance that this part supplements.* In implementing the OMB guidance in 2 CFR part 182, this part supplements four sections of the guidance, as shown in the following table. For each of those sections, you must follow the policies and procedures in the OMB guidance, as supplemented by this part.

Section of OMB guidance	Section in this part where supplemented	What the supplementation clarifies
(1) 2 CFR 182.225(a)	§ 782.225	Whom in USAID a recipient other than an individual must notify if an employee is convicted for a violation of a criminal drug statute in the workplace.
(2) 2 CFR 182.300(b)	§ 782.300	Whom in USAID a recipient who is an individual must notify if he or she is convicted of a criminal drug offense resulting from a violation occurring during the conduct of any award activity.
(3) 2 CFR 182.500	§ 782.500	Who in USAID is authorized to determine that a recipient other than an individual is in violation of the requirements of 2 CFR part 182, as implemented by this part.
(4) 2 CFR 182.505	§ 782.505	Who in USAID is authorized to determine that a recipient who is an individual is in violation of the requirements of 2 CFR part 182, as implemented by this part.

(c) *Sections of the OMB guidance that this part does not supplement.* For any section of OMB guidance in Subparts A through F of 2 CFR part 182 that is not listed in paragraph (b) of this section, USAID policies and procedures are the same as those in the OMB guidance.

Subpart A—Purpose and Coverage [Reserved]

Subpart B—Requirements for Recipients Other Than Individuals

§782.225 Whom in USAID does a recipient other than an individual notify about a criminal drug conviction?

A recipient other than an individual that is required under 2 CFR 182.225(a) to notify Federal agencies about an employee's conviction for a criminal drug offense must notify—

(a) Federal agencies if an employee who is engaged in the performance of an award informs you about a conviction, or you otherwise learn of the conviction. Your notification to the Federal agencies must—

(1) Be in writing;

(2) Include the employee's position title;

(3) Include the identification number(s) of each affected award;

(4) Be sent within ten calendar days after you learn of the conviction; and

(5) Be sent to every Federal agency on whose award the convicted employee was working. It must be sent to every awarding official or his or her official designee, unless the Federal agency has specified a central point for the receipt of the notices.

(b) Within 30 calendar days of learning about an employee's conviction, you must either—

(1) Take appropriate personnel action against the employee, up to and including termination, consistent with the requirements of the Rehabilitation Act of 1973 (29 U.S.C. 794), as amended; or

(2) Require the employee to participate satisfactorily in a drug abuse assistance or rehabilitation program approved for these purposes by a Federal, State or local health, law enforcement, or other appropriate agency.

Subpart C—Requirements for Recipients Who Are Individuals

§782.300 Whom in USAID does a recipient who is an individual notify about a criminal drug conviction?

A recipient who is an individual and is required under 2 CFR 182.300(b) to notify Federal agencies about a conviction for a criminal drug offense must notify each USAID office from which it currently has an award.

Subpart D—Responsibilities of Agency Awarding Officials

§782.400 What method do I use as an agency awarding official to obtain a recipient's agreement to comply with the OMB guidance?

To obtain a recipient's agreement to comply with applicable requirements in the OMB guidance at 2 CFR part 182, you must include the following term or condition in the award:

Drug-free workplace. You as the recipient must comply with drug-free workplace requirements in subpart B (or subpart C, if the recipient is an individual) of 782, which adopts the Government-wide implementation (2 CFR part 182) of sec. 5152–5158 of the Drug-Free Workplace Act of 1988 (Pub. L. 100–690, Title V, Subtitle D; 41 U.S.C. 701–707).

Subpart E—Violations of This Part and Consequences

§782.500 Who in USAID determines that a recipient other than an individual violated the requirements of this part?

The Director of the Office of Acquisition and Assistance is the official authorized to make the determination under 2 CFR 182.500.

§782.505 Who in USAID determines that a recipient who is an individual violated the requirements of this part?

The Director of the Office of Acquisition and Assistance is the official authorized to make the determination under 2 CFR 182.505.

Subpart F—Definitions

§ 782.605 Award (USAID supplement to Government-wide definition at 2 CFR 182.605)

Award means an award of financial assistance by the U.S. Agency for International Development or other Federal agency directly to a recipient.

(a) The term award includes:

(1) A Federal grant or cooperative agreement, in the form of money or property in lieu of money.

(2) A block grant or a grant in an entitlement program, whether or not the grant is exempted from coverage under the Government-wide rule that implements OMB Circular A-102 (for avail-ability, see 5 CFR 1310.3) and specifies uniform administrative requirements.

(b) The term award does not include:

(1) Technical assistance that provides services instead of money.

(2) Loans.

(3) Loan guarantees.

(4) Interest subsidies.

(5) Insurance.

(6) Direct appropriations.

(7) Veterans' benefits to individuals (i.e., any benefit to veterans, their families, or survivors by virtue of the service of a veteran in the Armed Forces of the United States).

(c) Notwithstanding paragraph (a)(2) of this section, this paragraph is not applicable to AID.

CHAPTER VIII—DEPARTMENT OF VETERANS AFFAIRS

PART 801—NONPROCUREMENT DEBARMENT AND SUSPENSION

Sec.
801.10   What does this part do?
801.20   Does this part apply to me?
801.30   What policies and procedures must I follow?

Subpart A—General

801.137   Who in the Department of Veterans Affairs may grant an exception to allow an excluded person to participate in a covered transaction?

Subpart B—Covered Transactions

801.220   What contracts and subcontracts, in addition to those listed in 2 CFR 180.220, are covered transactions?

Subpart C—Responsibilities of Participants Regarding Transactions

801.332   What methods must I use to pass requirements down to participants at lower tiers with whom I intend to do business?

Subpart D—Responsibilities of Federal Agency Officials Regarding Transactions

801.437   What method do I use to communicate to a participant the requirements described in the OMB guidance at 2 CFR 180.435?

Subparts E–H [Reserved]

Subpart I—Definitions

801.930   Debarring official (Department of Veterans Affairs supplement to government-wide definition at 2 CFR 180.930).
801.995   Principal (Department of Veterans Affairs supplement to government-wide definition at 2 CFR 180.995).
801.1010   Suspending official (Department of Veterans Affairs supplement to government-wide definition at 2 CFR 180.1010).

Subpart J—Limited Denial of Participation (Department of Veterans Affairs Optional Subpart for OMB Guidance at 2 CFR Part 180).

801.1100   General.
801.1105   Cause for a limited denial of participation.
801.1110   Scope and period of a limited denial of participation.
801.1111   Notice.
801.1112   Conference.
801.1113   Appeal.

AUTHORITY: Sec. 2455, Pub. L. 103–355, 108 Stat. 3327; E.O. 12549, 3 CFR, 1986 Comp., p.

189; E.O. 12689, 3 CFR, 1989 Comp., p. 235; 38 U.S.C. 501(a) and 3703(c).

SOURCE: 72 FR 30240, May 31, 2007, unless otherwise noted.

§ 801.10   What does this part do?

This part adopts the Office of Management and Budget (OMB) guidance in subparts A through I of 2 CFR part 180, as supplemented by this part, as the Department of Veterans Affairs (VA) policies and procedures for nonprocurement debarment and suspension. It thereby gives regulatory effect for the Department of Veterans Affairs to the OMB guidance as supplemented by this part. This part satisfies the requirements in section 3 of Executive Order 12549, "Debarment and Suspension" (3 CFR 1986 Comp., p. 189), Executive Order 12689, "Debarment and Suspension" (3 CFR 1989 Comp., p. 235) and 31 U.S.C. 6101 note (Section 2455, Pub. L. 103–355, 108 Stat. 3327).

§ 801.20   Does this part apply to me?

This part and, through this part, pertinent portions of the OMB guidance in subparts A through I of 2 CFR part 180 (see table at 2 CFR 180.100(b)) apply to you if you are a—

(a) Participant or principal in a "covered transaction" (see Subpart B of 2 CFR part 180 and the definition of "nonprocurement transaction" at 2 CFR 180.970, as supplemented by Subpart B of this part);

(b) Respondent in a Department of Veterans Affairs debarment or suspension action;

(c) Department of Veterans Affairs debarment or suspension official; or

(d) Department of Veterans affairs grants officer, agreements officer, or other official authorized to enter into any type of nonprocurement transaction that is a covered transaction.

§ 801.30   What policies and procedures must I follow?

For any section of OMB guidance in subparts A through I of 2 CFR part 180 that has no corresponding section in this part, Department of Veterans Affairs policies and procedures are those in the OMB guidance. For any such section where there is a corresponding section in this part, the Department of

Veterans Affairs policies and procedures that you must follow are the policies and procedures specified in each applicable section of the OMB guidance in subparts A through I of 2 CFR part 180, and as supplemented by the section in this part with the same section number. The contracts that are covered transactions, for example, are specified by § 180.220 of the OMB guidance (2 CFR 180.220) as supplemented by § 801.220 in this part (2 CFR 801.220).

Subpart A—General

§ 801.137 Who in the Department of Veterans Affairs may grant an exception to allow an excluded person to participate in a covered transaction?

Within the Department of Veterans Affairs, the Secretary of Veterans Affairs, the Under Secretary for Health, the Under Secretary for Benefits, and the Under Secretary for Memorial Affairs each has the authority to grant an exception to allow an excluded person to participate in a covered transaction, as provided in the OMB guidance at 2 CFR 180.135.

Subpart B—Covered Transactions

§ 801.220 What contracts and subcontracts, in addition to those listed in 2 CFR 180.220, are covered transactions?

VA does not extend coverage of nonprocurement suspension and debarment requirements beyond first-tier procurement contracts under a covered nonprocurement transaction, although the OMB guidance at 2 CFR 180.220(c) allows a Federal agency to do so (also see optional lower tier coverage in the figure in the appendix to 2 CFR part 180).

Subpart C—Responsibilities of Participants Regarding Transactions

§ 801.332 What methods must I use to pass requirements down to participants at lower tiers with whom I intend to do business?

You as a participant must include a term or condition in lower-tier transactions requiring lower-tier participants to comply with subpart C of the OMB guidance in 2 CFR part 180, as supplemented by this subpart.

Subpart D—Responsibilities of Federal Agency Officials Regarding Transactions

§ 801.437 What method do I use to communicate to a participant the requirements described in the OMB guidance at 2 CFR 180.435?

To communicate to a participant the requirements described in 2 CFR 180.435 of the OMB guidance, you must include a term or condition in the transaction that requires the participant's compliance with subpart C of 2 CFR part 180 (as supplemented by subpart C of this part) and requires the participant to include a similar term or condition in lower-tier covered transactions.

Subparts E–H [Reserved]

Subpart I—Definitions

§ 801.930 Debarring official (Department of Veterans Affairs supplement to government-wide definition at 2 CFR 180.930).

In addition to the debarring official listed at 2 CFR 180.930, the debarring official for the Department of Veterans Affairs is:

(a) For the Veterans Health Administration, the Under Secretary for Health;

(b) For the Veterans Benefits Administration, the Under Secretary for Benefits; and

(c) For the National Cemetery Administration, the Under Secretary for Memorial Affairs.

§ 801.995 Principal (Department of Veterans Affairs supplement to government-wide definition at 2 CFR 180.995.)

In addition to the principals identified at 2 CFR 180.995, for the Department of Veterans Affairs loan guaranty program, principals include, but are not limited to the following:

(a) Loan officers.

(b) Loan solicitors.

(c) Loan processors.

(d) Loan servicers.

(e) Loan supervisors.

(f) Mortgage brokers.

(g) Office managers.

(h) Staff appraisers and inspectors.

(i) Fee Appraisers and inspectors.

(j) Underwriters.

(k) Bonding companies.

(l) Real estate agents and brokers.

(m) Management and marketing agents.

(n) Accountants, consultants, investment bankers, architects, engineers, attorneys, and others in a business relationship with participants in connection with a covered transaction under the Department of Veterans Affairs loan guaranty program.

(o) Contractors involved in the construction, improvement or repair of properties financed with Department of Veterans Affairs guaranteed loans.

(p) Closing agents.

§801.1010 Suspending official (Department of Veterans Affairs supplement to government-wide definition at 2 CFR 180.1010).

In addition to the suspending official listed at 2 CFR 180.1010, the suspending official for the Department of Veterans Affairs is:

(a) For the Veterans Health Administration, the Under Secretary for Health;

(b) For the Veterans Benefits Administration, the Under Secretary for Benefits; and

(c) For the National Cemetery Administration, the Under Secretary for Memorial Affairs.

Subpart J—Limited Denial of Participation (Department of Veterans Affairs Optional Subpart for OMB Guidance at 2 CFR Part 180).

§801.1100 General.

Field facility directors are authorized to order a limited denial of participation affecting any participant or contractor and its affiliates except lenders and manufactured home manufacturers. In each case, even if the offense or violation is of a criminal, fraudulent or other serious nature, the decision to order a limited denial of participation shall be discretionary and in the best interests of the Government.

§801.1105 Cause for a limited denial of participation.

(a) *Causes.* A limited denial of participation shall be based upon adequate evidence of any of the following causes:

(1) Irregularities in a participant's or contractor's performance in the VA loan guaranty program;

(2) Denial of participation in programs administered by the Department of Housing and Urban Development or the Department of Agriculture, Rural Housing Service;

(3) Failure to satisfy contractual obligations or to proceed in accordance with contract specifications;

(4) Failure to proceed in accordance with VA requirements or to comply with VA regulations;

(5) Construction deficiencies deemed by VA to be the participant's responsibility;

(6) Falsely certifying in connection with any VA program, whether or not the certification was made directly to VA;

(7) Commission of an offense or other cause listed in §180.800;

(8) Violation of any law, regulation, or procedure relating to the application for guaranty, or to the performance of the obligations incurred pursuant to a commitment to guaranty;

(9) Making or procuring to be made any false statement for the purpose of influencing in any way an action of the Department.

(10) Imposition of a limited denial of participation by any other VA field facility.

(b) *Indictment.* A criminal indictment or information shall constitute adequate evidence for the purpose of limited denial of participation actions.

(c) *Limited denial of participation.* Imposition of a limited denial of participation by a VA field facility shall, at the discretion of any other VA field facility, constitute adequate evidence for a concurrent limited denial of participation. Where such a concurrent limited denial of participation is imposed, participation may be restricted on the same basis without the need for an additional conference or further hearing.

§ 801.1110 Scope and period of a limited denial of participation.

(a) *Scope and period.* The scope of a limited denial of participation shall be as follows:

(1) A limited denial of participation extends only to participation in the VA Loan Guaranty Program and shall be effective only within the geographic jurisdiction of the office or offices imposing it.

(2) The sanction may be imposed for a period not to exceed 12 months except for unresolved construction deficiencies. In cases involving construction deficiencies, the builder may be excluded for either a period not to exceed 12 months or for an indeterminate period which ends when the deficiency has been corrected or otherwise resolved in a manner acceptable to VA.

(b) *Effectiveness.* The sanction shall be effective immediately upon issuance and shall remain effective for the prescribed period. If the cause for the limited denial of participation is resolved before the expiration of the prescribed period, the official who imposed the sanction may terminate it. The imposition of a limited denial of participation shall not affect the right of the Department to suspend or debar any person under this part.

(c) *Affiliates.* An affiliate or organizational element may be included in a limited denial of participation solely on the basis of its affiliation, and regardless of its knowledge of or participation in the acts providing cause for the sanction. The burden of proving that a particular affiliate or organizational element is capable of meeting VA requirements and is currently a responsible entity and not controlled by the primary sanctioned party (or by an entity that itself is controlled by the primary sanctioned party) is on the affiliate or organizational element.

§ 801.1111 Notice.

(a) *Generally.* A limited denial of participation shall be initiated by advising a participant or contractor, and any specifically named affiliate, by certified mail, return receipt requested:

(1) That the sanction is effective as of the date of the notice;

(2) Of the reasons for the sanction in terms sufficient to put the participant or contractor on notice of the conduct or transaction(s) upon which it is based;

(3) Of the cause(s) relied upon under § 801.1105 for imposing the sanction;

(4) Of the right to request in writing, within 30 days of receipt of the notice, a conference on the sanction, and the right to have such conference held within 10 business days of receipt of the request;

(5) Of the potential effect of the sanction and the impact on the participant's or contractor's participation in Departmental programs, specifying the program(s) involved and the geographical area affected by the action.

(b) *Notification of action.* After 30 days, if no conference has been requested, the official imposing the limited denial of participation will notify VA Central Office of the action taken and of the fact that no conference has been requested. If a conference is requested within the 30-day period, VA Central Office need not be notified unless a decision to affirm all or a portion of the remaining period of exclusion is issued. VA Central Office will notify all VA field offices of sanctions imposed and still in effect under this subpart.

§ 801.1112 Conference.

Upon receipt of a request for a conference, the official imposing the sanction shall arrange such a conference with the participant or contractor and may designate another official to conduct the conference. The participant shall be given the opportunity to be heard within 10 business days of receipt of the request. This conference precedes, and is in addition to, the formal hearing provided if an appeal is taken under § 801.1113. Although formal rules of procedure do not apply to the conference, the participant or contractor may be represented by counsel and may present all relevant information and materials to the official or designee. After consideration of the information and materials presented, the official shall, in writing, advise the participant or contractor of the decision to withdraw, modify or affirm the limited denial of participation. If the decision is made to affirm all or a portion

262

of the remaining period of exclusion, the participant shall be advised of the right to request a formal hearing in writing within 30 days of receipt of the notice of decision. This decision shall be issued promptly, but in no event later than 20 days after the conference and receipt of materials.

§801.1113 Appeal.

Where the decision is made to affirm all or a portion of the remaining period of exclusion, any participant desiring an appeal shall file a written request for a hearing with the Under Secretary for Benefits, Department of Veterans Affairs, 810 Vermont Avenue, NW., Washington, DC 20420. This request shall be filed within 30 days of receipt of the decision to affirm. If a hearing is requested, it shall be held in accordance with the procedures in §§108.825 through 108.855. Where a limited denial of participation is followed by a suspension or debarment, the limited denial of participation shall be superseded and the appeal shall be heard solely as an appeal of the suspension or debarment.

CHAPTER IX—DEPARTMENT OF ENERGY

265

PART 901—NONPROCUREMENT DEBARMENT AND SUSPENSION

Sec.
901.10 What does this part do?
901.20 Does this part apply to me?
901.30 What policies and procedures must I follow?

Subpart A—General

901.137 Who in the Department of Energy may grant an exception to let an excluded person participate in a covered transaction?

Subpart B—Covered Transactions

901.220 What contracts and subcontracts, in addition to those listed in 2 CFR 180.220, are covered transactions?

Subpart C—Responsibilities of Participants Regarding Transactions

901.332 What methods must I use to pass requirements down to participants at lower tiers with whom I intend to do business?

Subpart D—Responsibilities of Federal Agency Officials Regarding Transactions

901.437 What method do I use to communicate to a participant the requirements described in the OMB guidance at 2 CFR 180.435?

Subparts E–H [Reserved]

Subpart I—Definitions

901.930 Debarring official (Department of Energy supplement to government-wide definition at 2 CFR 180.935).
901.950 Federal agency (Department of Energy supplement to government-wide definition at 2 CFR 180.910).
901.1010 Suspending official (Department of Energy supplement to government-wide definition at 2 CFR 180.1010).

Subpart J [Reserved]

AUTHORITY: Sec. 2455, Pub. L. 103–355, 108 Stat. 3327 (31 U.S.C. 6101 note); E.O. 12549 (3 CFR, 1986 Comp., p. 189); E.O. 12689 (3 CFR, 1989 Comp., p. 235); 42 U.S.C. 7101 *et seq.*; 50 U.S.C. 2401 *et seq.*

SOURCE: 71 FR 70459, Dec. 5, 2006, unless otherwise noted.

§ 901.10 What does this part do?

This part adopts the Office of Management and Budget (OMB) guidance in subparts A through I of 2 CFR part 180, as supplemented by this part, as the DOE policies and procedures for nonprocurement debarment and suspension. It thereby gives regulatory effect for DOE to the OMB guidance as supplemented by this part. This part satisfies the requirements in section 3 of Executive Order 12549, "Debarment and Suspension" (3 CFR 1986 Comp., p. 189); Executive Order 12689, "Debarment and Suspension" (3 CFR 1989 Comp., p. 235); and section 2455 of the Federal Acquisition Streamlining Act of 1994, Pub. L. 103–355 (31 U.S.C. 6101 note).

§ 901.20 Does this part apply to me?

This part and, through this part, pertinent portions of the OMB guidance in subparts A through I of 2 CFR part 180 (see table at 2 CFR 180.100(b)) apply to you if you are a—

(a) Participant or principal in a "covered transaction" (see subpart B of 2 CFR part 180 and the definition of "nonprocurement transaction" at 2 CFR 180.970);

(b) Respondent in a DOE suspension or debarment action;

(c) DOE debarment or suspension official; and

(d) DOE grants officer, agreements officer, or other official authorized to enter into any type of nonprocurement transaction that is a covered transaction.

§ 901.30 What policies and procedures must I follow?

The DOE policies and procedures that you must follow are the policies and procedures specified in each applicable section of the OMB guidance in subparts A through I of 2 CFR part 180 and any supplemental policies and procedures set forth in this part.

Subpart A—General

§ 901.137 Who in the Department of Energy may grant an exception to let an excluded person participate in a covered transaction?

The Director, Office of Procurement and Assistance Management, DOE, for DOE actions, and the Director, Office of Acquisition and Supply Management, NNSA, for NNSA actions, may grant an exception permitting an excluded person to participate in a particular covered transaction. If the Director, Office of Procurement and Assistance Management, DOE, for DOE actions, and Director, Office of Acquisition and Supply Management, NNSA, for NNSA actions, grants an exception, the exception must be in writing and state the reason(s) for deviating from the government-wide policy in Executive Order 12549.

Subpart B—Covered Transactions

§ 901.220 What contracts and subcontracts, in addition to those listed in 2 CFR 180.220, are covered transactions?

Although the OMB guidance at 2 CFR180.220(c) allows a Federal agency to do so (also see optional lower tier coverage in the figure in the appendix to 2 CFR part 180), DOE does not extend coverage of nonprocurement suspension and debarment requirements beyond first-tier procurement contracts under a covered nonprocurement transaction.

Subpart C—Responsibilities of Participants Regarding Transactions

§ 901.332 What methods must I use to pass requirements down to participants at lower tiers with whom I intend to do business?

You, as a participant, must include a term or condition in lower-tier transactions requiring lower-tier participants to comply with subpart C of the OMB guidance in 2 CFR part 180, as supplemented by this subpart.

Subpart D—Responsibilities of Federal Agency Officials Regarding Transactions

§ 901.437 What method do I use to communicate to a participant the requirements described in the OMB guidance at 2 CFR 180.435?

To communicate to a participant the requirements described in 2 CFR 180.435 of the OMB guidance, you must include a term or condition in the transaction that requires the participant's compliance with subpart C of 2 CFR part 180, as supplemented by subpart C of this part, and requires the participant to include a similar term or condition in lower-tier covered transactions.

Subparts E–H [Reserved]

Subpart I—Definitions

§ 901.930 Debarring official (Department of Energy supplement to government-wide definition at 2 CFR 180.930).

The Debarring Official for the Department of Energy, exclusive of NNSA, is the Director, Office of Procurement and Assistance Management, DOE. The Debarring Official for NNSA is the Director, Office of Acquisition and Supply Management, NNSA.

§ 901.950 Federal agency (Department of Energy supplement to government-wide definition at 2 CFR 180.950).

DOE means the U.S. Department of Energy, including the NNSA.

NNSA means the National Nuclear Security Administration.

§ 901.1010 Suspending official (Department of Energy supplement to government-wide definition at 2 CFR 180.1010).

The suspending official for the Department of Energy, exclusive of NNSA, is the Director, Office of Procurement and Assistance Management, DOE. The suspending official for NNSA is the Director, Office of Acquisition and Supply Management, NNSA.

Subpart J [Reserved]

PART 902—REQUIREMENTS FOR DRUG-FREE WORKPLACE (FINANCIAL ASSISTANCE)

Sec.
902.10   What does this part do?
902.20   Does this part apply to me?
902.30   What policies and procedures must I follow?

Subpart A—Purpose and Coverage [Reserved]

Subpart B—Requirements for Recipients Other Than Individuals

902.225   Whom in the DOE does a recipient other than an individual notify about a criminal drug conviction?

Subpart C—Requirements for Recipients Who Are Individuals

902.300   Whom in the DOE does a recipient who is an individual notify about a criminal drug conviction?

Subpart D—Responsibilities of Agency Awarding Officials

902.400   What method do I use as an agency awarding official to obtain a recipient's agreement to comply with the OMB guidance?

Subpart E—Violations of this Part and Consequences

902.500   Who in the DOE determines that a recipient other than an individual violated the requirements of this part?
902.505   Who in the DOE determines that a recipient who is an individual violated the requirements of this part?

Subpart F—Definitions

902.605   Award (DOE supplement to Governmentwide definition at 2 CFR 182.605).
902.645   Federal agency or agency.

AUTHORITY: 41 U.S.C. 701; 42 U.S.C. 7101 *et seq.*; 50 U.S.C. 2401 *et seq.*

SOURCE: 75 FR 39444, July 9, 2010, unless otherwise noted.

§902.10   What does this part do?

This part requires that the award and administration of DOE grants and cooperative agreements comply with Office of Management and Budget (OMB) guidance implementing the portion of the Drug-Free Workplace Act of 1988 (41 U.S.C. 701–707, as amended, hereafter referred to as "the Act") that applies to grants. It thereby—

(a) Gives regulatory effect to the OMB guidance (Subparts A through F of 2 CFR part 182) for the DOE's grants and cooperative agreements; and

(b) Establishes DOE policies and procedures for compliance with the Act that are the same as those of other Federal agencies, in conformance with the requirement in 41 U.S.C. 705 for Governmentwide implementing regulations.

§902.20   Does this part apply to me?

This part and, through this part, pertinent portions of the OMB guidance in Subparts A through F of 2 CFR part 182 (see table at 2 CFR 182.115(b)) apply to you if you are a—

(a) Recipient of a DOE grant or cooperative agreement; or

(b) DOE awarding official.

§902.30   What policies and procedures must I follow?

(a) *General.* You must follow the policies and procedures specified in applicable sections of the OMB guidance in Subparts A through F of 2 CFR part 182, as implemented by this part.

(b) *Specific sections of OMB guidance that this part supplements.* In implementing the OMB guidance in 2 CFR part 182, this part supplements four sections of the guidance, as shown in the following table. For each of those sections, you must follow the policies and procedures in the OMB guidance, as supplemented by this part.

Section of OMB guidance	Section in this part where supplemented	What the supplementation clarifies
(1) 2 CFR 182.225(a)	§ 902.225	Whom in the DOE a recipient other than an individual must notify if an employee is convicted for a violation of a criminal drug statute in the workplace.
(2) 2 CFR 182.300(b)	§ 902.300	Whom in the DOE a recipient who is an individual must notify if he or she is convicted of a criminal drug offense resulting from a violation occurring during the conduct of any award activity.

Section of OMB guidance	Section in this part where supplemented	What the supplementation clarifies
(3) 2 CFR 182.500	§ 902.500	Who in the DOE is authorized to determine that a recipient other than an individual is in violation of the requirements of 2 CFR part 182, as implemented by this part.
(4) 2 CFR 182.505	§ 902.505	Who in the DOE is authorized to determine that a recipient who is an individual is in violation of the requirements of 2 CFR part 182, as implemented by this part.
(5) 2 CFR 182.605	§ 902.605	Definition of "Award".
(6) 2 CFR 182.645	§ 902.645	Definition of "Federal agency or agency".

(c) *Sections of the OMB guidance that this part does not supplement.* For any section of OMB guidance in Subparts A through F of 2 CFR part 182 that is not listed in paragraph (b) of this section, DOE policies and procedures are the same as those in the OMB guidance.

Subpart A—Purpose and Coverage [Reserved]

Subpart B—Requirements for Recipients Other Than Individuals

§ 902.225 Whom in the DOE does a recipient other than an individual notify about a criminal drug conviction?

A recipient other than an individual that is required under 2 CFR 182.225(a) to notify Federal agencies about an employee's conviction for a criminal drug offense must notify each DOE office from which it currently has an award.

Subpart C—Requirements for Recipients Who Are Individuals

§ 902.300 Whom in the DOE does a recipient who is an individual notify about a criminal drug conviction?

A recipient who is an individual and is required under 2 CFR 182.300(b) to notify Federal agencies about a conviction for a criminal drug offense must notify each DOE office from which it currently has an award.

Subpart D—Responsibilities of Agency Awarding Officials

§ 902.400 What method do I use as an agency awarding official to obtain a recipient's agreement to comply with the OMB guidance?

To obtain a recipient's agreement to comply with applicable requirements in the OMB guidance at 2 CFR part 182, you must include the following term or condition in the award:

Drug-free workplace. You as the recipient must comply with drug-free workplace requirements in Subpart B (or Subpart C, if the recipient is an individual) of Part 902, which adopts the Governmentwide implementation (2 CFR part 182) of sec. 5152–5158 of the Drug-Free Workplace Act of 1988 (Pub. L. 100–690, Title V, Subtitle D; 41 U.S.C. 701–707).

Subpart E—Violations of this Part and Consequences

§ 902.500 Who in the DOE determines that a recipient other than an individual violated the requirements of this part?

The Secretary of the Department of Energy and the Secretary's designee or designees are authorized to make the determinations under 2 CFR 182.500 for DOE, including NNSA.

§ 902.505 Who in the DOE determines that a recipient who is an individual violated the requirements of this part?

The Secretary of the Department of Energy and the Secretary's designee or designees are authorized to make the determinations under 2 CFR 182.500 for DOE, including NNSA.

Subpart F—Definitions

§ 902.605 Award (DOE supplement to Governmentwide definition at 2 CFR 182.605).

The term *award* also includes Technology Investment Agreements (TIA). A TIA is a special type of assistance instrument used to increase the involvement of commercial firms in the Department's RD&D programs. A TIA may be either a type of cooperative agreement or a type of assistance transaction other than a cooperative agreement, depending on the intellectual property provisions. A TIA may be either expenditure based or fixed support.

§ 902.645 Federal agency or agency.

Department of Energy means the U.S. Department of Energy (DOE), including the National Nuclear Security Administration (NNSA).

CHAPTER XI—DEPARTMENT OF DEFENSE

PART 1125—NONPROCUREMENT DEBARMENT AND SUSPENSION

Sec.
1125.10 What does this part do?
1125.20 Does this part implement the OMB guidance in 2 CFR part 180 for all DoD nonprocurement transactions?
1125.30 Does this part apply to me?
1125.40 What policies and procedures must I follow?

Subpart A—General

1125.137 Who in the Department of Defense may grant an exception to let an excluded person participate in a covered transaction?

Subpart B—Covered Transactions

1125.220 What contracts and subcontracts, in addition to those listed in 2 CFR 180.220, are covered transactions?

Subpart C—Responsibilities of Participants Regarding Transactions

1125.332 What method must I use to pass requirements down to participants at lower tiers with whom I intend to do business?

Subpart D—Responsibilities of DoD Officials Regarding Transactions

1125.425 When do I check to see if a person is excluded or disqualified?
1125.437 What method do I use to communicate to a participant the requirements described in the OMB guidance at 2 CFR 180.435?

Subparts E–H [Reserved]

Subpart I—Definitions

1125.930 Debarring official (DoD supplement to Governmentwide definition at 2 CFR 180.930).
1125.937 DoD Component.
1125.1010 Suspending official (DoD supplement to Governmentwide definition at 2 CFR 180.1010).

AUTHORITY: Sec. 2455, Pub. L. 103–355, 108 Stat. 3327; E.O. 12549, 3 CFR, 1986 Comp., p. 189; E.O. 12689, 3 CFR, 1989 Comp., p. 235; 5 U.S.C. 301 and 10 U.S.C. 113.

SOURCE: 72 FR 34984, June 26, 2007, unless otherwise noted.

§ 1125.10 What does this part do?

This part adopts the Office of Management and Budget (OMB) guidance in subparts A through I of 2 CFR part 180, as supplemented by this part, as the Department of Defense (DoD) policies and procedures for nonprocurement debarment and suspension. It thereby gives regulatory effect for the Department of Defense to the OMB guidance as supplemented by this part. This part satisfies the requirements in section 3 of Executive Order 12549, "Debarment and Suspension" (3 CFR 1986 Comp., p. 189), Executive Order 12689, "Debarment and Suspension" (3 CFR 1989 Comp., p. 235) and 31 U.S.C. 6101 note (Section 2455, Public Law 103–355, 108 Stat. 3327).

§ 1125.20 Does this part implement the OMB guidance in 2 CFR part 180 for all DoD nonprocurement transactions?

This part implements the OMB guidelines in 2 CFR part 180 for most DoD nonprocurement transactions. However, it does not implement the guidelines as they apply to prototype projects under the authority of Section 845 of the National Defense Authorization Act for Fiscal Year 1994 (Pub. L. 103–160), as amended. The Director of Defense Procurement and Acquisition Policy maintains a DoD issuance separate from this part that addresses section 845 transactions.

§ 1125.30 Does this part apply to me?

This part and, through this part, pertinent portions of the OMB guidance in subparts A through I of 2 CFR part 180 (see table at 2 CFR 180.100(b)) apply to you if you are a—

(a) Participant or principal in a "covered transaction" (see subpart B of 2 CFR part 180 and the definition of "nonprocurement transaction" at 2 CFR 180.970, as supplemented by subpart B of this part), other than a section 845 transaction described in § 1125.20;

(b) Respondent in a DoD Component's nonprocurement suspension or debarment action;

(c) DoD Component's debarment or suspension official; or

(d) DoD Component's grants officer, agreements officer, or other official authorized to enter into a nonprocurement transaction that is a covered transaction.

§ 1125.40 What policies and procedures must I follow?

(a) *General.* You must follow the policies and procedures specified in applicable sections of the OMB guidance in subparts A through I of 2 CFR part 180, as implemented by this part.

(b) *Specific sections of OMB guidance that this part supplements.* In implementing the OMB guidance in 2 CFR part 180, this part supplements eight sections of the guidance, as shown in the following table. For each of those sections, you must follow the policies and procedures in the OMB guidance, as supplemented by this part.

Section of OMB guidance	Section in this part where supplemented	What the supplementation clarifies
(1) 2 CFR 180.135	§ 1125.137	Who in DoD may grant an exception for an excluded person to participate in a covered transaction.
(2) 2 CFR 180.220	§ 1125.220	Which lower-tier contracts under a nonprocurement transaction are covered transactions.
(3) 2 CFR 180.330	§ 1125.332	What method a participant must use to communicate requirements to a lower-tier participant.
(4) 2 CFR 180.425	§ 1125.425	When a DoD awarding official must check to see if a person is excluded or disqualified.
(5) 2 CFR 180.435	§ 1125.437	What method a DoD official must use to communicate requirements to a participant.
(6) 2 CFR 180.930	§ 1125.930	Which DoD officials are debarring officials.
(7) 2 CFR 180.1010	§ 1125.1010	Which DoD officials are suspending officials.

(c) *Sections of the OMB guidance that this part does not supplement.* For any section of OMB guidance in subparts A through I of 2 CFR 180 that is not listed in paragraph (b) of this section, DoD policies and procedures are the same as those in the OMB guidance.

Subpart A—General

§ 1125.137 Who in the Department of Defense may grant an exception to let an excluded person participate in a covered transaction?

Within the Department of Defense, the Secretary of Defense, Secretary of a Military Department, Head of a Defense Agency, Head of the Office of Economic Adjustment, and Head of the Special Operations Command have the authority to grant an exception to let an excluded person participate in a covered transaction, as provided in the OMB guidance at 2 CFR 180.135.

Subpart B—Covered Transactions

§ 1125.220 What contracts and subcontracts, in addition to those listed in 2 CFR 180.220, are covered transactions?

Although the OMB guidance at 2 CFR 180.220(c) allows a Federal agency to do so (also see optional lower tier coverage in the figure in the appendix to 2

CFR part 180), the Department of Defense does not extend coverage of nonprocurement suspension and debarment requirements beyond first-tier procurement contracts under a covered nonprocurement transaction.

Subpart C—Responsibilities of Participants Regarding Transactions

§ 1125.332 What method must I use to pass requirements down to participants at lower tiers with whom I intend to do business?

You as a participant in a covered transaction must include a term or condition in any lower-tier covered transaction into which you enter, to require the participant of that transaction to—

(a) Comply with subpart C of the OMB guidance in 2 CFR part 180; and

(b) Include a similar term or condition in any covered transaction into which it enters at the next lower tier.

Subpart D—Responsibilities of DoD Officials Regarding Transactions

§ 1125.425 When do I check to see if a person is excluded or disqualified?

In addition to the four instances identified in the OMB guidance at 2

CFR 180.425, you as a DoD Component official must check to see if a person is excluded or disqualified before you obligate additional funding (*e.g.*, through an incremental funding action) for a pre-existing grant or cooperative agreement with an institution of higher education, as provided in 32 CFR 22.520(e)(5).

§1125.437 What method do I use to communicate to a participant the requirements described in the OMB guidance at 2 CFR 180.435?

You as a DoD Component official must include a term or condition in each covered transaction into which you enter, to communicate to the participant the requirements to—

(a) Comply with subpart C of 2 CFR part 180, as supplemented by subpart C of this part; and

(b) Include a similar term or condition in any lower-tier covered transactions into which the participant enters.

Subparts E–H [Reserved]

Subpart I—Definitions

§1125.930 Debarring official (DoD supplement to Governmentwide definition at 2 CFR 180.930).

DoD Components' debarring officials for nonprocurement transactions are the same officials identified in 48 CFR part 209, subpart 209.4, as debarring officials for procurement contracts.

§1125.937 DoD Component.

In this part, DoD Component means the Office of the Secretary of Defense, a Military Department, a Defense Agency, a DoD Field Activity, or any other organizational entity of the Department of Defense that is authorized to award or administer grants, cooperative agreements, or other nonprocurement transactions.

§1125.1010 Suspending official (DoD supplement to Governmentwide definition at 2 CFR 180.1010).

DoD Components' suspending officials for nonprocurement transactions are the same officials identified in 48 CFR part 209, subpart 209.4, as suspending officials for procurement contracts.

CHAPTER XII—DEPARTMENT OF TRANSPORTATION

PART 1200—NONPROCUREMENT SUSPENSION AND DEBARMENT

Sec.
1200.10 What does this part do?
1200.20 Does this part apply to me?
1200.30 What policies and procedures must I follow?

Subpart A—General

1200.137 Who in the Department of Transportation may grant an exception to let an excluded person participate in a covered transaction?

Subpart B—Covered Transactions

1200.220 What contracts and subcontracts, in addition to those listed in 2 CFR 180.220, are covered transactions?

Subpart C—Responsibilities of Participants Regarding Transactions

1200.332 What methods must I use to pass requirements down to participants at lower tiers with whom I intend to do business?

Subpart D—Responsibilities of Federal Agency Officials Regarding Transactions

1200.437 What method do I use to communicate to a participant the requirements described in the OMB guidance at 2 CFR 180.435?

Subparts E–J [Reserved]

AUTHORITY: 49 U.S.C. 322; Sec. 2455, Public Law 103–355, 108 Stat. 3327 (31 U.S.C. 6101 note); E.O. 12549 (3 CFR, 1986 Comp., p. 189); E.O. 12689 (3 CFR, 1989 Comp., p. 235).

SOURCE: 73 FR 24140, May 2, 2008, unless otherwise noted.

§ 1200.10 What does this part do?

This part adopts the Office of Management and Budget (OMB) guidance in subparts A through I of 2 CFR part 180, as supplemented by this part, as the Department of Transportation policies and procedures for nonprocurement suspension and debarment. It thereby gives regulatory effect for the Department of Transportation to the OMB guidance as supplemented by this part. This part satisfies the requirements in section 3 of Executive Order 12549, "Supension and Debarment" (3 CFR 1986 Comp., p. 189), Executive Order 12689, "Suspension and Debarment" (3 CFR 1989 Comp., p. 235) and 31 U.S.C. 6101 note (Section 2455, Public Law 103–355, 108 Stat. 3327).

§ 1200.20 Does this part apply to me?

This part and, through this part, pertinent portions of the OMB guidance in subparts A through I of 2 CFR part 180 (see table at 2 CFR 180.100(b)) apply to you if you are a—

(a) Participant or principal in a "covered transaction" (see subpart B of 2 CFR part 180 and the definition of "nonprocurement transaction" at 2 CFR 180.970;

(b) Respondent in a Department of Transportation suspension or debarment action;

(c) Department of Transportation debarment or suspension official;

(d) Department of Transportation grants officer, agreements officer, or other official authorized to enter into any type of nonprocurement transaction that is a covered transaction.

§ 1200.30 What policies and procedures must I follow?

The Department of Transportation policies and procedures that you must follow are the policies and procedures specified in each applicable section of the OMB guidance in subparts A through I of 2 CFR part 180, as that section is supplemented by the section in this part with the same section number. The contracts that are covered transactions, for example, are specified by section 220 of the OMB guidance (i.e., 2 CFR 180.220), as supplemented by section 220 in this part (i.e., § 1200.220). For any section of OMB guidance in subparts A through I of 2 CFR 180 that has no corresponding section in this part, Department of Transportation policies and procedures are those in the OMB guidance.

Subpart A—General

§ 1200.137 Who in the Department of Transportation may grant an exception to let an excluded person participate in a covered transaction?

Within the Department of Transportation, Office of the Secretary, the Secretary or an official designated by the

Secretary may grant an exception permitting an excluded person to participate in a particular covered transaction. Within an Operating Administration of the Department of Transportation, the head of the operating administration may grant an exception permitting an excluded person to participate in a particular covered transaction. The head of an operating administration may delegate this function and authorize successive delegations.

Subpart B—Covered Transactions

§ 1200.220 What contracts and subcontracts, in addition to those listed in 2 CFR 180.220, are covered transactions?

In addition to the contracts covered under 2 CFR 180.220(b) of the OMB guidance, this part applies to any contract, regardless of tier, that is awarded by a contractor, subcontractor, supplier, consultant, or its agent or representative in any transaction, if the contract is to be funded or provided by the Department of Transportation under a covered nonprocurement transaction and the amount of the contract is expected to equal or exceed $25,000. This extends the coverage of the Department of Transportation nonprocurement suspension and debarment requirements to all lower tiers of subcontracts under covered nonprocurement transactions, as permitted under the OMB guidance at 2 CFR 180.220(c)

(see optional lower-tier coverage in the figure in the appendix to 2 CFR part 180).

Subpart C—Responsibilities of Participants Regarding Transactions

§ 1200.332 What methods must I use to pass requirements down to participants at lower tiers with whom I intend to do business?

You as a participant must include a term or condition in lower-tier transactions requiring lower-tier participants to comply with subpart C of the OMB guidance in 2 CFR part 180, as supplemented by this subpart.

Subpart D—Responsibilities of Federal Agency Officials Regarding Transactions

§ 1200.437 What method do I use to communicate to a participant the requirements described in the OMB guidance at 2 CFR 180.435?

To communicate to a participant the requirements described in 2 CFR 180.435 of the OMB guidance, you must include a term or condition in the transaction that requires the participant's compliance with subpart C of 2 CFR part 180 and requires the participant to include a similar term or condition in lower-tier covered transactions.

Subparts E–J [Reserved]

CHAPTER XIII—DEPARTMENT OF COMMERCE

PART 1326—NONPROCUREMENT DEBARMENT AND SUSPENSION

Sec.
1326.10 What does this part do?
1326.20 Does this part apply to me?
1326.30 What policies and procedures must I follow?

Subpart A—General

1326.137 Who in the Department of Commerce may grant an exception to let an excluded person participate in a covered transaction?

Subpart B—Covered Transactions

1326.215 Which nonprocurement transactions, in addition to those listed in 2 CFR 180.215, are not covered transactions?
1326.220 What contracts and subcontracts, in addition to those listed in 2 CFR 180.220, are covered transactions?

Subpart C—Responsibilities of Participants Regarding Transactions

1326.332 What methods must I use to pass requirements down to participants at lower tiers with whom I intend to do business?

Subpart D—Responsibilities of Federal Agency Officials Regarding Transactions

1326.437 What method do I use to communicate to a participant the requirements described in the OMB guidance at 2 CFR 180.435?

Subparts E–H [Reserved]

Subpart I—Definitions

1326.970 Nonprocurement transaction (Department of Commerce supplement to government-wide definition at 2 CFR 180.970).

Subpart J [Reserved]

AUTHORITY: 5 U.S.C. 301; Sec. 2455, Pub. L. 103–355, 108 Stat. 3327; E.O. 12549, 3 CFR, 1986 Comp., p. 189; E.O. 12689, 3 CFR, 1989 Comp., p. 235.

SOURCE: 71 FR 76574, Dec. 21, 2006, unless otherwise noted.

§ 1326.10 What does this part do?

This part adopts the Office of Management and Budget (OMB) guidance in subparts A through I of 2 CFR part 180, as supplemented by this part, as the Department of Commerce policies and procedures for nonprocurement debarment and suspension. It thereby gives regulatory effect to the OMB guidance as supplemented by this part. This part satisfies the requirements in section 3 of Executive Order 12549, "Debarment and Suspension" (3 CFR 1986 Comp., p. 189), Executive Order 12689, "Debarment and Suspension" (3 CFR 1989 Comp., p. 235) and 31 U.S.C. 6101 note (Section 2455, Public Law 103–355, 108 Stat. 3327).

§ 1326.20 Does this part apply to me?

This part and, through this part, pertinent portions of the OMB guidance in subparts A through I of 2 CFR part 180 (see table at 2 CFR 180.100(b)) apply to you if you are a—

(a) Participant or principal in a "covered transaction" (see subpart B of 2 CFR part 180 and the definition of "nonprocurement transaction" at 2 CFR 180.970, as supplemented by subpart B and § 1326.970 of this part).

(b) Respondent in a Department of Commerce suspension or debarment action.

(c) Department of Commerce debarment or suspension official;

(d) Department of Commerce grants officer, agreements officer, or other official authorized to enter into any type of nonprocurement transaction that is a covered transaction;

§ 1326.30 What policies and procedures must I follow?

The Department of Commerce policies and procedures that you must follow are the policies and procedures specified in each applicable section of the OMB guidance in subparts A through I of 2 CFR part 180, as that section is supplemented by the section in this part with the same section number. The contracts that are covered transactions, for example, are specified by section 220 of the OMB guidance (*i.e.*, 2 CFR 180.220) as supplemented by section 220 in this part (*i.e.*, § 1326.220). For any section of OMB guidance in subparts A through I of 2 CFR 180 that has no corresponding section in this part, Department of Commerce policies and procedures are those in the OMB guidance.

Subpart A—General

§ 1326.137 Who in the Department of Commerce may grant an exception to let an excluded person participate in a covered transaction?

Within the Department of Commerce, the Secretary of Commerce or designee has the authority to grant an exception to let an excluded person participate in a covered transaction, as provided in the OMB guidance at 2 CFR 180.135.

Subpart B—Covered Transactions

§ 1326.215 Which nonprocurement transactions, in addition to those listed in 2 CFR 180.215, are not covered transactions?

(a) For purposes of the Department of Commerce, a transaction that the Department needs to respond to a national or agency-recognized emergency or disaster includes the Fisherman's Contingency Fund.

(b) For purposes of the Department of Commerce, an incidental benefit that results from ordinary governmental operations includes:

(1) Export Promotion, Trade Information and Counseling, and Trade policy.

(2) Geodetic Surveys and Services (Specialized Services).

(3) Fishery Products Inspection Certification.

(4) Standard Reference Materials.

(5) Calibration, Measurement, and Testing.

(6) Critically Evaluated Data (Standard Reference Data).

(7) Phoenix Data System.

(8) The sale or provision of products, information, and services to the general public.

(c) For purposes of the Department of Commerce, any other transaction if the application of an exclusion to the transaction is prohibited by law includes:

(1) The Administration of the Antidumping and Countervailing Duty Statutes.

(2) The export Trading Company Act Certification of Review Program.

(3) Trade Adjustment Assistance Program Certification.

(4) Foreign Trade Zones Act of 1934, as amended.

(5) Statutory Import Program.

§ 1326.220 What contracts and subcontracts, in addition to those listed in 2 CFR 180.220, are covered transactions?

In addition to the contracts covered under 2 CFR 180.220(b) of the OMB guidance, this part applies to a subcontract that is awarded by a participant in a procurement transaction covered under 2 CFR 180.220(a), if the amount of the subcontract exceeds or is expected to exceed $25,000. This extends the coverage of the Department of Commerce nonprocurement suspension and debarment requirements to one additional tier of contracts under covered nonprocurement transactions, as permitted under the OMB guidance at 2 CFR 180.220(c) (see optional lower tier coverage in the figure in the appendix to 2 CFR part 180).

Subpart C—Responsibilities of Participants Regarding Transactions

§ 1326.332 What methods must I use to pass requirements down to participants at lower tiers with whom I intend to do business?

You as a participant must include a term or condition in lower-tier transactions requiring lower-tier participants to comply with subpart C of the OMB guidance in 2 CFR Part 180, as supplemented by this subpart.

Subpart D—Responsibilities of Federal Agency Officials Regarding Transactions

§ 1326.437 What method do I use to communicate to a participant the requirements described in the OMB guidance at 2 CFR 180.435?

To communicate to a participant the requirements described in 2 CFR 180.435 of the OMB guidance, you must include a term or condition in the transaction that requires the participant's compliance with subpart C of 2 CFR part 180, as supplemented by subpart C of this part, and requires the participant to include a similar term or condition in lower-tier covered transactions.

Subparts E–H [Reserved]

Subpart I—Definitions

§ 1326.970 Nonprocurement transaction (Department of Commerce supplement to government-wide definition at 2 CFR 180.970).

For purposes of the Department of Commerce, nonprocurement transaction includes the following:

(a) Joint project Agreements under 15 U.S.C. 1525.

(b) Cooperative research and development agreements.

(c) Joint statistical agreements.

(d) Patent licenses under 35 U.S.C. 207.

(e) NTIS joint ventures, 15 U.S.C. 3704b.

Subpart J [Reserved]

CHAPTER XIV—DEPARTMENT OF THE INTERIOR

PART 1400—NONPROCUREMENT DEBARMENT AND SUSPENSION

Sec.
1400.10 What does this part do?
1400.20 When does this part apply to me?
1400.30 What policies and procedures must I follow?

Subpart A—General

1400.137 Who in the Department of the Interior may grant an exception to let an excluded person participate in a covered transaction?

Subpart B—Covered Transactions

1400.215 Which nonprocurement transactions, in addition to those listed in 2 CFR 180.215, are not covered transactions?
1400.220 What contracts and subcontracts, in addition to those listed in 2 CFR 180.220, are covered transactions?

Subpart C—Responsibilities of Participants Regarding Transactions

1400.332 What methods must I use to pass requirements down to participants at lower tiers with whom I intend to do business?

Subpart D—Responsibilities of Federal Agency Officials Regarding Transactions

1400.437 What method do I use to communicate to a participant the requirements described in the OMB guidance at 2 CFR 180.435?

Subparts E–H [Reserved]

Subpart I—Definitions

1400.930 Debarring official (Department of the Interior supplement to the definition at 2 CFR 180.930).
1400.970 Nonprocurement transaction (Department of the Interior supplement to the definition at 2 CFR 180.970).
1400.1010 Suspending official (Department of the Interior supplement to the definition at 2 CFR 180.930).

AUTHORITY: E.O. 12549 (3 CFR, 1986 Comp., p. 189); E.O. 12689 (3 CFR, 1989 Comp., p. 235); sec. 2455 Pub. L. 103-355, 108 Stat. 3327 (31 U.S.C. 6101 note); 5 U.S.C. 301.

SOURCE: 72 FR 33384, June 18, 2007, unless otherwise noted.

§ 1400.10 What does this part do?

This part adopts the Office of Management and Budget (OMB) guidance in subparts A through I of 2 CFR part 180, as supplemented by this part, as the Department of the Interior policies and procedures for nonprocurement debarment and suspension. It thereby gives regulatory effect to the OMB guidance as supplemented by this part. This part satisfies the requirements in section 3 of Executive Order 12549, "Debarment and Suspension" (3 CFR 1986 Comp., p. 189), Executive Order 12689, "Debarment and Suspension" (3 CFR 1989 Comp., p. 235) and 31 U.S.C. 6101 note (Section 2455, Pub. L. 103–355, 108 Stat. 3327).

§ 1400.20 When does this part apply to me?

This part and, through this part, pertinent portions of the OMB guidance in subparts A through I of 2 CFR part 180 (see table at 2 CFR 180.100(b)) apply to you if you are—

(a) Participant or principal in a "covered transaction" (see subpart B of 2 CFR part 180 and the definition of "nonprocurement transaction" at 2 CFR 180.970, as supplemented by subpart B and § 1400.970);

(b) Respondent in a Department of the Interior suspension or debarment action;

(c) Department of the Interior debarment or suspension official, i.e., the Director, Office of Acquisition and Property Management; or

(d) Department of the Interior grants officer, agreements officer, or other official authorized to enter into any type of nonprocurement transaction that is a covered transaction.

§ 1400.30 What policies and procedures must I follow?

(a) The Department of the Interior policies and procedures that you must follow are specified in:

(1) Each applicable section of the OMB guidance in subparts A through I of 2 CFR part 180; and

(2) The supplement to each section of the OMB guidance that is found in this part under the same section number. (The contracts that are covered transactions, for example, are specified by section 220 of the OMB guidance (i.e., 2 CFR 180.220) as supplemented by section 220 in this part (i.e., Sec. 1400.220)).

(b) For any section of OMB guidance in subparts A through I of 2 CFR part 180 that has no corresponding section in this part, Department of the Interior policies and procedures are those in the OMB guidance.

Subpart A—General

§ 1400.137 Who in the Department of the Interior may grant an exception to let an excluded person participate in a covered transaction?

Within the Department of the Interior, the Director, Office of Acquisition and Property Management has the authority to grant an exception to let an excluded person participate in a covered transaction, as provided in the OMB guidance at 2 CFR 180.135.

Subpart B—Covered Transactions

§ 1400.215 Which nonprocurement transactions, in addition to those listed in 2 CFR 180.215, are not covered transactions?

(a) Transactions entered into pursuant to Public Law 93-638, 88 Stat. 2203.

(b) Under natural resource management programs, permits, licenses, exchanges, and other acquisitions of real property, rights-of-way, and easements.

(c) Transactions concerning mineral patent claims entered into pursuant to 30 U.S.C. 22 *et seq.*; and

(d) Water service contracts and repayments entered into pursuant to 43 U.S.C. 485.

§ 1400.220 What contracts and subcontracts, in addition to those listed in 2 CFR 180.220, are covered transactions?

Although the OMB guidance at 2 CFR 180.220(c) allows a Federal agency to do so (also see optional lower tier coverage in the figure in the appendix to 2 CFR part 180), the Department of the Interior does not extend coverage of nonprocurement suspension and debarment requirements beyond first-tier procurement contracts under a covered nonprocurement transaction.

Subpart C—Responsibilities of Participants Regarding Transactions

§ 1400.332 What methods must I use to pass requirements down to participants at lower tiers with whom I intend to do business?

You as a participant must include a term or condition in lower-tier transactions requiring lower-tier participants to comply with subpart C of the OMB guidance in 2 CFR part 180.

Subpart D—Responsibilities of Federal Agency Officials Regarding Transactions

§ 1400.437 What method do I use to communicate to a participant the requirements described in the OMB guidance at 2 CFR 180.435?

To communicate to a participant the requirements described in 2 CFR 180.435 of the OMB guidance, you must include a term or condition in the transaction that requires the participant's compliance with subpart C of 2 CFR part 180, as supplemented by subpart C of this part, and requires the participant to include a similar term or condition in lower-tier covered transactions.

Subparts E–H [Reserved]

Subpart I—Definitions

§ 1400.930 Debarring official (Department of the Interior supplement to the definition at 2 CFR 180.930).

The Debarring Official for the Department of the Interior is the Director, Office of Acquisition and Property Management.

§ 1400.970 Nonprocurement transaction (Department of the Interior supplement to the definition at 2 CFR 180.970).

In addition to those listed in 2 CFR 180.970, the Department of the Interior includes the following as nonprocurement transactions:

(a) Federal acquisition of a leasehold interest or any other interest in real property;

(b) Concession contracts;

(c) Disposition of Federal real and personal property and natural resources; and

(d) Any other nonprocurement transactions between the Department and a person.

§1400.1010 Suspending official (Department of the Interior supplement to the definition at 2 CFR 180.930).

The Suspending Official for the Department of the Interior is the Director, Office of Acquisition and Property Management.

Subpart J [Reserved]

PART 1401—REQUIREMENTS FOR DRUG-FREE WORKPLACE (FINANCIAL ASSISTANCE)

Subpart A—Purpose and Coverage

AUTHORITY: 5 U.S.C. 301; 31 U.S.C. 6101 note, 7501; 41 U.S.C. 252a; 41 U.S.C. 701–707.

SOURCE: 75 FR 71008, Nov. 22, 2010, unless otherwise noted.

Subpart A—Purpose and Coverage

§1401.100   What does this part do?

This part requires that the award and administration of the DOI grants and cooperative agreements comply with Office of Management and Budget (OMB) guidance implementing the portion of the Drug-Free Workplace Act of 1988, 41 U.S.C. 701–707, as amended (hereinafter, "the Act") that applies to grants. It thereby—

(a) Gives regulatory effect to the OMB guidance (Subparts A through F of 2 CFR Part 182) for DOI's grants and cooperative agreements; and

(b) Establishes DOI policies and procedures for compliance with the Act that are the same as those of other Federal agencies, in conformance with the requirement in 41 U.S.C. 705 for government-wide implementing regulations.

§ 1401.105   Does this part apply to me?

This part and, through this part, pertinent portions of the OMB guidance in Subparts A through F of 2 CFR part 182 apply if you are—

(a) A recipient of an assistance award from the Department of the Interior; or

(b) The Department of the Interior awarding official.

The following table (will be incorporated into 2 CFR part 182) shows the subparts that apply to you:

If you are	See subparts
(1) A recipient who is not an individual ...	A, C and F.
(2) A recipient who is an individual	A, D and F.
(3) A Department of the Interior awarding official.	A, E and F.

§ 1401.110   What policies and procedures must I follow?

(a) *General.* You must follow the policies and procedures specified in applicable sections of the OMB guidance in Subparts A through F of 2 CFR part 182, as implemented by this part.

(b) In implementing OMB guidance in 2 CFR part 182, this part supplements four sections of the guidance, as shown in the following table. For each of those sections, you must follow the policies and procedures set forth in the OMB guidance, as supplemented by this part.

Section of OMB guidance	Section in this part where supplemented	What the supplementation clarifies
(1) 2 CFR 182.225(a)	§ 1401.335	Whom in the DOI a recipient other than an individual must notify if an employee is convicted for a violation of a criminal drug statute in the workplace.
(2) 2 CFR 182.300(b)	§ 1401.401	Whom in the DOI a recipient who is an individual must notify if he or she is convicted of a criminal drug offense resulting from a violation occurring during the conduct of any award activity.
(3) 2 CFR 182.500	§ 1401.600	Who in the DOI is authorized to determine that a recipient other than an individual is in violation of the requirements of 2 CFR Part 182, as implemented by this part.
(4) 2 CFR 182.505	§ 1401.605	Who in the DOI is authorized to determine that a recipient who is an individual is in violation of the requirements of 2 CFR Part 182, as implemented by this part.

(c) *Sections of the OMB guidance that this part does not supplement.* For any section of OMB guidance in Subparts A through F of 2 CFR Part 182 that is not listed in paragraph (b) of this section, DOI policies and procedures are the same as those in the OMB guidance.

§ 1401.115   Are any of my Federal assistance awards exempt from this part?

This part does not apply to any award if the Director, Office of Acquisition and Property Management (PAM), determines that the application of this part would be inconsistent with the international obligations of the United States or the laws or regulations of a foreign government.

§ 1401.120   Does this part affect the Federal contracts that I receive?

It will affect future contract awards indirectly if you are debarred or suspended for a violation of the requirements of this part, as described in § 1401.610(c). However, this part does not directly apply to procurement contracts. The portion of the Drug-Free Workplace Act of 1988 that applies to Federal procurement contracts is carried out through the Federal Acquisition Regulation in 48 CFR part 23, subpart 23.5.

Subpart F—Definitions

§ 1401.205   Award.

Award means an award of financial assistance by DOI or other Federal agency directly to a recipient.

(a) The term award includes:

(1) A Federal grant or cooperative agreement, in the form of money or property in lieu of money.

(2) A block grant or a grant in an entitlement program, whether or not the grant is exempted from coverage under the Departmental rules at 43 CFR part 12, subpart C, "Uniform Administrative Requirements for Grants and Cooperative Agreements to State and Local Governments."

(b) The term award does not include:

(1) Technical assistance that provides services instead of money.

(2) Loans.

(3) Loan guarantees.

(4) Interest subsidies.

(5) Insurance.

(6) Direct appropriations.

(7) Veterans' benefits to individuals (*i.e.*, any benefit to veterans, their families, or survivors by virtue of the service of a veteran in the Armed Forces of the United States).

§ 1401.210 Controlled substance.

Controlled substance means any controlled substance identified in schedules I through V of the Controlled Substances Act, 21 U.S.C. 812, and as further defined by regulations at 21 CFR 1308.11 through 1308.15.

§ 1401.215 Conviction.

Conviction means a finding of guilt (including a plea of nolo contendere) or imposition of sentence, or both, by any judicial body charged with the responsibility to determine violations of the Federal or State criminal drug statutes.

§ 1401.220 Cooperative agreement.

Cooperative agreement means an award of financial assistance that, consistent with 31 U.S.C. 6305, is used to enter into the same kind of relationship as a grant (*see* definition of grant in section 1401.250), except that substantial involvement is expected between the Federal agency and the recipient when carrying out the activity contemplated by the award. The term does not include cooperative research and development agreements as defined in 15 U.S.C. 3710a.

§ 1401.225 Criminal drug statute.

Criminal drug statute means a Federal or non-Federal criminal statute involving the manufacture, distribution, dispensing, use, or possession of any controlled substance.

§ 1401.230 Debarment.

Debarment means an action taken by a Federal agency to prohibit a recipient from participating in Federal Government procurement contracts and covered non-procurement transactions. A recipient so prohibited is debarred, in accordance with the Federal Acquisition Regulation for procurement contracts (48 CFR part 9, subpart 9.4) and 2 CFR part 180.

§ 1401.235 Drug-free workplace.

Drug-free workplace means a site for the performance of work done in connection with a specific award at which employees of the recipient are prohibited from engaging in the unlawful manufacture, distribution, dispensing, possession, or use of a controlled substance.

§ 1401.240 Employee.

(a) *Employee* means the employee of a recipient directly engaged in the performance of work under the award, including—

(1) All direct charge employees;

(2) All indirect charge employees, unless their impact or involvement in the performance of work under the award is insignificant to the performance of the award; and

(3) Temporary personnel and consultants who are directly engaged in the performance of work under the award and who are on the recipient's payroll.

(b) This definition does not include workers not on the payroll of the recipient (*e.g.*, volunteers, even if used to meet a matching requirement; consultants or independent contractors not on the payroll; or employees of sub-recipients or subcontractors in covered workplaces).

§ 1401.245 Federal agency or agency.

Federal agency or *agency* means any United States executive department, military department, government corporation, government controlled corporation, any other establishment in the executive branch (including the Executive Office of the President), or any independent regulatory agency.

§ 1401.250   Grant.

Grant means an award of financial assistance that, consistent with 31 U.S.C. 6304, is used to enter into a relationship whereby—

(a) The principal purpose of which is to transfer a thing of value to the recipient to carry out a public purpose of support or stimulation authorized by a law of the United States, rather than to acquire property or services for the Federal Government's direct benefit or use; and

(b) In which substantial involvement is not expected between the Federal agency and the recipient when carrying out the activity contemplated by the award.

§ 1401.255   Individual.

Individual means a natural person.

§ 1401.260   Recipient.

Recipient means any individual, corporation, partnership, association, unit of government (except a Federal agency) or legal entity, however organized, that receives an award directly from a Federal agency.

§ 1401.265   State.

State means any of the States of the United States, the District of Columbia, the Commonwealth of Puerto Rico, or any territory or possession of the United States.

§ 1401.270   Suspension.

Suspension means an action taken by a Federal agency that immediately prohibits a recipient from participating in Federal Government procurement contracts and covered non-procurement transactions for a temporary period, pending completion of an investigation and any judicial or administrative proceedings that may ensue. A recipient so prohibited is suspended, in accordance with the Federal Acquisition Regulation Regulation for procurement contracts (48 CFR part 9, subpart 9.4) and 2 CFR part 180. Suspension of a recipient is a distinct and separate action from suspension of an award or suspension of payments under an award.

Subpart C—Requirements for Recipients Other Than Individuals

§ 1401.300   What must I do to comply with this part?

There are two general requirements if you are a recipient other than an individual.

(a) First, you must make a good faith effort, on a continuing basis, to maintain a drug-free workplace. You must agree to do so as a condition for receiving any award covered by this part. The specific measures that you must take in this regard are described in more detail in subsequent sections of this subpart. Briefly, those measures are to—

(1) Publish a drug-free workplace statement and establish a drug-free awareness program for your employees; and

(2) Take actions concerning employees who are convicted of violating drug statutes in the workplace.

(b) Second, you must identify all known workplaces under your Federal awards.

§ 1401.305   What must I include in my drug-free workplace statement?

You must publish a statement that—

(a) Tells your employees that the unlawful manufacture, distribution, dispensing, possession, or use of a controlled substance is prohibited in your workplace;

(b) Specifies the actions that you will take against employees for violating that prohibition; and

(c) Lets each employee know that, as a condition of employment under any award, he or she:

(1) Will abide by the terms of the statement; and

(2) Must notify you in writing if he or she is convicted for a violation of a criminal drug statute occurring in the workplace and must do so no more than five calendar days after the conviction.

§ 1401.310 To whom must I distribute my drug-free workplace statement?

You must require that a copy of the statement described in § 1401.305 be given to each employee who will be engaged in the performance of any Federal award.

§ 1401.315 What must I include in my drug-free awareness program?

You must establish an ongoing drug-free awareness program to inform employees about—

(a) The dangers of drug abuse in the workplace;

(b) Your policy of maintaining a drug-free workplace;

(c) Any available drug counseling, rehabilitation, and employee assistance programs; and

(d) The penalties that you may impose upon them for drug abuse violations occurring in the workplace.

§ 1401.320 By when must I publish my drug-free workplace statement and establish my drug-free awareness program?

If you are a new recipient that does not already have a policy statement as described in § 1401.305 and an ongoing awareness program as described in § 1401.315, you must publish the statement and establish the program by the time given in the following table:

If . . .	then you . . .
(a) The performance period of the award is less than 30 days	must have the policy statement and program in place as soon as possible, but before the date on which performance is expected to be completed.
(b) The performance period of the award is 30 days or more ...	must have the policy statement and program in place within 30 days after award.
(c) You believe there are extraordinary circumstances that will require more than 30 days for you to publish the policy statement and establish the awareness program.	may ask the Department of the Interior awarding official to give you more time to do so. The amount of additional time, if any, to be given is at the discretion of the awarding official.

§ 1401.325 What actions must I take concerning employees who are convicted of drug violations in the workplace?

There are two actions you must take if an employee is convicted of a drug violation in the workplace:

(a) First, you must notify Federal agencies if an employee who is engaged in the performance of an award informs you about a conviction, as required by § 1401.305(c)(2), or you otherwise learn of the conviction. Your notification to the Federal agencies must—

(1) Be in writing;

(2) Include the employee's position title;

(3) Include the identification number(s) of each affected award;

(4) Be sent within ten calendar days after you learn of the conviction; and

(5) Be sent to every Federal agency on whose award the convicted employee was working. It must be sent to every awarding official or his or her official designee, unless the Federal agency has specified a central point for the receipt of the notices.

(b) Second, within 30 calendar days of learning about an employee's conviction, you must either—

(1) Take appropriate personnel action against the employee, up to and including termination, consistent with the requirements of the Rehabilitation Act of 1973, 29 U.S.C. 794, as amended; or

(2) Require the employee to participate satisfactorily in a drug abuse assistance or rehabilitation program approved for these purposes by a Federal, State or local health, law enforcement, or other appropriate agency.

§ 1401.330 How and when must I identify workplaces?

(a) You must identify all known workplaces under each DOI award. A failure to do so is a violation of your drug-free workplace requirements. You may identify the workplaces—

(1) To the DOI official that is making the award, either at the time of application or upon award; or

(2) In documents that you keep on file in your offices during the performance of the award, in which case you must make the information available

for inspection upon request by DOI officials or their designated representatives.

(b) Your workplace identification for an award must include the actual address of buildings (or parts of buildings) or other sites where work under the award takes place. Categorical descriptions may be used (*e.g.*, all vehicles of a mass transit authority or State highway department while in operation, State employees in each local unemployment office, performers in concert halls or radio studios).

(c) If you identified workplaces to the DOI awarding official at the time of application or award, as described in paragraph (a)(1) of this section, and any workplace that you identified changes during the performance of the award, you must inform the DOI awarding official.

§ 1401.335 **Whom in the DOI does a recipient other than an individual notify about a criminal drug conviction?**

The DOI is not designating a central location for the receipt of these reports. Therefore you shall provide this report to every grant officer, or other designee within a bureau or office of the Department on whose grant activity the convicted employee was working.

Subpart D—Requirements for Recipients Who Are Individuals

§ 1401.400 **What must I do to comply with this part if I am an individual recipient?**

As a condition of receiving a DOI award, if you are an individual recipient, you must agree that—

(a) You will not engage in the unlawful manufacture, distribution, dispensing, possession, or use of a controlled substance in conducting any activity related to the award; and

(b) If you are convicted of a criminal drug offense resulting from a violation occurring during the conduct of any award activity, you will report the conviction:

(1) In writing.

(2) Within 10 calendar days of the conviction.

(3) To the Department of the Interior awarding official or other designee for each award that you currently have, unless § 1401.401 or the award document designates a central point for the receipt of the notices. When notice is made to a central point, it must include the identification number(s) of each affected award.

§ 1401.401 **Whom in the DOI does a recipient who is an individual notify about a criminal drug conviction?**

The DOI is not designating a central location for the receipt of these reports. Therefore you shall provide this report to every grant officer, or other designee within a bureau or office of the Department on whose grant activity the convicted employee was working.

Subpart E—Responsibilities of Department of Interior Awarding Officials

§ 1401.500 **What are my responsibilities as a DOI awarding official?**

To obtain a recipient's agreement to comply with applicable requirements in the OMB guidance at 2 CFR part 182, you must include the following term or condition in the award:

Drug-free workplace. You, as the recipient, must comply with drug-free workplace requirements in subpart B (or subpart C, if the recipient is an individual) of part 1401, which adopts the government-wide implementation of 2 CFR part 182; sections 5152–5158 of the Drug-Free Workplace Act of 1988, Pub. L. 100–690, Title V, Subtitle D; 41 U.S.C. 701–707.

Subpart F—Violations of this Part and Consequences

§ 1401.600 **How are violations of this part determined for recipients other than individuals?**

A recipient other than an individual is in violation of the requirements of this part if the Director, PAM determines, in writing, that—

(a) The recipient has violated the requirements of subpart B of this part; or

(b) The number of convictions of the recipient's employees for violating criminal drug statutes in the workplace is large enough to indicate that the recipient has failed to make a good faith effort to provide a drug-free workplace.

§1401.605 How are violations of this part determined for recipients who are individuals?

An individual recipient is in violation of the requirements of this part if the Director, PAM determines, in writing, that—

(a) The recipient has violated the requirements of subpart C of this part; or

(b) The recipient is convicted of a criminal drug offense resulting from a violation occurring during the conduct of any award activity.

§1401.610 What actions will the Federal Government take against a recipient determined to have violated this part?

If a recipient is determined to have violated this part, as described in §1401.600 or §1401.605, DOI may take one or more of the following actions—

(a) Suspension of payments under the award;

(b) Suspension or termination of the award; and

(c) Suspension or debarment of the recipient under 2 CFR part 180, for a period not to exceed five years.

§1401.615 Are there any exceptions to those actions?

The Secretary of the Interior may waive with respect to a particular award, in writing, a suspension of payments under an award, suspension or termination of an award, or suspension or debarment of a recipient if the Secretary of the Interior determines that such a waiver would be in the public interest. This exception authority cannot be delegated to any other official.

CHAPTER XV—ENVIRONMENTAL PROTECTION AGENCY

PART 1532—NONPROCUREMENT DEBARMENT AND SUSPENSION

Sec.
1532.10 What does this part do?
1532.20 Does this part apply to me?
1532.30 What policies and procedures must I follow?

Subpart A—General

1532.137 Who in the EPA may grant an exception to let an excluded person participate in a covered transaction?

Subpart B—Covered Transactions

1532.220 What contracts and subcontracts, in addition to those listed in 2 CFR 180.220, are covered transactions?

Subpart C—Responsibilities of Participants Regarding Transactions

1532.332 What methods must I use to pass requirements down to participants at lower tiers with whom I intend to do business?

Subpart D—Responsibilities of Federal Agency Officials Regarding Transactions

1532.437 What method do I use to communicate to a participant the requirements described in the OMB guidance at 2 CFR 180.435?

Subparts E-F [Reserved]

Subpart G—Suspension

1532.765 How may I appeal my EPA suspension?

Subpart H—Debarment

1532.890 How may I appeal my EPA debarment?

Subpart I—Definitions

1532.995 Principal (EPA supplement to government-wide definition at 2 CFR 180.995).

Subpart J—Statutory Disqualification and Reinstatement Under the Clean Air Act and Clean Water Act

1532.1100 What does this subpart do?
1532.1105 Does this subpart apply to me?
1532.1110 How will a CAA or CWA conviction affect my eligibility to participate in Federal contracts, subcontracts, assistance, loans and other benefits?
1532.1115 Can the EPA extend a CAA or CWA disqualification to other facilities?

1532.1120 What is the purpose of CAA or CWA disqualification?
1532.1125 How do award officials and others know if I am disqualified?
1532.1130 How does disqualification under the CAA or CWA differ from a Federal discretionary suspension or debarment action?
1532.1135 Does CAA or CWA disqualification mean that I must remain ineligible?
1532.1140 Can an exception be made to allow me to receive an award even though I may be disqualified?
1532.1200 How will I know if I am disqualified under the CAA or CWA?
1532.1205 What procedures must I follow to have my procurement and nonprocurement eligibility reinstated under the CAA or CWA?
1532.1210 Will anyone else provide information to the EPA debarring official concerning my reinstatement request?
1532.1215 What happens if I disagree with the information provided by others to the EPA debarring official on my reinstatement request?
1532.1220 What will the EPA debarring official consider in making a decision on my reinstatement request?
1532.1225 When will the EPA debarring official make a decision on my reinstatement request?
1532.1230 How will the EPA debarring official notify me of the reinstatement decision?
1532.1300 Can I resolve my eligibility status under terms of an administrative agreement without having to submit a formal reinstatement request?
1532.1305 What are the consequences if I mislead the EPA in seeking reinstatement or fail to comply with my administrative agreement?
1532.1400 How may I appeal a decision denying my request for reinstatement?
1532.1500 If I am reinstated, when will my name be removed from the EPLS?
1532.1600 What definitions apply specifically to actions under this subpart?

AUTHORITY: 33 U.S.C. 1251 et seq.; 42 U.S.C. 7401 et seq.; Sec. 2455, Pub. L. 103–355, 108 Stat. 3327 (31 U.S.C. 6101 note); E.O. 11738 (3 CFR, 1973 Comp., p. 799); E.O. 12549 (3 CFR, 1986 Comp., p. 189); E.O. 12689 (3 CFR, 1989 Comp., p. 235).

SOURCE: 72 FR 2422, Jan. 19, 2007, unless otherwise noted.

§ 1532.10 What does this part do?

This part adopts the Office of Management and Budget (OMB) guidance in subparts A through I of 2 CFR part 180, as supplemented by this part, as the Environmental Protection Agency

(EPA) policies and procedures for non-procurement debarment and suspension. It thereby gives regulatory effect for the EPA to the OMB guidance as supplemented by this part. This part satisfies the requirements in section 3 of Executive Order 12549, "Debarment and Suspension" (3 CFR 1986 Comp., p. 189), Executive Order 12689, "Debarment and Suspension" (3 CFR 1989 Comp., p. 235) and 31 U.S.C. 6101 note (Section 2455, Pub. L. 103-355, 108 Stat. 3327).

§ 1532.20 Does this part apply to me?

This part and, through this part, pertinent portions of the OMB guidance in subparts A through I of 2 CFR part 180 (see table at 2 CFR 180.100(b)) apply to you if you are a—

(a) Participant or principal in a "covered transaction" (see subpart B of 2 CFR part 180 and the definition of "nonprocurement transaction" at 2 CFR 180.970;

(b) Respondent in an EPA suspension or debarment action;

(c) EPA debarment or suspension official; or

(d) EPA grants officer, agreements officer, or other official authorized to enter into any type of nonprocurement transaction that is a covered transaction.

§ 1532.30 What policies and procedures must I follow?

The EPA policies and procedures that you must follow are the policies and procedures specified in each applicable section of the OMB guidance in subparts A through I of 2 CFR part 180, as that section is supplemented by the section in this part with the same section number. The contracts that are covered transactions, for example, are specified by section 220 of the OMB guidance (i.e., 2 CFR 180.220) as supplemented by section 220 in this part (i.e., § 1532.220). For any section of OMB guidance in subparts A through I of 2 CFR 180 that has no corresponding section in this part, EPA policies and procedures are those in the OMB guidance.

Subpart A—General

§ 1532.137 Who in the EPA may grant an exception to let an excluded person participate in a covered transaction?

The EPA Debarring Official has the authority to grant an exception to let an excluded person participate in a covered transaction, as provided in the OMB guidance at 2 CFR 180.135. If the EPA Debarring Official grants an exception, the exception must be in writing and state the reason(s) for deviating from the governmentwide policy in Executive Order 12549.

Subpart B—Covered Transactions

§ 1532.220 What contracts and sub-contracts, in addition to those listed in 2 CFR 180.220, are covered transactions?

In addition to the contracts covered under 2 CFR 180.220(b) of the OMB guidance, this part applies to any contract, regardless of tier, that is awarded by a contractor, subcontractor, supplier, consultant, or its agent or representative in any transaction, if the contract is to be funded or provided by the EPA under a covered nonprocurement transaction and the amount of the contract is expected to equal or exceed $25,000. This extends the coverage of the EPA nonprocurement suspension and debarment requirements to all lower tiers of subcontracts under covered nonprocurement transactions, as permitted under the OMB guidance at 2 CFR 180.220(c) (see optional lower tier coverage in the figure in the appendix to 2 CFR part 180).

Subpart C—Responsibilities of Participants Regarding Transactions

§ 1532.332 What methods must I use to pass requirements down to participants at lower tiers with whom I intend to do business?

You as a participant must include a term or condition in lower-tier transactions requiring lower-tier participants to comply with subpart C of the OMB guidance in 2 CFR part 180, as supplemented by this subpart.

Subpart D—Responsibilities of Federal Agency Officials Regarding Transactions

§1532.437 What method do I use to communicate to a participant the requirements described in the OMB guidance at 2 CFR 180.435?

To communicate to a participant the requirements described in 2 CFR 180.435 of the OMB guidance, you must include a term or condition in the transaction that requires the participant's compliance with subpart C of 2 CFR part 180, as supplemented by subpart C of this part, and requires the participant to include a similar term or condition in lower-tier covered transactions.

Subparts E–F [Reserved]

Subpart G—Suspension

§1532.765 How may I appeal my EPA suspension?

(a) If the EPA suspending official issues a decision under 2 CFR 180.755 to continue your suspension after you present information in opposition to that suspension under 2 CFR 180.720, you can ask for review of the suspending official's decision in two ways:

(1) You may ask the suspending official to reconsider the decision for material errors of fact or law that you believe will change the outcome of the matter; and/or

(2) You may request the Director, Office of Grants and Debarment (OGD Director), to review the suspending official's decision to continue your suspension within 30 days of your receipt of the suspending official's decision under 2 CFR 180.755 or paragraph (a)(1) of this section. However, the OGD Director can reverse the suspending official's decision only where the OGD Director finds that the decision is based on a clear error of material fact or law, or where the OGD Director finds that the suspending official's decision was arbitrary, capricious, or an abuse of discretion.

(b) A request for review under this section must be in writing; state the specific findings you believe to be in error; and include the reasons or legal bases for your position.

(c) A review under paragraph (a)(2) of this section is solely within the discretion of the OGD Director who may also stay the suspension pending review of the suspending official's decision.

(d) The EPA suspending official and the OGD Director must notify you of their decisions under this section, in writing, using the notice procedures at 2 CFR 180.615 and 180.975.

Subpart H—Debarment

§1532.890 How may I appeal my EPA debarment?

(a) If the EPA debarring official issues a decision under 2 CFR 180.870 to debar you after you present information in opposition to a proposed debarment under 2 CFR 180.815, you can ask for review of the debarring official's decision in two ways:

(1) You may ask the debarring official to reconsider the decision for material errors of fact or law that you believe will change the outcome of the matter; and/or

(2) You may request the Director, Office of Grants and Debarment (OGD Director), to review the debarring official's decision to debar you within 30 days of your receipt of the debarring official's decision under 2 CFR 180.870 or paragraph (a)(1) of this section. However, the OGD Director can reverse the debarring official's decision only where the OGD Director finds that the decision is based on a clear error of material fact or law, or where the OGD Director finds that the debarring official's decision was arbitrary, capricious, or an abuse of discretion.

(b) A request for review under this section must be in writing; state the specific findings you believe to be in error; and include the reasons or legal bases for your position.

(c) A review under paragraph (a)(2) of this section is solely within the discretion of the OGD Director who may also stay the debarment pending review of the debarring official's decision.

(d) The EPA debarring official and the OGD Director must notify you of their decisions under this section, in writing, using the notice procedures at 2 CFR 180.615 and 180.975.

Subpart I—Definitions

§ 1532.995 Principal (EPA supplement to government-wide definition at 2 CFR 180.995).

In addition to those listed in 2 CFR 180.995, other examples of individuals who are principals in EPA covered transactions include:

(a) Principal investigators;

(b) Technical or management consultants;

(c) Individuals performing chemical or scientific analysis or oversight;

(d) Professional service providers such as doctors, lawyers, accountants, engineers, etc.;

(e) Individuals responsible for the inspection, sale, removal, transportation, storage or disposal of solid or hazardous waste or materials;

(f) Individuals whose duties require special licenses;

(g) Individuals that certify, authenticate or authorize billings; and

(h) Individuals that serve in positions of public trust.

Subpart J—Statutory Disqualification and Reinstatement Under the Clean Air Act and Clean Water Act

§ 1532.1100 What does this subpart do?

This subpart explains how the EPA administers section 306 of the Clean Air Act (CAA) (42 U.S.C. 7606) and section 508 of the Clean Water Act (CWA) (33 U.S.C. 1368), which disqualify persons convicted for certain offenses under those statutes (see § 1532.1105), from eligibility to receive certain contracts, subcontracts, assistance, loans and other benefits (see coverage under the Federal Acquisition Regulation (FAR), 48 CFR part 9, subpart 9.4 and subparts A through I of 2 CFR part 180). It also explains: the procedures for seeking reinstatement of a person's eligibility under the CAA or CWA; the criteria and standards that apply to EPA's decision-making process; and requirements of award officials and others involved in Federal procurement and nonprocurement activities in carrying out their responsibilities under the CAA and CWA.

§ 1532.1105 Does this subpart apply to me?

(a) Portions of this subpart apply to you if you are convicted, or likely to be convicted, of any offense under section 7413(c) of the CAA or section 1319(c) of the CWA.

(b) Portions of this subpart apply to you if you are the EPA debarring official, a Federal procurement or nonprocurement award official, a participant in a Federal procurement or nonprocurement program that is precluded from entering into a covered transaction with a person disqualified under the CAA or CWA, or if you are a Federal department or agency anticipating issuing an exception to a person otherwise disqualified under the CAA or CWA.

§ 1532.1110 How will a CAA or CWA conviction affect my eligibility to participate in Federal contracts, subcontracts, assistance, loans and other benefits?

If you are convicted of any offense described in § 1532.1105, you are automatically disqualified from eligibility to receive any contract, subcontract, assistance, sub-assistance, loan or other nonprocurement benefit or transaction that is prohibited by a Federal department or agency under the Governmentwide debarment and suspension system (i.e. covered transactions under subpart A through I of 2 CFR part 180, or prohibited awards under 48 CFR part 9, subpart 9.4), if you:

(a) Will perform any part of the transaction or award at the facility giving rise to your conviction (called the violating facility); and

(b) You own, lease or supervise the violating facility.

§ 1532.1115 Can the EPA extend a CAA or CWA disqualification to other facilities?

The CAA specifically authorizes the EPA to extend a CAA disqualification to other facilities that are owned or operated by the convicted person. The EPA also has authority under subparts A through I of 2 CFR part 180, or under 48 CFR part 9, subpart 9.4, to take discretionary suspension and debarment actions on the basis of misconduct leading to a CAA or CWA conviction, or for activities that the EPA debarring official believes were designed to improperly circumvent a CAA or CWA disqualification.

§ 1532.1120 What is the purpose of CAA or CWA disqualification?

As provided for in Executive Order 11738 (3 CFR, 1973 Comp., p. 799), the purpose of CAA and CWA disqualification is to enforce the Federal Government's policy of undertaking Federal procurement and nonprocurement activities in a manner that improves and enhances environmental quality by promoting effective enforcement of the CAA or CWA.

§ 1532.1125 How do award officials and others know if I am disqualified?

If you are convicted under these statutes, the EPA enters your name and address and that of the violating facility into the Excluded Parties List System (EPLS) as soon as possible after the EPA learns of your conviction. In addition, the EPA enters other information describing the nature of your disqualification. Federal award officials and others who administer Federal programs consult the EPLS before entering into or approving procurement and nonprocurement transactions. Anyone may access the EPLS through the internet, currently at *http://www.epls.gov.*

§ 1532.1130 How does disqualification under the CAA or CWA differ from a Federal discretionary suspension or debarment action?

(a) CAA and CWA disqualifications are exclusions mandated by statute. In contrast, suspensions and debarments imposed under subparts A through I of 2 CFR part 180 or under 48 CFR part 9, subpart 9.4, are exclusions imposed at the discretion of Federal suspending or debarring officials. This means that if you are convicted of violating the CAA or CWA provisions described under § 1532.1105, ordinarily your name and that of the violating facility is placed into the EPLS before you receive a confirmation notice of the listing, or have the opportunity to discuss the disqualification with, or seek reinstatement from, the EPA.

(b) CAA or CWA disqualification applies to both the person convicted of the offense, and to the violating facility during performance of an award or covered transaction under the Federal procurement and nonprocurement suspension and debarment system. It is the EPA's policy to carry out CAA and CWA disqualifications in a manner which integrates the disqualifications into the Governmentwide suspension and debarment system. Whenever the EPA determines that the risk presented to Federal procurement and nonprocurement activities on the basis of the misconduct which gives rise to a person's CAA or CWA conviction exceeds the coverage afforded by mandatory disqualification, the EPA may use its discretionary authority to suspend or debar a person under subparts A through I of 2 CFR part 180, or under 48 CFR part 9, subpart 9.4.

§ 1532.1135 Does CAA or CWA disqualification mean that I must remain ineligible?

You must remain ineligible until the EPA debarring official certifies that the condition giving rise to your conviction has been corrected. If you desire to have your disqualification terminated, you must submit a written request for reinstatement to the EPA debarring official and support your request with persuasive documentation. For information about the process for reinstatement see §§ 1532.1205 and 1532.1300.

§ 1532.1140 Can an exception be made to allow me to receive an award even though I may be disqualified?

(a) After consulting with the EPA debarring official, the head of any Federal department or agency (or designee) may exempt any particular award or a class of awards with that department or agency from CAA or CWA disqualification. In the event an exemption is granted, the exemption must:

(1) Be in writing; and

(2) State why the exemption is in the paramount interests of the United States.

(b) In the event an exemption is granted, the exempting department or agency must send a copy of the exemption decision to the EPA debarring official for inclusion in the official record.

§ 1532.1200 How will I know if I am disqualified under the CAA or CWA?

There may be several ways that you learn about your disqualification. You are legally on notice by the statutes that a criminal conviction the CAA or CWA automatically disqualifies you. As a practical matter, you may learn about your disqualification from your defense counsel, a Federal contract or award official, or from someone else who sees your name in the EPLS. As a courtesy, the EPA will attempt to notify you and the owner, lessor or supervisor of the violating facility that your names have been entered into the EPLS. The EPA will inform you of the procedures for seeking reinstatement and give you the name of a person you can contact to discuss your reinstatement request.

§ 1532.1205 What procedures must I follow to have my procurement and nonprocurement eligibility reinstated under the CAA or CWA?

(a) You must submit a written request for reinstatement to the EPA debarring official stating what you believe the conditions were that led to your conviction, and how those conditions have been corrected, relieved or addressed. Your request must include documentation sufficient to support all material assertions you make. The debarring official must determine that all the technical and non-technical causes, conditions and consequences of your actions have been sufficiently addressed so that the Government can confidently conduct future business activities with you, and that your future operations will be conducted in compliance with the CAA and CWA.

(b) You may begin the reinstatement process by having informal discussions with the EPA representative named in your notification of listing. Having informal dialogue with that person will make you aware of the EPA concerns that must be addressed. The EPA representative is not required to negotiate conditions for your reinstatement. However, beginning the reinstatement process with informal dialogue increases the chance of achieving a favorable outcome, and avoids unnecessary delay that may result from an incomplete or inadequate reinstatement request. It may also allow you to resolve your disqualification by reaching an agreement with the EPA debarring official under informal procedures. Using your informal option first does not prevent you from submitting a formal reinstatement request with the debarring official at any time.

§ 1532.1210 Will anyone else provide information to the EPA debarring official concerning my reinstatement request?

If you request reinstatement under § 1532.1205, the EPA debarring official may obtain review and comment on your request by anyone who may have information about, or an official interest in, the matter. For example, the debarring official may consult with the EPA Regional offices, the Department of Justice or other Federal agencies, or state, tribal or local governments. The EPA debarring official will make sure that you have an opportunity to address important allegations or information contained in the administrative record before making a final decision on your request for reinstatement.

§ 1532.1215 What happens if I disagree with the information provided by others to the EPA debarring official on my reinstatement request?

(a) If your reinstatement request is based on factual information (as opposed to a legal matter or discretionary conclusion) that is different from the information provided by others or otherwise contained in the administrative record, the debarring official will decide whether those facts are genuinely in dispute, and material to making a decision. If so, a fact-finding proceeding will be conducted in accordance with 2 CFR 180.830 through 180.840, and the debarring official will consider the findings when making a decision on your reinstatement request.

(b) If the basis for your disagreement with the information contained in the administrative record relates to a legal issue or discretionary conclusion, or is not a genuine dispute over a material fact, you will not have a fact-finding proceeding. However, the debarring official will allow you ample opportunity to support your position for the record and present matters in opposition to your continued disqualification. A summary of any information you provide orally, if not already recorded, should also be submitted to the debarring official in writing to assure that it is preserved for the debarring official's consideration and the administrative record.

§ 1532.1220 What will the EPA debarring official consider in making a decision on my reinstatement request?

(a) The EPA debarring official will consider all information and arguments contained in the administrative record in support of, or in opposition to, your request for reinstatement, including any findings of material fact.

(b) The debarring official will also consider any mitigating or aggravating factors that may relate to your conviction or the circumstances surrounding it, including any of those factors that appear in 2 CFR 180.860 that may apply to your situation.

(c) Finally, if disqualification applies to a business entity, the debarring official will consider any corporate or business attitude, policies, practices and procedures that contributed to the events leading to conviction, or that may have been implemented since the date of the misconduct or conviction. You can obtain any current policy directives issued by the EPA that apply to CAA or CWA disqualification or reinstatement by contacting the Office of the EPA Debarring Official, U.S. EPA, Office of Grants and Debarment (3901R), 1200 Pennsylvania Avenue, NW., Washington, DC 20460.

§ 1532.1225 When will the EPA debarring official make a decision on my reinstatement request?

(a) The EPA debarring official will make a decision regarding your reinstatement request under § 1532.1205(a), when the administrative record is complete, and he or she can determine whether the condition giving rise to the CAA or CWA conviction has been corrected-usually within 45 days of closing the administrative record.

(b) A reinstatement request is not officially before the debarring official while you are having informal discussions under § 1532.1205(b).

§ 1532.1230 How will the EPA debarring official notify me of the reinstatement decision?

The EPA debarring official will notify you of the reinstatement decision in writing, using the same methods for communicating debarment or suspension action notices under 2 CFR 180.615.

§ 1532.1300 Can I resolve my eligibility status under terms of an administrative agreement without having to submit a formal reinstatement request?

(a) The EPA debarring official may, at any time, resolve your CAA or CWA eligibility status under the terms of an administrative agreement. Ordinarily, the debarring official will not make an offer to you for reinstatement until after the administrative record for decision is complete, or contains enough information to enable him or her to make an informed decision in the matter.

(b) Any resolution of your eligibility status under the CAA or CWA resulting from an administrative agreement must include a certification that the condition giving rise to the conviction has been corrected.

(c) The EPA debarring official may enter into an administrative agreement to resolve CAA or CWA disqualification issues as part of a comprehensive criminal plea, civil or administrative agreement when it is in the best interest of the United States to do so.

§ 1532.1305 What are the consequences if I mislead the EPA in seeking reinstatement or fail to comply with my administrative agreement?

(a) Any certification of correction issued by the EPA debarring official whether the certification results from a reinstatement decision under §§ 1532.1205(a) and 1532.1230, or from an administrative agreement under §§ 1532.1205(b) and 1532.1300, is conditioned upon the accuracy of the information, representations or assurances made during development of the administrative record.

(b) If the EPA debarring official finds that he or she has certified correction of the condition giving rise to a CAA or CWA conviction or violation on the basis of a false, misleading, incomplete or inaccurate information; or if a person fails to comply with material condition of an administrative agreement, the EPA debarring official may take suspension or debarment action against the person(s) responsible for the misinformation or noncompliance with the agreement as appropriate. If anyone provides false, inaccurate, incomplete or misleading information to EPA in an attempt to obtain reinstatement, the EPA debarring official will refer the matter to the EPA Office of Inspector General for potential criminal or civil action.

§ 1532.1400 How may I appeal a decision denying my request for reinstatement?

(a) If the EPA debarring official denies your request for reinstatement under the CAA or CWA, you can ask for review of the debarring official's decision in two ways:

(1) You may ask the debarring official to reconsider the decision for material errors of fact or law that you believe will change the outcome of the matter; and/or

(2) You may request the Director, Office of Grants and Debarment (OGD Director), to review the debarring official's denial within 30 days of your receipt of the debarring official's decision under § 1532.1230 or paragraph (a)(1) of this section. However, the OGD Director can reverse the debarring official's decision denying reinstatement only where the OGD Director finds that there is a clear error of material fact or law, or where the OGD Director finds that the debarring official's decision was arbitrary, capricious, or an abuse of discretion.

(b) A request for review under this section must be in writing and state the specific findings you believe to be in error and include the reasons or legal bases for your position.

(c) A review under this section is solely within the discretion of the OGD Director.

(d) The OGD Director must notify you of his or her decision under this section, in writing, using the notice procedures at 2 CFR 180.615 and 180.975.

§ 1532.1500 If I am reinstated, when will my name be removed from the EPLS?

If your eligibility for procurement and nonprocurement participation is restored under the CAA or CWA, whether by decision, appeal, or by administrative agreement, the EPA will remove your name and that of the violating facility from the EPLS, generally within 5 working days of your reinstatement.

§ 1532.1600 What definitions apply specifically to actions under this subpart?

In addition to definitions under subpart A through I of 2 CFR part 180 that apply to this part as a whole, the following two definitions apply specifically to CAA and CWA disqualifications under this subpart:

(a) Person means an individual, corporation, partnership, association, state, municipality, commission, or political subdivision of a state, or any interstate body.

(b) Violating facility means any building, plant, installation, structure, mine, vessel, floating craft, location or site of operations that gives rise to a CAA or CWA conviction, and is a location at which or from which a Federal contract, subcontract, loan, assistance award or other covered transactions may be performed. If a site of operations giving rise to a CAA or CWA conviction contains or includes more than one building, plant, installation, structure, mine, vessel, floating craft, or other operational element, the entire location or site of operation is regarded as the violating facility unless otherwise limited by the EPA.

PART 1536—REQUIREMENTS FOR DRUG-FREE WORKPLACE (FINANCIAL ASSISTANCE)

Sec.
1536.10 What does this part do?
1536.20 Does this part apply to me?
1536.30 What policies and procedures must I follow?

Subpart A—Purpose and Coverage
[Reserved]

Subpart B—Requirements for Recipients Other Than Individuals

1536.225 Whom in the Environmental Protection Agency does a recipient other than an individual notify about a criminal drug conviction?

Subpart C—Requirements for Recipients Who Are Individuals

1536.300 Whom in the Environmental Protection Agency does a recipient who is an individual notify about a criminal drug conviction?

Subpart D—Responsibilities of Agency Awarding Officials

1536.400 What method do I use as an agency awarding official to obtain a recipient's agreement to comply with the OMB guidance?

Subpart E—Violations of This Part and Consequences

1536.500 Who in the Environmental Protection Agency determines that a recipient other than an individual violated the requirements of this part?
1536.505 Who in the Environmental Protection Agency determines that a recipient who is an individual violated the requirements of this part?

AUTHORITY: 41 U.S.C. 701–707.

SOURCE: 75 FR 80288, Dec. 22, 2010, unless otherwise noted.

§ 1536.10 What does this part do?

This part requires that the award and administration of Environmental Protection Agency grants and cooperative agreements comply with Office of Management and Budget (OMB) guidance implementing the portion of the Drug-Free Workplace Act of 1988 (41 U.S.C. 701–707, as amended, hereafter referred to as "the Act") that applies to grants. It thereby—

(a) Gives regulatory effect to the OMB guidance (Subparts A through F of 2 CFR part 182) for the Environmental Protection Agency's grants and cooperative agreements; and

(b) Establishes Environmental Protection Agency policies and procedures for compliance with the Act that are the same as those of other Federal agencies, in conformance with the requirement in 41 U.S.C. 705 for Governmentwide implementing regulations.

§ 1536.20 Does this part apply to me?

This part and, through this part, pertinent portions of the OMB guidance in Subparts A through F of 2 CFR part 182 (*see* table at 2 CFR 182.115(b)) apply to you if you are a—

(a) Recipient of a Environmental Protection Agency grant or cooperative agreement; or

(b) Environmental Protection Agency awarding official.

§ 1536.30 What policies and procedures must I follow?

(a) *General.* You must follow the policies and procedures specified in applicable sections of the OMB guidance in Subparts A through F of 2 CFR part 182, as implemented by this part.

(b) *Specific sections of OMB guidance that this part supplements.* In implementing the OMB guidance in 2 CFR part 182, this part supplements four sections of the guidance, as shown in the following table. For each of those sections, you must follow the policies and procedures in the OMB guidance, as supplemented by this part.

Section of OMB guidance	Section in this part where supplemented	What the supplementation clarifies
(1) 2 CFR 182.225(a)	§ 1536.225	Whom in the Environmental Protection Agency a recipient other than an individual must notify if an employee is convicted for a violation of a criminal drug statute in the workplace.
(2) 2 CFR 182.300(b)	§ 1536.300	Whom in the Environmental Protection Agency a recipient who is an individual must notify if he or she is convicted of a criminal drug offense resulting from a violation occurring during the conduct of any award activity.
(3) 2 CFR 182.500	§ 1536.500	Who in the Environmental Protection Agency is authorized to determine that a recipient other than an individual is in violation of the requirements of 2 CFR part 182, as implemented by this part.

Section of OMB guidance	Section in this part where supplemented	What the supplementation clarifies
(4) 2 CFR 182.505	§ 1536.505	Who in the Environmental Protection Agency is authorized to determine that a recipient who is an individual is in violation of the requirements of 2 CFR part 182, as implemented by this part.

(c) *Sections of the OMB guidance that this part does not supplement.* For any section of OMB guidance in Subparts A through F of 2 CFR part 182 that is not listed in paragraph (b) of this section, Environmental Protection Agency policies and procedures are the same as those in the OMB guidance.

Subpart A—Purpose and Coverage [Reserved]

Subpart B—Requirements for Recipients Other Than Individuals

§ 1536.225 Whom in the Environmental Protection Agency does a recipient other than an individual notify about a criminal drug conviction?

A recipient other than an individual that is required under 2 CFR 182.225(a) to notify Federal agencies about an employee's conviction for a criminal drug offense must notify the EPA award official from each Environmental Protection Agency office from which it currently has an award.

Subpart C—Requirements for Recipients Who Are Individuals

§ 1536.300 Whom in the Environmental Protection Agency does a recipient who is an individual notify about a criminal drug conviction?

A recipient who is an individual and is required under 2 CFR 182.300(b) to notify Federal agencies about a conviction for a criminal drug offense must notify the EPA award official from each Environmental Protection Agency office from which it currently has an award.

Subpart D—Responsibilities of Agency Awarding Officials

§ 1536.400 What method do I use as an agency awarding official to obtain a recipient's agreement to comply with the OMB guidance?

To obtain a recipient's agreement to comply with applicable requirements in the OMB guidance at 2 CFR part 182, you must include the following term or condition in the award:

Drug-free workplace. You as the recipient must comply with drug-free workplace requirements in Subpart B (or Subpart C, if the recipient is an individual) of 2 CFR Subtitle B, Chapter XV, Part 1536, which adopts the Governmentwide implementation (2 CFR part 182) of sec. 5152–5158 of the Drug-Free Workplace Act of 1988 (Pub. L. 100–690, Title V, Subtitle D; 41 U.S.C. 701–707).

Subpart E—Violations of This Part and Consequences

§ 1536.500 Who in the Environmental Protection Agency determines that a recipient other than an individual violated the requirements of this part?

The EPA Administrator or designee is the official authorized to make the determination under 2 CFR 182.500.

§ 1536.505 Who in the Environmental Protection Agency determines that a recipient who is an individual violated the requirements of this part?

The EPA Administrator or designee is the official authorized to make the determination under 2 CFR 182.505.

CHAPTER XVIII—NATIONAL AERONAUTICS AND SPACE ADMINISTRATION

PART 1880—NONPROCUREMENT DEBARMENT AND SUSPENSION

Sec.
1880.10 What does this part do?
1880.20 Does this part apply to me?
1880.30 What policies and procedures must I follow?

Subpart A—General

1880.137 Who in NASA may grant an exception to let an excluded person participate in a covered transaction?

Subpart B—Covered Transactions

1880.220 What contracts and subcontracts, in addition to those listed in 2 CFR 180.220, are covered transactions?

Subpart C—Responsibilities of Participants Regarding Transactions

1880.332 What methods must I use to pass requirements down to participants at lower tiers with whom I intend to do business?

Subpart D—Responsibilities of Federal Agency Officials Regarding Transactions

1880.437 What method do I use to communicate to a participant the requirements described in the OMB guidance at 2 CFR 180.435?

Subparts E–J [Reserved]

AUTHORITY: Sec. 2455, Pub. L. 103–355, 108 Stat. 3327; E.O. 12549, 3 CFR, 1986 Comp., p. 189; E.O. 12689, 3 CFR, 1989 Comp., p. 235; 42 U.S.C. 2473(c)(1).

SOURCE: 72 FR 19783, Apr. 20, 2007, unless otherwise noted.

§ 1880.10 What does this part do?

This part adopts the Office of Management and Budget (OMB) guidance in subparts A through I of 2 CFR part 180, as supplemented by this part, as the NASA policies and procedures for nonprocurement debarment and suspension. It thereby gives regulatory effect for NASA to the OMB guidance as supplemented by this part. This part satisfies the requirements in section 3 of Executive Order 12549, "Debarment and Suspension" (3 CFR 1986 Comp., p. 189), Executive Order 12689, "Debarment and Suspension" (3 CFR 1989 Comp., p. 235) and 31 U.S.C. 6101 note (Section 2455, Public Law 103–355, 108 Stat. 3327).

§ 1880.20 Does this part apply to me?

This part and, through this part, pertinent portions of the OMB guidance in subparts A through I of 2 CFR part 180 (see table at 2 CFR 180.100(b)) apply to you if you are a—

(a) Participant or principal in a "covered transaction" (see subpart B of 2 CFR part 180 and the definition of "nonprocurement transaction" at 2 CFR 180.970);

(b) Respondent in a NASA suspension or debarment action;

(c) NASA debarment or suspension official; or

(d) NASA grants officer, agreements officer, or other official authorized to enter into any type of nonprocurement transaction that is a covered transaction.

§ 1880.30 What policies and procedures must I follow?

The NASA policies and procedures that you must follow are the policies and procedures specified in each applicable section of the OMB guidance in subparts A through I of 2 CFR part 180, as that section is supplemented by the section in this part with the same section number. The contracts that are covered transactions, for example, are specified by section 220 of the OMB guidance (i.e., 2 CFR 180.220) as supplemented by section 220 in this part (i.e., § 1880.220). For any section of OMB guidance in subparts A through I of 2 CFR 180 that has no corresponding section in this part, NASA policies and procedures are those in the OMB guidance.

Subpart A—General

§ 1880.137 Who in NASA may grant an exception to let an excluded person participate in a covered transaction?

The Chief Acquisition Officer has the authority to grant an exception to let an excluded person participate in a covered transaction, as provided in the OMB guidance at 2 CFR 180.135.

Subpart B—Covered Transactions

§ 1880.220 What contracts and subcontracts, in addition to those listed in 2 CFR 180.220, are covered transactions?

NASA extends coverage of nonprocurement suspension and debarment requirements beyond first-tier procurement contracts under a covered nonprocurement action, to all lower tier subcontracts, at all dollar values, consistent with OMB guidance at 2 CFR 180.220(c) and the figure in the appendix at 2 CFR part 180. NASA does not permit subcontracting to suspended or debarred entities at any tier, at any dollar amount.

[78 FR 13211, Feb. 27, 2013]

Subpart C—Responsibilities of Participants Regarding Transactions

§ 1880.332 What methods must I use to pass requirements down to participants at lower tiers with whom I intend to do business?

You as a participant must include a term or condition in lower-tier transactions requiring lower-tier participants to comply with subpart C of the OMB guidance in 2 CFR part 180, as supplemented by this subpart.

Subpart D—Responsibilities of Federal Agency Officials Regarding Transactions

§ 1880.437 What method do I use to communicate to a participant the requirements described in the OMB guidance at 2 CFR 180.435?

To communicate to a participant the requirements described in 2 CFR 180.435 of the OMB guidance, you must include a term or condition in the transaction that requires the participant's compliance with subpart C of 2 CFR part 180, as supplemented by subpart C of this part, and requires the participant to include a similar term or condition in lower-tier covered transactions.

Subparts E–J [Reserved]

CHAPTER XX—UNITED STATES NUCLEAR REGULATORY COMMISSION

PART 2000—NONPROCUREMENT DEBARMENT AND SUSPENSION

Subpart A—General

Sec.
2000.10 What does this part do?
2000.20 Does this part apply to me?
2000.30 What policies and procedures must I follow?
2000.135 Who in the Nuclear Regulatory Commission may grant an exception to let an excluded person participate in a covered transaction?

Subpart B—Covered Transactions

2000.220 What contracts and subcontracts, in addition to those listed in 2 CFR 180.220, are covered transactions?

Subpart C—Responsibilities of Participants Regarding Transactions

2000.330 What method must be used to pass requirements down to participants at lower tiers?

Subparts D–H [Reserved]

Subpart I—Definitions

2000.930 Debarring official.
2000.1010 Suspending official.

AUTHORITY: Sec. 2455, Pub. L. 103–355, 108 Stat. 3327; E.O. 12549, 3 CFR, 1986 Comp., p. 189; E.O. 12689, 3 CFR, 1989 Comp., p. 235; 5 U.S.C. 301 and 10 U.S.C. 113.

SOURCE: 75 FR 27924, May 19, 2010, unless otherwise noted.

Subpart A—General

§ 2000.10 What does this part do?

This part promulgates a regulation adopting the Office of Management and Budget (OMB) guidance in subparts A through I of 2 CFR part 180, establishing the United States Nuclear Regulatory Commission (NRC) policies and procedures for nonprocurement debarment and suspension. NRC thereby gives regulatory effect to the OMB guidance. It also supplements the OMB guidance by identifying NRC implementing officials and identifying how to pass these requirements through to other entities.

§ 2000.20 Does this part apply to me?

This part and, through this part, pertinent portions of the OMB guidance in subparts A through I of 2 CFR part 180 (see table at 2 CFR 180.100(b)) apply to:

(a) Participant or principal in a "covered transaction";

(b) Respondent in an NRC nonprocurement suspension or debarment action;

(c) NRC debarment or suspension official; or

(d) NRC grants officer, agreements officer, or other official authorized to enter into a covered nonprocurement transaction.

§ 2000.30 What policies and procedures must I follow?

(a) The NRC policies and procedures that you must follow are the policies and procedures specified in each applicable section of the OMB guidance in Subparts A through I of 2 CFR part 180, and those in this part. The NRC has closely tracked OMB's numbering scheme. For example, the contracts under a nonprocurement transaction that are covered transactions that are in section 220 of the OMB guidance (i.e., 2 CFR 180.220) are found in § 2000.220.

(b) For any section of OMB guidance in subparts A through I of 2 CFR part 180 that has no corresponding section in this part, NRC requirements are those in the OMB guidance at 2 CFR part 180.

§ 2000.135 Who in the Nuclear Regulatory Commission may grant an exception to let an excluded person participate in a covered transaction?

The Director, Office of Administration or another official designated by the Director, has the authority to grant a written exception to let an excluded person participate in a covered transaction, as provided in guidance at 2 CFR 180.135. The Director or other official designated by the Director shall explain the reason(s) for deviating from the governmentwide policy.

Subpart B—Covered Transactions

§ 2000.220 What contracts and subcontracts, in addition to those listed in 2 CFR 180.220, are covered transactions?

The NRC nonprocurement suspension and debarment requirements apply

319

only to first-tier procurement contracts under a covered nonprocurement transaction.

Subpart C—Responsibilities of Participants Regarding Transactions

§ 2000.330 What method must be used to pass requirements down to participants at lower tiers?

A participant in a covered transaction must include a term or condition in any lower-tier covered transaction to require the participant of that transaction to—

(a) Comply with subpart C of the OMB guidance in 2 CFR part 180; and

(b) Include a similar term or condition in any covered transaction into which it enters at the next lower tier.

Subparts E–H [Reserved]

Subpart I—Definitions

§ 2000.930 Debarring official.

The Debarring Official for the United States Nuclear Regulatory Commission is the Director, Office of Administration.

§ 2000.1010 Suspending official.

The suspending official for the United States Nuclear Regulatory Commission is the Director, Office of Administration.

CHAPTER XXII—CORPORATION FOR NATIONAL AND COMMUNITY SERVICE

PART 2200—NONPROCUREMENT DEBARMENT AND SUSPENSION

Sec.
2200.10 What does this part do?
2200.20 Does this part apply to me?
2200.30 What policies and procedures must I follow?
2200.137 Who in the Corporation for National and Community Service may grant an exception to let an excluded person participate in a covered transaction?
2200.220 What contracts and subcontracts, in addition to those listed in 2 CFR 180.220, are covered transactions?
2200.332 What methods must I use to pass requirements down to participants at lower tiers with whom I intend to do business?
2200.437 What method do I use to communicate to a participant the requirements described in the OMB guidance at 2 CFR 180.435?

AUTHORITY: Sec. 2455, Pub. L. 103–355, 108 Stat. 3327; E.O. 12549, 3 CFR, 1986 Comp., p. 189; E.O. 12689, 3 CFR, 1989 Comp., p. 235; 22 U.S.C. 2503(b).

SOURCE: 72 FR 28826, May 23, 2007, unless otherwise noted.

§ 2200.10   What does this part do?

This part adopts the Office of Management and Budget (OMB) guidance in subparts A through I of 2 CFR part 180, as supplemented by this part, as the Corporation for National and Community Service policies and procedures for nonprocurement debarment and suspension. It thereby gives regulatory effect for the Corporation for National and Community Service to the OMB guidance as supplemented by this part. This part satisfies the requirements in section 3 of Executive Order 12549, "Debarment and Suspension" (3 CFR 1986 Comp., p. 189), Executive Order 12689, "Debarment and Suspension" (3 CFR 1989 Comp., p. 235) and 31 U.S.C. 6101 note (Section 2455, Pub. L. 103–355, 108 Stat. 3327).

§ 2200.20   Does this part apply to me?

This part and, through this part, pertinent portions of the OMB guidance in subparts A through I of 2 CFR part (see table at 2 CFR 180.100(b)) apply to you if you are a—

(a) Participant or principal in a "covered transaction." (see subpart B of 2 CFR part 180 and the definition of

"nonprocurement transaction" at 2 CFR 180.970.

(b) Respondent in a Corporation for National and Community Service suspension or debarment action;

(c) Corporation for National and Community Service debarment or suspension official; or

(d) Corporation for National and Community Service grants officer, agreements officer, or other official authorized to enter into any type of nonprocurement transaction that is a covered transaction.

§ 2200.30   What policies and procedures must I follow?

The Corporation for National and Community Service policies and procedures that you must follow are the policies and procedures specified in each applicable section of the OMB guidance in subparts A through I of 2 CFR part 180, as that section is supplemented by the section in this part with the same section number. The contracts that are covered transactions, for example, are specified by section 220 of the OMB guidance (i.e., 2 CFR 180.220) as supplemented by section 220 in this part (i.e., Sec. 2200.220). For any section of OMB guidance in subparts A through I of 2 CFR part 180 that has no corresponding section in this part, Corporation for National and Community Service policies and procedures are those in the OMB guidance.

§ 2200.137   Who in the Corporation for National and Community Service may grant an exception to let an excluded person participate in a covered transaction?

The Chief Executive Officer (or another official designated by the Chief Executive Officer) has the authority to grant an exception to let an excluded person participate in a covered transaction, as provided in the OMB guidance at 2 CFR 180.135.

§ 2200.220   What contracts and subcontracts, in addition to those listed in 2 CFR 180.220, are covered transactions?

Although the OMB guidance at 2 CFR 180.220(c) allows a Federal agency to do so (also see optional lower tier coverage in the figure in the appendix to 2 CFR part 180), Corporation for National

323

and Community Service does not extend coverage of nonprocurement suspension and debarment requirements beyond first-tier procurement contracts under a covered nonprocurement transaction.

§ 2200.332 What methods must I use to pass requirements down to participants at lower tiers with whom I intend to do business?

You as a participant must include a term or condition in lower-tier transactions requiring lower-tier participants to comply with Subpart C of the OMB guidance in 2 CFR part 180.

§ 2200.437 What method do I use to communicate to a participant the requirements described in the OMB guidance at 2 CFR 180.435?

To communicate to a participant the requirements described in 2 CFR 180.435 of the OMB guidance, you as an agency official must include a term or condition in the transaction that requires the participant's compliance with subpart C of 2 CFR part 180, and requires the participant to include a similar term or condition in lower-tier covered transactions.

PART 2245—REQUIREMENTS FOR DRUG-FREE WORKPLACE (FINANCIAL ASSISTANCE)

Sec.
2245.10 What does this part do?
2245.20 Does this part apply to me?
2245.30 What policies and procedures must I follow?

Subpart A—Purpose and Coverage [Reserved]

Subpart B—Requirements for Recipients Other Than Individuals

2245.225 Whom in the Corporation does a recipient other than an individual notify about a criminal drug conviction?

Subpart C—Requirements for Recipients Who Are Individuals

2245.300 Whom in the Corporation does a recipient who is an individual notify about a criminal drug conviction?

Subpart D—Responsibilities of Agency Awarding Officials

2245.400 What method do I use as an agency awarding official to obtain a recipient's agreement to comply with the OMB guidance?

Subpart E—Violations of this Part and Consequences

2245.500 Who in the Corporation determines that a recipient other than an individual violated the requirements of this part?
2245.505 Who in the Corporation determines that a recipient who is an individual violated the requirements of this part?

Subpart F [Reserved]

AUTHORITY: 41 U.S.C. 701–707; 42 U.S.C. 12644.

SOURCE: 75 FR 22206, Apr. 28, 2010, unless otherwise noted.

§ 2245.10 What does this part do?

This part requires that the award and administration of the Corporation's grants and cooperative agreements comply with Office of Management and Budget (OMB) guidance implementing the portion of the Drug-Free Workplace Act of 1988 (41 U.S.C. 701–707, as amended, hereafter referred to as "the Act") that applies to grants. It thereby—

(a) Gives regulatory effect to the OMB guidance (Subparts A through F of 2 CFR part 182) for the Corporation's grants and cooperative agreements; and

(b) Establishes the Corporation's policies and procedures for compliance with the Act that are the same as those of other Federal agencies, in conformance with the requirement in 41 U.S.C. 705 for Government-wide implementing regulations.

§ 2245.20 Does this part apply to me?

This part and, through this part, pertinent portions of the OMB guidance in Subparts A through F of 2 CFR part 182 (see table at 2 CFR 182.115(b)) apply to you if you are a—

(a) Recipient of a Corporation grant or cooperative agreement; or

(b) A Corporation awarding official.

§2245.30 What policies and procedures must I follow?

(a) *General.* You must follow the policies and procedures specified in applicable sections of the OMB guidance in Subparts A through F of 2 CFR part 182, as implemented by this part.

(b) *Specific sections of OMB guidance that this part supplements.* In implementing the OMB guidance in 2 CFR part 182, this part supplements four sections of the guidance, as shown in the following table. For each of those sections, you must follow the policies and procedures in the OMB guidance, as supplemented by this part.

Section of OMB guidance	Section in this part where supplemented	What the supplementation clarifies
(1) 2 CFR 182.225(a)	§2245.225	Whom in the Corporation a recipient other than an individual must notify if an employee is convicted for a violation of a criminal drug statute in the workplace.
(2) 2 CFR 182.300(b)	§2245.300	Whom in the Corporation a recipient who is an individual must notify if he or she is convicted of a criminal drug offense resulting from a violation occurring during the conduct of any award activity.
(3) 2 CFR 182.500 ...	§2245.500	Who in the Corporation is authorized to determine that a recipient other than an individual is in violation of the requirements of 2 CFR part 182, as implemented by this part.
(4) 2 CFR 182.505 ...	§2245.505	Who in the Corporation is authorized to determine that a recipient who is an individual is in violation of the requirements of 2 CFR part 182, as implemented by this part.

(c) *Sections of the OMB guidance that this part does not supplement.* For any section of OMB guidance in Subparts A through F of 2 CFR part 182 that is not listed in paragraph (b) of this section, the Corporation's policies and procedures are the same as those in the OMB guidance.

Subpart A—Purpose and Coverage [Reserved]

Subpart B—Requirements for Recipients Other Than Individuals

§2245.225 Whom in the Corporation does a recipient other than an individual notify about a criminal drug conviction?

A recipient other than an individual that is required under 2 CFR 182.225(a) to notify Federal agencies about an employee's conviction for a criminal drug offense must notify the Corporation's awarding official or other designee.

Subpart C—Requirements for Recipients Who Are Individuals

§2245.300 Whom in the Corporation does a recipient who is an individual notify about a criminal drug conviction?

A recipient who is an individual and is required under 2 CFR 182.300(b) to notify Federal agencies about a conviction for a criminal drug offense must notify the Corporation's awarding official or other designee.

Subpart D—Responsibilities of Agency Awarding Officials

§2245.400 What method do I use as an agency awarding official to obtain a recipient's agreement to comply with the OMB guidance?

To obtain a recipient's agreement to comply with applicable requirements in the OMB guidance at 2 CFR part 182, you must obtain each recipient's agreement, as a condition of the award, to comply with the requirements in subpart B (or subpart C, if the recipient is an individual) of 2245, which adopts the Government-wide implementation (2 CFR part 182) of sec. 5152–5158 of the Drug-Free Workplace Act of 1988 (Pub. L. 100–690, Title V, Subtitle D; 41 U.S.C. 701–707).

Subpart E—Violations of this Part and Consequences

§ 2245.500 Who in the Corporation determines that a recipient other than an individual violated the requirements of this part?

The Corporation's Chief Executive Officer or designee is authorized to make the determination under 2 CFR 182.500.

§ 2245.505 Who in the Corporation determines that a recipient who is an individual violated the requirements of this part?

The Corporation's Chief Executive Officer or designee is authorized to make the determination under 2 CFR 182.500.

Subpart F [Reserved]

CHAPTER XXIII—SOCIAL SECURITY ADMINISTRATION

PART 2336—NONPROCUREMENT DEBARMENT AND SUSPENSION

Sec.
2336.10   What does this part do?
2336.20   Does this part apply to me?
2336.30   What policies and procedures must I follow?

Subpart A—General

2336.137   Who in the SSA may grant an exception to let an excluded person participate in a covered transaction?

Subpart B—Covered Transactions

2336.220   What contracts and subcontracts, in addition to those listed in 2 CFR 180.220, are covered transactions?

Subpart C—Responsibilities of Participants Regarding Transactions

2336.332   What methods must I use to pass requirements down to participants at lower tiers with whom I intend to do business?

Subpart D—Responsibilities of Federal Agency Officials Regarding Transactions

2336.437   What method do I use to communicate to a participant the requirements described in the OMB guidance at 2 CFR 180.435?

Subparts E–J [Reserved]

AUTHORITY: 42 U.S.C. 902(a)(5); Sec. 2455, Pub. L. 103–355, 108 Stat. 3327; E.O. 12549 (3 CFR, 1986 Comp., p. 189); E.O. 12689 (3 CFR, 1989 Comp., p. 235).

SOURCE: 72 FR 46140, Aug. 17, 2007, unless otherwise noted.

§ 2336.10   What does this part do?

This part adopts the Office of Management and Budget (OMB) guidance in subparts A through I of 2 CFR part 180, as supplemented by this part, as the SSA policies and procedures for nonprocurement debarment and suspension. This part satisfies the requirements in section 3 of Executive Order 12549, "Debarment and Suspension" (3 CFR 1986 Comp., p. 189), Executive Order 12689, "Debarment and Suspension" (3 CFR 1989 Comp., p. 235) and 31 U.S.C. 6101 note (Section 2455, Pub. L. 103–355, 108 Stat. 3327).

§ 2336.20   Does this part apply to me?

This part and, through this part, pertinent portions of the OMB guidance in subparts A through I of 2 CFR part 180 (see table at 2 CFR 180.100(b)) apply to you if you are a—

(a) Participant or principal in a "covered transaction" (see subpart B of 2 CFR part 180 and the definition of "nonprocurement transaction" at 2 CFR 180.970);

(b) Respondent in an SSA suspension or debarment action;

(c) SSA debarment or suspension official; or

(d) SSA grants officer, agreements officer, or other official authorized to enter into any type of nonprocurement transaction that is a covered transaction.

§ 2336.30   What policies and procedures must I follow?

The SSA policies and procedures that you must follow are the policies and procedures specified in each applicable section of the OMB guidance in subparts A through I of 2 CFR part 180, as supplemented by the section in this part with the same section number. The contracts that are covered transactions, for example, are specified by section 220 of the OMB guidance (i.e., 2 CFR 180.220), as supplemented by section 220 in this part (i.e., § 2336.220). For any section of OMB guidance in subparts A through I of 2 CFR 180 that has no corresponding section in this part, SSA policies and procedures are those in the OMB guidance.

Subpart A—General

§ 2336.137   Who in the SSA may grant an exception to let an excluded person participate in a covered transaction?

(a) Within the Social Security Administration, the Commissioner or the designated agency debarment official may grant an exception permitting an excluded person to participate in a particular covered transaction. If the Commissioner or the designated agency debarment official grants an exception, the exception must be in writing and state the reason(s) for deviating from the OMB guidance at 2 CFR 180.135.

(b) An exception granted by one agency for an excluded person does not extend to the covered transactions of another agency.

Subpart B—Covered Transactions

§ 2336.220 What contracts and subcontracts, in addition to those listed in 2 CFR 180.220, are covered transactions?

Although the OMB guidance at 2 CFR 180.220(c) allows a Federal agency to do so (also see option lower tier coverage in the figure in the appendix to 2 CFR part 180), SSA does not extend coverage of nonprocurement suspension and debarment requirements beyond first-tier procurement contracts under a covered nonprocurement transaction.

Subpart C—Responsibilities of Participants Regarding Transactions

§ 2336.332 What methods must I use to pass requirements down to participants at lower tiers with whom I intend to do business?

You as a participant must include a term or condition in lower-tier transactions requiring lower-tier participants to comply with subpart C of the OMB guidance in 2 CFR part 180, as supplemented by this subpart.

Subpart D—Responsibilities of Federal Agency Officials Regarding Transactions

§ 2336.437 What method do I use to communicate to a participant the requirements described in the OMB guidance at 2 CFR 180.435?

To communicate to a participant the requirements described in 2 CFR 180.435 of the OMB guidance, you must include a term or condition in the transaction that requires the participant's compliance with subpart C of 2 CFR part 180, as supplemented by subpart C of this part, and requires the participant to include a similar term or condition in lower-tier covered transactions.

Subparts E–J [Reserved]

PART 2339—REQUIREMENTS FOR DRUG-FREE WORKPLACE (FINANCIAL ASSISTANCE)

AUTHORITY: 41 U.S.C. 701–707.

SOURCE: 75 FR 31274, June 3, 2010, unless otherwise noted.

§ 2339.10 What does this part do?

This part requires that the award and administration of Social Security Administration (SSA) grants and cooperative agreements comply with Office of Management and Budget (OMB) guidance implementing the portion of the Drug-Free Workplace Act of 1988 (41 U.S.C. 701–707, as amended, hereafter referred to as "the Act") that applies to grants. It thereby—

(a) Gives regulatory effect to the OMB guidance (subparts A through F of 2 CFR part 182) for SSA's grants and cooperative agreements; and

(b) Establishes SSA's policies and procedures for compliance with the Act that are the same as those of other Federal agencies, in conformance with the requirement in 41 U.S.C. 705 for Government-wide implementing regulations.

§ 2339.20 Does this part apply to me?

This part and, through this part, pertinent portions of the OMB guidance in subparts A through F of 2 CFR part 182 (see table at 2 CFR 182.115(b)) apply to you if you are—

(a) A recipient of an SSA grant or cooperative agreement; or

(b) An SSA awarding official.

§ 2339.30 What policies and procedures must I follow?

(a) *General.* You must follow the policies and procedures specified in applicable sections of the OMB guidance in Subparts A through F of 2 CFR part 182, as implemented by this part.

(b) *Specific sections of OMB guidance that this part supplements.* In implementing the OMB guidance in 2 CFR part 182, this part supplements four sections of the guidance, as shown in the following table.

Section of OMB guidance in 2 CFR	Section in this part where supplemented, 2 CFR	What the supplementation clarifies
(1) 182.225(a)	§ 2339.225	Who in SSA a recipient other than an individual must notify if an employee is convicted for a violation of a criminal drug statute in the workplace.
(2) 182.300(b)	§ 2339.300	Who in SSA a recipient who is an individual must notify if he or she is convicted of a criminal drug offense resulting from a violation occurring during the conduct of any award activity.
(3) 182.500	§ 2339.500	Who in SSA is authorized to determine that a recipient other than an individual is in violation of the requirements of 2 CFR part 182, as implemented by this part.
(4) 182.505	§ 2339.505	Who in SSA is authorized to determine that a recipient who is an individual is in violation of the requirements of 2 CFR part 182, as implemented by this part.

(c) *Sections of the OMB guidance that this part does not supplement.* Our policies and procedures are the same as those in the OMB guidance for any section not included in the table in paragraph (b) of this section.

Subpart A [Reserved]

Subpart B—Requirements for Recipients Other Than Individuals

§ 2339.225 Who in the Social Security Administration does a recipient other than an individual notify about a criminal drug conviction?

A recipient other than an individual that is required under 2 CFR 182.225(a) to notify Federal agencies about an employee's conviction for a criminal drug offense must notify the Commissioner of Social Security or designee.

Subpart C [Reserved]

Subpart D—Responsibilities of Agency Awarding Officials

§ 2339.400 What method do I use as an agency awarding official to obtain a recipient's agreement to comply with the OMB guidance?

You must include the following term or condition in the award:

Drug-free workplace. You, as the recipient, must comply with drug-free workplace requirements in Subpart B, which adopts the Government-wide implementation (2 CFR part 182) of sec. 5152–5158 of the Drug-Free Workplace Act of 1988 (Pub. L. 100–690, Title V, Subtitle D; 41 U.S.C. 701–707).

Subpart E—Violations of this Part and Consequences

§ 2339.500 Who in the Social Security Administration determines that a recipient other than an individual violated the requirements of this part?

The Commissioner of Social Security or designee will make the determination.

Subpart F [Reserved]

CHAPTER XXIV—DEPARTMENT OF HOUSING AND URBAN DEVELOPMENT

PART 2424—NONPROCUREMENT DEBARMENT AND SUSPENSION

Sec.
2424.10 What does this part do?
2424.20 Does this part apply to me?
2424.30 What policies and procedures must I follow?

Subpart A—General

2424.137 Who in HUD may grant an exception to let an excluded person participate in a covered transaction?

Subpart B—Covered Transactions

2424.220 What contracts and subcontracts, in addition to those listed in 2 CFR 180.220, are covered transactions?

Subpart C—Responsibilities of Participants Regarding Transactions

2424.300 What must I do before I enter into a covered transaction with another person at the next lower tier (HUD supplement to governmentwide definition at 2 CFR 180.300)?
2424.332 What methods must I use to pass requirements down to participants at lower tiers with whom I intend to do business?

Subpart D—Responsibilities of Federal Agency Officials Regarding Transactions

2424.437 What method do I use to communicate to a participant the requirements described in the OMB guidance at 2 CFR 180.435?

Subparts E–F [Reserved]

Subpart G—Suspension

2424.747 Who conducts fact finding for HUD suspensions?

Subpart H—Debarment

2424.842 Who conducts fact finding for HUD debarments?

Subpart I—Definitions

2424.952 Hearing officer.
2424.970 Nonprocurement transaction (HUD supplement to governmentwide definition at 2 CFR 180.970).
2424.995 Principal (HUD supplement to governmentwide definition at 2 CFR 180.995).
2424.1017 Ultimate beneficiary.

Subpart J—Limited Denial of Participation

2424.1100 What is a limited denial of participation?
2424.1105 Who may issue a limited denial of participation?
2424.1110 When may a HUD official issue a limited denial of participation?
2424.1115 When does a limited denial of participation take effect?
2424.1120 How long may a limited denial of participation last?
2424.1125 How does a limited denial of participation start?
2424.1130 How may I contest my limited denial of participation?
2424.1135 Do Federal agencies coordinate limited denial of participation actions?
2424.1140 What is the scope of a limited denial of participation?
2424.1145 May HUD impute the conduct of one person to another in a limited denial of participation?
2424.1150 What is the effect of a suspension or debarment on a limited denial of participation?
2424.1155 What is the effect of a limited denial of participation on a suspension or a debarment?
2424.1160 May a limited denial of participation be terminated before the term of the limited denial of participation expires?
2424.1165 How is a limited denial of participation reported?

AUTHORITY: Sec. 2455, Pub. L. 103–355, 108 Stat. 3327; E.O. 12549, 3 CFR, 1986 Comp., p. 189; E.O. 12689, 3 CFR, 1989 Comp., p. 235.

SOURCE: 72 FR 73487, Dec. 27, 2007, unless otherwise noted.

§ 2424.10 What does this part do?

In this part, HUD adopts, as HUD policies, procedures, and requirements for nonprocurement debarment and suspension, the OMB guidance in subparts A through I of 2 CFR part 180, as supplemented by this part. This adoption thereby gives regulatory effect for HUD to the OMB guidance, as supplemented by this part. This part satisfies the requirements in section 3 of Executive Order 12549, "Debarment and Suspension" (3 CFR 1986 Comp., p. 189), Executive Order 12689, "Debarment and Suspension" (3 CFR 1989 Comp., p. 235) and 31 U.S.C. 6101 note (Section 2455, Pub. L. 103–355, 108 Stat. 3327).

§ 2424.20 Does this part apply to me?

This part and, through this part, pertinent portions of subparts A through I of 2 CFR part 180 (see table at 2 CFR 180.100(b)), apply to you if you are a—
(a) Participant or principal in a "covered transaction" (see subpart B of 2 CFR part 180 and the definition of

335

"nonprocurement transaction" at 2 CFR 180.970, as supplemented by § 2424.970 of this part);

(b) Respondent in a HUD suspension or debarment action;

(c) HUD debarment or suspension official; or

(d) HUD grants officer, agreements officer, or other official authorized to enter into any type of nonprocurement transaction that is a covered transaction.

§ 2424.30 What policies and procedures must I follow?

The HUD policies and procedures that you must follow are the policies and procedures specified in each applicable section of the OMB guidance in subparts A through I of 2 CFR part 180, as that section is supplemented by the section in this part with the same section number. The contracts that are covered transactions, for example, are specified by section 220 of the OMB guidance (i.e., 2 CFR 180.220), as supplemented by section 220 in this part (i.e., § 2424.220). For any section of OMB guidance in subparts A through I of 2 CFR 180 that has no corresponding section in this part, HUD policies and procedures are those in the OMB guidance.

Subpart A—General

§ 2424.137 Who in HUD may grant an exception to let an excluded person participate in a covered transaction?

The Secretary or designee may grant an exception permitting an excluded person to participate in a particular covered transaction. If the Secretary or a designee grants an exception, the exception must be in writing and state the reason(s) for deviating from the governmentwide policy in Executive Order 12549.

Subpart B—Covered Transactions

§ 2424.220 What contracts and subcontracts, in addition to those listed in 2 CFR 180.220, are covered transactions?

In addition to the contracts covered under 2 CFR 180.220(b) of the OMB guidance, this part applies to any contract, regardless of tier, that is awarded by a contractor, subcontractor, supplier, consultant, or its agent or representative in any transaction, if the contract is to be funded or provided by HUD under a covered nonprocurement transaction and the amount of the contract is expected to equal or exceed $25,000. This extends the coverage of the HUD nonprocurement suspension and debarment requirements to all lower tiers of subcontracts under covered nonprocurement transactions, as permitted under the OMB guidance at 2 CFR 180.220(c) (see optional lower-tier coverage in the figure in the appendix to 2 CFR part 180).

Subpart C—Responsibilities of Participants Regarding Transactions

§ 2424.300 What must I do before I enter into a covered transaction with another person at the next lower tier (HUD supplement to governmentwide definition at 2 CFR 180.300)?

(a) You, as a participant, are responsible for determining whether you are entering into a covered transaction with an excluded or disqualified person. You may decide the method by which you do so.

(1) You may, but are not required to, check the Excluded Parties List System (EPLS).

(2) You may, but are not required to, collect a certification from that person.

(b) In the case of an employment contract, HUD does not require employers to check the EPLS prior to making salary payments pursuant to that contract.

§ 2424.332 What methods must I use to pass requirements down to participants at lower tiers with whom I intend to do business?

To communicate the requirements to lower-tier participants, you must include a term or condition in the transaction requiring compliance with subpart C of the OMB guidance in 2 CFR part 180, as supplemented by this subpart.

Subpart D—Responsibilities of Federal Agency Officials Regarding Transactions

§2424.437 What method do I use to communicate to a participant the requirements described in the OMB guidance at 2 CFR 180.435?

To communicate to a participant the requirements described in 2 CFR 180.435 of the OMB guidance, you must include a term or condition in the transaction that requires the participant to: comply with subpart C of 2 CFR part 180, as supplemented by subpart C of this part, and include a similar term or condition in lower-tier covered transactions.

Subparts E-F [Reserved]

Subpart G—Suspension

§2424.747 Who conducts fact finding for HUD suspensions?

In all HUD suspensions, the official who shall conduct additional proceedings where disputed material facts are challenged shall be a hearing officer.

Subpart H—Debarment

§2424.842 Who conducts fact finding for HUD debarments?

In all HUD debarments, the official who shall conduct additional proceedings where disputed material facts are challenged shall be a hearing officer.

Subpart I—Definitions

§2424.952 Hearing officer.

Hearing Officer means an Administrative Law Judge or Office of Appeals Judge authorized by HUD's Secretary or by the Secretary's designee to conduct proceedings under this part.

§2424.970 Nonprocurement transaction (HUD supplement to governmentwide definition at 2 CFR 180.970).

In the case of employment contracts that are covered transactions, each salary payment under the contract is a separate covered transaction.

§2424.995 Principal (HUD supplement to governmentwide definition at 2 CFR 180.995).

A person who has a critical influence on, or substantive control over, a covered transaction, whether or not employed by the participant. Persons who have a critical influence on, or substantive control over, a covered transaction may include, but are not limited to:

(a) Loan officers;

(b) Staff appraisers and inspectors;

(c) Underwriters;

(d) Bonding companies;

(e) Borrowers under programs financed by HUD or with loans guaranteed, insured, or subsidized through HUD programs;

(f) Purchasers of properties with HUD-insured or Secretary-held mortgages;

(g) Recipients under HUD assistance agreements;

(h) Ultimate beneficiaries of HUD programs;

(i) Fee appraisers and inspectors;

(j) Real estate agents and brokers;

(k) Management and marketing agents;

(l) Accountants, consultants, investment bankers, architects, engineers, and attorneys who are in a business relationship with participants in connection with a covered transaction under a HUD program;

(m) Contractors involved in the construction or rehabilitation of properties financed by HUD, with HUD-insured loans or acquired properties, including properties held by HUD as mortgagee-in-possession;

(n) Closing agents;

(o) Turnkey developers of projects financed by or with financing insured by HUD;

(p) Title companies;

(q) Escrow agents;

(r) Project owners;

(s) Administrators of hospitals, nursing homes, and projects for the elderly financed or insured by HUD; and

(t) Developers, sellers, or owners of property financed with loans insured under Title I or Title II of the National Housing Act.

§ 2424.1017 Ultimate beneficiary.

Ultimate beneficiaries of HUD programs include, but are not limited to, subsidized tenants and subsidized mortgagors, such as those assisted under Section 8 Housing Assistance Payment contracts, by Section 236 Rental Assistance, or by Rent Supplement payments.

Subpart J—Limited Denial of Participation

§ 2424.1100 What is a limited denial of participation?

A limited denial of participation excludes a specific person from participating in a specific program, or programs, within a HUD field office's geographic jurisdiction, for a specific period of time. A limited denial of participation is normally issued by a HUD field office, but may be issued by a Headquarters office. The decision to impose a limited denial of participation is discretionary and based on the best interests of the federal government.

§ 2424.1105 Who may issue a limited denial of participation?

The Secretary designates HUD officials who are authorized to impose a limited denial of participation, affecting any participant and/or their affiliates, except mortgagees approved by the Federal Housing Administration (FHA).

§ 2424.1110 When may a HUD official issue a limited denial of participation?

(a) An authorized HUD official may issue a limited denial of participation against a person, based upon adequate evidence of any of the following causes:

(1) Approval of an applicant for insurance would constitute an unsatisfactory risk;

(2) There are irregularities in a person's past performance in a HUD program;

(3) The person has failed to maintain the prerequisites of eligibility to participate in a HUD program;

(4) The person has failed to honor contractual obligations or to proceed in accordance with contract specifications or HUD regulations;

(5) The person has failed to satisfy, upon completion, the requirements of an assistance agreement or contract;

(6) The person has deficiencies in ongoing construction projects;

(7) The person has falsely certified in connection with any HUD program, whether or not the certification was made directly to HUD;

(8) The person has committed any act or omission that would be cause for debarment under 2 CFR 180.800;

(9) The person has violated any law, regulation, or procedure relating to the application for financial assistance, insurance, or guarantee, or to the performance of obligations incurred pursuant to a grant of financial assistance or pursuant to a conditional or final commitment to insure or guarantee;

(10) The person has made or procured to be made any false statement for the purpose of influencing in any way an action of the Department; or

(11) Imposition of a limited denial of participation by any other HUD office.

(b) Filing of a criminal Indictment or Information shall constitute adequate evidence for the purpose of limited denial of participation actions. The Indictment or Information need not be based on offenses against HUD.

(c) Imposition of a limited denial of participation by any other HUD office shall constitute adequate evidence for a concurrent limited denial of participation. Where such a concurrent limited denial of participation is imposed, participation may be restricted on the same basis without the need for an additional conference or further hearing.

(d) An affiliate or organizational element may be included in a limited denial of participation solely on the basis of its affiliation, and regardless of its knowledge of or participation in the acts providing cause for the sanction. The burden of proving that a particular affiliate or organizational element is currently responsible and not controlled by the primary sanctioned party (or by an entity that itself is controlled by the primary sanctioned party) is on the affiliate or organizational element.

§2424.1115 When does a limited denial of participation take effect?

A limited denial of participation is effective immediately upon issuance of the notice.

§2424.1120 How long may a limited denial of participation last?

A limited denial of participation may remain in effect up to 12 months.

§2424.1125 How does a limited denial of participation start?

A limited denial of participation is made effective by providing the person, and any specifically named affiliate, with notice:

(a) That the limited denial of participation is being imposed;

(b) Of the cause(s) under §2424.1110 for the sanction;

(c) Of the potential effect of the sanction, including the length of the sanction and the HUD program(s) and geographic area affected by the sanction;

(d) Of the right to request, in writing, within 30 days of receipt of the notice, a conference under §2424.1130; and

(e) Of the right to contest the limited denial of participation under §2424.1130.

§2424.1130 How may I contest my limited denial of participation?

(a) Within 30 days after receiving a notice of limited denial of participation, you may request a conference with the official who issued such notice. The conference shall be held within 15 days after the Department's receipt of the request for a conference, unless you waive this time limit. The official or designee who imposed the sanction shall preside. At the conference, you may appear with a representative and may present all relevant information and materials to the official or designee. Within 20 days after the conference, or within 20 days after any agreed-upon extension of time for submission of additional materials, the official or designee shall, in writing, advise you of the decision to terminate, modify, or affirm the limited denial of participation. If all or a portion of the remaining period of exclusion is affirmed, the notice of affirmation shall advise you of the opportunity to contest the notice and to request a hearing before a Departmental

Hearing Officer. You have 30 days after receipt of the notice of affirmation to request this hearing. If the official or designee does not issue a decision within the 20-day period, you may contest the sanction before a Departmental Hearing Officer. Again, you have 30 days from the expiration of the 20-day period to request this hearing. If you request a hearing before the Departmental Hearing Officer, you must submit your request to the Debarment Docket Clerk, Department of Housing and Urban Development, 451 Seventh Street, SW., B–133 Portals 200, Washington DC 20410–0500.

(b) You may skip the conference with the official and you may request a hearing before a Departmental Hearing Officer. This must also be done within 30 days after receiving a notice of limited denial of participation. If you opt to have a hearing before a Departmental Hearing Officer, you must submit your request to the Debarment Docket Clerk, Department of Housing and Urban Development, 451 Seventh Street, SW., B–133 Portals 200, Washington DC 20410–0500. The hearing before the Departmental Hearing Officer is more formal than the conference before the sanctioning official described above. The Departmental Hearing Officer will conduct the hearing in accordance with 24 CFR part 26, subpart A. The Departmental Hearing Officer will issue findings of fact and make a recommended decision. The sanctioning official will then make a final decision, as promptly as possible, after the Departmental Hearing Officer's recommended decision is issued. The sanctioning official may reject the recommended decision or any findings of fact, only after specifically determining that the decision or any of the facts are arbitrary, capricious, or clearly erroneous.

(c) In deciding whether to terminate, modify, or affirm a limited denial of participation, the Departmental official or designee may consider the factors listed at 2 CFR 180.860. The Departmental Hearing Officer may also consider the factors listed at 2 CFR 180.860 in making any recommended decision.

§ 2424.1135　Do Federal agencies coordinate limited denial of participation actions?

Federal agencies do not coordinate limited denial of participation actions. As stated in § 2424.1100, a limited denial of participation is a HUD-specific action and applies only to HUD activities.

§ 2424.1140　What is the scope of a limited denial of participation?

The scope of a limited denial of participation is as follows:

(a) A limited denial of participation generally extends only to participation in the program under which the cause arose. A limited denial of participation may, at the discretion of the authorized official, extend to other programs, initiatives, or functions within the jurisdiction of an Assistant Secretary. The authorized official, however, may determine that where the sanction is based on an indictment or conviction, the sanction shall apply to all programs throughout HUD.

(b) For purposes of this subpart, participation includes receipt of any benefit or financial assistance through grants or contractual arrangements; benefits or assistance in the form of loan guarantees or insurance; and awards of procurement contracts.

(c) The sanction may be imposed for a period not to exceed 12 months, and shall be effective within the geographic jurisdiction of the office imposing it, unless the sanction is imposed by an Assistant Secretary or Deputy Assistant Secretary, in which case the sanction may be imposed on either a nationwide or a more restricted basis.

§ 2424.1145　May HUD impute the conduct of one person to another in a limited denial of participation?

For purposes of determining a limited denial of participation, HUD may impute conduct as follows:

(a) *Conduct imputed from an individual to an organization.* HUD may impute the fraudulent, criminal, or other improper conduct of any officer, director, shareholder, partner, employee, or other individual associated with an organization, to that organization when the improper conduct occurred in connection with the individual's performance of duties for or on behalf of that organization, or with the organization's knowledge, approval, or acquiescence. The organization's acceptance of the benefits derived from the conduct is evidence of knowledge, approval, or acquiescence.

(b) *Conduct imputed from an organization to an individual or between individuals.* HUD may impute the fraudulent, criminal, or other improper conduct of any organization to an individual, or from one individual to another individual, if the individual to whom the improper conduct is imputed participated in, had knowledge of, or had reason to know of the improper conduct.

(c) *Conduct imputed from one organization to another organization.* HUD may impute the fraudulent, criminal, or other improper conduct of one organization to another organization when the improper conduct occurred in connection with a partnership, joint venture, joint application, association, or similar arrangement, or when the organization to whom the improper conduct is imputed has the power to direct, manage, control, or influence the activities of the organization responsible for the improper conduct. Acceptance of the benefits derived from the conduct is evidence of knowledge, approval, or acquiescence.

§ 2424.1150　What is the effect of a suspension or debarment on a limited denial of participation?

If you have submitted a request for a hearing pursuant to § 2424.1130 of this subpart, and you also receive, pursuant to subpart G or H of this part, a notice of proposed debarment or suspension that is based on the same transaction(s) or the same conduct as the limited denial of participation, as determined by the debarring or suspending official, the following rules shall apply:

(a) During the 30-day period after you receive a notice of proposed debarment or suspension, during which you may elect to contest the debarment under 2 CFR 180.815, or the suspension pursuant to 2 CFR 180.720, all proceedings in the limited denial of participation, including discovery, are automatically stayed.

(b) If you do not contest the proposed debarment pursuant to 2 CFR 180.815, or the suspension pursuant to 2 CFR 180.720, the final imposition of the debarment or suspension shall also constitute a final decision with respect to the limited denial of participation, to the extent that the debarment or suspension is based on the same transaction(s) or conduct as the limited denial of participation.

(c) If you contest the proposed debarment pursuant to 2 CFR 180.815, or the suspension pursuant to 2 CFR 180.720, then:

(1) Those parts of the limited denial of participation and the debarment or suspension based on the same transaction(s) or conduct, as determined by the debarring or suspending official, shall be immediately consolidated before the debarring or suspending official;

(2) Proceedings under the consolidated portions of the limited denial of participation shall be stayed before the hearing officer until the suspending or debarring official makes a determination as to whether the consolidated matters should be referred to a hearing officer. Such a determination must be made within 90 days of the date of the issuance of the suspension or proposed debarment, unless the suspending/debarring official extends the period for good cause.

(i) If the suspending or debarring official determines that there is a genuine dispute as to material facts regarding the consolidated matter, the entire consolidated matter will be referred to the hearing officer hearing the limited denial of participation, for additional proceedings pursuant to 2 CFR 180.750 or 180.845.

(ii) If the suspending or debarring official determines that there is no dispute as to material facts regarding the consolidated matter, jurisdiction of the hearing officer under 2 CFR part 2424, subpart J, to hear those parts of the limited denial of participation based on the same transaction[s] or conduct as the debarment or suspension, as determined by the debarring or suspending official, will be transferred to the debarring or suspending official, and the hearing officer responsible for hearing the limited denial of participation

shall transfer the administrative record to the debarring or suspending official.

(3) The suspending or debarring official shall hear the entire consolidated case under the procedures governing suspensions and debarments, and shall issue a final decision as to both the limited denial of participation and the suspension or debarment.

§ 2424.1155　What is the effect of a limited denial of participation on a suspension or a debarment?

The imposition of a limited denial of participation does not affect the right of the Department to suspend or debar any person under this part.

§ 2424.1160　May a limited denial of participation be terminated before the term of the limited denial of participation expires?

If the cause for the limited denial of participation is resolved before the expiration of the 12-month period, the official who imposed the sanction may terminate it.

§ 2424.1165　How is a limited denial of participation reported?

When a limited denial of participation has been made final, or the period for requesting a conference pursuant to § 2424.1130 has expired without receipt of such a request, the official imposing the limited denial of participation shall notify the Director of the Compliance Division in the Departmental Enforcement Center of the scope of the limited denial of participation.

PART 2429—REQUIREMENTS FOR DRUG-FREE WORKPLACE (FINANCIAL ASSISTANCE)

Sec.
2429.10　What does this part do?
2429.20　Does this part apply to me?
2429.30　What policies and procedures must I follow?

Subpart A [Reserved]

Subpart B—Requirements for Recipients Other Than Individuals

2429.225　Whom in HUD does a recipient other than an individual notify about a criminal drug conviction?

Subpart C—Requirements for Recipients Who Are Individuals

2429.300　Whom in HUD does a recipient who is an individual notify about a criminal drug conviction?

Subpart D—Responsibilities of Agency Awarding Officials

2429.400　What method do I use as an agency awarding official to obtain a recipient's agreement to comply with the OMB guidance?

Subpart E—Violations of This Part and Consequences

2429.500　Who in HUD determines that a recipient other than an individual violated the requirements of this part?
2429.505　Who in HUD determines that a recipient who is an individual violated the requirements of this part?

Subpart F [Reserved]

AUTHORITY: 41 U.S.C. 701–707; 42 U.S.C. 3535(d).

SOURCE: 76 FR 45166, July 28, 2011, unless otherwise noted.

§ 2429.10　What does this part do?

This part requires that the award and administration of HUD grants and cooperative agreements comply with Office of Management and Budget (OMB) guidance implementing the portion of the Drug-Free Workplace Act of 1988 (41 U.S.C. 701–707) (referred to as the Act in this part) that applies to grants. This part:

(a) Gives regulatory effect to the OMB guidance (Subparts A through F of 2 CFR part 182) for HUD grants and cooperative agreements; and

(b) Establishes HUD policies and procedures for compliance with the Act that are the same as those of other Federal agencies, in conformance with the requirement in 41 U.S.C. 705 for governmentwide implementing regulations.

§ 2429.20　Does this part apply to me?

This part, and through this part, pertinent portions of the OMB guidance in subparts A through F of 2 CFR part 182 (see table at 2 CFR 182.115(b)) apply to you if you are a:

(a) Recipient of a HUD grant or cooperative agreement; or

(b) HUD awarding official.

§ 2429.30　What policies and procedures must I follow?

(a) *General.* You must follow the policies and procedures specified in applicable sections of the OMB guidance in Subparts A through F of 2 CFR part 182, as implemented by this part.

(b) *Specific sections of OMB guidance that this part supplements.* In implementing the OMB guidance in 2 CFR part 182, this part supplements four sections of the guidance, as shown in the following table. For each of those sections, you must follow the policies and procedures of the OMB guidance, as supplemented by this part.

Section of OMB guidance	Section in this part where supplemented	What the supplementation clarifies
(1) 2 CFR 182.225(a)	§ 2429.225	Whom in HUD must a recipient other than an individual notify if an employee is convicted for a violation of a criminal drug statute in the workplace?
(2) 2 CFR 182.300(b)	§ 2429.300	Whom in HUD must a recipient who is an individual notify if he or she is convicted of a criminal drug offense resulting from a violation occurring during the conduct of any award activity?
(3) 2 CFR 182.500	§ 2429.500	Who in HUD is authorized to determine that a recipient other than an individual is in violation of the requirements of 2 CFR part 182, as implemented by this part?
(4) 2 CFR 182.505	§ 2429.505	Who in HUD is authorized to determine that a recipient who is an individual is in violation of the requirements of 2 CFR part 182, as implemented by this part?

(c) *Sections of the OMB guidance that this part does not supplement.* For any section of OMB guidance in Subparts A through F of 2 CFR part 182 that is not listed in paragraph (b) of this section, HUD policies and procedures are the same as those in the OMB guidance.

Subpart A [Reserved]

Subpart B—Requirements for Recipients Other Than Individuals

§ 2429.225 Whom in HUD does a recipient other than an individual notify about a criminal conviction?

A recipient other than an individual who is required under 2 CFR 182.225(a) to notify Federal agencies about an employee's conviction for a criminal drug offense must notify each HUD office with which it currently has an award.

Subpart C—Requirements for Recipients Who Are Individuals

§ 2429.300 Whom in HUD does a recipient who is an individual notify about a criminal conviction?

A recipient who is an individual and is required under 2 CFR 182.300(b) to notify Federal agencies about a conviction for a criminal drug offense must notify each HUD office with which he or she currently has an award.

Subpart D—Responsibilities of Agency Awarding Officials

§ 2429.400 What method do I use as an agency awarding official to obtain a recipient's agreement to comply with the OMB guidance?

To obtain a recipient's agreement to comply with applicable requirements in the OMB guidance at 2 CFR part 182, you must include the following term or condition in the award:

Drug-free workplace. You as the recipient must comply with drug-free workplace requirements in Subpart B (or Subpart C, if the recipient is an individual) of part 2429, which adopts the governmentwide implementation (2 CFR part 182) of sections 5152–5158 of the Drug-Free Workplace Act of 1988 (Pub. L. 100–690, Title V, Subtitle D; 41 U.S.C. 701–707).

Subpart E—Violations of This Part and Consequences

§ 2429.500 Who in HUD determines that a recipient other than an individual violated the requirements of this part?

The Secretary or designee is the official authorized to make the determination under 2 CFR 182.500.

§ 2429.505 Who in HUD determines that a recipient who is an individual violated the requirements of this part?

The Secretary or designee is the official authorized to make the determination under 2 CFR 182.505.

Subpart F [Reserved]

343

CHAPTER XXV—NATIONAL SCIENCE FOUNDATION

PART 2520—NONPROCUREMENT DEBARMENT AND SUSPENSION

AUTHORITY: 42 U.S.C. 1870(a); Sec. 2455, Pub. L. 103–355, 108 Stat. 3327; E.O. 12549, 3 CFR, 1986 Comp., p. 189; E.O. 12689, 3 CFR, 1989 Comp., p. 235.

SOURCE: 72 FR 4944, Feb. 2, 2007, unless otherwise noted.

§ 2520.10 What does this part do?

This part adopts the Office of Management and Budget (OMB) guidance in subparts A through I of 2 CFR part 180, as supplemented by this part, as the NSF policies and procedures for nonprocurement debarment and suspension. It thereby gives regulatory effect for NSF to the OMB guidance as supplemented by this part. This part satisfies the requirements in section 3 of Executive Order 12549, "Debarment and Suspension" (3 CFR 1986 Comp., p. 189), Executive Order 12689, "Debarment and Suspension" (3 CFR 1989 Comp., p. 235) and 31 U.S.C. 6101 note (Section 2455, Public Law 103–355, 108 Stat. 3327).

§ 2520.20 Does this part apply to me?

This part and, through this part, pertinent portions of the OMB guidance in subparts A through I of 2 CFR part 180 (see table at 2 CFR 180.100(b)) apply to you if you are a—

(a) Participant or principal in a "covered transaction" (see Subpart B of 2 CFR part 180 and the definition of "nonprocurement transaction" at 2 CFR 180.970).

(b) Respondent in an NSF suspension or debarment action.

(c) NSF debarment or suspension official.

(d) NSF grants officer, agreements officer, or other official authorized to enter into any type of nonprocurement transaction that is a covered transaction.

§ 2520.30 What policies and procedures must I follow?

The NSF policies and procedures that you must follow are the policies and procedures specified in each applicable section of the OMB guidance in subparts A through I of 2 CFR part 180, as that section is supplemented by the section in this part with the same section number. The contracts that are covered transactions, for example, are specified by section 220 of the OMB guidance (i.e., 2 CFR 180.220) as supplemented by section 220 in this part (i.e., § 2520.220). For any section of OMB guidance in subparts A through I of 2 CFR 180 that has no corresponding section in this part, NSF policies and procedures are those in the OMB guidance.

Subpart A—General

§ 2520.137 Who in NSF may grant an exception to let an excluded person participate in a covered transaction?

The NSF Director and the Deputy Director have the authority to grant an exception to let an excluded person participate in a covered transaction.

Subpart B—Covered Transactions

§ 2520.220 What contracts and subcontracts, in addition to those listed in 2 CFR 180.220, are covered transactions?

Although the OMB guidance at 2 CFR 180.220(c) allows a Federal agency to do so (also see optional lower tier coverage in the figure in the appendix to 2 CFR part 180), NSF does not extend coverage of nonprocurement suspension and debarment requirements beyond first-tier procurement contracts under a covered nonprocurement transaction.

Subpart C—Responsibilities of Participants Regarding Transactions

§ 2520.332 What methods must I use to pass requirements down to participants at lower tiers with whom I intend to do business?

You as a participant must include a term or condition in lower-tier transactions requiring lower-tier participants to comply with subpart C of the OMB guidance in 2 CFR part 180, as supplemented by this subpart.

Subpart D—Responsibilities of Federal Agency Officials Regarding Transactions

§ 2520.437 What method do I use to communicate to a participant the requirements described in the OMB guidance at 2 CFR 180.435?

To communicate to a participant the requirements described in 2 CFR 180.435 of the OMB guidance, you must include a term or condition in the transaction that requires the participant's compliance with subpart C of 2 CFR's part 180, as supplemented by subpart C of this part, and requires the participant to include a similar term or condition in lower-tier covered transactions.

Subparts E–I [Reserved]

CHAPTER XXVI—NATIONAL ARCHIVES AND RECORDS ADMINISTRATION

PART 2600—NONPROCUREMENT DEBARMENT AND SUSPENSION

Sec.
2600.10 What does this part do?
2600.20 Does this part apply to me?
2600.30 What policies and procedures must I follow?

Subpart A—General

2600.137 Who in NARA may grant an exception to let an excluded person participate in a covered transaction?

Subpart B—Covered Transactions

2600.220 What contracts and subcontracts, in addition to those listed in 2 CFR 180.220, are covered transactions?

Subpart C—Responsibilities of Participants Regarding Transactions

2600.332 What methods must I use to pass requirements down to participants at lower tiers with whom I intend to do business?

Subpart D—Responsibilities of Federal Agency Officials Regarding Transactions

2600.437 What method do I use to communicate to a participant the requirements described in the OMB guidance at 2 CFR 180.435?

Subparts E–J [Reserved]

AUTHORITY: Sec. 2455, Pub. L. 103–355, 108 Stat. 3327; E.O. 12549, 3 CFR, 1986 Comp., p. 189; E.O. 12689, 3 CFR, 1989 Comp., p. 235; 44 U.S.C. 2104(a).

SOURCE: 72 FR 2768, Jan. 23, 2007, unless otherwise noted.

§ 2600.10 What does this part do?

This part adopts the Office of Management and Budget (OMB) guidance in subparts A through I of 2 CFR part 180, as supplemented by this part, as NARA's policies and procedures for nonprocurement debarment and suspension. It thereby gives regulatory effect for NARA to the OMB guidance as supplemented by this part. This part satisfies the requirements in section 3 of Executive Order 12549, "Debarment and Suspension" (3 CFR 1986 Comp., p. 189), Executive Order 12689, "Debarment and Suspension" (3 CFR 1989 Comp., p. 235) and 31 U.S.C. 6101 note (Section 2455, Pub. L. 103–355, 108 Stat. 3327).

§ 2600.20 Does this part apply to me?

This part and, through this part, pertinent portions of the OMB guidance in subparts A through I of 2 CFR part 180 (see table at 2 CFR 180.100(b)) apply to you if you are a—

(a) Participant or principal in a "covered transaction" (see subpart B of 2 CFR part 180 and the definition of "nonprocurement transaction" at 2 CFR 180.970.

(b) Respondent in a NARA suspension or debarment action.

(c) NARA debarment or suspension official;

(d) NARA grants officer, agreements officer, or other official authorized to enter into any type of nonprocurement transaction that is a covered transaction;

§ 2600.30 What policies and procedures must I follow?

NARA policies and procedures that you must follow are the policies and procedures specified in each applicable section of the OMB guidance in subparts A through I of 2 CFR part 180, as that section is supplemented by the section in this part with the same section number. The contracts that are covered transactions, for example, are specified by section 220 of the OMB guidance (i.e., 2 CFR 180.220) as supplemented by section 220 in this part (i.e., § 2600.220). For any section of OMB guidance in subparts A through I of 2 CFR 180 that has no corresponding section in this part, NARA policies and procedures are those in the OMB guidance.

Subpart A—General

§ 2600.137 Who in NARA may grant an exception to let an excluded person participate in a covered transaction?

The Archivist of the United States or designee may grant an exception permitting an excluded person to participate in a particular covered transaction as provided in the OMB guidance at 2 CFR 180.135.

Subpart B—Covered Transactions

§ 2600.220 What contracts and subcontracts, in addition to those listed in 2 CFR 180.220, are covered transactions?

Although the OMB guidance at 2 CFR 180.220(c) allows a Federal agency to do so (also see optional lower tier coverage in the figure in the appendix to 2 CFR part 180), NARA does not extend coverage of nonprocurement suspension and debarment requirements beyond first-tier procurement contracts under a covered nonprocurement transaction.

Subpart C—Responsibilities of Participants Regarding Transactions

§ 2600.332 What methods must I use to pass requirements down to participants at lower tiers with whom I intend to do business?

You as a participant must include a term or condition in lower-tier transactions requiring lower-tier participants to comply with subpart C of the OMB guidance in 2 CFR part 180.

Subpart D—Responsibilities of Federal Agency Officials Regarding Transactions

§ 2600.437 What method do I use to communicate to a participant the requirements described in the OMB guidance at 2 CFR 180.435?

To communicate to a participant the requirements described in 2 CFR 180.435 of the OMB guidance, you must include a term or condition in the transaction that requires the participant's compliance with subpart C of 2 CFR part 180 and requires the participant to include a similar term or condition in lower-tier covered transactions.

Subparts E–J [Reserved]

CHAPTER XXVII—SMALL BUSINESS ADMINISTRATION

PART 2700—NONPROCUREMENT DEBARMENT AND SUSPENSION

Sec.
2700.10   What does this part do?
2700.20   Does this part apply to me?
2700.30   What policies and procedures must I follow?

Subpart A—General

2700.137   Who in the Small Business Administration may grant an exception to let an excluded person participate in a covered transaction?

Subpart B—Covered Transactions

2700.220   What contracts and subcontracts, in addition to those listed in 2 CFR 180.220, are covered transactions?

Subpart C—Responsibilities of Participants Regarding Transactions

2700.332   What methods must I use to pass requirements down to participants at lower tiers with whom I intend to do business?

Subpart D—Responsibilities of Federal Agency Officials Regarding Transactions

2700.437   What method do I use to communicate to a participant the requirements described in the OMB guidance at 2 CFR 180.435?

Subparts E–F [Reserved]

Subpart G—Suspension

2700.765   How may I appeal my suspension?

Subpart H—Debarment

2700.890   How may I appeal my debarment?

Subpart I—Definitions

2700.930   Debarring official (SBA supplement to government-wide definition at 2 CFR 180.930).
2700.995   Principal (SBA supplement to government-wide definition at 2 CFR 180.995).
2700.1010   Suspending official (SBA supplement to government-wide definition at 2 CFR 180.1010).

Subpart J [Reserved]

AUTHORITY: Sec. 2455, Pub. L. 103–355, 108 Stat. 3327 (31 U.S.C. 6101 note); E.O. 12549 (3 CFR, 1986 Comp., p. 189); E.O. 12689 (3 CFR, 1989, 1986 Comp., p. 235); 15 U.S.C. 634(b)(6).

SOURCE: 72 FR 39728, July 20, 2007, unless otherwise noted.

§ 2700.10   What does this part do?

This part adopts the Office of Management and Budget (OMB) guidance in subparts A through I of 2 CFR part 180, as supplemented by this part, as the SBA policies and procedures for nonprocurement debarment and suspension. It thereby gives regulatory effect for SBA to the OMB guidance as supplemented by this part. This part satisfies the requirements in section 3 of Executive Order 12549, "Debarment and Suspension" (3 CFR 1986 Comp., p. 189); Executive Order 12689, "Debarment and Suspension" (3 CFR 1989 Comp., p. 235); and section 2455 of the Federal Acquisition Streamlining Act of 1994, Pub. L. 103–355 (31 U.S.C. 6101 note).

§ 2700.20   Does this part apply to me?

This part and, through this part, pertinent portions of the OMB guidance in subparts A through I of 2 CFR part 180 (see table at 2 CFR 180.100(b)) apply to you if you are a—

(a) Participant or principal in a "covered transaction" (see subpart B of 2 CFR part 180 and the definition of "nonprocurement transaction" at 2 CFR 180.970);

(b) Respondent in an SBA suspension or debarment action;

(c) SBA debarment or suspension official; or

(d) SBA grants officer, agreements officer, or other official authorized to enter into any type of nonprocurement transaction that is a covered transaction.

§ 2700.30   What policies and procedures must I follow?

The SBA policies and procedures you must follow are the policies and procedures specified in each applicable section of the OMB guidance in subparts A through I of 2 CFR part 180, as that section is supplemented by the section in this part with the same section number. The contracts that are covered transactions, for example, are specified by section 220 of the OMB guidance (i.e., 2 CFR 180.220) as supplemented by section 220 of this part (i.e., § 2700.220). For any section of OMB guidance in subparts A through I of 2 CFR 180 that has no corresponding section in this part, SBA policies and procedures are those in the OMB guidance.

Subpart A—General

§ 2700.137 Who in the Small Business Administration may grant an exception to let an excluded person participate in a covered transaction?

The Director of the Office of Credit Risk Management may grant an exception permitting an excluded person to participate in a particular covered transaction under SBA's financial assistance programs. For all other Agency programs, the Associate General Counsel for Procurement Law may grant such an exception.

[72 FR 39728, July 20, 2007, as amended at 73 FR 43348, July 25, 2008]

Subpart B—Covered Transactions

§ 2700.220 What contracts and subcontracts, in addition to those listed in 2 CFR 180.220, are covered transactions?

In addition to the contracts covered under 2 CFR 180.22(b) of the OMB guidance, this part applies to any contract, regardless of tier, that is awarded by a contractor, subcontractor, supplier, consultant, or its agent or representative in any transaction, if the contract is to be funded or provided by the SBA under a covered nonprocurement transaction and the amount of the contract is expected to equal or exceed $25,000. This extends the coverage of the SBA nonprocurement suspension and debarment requirements to all lower tiers of subcontracts under covered nonprocurement transactions, as permitted under the OMB guidance at 2 CFR 180.200(c) (see optional lower tier coverage in the figure in the appendix to 2 CFR part 180)

Subpart C—Responsibilities of Participants Regarding Transactions

§ 2700.332 What methods must I use to pass requirements down to participants at lower tiers with whom I intend to do business?

You, as a participant, must include a term or condition in lower-tier trans-actions requiring lower-tier participants to comply with subpart C of the OMB guidance in 2 CFR part 180, as supplemented by this part.

Subpart D—Responsibilities of Federal Agency Officials Regarding Transactions

§ 2700.437 What method do I use to communicate to a participant the requirements described in the OMB guidance at 2 CFR 180.435?

To communicate to a participant the requirements described in 2 CFR 180.435 of the OMB guidance, you must include a term or condition in the transaction that requires the participant's compliance with subpart C of 2 CFR part 180, as supplemented by subpart C of this part, and requires the participant to include a similar term or condition in lower-tier covered transactions.

Subparts E–F [Reserved]

Subpart G—Suspension

§ 2700.765 How may I appeal my suspension?

(a) If the SBA suspending official issues a decision under § 180.755 to continue your suspension after you present information in opposition to that suspension under § 180.720, you may ask for review of the suspending official's decision in two ways:

(1) You may ask the suspending official to reconsider the decision for material errors of fact or law that you believe will change the outcome of the matter; or

(2) You may request that the SBA Office of Hearings and Appeals (OHA) review the suspending official's decision to continue your suspension within 30 days of your receipt of the suspending official's decision under § 180.755 or paragraph (a)(1) of this section. However, OHA may reverse the suspending official's decision only where OHA finds that the decision is based on a clear error of material fact or law, or where OHA finds that the suspending official's decision was arbitrary, capricious, or an abuse of discretion. You may appeal the suspending official's decision without requesting reconsideration, or you may appeal the decision

of the suspending official on reconsideration. The procedures governing OHA appeals are set forth in 13 CFR part 134.

(b) A request for review under this section must be in writing; state the specific findings you believe to be in error; and include the reasons or legal bases for your position.

(c) OHA, in its discretion, may stay the suspension pending review of the suspending official's decision.

(d) The SBA suspending official and OHA must notify you of their decision under this section, in writing, using the notice procedures set forth at §§ 180.615 and 180.975.

Subpart H—Debarment

§ 2700.890 How may I appeal my debarment?

(a) If the SBA debarring official issues a decision under § 180.870 to debar you after you present information in opposition to a proposed debarment under § 180.815, you may ask for review of the debarring official's decision in two ways:

(1) You may ask the debarring official to reconsider the decision for material errors of fact or law that you believe will change the outcome of the matter; or

(2) You may request that the SBA Office of Hearings and Appeals (OHA) review the debarring official's decision to debar you within 30 days of your receipt of the debarring official's decision under § 180.870 or paragraph (a)(1) of this section. However, OHA may reverse the debarring official's decision only where OHA finds that the decision is based on a clear error of material fact or law, or where OHA finds that the debarring official's decision was arbitrary, capricious, or an abuse of discretion. You may appeal the debarring official's decision without requesting reconsideration, or you may appeal the decision of the debarring official on reconsideration. The procedures governing OHA appeals are set forth in 13 CFR part 134.

(b) A request for review under this section must be in writing; state the specific findings you believe to be in error; and include the reasons or legal bases for your position.

(c) OHA, in its discretion, may stay the debarment pending review of the debarring official's decision.

(d) The SBA debarring official and OHA must notify you of their decision under this section, in writing, using the notice procedures set forth at §§ 180.615 and 180.975.

Subpart I—Definitions

§ 2700.930 Debarring official (SBA supplement to government-wide definition at 2 CFR 180.930).

For SBA, the debarring official for financial assistance programs is the Director of the Office of Credit Risk Management; for all other programs, the debarring official is the Associate General Counsel for Procurement Law.

[72 FR 39728, July 20, 2007, as amended at 73 FR 43348, July 25, 2008]

§ 2700.995 Principal (SBA supplement to government-wide definition at 2 CFR 180.995).

Principal means—

(a) Other examples of individuals who are principals in SBA covered transactions include:

(1) Principal investigators.

(2) Securities brokers and dealers under the section 7(a) Loan, Certified Development Company (CDC) and Small Business Investment Company (SBIC) programs.

(3) Applicant representatives under the section 7(a) Loan, CDC, SBIC, Small Business Development Center (SBDC), and section 7(j) programs.

(4) Providers of professional services under the section 7(a) Loan, CDC, SBIC, SBDC, and section 7(j) programs.

(5) Individuals that certify, authenticate or authorize billings.

(b) [Reserved]

§ 2700.1010 Suspending official (SBA supplement to government-wide definition at 2 CFR 180.1010).

For SBA, the suspending official for financial assistance programs is the Director of the Office of Credit Risk Management; for all other programs, the suspending official is the Associate General Counsel for Procurement Law.

[72 FR 39728, July 20, 2007, as amended at 73 FR 43348, July 25, 2008]

Subpart J [Reserved]

CHAPTER XXVIII—DEPARTMENT OF JUSTICE

PART 2867—NONPROCUREMENT DEBARMENT AND SUSPENSION

Sec.
2867.10   What does this part do?
2867.20   To whom does this part apply?
2867.30   What policies and procedures must be followed?

Subpart A—General

2867.137   Who in the Department of Justice may grant an exception to let an excluded person participate in a covered transaction?

Subpart B—Covered Transactions

2867.220   What contracts and subcontracts, in addition to those listed in 2 CFR 180.220, are covered transactions?

Subpart C—Responsibilities of Participants Regarding Transactions

2867.332   What method must a participant use to pass requirements down to participants at lower tiers with whom the participant intends to do business?

Subpart D—Responsibilities of Federal Agency Officials Regarding Transactions

2867.437   What method must be used to communicate to a participant the requirements described in the OMB guidance at 2 CFR 180.435?

Subparts E–J [Reserved]

AUTHORITY: Sec. 2455, Pub. L. 103–355, 108 Stat. 3327; E.O. 12549, 3 CFR, 1986 Comp., p. 189; E.O. 12689, 3 CFR, 1989 Comp., p. 235; 5 U.S.C. 301; 28 U.S.C. 509, 510, 515–519.

SOURCE: 72 FR 11286, Mar. 13, 2007, unless otherwise noted.

§ 2867.10   What does this part do?

This part adopts the Office of Management and Budget (OMB) guidance in subparts A through I of 2 CFR part 180, as supplemented by this part, as the Department of Justice policies and procedures for nonprocurement debarment and suspension. It thereby gives regulatory effect for the Department of Justice to the OMB guidance as supplemented by this part. This part satisfies the requirements in section 3 of Executive Order 12549, "Debarment and Suspension" (3 CFR 1986 Comp., p. 189), Executive Order 12689, "Debarment and Suspension" (3 CFR 1989 Comp., p. 235)

and 31 U.S.C. 6101 note (Section 2455, Pub. L. 103–355, 108 Stat. 3327).

§ 2867.20   To whom does this part apply?

This part and, through this part, pertinent portions of the OMB guidance in subparts A through I of 2 CFR part 180 (see table at 2 CFR 180.100(b)) apply to any—

(a) Participant or principal in a "covered transaction" (sees subpart B of 2 CFR part 180 and the definition of "nonprocurement transaction" at 2 CFR 180.970 (as supplemented by subpart B of this part));

(b) Respondent in a Department of Justice suspension or debarment action;

(c) Department of Justice debarment or suspension official;

(d) Department of Justice grants officer, agreements officer, or other official authorized to enter into any type of nonprocurement transaction that is a covered transaction.

§ 2867.30   What policies and procedures must be followed?

The Department of Justice policies and procedures that must be followed are the policies and procedures specified in each applicable section of the OMB guidance in subparts A through I of 2 CFR part 180, as that section is supplemented by the section in this part with the same section number. The contracts that are covered transactions, for example, are specified by section 220 of the OMB guidance (i.e., 2 CFR 180.220) as supplemented by section 220 in this part (i.e., § 2867.220). For any section of OMB guidance in subparts A through I of 2 CFR 180 that has no corresponding section in this part, Department of Justice policies and procedures are those in the OMB guidance.

Subpart A—General

§ 2867.137   Who in the Department of Justice may grant an exception to let an excluded person participate in a covered transaction?

Within the Department of Justice, the Attorney General or designee has the authority to grant an exception to let an excluded person participate in a covered transaction, as provided in the OMB guidance at 2 CFR 180.135.

Subpart B—Covered Transactions

§ 2867.220 What contracts and subcontracts, in addition to those listed in 2 CFR 180.220, are covered transactions?

Although the OMB guidance at 2 CFR 180.220(c) allows a Federal agency to do so (also see optional lower tier coverage in the figure in the appendix to 2 CFR part 180), the Department of Justice does not extend coverage of nonprocurement suspension and debarment requirements beyond first-tier procurement contracts under a covered nonprocurement transaction.

Subpart C—Responsibilities of Participants Regarding Transactions

§ 2867.332 What method must a participant use to pass requirements down to participants at lower tiers with whom the participant intends to do business?

A participant must include a term or condition in lower-tier transactions requiring lower-tier participants to comply with subpart C of the OMB guidance in 2 CFR part 180, as supplemented by this subpart.

Subpart D—Responsibilities of Federal Agency Officials Regarding Transactions

§ 2867.437 What method must be used to communicate to a participant the requirements described in the OMB guidance at 2 CFR 180.435?

To communicate to a participant the requirements described in 2 CFR 180.435 of the OMB guidance, the communication must include a term or condition in the transaction that requires the participant's compliance with subpart C of 2 CFR part 180, as supplemented by subpart C of this part, and requires the participant to include a similar term or condition in lower-tier covered transactions.

Subparts E–J [Reserved]

CHAPTER XXX—DEPARTMENT OF HOMELAND SECURITY

PART 3000—NONPROCUREMENT DEBARMENT AND SUSPENSION

Sec.
3000.10   What does this part do?
3000.20   Does this part apply to me?
3000.30   What policies and procedures must I follow?

Subpart A—General

3000.137   Who in the Department of Homeland Security may grant an exception to let an excluded person participate in a covered transaction?

Subpart B—Covered Transactions

3000.220   What contracts and subcontracts, in addition to those listed in 2 CFR 180.220, are covered transactions?

Subpart C—Responsibilities of Participants Regarding Transactions

3000.332   What methods must I use to pass requirements down to participants at lower tiers with whom I intend to do business?

Subpart D—Responsibilities of Department of Homeland Security Officials Regarding Transactions

3000.437   What method do I use to communicate to a participant the requirements described in the Office of Management and Budget guidance at 2 CFR 180.435?

Subpart E–I [Reserved]

AUTHORITY: Sec. 2455, Public Law 103–355, 108 Stat. 3327; E.O. 12549, 3 CFR, 1986 Comp., p. 189; E.O. 12689, 3 CFR, 1989 Comp., p. 235; Public Law 107–296, 116 Stat. 2135.

SOURCE: 74 FR 34497, July 16, 2009, unless otherwise noted.

§ 3000.10   What does this part do?

This part adopts the Office of Management and Budget (OMB) guidance in Subparts A through I of 2 CFR part 180, as supplemented by this part, as the Department of Homeland Security policies and procedures for nonprocurement debarment and suspension. It thereby gives regulatory effect for the Department of Homeland Security to the OMB guidance as supplemented by this part. This part satisfies the requirements in section 3 of Executive Order 12549, "Debarment and Suspension" (3 CFR 1986 Comp., p. 189), Execu-

tive Order 12689, "Debarment and Suspension" (3 CFR 1989 Comp., p. 235) and 31 U.S.C. 6101 note (Section 2455, Pub. L. 103–355, 108 Stat. 3327).

§ 3000.20   Does this part apply to me?

This part and, through this part, pertinent portions of the OMB guidance in Subparts A through I of 2 CFR part 180 (see table at 2 CFR 180.100(b)) apply to you if you are a—

(a) Participant or principal in a "covered transaction" (see Subpart B of 2 CFR Part 180 and the definition of "nonprocurement transaction" at 2 CFR 180.970);

(b) Respondent in a Department of Homeland Security suspension or debarment action;

(c) Department of Homeland Security debarment or suspension official;

(d) Department of Homeland Security grants officer, agreements officer, or other official authorized to enter into any type of nonprocurement transaction that is a covered transaction.

§ 3000.30   What policies and procedures must I follow?

The Department of Homeland Security policies and procedures that you must follow are the policies and procedures specified in each applicable section of the OMB guidance in Subparts A through I of 2 CFR Part 180, as that section is supplemented by the section in this part with the same section number. The contracts that are covered transactions, for example, are specified by section 220 of the OMB guidance (i.e., 2 CFR 180.220) as supplemented by section 220 in this part (i.e., § 3000.220). For any section of OMB guidance in Subparts A through I of 2 CFR Part 180 that has no corresponding section in this part, Department of Homeland Security policies and procedures are those in the OMB guidance.

Subpart A—General

§ 3000.137   Who in the Department of Homeland Security may grant an exception to let an excluded person participate in a covered transaction?

Within the Department of Homeland Security, the Secretary of Homeland Security has delegated the authority

365

to grant an exception to let an excluded person participate in a covered transaction to the Head of the Contracting Activity for each DHS component as provided in the OMB guidance at 2 CFR 180.135.

Subpart B—Covered Transactions

§ 3000.220 What contracts and subcontracts, in addition to those listed in 2 CFR 180.220, are covered transactions?

Department of Homeland Security extends coverage of nonprocurement suspension and debarment requirements beyond first-tier procurement contracts under a covered nonprocurement transaction.

Subpart C—Responsibilities of Participants Regarding Transactions

§ 3000.332 What methods must I use to pass requirements down to participants at lower tiers with whom I intend to do business?

You as a participant in a covered transaction must include a term or condition in any lower-tier covered transaction into which you enter, to require the participant of that transaction to—

(a) Comply with Subpart C of the OMB guidance in 2 CFR part 180; and

(b) Include a similar term or condition in any covered transaction into which it enters at the next lower tier.

Subpart D—Responsibilities of Department of Homeland Security Officials Regarding Transactions

§ 3000.437 What method do I use to communicate to a participant the requirements described in the Office of Management and Budget guidance at 2 CFR 180.435?

You as a DHS component official must include a term or condition in each covered transaction into which you enter, to communicate to the participant the requirements to—

(a) Comply with subpart C of the OMB guidance in 2 CFR part 180; and

(b) Include a similar term or condition in any lower-tier covered transactions into which the participant enters.

Subparts E–I [Reserved]

PART 3001—REQUIREMENTS FOR DRUG-FREE WORKPLACE (FINANCIAL ASSISTANCE)

Sec.
3001.10   What does this part do?
3001.20   Does this part apply to me?
3001.30   What policies and procedures must I follow?

Subpart A—Purpose and Coverage [Reserved]

Subpart B—Requirements for Recipients Other Than Individuals

3001.225   Who in DHS does a recipient other than an individual notify about a criminal drug conviction?

Subpart C—Requirements for Recipients Who Are Individuals

3001.300   Who in DHS does a recipient who is an individual notify about a criminal drug conviction?

Subpart D—Responsibilities of Agency Awarding Officials

3001.400   What method do I use as an agency awarding official to obtain a recipient's agreement to comply with the OMB guidance?

Subpart E—Violations of This Part and Consequences

3001.500   Who in DHS determines that a recipient other than an individual violated the requirements of this part?
3001.505   Who in DHS determines that a recipient who is an individual violated the requirements of this part?
3001.510   What actions will the Federal Government take against a recipient determined to have violated this part?

Subpart F—Definitions

3001.605   Award.
3001.661   Reimbursable Agreement.

AUTHORITY: 5 U.S.C. 301; 41 U.S.C. 701–707; OMB Guidance for Drug-Free Workplace Requirements, codified at 2 CFR part 182.

SOURCE: 76 FR 10207, Feb. 24, 2011, unless otherwise noted.

§3001.10 What does this part do?

This part requires that the award and administration of Department of Homeland Security (DHS) grants and cooperative agreements comply with Office of Management and Budget (OMB) guidance implementing the portion of the Drug-Free Workplace Act of 1988 (41 U.S.C. 701–707, as amended, hereafter referred to as "the Act") that applies to grants. It thereby—

(a) Gives regulatory effect to the OMB guidance, as supplemented by this part (Subparts A through F of 2 CFR part 182) for DHS's grants and cooperative agreements; and

(b) Establishes DHS policies and procedures, as supplemented by this part, for compliance with the Act that are the same as those of other Federal agencies, in conformance with the requirement in 41 U.S.C. 705 for Government-wide implementing regulations.

§3001.20 Does this part apply to me?

This part and, through this part, pertinent portions of the OMB guidance in Subparts A through F of 2 CFR part 182 (*see* table at 2 CFR 182.115(b)) apply to you if you are a—

(a) Recipient of a DHS grant or cooperative agreement; or

(b) DHS awarding official.

§3001.30 What policies and procedures must I follow?

(a) *General.* You must follow the policies and procedures specified in applicable sections of the OMB guidance in Subparts A through F of 2 CFR part 182, as implemented by this part.

(b) *Specific sections of OMB guidance that this part supplements.* This part supplements the OMB guidance in 2 CFR part 182 as shown in the following table. For each of those sections, you must follow the policies and procedures in the OMB guidance, as supplemented by this part.

Section of OMB guidance	Section in this part where supplemented	What the supplementation clarifies
2 CFR 182.225(a)	§3001.225	Who in DHS a recipient other than an individual must notify if an employee is convicted for a violation of a criminal drug statute in the workplace.
2 CFR 182.300(b)	§3001.300	Who in DHS a recipient who is an individual must notify if he or she is convicted of a criminal drug offense resulting from a violation occurring during the conduct of any award activity.
2 CFR 182.400	§3001.400	What method do I use as an agency awarding official to obtain a recipient's agreement to comply with the OMB guidance.
2 CFR 182.500	§3001.500	Who in DHS is authorized to determine that a recipient other than an individual is in violation of the requirements of 2 CFR part 182, as implemented by this part.
2 CFR 182.505	§3001.505	Who in DHS is authorized to determine that a recipient who is an individual is in violation of the requirements of 2 CFR part 182, as implemented by this part.
2 CFR 182.510	§3001.510	What actions the Federal Government will take against a recipient determined to have violated 2 CFR part 182, as implemented by this part.
2 CFR 182.605	§3001.605	What types of assistance are included in the definition of "award."
None	§3001.661	What types of assistance are included in the definition of "reimbursable agreement."

(c) *Sections of the OMB guidance that this part does not supplement.* For any section of OMB guidance in Subparts A through F of 2 CFR part 182 that is not listed in paragraph (b) of this section, DHS policies and procedures are the same as those in the OMB guidance.

Subpart A—Purpose and Coverage [Reserved]

Subpart B—Requirements for Recipients Other Than Individuals

§3001.225 Who in DHS does a recipient other than an individual notify about a criminal drug conviction?

A recipient other than an individual that is required under 2 CFR 182.225(a) to notify Federal agencies about an employee's conviction for a criminal drug offense must notify the DHS Office of Inspector General and each DHS office from which the recipient currently has an award.

Subpart C—Requirements for Recipients Who Are Individuals

§ 3001.300 Who in DHS does a recipient who is an individual notify about a criminal drug conviction?

A recipient who is an individual and is required under 2 CFR 182.300(b) to notify Federal agencies about a conviction for a criminal drug offense must notify the DHS Office of Inspector General and each DHS office from which the recipient currently has an award.

Subpart D—Responsibilities of Agency Awarding Officials

§ 3001.400 What method do I use as an agency awarding official to obtain a recipient's agreement to comply with the OMB guidance?

To obtain a recipient's agreement to comply with applicable requirements in the OMB guidance at 2 CFR part 182, you must include the following term or condition in the award:

Drug-free workplace. You as the recipient must comply with drug-free workplace requirements in Subpart B (or Subpart C, if the recipient is an individual) of 2 CFR part 3001, which adopts the Government-wide implementation (2 CFR part 182) of sec. 5152–5158 of the Drug-Free Workplace Act of 1988 (Pub. L. 100–690, Title V, Subtitle D; 41 U.S.C. 701–707).

Subpart E—Violations of This Part and Consequences

§ 3001.500 Who in DHS determines that a recipient other than an individual violated the requirements of this part?

The Secretary of Homeland Security, or his or her official designee, will make the determination that a recipient other than an individual violated the requirements of this part.

§ 3001.505 Who in DHS determines that a recipient who is an individual violated the requirements of this part?

The Secretary of Homeland Security, or his or her official designee, will make the determination that a recipient who is an individual violated the requirements of this part.

§ 3001.510 What actions will the Federal Government take against a recipient determined to have violated this part?

If a recipient is determined to have violated 2 CFR part 182, as implemented by this part, the agency will take one or more of the following actions—

(a) Suspension of payments under the award;

(b) Suspension or termination of the award; and

(c) Suspension or debarment of the recipient under 2 CFR part 180 and 2 CFR part 3000, for a period not to exceed five years.

Subpart F—Definitions

§ 3001.605 Award.

Award means an award of financial assistance by a Federal agency directly to a recipient.

(a) The term award includes:

(1) A Federal grant, cooperative agreement or reimbursable agreement, in the form of money or property in lieu of money.

(2) A block grant or a grant in an entitlement program, whether or not the grant is exempted from coverage under 2 CFR part 182 and specifies uniform administrative requirements.

(b) The term "award" does not include:

(1) Technical assistance that provides services instead of money.

(2) Loans.

(3) Loan guarantees.

(4) Interest subsidies.

(5) Insurance.

(6) Direct appropriations.

(7) Veterans' benefits to individuals (*i.e.*, any benefit to veterans, their families, or survivors by virtue of the service of a veteran in the Armed Forces of the United States).

(8) Other Transactional Authority Award.

§3001.661   **Reimbursable Agreement.**

Reimbursable Agreement means an award in which the recipient is reimbursed for expenditures only, and is not eligible for advance payments.

CHAPTER XXXI—INSTITUTE OF MUSEUM AND LIBRARY SERVICES

PART 3185—NONPROCUREMENT DEBARMENT AND SUSPENSION

Sec.
3185.10   What does this part do?
3185.20   Does this part apply to me?
3185.30   What policies and procedures must I follow?

Subpart A—General

3185.137   Who in IMLS may grant an exception to let an excluded person participate in a covered transaction?

Subpart B—Covered Transactions

3185.220   What contracts and subcontracts, in addition to those listed in 2 CFR 180.220, are covered transactions?

Subpart C—Responsibilities of Participants Regarding Transactions

3185.332   What methods must I use to pass requirements down to participants at lower tiers with whom I intend to do business?

Subpart D—Responsibilities of Federal Agency Officials Regarding Transactions

3185.437   What method do I use to communicate to a participant the requirements described in the OMB guidance at 2 CFR 180.435?

Subparts E–I [Reserved]

AUTHORITY: 20 U.S.C. 9103(f); Sec. 2455, Pub. L. 103–355, 108 Stat. 3327; E.O. 12549, 3 CFR, 1986 Comp., p. 189; E.O. 12689, 3 CFR, 1989 Comp., p. 235.

SOURCE: 73 FR 46529, Aug. 11, 2008, unless otherwise noted.

§ 3185.10   What does this part do?

This part adopts the Office of Management and Budget (OMB) guidance in subparts A through I of 2 CFR part 180, as supplemented by this part, as the Institute of Museum and Library Services (IMLS) policies and procedures for nonprocurement debarment and suspension. It thereby gives regulatory effect for IMLS to the OMB guidance as supplemented by this part. This part satisfies the requirements in section 3 of Executive Order 12549, "Debarment and Suspension" (3 CFR 1986 Comp., p. 189), Executive Order 12689, "Debarment and Suspension" (3 CFR 1989 Comp., p. 235) and 31 U.S.C. 6101 note

(Section 2455, Pub. L. 103–355, 108 Stat. 3327).

§ 3185.20   Does this part apply to me?

This part and, through this part, pertinent portions of the OMB guidance in subparts A through I of 2 CFR part 180 (see table at 2 CFR 180.100(b)) apply to you if you are a—

(a) Participant or principal in a "covered transaction" (see subpart B of 2 CFR part 180 and the definition of "nonprocurement transaction" at 2 CFR 180.970.

(b) Respondent in an IMLS suspension or debarment action.

(c) IMLS debarment or suspension official;

(d) IMLS grants officer, agreements officer, or other official authorized to enter into any type of nonprocurement transaction that is a covered transaction.

§ 3185.30   What policies and procedures must I follow?

The IMLS policies and procedures that you must follow are the policies and procedures specified in each applicable section of the OMB guidance in subparts A through I of 2 CFR part 180, as that section is supplemented by the section in this part with the same section number. The contracts that are covered transactions, for example, are specified by section 220 of the OMB guidance (i.e., 2 CFR 180.220) as supplemented by section 220 in this part (i.e., § 3185.220). For any section of OMB guidance in subparts A through I of 2 CFR 180 that has no corresponding section in this part, IMLS policies and procedures are those in the OMB guidance.

Subpart A—General

§ 3185.137   Who in the IMLS may grant an exception to let an excluded person participate in a covered transaction?

The IMLS Director has the authority to grant an exception to let an excluded person participate in a covered transaction, as provided in the OMB guidance at 2 CFR 180.135.

373

Subpart B—Covered Transactions

§ 3185.220 What contracts and subcontracts, in addition to those listed in 2 CFR 180.220, are covered transactions?

Although the OMB guidance at 2 CFR 180.220(c) allows a Federal agency to do so (also see optional lower-tier coverage in the figure in the appendix to 2 CFR part 180), IMLS does not extend coverage of nonprocurement suspension and debarment requirements beyond first-tier procurement contracts under a covered nonprocurement transaction.

Subpart C—Responsibilities of Participants Regarding Transactions

§ 3185.332 What methods must I use to pass requirements down to participants at lower tiers with whom I intend to do business?

You as a participant must include a term or condition in lower-tier transactions requiring lower-tier participants to comply with subpart C of the OMB guidance in 2 CFR part 180, as supplemented by this subpart.

Subpart D—Responsibilities of Federal Agency Officials Regarding Transactions

§ 3185.437 What method do I use to communicate to a participant the requirements described in the OMB guidance at 2 CFR 180.435?

To communicate to a participant the requirements described in 2 CFR 180.435 of the OMB guidance, you must include a term or condition in the transaction that requires the participant's compliance with subpart C of 2 CFR part 180, as supplemented by subpart C of this part, and requires the participant to include a similar term or condition in lower-tier covered transactions.

Subparts E–I [Reserved]

PART 3186—REQUIREMENTS FOR DRUG-FREE WORKPLACE (FINANCIAL ASSISTANCE)

Sec.
3186.10   What does this part do?
3186.20   Does this part apply to me?
3186.30   What policies and procedures must I follow?

Subpart A—Purpose and Coverage [Reserved]

Subpart B—Requirements for Recipients Other Than Individuals

3186.225   Whom in the IMLS does a recipient other than an individual notify about a criminal drug conviction?

Subpart C—Requirements for Recipients Who Are Individuals

3186.300   Whom in the IMLS does a recipient who is an individual notify about a criminal drug conviction?

Subpart D—Responsibilities of Agency Awarding Officials

3186.400   What method do I use as an agency awarding official to obtain a recipient's agreement to comply with the OMB guidance?

Subpart E—Violations of this Part and Consequences

3186.500   Who in the IMLS determines that a recipient other than an individual violated the requirements of this part?
3186.505   Who in the IMLS determines that a recipient who is an individual violated the requirements of this part?

AUTHORITY: 41 U.S.C. 701–707.

SOURCE: 75 FR 39134, July 8, 2010, unless otherwise noted.

§ 3186.10   What does this part do?

This part requires that the award and administration of IMLS grants and cooperative agreements comply with Office of Management and Budget (OMB) guidance implementing the portion of the Drug-Free Workplace Act of 1988 (41 U.S.C. 701–707, as amended, hereafter referred to as "the Act") that applies to grants. It thereby—

(a) Gives regulatory effect to the OMB guidance (Subparts A through F of 2 CFR part 182) for the IMLS's grants and cooperative agreements; and

(b) Establishes IMLS policies and procedures for compliance with the Act that are the same as those of other Federal agencies, in conformance with the requirement in 41 U.S.C. 705 for Governmentwide implementing regulations.

§3186.20 Does this part apply to me?

This part and, through this part, pertinent portions of the OMB guidance in Subparts A through F of 2 CFR part 182 (see table at 2 CFR 182.115(b)) apply to you if you are a—

(a) Recipient of an IMLS grant or cooperative agreement; or

(b) IMLS awarding official.

§3186.30 What policies and procedures must I follow?

(a) *General.* You must follow the policies and procedures specified in applicable sections of the OMB guidance in Subparts A through F of 2 CFR part 182, as implemented by this part.

(b) *Specific sections of OMB guidance that this part supplements.* In implementing the OMB guidance in 2 CFR part 182, this part supplements four sections of the guidance, as shown in the following table. For each of those sections, you must follow the policies and procedures in the OMB guidance, as supplemented by this part.

Section of OMB guidance	Section in this part where supplemented	What the supplementation clarifies
(1) 2 CFR 182.225(a)	§3186.225	Whom in the IMLS a recipient other than an individual must notify if an employee is convicted for a violation of a criminal drug statute in the workplace.
(2) 2 CFR 182.300(b)	§3186.300	Whom in the IMLS a recipient who is an individual must notify if he or she is convicted of a criminal drug offense resulting from a violation occurring during the conduct of any award activity.
(3) 2 CFR 182.500	§3186.500	Who in the IMLS is authorized to determine that a recipient other than an individual is in violation of the requirements of 2 CFR part 182, as implemented by this part.
(4) 2 CFR 182.505	§3186.505	Who in the IMLS is authorized to determine that a recipient who is an individual is in violation of the requirements of 2 CFR part 182, as implemented by this part.

(c) *Sections of the OMB guidance that this part does not supplement.* For any section of OMB guidance in Subparts A through F of 2 CFR part 182 that is not listed in paragraph (b) of this section, IMLS policies and procedures are the same as those in the OMB guidance.

Subpart A—Purpose and Coverage [Reserved]

Subpart B—Requirements for Recipients Other Than Individuals

§3186.225 Whom in the IMLS does a recipient other than an individual notify about a criminal drug conviction?

A recipient other than an individual that is required under 2 CFR 182.225(a) to notify Federal agencies about an employee's conviction for a criminal drug offense must notify each IMLS office from which it currently has an award.

Subpart C—Requirements for Recipients Who Are Individuals

§3186.300 Whom in the IMLS does a recipient who is an individual notify about a criminal drug conviction?

A recipient who is an individual and is required under 2 CFR 182.300(b) to notify Federal agencies about a conviction for a criminal drug offense must notify each IMLS office from which it currently has an award.

Subpart D—Responsibilities of Agency Awarding Officials

§3186.400 What method do I use as an agency awarding official to obtain a recipient's agreement to comply with the OMB guidance?

To obtain a recipient's agreement to comply with applicable requirements in the OMB guidance at 2 CFR part 182, you must include the following term or condition in the award:

Drug-free workplace. You as the recipient must comply with drug-free workplace requirements in Subpart B (or Subpart C, if the recipient is an individual) of 2 CFR part 3186, which adopts the Governmentwide implementation (2 CFR part 182) of sec. 5152–5158 of the Drug-Free Workplace Act of 1988 (Pub. L. 100–690, Title V, Subtitle D; 41 U.S.C. 701–707).

Subpart E—Violations of this Part and Consequences

§ 3186.500 Who in the IMLS determines that a recipient other than an individual violated the requirements of this part?

The IMLS Chief Financial Officer is the official authorized to make the determination under 2 CFR 182.500.

§ 3186.505 Who in the IMLS determines that a recipient who is an individual violated the requirements of this part?

The IMLS Chief Financial Officer is the official authorized to make the determination under 2 CFR 182.505.

CHAPTER XXXII—NATIONAL ENDOWMENT FOR THE ARTS

PART 3254—NONPROCUREMENT DEBARMENT AND SUSPENSION

Sec.
3254.10   What does this part do?
3254.20   Does this part apply to me?
3254.30   What policies and procedures must I follow?

Subpart A—General

3254.137   Who in the NEA may grant an exception to let an excluded person participate in a covered transaction?

Subpart B—Covered Transactions

3254.220   What contracts and subcontracts, in addition to those listed in 2 CFR 180.220, are covered transactions?

Subpart C—Responsibilities of Participants Regarding Transactions

3254.332   What methods must I use to pass requirements down to participants at lower tiers with whom I intend to do business?

Subpart D—Responsibilities of Federal Agency Officials Regarding Transactions

3254.437   What method do I use to communicate to a participant the requirements described in the OMB guidance at 2 CFR 180.435?

Subparts E–I [Reserved]

AUTHORITY: Sec. 2455, Pub. L. 103–355, 108 Stat. 3327; E.O. 12549, 3 CFR, 1986 Comp., p. 189; E.O. 12689, 3 CFR, 1989 Comp., p. 235.

SOURCE: 72 FR 6141, Feb. 9, 2007, unless otherwise noted.

§ 3254.10   What does this part do?

This part adopts the Office of Management and Budget (OMB) guidance in subparts A through I of 2 CFR part 180, as supplemented by this part, as the National Endowment for the Arts (NEA) policies and procedures for nonprocurement debarment and suspension. It thereby gives regulatory effect for the NEA to the OMB guidance as supplemented by this part. This part satisfies the requirements in section 3 of Executive Order 12549, "Debarment and Suspension" (3 CFR 1986 Comp., p. 189), Executive Order 12689, "Debarment and Suspension" (3 CFR 1989 Comp., p. 235) and 31 U.S.C. 6101 note (Section 2455, Public Law 103–355, 108 Stat. 3327).

§ 3254.20   Does this part apply to me?

This part and, through this part, pertinent portions of the OMB guidance in subparts A through I of 2 CFR part 180 (see table at 2 CFR 180.100(b)) apply to you if you are a—

(a) Participant or principal in a "covered transaction" (see subpart B of 2 CFR part 180 and the definition of "nonprocurement transaction" at 2 CFR 180.970.

(b) Respondent in a NEA suspension or debarment action.

(c) NEA debarment or suspension official;

(d) NEA grants officer, agreements officer, or other official authorized to enter into any type of nonprocurement transaction that is a covered transaction;

§ 3254.30   What policies and procedures must I follow?

The NEA policies and procedures that you must follow are the policies and procedures specified in each applicable section of the OMB guidance in subparts A through I of 2 CFR part 180, as that section is supplemented by the section in this part with the same section number. The contracts that are covered transactions, for example, are specified by section 220 of the OMB guidance (i.e., 2 CFR 180.220) as supplemented by section 220 in this part (i.e., § 3254.220). For any section of OMB guidance in subparts A through I of 2 CFR 180 that has no corresponding section in this part, NEA policies and procedures are those in the OMB guidance.

Subpart A—General

§ 3254.137   Who in the NEA may grant an exception to let an excluded person participate in a covered transaction?

The NEA Chairman has the authority to grant an exception to let an excluded person participate in a covered transaction, as provided in the OMB guidance at 2 CFR 180.135.

Subpart B—Covered Transactions

§ 3254.220 What contracts and subcontracts, in addition to those listed in 2 CFR 180.220, are covered transactions?

Although the OMB guidance at 2 CFR 180.220(c) allows a Federal agency to do so (also see options lower tier coverage in the figure in the appendix to 2 CFR part 180), NEA does not extend coverage of nonprocurement suspension and debarment requirements beyond first-tier procurement contracts under a covered nonprocurement transaction.

Subpart C—Responsibilities of Participants Regarding Transactions

§ 3254.332 What methods must I use to pass requirements down to participants at lower tiers with whom I intend to do business?

You as a participant must include a term or condition in lower-tier transactions requiring lower-tier participants to comply with subpart C of the OMB guidance in 2 CFR part 180, as supplemented by this subpart.

Subpart D—Responsibilities of Federal Agency Officials Regarding Transactions

§ 3254.437 What method do I use to communicate to a participant the requirements described in the OMB guidance at 2 CFR 180.435?

To communicate to a participant the requirements described in 2 CFR 180.435 of the OMB guidance, you must include a term or condition in the transaction that requires the participant's compliance with subpart C of 2 CFR part 180, as supplemented by subpart C of this part, and requires the participant to include a similar term or condition in lower-tier covered transactions.

Subparts E–I [Reserved]

CHAPTER XXXIII—NATIONAL ENDOWMENT FOR THE HUMANITIES

PART 3369—NONPROCUREMENT DEBARMENT AND SUSPENSION

Sec.
3369.10 What does this part do?
3369.20 Does this part apply to me?
3369.30 What policies and procedures must I follow?

Subpart A—General

3369.137 Who in the NEH may grant an exception to let an excluded person participate in a covered transaction?

Subpart B—Covered Transactions

3369.220 What contracts and subcontracts, in addition to those listed in 2 CFR 180.220, are covered transactions?

Subpart C—Responsibilities of Participants Regarding Transactions

3369.332 What methods must I use to pass requirements down to participants at lower tiers with whom I intend to do business?

Subpart D—Responsibilities of Federal Agency Officials Regarding Transactions

3369.437 What method do I use to communicate to a participant the requirements described in the OMB guidance at 2 CFR 180.435?

Subparts E–I [Reserved]

AUTHORITY: 20 U.S.C. 959(a)(1); Sec. 2455, Pub. L. 103–355, 108 Stat. 3327; E.O. 12549, 3 CFR, 1986 Comp., p. 189; E.O. 12689, 3 CFR, 1989 Comp., p. 235.

SOURCE: 72 FR 9236, Mar. 1, 2007, unless otherwise noted.

§ 3369.10   What does this part do?

This part adopts the Office of Management and Budget (OMB) guidance in subparts A through I of 2 CFR part 180, as supplemented by this part, as the National Endowment for the Humanities (NEH) policies and procedures for nonprocurement debarment and suspension. It thereby gives regulatory effect for the NEH to the OMB guidance as supplemented by this part. This part satisfies the requirements in section 3 of Executive Order 12549, "Debarment and Suspension" (3 CFR 1986 Comp., p. 189), Executive Order 12689, "Debarment and Suspension" (3 CFR 1989 Comp., p. 235) and 31 U.S.C. 6101 note (Section 2455, Public Law 103–355, 108 Stat. 3327).

§ 3369.20   Does this part apply to me?

This part and, through this part, pertinent portions of the OMB guidance in subparts A through I of 2 CFR part 180 (see table at 2 CFR 180.100(b)) apply to you if you are a—

(a) Participant or principal in a "covered transaction" (see subpart B of 2 CFR part 180 and the definition of "nonprocurement transaction" at 2 CFR 180.970).

(b) Respondent in a NEH suspension or debarment action.

(c) NEH debarment or suspension official;

(d) NEH grants officer, agreements officer, or other official authorized to enter into any type of nonprocurement transaction that is a covered transaction;

§ 3369.30   What policies and procedures must I follow?

The NEH policies and procedures that you must follow are the policies and procedures specified in each applicable section of the OMB guidance in subparts A through I of 2 CFR part 180, as that section is supplemented by the section in this part with the same section number. The contracts that are covered transactions, for example, are specified by section 220 of the OMB guidance (i.e., 2 CFR 180.220) as supplemented by section 220 in this part (i.e., § 3369.220). For any section of OMB guidance in subparts A through I of 2 CFR 180 that has no corresponding section in this part, NEH policies and procedures are those in the OMB guidance.

Subpart A—General

§ 3369.137   Who in the NEH may grant an exception to let an excluded person participate in a covered transaction?

The NEH Chairman has the authority to grant an exception to let an excluded person participate in a covered transaction, as provided in the OMB guidance at 2 CFR 180.135.

Subpart B—Covered Transactions

§ 3369.220 What contracts and subcontracts, in addition to those listed in 2 CFR 180.220, are covered transactions?

Although the OMB guidance at 2 CFR 180.220(c) allows a Federal agency to do so (also see optional lower tier coverage in the figure in the appendix to 2 CFR part 180), NEH does not extend coverage of nonprocurement suspension and debarment requirements beyond first-tier procurement contracts under a covered nonprocurement transaction.

Subpart C—Responsibilities of Participants Regarding Transactions

§ 3369.332 What methods must I use to pass requirements down to participants at lower tiers with whom I intend to do business?

You as a participant must include a term or condition in lower-tier transactions requiring lower-tier participants to comply with subpart C of the OMB guidance in 2 CFR part 180, as supplemented by this subpart.

Subpart D—Responsibilities of Federal Agency Officials Regarding Transactions

§ 3369.437 What method do I use to communicate to a participant the requirements described in the OMB guidance at 2 CFR 180.435?

To communicate to a participant the requirements described in 2 CFR 180.435 of the OMB guidance, you must include a term or condition in the transaction that requires the participant's compliance with subpart C of 2 CFR part 180, as supplemented by subpart C of this part, and requires the participant to include a similar term or condition in lower-tier covered transactions.

Subparts E–I [Reserved]

PART 3373—REQUIREMENTS FOR DRUG-FREE WORKPLACE (FINANCIAL ASSISTANCE)

Sec.
3373.10   What does this part do?
3373.20   Does this part apply to me?
3373.30   What policies and procedures must I follow?

Subpart A—Purpose and Coverage [Reserved]

Subpart B—Requirements for Recipients Other Than Individuals

3373.225   Whom in the NEH does a recipient other than an individual notify about a criminal drug conviction?

Subpart C—Requirements for Recipients Who Are Individuals

3373.300   Whom in the NEH does a recipient who is an individual notify about a criminal drug conviction?

Subpart D—Responsibilities of Agency Awarding Officials

3373.400   What method do I use as an agency awarding official to obtain a recipient's agreement to comply with the OMB guidance?

Subpart E—Violations of This Part and Consequences

3373.500   Who in the NEH determines that a recipient other than an individual violated the requirements of this part?
3373.505   Who in the NEH determines that a recipient who is an individual violated the requirements of this part?

Subpart F—Definitions [Reserved]

AUTHORITY: 41 U.S.C. 701–707.

SOURCE: 75 FR 52858, Aug. 30, 2010, unless otherwise noted.

§ 3373.10   What does this part do?

This part requires that the award and administration of NEH grants and cooperative agreements comply with Office of Management and Budget (OMB) guidance implementing the portion of the Drug-Free Workplace Act of 1988 (41 U.S.C. 701–707, as amended, hereafter referred to as "the Act") that applies to grants. It thereby—

(a) Gives regulatory effect to the OMB guidance (Subparts A through F of 2 CFR part 182) for the NEH's grants and cooperative agreements; and

(b) Establishes NEH policies and procedures for compliance with the Act that are the same as those of other Federal agencies, in conformance with the requirement in 41 U.S.C. 705 for Governmentwide implementing regulations.

§ 3373.20 Does this part apply to me?

This part and, through this part, pertinent portions of the OMB guidance in Subparts A through F of 2 CFR part 182 (*see* table at 2 CFR 182.115(b)) apply to you if you are a—

(a) Recipient of a NEH grant or cooperative agreement; or

(b) NEH awarding official.

§ 3373.30 What policies and procedures must I follow?

(a) *General.* You must follow the policies and procedures specified in applicable sections of the OMB guidance in Subparts A through F of 2 CFR part 182, as implemented by this part.

(b) *Specific sections of OMB guidance that this part supplements.* In implementing the OMB guidance in 2 CFR part 182, this part supplements four sections of the guidance, as shown in the following table. For each of those sections, you must follow the policies and procedures in the OMB guidance, as supplemented by this part.

Section of OMB guidance	Section in this part where supplemented	What the supplementation clarifies
(1) 2 CFR 182.225(a)	§ 3373.225	Whom in the NEH a recipient other than an individual must notify if an employee is convicted for a violation of a criminal drug statute in the workplace.
(2) 2 CFR 182.300(b)	§ 3373.300	Whom in the NEH a recipient who is an individual must notify if he or she is convicted of a criminal drug offense resulting from a violation occurring during the conduct of any award activity.
(3) 2 CFR 182.500	§ 3373.500	Who in the NEH is authorized to determine that a recipient other than an individual is in violation of the requirements of 2 CFR part 182, as implemented by this part.
(4) 2 CFR 182.505	§ 3373.505	Who in the NEH is authorized to determine that a recipient who is an individual is in violation of the requirements of 2 CFR part 182, as implemented by this part.

(c) *Sections of the OMB guidance that this part does not supplement.* For any section of OMB guidance in Subparts A through F of 2 CFR part 182 that is not listed in paragraph (b) of this section, NEH policies and procedures are the same as those in the OMB guidance.

Subpart A—Purpose and Coverage [Reserved]

Subpart B—Requirements for Recipients Other Than Individuals

§ 3373.225 Whom in the NEH does a recipient other than an individual notify about a criminal drug conviction?

A recipient other than an individual that is required under 2 CFR 182.225(a) to notify Federal agencies about an employee's conviction for a criminal drug offense must notify the Director, Office of Grant Management, NEH.

Subpart C—Requirements for Recipients Who Are Individuals

§ 3373.300 Whom in the NEH does a recipient who is an individual notify about a criminal drug conviction?

A recipient who is an individual and is required under 2 CFR 182.300(b) to notify Federal agencies about a conviction for a criminal drug offense must notify the Director, Office of Grant Management, NEH.

Subpart D—Responsibilities of Agency Awarding Officials

§ 3373.400 What method do I use as an agency awarding official to obtain a recipient's agreement to comply with the OMB guidance?

To obtain a recipient's agreement to comply with applicable requirements in the OMB guidance at 2 CFR part 182, you must include the following term or condition in the award:

Drug-free workplace. You as the recipient must comply with drug-free workplace requirements in Subpart B (or Subpart C, if the recipient is an individual) of 2 CFR Part 3373, which adopts the Governmentwide implementation (2 CFR part 182) of sec. 5152–5158 of the Drug-Free Workplace Act of 1988 (Pub. L. 100–690, Title V, Subtitle D; 41 U.S.C. 701–707).

Subpart E—Violations of This Part and Consequences

§ 3373.500 Who in the NEH determines that a recipient other than an individual violated the requirements of this part?

The NEH General Counsel is the agency official authorized to make the determination under 2 CFR 182.500.

§ 3373.505 Who in the NEH determines that a recipient who is an individual violated the requirements of this part?

The NEH General Counsel is the agency official authorized to make the determination under 2 CFR 182.505.

Subpart F—Definitions [Reserved]

CHAPTER XXXIV—DEPARTMENT OF EDUCATION

PART 3485—NONPROCUREMENT DEBARMENT AND SUSPENSION

Sec.
3485.12 What does this part do?
3485.22 Does this part apply to me?
3485.32 What policies and procedures must I follow?

Subpart A—General

3485.137 May the Department grant an exception to let an excluded person participate in a covered transaction?

Subpart B—Covered Transactions

3485.220 Are any procurement contracts included as covered transactions?

Subpart C—Responsibilities of Participants Regarding Transactions

3485.310 What must I do if a Federal agency excludes a person with whom I am already doing business in a covered transaction?
3485.315 May I use the services of an excluded person as a principal under a covered transaction?
3485.330 What methods must I use to pass requirements down to participants at lower tiers with whom I intend to do business?

Subpart D—Responsibilities of the Department's Officials Regarding Transactions

3485.415 What must I do if a Federal agency excludes the participant or a principal after I enter into a covered transaction?
3485.437 What method do I use to communicate to a participant the requirements described in § 180.435 of this title?

Subpart E [Reserved]

Subpart F—General Principles Relating to Suspension and Debarment Actions

3485.611 What procedures do we use for a suspension or debarment action involving title IV, HEA transactions?
3485.612 When does an exclusion by another agency affect the ability of the excluded person to participate in a title IV, HEA transaction?

Subpart G—Suspension

3485.711 When does a suspension affect title IV, HEA transactions?

Subpart H—Debarment

3485.811 When does a debarment affect title IV, HEA transactions?

Subpart I—Definitions

3485.937 ED Deciding Official.
3485.952 HEA.
3485.995 Principal.
3485.1016 Title IV, HEA participant.
3485.1017 Title IV, HEA program.
3485.1018 Title IV, HEA transaction.

Subpart J [Reserved]

APPENDIX A TO PART 3485—COVERED TRANSACTIONS

AUTHORITY: E.O. 12549 (3 CFR 1986 Comp., p. 189); E.O. 12689 (3 CFR 1989 Comp., p. 235); sec. 2455, Pub. L. 103–355, 108 Stat. 3327 (31 U.S.C. 6101 note); 20 U.S.C. 1082, 1094, 1221e–3, and 3474, unless otherwise noted.

SOURCE: 77 FR 18673, Mar. 28, 2012, unless otherwise noted.

§ 3485.12 What does this part do?

(a)(1) The Department of Education (the "Department" or "ED") adopts subparts A through I of the Office of Management and Budget guidance in 2 CFR part 180. Thus, this part gives regulatory effect to the OMB guidance and supplements the guidance as needed for the Department. This part satisfies the requirements in section 3 of Executive Order 12549, "Debarment and Suspension" (3 CFR part 1986 Comp., p. 189), Executive Order 12689, "Debarment and Suspension" (3 CFR part 1989 Comp., p. 235) and 31 U.S.C. 6101 note (Section 2455, Pub. L. 103–355, 108 Stat. 3327).

(2) The table of contents for this part contains only those sections in part 3485 that include supplements to the guidance in part 180 and new sections needed to implement the guidance for the Department's programs. In those sections of the OMB guidance that are supplemented, the section in part 3485 includes both the text of the OMB guidance that is not affected by the change and any additional paragraphs that need to be added to the OMB guidance. For example, § 180.220 of this title contains only paragraphs (a) and (b). The text of § 3485.220, which supplements § 180.220 to extend lower-tier transactions to certain transactions below the primary tier, includes both the text of paragraph (a) and (b) of § 180.220 and the text of added paragraph (c).

(3) In those sections in part 180 that do not have paragraph designations and that the Department supplements, the section in this part implementing

389

the OMB guidance designates the undesignated paragraph from part 180 as paragraph (a) and the first supplemental paragraph as paragraph (b). For example, 2 CFR 180.330 includes an undesignated lead in paragraph and two subparagraphs designated (a) and (b). In § 3485.330, the undesignated paragraph in 2 CFR 180.330 is designated paragraph (a) and the two subparagraphs are designated paragraphs (1) and (2). The added paragraphs are designated paragraph (b) and (c).

(b) The authority for all the provisions in 2 CFR part 180 as adopted in this part is listed as follows.

AUTHORITY: E.O. 12549 (3 CFR 1986 Comp., p. 189); E.O. 12689 (3 CFR 1989 Comp., p. 235); sec. 2455, Pub. L. 103–355, 108 Stat. 3327 (31 U.S.C. 6101 note); 20 U.S.C. 1082, 1094, 1221e–3, and 3474.

(Authority: E.O. 12549 (3 CFR 1986 Comp., p. 189); E.O. 12689 (3 CFR 1989 Comp., p. 235); sec. 2455, Pub. L. 103–355, 108 Stat. 3327 (31 U.S.C. 6101 note); 20 U.S.C. 1082, 1094, 1221e–3, and 3474, unless otherwise noted.)

§ 3485.22 Does this part apply to me?

This part applies to you if you are—

(a) A participant or principal in a "covered transaction" (see subpart B of this part and the definition of "nonprocurement transaction" in § 180.970 of this title).

(b) A respondent in a suspension or debarment action of the Department.

(c) An ED deciding official; or

(d) An ED officer authorized to enter into any type of nonprocurement transaction that is a covered transaction.

(Authority: E.O. 12549 (3 CFR 1986 Comp., p. 189); E.O. 12689 (3 CFR 1989 Comp., p. 235); sec. 2455, Pub. L. 103–355, 108 Stat. 3327 (31 U.S.C. 6101 note); 20 U.S.C. 1082, 1094, 1221e–3, and 3474)

§ 3485.32 What policies and procedures must I follow?

The Department's policies and procedures that you must follow are the policies and procedures specified in this part and in Subparts A through I of 2 CFR part 180. The contracts that are covered transactions, for example, are specified in § 3485.220. Section 180.205 of this title does not require supplementation, so it is not included in the table of contents for this part

and is not separately stated in this part.

(Authority: E.O. 12549 (3 CFR 1986 Comp., p. 189); E.O. 12689 (3 CFR 1989 Comp., p. 235); sec. 2455, Pub. L. 103–355, 108 Stat. 3327 (31 U.S.C. 6101 note); 20 U.S.C. 1082, 1094, 1221e–3, and 3474)

Subpart A—General

§ 3485.137 May the Department grant an exception to let an excluded person participate in a covered transaction?

(a) Yes, the Secretary delegates to the ED Deciding Official the authority under this section to grant an exception permitting an excluded person to participate in a particular covered transaction.

(b) If the ED Deciding Official grants an exception, the exception must be in writing and state the reason(s) for deviating from the Governmentwide policy in Executive Order 12549.

(Authority: E.O. 12549 (3 CFR 1986 Comp., p. 189); E.O. 12689 (3 CFR 1989 Comp., p. 235); sec. 2455, Pub. L. 103–355, 108 Stat. 3327 (31 U.S.C. 6101 note); 20 U.S.C. 1082, 1094, 1221e–3, and 3474)

Subpart B—Covered Transactions

§ 3485.220 Are any procurement contracts included as covered transactions?

(a) Covered transactions under this part—

(1) Do not include any procurement contracts awarded directly by a Federal agency; but

(2) Do include some procurement contracts awarded by non-Federal participants in nonprocurement covered transactions.

(b) Specifically, a contract for goods or services is a covered transaction if any of the following applies:

(1) The contract is awarded by a participant in a nonprocurement transaction that is covered under § 180.210 of this title, and the amount of the contract is expected to equal or exceed $25,000.

(2) The contract requires the consent of an official of a Federal agency. In that case, the contract, regardless of the amount, always is a covered transaction, and it does not matter who

awarded it. For example, it could be a subcontract awarded by a contractor at a tier below a nonprocurement transaction, as shown in the Appendix to Part 3485—Covered Transactions.

(3) The contract is for Federally-required audit services.

(4) The contract is to perform services as a third party servicer in connection with a title IV, HEA program.

(c) In addition to the contracts covered under 2 CFR 180.220(b) of the OMB guidance, this part applies to any contract, regardless of tier, that is awarded by a contractor, subcontractor, supplier, consultant, or its agent or representative in any transaction, if the contract is to be funded or provided by ED under a covered nonprocurement transaction and the amount of the contract is expected to equal or exceed $25,000. This extends the coverage of the ED nonprocurement suspension and debarment requirements to all lower tiers of subcontracts under covered nonprocurement transactions, as permitted under the OMB guidance at 2 CFR 180.220(c) (see optional lower tier coverage in the figure in Appendix A to Part 3485—Covered Transactions).

(Authority: E.O. 12549 (3 CFR 1986 Comp., p. 189); E.O. 12689 (3 CFR 1989 Comp., p. 235); sec. 2455, Pub. L. 103–355, 108 Stat. 3327 (31 U.S.C. 6101 note); 20 U.S.C. 1082, 1094, 1221e–3, and 3474)

Subpart C—Responsibilities of Participants Regarding Transactions

§ 3485.310 What must I do if a Federal agency excludes a person with whom I am already doing business in a covered transaction?

(a) You as a participant may continue covered transactions with an excluded person if the transactions were in existence when the agency excluded the person. However, you are not required to continue the transactions, and you may consider termination. You should make a decision about whether to terminate and the type of termination action, if any, only after a thorough review to ensure that the action is proper and appropriate.

(b) You may not renew or extend covered transactions (other than no-cost time extensions) with any excluded person, unless another Federal agency responsible for the transaction grants an exception under § 180.135 of this title or ED grants an exception under § 3485.137.

(c) If you are a title IV, HEA participant, you may not continue a title IV, HEA transaction with an excluded person after the effective date of the exclusion unless permitted by 34 CFR 668.26, 682.702, or 668.94, as applicable.

(Authority: E.O. 12549 (3 CFR 1986 Comp., p. 189); E.O. 12689 (3 CFR 1989 Comp., p. 235); sec. 2455, Pub. L. 103–355, 108 Stat. 3327 (31 U.S.C. 6101 note); 20 U.S.C. 1082, 1094, 1221e–3, and 3474)

§ 3485.315 May I use the services of an excluded person as a principal under a covered transaction?

(a) You as a participant may continue to use the services of an excluded person as a principal under a covered transaction if you were using the services of that person in the transaction before the person was excluded. However, you are not required to continue using that person's services as a principal. You should make a decision about whether to discontinue that person's services only after a thorough review to ensure that the action is proper and appropriate.

(b) You may not begin to use the services of an excluded person as a principal under a covered transaction unless another Federal agency responsible for the transaction grants an exception under § 180.135 of this title or, if ED took the action, an ED deciding official grants an exception under § 3485.137.

(c) If you are a title IV, HEA participant—

(1) You may not renew or extend the term of any contract or agreement for the services of an excluded person as a principal with respect to a title IV, HEA transaction; and

(2) You may not continue to use the services of that excluded person as a principal under this kind of an agreement or arrangement more than 90 days after you learn of the exclusion or after the close of the Federal fiscal

year in which the exclusion takes effect, whichever is later.

(Authority: E.O. 12549 (3 CFR 1986 Comp., p. 189); E.O. 12689 (3 CFR 1989 Comp., p. 235); sec. 2455, Pub. L. 103–355, 108 Stat. 3327 (31 U.S.C. 6101 note); 20 U.S.C. 1082, 1094, 1221e–3, and 3474)

§ 3485.330 What methods must I use to pass requirements down to participants at lower tiers with whom I intend to do business?

(a) Before entering into a covered transaction with a participant at the next lower tier, you must require that participant to—

(1) Comply with this subpart as a condition of participation in the transaction. You must do so using the method specified in paragraph (b) of this section; and

(2) Pass the requirement to comply with this subpart to each person with whom the participant enters into a covered transaction at the next lower tier.

(b) To communicate the requirements in this part to a participant, you must include a term or condition in the transaction that requires the participant's compliance with part 180, subpart C, of this title, as adopted at § 3485.12, and requires the participant to include a similar term or condition in lower-tier covered transactions.

(c) The failure of a participant to include a requirement to comply with Subpart C of 2 CFR part 180 in the agreement with a lower tier participant does not affect the lower tier participant's responsibilities under this part.

(Authority: E.O. 12549 (3 CFR 1986 Comp., p. 189); E.O. 12689 (3 CFR 1989 Comp., p. 235); sec. 2455, Pub. L. 103–355, 108 Stat. 3327 (31 U.S.C. 6101 note); 20 U.S.C. 1082, 1094, 1221e–3, and 3474)

Subpart D—Responsibilities of the Department's Officials Regarding Transactions

§ 3485.415 What must I do if a Federal agency excludes the participant or a principal after I enter into a covered transaction?

(a) You as a Federal agency official may continue covered transactions with an excluded person, or under which an excluded person is a principal, if the transactions were in existence when the person was excluded. You are not required to continue the transactions, however, and you may consider termination. You should make a decision about whether to terminate and the type of termination action, if any, only after a thorough review to ensure that the action is proper.

(b) You may not renew or extend covered transactions (other than no-cost time extensions) with any excluded person, or under which an excluded person is a principal, unless you obtain an exception under § 3485.137.

(c) *Title IV, HEA transactions.* If you are a title IV, HEA participant—

(1) You may not renew or extend the term of any contract or agreement for the services of an excluded person as a principal with respect to a title IV, HEA transaction; and

(2) You may not continue to use the services of that excluded person as a principal under this kind of an agreement or arrangement more than 90 days after you learn of the exclusion or after the close of the Federal fiscal year in which the exclusion takes effect, whichever is later.

(Authority: E.O. 12549 (3 CFR 1986 Comp., p. 189); E.O. 12689 (3 CFR 1989 Comp., p. 235); sec. 2455, Pub. L. 103–355, 108 Stat. 3327 (31 U.S.C. 6101 note); 20 U.S.C. 1082, 1094, 1221e–3, and 3474)

§ 3485.437 What method do I use to communicate to a participant the requirements described in § 180.435 of this title?

To communicate the requirements in this part to a participant, you must include a term or condition in the transaction that requires the participant's compliance with part 180, subpart C, of this title, as adopted at § 3485.12 and requires the participant to include a similar term or condition in lower-tier covered transactions.

(Authority: E.O. 12549 (3 CFR 1986 Comp., p. 189); E.O. 12689 (3 CFR 1989 Comp., p. 235); sec. 2455, Pub. L. 103–355, 108 Stat. 3327 (31 U.S.C. 6101 note); 20 U.S.C. 1082, 1094, 1221e–3, and 3474)

Subpart E [Reserved]

Subpart F—General Principles Relating to Suspension and Debarment Actions

§3485.611 What procedures do we use for a suspension or debarment action involving a title IV, HEA transaction?

(a) If we suspend a title IV, HEA participant under Executive Order 12549, we use the following procedures to ensure that the suspension prevents participation in title IV, HEA transactions:

(1) The notification procedures in §180.715 of this title.

(2) Instead of the procedures in §§180.720 through 180.760 of this title, the procedures in 34 CFR part 668, subpart G, or 34 CFR part 682, subpart D or G, as applicable.

(3) In addition to the findings and conclusions required by 34 CFR part 668, subpart G, or 34 CFR part 682, subpart D or G, the suspending official, and, on appeal, the Secretary determines whether there is sufficient cause for suspension as explained in §180.700 of this title.

(b) If we debar a title IV, HEA participant under E.O. 12549, we use the following procedures to ensure that the debarment also precludes participation in title IV, HEA transactions:

(1) The notification procedures in §§180.805 and 180.870 of this title.

(2) Instead of the procedures in §§180.810 through 180.885 of this title, the procedures in 34 CFR part 668, subpart G, or 34 CFR part 682, subpart D or G, as applicable.

(3) On appeal from a decision debarring a title IV, HEA participant, we issue a final decision after we receive any written materials from the parties.

(4) In addition to the findings and conclusions required by 34 CFR part 668, subpart G, or 34 CFR part 682, subpart D or G, the debarring official, and, on appeal, the Secretary determines whether there is sufficient cause for debarment as explained in §180.800 of this title.

(Authority: E.O. 12549 (3 CFR 1986 Comp., p. 189); E.O. 12689 (3 CFR 1989 Comp., p. 235); sec. 2455, Pub. L. 103–355, 108 Stat. 3327 (31 U.S.C. 6101 note); 20 U.S.C. 1082, 1094, 1221e–3, and 3474)

§3485.612 When does an exclusion by another agency affect the ability of the excluded person to participate in a title IV, HEA transaction?

(a) If a title IV, HEA participant is debarred by another agency under E.O. 12549, using procedures described in paragraph (d) of this section, that party is not eligible to enter into title IV, HEA transactions for the duration of the debarment.

(b)(1) If a title IV, HEA participant is suspended by another agency under E.O. 12549 or under a proposed debarment under the Federal Acquisition Regulation (FAR) (48 CFR part 9, subpart 9.4), using procedures described in paragraph (d) of this section, that party is not eligible to enter into title IV, HEA transactions for the duration of the suspension.

(2)(i) The suspension of title IV, HEA eligibility as a result of suspension by another agency lasts for at least 60 days.

(ii) If the excluded party does not object to the suspension, the 60-day period begins on the 35th day after that agency issues the notice of suspension.

(iii) If the excluded party objects to the suspension, the 60-day period begins on the date of the decision of the suspending official.

(3) The suspension of title IV, HEA eligibility does not end on the 60th day if—

(i) The excluded party agrees to an extension; or

(ii) Before the 60th day we begin a limitation or termination proceeding against the excluded party under 34 CFR part 668, subpart G, or part 682, subpart D or G.

(c)(1) If a title IV, HEA participant is debarred or suspended by another Federal agency—

(i) We notify the participant whether the debarment or suspension prohibits participation in title IV, HEA transactions; and

(ii) If participation is prohibited, we state the effective date and duration of the prohibition.

(2) If a debarment or suspension by another agency prohibits participation in title IV, HEA transactions, that prohibition takes effect 20 days after we mail notice of our action.

(3) If the Department or another Federal agency suspends a title IV, HEA participant, we determine whether grounds exist for an emergency action against the participant under 34 CFR part 668, subpart G, or part 682, subpart D or G, as applicable.

(4) We use the procedures in § 3485.611 to exclude a title IV, HEA participant excluded by another Federal agency using procedures that did not meet the standards in paragraph (d) of this section.

(d) If a title IV, HEA participant is excluded by another agency, we debar, terminate, or suspend the participant—as provided under this part, 34 CFR part 668, or 34 CFR part 682, as applicable—if that agency followed procedures that gave the excluded party—

(1) Notice of the proposed action;

(2) An opportunity to submit and have considered evidence and argument to oppose the proposed action;

(3) An opportunity to present its objection at a hearing—

(i) At which the agency has the burden of persuasion by a preponderance of the evidence that there is cause for the exclusion; and

(ii) Conducted by an impartial person who does not also exercise prosecutorial or investigative responsibilities with respect to the exclusion action;

(4) An opportunity to present witness testimony, unless the hearing official finds that there is no genuine dispute about a material fact;

(5) An opportunity to have agency witnesses with personal knowledge of material facts in genuine dispute testify about those facts, if the hearing official determines their testimony to be needed, in light of other available evidence and witnesses; and

(6) A written decision stating findings of fact and conclusions of law on which the decision is rendered.

(Authority: E.O. 12549 (3 CFR 1986 Comp., p. 189); E.O. 12689 (3 CFR 1989 Comp., p. 235); sec. 2455, Pub. L. 103–355, 108 Stat. 3327 (31 U.S.C. 6101 note); 20 U.S.C. 1082, 1094, 1221e–3, and 3474)

Subpart G—Suspension

§ 3485.711 When does a suspension affect title IV, HEA transactions?

(a) A suspension under § 3485.611(a) takes effect immediately if the Secretary takes an emergency action under 34 CFR part 668, subpart G, or 34 CFR part 682, subpart D or G, at the same time the Secretary issues the suspension.

(b)(1) Except as provided under paragraph (a) of this section, a suspension under § 3485.611(a) takes effect 20 days after those procedures are complete.

(2) If the respondent appeals the suspension to the Secretary before the expiration of the 20 days under paragraph (b)(1) of this section, the suspension takes effect when the respondent receives the Secretary's decision.

(Authority: E.O. 12549 (3 CFR 1986 Comp., p. 189); E.O. 12689 (3 CFR 1989 Comp., p. 235); sec. 2455, Pub. L. 103–355, 108 Stat. 3327 (31 U.S.C. 6101 note); 20 U.S.C. 1082, 1094, 1221e–3, and 3474)

Subpart H—Debarment

§ 3485.811 When does a debarment affect title IV, HEA transactions?

(a) A debarment under § 3485.611(b) takes effect 30 days after those procedures are complete.

(b) If the respondent appeals the debarment to the Secretary before the expiration of the 30 days under paragraph (a) of this section, the debarment takes effect when the respondent receives the Secretary's decision.

(Authority: E.O. 12549 (3 CFR 1986 Comp., p. 189); E.O. 12689 (3 CFR 1989 Comp., p. 235); sec. 2455, Pub. L. 103–355, 108 Stat. 3327 (31 U.S.C. 6101 note); 20 U.S.C. 1082, 1094, 1221e–3, and 3474)

Subpart I—Definitions

§ 3485.937 ED Deciding Official.

The ED Deciding Official is an officer of the Department who has delegated authority under the procedures of the Department of Education to decide whether to affirm a suspension or enter a debarment.

(Authority: E.O. 12549 (3 CFR 1986 Comp., p. 189); E.O. 12689 (3 CFR 1989 Comp., p. 235); sec. 2455, Pub. L. 103–355, 108 Stat. 3327 (31 U.S.C. 6101 note); 20 U.S.C. 1082, 1094, 1221e–3, and 3474)

§3485.952 HEA.

HEA means the Higher Education Act of 1965, as amended.

(Authority: E.O. 12549 (3 CFR 1986 Comp., p. 189); E.O. 12689 (3 CFR 1989 Comp., p. 235); sec. 2455, Pub. L. 103–355, 108 Stat. 3327 (31 U.S.C. 6101 note); 20 U.S.C. 1082, 1094, 1221e–3, and 3474)

§3485.995 Principal.

Principal means—

(a) An officer, director, owner, partner, principal investigator, or other person within a participant with management or supervisory responsibilities related to a covered transaction; or

(b) A consultant or other person, whether or not employed by the participant or paid with Federal funds, who—

(1) Is in a position to handle Federal funds;

(2) Is in a position to influence or control the use of those funds; or

(3) Occupies a technical or professional position capable of substantially influencing the development or outcome of an activity required to perform the covered transaction.

(c) For the purposes of Department of Education title IV, HEA transactions—

(1) A third-party servicer, as defined in 34 CFR 668.2 or 682.200; or

(2) Any person who provides services described in 34 CFR 668.2 or 682.200 to a title IV, HEA participant, whether or not that person is retained or paid directly by the title IV, HEA participant.

(Authority: E.O. 12549 (3 CFR 1986 Comp., p.189); E.O. 12689 (3 CFR 1989 Comp., p.235); sec. 2455, Pub. L. 103–355, 108 Stat. 3327 (31 U.S.C. 6101 note); 20 U.S.C. 1082, 1094, 1221e–3, and 3474)

§3485.1016 Title IV, HEA participant.

A title IV, HEA participant is—

(a) An institution described in 34 CFR 600.4, 600.5, or 600.6 that provides postsecondary education; or

(b) A lender, third-party servicer, or guaranty agency, as those terms are defined in 34 CFR 668.2 or 682.200.

(Authority: E.O. 12549 (3 CFR 1986 Comp., p.189); E.O. 12689 (3 CFR 1989 Comp., p.235); sec. 2455, Pub. L. 103–355, 108 Stat. 3327 (31 U.S.C. 6101 note); 20 U.S.C. 1082, 1094, 1221e–3, and 3474)

§3485.1017 Title IV, HEA program.

A title IV, HEA program includes any program listed in 34 CFR 668.1(c).

(Authority: E.O. 12549 (3 CFR 1986 Comp., p.189); E.O. 12689 (3 CFR 1989 Comp., p. 235); sec. 2455, Pub. L. 103–355, 108 Stat. 3327 (31 U.S.C. 6101 note); 20 U.S.C. 1082, 1094, 1221e–3, and 3474)

§3485.1018 Title IV, HEA transaction.

A title IV, HEA transaction includes—

(a) A disbursement or delivery of funds provided under a title IV, HEA program to a student or borrower;

(b) A certification by an educational institution of eligibility for a loan under a title IV, HEA program;

(c) Guaranteeing a loan made under a title IV, HEA program; and

(d) The acquisition or exercise of any servicing responsibility for a grant, loan, or work study assistance under a title IV, HEA program.

(Authority: E.O. 12549 (3 CFR 1986 Comp., p.189); E.O. 12689 (3 CFR 1989 Comp., p.235); sec. 2455, Pub. L. 103–355, 108 Stat. 3327 (31 U.S.C. 6101 note); 20 U.S.C. 1082, 1094, 1221e–3, and 3474)

Subpart J [Reserved]

APPENDIX A TO PART 3485—COVERED TRANSACTIONS

Appendix A to Part 3485--Covered Transactions

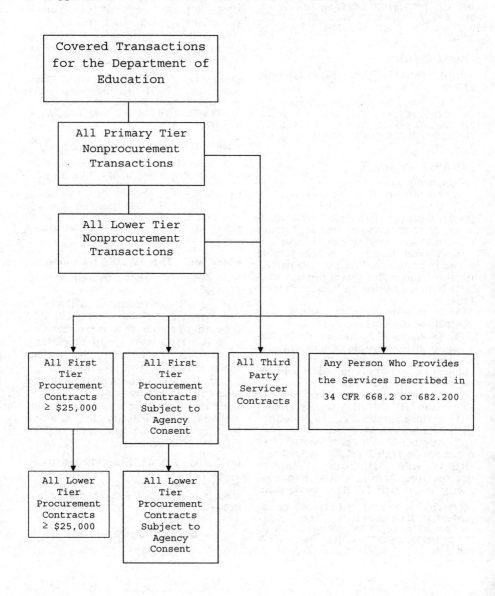

CHAPTER XXXV—EXPORT-IMPORT BANK OF THE UNITED STATES

PART 3513—NONPROCUREMENT DEBARMENT AND SUSPENSION

Sec.
3513.10 What does this part do?
3513.20 Does this part apply to me?
3513.30 What policies and procedures must I follow?

Subpart A—General

3513.137 Who at Ex-Im Bank may grant an exception to let an excluded person participate in a covered transaction?

Subpart B—Covered Transactions

3513.220 What contracts and subcontracts, in addition to those listed in 2 CFR 180.220, are covered transactions?

Subpart C—Responsibilities of Participants Regarding Transactions

3513.332 What methods must I use to pass requirements down to participants at lower tiers with whom I intend to do business?

Subpart D—Responsibilities of Federal Agency Officials Regarding Transactions

3513.437 What method do I use to communicate to a participate the requirements described in the OMB guidance at 2 CFR 180.435?

Subparts E–J [Reserved]

AUTHORITY: Sec. 2455, Pub. L. 103–355, 108 Stat. 3327; E.O. 12549, 3 CFR, 1986 Comp., p. 189; E.O. 12689, 3 CFR, 1989 Comp., p. 235.

SOURCE: 72 FR 30244, May 31, 2007, unless otherwise noted.

§ 3513.10 What does this part do?

This part adopts the Office of Management and Budget (OMB) guidance in subparts A through I of 2 CFR part 180, as supplemented by this part, as the Export Import Bank of the United States (Ex-Im Bank) policies and procedures for nonprocurement debarment and suspension. It thereby gives regulatory effect for Ex-Im Bank to the OMB guidance as supplemented by this part. This part satisfies the requirements in section 3 of Executive Order 12549, "Debarment and Suspension" (3 CFR 1986 Comp., p. 189), Executive Order 12689, "Debarment and Suspension" (3 CFR 1989 Comp., p. 235) and 31

U.S.C. 6101 note (Section 2455, Pub. L. 103–355, 108 Stat. 3327).

§ 3513.20 Does this part apply to me?

This part and, through this part, pertinent portions of the OMB guidance in subparts A through I of 2 CFR part 180 (see table at 2 CFR 180.100(b)) apply to you if you are a—

(a) Participant or principal in a "covered transaction" (see subpart B of 2 CFR part 180 and the definition of "nonprocurement transaction" at 2 CFR 180.970, as supplemented by subpart B of this part).

(b) Respondent in an Ex-Im Bank suspension or debarment action.

(c) Ex-Im Bank debarment or suspension official;

(d) Ex-Im Bank grants officer, agreements officer, or other official authorized to enter into any type of nonprocurement transaction that is a covered transaction;

§ 3513.30 What policies and procedures must I follow?

Ex-Im Bank policies and procedures that you must follow are the policies and procedures specified in each applicable section of the OMB guidance in subparts A through I of 2 CFR part 180, as that section is supplemented by the section in this part with the same section number. The contracts that are covered transactions, for example, are specified by section 220 of the OMB guidance (i.e., 2 CFR 180.220) as supplemented by section 220 in this pat (i.e., § 3513.220). For any section of OMB guidance in subparts A through I of 2 CFR 180 that has no corresponding section in this part, Ex-Im Bank policies and procedures are those in the OMB guidance.

Subpart A—General

§ 3513.137 Who in Ex-Im Bank may grant an exception to let an excluded person participate in a covered transaction?

(a) The Ex-Im Bank agency head or designee may grant an exception permitting an excluded person to participate in a particular covered transacting. If the Ex-Im Bank agency head or designee grants an exception, the exception must be in writing and

399

state the reason(s) for deviating from the government wide policy in Executive Order 12549.

(b) An exception granted by one agency for an excluded person does not extend to the covered transactions of another agency.

Subpart B—Covered Transactions

§ 3513.220 What contracts and subcontracts, in addition to those listed in 2 CFR 180.220, are covered transactions?

Although the OMB guidance at 2 CFR 180.220(c) allows a Federal agency to do so (also see optional lower tier coverage in the figure in the appendix to 2 CFR part 180), Ex-Im Bank does not extend coverage of nonprocurement suspension and debarment requirements beyond first-tier procurement under a covered nonprocurement transaction.

Subpart C—Responsibilities of Participants Regarding Transactions

§ 3513.332 What methods must I use to pass requirements down to participants at lower tiers with whom I intend to do business?

To communicate the requirements, you must include a term or condition in the transaction requiring the participants' compliance with subpart C of this part and requiring them to include a similar term or condition in lower-tiered covered transactions.

Subpart D—Responsibilities of Federal Agency Officials Regarding Transactions

§ 3513.437 What method do I use to communicate to a participant the requirements described in the OMB guidance at 2 CFR 180.435?

To communicate to a participant the requirements described in 2 CFR 180.435 of the OMB guidance, you must include a term or condition in the transaction that requires the participant's compliance with subpart C of 2 CFR part 180, as supplemented by subpart C of this part, and requires the participant to include a similar term or condition in lower-tier covered transactions.

Subparts E–J [Reserved]

CHAPTER XXXVII—PEACE CORPS

PART 3700—NONPROCUREMENT DEBARMENT AND SUSPENSION

Sec.
3700.10   What does this part do?
3700.20   Does this part apply to me?
3700.30   What policies and procedures must I follow?
3700.137 Who in the Peace Corps may grant an exception to let an excluded person participate in a covered transaction?
3700.220 What contracts and subcontracts, in addition to those listed in 2 CFR 180.220, are covered transactions?
3700.332 What methods must I use to pass requirements down to participants at lower tiers with whom I intend to do business?
3700.437 What method do I use to communicate to a participant the requirements described in the OMB guidance at 2 CFR 180.435?

AUTHORITY: Sec. 2455, Pub. L. 103–355, 108 Stat. 3327; E.O. 12549, 3 CFR, 1986 Comp., p. 189; E.O. 12689, 3 CFR, 1989 Comp., p. 235; 22 U.S.C. 2503(b).

SOURCE: 71 FR 64731, Nov. 22, 2006, unless otherwise noted.

§ 3700.10   What does this part do?

This part adopts the Office of Management and Budget (OMB) guidance in subparts A through I of 2 CFR part 180, as supplemented by this part, as the Peace Corps policies and procedures for nonprocurement debarment and suspension. It thereby gives regulatory effect for the Peace Corps to the OMB guidance as supplemented by this part. This part satisfies the requirements in section 3 of Executive Order 12549, "Debarment and Suspension" (3 CFR 1986 Comp., p. 189), Executive Order 12689, "Debarment and Suspension" (3 CFR 1989 Comp., p. 235) and 31 U.S.C. 6101 note (Section 2455, Pub. L. 103–355, 108 Stat. 3327).

§ 3700.20   Does this part apply to me?

This part and, through this part, pertinent portions of the OMB guidance in subparts A through I of 2 CFR part (see table at 2 CFR 180.100(b)) apply to you if you are a—

(a) Participant or principal in a "covered transaction" (see subpart B of 2 CFR part 180 and the definition of "nonprocurement transaction" at 2 CFR 180.970);

(b) Respondent in a Peace Corps suspension or debarment action;

(c) Peace Corps debarment or suspension official; or

(d) Peace Corps grants officer, agreements officer, or other official authorized to enter into any type of nonprocurement transaction that is a covered transaction.

§ 3700.30   What policies and procedures must I follow?

The Peace Corps policies and procedures that you must follow are the policies and procedures specified in each applicable section of the OMB guidance in subparts A through I of 2 CFR part 180, as that section is supplemented by the section in this part with the same section number. The contracts that are covered transactions, for example, are specified by section 220 of the OMB guidance (i.e., 2 CFR 180.220) as supplemented by section 220 in this part (i.e., § 3700.220). For any section of OMB guidance in subparts A through I of 2 CFR 180 that has no corresponding section in this part, Peace Corps policies and procedures are those in the OMB guidance.

§ 3700.137   Who in the Peace Corps may grant an exception to let an excluded person participate in a covered transaction?

The Director of the Peace Corps has the authority to grant an exception to let an excluded person participate in a covered transaction, as provided in the OMB guidance at 2 CFR 180.135.

§ 3700.220   What contracts and subcontracts, in addition to those listed in 2 CFR 180.220, are covered transactions?

Although the OMB guidance at 2 CFR 180.220(c) allows a Federal agency to do so (also see optional lower tier coverage in the figure in the appendix to 2 CFR part 180), Peace Corps does not extend coverage of nonprocurement suspension and debarment requirements beyond first-tier procurement contracts under a covered nonprocurement transaction.

403

§ 3700.332 What methods must I use to pass requirements down to participants at lower tiers with whom I intend to do business?

You as a participant must include a term or condition in lower-tier transactions requiring lower-tier participants to comply with subpart C of the OMB guidance in 2 CFR part 180.

§ 3700.437 What method do I use to communicate to a participant the requirements described in the OMB guidance at 2 CFR 180.435?

To communicate to a participant the requirements described in 2 CFR 180.435 of the OMB guidance, you as an agency official must include a term or condition in the transaction that requires the participant's compliance with subpart C of 2 CFR part 180, and requires the participant to include a similar term or condition in lower-tier covered transactions.

CHAPTER LVIII—ELECTION ASSISTANCE COMMISSION

PART 5800—NONPROCUREMENT DEBARMENT AND SUSPENSION

Sec.
5800.10 What does this part do?
5800.20 Does this part apply to me?
5800.30 What policies and procedures must I follow?

Subpart A—General

5800.137 Who at the Commission may grant an exception to let an excluded person participate in a covered transaction?

Subpart B—Covered Transactions

5800.220 What contracts and subcontracts, in addition to those listed in 2 CFR 180.220, are covered transactions?

Subpart C—Responsibilities of Participants Regarding Transactions

5800.332 What methods must I use to pass requirements down to participants at lower tiers with whom I intend to do business?

Subpart D—Responsibilities of Federal Agency Officials Regarding Transactions

5800.437 What method do I use to communicate to a participant the requirements described in the OMB guidance at 2 CFR 180.435?
5800.765 May I ask the suspending official to reconsider a decision to suspend me?
5800.875 May I ask the debarring official to reconsider a decision to debar me?
5800.880 What factors may influence the debarring official during reconsideration?
5800.890 How may I appeal my debarment?

Subpart E—H [Reserved]

Subpart I—Definitions

5800.930   Debarring official.
5800.970   Nonprocurement transaction.
5800.1010 Suspending official.

Subpart J [Reserved]

AUTHORITY: Sec. 2455, Pub. L. 103–355, 108; Stat. 3327 (31 U.S.C. 6101 note); E.O. 12549; (3 CFR, 1986 Comp., p. 189); E.O. 12689 (3); CFR, 1989 Comp., p. 235).

SOURCE: 75 FR 41692, July 19, 2010, unless otherwise noted.

§ 5800.10   What does this part do?

This part adopts the Office of Management and Budget (OMB) guidance in Subparts A through I of 2 CFR part 180, as supplemented by this part, as the U.S. Election Assistance Commission ("the Commission" or "EAC") policies and procedures for nonprocurement debarment and suspension. It thereby gives regulatory effect for the Commission to the OMB guidance as supplemented by this part. This part satisfies the requirements in section 3 of Executive Order 12549, "Debarment and Suspension" and 31 U.S.C. 6101 note.

§ 5800.20   Does this part apply to me?

This part and, through this part, pertinent portions of the OMB guidance in subparts A through I of 2 CFR part (see table at 2 CFR 180.100(b)) apply to you if you are a—

(a) Participant or principal in a "covered transaction" (see subpart B of 2 CFR part 180 and the definition of "nonprocurement transaction" at 2 CFR 180.970);

(b) Respondent in a Commission suspension or debarment action;

(c) Commission debarment or suspension official; or

(d) Commission grants officer, agreements officer, or other official authorized to enter into any type of nonprocurement transaction that is a covered transaction.

§ 5800.30   What policies and procedures must I follow?

The Commission policies and procedures that you must follow are the policies and procedures specified in each applicable section of the OMB guidance in Subparts A through I of 2 CFR part 180, as that section is supplemented by the section in this part with the same section number. The contracts that are covered transactions, for example, are specified by section 220 of the OMB guidance (i.e., 2 CFR 180.220) as supplemented by section 220 in this part (i.e., §____.220). For any section of OMB guidance in Subparts A through I of 2 CFR 180 that has no corresponding section in this part, Commission policies and procedures are those in the OMB guidance.

Subpart A—General

§ 5800.137 Who at the Commission may grant an exception to let an excluded person participate in a covered transaction?

The Commission's Contracting Officer has the authority to grant an exception to let an excluded person participate in a covered transaction, as provided in the OMB guidance at 2 CFR 180.135.

Subpart B—Covered Transactions

§ 5800.220 What contracts and subcontracts, in addition to those listed in 2 CFR 180.220, are covered transactions?

Pursuant to 2 CFR 180.220(c), the Commission extends coverage of nonprocurement suspension and debarment requirements beyond first-tier procurement contracts to include any subcontract to be funded by the Commission, the value of which is expected to equal to or exceed $25,000 or 30 percent of the value of first-tier transaction, whichever is lesser.

Subpart C—Responsibilities of Participants Regarding Transactions

§ 5800.332 What methods must I use to pass requirements down to participants at lower tiers with whom I intend to do business?

If a lower-tier transaction is covered pursuant to § 5800.220, you as a participant must include a term or condition in lower-tier transactions requiring lower-tier participants to comply with Subpart C of the OMB guidance in 2 CFR part 180.

Subpart D—Responsibilities of Federal Agency Officials Regarding Transactions

§ 5800.437 What method do I use to communicate to a participant the requirements described in the OMB guidance at 2 CFR 180.435?

To communicate to a participant the requirements described in 2 CFR 180.435 of the OMB guidance, you as an agency official must include a term or condition in the transaction that requires the participant's compliance with subpart C of 2 CFR part 180, and requires the participant to include a similar term or condition in lower-tier covered transactions.

§ 5800.765 May I ask the suspending official to reconsider a decision to suspend me?

Yes. Within 30 days of receiving a final notice of suspension, you may make a written request for the suspending official to reconsider your suspension.

§ 5800.875 May I ask the debarring official to reconsider a decision to debar me?

Yes. Within 30 days of receiving a final notice of debarment, you may make a written request for the debarring official to reconsider your debarment pursuant to § 5800.880. The disposition of your request for reconsideration; or the result of your appeal; shall be considered a final agency action.

§ 5800.880 What factors may influence the debarring official during reconsideration?

The debarring official may reduce or terminate your debarment based on:

(a) Newly discovered material evidence;

(b) A reversal of the conviction or civil judgment upon which your debarment was based;

(c) A bona fide change in ownership or management;

(d) Elimination of other causes for which the debarment was imposed; or

(e) Other reasons the debarring official finds appropriate.

§ 5800.890 How may I appeal my debarment?

(a) If the Commission debarring official issues a decision under 2 CFR 180.870 to debar you after you present information in opposition to a proposed debarment under § 180.815, you may ask for review of the debarring official's decision in two ways:

(1) You may ask the debarring official under § 875 to reconsider the decision for material errors of fact or law that you believe will change the outcome of the matter; or

(2) You may request a review by the EAC's debarment appeals body (DAP), which is composed of the Executive Director, Chief Financial Officer, and Chief Operating Officer. The DAP will review your appeal and make a determination on whether to sustain or reverse the decision of the debarring official. The DAP will then make a recommendation to the EAC Commissioners who will vote by circulation on whether to accept or reject the recommendation of the DAP. A request to review the debarring official's decision to debar you must be made within 30 days of your receipt of the debarring official's decision under §180.870 or paragraph (a)(1) of this section. However, the DAP may recommend to the EAC Commissioners that the debarring official's decision be reversed, based on a majority vote of the DAP, only where the DAP finds that the decision is based on a clear error of material fact or law, or where DAP finds that the debarring official's decision was arbitrary, capricious, or an abuse of discretion. You may appeal the debarring official's decision without requesting reconsideration, or you may appeal the decision of the debarring official on reconsideration.

(b) A request for review under this section must be in writing; prominently state on the envelope or other cover and at the top of the first page "Debarment Appeal;" state the specific findings you believe to be in error; and include the reasons or legal bases for your position. The appeal request should be delivered or addressed to the U.S. Election Assistance Commission, 1201 New York Avenue, NW., Suite 300, Washington, DC 20005.

(c) After the circulation vote of the EAC Commissioners has been certified, either the Commission debarring official or the DAP must notify you of their decision under this section, in writing, using the notice procedures set forth at §§180.615 and 180.975.

(d) [Reserved]

(e) Nothing in this part prohibits the EAC from delegating the appeal review process to another Federal agency through a memorandum of understanding or interagency agreement.

Subparts E—H [Reserved]

Subpart I—Definitions

§5800.930 Debarring official.

For the Commission, the debarring official for all nonprocurement transactions is the Commission's Contracting Officer. In the case of a vacancy in the position of the Contracting Officer, the alternate debarring official is the Chief Financial Officer.

§5800.970 Nonprocurement transaction.

While the Commission treats all payments made to states under 42 U.S.C. 15301, 15302 and 15401 as grants, this part does not apply to grants made to states and political subdivisions therein.

§5800.1010 Suspending official.

For the Commission, the debarring official for all nonprocurement transactions is the Commission's Contracting Officer. In the case of a vacancy in the position of the Contracting Officer, the alternate debarring official is the Chief Financial Officer.

Subpart J [Reserved]

FINDING AIDS

A list of CFR titles, subtitles, chapters, subchapters and parts and an alphabetical list of agencies publishing in the CFR are included in the CFR Index and Finding Aids volume to the Code of Federal Regulations which is published separately and revised annually.

Table of CFR Titles and Chapters
Alphabetical List of Agencies Appearing in the CFR
List of CFR Sections Affected

Table of CFR Titles and Chapters

(Revised as January 1, 2014)

Title 1—General Provisions

I   Administrative Committee of the Federal Register (Parts 1—49)
II   Office of the Federal Register (Parts 50—299)
III   Administrative Conference of the United States (Parts 300—399)
IV   Miscellaneous Agencies (Parts 400—500)

Title 2—Grants and Agreements

     SUBTITLE A—OFFICE OF MANAGEMENT AND BUDGET GUIDANCE FOR GRANTS AND AGREEMENTS

I   Office of Management and Budget Governmentwide Guidance for Grants and Agreements (Parts 2—199)
II   Office of Management and Budget Guidance (Parts 200—299)
     SUBTITLE B—FEDERAL AGENCY REGULATIONS FOR GRANTS AND AGREEMENTS

III   Department of Health and Human Services (Parts 300— 399)
IV   Department of Agriculture (Parts 400—499)
VI   Department of State (Parts 600—699)
VII   Agency for International Development (Parts 700—799)
VIII   Department of Veterans Affairs (Parts 800—899)
IX   Department of Energy (Parts 900—999)
XI   Department of Defense (Parts 1100—1199)
XII   Department of Transportation (Parts 1200—1299)
XIII   Department of Commerce (Parts 1300—1399)
XIV   Department of the Interior (Parts 1400—1499)
XV   Environmental Protection Agency (Parts 1500—1599)
XVIII   National Aeronautics and Space Administration (Parts 1800—1899)
XX   United States Nuclear Regulatory Commission (Parts 2000—2099)
XXII   Corporation for National and Community Service (Parts 2200—2299)
XXIII   Social Security Administration (Parts 2300—2399)
XXIV   Housing and Urban Development (Parts 2400—2499)
XXV   National Science Foundation (Parts 2500—2599)
XXVI   National Archives and Records Administration (Parts 2600—2699)
XXVII   Small Business Administration (Parts 2700—2799)
XXVIII   Department of Justice (Parts 2800—2899)

413

Title 2—Grants and Agreements—Continued

Title 3—The President

Title 4—Accounts

Title 5—Administrative Personnel

Title 5—Administrative Personnel—Continued

415

Title 5—Administrative Personnel—Continued

Title 6—Domestic Security

Title 7—Agriculture

Title 7—Agriculture—Continued

Title 8—Aliens and Nationality

Title 9—Animals and Animal Products

Title 10—Energy

Title 11—Federal Elections

Title 12—Banks and Banking

420

Title 25—Indians

Title 25—Indians—Continued

Title 26—Internal Revenue

Title 27—Alcohol, Tobacco Products and Firearms

Title 28—Judicial Administration

Title 29—Labor

Title 29—Labor—Continued

Title 30—Mineral Resources

Title 31—Money and Finance: Treasury

Title 32—National Defense

Title 35 [Reserved]

Title 36—Parks, Forests, and Public Property

I   National Park Service, Department of the Interior (Parts 1—199)
II   Forest Service, Department of Agriculture (Parts 200—299)
III   Corps of Engineers, Department of the Army (Parts 300—399)
IV   American Battle Monuments Commission (Parts 400—499)
V   Smithsonian Institution (Parts 500—599)
VI   [Reserved]
VII   Library of Congress (Parts 700—799)
VIII Advisory Council on Historic Preservation (Parts 800—899)
IX   Pennsylvania Avenue Development Corporation (Parts 900—999)
X   Presidio Trust (Parts 1000—1099)
XI   Architectural and Transportation Barriers Compliance Board (Parts 1100—1199)
XII   National Archives and Records Administration (Parts 1200—1299)
XV   Oklahoma City National Memorial Trust (Parts 1500—1599)
XVI   Morris K. Udall Scholarship and Excellence in National Environmental Policy Foundation (Parts 1600—1699)

Title 37—Patents, Trademarks, and Copyrights

I   United States Patent and Trademark Office, Department of Commerce (Parts 1—199)
II   U.S. Copyright Office, Library of Congress (Parts 200—299)
III   Copyright Royalty Board, Library of Congress (Parts 300—399)
IV   Assistant Secretary for Technology Policy, Department of Commerce (Parts 400—599)

Title 38—Pensions, Bonuses, and Veterans' Relief

I   Department of Veterans Affairs (Parts 0—199)
II   Armed Forces Retirement Home (Parts 200—299)

Title 39—Postal Service

I   United States Postal Service (Parts 1—999)
III   Postal Regulatory Commission (Parts 3000—3099)

Title 40—Protection of Environment

I   Environmental Protection Agency (Parts 1—1099)
IV   Environmental Protection Agency and Department of Justice (Parts 1400—1499)
V   Council on Environmental Quality (Parts 1500—1599)
VI   Chemical Safety and Hazard Investigation Board (Parts 1600—1699)

Title 45—Public Welfare—Continued

Title 46—Shipping

Title 47—Telecommunication

Title 48—Federal Acquisition Regulations System

Title 49—Transportation

Title 49—Transportation—Continued

V National Highway Traffic Safety Administration, Department of Transportation (Parts 500—599)

VI Federal Transit Administration, Department of Transportation (Parts 600—699)

VII National Railroad Passenger Corporation (AMTRAK) (Parts 700—799)

VIII National Transportation Safety Board (Parts 800—999)

X Surface Transportation Board, Department of Transportation (Parts 1000—1399)

XI Research and Innovative Technology Administration, Department of Transportation (Parts 1400—1499) [Reserved]

XII Transportation Security Administration, Department of Homeland Security (Parts 1500—1699)

Title 50—Wildlife and Fisheries

I United States Fish and Wildlife Service, Department of the Interior (Parts 1—199)

II National Marine Fisheries Service, National Oceanic and Atmospheric Administration, Department of Commerce (Parts 200—299)

III International Fishing and Related Activities (Parts 300—399)

IV Joint Regulations (United States Fish and Wildlife Service, Department of the Interior and National Marine Fisheries Service, National Oceanic and Atmospheric Administration, Department of Commerce); Endangered Species Committee Regulations (Parts 400—499)

V Marine Mammal Commission (Parts 500—599)

VI Fishery Conservation and Management, National Oceanic and Atmospheric Administration, Department of Commerce (Parts 600—699)

Alphabetical List of Agencies Appearing in the CFR
(Revised as of January 1, 2014)

Agency	CFR Title, Subtitle or Chapter
Administrative Committee of the Federal Register	1, I
Administrative Conference of the United States	1, III
Advisory Council on Historic Preservation	36, VIII
Advocacy and Outreach, Office of	7, XXV
Afghanistan Reconstruction, Special Inspector General for	22, LXXXIII
African Development Foundation	22, XV
Federal Acquisition Regulation	48, 57
Agency for International Development	2, VII; 22, II
Federal Acquisition Regulation	48, 7
Agricultural Marketing Service	7, I, IX, X, XI
Agricultural Research Service	7, V
Agriculture Department	2, IV; 5, LXXIII
Advocacy and Outreach, Office of	7, XXV
Agricultural Marketing Service	7, I, IX, X, XI
Agricultural Research Service	7, V
Animal and Plant Health Inspection Service	7, III; 9, I
Chief Financial Officer, Office of	7, XXX
Commodity Credit Corporation	7, XIV
Economic Research Service	7, XXXVII
Energy Policy and New Uses, Office of	2, IX; 7, XXIX
Environmental Quality, Office of	7, XXXI
Farm Service Agency	7, VII, XVIII
Federal Acquisition Regulation	48, 4
Federal Crop Insurance Corporation	7, IV
Food and Nutrition Service	7, II
Food Safety and Inspection Service	9, III
Foreign Agricultural Service	7, XV
Forest Service	36, II
Grain Inspection, Packers and Stockyards Administration	7, VIII; 9, II
Information Resources Management, Office of	7, XXVII
Inspector General, Office of	7, XXVI
National Agricultural Library	7, XLI
National Agricultural Statistics Service	7, XXXVI
National Institute of Food and Agriculture	7, XXXIV
Natural Resources Conservation Service	7, VI
Operations, Office of	7, XXVIII
Procurement and Property Management, Office of	7, XXXII
Rural Business-Cooperative Service	7, XVIII, XLII, L
Rural Development Administration	7, XLII
Rural Housing Service	7, XVIII, XXXV, L
Rural Telephone Bank	7, XVI
Rural Utilities Service	7, XVII, XVIII, XLII, L
Secretary of Agriculture, Office of	7, Subtitle A
Transportation, Office of	7, XXXIII
World Agricultural Outlook Board	7, XXXVIII
Air Force Department	32, VII
Federal Acquisition Regulation Supplement	48, 53
Air Transportation Stabilization Board	14, VI
Alcohol and Tobacco Tax and Trade Bureau	27, I
Alcohol, Tobacco, Firearms, and Explosives, Bureau of	27, II
AMTRAK	49, VII
American Battle Monuments Commission	36, IV
American Indians, Office of the Special Trustee	25, VII

435

437

438

Agency	CFR Title, Subtitle or Chapter
National Railroad Passenger Corporation (AMTRAK)	49, VII
National Science Foundation	2, XXV; 5, XLIII; 45, VI
Federal Acquisition Regulation	48, 25
National Security Council	32, XXI
National Security Council and Office of Science and Technology Policy	47, II
National Telecommunications and Information Administration	15, XXIII; 47, III, IV
National Transportation Safety Board	49, VIII
Natural Resources Conservation Service	7, VI
Natural Resource Revenue, Office of	30, XII
Navajo and Hopi Indian Relocation, Office of	25, IV
Navy Department	32, VI
Federal Acquisition Regulation	48, 52
Neighborhood Reinvestment Corporation	24, XXV
Northeast Interstate Low-Level Radioactive Waste Commission	10, XVIII
Nuclear Regulatory Commission	2, XX; 5, XLVIII; 10, I
Federal Acquisition Regulation	48, 20
Occupational Safety and Health Administration	29, XVII
Occupational Safety and Health Review Commission	29, XX
Ocean Energy Management, Bureau of	30, V
Offices of Independent Counsel	28, VI
Office of Workers' Compensation Programs	20, VII
Oklahoma City National Memorial Trust	36, XV
Operations Office	7, XXVIII
Overseas Private Investment Corporation	5, XXXIII; 22, VII
Patent and Trademark Office, United States	37, I
Payment From a Non-Federal Source for Travel Expenses	41, 304
Payment of Expenses Connected With the Death of Certain Employees	41, 303
Peace Corps	2, XXXVII; 22, III
Pennsylvania Avenue Development Corporation	36, IX
Pension Benefit Guaranty Corporation	29, XL
Personnel Management, Office of	5, I, XXXV; 45, VIII
Human Resources Management and Labor Relations Systems, Department of Homeland Security	5, XCVII
Federal Acquisition Regulation	48, 17
Federal Employees Group Life Insurance Federal Acquisition Regulation	48, 21
Federal Employees Health Benefits Acquisition Regulation	48, 16
Pipeline and Hazardous Materials Safety Administration	49, I
Postal Regulatory Commission	5, XLVI; 39, III
Postal Service, United States	5, LX; 39, I
Postsecondary Education, Office of	34, VI
President's Commission on White House Fellowships	1, IV
Presidential Documents	3
Presidio Trust	36, X
Prisons, Bureau of	28, V
Privacy and Civil Liberties Oversight Board	6, X
Procurement and Property Management, Office of	7, XXXII
Productivity, Technology and Innovation, Assistant Secretary	37, IV
Public Contracts, Department of Labor	41, 50
Public and Indian Housing, Office of Assistant Secretary for	24, IX
Public Health Service	42, I
Railroad Retirement Board	20, II
Reclamation, Bureau of	43, I
Recovery Accountability and Transparency Board	4, II
Refugee Resettlement, Office of	45, IV
Relocation Allowances	41, 302
Research and Innovative Technology Administration	49, XI
Rural Business-Cooperative Service	7, XVIII, XLII, L
Rural Development Administration	7, XLII
Rural Housing Service	7, XVIII, XXXV, L
Rural Telephone Bank	7, XVI
Rural Utilities Service	7, XVII, XVIII, XLII, L

Agency	CFR Title, Subtitle or Chapter
Saint Lawrence Seaway Development Corporation	33, IV
Science and Technology Policy, Office of	32, XXIV
Science and Technology Policy, Office of, and National Security Council	47, II
Secret Service	31, IV
Securities and Exchange Commission	5, XXXIV; 17, II
Selective Service System	32, XVI
Small Business Administration	2, XXVII; 13, I
Smithsonian Institution	36, V
Social Security Administration	2, XXIII; 20, III; 48, 23
Soldiers' and Airmen's Home, United States	5, XI
Special Counsel, Office of	5, VIII
Special Education and Rehabilitative Services, Office of	34, III
State Department	2, VI; 22, I; 28, XI
Federal Acquisition Regulation	48, 6
Surface Mining Reclamation and Enforcement, Office of	30, VII
Surface Transportation Board	49, X
Susquehanna River Basin Commission	18, VIII
Technology Administration	15, XI
Technology Policy, Assistant Secretary for	37, IV
Tennessee Valley Authority	5, LXIX; 18, XIII
Thrift Supervision Office, Department of the Treasury	12, V
Trade Representative, United States, Office of	15, XX
Transportation, Department of	2, XII; 5, L
Commercial Space Transportation	14, III
Contract Appeals, Board of	48, 63
Emergency Management and Assistance	44, IV
Federal Acquisition Regulation	48, 12
Federal Aviation Administration	14, I
Federal Highway Administration	23, I, II
Federal Motor Carrier Safety Administration	49, III
Federal Railroad Administration	49, II
Federal Transit Administration	49, VI
Maritime Administration	46, II
National Highway Traffic Safety Administration	23, II, III; 47, IV; 49, V
Pipeline and Hazardous Materials Safety Administration	49, I
Saint Lawrence Seaway Development Corporation	33, IV
Secretary of Transportation, Office of	14, II; 49, Subtitle A
Surface Transportation Board	49, X
Transportation Statistics Bureau	49, XI
Transportation, Office of	7, XXXIII
Transportation Security Administration	49, XII
Transportation Statistics Bureau	49, XI
Travel Allowances, Temporary Duty (TDY)	41, 301
Treasury Department	5, XXI; 12, XV; 17, IV; 31, IX
Alcohol and Tobacco Tax and Trade Bureau	27, I
Community Development Financial Institutions Fund	12, XVIII
Comptroller of the Currency	12, I
Customs and Border Protection	19, I
Engraving and Printing, Bureau of	31, VI
Federal Acquisition Regulation	48, 10
Federal Claims Collection Standards	31, IX
Federal Law Enforcement Training Center	31, VII
Financial Crimes Enforcement Network	31, X
Fiscal Service	31, II
Foreign Assets Control, Office of	31, V
Internal Revenue Service	26, I
Investment Security, Office of	31, VIII
Monetary Offices	31, I
Secret Service	31, IV
Secretary of the Treasury, Office of	31, Subtitle A
Thrift Supervision, Office of	12, V
Truman, Harry S. Scholarship Foundation	45, XVIII
United States and Canada, International Joint Commission	22, IV
United States and Mexico, International Boundary and Water Commission, United States Section	22, XI

Agency	CFR Title, Subtitle or Chapter
U.S. Copyright Office	37, II
Utah Reclamation Mitigation and Conservation Commission	43, III
Veterans Affairs Department	2, VIII; 38, I
Federal Acquisition Regulation	48, 8
Veterans' Employment and Training Service, Office of the Assistant Secretary for	41, 61; 20, IX
Vice President of the United States, Office of	32, XXVIII
Vocational and Adult Education, Office of	34, IV
Wage and Hour Division	29, V
Water Resources Council	18, VI
Workers' Compensation Programs, Office of	20, I
World Agricultural Outlook Board	7, XXXVIII

List of CFR Sections Affected

All changes in this volume of the Code of Federal Regulations (CFR) that were made by documents published in the FEDERAL REGISTER since January 1, 2009 are enumerated in the following list. Entries indicate the nature of the changes effected. Page numbers refer to FEDERAL REGISTER pages. The user should consult the entries for chapters, parts and subparts as well as sections for revisions.

For changes to this volume of the CFR prior to this listing, consult the annual edition of the monthly List of CFR Sections Affected (LSA). The LSA is available at *www.fdsys.gov.* For changes to this volume of the CFR prior to 2001, see the "List of CFR Sections Affected, 1949–1963, 1964–1972, 1973–1985, and 1986–2000" published in 11 separate volumes. The "List of CFR Sections Affected 1986–2000" is available at *www.fdsys.gov.*

○